Social History of Africa

HISTORY AND MEMORY IN THE AGE OF ENSLAVEMENT

Recent Titles in
Social History of Africa Series
Series Editors: Allen Isaacman and Jean Allman

HISTORY AND MEMORY
IN THE AGE
OF ENSLAVEMENT

BECOMING MERINA
IN HIGHLAND MADAGASCAR,
1770–1822

Pier M. Larson

HEINEMANN
Portsmouth, NH

JAMES CURREY
Oxford

DAVID PHILIP
Cape Town

Heinemann
A division of Reed Elsevier Inc.
361 Hanover Street
Portsmouth, NH 03801-3912
USA
www.heinemann.com

James Currey Ltd.
73 Botley Road
Oxford OX2 0BS
United Kingdom

David Philip Publishers (Pty) Ltd.
208 Werdmuller Centre
Claremont 7708
Cape Town, South Africa

Offices and agents throughout the world

ISBN 0–325–00217–7 (Heinemann cloth)
ISBN 0–325–00216–9 (Heinemann paper)
ISBN 0–85255–689–6 (James Currey cloth)
ISBN 0–85255–639–X (James Currey paper)

British Library Cataloguing in Publication Data

Larson, Pier M.
  History and memory in the age of enslavement : becoming Merina in highland Madagascar, 1770–1822.—(Social history of Africa)
  1. Slave-trade—Madagascar—History 2. Merina (Malagasy people)—History—18th century 3. Merina (Malagasy people)—History—19th century 4. Madagascar—Social condtitions—18th century 5. Madagascar—Social condtitions—19th century 6. Madagascar—History—To 1810
  I. Title
  306.3'62'09691'09033

Library of Congress Cataloging-in-Publication Data

Larson, Pier Martin.
  History and memory in the age of enslavement : becoming Merina in highland Madagascar, 1770–1822 / Pier M. Larson.
    p. cm.—(Social history of Africa, ISSN 1099–8098)
    Includes bibliographical references and index.
    ISBN 0–325–00217–7 (alk. paper)—ISBN 0–325–00216–9 (pbk. : alk. paper)
    1. Merina (Malagasy people)—Ethnic identity. 2. Merina (Malagasy people)—History. 3. Slavery—Madagascar. 4. Slave trade—Indian Ocean Region. I. Title. II. Series.
  DT469.M277 M475 2000
  969.1004'993—dc21   99–049241

Paperback cover photo: Embroidered image of Andrianampoinimerina modeled after Ramanankirahina's imaginary painting of 1905 (see Figure 5.1). The author purchased this rich embroidery of colored thread in a craft market of Antananarivo in September 1999. Memories of Andrianampoinimerina, very much alive in modern highland Madagascar, are wedded to this stereotypical image. The artist is unknown.

Printed in the United States of America on acid-free paper.

04 03 02 01 00 SB 1 2 3 4 5 6 7 8 9

ho fahatsiarovana ny hadino

in memory of the forgotten

CONTENTS

ILLUSTRATIONS

PHOTOGRAPHS

TABLES

TEXTUAL NOTES

Dates in the notes are represented in the day/month/year format, such that 03/06/11 means June 3, 1811. The century to which double-year digits belong should be clear from the context. For some citations, no specific day in a month is available, and this is indicated in the following manner: 06/11, or June 1811.

Translations from French, Malagasy, and Norwegian into English are the author's, except where explicitly stated in the notes. Paraphrase in translation has been employed especially in the case of Malagasy historical narratives, where literal translations often come out meaningless in English.

Orthography for nineteenth-century Malagasy words reproduced in quotations has not been modified from the original, except where explicitly stated in the text or notes.

Errors and deviations from modern usage, punctuation, and spelling in the quotations has not been modified with a "[sic]."

PREFACE

This book is a story of the cultural impact of the slave trade on an insular African society. In it I explore how the people of highland Madagascar* reshaped their social identity and some of their cultural practices through encounter with European merchants, diplomats, and commercial economies in Madagascar's early modern era.[1] Cultural transformations issued from the various behaviors of highland Malagasy and foreigners in a time of social crisis. That time of crisis, the late eighteenth and early nineteenth centuries, was characterized by enslavement of persons in highland Madagascar and their export eastward out of the great island into the Mascarene islands of the western Indian Ocean. My principal argument is that the modern Merina ethnic identity and some of its key cultural traditions were fashioned and refashioned through localized experiences of enslavement and mercantile capitalism and by a tension-filled political dialogue between common highland Malagasy and their rulers. In becoming Merina, highland Malagasy articulated historical narratives of their common past that they employed in political struggles over citizenship and royal sovereignty. The production of historical narrative and its accompanying ethnic identity was a form of social action, an intervention into the political life of highland Madagascar that influenced how highlanders both remembered and forgot the role of enslavement in their past.

Secondarily and more broadly, I argue that the African diaspora includes the African continent as well as areas external to it. As many African slaves as were forcibly exiled from the continent were captured and

*By highland Madagascar and central Madagascar I refer to the area commonly known as Imerina *enin-toko* ("of six districts"; see Map 5.1), roughly the current province of Antananarivo. Likewise, highlanders and highland Malagasy are the people who inhabit that area.

moved to new destinations within the continent itself. For a variety of reasons these individuals and their experiences are usually excluded from studies of the African diaspora, which are primarily concerned with the experiences of Africans and their descendants in the western Atlantic. In addition to enslaved Africans held within African destination societies, however, source societies for slaves entering forced migrations in Africa and elsewhere merit inclusion in the diverse range of human experiences of African dispersion. Placing source societies within the African diaspora entails expanding the concept of diaspora to encompass both spatial and social displacements. Historians of Africa who work on slavery, displacement, trauma, and cultural change during the era of the slave trade, in both destination and source African societies, should claim the African diaspora as their intellectual field.[2] Attention to the experiences of Africans within the African diaspora of the mother continent and within other traditionally overlooked areas such as the Indian Ocean and the Mediterranean world will necessarily transform and complicate how scholars theorize identity transformations in the grand dispersion more generally, and in the Americas in particular. Specifically, the rise of new social identities in the African continental portion of the diaspora during the age of enslavement was in many cases linked to a social amnesia of enslavement, differing from the formation of African American identities in the western Atlantic and their link to memorialization of trauma and victimization by enslavement. Understanding ethnogenesis in the "Black Atlantic" and elsewhere in the great modern diaspora of Africans requires attention to both vernacular expressions of identity and the ways in which many Africans purposely remembered and forgot experiences of enslavement.[3]

Third, this case study of commercial capitalism and cultural transformation in highland Madagascar offers a specific example of how Indian Ocean maritime history may be linked to the sociocultural transformation of hinterland societies. A survey of historical literature on the Indian Ocean reveals how challenging it has been for historians to join maritime commercial histories to those of the production systems of the interior that supplied ocean-based markets.[4] Among scholars of the Indian Ocean region, historians of east Africa have most successfully struggled "to bring the ocean closer to the land" in their studies of the export ivory and slave trades of the eighteenth and nineteenth centuries.[5] Lying as it does at the geographic and human crossroads of east Africa and the Indian Ocean, Madagascar shares a common economic past with east Africa and serves as an example of how maritime-oriented Indian Ocean histories can be joined to those of social change in export-producing societies of the hinterland. As Sinnappah Arasaratnam argued in a recent review of Indian

Ocean historiography, the most enlightening studies of linkages between the hinterland and the ocean are microhistories that explore the effects of international commerce and European empire on local societies.[6] This book is such a study.

Fourth, I argue that history and memory are distinct yet complementary ways of apprehending the past and ascribing meaning to it. While most historians have understood history and memory as opposed to each other, I see them as interconnected. This interconnection is abundantly clear in highland Madagascar, where people employed popular historical memories during the early nineteenth century to shape the course of historical events. Those social memories took the concrete form of historical narratives that have subsequently and powerfully molded the professional historiography of highland Madagascar. Thus, history, in its double meaning as things that happened in the past and as professional historiography, has enjoyed and continues to enjoy a deep and meaningfully productive interaction with memory in highland Madagascar. Beyond the specific case of highland Madagascar, I argue that professional historians of the African slave trade ought to work more seriously with African historical memories than they have heretofore done. Guild history must engage popular memories and draw from their interpretations of the past, contextualizing those interpretations with other forms of available evidence. By eschewing the validity and usefulness of African historical memories in favor of contemporary European observations, historians of the slave trade impoverish their reconstructions of the human commerce and disembody knowledge of Africa's traumatic past. Pathways to awareness of the pervasive and lasting cultural impact of the slave trade in Africa and elsewhere lead through history's reflective and intensive engagement with memory.

Finally, through this study I explore the making of concepts and practices of sovereignty in a precolonial African polity. As elsewhere in Africa and beyond, highland Malagasy royalty and its strategies of power did not appear fully mature when the Merina kingdom was fashioned in the late eighteenth century but emerged over time as rulers and their subject-citizens collaborated and confronted one another over important political issues. If colonialism marked a fundamental transformation in the practices and ideas of sovereignty in Africa, the age of enslavement likewise generated conditions in which Africans transformed their political relationships, particularly those with their rulers.[7] As is well known, making and trading slaves was in many instances closely associated with state formation in certain areas of Africa, especially in slaving societies, and the destruction of institutions of the state in others, particularly in areas targeted by slavers.[8] To understand African sovereignty during this period of sociopolitical upheaval well before the arrival of European colonial rulers, historians must pay especial attention to subjects as citizens and state transformations as "cultural revolutions" that shifted social practices and relationships between Africans and their leaders.[9] In highland Madagascar the sociopolitical "effects" of enslavement and the slave trade nurtured a political populism among common citizens. In turn, this populism reinforced royal power at the turn of the nineteenth century, rooting it in the historical experiences, cultural languages, and routine practices of highland people. Frequently interpreted as either an epitome of authoritarianism or an instance of culturally authentic democracy, precolonial African government could be variously founded in popular opinion and despotic rule. Highland Madagascar offers a remarkable case of the early foundation of royal power in populist politics and its later authoritarian consolidation against public will. Enmeshed in multiple relationships of subordination to monarchical and local power yet active in the political life of their nation, highland Malagasy were simultaneously citizens and subjects. A lesson emerging from this history is that the languages and practices of political sovereignty in Africa as elsewhere are neither inherently popular nor authoritarian, but enable the development of competing claims as they are deployed in specific political conflicts.

Madagascar is often considered a world apart, a minicontinent unto itself. While this popular idea of insular exceptionalism nurtures a modern sense of Malagasy national identity that enables islanders to emphasize similarities among themselves and foreigners to recognize what is distinctive about islanders as a related people, it is nevertheless a stumbling block to understanding the Malagasy in relation to each other and to the world in which they live. Because of their varied origins in the expansion of Bantu and Austronesian language speakers into the western Indian Ocean, Malagasy have long and vigorously debated their identities as island peoples.[10] With this work I contribute to that debate by proposing an identity history for the Merina of highland central Madagascar and by locating that history within wider narratives of merchant capitalism, African history, African diaspora, and Indian Ocean history. This is a history specific to time and place, yet one which argues that while culturally unique, highland Malagasy share fundamental historical experiences of enslavement and response to its ensuing crises with tens of millions of persons on the African continent. Through the unique past of highland Malagasy, I propose one example of how Africans across the mother continent responded to the opportunities and tragedies of enslavement and through them sought to transform their cultural practices, collective identities, and understandings of the past. A micro-study of enslavement in a society simultaneously of east Africa and the Indian Ocean, this book suggests new directions and intellectual challenges for the history of African identities and cultural innovation in the diaspora of slavery. These pages also embody a cautionary tale for scholars interested in the transformation of African cultures in the diaspora. In recent years, some scholars of the African American experience (and even Africanists themselves) have projected modern African ethnic identities back into the past, when they may have been expressed altogether differently than in the present or even failed to exist.[11] Many of these identities, as many scholars are now discovering, were molded by the very socioeconomic forces that consigned tens of millions into the bitter experiences of bondage.

Because its primary focus is the impact of the slave trade on societies within the Malagasy interior, this study is neither a history of slaves nor of slavery, but of those who were left behind in communities from which export slaves were taken. This bears clarifying at the outset, for Madagascar lay at a cultural and economic crossroads in the western Indian Ocean and its peoples experienced a variety of slave trades between the fifteenth and nineteenth centuries as both captives and captors. Malagasy participation in slave trades as suppliers and purchasers increased the incidence of slavery and other forms of social subordination (such as pawnship, or the position of *zazahova*) within Malagasy societies. The rise of slavery within highland Madagascar is among the salient effects of the slave trade from Madagascar to the Mascarenes, but one only peripherally treated here. Internal slavery (*fanandevozana*) became increasingly significant toward the end of the period considered in this book, primarily after 1809, the abolition of the export slave trade from the Merina kingdom in 1820, and the formation of King Radama's professional army in early 1822. Coming toward the end of a half-century of enslavements mainly within highland Madagascar itself, the influx of non-Merina slaves that swelled the highland population after 1809 dramatically expanded the modern category of *mainty*, or "black" highlanders, composed of royal servants, slaves, and their descendants.[12] Captives from beyond the periphery of the Merina kingdom came in large measure to replace highlanders who had experienced the misfortune of forced exile to the Mascarenes over the preceding decades, many of them becoming attached to households themselves previously victimized by enslavement. A comprehensive history of Malagasy slavery that considers how highlanders rationalized such an ironic twist of fate remains to be written.[13] That experiences of enslavement were followed so rapidly by active and widespread participation in slaving and slaveholding within highland Madagascar (by the mid-nineteenth century only a third to a fifth of highland households did not have any claim to slave labor) demonstrates how flexible highlanders' attitudes toward enslavement were.[14] This flexibility is both the irony and the tragedy of slavery; it confronts us with what it means to be human. It is a key interest in the chapters that follow.

This work, then, explores one subset of Malagasy experiences among the many slave trades over the years: that of the *fotsy,* or nonslave (i.e., non-

mainty) population of highland Madagascar at the beginning of the nineteenth century.[15] Here an explanation of vernacular terminology employed throughout the text is necessary. Nineteenth-century highlanders made a fundamental distinction between generally free persons (*fotsy*) and generally unfree persons (*mainty*). The *fotsy* were further divided into the *andriana*, commonly glossed "nobility," and the *hova*, usually translated as "commoners."[16] Few of the *andriana*, however, enjoyed the material privileges of the monarchy, the "landed aristocracy" (a subgroup of *andriana* known as *tompomenakely*), or other resource-rich persons, and neither the *hova* nor the *andriana* ever functioned as a single community or cohesive corporate group. Throughout this text I employ "common people" and "commoners" to refer to the majority of both *hova* and *andriana* who, unlike the few of their number, did not enjoy the many socioeconomic privileges potentially accorded by status title, wealth, or political power. By doing so I do not wish to suggest that social status differences (*hova*, *andriana*) were immaterial, only that they are less important to the substance and argument of this particular book with its emphasis on economic differentiation, administrative subordination to monarchy, and historical memory. In nineteenth-century highland Madagascar, as today, status title is important to understanding potential networks and possibilities but does not predict socioeconomic position or actual privilege, both of which issue from achievement as well as ascription.[17] Finally, by "royalty" I mean the reigning sovereign and his or her close relatives and contenders, not the totality of the *andriana* (who are better conceived in translation, as I have noted, as a type of nobility). When I refer separately to all the *hova* or all the *andriana*, I favor the appropriate Malagasy language terms to their more imprecise English equivalents. The reader should pay careful attention to these usages, especially to the fact that by "commoners" I am not talking about the *hova* but about most nonslave highland Malagasy of the period.

From their earliest attempts to understand the nature of servitude within Africa, historians have debated the appropriateness of the terms *slave* and *slavery* in reference to variant forms of African social and economic subordination.[18] Despite certain generally universal features of African bondage on the mother continent and elsewhere—capture, natal alienation, general dishonor, deprivation of kinship and citizenship rights, reduction to salable and controllable property (at least for a period)—African slavery within Africa and about the Atlantic, Mediterranean, and Indian oceans was exceptionally diverse. This diversity defies easy generalization. Experiences of subordination, for example, were mediated by the way in which individuals were captured, demography and geography at points of capture and subsequent transfer, slaves' and masters' relationships to the means of production, slaves' ability to seek social and economic advancement in the societies of their capture, and by the particularities of local culture and ideology. Personal narratives of enslavement, especially those offered by individuals who experienced servitude on separate continents in their lifetimes, testify most powerfully to these considerable differences. Despite profound discontinuities in the nature of slavery within Africa and elsewhere, I retain the term *slavery* here for two specific reasons. First, this work concerns the kin, neighbors, and rulers of individuals captured for sale across the sea into a European system of plantation agriculture. Forcibly exported individuals were bought and sold in commercial transactions between Malagasy and foreigners, the most fundamental indication of their condition as chattel property, as slaves. Second, and more important, employing a single term for diverse forms of servitude resulting from capture and forced natal alienation accentuates structural interconnections within a world economy. It was the expansion of Europe and its mercantile capitalist economy from the fifteenth century, and the functioning of many other external markets for human beings over a longer time span, that generated an external demand for slaves as labor, kin, and social prestige and that encouraged Africans to capture millions of new slaves, simultaneously increasing servitude on the African continent and elsewhere.[19] Though each unique, forms of African bondage in Africa, the Atlantic, the Mediterranean and Islamic worlds, and in the Indian Ocean were fundamentally linked by intersecting commercial economies. To multiply a vocabulary of reference for an intercontinentally joined system of forced labor to emphasize its diversity is to lose sight of the interconnections. While I recognize and underscore the significance of diversity, I wish to highlight structural connections.

Finally, in writing this book I have been acutely aware of walking an intellectual tightrope. Given the geographical location of Madagascar and my own scholarly interests, the audience for this work includes Africanists, Malgachisants (scholars of Madagascar), Indian Ocean specialists, and students of the African diaspora. This diverse audience has less in common than it ought to. Africanists, even specialists of east Africa, are generally unfamiliar and uncomfortable with Madagascar, east Africa's "British Isles." This stems partly from linguistic discontinuities: Madagascar is a francophone country in a modern anglophone zone of influence and the native Malagasy language is Austronesian, not Bantu (the language subfamily that predominates in east Africa). Due to a blossoming and influential scholarship on Africans in the Atlantic, scholars of west Africa are generally far more attuned to Atlantic history than east Africanists are to Indian Ocean history, a field of inquiry still in its intellectual formation.[20] Scholars of the African diaspora have unfortunately limited themselves primarily to the history of African peoples in the Atlantic, particularly in its western portions. For them, the Indian Ocean is a world apart. For their part, historians of the Indian Ocean mostly hail from South Asian history (the Indian subcontinent sits astride the great ocean), rather than from among the ranks of Africanists, and are only secondarily familiar with Africanist historiographical debates, including those about slavery and African dispersion. Malgachisants tend to know more about Africa and the Indian Ocean than east Africanists and Indian Oceanists know about Madagascar, but most Malgachisants are francophone while the primary audience for this book, as well as my academic training, is anglophone. These multiple discontinuities in experience, expertise, and audience oblige me to steer the present narrative between disparate historiographies and languages in an attempt to appeal to specialists and generalists in largely fragmented fields. For Africanists, diaspora scholars, and experts on the Indian Ocean, the detail on Madagascar, including the Malagasy language terms, may be overwhelming at times; for Malgachisants, Indian Ocean specialists, and scholars of the New World diaspora the predominantly anglophone historiography of Africa engaged in these chapters may seem far removed from their usual experiences and concerns. Both intellectually and experientially, I inhabit the interstices of this unfortunate yet stimulating fragmentation. I hope that my attempt to draw diverse intellectual worlds together will prove insightful for all who indulge my effort.

ACKNOWLEDGMENTS

My intellectual and personal debts are legion. First, I would like to express my appreciation to Ernest and Cecelia Dumor, who tantalized me with African history as an undergraduate. That interest was nourished by Allen Isaacman and Lansiné Kaba at the University of Minnesota. Bill Brown, Steve Feierman, and Jan Vansina at the University of Wisconsin trained me as an apprentice to the historical guild. I would like to thank Jan for reading the manuscript and offering advice in the early stages of production (as a dissertation) and Steve for his attention as the project neared completion. The initial inspiration for this study was kindled by the stimulating visions of Steve Stern and Florencia Mallon, historians of Latin America with whom I studied comparative slavery and Andean history in Madison. Their insights on the local experiences of global capitalism in the Americas have left an indelible mark on these pages. I would also like to thank Allen Isaacman, Richard Roberts, and Ned Alpers for their guidance, support, and incisive criticisms of the manuscript; they have very significantly improved the book. Joseph Miller commented on parts of chapters 3 and 4 in a much earlier article version. His ideas were valuable in the process of revising. Research was conducted over nearly a decade and financed variously by the Mellon Foundation, the Social Science Research Council, the Fulbright-Hays Doctoral Dissertation Research Abroad Fellowship Program, the Scandinavian American Foundation, the Pennsylvania State University Liberal Arts Office for Research and Graduate Studies, and the dean's office of The Johns Hopkins University's Krieger School of Arts and Sciences. I would also like to acknowledge the *William and Mary Quarterly* for permission to republish here modified parts of an article that recently appeared there.*

---
* Larson, 1999.

I have been especially inspired by the important work of several pre-decessors and colleagues in Malagasy studies. In particular I would like to acknowledge the influence of Gerald M. Berg, Maurice Bloch, Gwyn Campbell, Stephen Ellis, Gillian Feeley-Harnik, Jean-Claude Hébert, Françoise Raison-Jourde, and Gilbert Ratsivalaka. Without their insight-ful and provocative work before me I could not have written—much less conceptualized—this book. If my interpretation of Malagasy history dif-fers at points from theirs, it is because their solid work provided a foun-dation and inspiration for my own interests. Jean-Claude Hébert has been extraordinarily generous over the last years with his attention to detail, frank criticisms, and copious unpublished manuscripts. Nancy Hunt and Paul Landau, fellow historians from Wisconsin, have been friends and inspirations since we first met more than a decade ago. To my research cohorts David Graeber, Jennifer Cole, and Rebecca Green I owe both intellectual stimulation and the joys of diversion from investigation. David and I, who both developed intellectual interests in highland Madagascar (and, indeed, in two separate towns called Betafo), shared many conver-sations together while slogging through series IIICC in the Malagasy National Archives at Tsaralalana. I have benefited from his wit, incisive mind, and moral support. Jennifer Cole provided invaluable assistance by perceptively commenting on several chapters when she was very busy. Cole, Green, and Graeber all graciously answered multiple queries by e-mail over the years, sharing their ideas and work with me. Susan Kus and Kim Raharijaona dispatched copies of unpublished works and offered their expertise on various matters. Both Richard Allen and Richard Barker shared parts of their unpublished research on Mauritius with me. Walter Hawthorne gave the complete manuscript a careful reading and offered detailed comments that assisted with final revisions. I owe particular thanks to Lee Carpenter for editorial advice as the work neared comple-tion. I will never forget the valuable assistance Thaddeus Sunseri ren-dered me while I was conducting research in Madagascar and east Africa. Thank you.

I owe a substantial debt to the international Lutheran mission community, out of which I emerged. Nils Kristian Høimyr graciously hosted me at the Norwegian Missionary Society archives in Stavanger and facilitated my re-search there, tolerating my continual presence in his space for over six months. The Norwegian Lutheran Mission and its missionaries at Antsirabe were welcoming and allowed me to employ their impressive library. In Antananarivo, Tom Krohn assisted me in multiple ways and on several occa-sions, as did Tom Berkas during the early stages of my work. The missionar-ies of the American Evangelical Lutheran Church in Antananarivo and

Antsirabe have consistently provided me with many favors and places to stay over the years.

Manassé Esoavelomandroso's support was instrumental to the acquisition of research clearance and a residence visa for Madagascar. I would especially like to thank Rajaonesy Benjamin and Razanamanana Abéline of Betafo, who hosted me in the Vakinankaratra and always saw to my comfort and culinary interests. I enjoyed sharing in the lives of their family. I would also like to thank the Rakotonjohany family of Betafo, especially the late Pamphille Rakotonjohany, my research assistant, who transcribed the interviews I recorded while he was a law student in Antananarivo. May his soul rest in peace. Dieudonné Pascal Rasolonjatovo, who eked out a miserable living selling rice cakes in Antsirabe, introduced me to a cultural world I did not know. I also mourn his death. The untimely and tragic deaths of those closest to me during research in the Malagasy countryside testify to a continuing and nefarious legacy of historically generated poverty. To Mme. Razoharinoro, director of the National Archives in Antananarivo-Tsaralalana, I give my thanks for continued support during multiple visits to the archives. The staff of the archives—Nicomédine, Anisolo, Hary-Lanto, and Héline—always proved helpful, and by their friendly and witty conversation assured that my visits to Tsaralalana were more than shuffling through piles of decaying and dusty papers. Ignace Rakoto of the Musée d'Art et d'Archéologie conveyed information to me from Antananarivo and has long promoted my work in Madagascar. Solofo Randrianja of the University of Toamasina assisted me with numerous problems and is always a friend. Most of all, I cannot sufficiently thank the hundreds of men and women who took time to speak with me and feed me while I was conducting research in the countryside of central Imerina, and especially in the Vakinankaratra. Although this work is not the one I first promised them, I hope to fulfill that promise in the near future.

How can I ever forget *Blue Velvet* on those nights in Madison with Jean-Louis Ratsimihah, Kathleen Heiman, Jay Bradbury, and Adrienne Pressman? For a short time in our lives we shared joy and sorrow together. Antony Scott and Marina van Vessem, along with their families, kept me many times as I passed through England. I will always remember the drinks Ant stole into my room at the Royal Free Hospital in London. It was a terribly kind gesture at a most propitious moment. John Robertson and Karla Herman assisted me with advice and moral support through a personal crisis.

If not for the adventuresome spirit of Milton and Jean Larson, who gave up nearly everything they knew for the unknown some four decades ago, I would never have developed an intellectual interest in Madagascar. The sacrifices they made for our family and for countless others over the years have enriched my life and are the deepest roots of this book. My sister Carolyn cheerfully donated her left kidney to me as this book was completed. I owe her the ineffable gift of mobility and quality of life. Her act of selfless generosity will never be forgotten; may it encourage others to donate what they can. Special thanks to Sheryl McCurdy for offering me both intellectual and moral support throughout this project, and to Anthony, who infused us with energy.

GLOSSARY

agent commercial: A trade representative of the French government on Madagascar's east coast.

ambaniandro: A term commonly employed to denote citizen-subjects of the sovereign of highland Madagascar (also *ambanilanitra*).

ambanilanitra: A term commonly employed to denote citizen-subjects of the sovereign of highland Madagascar (also *ambaniandro*).

andevo: Slaves who could be bought and sold, usually cultural outsiders to the location of their servitude.

andriambaventy: Civilian judges of the Merina kingdom resident at Antananarivo and appointed by king Radama.

andriana: Highland Malagasy enjoying high status and a variety of social privileges; roughly equivalent to nobility.

famadihana: A mortuary ritual of secondary burial practiced by highland Malagasy.

fanandevozana: Slavery, derived from the term *andevo*, slave.

fanjakan'andriana: "Government by *andriana*," a metaphor for powerful and orderly authority over a single polity by a single sovereign of *andriana* status.

fanjakana: Kingdom, government, authority, privilege, dignity.

fanjakana hova: "Government by *hova*," a metaphor for chaotic authority, political division, and multiple vying leaders.

fanompoana: Unremunerated labor service performed for royalty, especially sovereigns.

fatidra: Blood brotherhood.

firenena: From *reny*, mother; term employed by highland Malagasy to denote descent groups composed of multiple *teraky*, which see.

fokonolona: A council of elders empowered by the sovereign to decide local judicial cases and maintain social control in local communities.

fotsy: Whites, designating all highland Malagasy who were neither servants nor slaves; the "free," including both *hova* and *andriana*.

gamella: A local variety of rice grown along Madagascar's east coast.

gamelle: A fluctuating measure of weight employed in the rice trade of Madagascar's east coast.

hasina: A complex notion denoting efficacious power, sacred life force, and blessing; the premier mystical quality of sovereigns.

hetra: A measure of rice land theoretically allocated to all highland Malagasy.

hova: Highland Malagasy of neither servant-slave (*andevo*) nor royal (*andriana*) status, roughly equivalent to commoners.

kabary: Speeches delivered at formal meetings and assemblies.

mainty: Blacks, refers in modern usage to highland Malagasy of servant-slave origin and their descendants.

maroseranina: The advisers, highest-level administrators, and consorts of king Radama; individuals who displaced the "friends" of Andrianampoinimerina after 1809.

orimbato: An obelisk or, metaphorically, a solemn agreement.

palissade: The walled settlement of the French trade representative on the east coast of Madagascar.

razzia: A slave raid.

régisseur des traites: A French trade representative on the east coast of Madagascar.

salaisons: Salted beef preserves.

sampy: Royal talismans, key emblems of royal power.

tanety: Hillside farmland, as opposed to rice fields in the valleys.

tanindrazana: Literally, "ancestral land," a descent-group homeland.

Tantara or *Tantara ny Andriana*:   Historical narratives, once oral, set to writing and published as a compendium during the second half of the nineteenth century.

teraky: [Author's term] A local-level ancestry composed of individuals likely to be buried in the same tomb and claiming descent from a single ancestor two to three generations ascendant.

toko: A district of the Merina kingdom.

tompomenakely: An *andriana* (which see) of high status granted control over a rural estate, part of the tax revenue flowing therefrom, and privileges to the labor of resident farmers.

traitant: A francophone merchant of slaves.

tsena: A weekly market.

vadinebazaha: A female business and sexual partner of a European merchant.

zazahova: A pawn, or nonkin social dependent, born in highland Madagascar.

ABBREVIATIONS

ADC/FD	Archives Départementales de Caen, Fonds Decaen
AN/CAOM/AGGM	Archives Nationales, Centre des Archives d'Outre-Mer (Aix-en-Provence), Archives du Gouvernement Général de Madagascar
AN/CAOM/SG	Archives Nationales, Centre des Archives d'Outre-Mer (Aix-en-Provence), Série Géographique
AN/P/COL	Archives Nationales (Paris), Série Colonies
ARDM/AR/IIICC	Archives de la République Démocratique de Madagascar (Tsaralalana, Antananarivo), Archives Royales, Série IIICC
BL/MD	British Library (London), Manuscripts Division
Firaketana	*Firaketana ny Teny sy ny Zavatra Malagasy: dictionnaire encyclopédique malgache.* Published serially from 1937 to 1970.
HOM	*History of Madagascar*, William Ellis, ed., 2 vols. (London, 1838)
LFC/SR	Larson Fieldwork Collection, Sound Recording
LMS	London Missionary Society Archives, School of Oriental and African Studies (London), Madagascar Incoming Letters
LMS/J	London Missionary Society Archives, School of Oriental and African Studies (London), Journals, Madagascar and Mauritius
MNA/HB	Mauritius National Archives (Coromandel), Series HB

MNA/IG   Mauritius National Archives, claims for compensation submitted to the Compensation Committee

NMS/HA   Archives of the Norwegian Missionary Society (Det Norske Misjonsselskapet), Stavanger, Hjemme Arkiv (Inkomne Brev), Madagaskar

NMT   *Norsk Misjonstidende* (Stavanger)

PRO/CO   Public Record Office (London, Kew), Colonial Office

PRO/FO   Public Record Office (London, Kew), Foreign Office

RH   Raombana, *Histoires*

Tantara   *Tantara ny Andriana* (Antananarivo: Trano Pirintim-Pirenena, 1981). Two volumes successively paginated. A collection of nineteenth-century oral tradition.

1

ENSLAVEMENT AND CULTURE

Culture is logic with a history.

—Johannes Fabian[1]

[I]t is totally misleading to refer to African society at the end of the slave trade as "traditional."

—Walter Rodney[2]

THREE STORIES

During the austral winter of 1777, French *traitant* (merchant of slaves) Nicolas Mayeur, accompanied by Malagasy guides and porters, marched westward from Madagascar's eastern coastal town of Mahanoro, through the island's thick rain forest, and over its backbone of mountains. On July 12 the party emerged from the forest and entered the Andrantsay kingdom in the grassy highlands of central Madagascar, a loosely integrated federation of chiefdoms extending some 70 kilometers from east to west in an area known today as the Vakinankaratra. At the kingdom's border town of Ambohidrainandriana, the company of travelers dispatched a message by runner to king Andrianony, who lived two days' journey further west at the Andrantsay capital of Ifandanana.[3] Mayeur and his entourage were gathering intelligence under the orders of the governor of a small and languishing French colony of settlement and trade deep in the Bay of Antongil on the northwest coast of Madagascar. Mayeur had been engaged by the colony's leader to search out rulers within the Malagasy interior who might supply slaves and cattle to both that settlement and plantations on the French Indian Ocean island colonies of Île de France and Bourbon (collectively known as the Mascarene islands or the Mascarenes; see Maps 1.1 and 1.2).

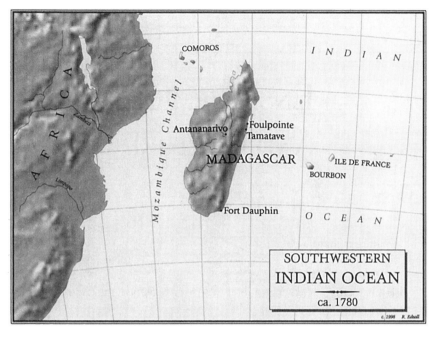

Map 1.1   The Southwestern Indian Ocean, ca. 1780

Over the next week Mayeur and his entourage made their way westward across the heavily populated heart of the Andrantsay kingdom. Mayeur noted that Andrantsay was densely populated, an observation of particular encouragement to an emissary seeking slaves. However, after repeated inquiry Mayeur and his party also ascertained that Andrantsay was a kingdom at peace with its neighbors. This was a disappointment. Peaceable kingdoms were unlikely sources of war captives who could be purchased as slaves. It also became apparent as the party traveled through the country that the inhabitants were not rich in cattle, having little uncultivated land on which to pasture their animals. During his lengthy stay at the Andrantsay capital of Ifandanana, Mayeur conversed frequently with king Andrianony. Despite Andrianony's avid desire to attract European traders to his court and his assurances that he could supply cattle and slaves in modest numbers, Mayeur was discouraged with the poor prospects for opening a lucrative trade in captives with Andrantsay.

Then something remarkable happened. One afternoon during his sojourn at Ifandanana, Mayeur was visited secretly by a messenger from a smaller kingdom, Antananarivo, lying more than 150 kilometers to the north. After welcoming the emissary and conversing with him for some time, Mayeur began to suspect that the envoy had misrepresented his identity. He eventu-

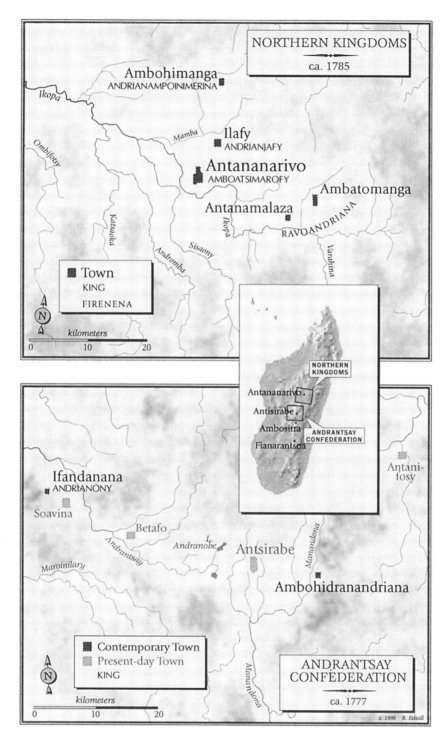

Map 1.2   Highland Madagascar, ca. 1777 and 1785

ally realized—to his utter astonishment—that the messenger was none other than Andrianamboatsimarofy, the king of Antananarivo in person! Disguised in the garb of a common farmer, Andrianamboatsimarofy risked his life by traveling far southward and slipping surreptitiously into the capital of a commercial competitor. His identity revealed to Mayeur, the adventurous Andrianamboatsimarofy explained that he had dangerously stolen into the heart of the Andrantsay to lure Mayeur with abundant trade opportunities further north. There, he emphasized, Mayeur would find plentiful supplies of slaves for export. Mayeur readily agreed to Andrianamboatsimarofy's attractive invitation and within a few days bid farewell to his host, Andrianony. Secretly—so as not to alert the Andrantsay king to his clandestine destination—Mayeur repaired eastward along the same route he had employed during his advance into Andrantsay. Once beyond the kingdom's borders, however, Mayeur and Andrianamboatsimarofy turned northward and traveled three days to Antananarivo, where Mayeur entered negotiations for the delivery of slaves.[4]

In 1785 a struggle for the kingship of Ilafy, a minikingdom some 15 kilometers northwest of Antananarivo, broke into the open. The leaders of a descent group named Ravoandriana, subject to that kingdom but living southeast of Antananarivo, abandoned their reigning king, Andrianjafy, and proffered their support to his competitor, Ramboasalama, who ruled at Ambohimanga.[5] Enraged at an act he considered exceedingly treacherous, king Andrianjafy cooked up a plan to avenge the betrayal and to rid himself of the Ravoandriana altogether. He secretly contacted king Andrianamboatsimarofy at Antananarivo (who in the previous story dared sneak incognito into his southern competitor's kingdom) and offered to transfer the "impudent" Ravoandriana and their lands to him, a prerogative of kings, on the condition that Andrianamboatsimarofy would enslave some of the Ravoandriana and sell them to French merchants for export. As suggested in the preceding story, Andrianamboatsimarofy was enthusiastic about the lucrative opportunities for an external commerce in slaves. He assented to Andrianjafy's vengeful scheme.

Confronted with the royal transfer of their sovereignty from Andrianjafy at Ilafy to Andrianamboatsimarofy at Antananarivo, the Ravoandriana conveyed a delegation of messengers to submit their collective allegiance to their new king. While on the road to Antananarivo, however, the Ravoandriana delegation was fallen upon by toughs of their new sovereign, Andrianamboatsimarofy. The kidnappers captured some twenty-five Ravoandriana and immediately sold them to a French slave trader named Savoureux. The captured Ravoandriana were of a nonslave social rank (they were *fotsy*) of whom arbitrary enslavement—even when ordered by a king to whom they had not yet sworn allegiance—was something they considered illegitimate. Obliged to take the offensive to save their kins-people from the grim fate of enslavement and to prevent future abuses of royal power, 6,000 Ravoandriana ransacked Antananarivo searching for their perfidious new sovereign and seeking to release their kinspeople from Savoureux's caravan. Fearing for his life at the hands of the en-raged Ravoandriana, king Andrianamboatsimarofy fled his capital in the company of Savoureux, to whom he had sold the captured Ravoandriana (Savoureux was probably well armed). Knowing that without a king and protector they would at length expose themselves to the many perils of late eighteenth-century highland Madagascar, the Ravoandriana eventu-ally affirmed their allegiance to the treacherous and runaway Andrianam-boatsimarofy but condemned his actions and vowed to use all means at their disposal to rescue their kinspeople from illegitimate enslavement. They were largely successful. Over the next several days Ravoandriana forcibly wrested most of their kinspeople from Savoureux's caravan and even threatened the French *traitant*'s life.[6]

Thirty-six years after the Ravoandriana protest over illegitimate enslave-ment, in 1822, all central Madagascar was united politically under a single king, Radama. Radama had two years earlier concluded a treaty with the British (who had displaced the French in Île de France/Mauritius in 1810) to discontinue the export of slaves from central Madagascar. With the assis-tance of British officers and weaponry, Radama was in the process of ex-panding his kingdom islandwide. As commander-in-chief of a newly profes-sional standing army of fresh recruits trained in European fighting techniques and partially armed with foreign weapons, Radama determined to cut away the customary plaits of hair that graced his head and crop it short in the Eu-ropean military fashion. This he did in private on April 3, 1822. He appeared shortly thereafter to his people.

The royal haircut electrified the kingdom. Its symbolism was rich and immediate. Highland Malagasy customarily shaved away the plaits of newly captured slaves and cropped their hair short, emblems of newfound subordination and social disrespect. "Now he [Radama] has become a slave of the British," people began to murmur of their king, commenting on his astonishing crewcut. In the metaphoric language of highland Malagasy politics, the highland kingdom was conceived as a head of hair, its vari-ous strands and communities woven together to form a complex and or-dered political coiffure. Viewed through this metaphor, Radama's neatly parted and plaited hair served as an emotional and potent cultural symbol for the social structure of the kingdom and the relationships among its diverse rural communities and the royal court. All were joined by and to royalty, just as the king's many plaits were centrally joined at his head. By ridding himself of his patrimonial hairdo, Radama threw the customary political order of his kingdom into question. This was the primary concern of highland Malagasy when on April 16 some 5,000 women from the region of Ambohimanga gathered at a village east of Antananarivo and notified Radama they were displeased with his decision to clip his hair. They demanded he sever his alliance with the British, whom they identified as the ultimate source of the displeasing cultural innovation.

Radama was furious. "Was he not King and could not he do as he pleased in these things without consulting them?" Rankled by an extraordinarily open challenge to his authority, Radama resolved to reply with raw force. A British missionary resident in Antananarivo explained what happened next.

> The next orders issued, were to select the principal people out of the crowd, & ask all who were the first instigators of this mutiny. Were there any men that excited them to this, or was it merely their own inventions &c &c. They boldly replied they and they alone were the only instigators of it, and said that every woman of note, even the King's own mother, should be fined a spanish dollar [a silver currency used in Madagascar at the time] that would refuse to join them. The next orders delivered were to set 4 of the principal ones apart and as soon as the gun fired, the soldiers of the very same district [as the women] ran with great speed and put these four women to death with the point of their bayonets.[7]

ENCULTURING ENSLAVEMENT

The three preceding historical vignettes span the era considered in this book and introduce some of its principal concerns. I will revisit each of the stories in the chapters that follow. Like the voyage of Nicolas Mayeur, this historical inquiry begins in about 1770 when highland Madagascar emerged as an important source of slaves for the Mascarenes. It closes with a protest by women against Radama's haircut and his symbolic enslavement to European custom in mid-1822. The three extraordinary stories frame a progression of human experience in central Madagascar. Each reveals a complex set of ramifications of the external trade in slaves. As demonstrated in the first story, that trade originated through European expansion and mercantile demand for unfree labor, on the one hand, and the willingness of Malagasy royalty to enslave human beings, on the other. The commercial associations developed between highland Malagasy rulers, who generated slaves, and European merchants, who transported them to the coast, also emerges in the story. So too do the creative politics of highland Madagascar's rural descent groups in a time of political insecurity and social crisis. The Ravoandriana's protest against illegitimate enslavement testifies to the readiness and capacity of highland Malagasy to collectively challenge enslavement of their kin and to the shifting political alliances of late eighteenth-century highland Madagascar. From the way the Ravoandriana confronted what they considered the illegitimate actions of Andrianamboatsimarofy in 1785, it is clear that highland Malagasy did not always willingly give their kinspeople over to enslavement. As citizens, they claimed certain rights and expected their leaders to respect them. Common people were not putty in the hands of their rulers. Yet at the same time, export commerce fostered considerable social strife *within* local communities. That dissention crystallized along fault lines of social rank, class, and gender. The women's revolt against king Radama in 1822 testifies to this internal social stratification. Protest over illegitimate enslavement and hair cropping suggests that experiences of enslavement in central Madagascar were varied, culturally meaningful, deeply painful, and structured by one's economic and social position.

These rich stories of people and enslavement turn me to the key question I explore in this book: how did individuals and collective groups in central Madagascar respond to the challenges and opportunities of the "slave trade" and what consequences did their actions bear for their society and culture? What, in short, was the cultural "impact" of the "slave trade" in highland Madagascar, a source society for export slaves? To answer this question, I must first examine how scholars have conceptualized enslavement and its African "impact."

The entanglement of relationships, expectations, and actions emerging from the three stories illustrates how specific and wide-ranging an understanding of the "impact" of the "slave trade" must be. I have enclosed both "impact" and "slave trade" in quotation marks up to this point because they are critical words in this book. They are intellectual departures rather than destinations, human experiences to be explored rather than assumed, and exceedingly complex phenomena rather than the mechanical and direct results of capture and sale of human beings. The slave trade and its impact were considerably more multifaceted and embedded within African society, economy, and culture than both the words themselves and most recent literature on the effects of the slave trade convey. Scholars have developed a variety of positions concerning the impact of the external and domestic slave trades on Africa, many heavy with simplistic judgment, often arguing a positive, negative, or even a neutral influence, and frequently generalizing local findings to the continent as a whole.[8] The value of sweeping pronouncements—especially those couched in the dualistic terms of winners and losers—is limited by the diversity of African experiences in economies of enslavement and by the contradictory social tensions always inherent in strategies of participation in or abstention from slaving.[9] Philip Curtin's cautions about variability in the consequences of the slave trade across the continent have been supported by an increasingly sophisticated and voluminous literature on Africa and the domestic influences of international commerce.[10]

Among the most frequently explored effects of the slave trade on Africa and Africans are war and armed conflict,[11] economic growth,[12] economic underdevelopment,[13] expansion of political scale,[14] political disintegration,[15] imbalances of wealth and power,[16] shifts in demography,[17] and an increase in slavery and servitude.[18] Most studies identify two or more of these processes operating simultaneously in any one location. Two debates in particular have occupied much scholarly attention. The first concerns whether slavery was widespread in Africa before the transatlantic slave trade and whether fresh European demands for slaves in the Americas substantially increased enslavements within Africa.[19] The second considers whether the slave trade was beneficial, detrimental, or without influence for African economies.[20] I suggest answers to some of the preceding issues with respect to highland Madagascar, but none of them is of paramount concern here. This case study of highland Madagascar seeks to build on existing scholarship to expand and complicate scholarly understanding of the impact of the slave trade by venturing into the realm of cultural transformation, or "other issues" in the words of Paul Lovejoy.[21]

Enslavement, commerce in captives, and their effects can be adequately understood only by venturing into locally rooted African social, cultural, and intellectual history, and by taking African languages and rhetoric seriously. Here, effects are more subtle, less immediate, and secondarily tied to what people did to participate in or to protect themselves from enslavement, even years after capture for export had terminated. Judgments of positive and negative effects in the cultural realm also are much less clear than in other areas, more subjective, and, it could be provocatively argued, mostly irrelevant. To classify sociocultural changes as generally beneficial or detrimental is to measure diverse human actions and experiences with a largely meaningless instrument. As with any transformation, the most relevant questions to ask are, How did sociocultural change differentially affect various categories of people and shift their mutual relationships? and, For *whom* were transformations generally positive or negative? In complex and socially stratified societies such as most of those that supplied or consumed slaves in Africa, individuals in different social stations did not share the same interests and experiences. Although it is often possible to identify local winners and losers in the context of social and economic change, the ultimate beneficiaries of transformations in cultural practice and identity emerge less clearly from the evidence. In highland Madagascar, for example, transformations in identity and cultural practice benefited no one in and of themselves; it was the purposes to which those new cultural changes were later deployed that mattered.

To assess the connections between enslavement and culture change in Africa is to explore the ebb and flow of human relationships and population movements. It is helpful to begin this task by viewing the slave trade as an example of a complex and coercive human diaspora of multiple dimensions, including forced domestic migrations from one region of Africa to other regions, involuntary external movements of people from Africa to other continents, and transformations in the lives of those remaining at home. The African diaspora was composed of several interlinked human dispersions separated in time and space, each associated with the others but usually and unfortunately studied in isolation from them. For purposes of illustration, let me consider the life history of a single slave in the transatlantic system, an African-born woman from the interior of west central Africa. The end point of that slave's experience—let me call her Guilhermina—is life and labor on a Bahian plantation (Brazil), where she may die within a decade of arrival. The most voluminous literature on slavery in the Atlantic focuses on such experiences of slave labor and life in the Americas, the economics of slavery, resistance, emancipation, the making of African American cultures, interactions among different social groups in slave societies, and the transition to freedom.[22]

Guilhermina arrived in Brazil after experiencing the infamous middle passage of transport across the Atlantic Ocean stuffed into the bowels of a stinking European ship. Here too, much work has been conducted on the organization, financing, and experience of the oceanic portion of the Atlantic slave trade, mortality on board ship, the demographic composition of slave cargoes, the relative importance of demand and supply to this composition, and the like, although much still remains to be done.[23] Because Guilhermina, like most slaves forcibly transported across the Atlantic, was not first enslaved on the African coast, her experience of enslavement did not commence on board a European-owned vessel. Like many others, she languished for several years in bondage within west central Africa and was eventually "sold down to the coast" for recalcitrance with her African mistress. A growing body of literature examines the unique experience of slaves' lives and labors within Africa, focusing on the economic organization of African slavery and, increasingly, on issues of culture, hegemony, and resistance, offering fascinating comparisons to parallel studies in the Americas.[24] The volume of literature on African slavery is considerably less than that for the Americas, however, and not because there were fewer slaves in the Africas* (there were as many slaves in the Africas as in the Americas at any one time), but because evidence for African slavery is thinner and for a variety of reasons Western scholars and their publics are less interested in slavery in the eastern Atlantic than in its western portions.[25]

Before she served her mistress near the African coast, Guilhermina was transported away from her point of capture several hundred kilometers within the African interior and resold six times to intermediate speculators along the way. Scholars are also interested in this domestic portion of the African diaspora experience—movement along the internal "way of death" from the African interior to the coast—where mortality rates sometimes waxed higher than on the oceanic middle passage.[26] Life histories of captured persons have proved especially helpful to understanding the African portion of this complex "route of the slave."[27] Finally, of course, Guilhermina was captured at home in the heart of Africa, perhaps entangled in a web of debt, seized and sold away by her creditors, or accused of witchcraft and condemned to death, but reprieved of the gruesome sentence only to be handed over to her first master by the judge who condemned her in exchange for a length of imported cotton cloth, several bottles of rum, and some gunpowder.

Guilhermina's original misfortune of capture within Africa is "one of the most perplexing problems in the Atlantic slave trade,"[28] the single part of the mosaic diaspora experience about which scholars know least.[29] "There is no topic in African history on which so much has been written and yet so little known as the Atlantic slave trade," noted Kwame Yeboa Daaku in 1968.[30] Despite a proliferation of fundamental and illuminating research since that time, his statement still rings true today. Comprehensive histories of slavery and the slave trade tend to say little about enslavement,[31] and even specialized studies of African slavery and its associated human commerce are almost universally weak on the process of making slaves, the fundamental human experience laying at the very origin of slavery, the slave trade, and the modern African diaspora.[32] Of all the dimensions of slavery, the production of slaves in the African interior and its linkage to social transformations is the least well known. Again Daaku: "If such large numbers of Africans could be sold out as slaves there is the need to find out how these people were procured."[33] In most works, methods and experiences of enslavement are summarized in general and abbreviated terms, while analytical lenses are

---

*It is a well-established practice to denote the American continents in all their diversity by referring to "the Americas." Although Africa is a single continent, I employ the plural here and elsewhere in this book to emphasize the cultural diversity of Africans and the variance of the slave trade in particular areas of the continent.

more sharply focused on individuals as they pass into transportation networks, especially the putrid bowels of vessels plying the westward-running oceanic middle passage. The significance of enslavement for Africa and Africans fades into an overriding interest with the Atlantic and the Americas, the final destination of considerably less than one-half of those enslaved on the African continent between the sixteenth and nineteenth centuries.[34] Slaves' "origin and the manner in which they were obtained," notes Herbert Klein in his new survey of the Atlantic slave trade, "are among the more difficult areas to detail."[35] The further eastward one peers along Guilhermina's bitter path of Atlantic exile, the less clearly one sees. The same holds true of African exile to other destinations.

This study explores the historiographically obscure early stages in Guilhermina's complex life of enslavement. It is not, however, primarily an examination of Guilhermina's own experiences, although such a focus would prove both an important and a relevant one. Unlike most histories of slavery and the slave trade, this inquiry is concerned with the impact of Guilhermina's enslavement upon the community from which she hailed: her captors, her siblings, her parents, her extended kin, her descent group, and her sovereign—all those left behind. What did slavers do with their commercial wealth? How did uses of that wealth further reinforce enslavement and sociopolitical subordination? How did Guilhermina's kin react to her capture? Did they blame Guilhermina's creditors, the judge, the reigning chief, themselves, anybody? What did they do about Guilhermina's enslavement? How did Guilhermina's capture change their relationships with her captors and with their local leaders? What did they do to protect additional family members from enslavement? And, most important, what were the political and cultural consequences of all the things Guilhermina's slavers, kith, kin, and leaders did because of the social disruptions caused by her capture? How, for example, did enslavement shape political rhetoric and the careers of rulers? Did enslavement curtail the citizenship rights of subjects, or expand them? Such questions have proved exceedingly difficult for historians of Africa to answer, first and foremost because of a paucity of contemporary documentation, but also in that they have not sought in the right places, taken a long-term view, nor consulted all the available evidence. Many enslavements took place far beyond the observation of literate people or, as in the case of the Islamic regions of Africa, they were seldom recorded in writing by the literate individuals who observed them. Public memory of enslavement, too, has generally faded with time and inclination, particularly among the descendants of slavers and slaveholders.[36] Many individuals were captured within and behind what historians have come to call a dynamic "slaving frontier," a zone of slaving progressing like a wave from the coast into the interior of the continent.[37] Slaving frontiers were normally areas of pervasive conflict and considerable social upheaval. They have attracted little serious historical attention because European merchants, who supply much of our contemporary knowledge about the slave trade, seldom ventured into them.[38]

Despite the forces of social amnesia and the scantiness of contemporary evidence (especially reliable quantitative evidence), historians have pointed to a variety of ways in which slaves were created from nonslave persons within Africa. Although the relative mix of means of enslavement clearly varied over time and place, an emphasis on armed conflict and the linked generation of slaves as prisoners of war has long held sway in scholarly interpretations of enslavement. From Senegambia, for example, Curtin has argued that possibly as many as 80 percent of the slaves exported into the Atlantic were victims of armed capture.[39] While actual proportions of war captives among the mix of African export slaves from this and other regions are seldom adduced with such certainty, the assumption that warfare was the primary generator of bondpeople has been argued for most of west Africa, and especially for the Sahelian belt with its heavy Islamicization (according to Islamic ideology, only non-Muslim prisoners of war could legitimately be enslaved; as a result, most captives from Islamic areas, it is argued, were men).[40] The assumption that most newly enslaved Africans were prisoners of war is developed explicitly by Claude Meillassoux, who writes that "In West Africa, neither free commoners nor slaves born in captivity could be alienated. The only persons who could be sold were those snatched from their homes and families through capture. Communities could not sell their own members nor their domestic slaves, nor breed slaves for sale. In these circumstances slaves were only produced through war or plunder."[41]

Developing an emphasis on prisoners of war snatched from cultural groups different from their captors as the primary category of African captives, scholars generally associate the slave trade with depersonalized physical violence, generalized armed conflict, and unspecified infrastructural devastation. For example, in his recent study of Senegambia, Boubacar Barry, like many of his colleagues, explores what he terms "the generalized violence and chaos caused by the slave trade."[42] Considering enslavement before the eighteenth century, John Thornton notes that "military enslavement was by far the most significant method" for making slaves.[43] In his synthesis of the secondary literature on slavery in Africa, Paul Lovejoy writes that the era of the slave trade up to 1800 is best characterized as a time of "war-lord-ism" across the continent. "In this situation of political fragmentation," he writes, "the characteristic figure was the soldier, who lived as a parasite off the turmoil of the continent." Likewise during the nineteenth century, enslavement in most areas of the continent (with the notable exception of the hinterland of the Bight of Biafra), he notes, was primarily the result of warfare.[44] Summing up the process of African enslavement in his recent historical synthesis of the slave trade heavily dependent upon the secondary literature, Hugh Thomas emphasizes warfare as a source of slaves, remarking that kings made slaves from their own subjects only "occasionally" and that such forms of enslavement were "unusual."[45]

The image of war, unspecific infrastructural spoliation, and a concomitant depersonalized and disembodied process in the generation of prisoners also has been carried over into central and eastern Africa, where armed conflict was likely secondary in the creation of new slaves. Joseph Miller, who has written most extensively on the external trade from Angola, employs a paradigm of civil war to characterize the slaving frontier, emphasizing armed conflict during brief periods (violent slaving) though indicating that most slaves were seized by their own rulers outside of a warring situation once the slaving frontier had moved onward (mercantilistic slaving).[46] Writing about the east African trade, R.W. Beachey and Edward Alpers focus their respective discussions of enslavement on war, destruction of institutions, and generalized depopulation. Concluding his study of the export trade from northern Mozambique, Alpers observes that the interior was "depopulated by the ravages of the slave trade."[47] This may be an accurate description, yet it calls for further research into the specific methods and experiences of enslavement and their connection to the remaking of northern Mozambiquean societies. The same observation holds true for much writing about the domestic impact of the slave trade. Enslavement was not a "mass phenomenon," Patrick Manning once appropriately cautioned, but the sum of tens of millions of specific and individual experiences of capture distributed in time and space.[48] Only through an appreciation of the cumulative influence of individual experiences will historians more fully understand the impact of the slave trade on Africa, especially in its cultural dimensions.[49]

When individual experiences are made the departure point for studies of the impact of the slave trade, reasons for modifying, qualifying, and nuancing the emphasis on warfare, depersonalized violence, and infrastructural despoliation suggest themselves. Ferreting out particular human transactions in a welter of slavemaking that looks fuzzy from afar enables greater appreciation for sociocultural transformation and requires attention to a diversity of issues. First of all, the number of export slaves generated by "war" depends upon how one chooses to classify the slave raids, termed *razzia* in the francophone literature, that were characteristic of much of the Islamic Sahelian belt.[50] If victims of the *razzia* are prisoners of war to some historians, they slide over into the kidnapped in the estimation of others. Because of the fuzziness of these imperfect classifications of modes of enslavement, the approximate percentages of slaves assigned to the misleadingly discrete categories of "prisoners of war" and "kidnapped" differ dramatically in characterizations of enslavement in west Africa.[51]

More important though, the extant (admittedly very sparse) quantitative data concerning the means by which slaves were created within the African interior do not unambiguously support an emphasis on warfare. While conducting linguistic research in Liberia, Church Missionary Society emissary Sigismund Koelle interviewed 179 "recaptives," slaves captured by British antislave trade patrols off the coast of west Africa and resettled in Sierra Leone during the first half of the nineteenth century. Most of these individuals, who had been enslaved between 1810 and 1847 and embarked from the African coast between the River Gambia and northern Cameroon, were chosen by Koelle to represent a wide variety of languages spoken in the west African interior.[52] Using Koelle's data, which indicate how each of the former slaves had been captured, P.E.H. Hair found that only 34% of Koelle's informants from all Africa had been "taken in war," while the balance were kidnapped (30%), sold by relatives or superiors (7%), sold to pay debts (7%), or enslaved through the judicial process (11%) and by other means (11%).[53] Roughly a third, therefore, were taken as prisoners of war, a third kidnapped, and a third reduced to slavery by family, social superiors, and by other means.[54] Stated in other terms, while two-thirds were forcibly snatched by outsiders to their lineages, a full one-third were probably ejected from within.[55]

David Northrup further analyzed this data by breaking it into a northern, Sahelian cluster and a southern one centering on the Niger-Cross River deltas. He found that while 38% of Koelle's informants from the northern zone had been captured in armed conflict, none from the southern zone had. Northrup concluded that historians of the Niger Delta had dramatically overestimated warfare as the origin of slaves.[56] Because Koelle sought to interview persons representing as many different languages as possible, his data do not accurately reflect the proportions of individuals actually enslaved from each language group. Furthermore, the data cannot be considered a perfectly random sample, dependent as they were on which vessels British cruisers intercepted and who Koelle chose to interview. Despite these important qualifications, however, Koelle's data on enslavement were collected from a single population of export slaves who, speaking different languages, represented a broad spectrum of African societies in the west African interior. The multiple ways in which Koelle's informants were enslaved suggest that warfare was an important means of capture, yet not as predominant as is conventionally assumed, even in the Sahelian zone during the early nineteenth-century era of Islamic jihads.

Data about means of enslavement can be gleaned from many biographical sources available in the Americas. While some of these confirm the overwhelming importance of capture in war, others suggest exactly the opposite. Take, for example, the biographies of captives aboard the famous ship *Amistad*, commandeered by enslaved Africans off the coast of Cuba in 1839. The Africans attempted to sail the schooner toward the west African coast but washed up near Long Island, New York, instead. When the African's biographies were recorded in New Haven, Connecticut, as part of the legal procedures that ensued after the incident, most noted how each individual had been enslaved. An examination of the biographies reveals that of the 37 captives and their interpreter still alive in mid-1840 46% (seventeen persons) had been kidnapped, generally on deserted roads by two to six men. Fourteen percent (five persons) had been enslaved for "criminal conduct" or "taken by a king," and 10% (four persons) sold by kin or pawned and subsequently enslaved. Finally, while date on enslavement are missing for five of the captives (14%), only six (16%) had been captured as prisoners of war or through large-scale raids on their villages of residence. Nearly all the captives were Mende speakers originating from the hinterland of what is now the upper coast of Sierra Leone and were enslaved during the early nineteenth century.[57]

Part of the bias favoring prisoners of war as the most numerous victims of enslavement stems from a nearly exclusive focus on slaves moved across the Atlantic and on Africans as suppliers rather than as users of servile labor. It is slaves destined for export into the western Atlantic who are most easily countable and most often counted to ascertain how individuals were enslaved within the African interior. Yet the transatlantic commerce was but one of Africa's many trades in slaves. Koelle's informants, for example, were all individuals who had entered the transatlantic slave trade but were captured by British vessels and subsequently resettled in and about Freetown. The *Amistad* captives had likewise entered the Atlantic. Data concerning means of enslavement based on slaves actually entering the Atlantic commerce, however, will likely overestimate the number of slaves captured in violent acts of warfare, and this must be true of Koelle's informants. Prisoners of war were among the African slaves most likely to be sent away from the continent, and most of these individuals were men.[58] Paul Lovejoy's recently compiled database of 108 slaves from the central Sudan who entered the transatlantic slave trade between 1805 and 1850 illustrates this point. Sixty-six of the slaves in Lovejoy's dataset are derived from Koelle's list of recaptive informants, so there is significant overlap between his collection and Koelle's. Seventy-six percent of the 108 slaves whose means of enslavement were known, Lovejoy writes, were taken in "war/jihad/raiding" and another 15% kidnapped. Of the 108, then, some 90% were violently seized. Men constituted the overwhelming majority of Lovejoy's list of export slaves, for there were only five women among them. Extrapolating from the histories of the export slaves on his list, Lovejoy notes that "The overwhelming majority of slaves from the Central Sudan were not only prime adult males, but most were also seized in war or raids associated with the jihad."[59] This demographic pattern of captive populations destined for export matches that identified by Sylviane Diouf for Islamic regions; women, she argues, constituted only about 15 to 20 percent of the Islamic population exported to the Americas.[60] A similar pattern is suggested by John Thornton for the kingdom of Kongo in the early eighteenth century.[61] Lovejoy characterizes the central Sudan as exceptional among African regions in the high percentage of men among its export slaves, yet his conclusions about means of enslavement in the central Sudan do not distinguish between slaves destined for export and those retained within Africa.[62] Much slave trading in the central Sudan during the nineteenth century, it is known, occurred on a small scale with merchants moving only two or three slaves and conducting many small transactions.[63] Behind the eminently visible raids and threats of raids in the early nineteenth-century central Sudan lay a variety of other less violent methods of enslavement recently described by Abdullahi Mahadi and Sylviane Diouf.[64] Contrary to what populations of slaves entering the transatlantic trade would suggest, many captives retained in the central Sudan, as elsewhere in Africa, may not have been prisoners of war but persons "harvested" from the population by more decentralized and less violent means of enslavement in a time of social and political insecurity when social disincentives against such otherwise illegitimate activity were lowered.[65]

Africa, then, supplied a variety of foreign and domestic markets for slaves, and these markets were differently structured, most notably in the demographic composition of slaves they consumed and in the means by which those individuals were captured. In the transatlantic trade, Africans retained as many new slaves as they exported; African consumers preferred female slaves and retained them in higher proportions than men (well illustrated by Lovejoy's census examined in the two previous paragraphs).[66] Despite their stated preference for adult male captives in the ideal proportions of two men for each woman, however, American slaveowners were constrained by the structure of African export markets to compromise their goals for the demographic composition of slave imports. To accommodate their preference for men, American consumers of servile labor had to accept large numbers of boys (nearly 16% of all slaves carried westward across the Atlantic), whom they found less desirable than prime-aged men. At the same time American purchasers were obliged to settle for a larger number of females than they desired among the mix of imported slaves (some 26% of all newly imported American slaves were women and another 9% were girls). As a result of these patterns of human commerce, forced exile of Africans in the transatlantic trade more resembled (in demographic terms) free European transatlantic migrations in family groups than the primarily adult male composition of migrating populations of European indentured laborers. In total, about 64%

of Africans forced to cross the Atlantic in bondage were male, but only 49% of that total were men; women and children comprised more than half of all slaves moved across the Atlantic to the Americas. Fewer men and more women and children entered the transatlantic slave trade than has long been assumed.[67]

While much evidence suggests that Africans retained as many slaves domestically as they exported across the Atlantic, the Sahara, and the Indian Ocean, female slaves outnumbered male captives in the last two of these three interconnected export trades.[68] Within the domestic trades of Africa and in African destination societies, female slaves usually also outnumbered male captives.[69] In short, the aggregate evidence for the various slave trades from and within Africa all point to the preponderance of women and children among newly enslaved persons. Less well explored than the demographic composition of the various slave trades is the proposition that men tended to be captured differently than women and children.[70] Although women and children were often enslaved in large numbers during times of war—warriors often were executed, sold away, or managed to escape while their women and children were enslaved—women and children were more likely than men to be ejected from their lineages as a result of the actions of kinspeople, neighbors, and rulers, often in surreptitious circumstances.[71] All of the pawns in the *Amistad* case, for example, were girls. Enslavement in nineteenth-century east and central Africa is especially illustrative of this pattern of social capture. Always high, the proportion of women and children in the transatlantic slave trade from west central Africa rose to an apex of just over 60 percent during the early nineteenth century.[72] In southeast Africa this figure was even higher, calculated by David Eltis at near 66% between 1811 and 1867.[73]

Employing mission records, Marcia Wright concludes that east and central African slaves during the same period were most frequently victims of internal social conflict and the product of social transfers and negotiation. "A listing of thirty-six women and children freed at the north end of Lake Nyasa in the early 1890s," she finds, demonstrates that "Slave raiding per se played a relatively small part in creating a pool of slaves. . . . The victims were most often kidnapped or taken in compensation for offenses by male relatives."[74] Joseph Miller's conclusion that kings in the Angolan hinterland abandoned violence for "more peaceful, mercantilistic methods of extracting the captives needed to buy imports" supports this conclusion.[75] If female captives tended to predominate where enslavement occurred by social or nonviolent means, future research should disaggregate the ways in which men and women were captured within the same areas. The preponderance of women among new African captives for nearly all destinations, excepting the Americas, however, suggests that enslavement within moral communities may have been considerably underestimated by historians of the slave trade.

An overemphasis on warfare as a means of enslavement in modern studies may additionally stem from both modern and contemporary notions that armed confrontation was the most socially acceptable way in which persons could be enslaved. The most dramatic form of enslavement, armed capture symbolizes the violence that underlay depriving individuals of their kinship and citizenship rights and forcibly moving them to distant places. It also lessens the responsibility of captors, for selling prisoners rather than killing them can be interpreted as a merciful act (explicitly so in the context of Islamic ideology and many ceremonies of enslavement). Claiming that captives in their power were prisoners of war was one way in which African slavers sought to lay a legitimate claim to ill-gotten human merchandise. Among African slaves, victims of armed conflict are the most visible in surviving historical sources because the hostilities that led to their capture were more likely than individualized and surreptitious forms of enslavement to be registered in writing by foreign and Islamic African contemporaries or retained in African collective memories. While at many times and places a majority of slaves must have been prisoners of war—and the Islamic regions of west Africa are clearly the best candidates for this pattern—other forms of enslavement including kidnapping, sale by kin, capture for debt, and judicial punishment tended to predominate or were at least very significant in other areas, even during the nineteenth century. These "uncoordinated activities by individual entrepreneurs" and their capacity to shift human relationships and alter local cultural practices and identities should not be underestimated.[76]

When enslavement occurred *within* lineage, ethnic, and political communities supposedly bound together by moral ties, it refashioned relationships, often pitting neighbor, kin, and patron-client against one another and throwing the security of kinship and dependency into doubt. Some scholars have noted the importance of enslavement as social "harvesting" or "fishing for men" but have not sufficiently developed these ideas.[77] In his study of trade along the upper Guinea Coast, for example, Walter Rodney found "personal rivalries," "personal struggles," "personal vendettas," "vengeance and retribution," "class exploitation," "deterioration in the customary law," and "deceits, treachery or stratagems" among the many reasons for enslavement. "Kings," he wrote, "were just as likely to rob their own people as to attack their neighbours."[78] Others have noted that slaves were produced through "local disturbances,"[79] "trickery,"[80] "cruel distortions,"[81] "crimes, revenge, kidnapping," "considerable perversion of justice,"[82] conversions of coercive institutions,[83] "organized gangs, unscrupulous traders, bandits, roaming soldiers, and occasional kidnappers,"[84] or "the raw fact of negotiability."[85] The Aro Chukwu oracle of the Cross River area, a classic example of the domestic social tensions that generated captives, "ate" prisoners demanded in payment of fines imposed upon persons judged in its court of last resort. Most of these individuals disappeared into the export commerce, sent plodding away along the paths that led from the Aro Chukwu shrine toward the coast.[86]

In a wide belt across west central and east Africa, and to some extent in west Africa, a significant proportion of slaves began their march toward the coast as a result of their own or their kinfolk's inability to liquidate debts.[87] The story of Swema, who was enslaved in Yaoland near Lake Malawi and marched in a caravan to Zanzibar during the 1860s, poignantly demonstrates how indebtedness could lead to enslavement within a local community. Following the death of her father in a lion attack, an infestation of locusts that devoured all the family's crops, the demise of their livestock by starvation, and an epidemic that killed her two sisters and brother, Swema and her mother decamped to the countryside in a bid to restart their tattered lives. A neighbor lent them two sacks of sorghum (*mtama*) to get them started, but when the harvest failed they could not repay the loan. Swema's mother asked for more time to settle the debt and set herself to making pottery for sale. When her efforts to raise cash did not pan out, a passing Zanzibari caravan put the vulnerable mother and child in grave danger. That morning, their creditor and neighbor approached the house with two local elders and a Zanzibari merchant from the passing caravan.

> Without asking permission, he entered our hut and said with severity to my mother: "Mother of Swema, you haven't anything to pay in return for my two sacks of *mtama*: for that reason I am seizing your child. You are my witnesses," he said to the elders. Then turning towards the Arab [Zanzibari] he said to him: "Well, Sir, it's settled, six coudées of American cloth for this little girl." The Arab took me by the hand, made me stand up and walk; examined my teeth, and after several moments of thought responded: "It's fine; come take the six coudées of cloth."

Devastated, Swema's mother then desperately entreated the merchant who had purchased her daughter to allow her to accompany the caravan so as not to be separated from Swema, the only member of her immediate family still alive. She would bear an ivory tusk for her new master, she pledged. After some days, however, Swema's mother could no longer endure the crushing burden of the tusk and was relieved of it. Because she was no longer materially contributing to the caravan, the merchant denied her food. She continued to follow the grisly cortege, starving, but Swema was prevented from sharing rations with her sickened and weakened mother. On orders of the Zanzibari merchant, guards pushed Swema's mother away from camp in the evening and eventually beat her back, wrenching Swema from her arms. The emaciated woman was left to perish alone by the roadside. When the caravan reached Zanzibar, Swema, heartbroken and perilously ill, was herself taken for dead and buried in a shallow grave. She was discovered under a thin layer of earth by a young man who brought her to the local Catholic mission. She survived her ordeal to bring us her story.[88]

Arresting narratives of enslavement like Swema's poignantly illustrate how social fabric could be rent and lives forfeited through "civil" forms of enslavement. But even when slaves were captured through warfare, organized raids, or individualized kidnapping—when they were violently snatched from lineages by outsiders as a majority of African slaves likely were—a complete understanding of the circumstances and impact of their enslavement likewise requires an exploration of the precise social tensions that nourished aggression and the cultural principles that structured violent encounters between aggressors and their victims. As Paul Lovejoy has recently argued, historians of the African diaspora ought to shift their work from generalized, abstract, and depersonalized characterizations of forced African migration to consider individual experiences and the many contributions of Africans captured in specific circumstances and from precise cultural areas.[89] Behind the abstract social chaos, depopulation, and infrastructural destruction of the slave trade—even armed capture— lay real people and a concrete perversion of civil relationships.

When they targeted speakers of their own languages, but even when they waged war against cultural others, slavers became entangled in messy and conflict-ridden social relationships with victims and their kin. Refusing to allow captors anonymity, individual narratives of enslavement richly demonstrate the importance of the nitty-gritty details of social conflict to the generation of bondpeople, even in cases where victims were snatched by armed gangs and warriors.[90] Nuancing historians' broad categories and quantitative assessments of enslavement by recounting individual experiences of capture behind the translucent curtain of slaving frontiers, slaves' narratives of armed capture suggest that victims, kin, and slavers encountered one another with expectations that were usually broken. Scholars must take these fractured relationships in a time of personal crisis seriously if they are to fully comprehend what armed capture meant for victims, for kin, for their neighbors left behind, and for the sociocultural transformation of daily life in African societies.[91]

Taken by an enemy army far in the interior of east Africa, Msatulwa Mwachitete recounted how the conflict that left him a slave built up over months when violated clientage relationships between his father (a chief)

Figure 1.1 A "Gang of Captives." Images such as this popular woodcut of a coffle of slaves in east Africa published in a book by David and Charles Livingstone depict the human indignities and the suffering of the infamous march to the coast but offer little insight into the varied individual experiences of capture. Slaves appear in the illustration as an indiscriminate "gang" already separated from kin and community. Out of sight, the latter and the impact of enslavement upon them and their mutual relationships are seldom considered. Like the Livingstones, professional historians view human commerce from an exterior vantage point (chronologically, culturally, quantitatively), focusing primarily on the postcapture experiences of the enslaved rather than the communities from which they came. (*Source*: David and Charles Livingstone, *Narrative of an Expedition to the Zambesi and its Tributaries* [New York, 1866], 376.)

and a wandering stranger led to a surprise attack on his village.[92] The capture of Job (Ayuba Suleiman Diallo, a merchant) and his interpreter along the Gambia River of west Africa in 1730 suggests that armed capture subsequently entailed a violation of commonly recognized social principles.

> It happened that a company of the Mandingoes, who live upon plunder, passing by at that time, and observing him unarmed, rushed in, to the number of seven or eight at once, at a back door, and pinioned Job, before he could get to his arms, together with his interpreter, who is a slave in Maryland still. They then shaved their heads and beards, which Job and his man resented as the highest indignity; tho' the Mandingoes meant no more by it, than to make them appear like Slaves taken in war.[93]

Dismayed by their surprise capture, Job and his interpreter were most disturbed at having their heads and beards shaved, a practice legitimately reserved for true prisoners of war, which they were not. By shearing away their captives' hair, the slaving Mandingos performed an illegitimate social act, yet one necessary to concealing their self-recognized feat of illicit enslavement and making it stick. With their heads shaved, Job and his assistant were less likely to escape their misfortune. Snatched at an early age by Maviti raiders near his home in the region of Lake Bangweulu, central Africa, Petro Kilekwa was bound and immediately sold, but kept overnight in his natal town by the coastal traders who purchased him from his raiders. He was espied that evening among the slaves, whereupon his mother entered into ransom negotiations with the merchant to whom he had been sold by the marauding Maviti. "My mother," he writes, "went to relations to get cloth on credit and she got three yards of calico, but my master demanded eight. Mother could not get eight yards, so she was unable to ransom me. She was very sad and cried bitterly and I cried bitterly too, 'Woe is me, mother,' because I was leaving my mother and my relations and my country."[94]

The social complexity of individual experiences of enslavement, the broken expectations, and the concepts of proper social relationships that render them meaningful suggest that historians need to distinguish between macrocosmic and microcosmic views of enslavement. The nineteenth-century jihads of the central Sudan or the decline of old Oyo, for example, produced much armed conflict and upheaval that generated slaves as prisoners of war or kidnappees, but each of these larger processes was further characterized by what Curtin has termed a "microcosmic web of family and personal relations" that lent social texture and a complex array of human decisions to large-scale events.[95] Examining narratives of violent enslavement from nineteenth-century Islamic Hausa literature, M. Hiskett suggests that when scholars scrutinize the circumstances of violent capture in individual cases they find "that magic, sorcery and witchcraft were closely involved in the whole business of slave hunting and catching."[96] In other words, the broad political and social transformations of African societies that produced export captives as prisoners of war or kidnappees become far more complicated and culturally embedded when historians search beyond quantifiable data to peer into the elaborate interpersonal tensions and relationships that encouraged armed conflict and structured particular encounters. For the tens of millions who were victimized, as well as their friends and families left behind, enslavement was neither faceless nor routine. It tore into the fabric of local societies and personal lives in very specific ways. If armed conflict was prevalent in precolonial Africa and responsible for the collection of a majority of export slaves, the circumstances and specific practices of enslavement reveal the convoluted social transactions that started tens of millions along their way of death and remade African societies from the inside.[97] The lasting impact of the slave trade on African cultures, resulting as it did from the accumulation of individual social transactions, remains largely to be discovered.[98]

To explore the relationship between enslavement and African cultural transformations is also to broaden existing studies of slavery, culture, and identity transformation in the African diaspora. Most such studies focus on cultural change and expression in the destination societies of slaves, whether in the Africas or the Americas.[99] "If African history holds the key to the diaspora," Paul Lovejoy aptly remarked in a recent article, "then the study of the diaspora must begin in Africa, not in the Americas or elsewhere."[100] While many scholars of Africa have worked on slavery and its accompanying internal displacement of Africans, both they and their colleagues in the Americas customarily define the diaspora as commencing at the African coast or applying only to those slaves who eventually ended up beyond Africa's continental borders.[101] (I return to this point in chapter 7.)

To diversify their study of the cultural impact of enslavement beyond the experiences of slaves held in destination societies, scholars need to consider cultural transformation among the networks of persons who transported slaves from place to place and within the continental source societies from which African slaves were wrenched.[102] Slaves usually acquired value in direct proportion to the distance they were alienated from their places of birth within frontiers of enslavement, geographically separating source, destination, and transit zones. Yet these zones were connected in captives' experiences and all of them form part of the African diaspora, the great dispersion and displacement of African peoples over the last several centuries. The present study focuses on sociocultural change within a slaving frontier, the homeland of victims. In highland Madagascar, as elsewhere in Africa linked to the export commerce, cultural traditions and stratified social structures were productive of slaves but were in turn revised through practices of enslavement and the many human dimensions of its associated commerce. Understanding the consequences of enslavement and commercial capitalism in highland Madagascar is central to identifying the origins of Merina ethnicity and many of its cultural practices. Behind modern Merina identity and its culture lies a forgotten, or "secret," history of the slave trade.[103]

BECOMING MERINA

The Merina are the most numerous ethnic group in modern Madagascar, today numbering approximately 3.5 million individuals.[104] Merina live primarily in the province of Madagascar's capital, Antananarivo, and owe their collective identity to the rise of a unified kingdom in highland central Madagascar at the end of the eighteenth century. Founded by a popular cultural hero named Andrianampoinimerina who ruled from about 1780 until his death in 1809, the kingdom consolidated several modest town-states within the Malagasy highlands and has come to be known as the "Merina kingdom."[105] During the second and third decades of the nineteenth century, Andrianampoinimerina's son and successor, Radama, expanded the Merina kingdom outward in all directions from its landlocked position in the highlands of central Madagascar. This was accomplished in diplomatic alliance with Britain, which offered military assistance to Radama's armies, and through the support of missionaries of the London Missionary Society, who created a written form of the Malagasy language in Latin script, opened schools, and supplied Radama with literate administrators and secretaries. By military and bureaucratic expansion, the Merina kingdom emerged as a multicultural polity. At the center of the polity lay the Merina and their homeland, called Imerina; at its periphery, the conquered provinces and peoples. At its apogee in the mid-nineteenth century, the Merina kingdom nominally controlled some two-thirds of Madagascar's territory. Ruled at first by *andriana* sovereigns and then by *hova* prime ministers, the Merina kingdom endured until French colonial troops occupied Madagascar in late 1895.[106]

Historians of central Madagascar have long assumed, often implicitly, that the Merina existed as a coherent and named ethnic group far into the island's past.[107] Works treating the eighteenth century and earlier, for example, routinely identify highland peoples as Merina.[108] This common misunderstanding of Merina ethnicity assumes that highland Malagasy identity is genetically determined: if people in highland Madagascar today call themselves Merina, their ancestors were by definition Merina too. Yet contemporary historical sources concerning central Madagascar do not speak of a people called Merina until the beginning of the nineteenth century, just as the trade in slaves from central Madagascar was coming to an end. The historically recent appearance of Merina as an ethnonym suggests that becoming and being Merina was a social and time-bound phenomenon, a process worthy of inquiry rather than a given or physically and culturally fixed characteristic. A small portion of highland Madagascar, probably the direct environs of Antananarivo, was known as Imerina (from *erinerina*, "conspicuous place, prominency") from at least the mid-seventeenth century. The ethnic term Merina that came into use more than a century later was a shortened form of *Antaimerina*, people of Imerina."[109]

Well into the nineteenth century, coastal Malagasy frequently referred to people living in the highlands as Amboalambo (literally: "wild dog–wild pig"), a slur that assimilated highland Malagasy to the ritually unclean animals of Islam.[110] From their earliest contacts with Madagascar, Europeans employed the term Hove (also written Hova, Ove, Ova) to designate people from highland Madagascar.[111] They may have adopted this usage from coastal Malagasy, who even today frequently designate all highlanders as "*hova*." Converting Ove into the name of the place highlanders inhabited, Europeans called highland Madagascar Ancove rather than Imerina (also Hancove, Hancova, Ankove, Ankova), meaning "at the place of the Hova." Readers will encounter these persistent terms in European evidence cited throughout this book. European authors employed Hove and Ankove for highland Madagascar and its people well into the twentieth century, but these were not terms highland Malagasy themselves utilized in precisely the same way. To be *hova* in highland Madagascar, as I wrote in the preface to this book, was to be socially classified as neither of *andriana* nor of servant-slave status; it was to be what is most conveniently translated into English as a commoner.[112] Lacking a unified political or ethnic identity during the eighteenth century, the people of highland Madagascar were designated by European and Malagasy others through the status-group term applying to the largest proportion of their population (most highland Malagasy at the time were of *hova* status). But *hova*, like *andriana* and *andevo* (slaves), was not an ethnonym—it was a status-group designation of a subset of highland Malagasy. Europeans and Malagasy from the coastal regions were mistaken in their use of *hova* as ethnonym, and highland Malagasy refused to adopt the incorrect ethnic taxonomy.[113]

If being Merina is a comparatively modern identity dating to the beginning of the nineteenth century, how and why did the people of highland Madagascar come to consider themselves as Merina at that time? Most research on ethnicity suggests scholars look to interethnic relations for answers to this question. Since the end of the Second World War, humanists and social scientists have developed theories of ethnicity that consider how collective identities crystallize in opposition to "other" identities in multiethnic contexts. The history and etymology of ethnicity helps to understand why the term has channeled research in this direction. The terms *ethnic* and *ethnical* entered the English language in the mid-fourteenth century, when they were employed in biblical translations from Greek to gloss *ethnikos*, "gentile, heathen, pagan, cultural other."[114] In turn, *ethnikos* was derived from *ethnos*, which, traced to its earliest documented use by Homer, designated a "large, undifferentiated group of either animals or warriors," such as a swarm of bees or a throng of foot soldiers.[115] In later Greek usage *ethnos* became more polyvalent, meaning "number of people living together, company, body of men, band, host (used of particular tribes and animals), nation, people, class of men, caste, tribe."[116] From its origins in Greek and English, then, to be ethnic has meant to be culturally other, and ethnic identity implies dual or multiethnic interactions.

Derived from the adjective *ethnic*, the noun *ethnicity* first emerged in the North American academy only in the 1940s and flourished there during the following decades as urban sociologists sought to explain why

Americans of various cultural and national backgrounds failed to homogenize into the hypothesized social melting pot.[117] Born in the study of polyculturalism, *ethnicity* (the term and concept) was introduced to African studies in 1960 by Columbia-trained sociologist Immanuel Wallerstein as a way to understand "the feeling of loyalty to" urban ethnic groups (so-called "tribes") which—counterintuitively, Wallerstein argued—helped to foster national integration in the early period of African independence.[118] Among Africanists the term was quickly assimilated by urban anthropologists who, like their Americanist counterparts, were interested in explaining why existing theories of "detribalization" failed to explain the retention, invention, and celebration of parochial cultural traditions in largely urban places of wage labor.[119] By the mid-1970s Africanists from a variety of disciplines had adopted *ethnicity* as a more polite way to name tribalism and usually considered ethnicity to be a product of the *interaction* of distinct cultural—ethnic—groups, especially in the circumstances of colonization.[120] From both its historical and academic origins, then, ethnicity has privileged interethnic studies of formation and transformation in collective identities. Through such "externally oriented" paradigms of ethnicity, historians have identified the shifting cultural boundaries that separate ethnic groups one from the other as the most likely sites of ethnic identity formation. The emergence of a collective identity is, therefore, usually seen to be dependent upon the simultaneous definition of cultural others, including foreign slaves held locally, or upon subordination within a colonial administrative framework.[121]

At first glance the theoretically predominant approach to ethnogenesis seemed to make sense when applied to highland Madagascar. During the course of the early nineteenth century armies from central Madagascar expanded toward the island's coasts, conquering and enslaving widely dispersed peoples and creating a hierarchical, pluricultural realm. In the process of subjugating and administering the various regions of Madagascar, people from Imerina generated stereotypes of dominated cultural others that emphasized the uniqueness of being Merina.[122] In Merina historical narratives of the nineteenth century, for example, Betsileo (the people to the immediate south of the Merina) are represented as paragons of stupidity and inveterate practitioners of bad magic in contrast to more intelligent, enlightened, and refined Merina selves.[123] Coastward expansion of the highland Malagasy kingdom during the nineteenth century was clearly a key component in the making of Madagascar's modern configuration of ethnic categories, as scholars working on various parts of the island have demonstrated.[124] Although the frontiers between those ethnic categories could be both fluid and porous, boundaries between Merina and their others—often collectively designated as *tanindrana*, or "strangers"—there clearly were.[125]

For the people of highland Madagascar themselves, however, political dominance over cultural others was not the primary process underpinning the early formation of an identity during the first decades of the nineteenth century.[126] The more I scrutinized the evidence for Merina ethnogenesis, the more I realized that the most significant relationships fostering the rise of an ethnic identity termed Merina were not those that erected boundaries with cultural others either within or outside highland Madagascar, but relationships among highland Malagasy themselves within an international economy of mercantile capitalism. As the politically dominant and most privileged of persons within the Merina kingdom, highland Malagasy did not have a collective identity thrust upon them from the outside. Merina ethnic identity crystallized among highlanders at the heart of their homeland—around the royal court at Antananarivo—and moved outward from there across Imerina. As an "identity for itself" whose primary set of articulating relationships was intraethnic struggle over citizenship and the sovereign's prerogatives, Merina identity originated as a political loyalty to the kingdom of Andrianampoinimerina at the beginning of the nineteenth century.[127] That political loyalty was undergoing internal metamorphosis into an ethnicity by 1822 as rural communities appropriated it to press demands upon their new king, Radama. In the process of embracing the political identity that bound commoners to their king (and, most important, the king to his commoners), highland Malagasy shifted Merina identity in a new direction. By turning political identity back upon the royal court as a cultural resource in their political struggle with a new king, highland Malagasy ethnicized it, appropriating it from royalty and placing it in the service of popular aspirations.

To say that highland Malagasy transformed a political identity into an ethnic one is to talk about that identity with a modern academic vocabulary and only in the broadest terms. Ethnicity is, after all, an abstraction that poorly conveys the particular ways in which a group conceives of its identity, the language in which it speaks about the human relationships underpinning that identity, and the contexts in which the identity becomes relevant. Malagasy language texts of the nineteenth century (among which are the *Tantara*, discussed below) identify Merina identity among a series of overlapping categories signifying people belonging to Andrianampoinimerina's kingdom. In speeches addressing their people reproduced in nineteenth-century texts, highland rulers frequently employed three terms to designate their subjects: *ambanilanitra*, *ambaniandro*, and Merina.[128] Each referring to the nonslave or *fotsy* people of the kingdom, these terms were frequently interchanged one with the other yet differed in their meaning. As employed by highland Malagasy, *ambaniandro* (beneath the sun) and *ambanilanitra* (beneath the heavens) designated those highlanders who pledged allegiance to the sovereign, conceived metaphorically as the sun and the heavens.[129] These terms emphasized highlanders' political subordination to a single ruler as necessary to a unified identity; both can be translated as "citizens," or individuals who, offering allegiance to a sovereign, expected certain behaviors of that sovereign and of each other (the terms are further discussed in chapter 5). By contrast, the ethnonym *Merina* associated highlanders' identity with the place they lived, Imerina. While Merina was employed to designate a community of people, it was equally utilized as a toponym.[130] When Merina appears in nineteenth-century texts in the form *i Merina* or *Imerina*, a grammatical construction that may designate either a place or a person, it is often ambiguous which of these two meanings is intended.[131] This ambiguous usage is the one most frequently appearing in nineteenth-century Malagasy language texts. The double meanings of *i Merina* suggest that highland Malagasy did not make significant distinctions between *Merina* as ethnonym and *Merina* as toponym, associating themselves with the land on which they lived. Polyvalent usage of this sort is not unique to the term *Merina*, for highland Malagasy routinely employed such metonymic nouns by substituting place names and collective identity terms for each other.[132]

Merina as ethnonym in highland Malagasy language texts of the nineteenth century usually appears in speeches reported to have been delivered before large groups of people, as when the famous founder king Andrianampoinimerina addressed his assembled subjects saying, "And this is what I have to say to you O Merina" (*Ary izany ho lazai'ko amy nareo ry Merina*).[133] Consistent with this usage, the term *Merina* never appears in nineteenth-century texts as an adjective (a Merina man, a Merina custom). Some texts modify Imerina with *ambanilanitra*, as if employing the latter term as an adjective (*veloma, ray Imerina ambanilanitra*; adieu, you Merina ambanilanitra).[134] This construction elicits the sense of "you citizen Merina" without clearly transforming *ambanilanitra* into an adjective. The only identity term clearly employed as an adjective in nineteenth-century texts is probably an introduction of European compilers and editors, who were accustomed to employing such adjectives of identity in their mother tongues (an English house, *la cuisine française*). Because such compilers understood enough of local Malagasy language usage to know they could not turn Merina into an adjective, they were constrained to introduce a new European-derived identity adjective—Malagasy. In the *Tantara*, for example, the French editor inserts "Gasy" and "Malagasy" as adjectives, although the noun each adjective modifies refers to central Madagascar in particular rather than the entire island and its people.[135] Nineteenth-century Merina identity was conceptually tied to highland people as a political unity under a single sovereign, whose state, we shall learn, was also called Imerina (and not some equivalent of "the Merina kingdom," a grammatically impossible construction in the early nineteenth-century vernacular). Merina identity was originally the characteristic of a political community and could not inhere separately in individuals nor exist as an abstract quality or essence in the same way, for example, that English-ness might in an English woman.

Because nineteenth-century Merina identity was the characteristic of an entire group, struggles over that identity entailed conflict over social rela-tionships and behavior, over ethnic performance, within the community of identity.[136] The rhetoric employed in those struggles tended to emphasize cultural practices and political hierarchy and to prescribe their associated behaviors. During the first decades of the nineteenth century, highlanders made frequent appeals to the politico-ethnic identity that connected them, but they did so infrequently through explicit invocation of the term *Merina*, for they often referred to themselves as citizens of their polity, as *ambaniandro* and *ambanilanitra*. Each of these three terms—*Merina*, *ambaniandro*, and *ambanilanitra*—invoked the same unity but with differ-ent meanings, as we have seen. It was not the ethnonym *Merina* that was so important to highland Malagasy, then, but the moral unity it designated and what that unity meant in practical terms. Appeals to a variety of overlapping terms to express the same internal unity is consistent with the way in which Merina identity developed; the reification of identity into a single and fre-quently invoked ethnic name is characteristic of expressions of ethnicity within the context of the modern nation-state, in which self-identity is usu-ally framed in opposition to ethnic others (and in which context current aca-demic theories of ethnicity have been formulated). A "vernacular identity" highland Malagasy politico-ethnic identity of the early nineteenth century was unique and did not conform to many of the commonly assumed norms of modern ethnicity.

Since Merina identity was the outcome of highlanders' attempts to define and produce virtuous behavior, it was akin to what John Lonsdale in his study of Kikuyu history has called a moral ethnicity. "Moral ethnicity," he writes, "creates communities from within through domestic controversy over civic virtue." Like the unity of Kikuyu, the imagined Merina community during the early nineteenth century was a "crowded debating hall" where a new and broadly conceived community of interest crystallized, claiming autonomy from its leadership by espousing an independent vision of royal power and interpreting that vision as socially virtuous.[137] Indeed, all modern identities (and probably ancient ones too) embody moral visions of virtuous behavior, for to be is to behave in certain culturally and socially distinctive ways and not in others.[138] Conflict over virtuous behavior, the ideal for citizen mem-bers of the body politic, lay at the heart of relationships among highland Malagasy in the age of enslavement. Kings and commoners both espoused civic virtue, but their interpretations of virtuous behavior often differed. The tensions inherent in their disparate interests and mutual relationships were productive of Merina ethnicity and its cultural traditions. What was unique about ethnogenesis in nineteenth-century highland Madagascar was the fundamental role of common people and popular opinion in the process. Expressed through a moralized popular ethos, Merina ethnicity was an "evolving consciousness," as T.H. Breen has written in the context of early American history, which derived from "the transformation of personal experience into public opinion." Merina identity was a consciousness founded upon a multiplicity of "local and personal histories" in the age of enslavement.[139]

People who imagine themselves as a moral community, such as an ethnic one, usually claim to share a common past. Highland Malagasy articulated their shared past primarily through historical narrative and ritual.[140] By the mid-nineteenth century nearly all highlanders shared a common set of stories about their past. Gathered into the *Tantara* as described in the next section of this chapter, these stories recounted the lives and deeds of the founder king, his predecessors, and subsequent rulers of the Merina kingdom; transcribed and published during the course of the nineteenth century, the stories became shared transcripts of Merina identity. Because they shared a set of historical narratives articulated verbally and set to print in the course of the nineteenth century, highland Malagasy constituted what Joanne Rappaport calls a "textual community," drawing on a common stock of narratives both to explain their collective moral connection to the past and to publicly justify their present actions.[141] Central to highlanders' self-definition as Merina, shared historical narratives overlay locally produced histories most highlanders preserved about the past of their particular descent groups. Joined to the Merina community, descent groups, termed *firenena*, retained their own distinctive histories and identities, many of them originating well before the late eighteenth century. Highlanders thus shared a new pan-Merina identity associated with historical narratives about common rulers while simultaneously nourishing a keen sense of old local diversity through narratives concerned with local descent groups. For Merina identity, this local diversity worked in potentially contradictory ways: it might either accentuate the value and usefulness of Merina identity or provide the difference with which to undermine it.

By imagining themselves as Merina and employing historical narratives to define that identity, highland Malagasy fashioned an ethnicity and its related traditions a century before colonization. The experience of highland Malagasy throws into question a common notion that the emergence of African ethnic consciousness or "tribes" was largely tied to the process of European colonization and administration during the twentieth century, and that such identities crystallized primarily as a result of the political-cultural work of European administrators and African elites.[142] An increasing number of studies about the nineteenth century demonstrate that Africans were fully capable of expressing their cultural identities as distinct groups well before European colonization, although ethnic identity before and after colonization might differ significantly.[143] This study joins that work. Precolonial ethnic identities, moreover, were not characterized by stability nor by fixed cultural traditions. Like ethnic identities of the twentieth century, those in earlier periods were in constant flux, shaped by the unique needs of the people who produced them.[144] To employ the terminology of Hobsbawm and Ranger, Africans were skilled at "inventing" new traditions and in discarding others to manage their lives and bring meaning and order to their changing circumstances.[145] This was especially true of Africans in the age of enslavement.

In many African societies, for example, witchcraft emerged as a frequent idiom through which people made sense of the creation and delivery of slaves.[146] Among the Temne of Sierra Leone, witchcraft accusations and witch finding produced an abundance of slaves for export, linking the Atlantic economy of mercantile capitalism to the redefinition of witchcraft and to a modification of techniques for rooting out evil within the African interior.[147] If witchcraft was tradition, it underwent significant transformations as a result of the slave trade. A fraternity of slave traders in west central Africa created a healing society known as Lemba to cure its members of the physical and social ailments acquired through slaving. While Lemba safeguarded their health, society members forged a cultural bond among themselves that lent cohesion and organization to their trade diaspora, ironically hastening the movement of slaves along their way of exile.[148] Among the Diola of Senegambia, family shrines protected individuals from enslavement and served to enforce the "rules" of enslavement that limited export sale to captives whose relatives could not ransom them. As enslavement intensified, however, some families introduced new types of shrines that insured them success in slaving enterprises and protected them from spiritual and social retribution when they broke social convention by selling persons illegitimately enslaved or never publicly offered for ransom. Through a complex interaction between slaving and shrines, the Diola retailored their religious culture during the era of the slave trade.[149]

Like Africans on the mother continent, highland Malagasy were active in remodeling their cultural practices as well as their identities in the era of the slave trade. Highland Malagasy dropped some traditions from their repertoire during the early nineteenth century. Most notable among these were ear piercing and scarification. The former entailed cutting the ear lobe, stretching it out, and placing metal rings in it; the latter, cosmetic cutting on the upper part of the arms and stomach.[150] Other traditions were modified. Highland Malagasy of the early nineteenth century altered mortuary practices, including the architecture of their tombs and the rituals they performed there.

Because tombs and collective identities were intimately intertwined in highland Madagascar, changes in one of these domains were reflected in the other. Transformations in collective identity and cultural practice were closely related to each other and to commerce and state formation, and they embodied the social concerns of highland Malagasy, imparting a distinctively historical and popular character to Merina identity. In the process of creating a new collective identity, common highland Malagasy participated integrally in re-creating Malagasy royalty, building a modern kingdom, and transforming their cultural practices.

ACTORS, WITNESSES, MEMORIES

Historians customarily reflect on the nature and limitations of their historical sources. For a study of the impact of enslavement on an eighteenth- and nineteenth-century African society, such an exercise is especially pressing. Africanists interested in slavery read with envy the richly documented works now appearing in impressive number on the experiences of enslaved Africans and their descendants in the Americas. Most of these studies draw on a wide variety of written and oral sources, including newspaper articles, editorials, advertisements, censuses, pamphlets and other contemporary publications, account books, parish records, legislation, and early twentieth-century interviews of once-enslaved individuals and their descendants. The literacy of a significant proportion of slaveholders, and even some slaves, in the Americas and an ethos among them that encouraged and valued writing, publication, and preservation of experiences in forms such as the personal diary has nourished the scholarly imagination and primed many Americans' memories about the significance and impact of enslavement on their common history.[151]

By contrast, scholarly and public commemorations of enslavement in Africa are infrequent. The paucity of contemporary evidence is one of the reasons for the generally weak public historical memory of enslavement on the eastern side of the Atlantic. Politics is another. Where memories of enslavement tend to emerge most saliently—in the oral narratives Africans spin for the most local (and even secret) of audiences—professional historians have little extensive or systematic access.[152] How many inquisitive historians have elicited an uncomfortable silence from their interlocutors when they asked about slavery, especially when employing the appropriate vernacular terminology for it? When I spoke with highland Malagasy about servitude, for example, the conversations were often surreptitious and hushed. Many of my hosts in the Vakinankaratra rose to close windows and doors and required me to stop my recording device before agreeing to speak. If the descendants of slaves are reluctant to acknowledge their servile history, descendants of the free often speak about slavery in euphemisms.[153] The numerous social taboos surrounding slavery were reinforced by a national law which, I was assured, had been enacted during the 1980s making it punishable to identify someone's slave origins. While the modern traces of enslavement are everywhere present in highland Malagasy society as elsewhere in Africa, structuring social relations and everyday life, historical narratives and other publicly available discourses must be carefully "combed" for evidence of this fundamental experience about which so many silences have developed. A form of writing in Arabic script called *sorabe* was employed in highland Madagascar during the eighteenth century but it was restricted to a handful of individuals who refused to teach it widely.[154] *Sorabe* manuscripts do not shed much light on enslavement, focused as they are on other issues. As a result, for strictly contemporary accounts of enslavement and its impact, historians of the island are largely dependent upon the written accounts of Europeans who recorded their personal experiences in a foreign land.

Unlike in most regions of Africa where Europeans were confined by local merchants and rulers to restricted areas along the coast, foreign slave traders, diplomats, and other travelers ventured into the Malagasy interior in search of captives, political alliances, adventure, and self-aggrandizement. Some of these individuals have left written accounts of their experiences. From 1820, toward the end of the period covered in this work, British missionaries of the London Missionary Society entered highland Madagascar to begin evangelizing and teaching Christian literacy. Their dispatches to directors of the society in London are invaluable evidence in the latter chapters of this book. Many key manuscripts on the history of highland Madagascar during the late eighteenth and early nineteenth centuries have been published in colonial and postcolonial scholarly journals on Madagascar, especially in the *Bulletin de l'Académie Malgache* and the *Bulletin de Madagascar*, while some entered publication in their own time well before the twentieth century. For this reason, many contemporarily produced works are cited in the notes with dates of publication several decades (and in some cases more than a century) after the time of their first production. Other contemporary documents were consulted in manuscript version. Archival papers concerning late eighteenth- and early nineteenth-century highland Madagascar are widely dispersed in Paris, Caen, Aix-en-Provence, London, Coromandel (Mauritius), and Antananarivo. The list of manuscript sources at the end of the book contains an overview of archived papers considered in this study. These are cited in the relevant notes.

Some important consequences result from my reliance on historical evidence stemming primarily from a foreign elite, many of whom were slave traders. While kings and merchants frequently emerge as named individuals in the contemporary historical sources, common highland Malagasy, most of whom were small-scale rice farmers, tend to appear as collectively acting descent groups (such as the Ravoandriana). Throughout this work, I employ the words *community* and *rural community* in a general way to designate descent/political groups like the *firenena* of the late eighteenth and early nineteenth centuries.[155] Differences in the historical visibility of rural communities, on the one hand, and kings and slave merchants, on the other, reflect the asymmetrical balances of power in highland Madagascar during the age of the slave trade. Because of their greater social power, their ability to act with significant autonomy, and their alliances with Europeans who produced written documents, the elite men who created slaves and traded them attain greater individuality in this history than do more humble slavers and many of those who were the actual and potential victims of enslavement. This social imbalance in historical visibility which lasted into the first decades of the nineteenth century is a practical limitation of the available evidence—the dead cannot now be interviewed—and I am obliged to maneuver through it.

That historical agency resides in the individual is virtually axiomatic in modern Western social theory.[156] This principle has underpinned much recent research into the multiple divisions crosscutting corporate groups and undermining the social solidarity of crowds.[157] Studies of rural communities, for example, have been extensively criticized for failing to sufficiently explore the heterogeneity and social diversity that characterize them. Facile symbols of social solidarity to the urbane, rural communities are riven by multifaceted and profound internal conflicts. People do not act collectively to protect community, it is argued; they struggle among themselves to determine what kind of a community they will live in.[158] Yet it is not altogether out of Malagasy cultural character that common highland Malagasy usually emerge in eighteenth- and early nineteenth-century historical narratives as collectively named and collectively acting descent groups. Even today, rural highland Malagasy consider descent groups to be the most historically relevant social units and they fashion narratives to comment upon the experiences of those groups.[159] Such descent groups demonstrated even greater social cohesion at the turn of the nineteenth century than they do today. In times of crisis they sometimes acted collectively and decisively to promote common interests, as the Ravoandriana did in 1785. Highland Malagasy rulers created their kingdoms when they negotiated political relationships with descent groups as collectivities. During the era of the export slave trade, rural communities sometimes drew together in social solidarity while at the same time they were crosscut by tensions that differentiated them from within. Descent groups, and the individuals, households, and miniancestries that composed them must therefore be examined from differing perspectives: as potentially cohesive entities whose members sometimes shared common interests and as distressed groups often fractured by tensions of kin, class, generation, and gender. To the extent available historical evidence permits, I explore these social tensions in this study.

When scholars of eighteenth- and nineteenth-century highland Madagascar turn away from foreign-produced records to Malagasy historical memories they encounter an immediate paradox. In contrast to European accounts of the sort described above, the extant Malagasy historical narratives, as I noted earlier, reveal comparatively little in a direct fashion about enslavement and the export trade in captives (some exceptions are examined in chapter 3). Highland Malagasy historical narratives are conspicuously silent about the formative role of external trade in highland Malagasy history, viewing state formation primarily in domestic terms.[160] This silence about Imerina's transformation by merchant capitalism is not due to a lack of Malagasy language sources. Working from verbal accounts, highland Malagasy who learned to write their language in Latin script in missionary schools after 1820 created a range of historical and cultural texts. Most of these were histories of royalty, others were descent group histories, and still others descriptions and justifications of highland cultural practices. In the mid-1860s a French Jesuit priest named François Callet recognized the practical value of these manuscripts and began to collect them. Supplemented by his own inquiries among elderly male historians, Callet gathered a large body of manuscript "inheritance of the ears" (*lovan-tsofina*) and published them on the presses of the Catholic mission at Antananarivo. The resulting work has come to be known as the *Tantara ny Andriana* (the "history of sovereigns," abbreviated throughout this book simply as the *Tantara*, with a capital T) and in its most recent reference edition has been issued by the Malagasy government press in two volumes of more than 1,200 pages.[161]

Tantara narratives portray the highland Malagasy past in local cultural and political terms, seldom connecting insular developments to international trade. Rather, as the name Callet chose for the collection of texts indicates, its narratives concerning the period between 1770 and 1820 are focused largely on Malagasy sovereigns, especially founder-king Andrianampoinimerina, his ancestors, his military conquests, and the domestic organization of his kingdom. In reflecting on their history, why did nineteenth-century highland Malagasy remember their first king in greatest detail and at greatest length while devoting so little attention to those sovereigns who reigned closest to their time? (Some 640 pages, or more than half of the *Tantara*, is devoted to Andrianampoinimerina; less than 200 pages describe the reigns of the founder king's six successors.) And while contemporary European documents identify Andrianampoinimerina as an astute slave merchant whose political success was predicated upon wealth generated through participation in the external slave trade, why do *Tantara* narratives reveal so little about Andrianampoinimerina's export slaving activities, especially since foreign

TOKO IV

NY NANOKOAN' ANDRIANAMPOINIMERINA NY DIDIMPANJAKANA SY
NY. LALÀNA AMINY FITSARANA.

§ I. NY HELOKA 12 LOHA.

Ny namoahan' Andrianampoinimerina ny didy, dia namory ny ambanilanitra Andrianampoinimerina teto Antananarivo (teo Ambohimanga, hoy ny sasany), dia hoy izy : « Ny anarany ny basy ko, ny iray *Bedoaka :* tsy misy basy midoàka afatsy ny ahy, tsy misy hidoàka afatsy ny teny aminy fanjaka' ko f' izaho manjaka tokana ka tsy mahazo midoàka roa raha olona hafa raha tsy izaho ; ary ny anarany ny basy ko iray atao ko *Tsi-mahaka :* izaho tsy mahàka ny an' olona, tia' ko tsy haka ny an' olona hianareo : ary ny iray atao ko *Aka-no-maty :* raha manao ho aka loatra mitoky aminy fitiavan' andriana k' andeha manota ny didimpanjaka' ko, maty ko raha manao izany, kanefa izaho tsy mba miady amam-paty na manondro basy ahy aza, nony maty ny ai' ny (ley manao aka loatra) dia ome' ko ny hava' ny ny faty ny alevina eo am-pasana aminy razana, (raha maty ny ady, asai' ny alaina ny faty antsoina aminy fihaonana *atao ny faty* ny hava' nareo fa maty ny ady ; raha maty meloka, dia ome' ny ny amboa ny faty ; raha maty mamosavy, alevina anatsinomindoha) ; koa izao no anaova' ko anarany ny basy ko telo, hoy Andrianampoinimerina. » Tahirizina eto Ambohimanga ireo basy telo ireo. Ary hoy Andrianampoinimerina : « Ary izaho mamory anareo ambanilanitra, na ny be ny tany, na ny zaza, na ny vehivavy, ary hampifidy anareo, hoy izy. » Dia nalai' ny ny tsiraka naseho ny tamy ·ny ambanilanitra ary nampifidy hoe : « Inona no tia' nareo ?

Photograph 1.1   "Andrianampoinimerina Issues Decrees and Laws Concerning Justice." The beginning of a chapter from the 1981 reference edition of the *Tantara ny Andriana*, compiled by Jesuit priest François Callet during the later nineteenth century. In this passage, Andrianampoinimerina discusses the names of his three muskets: Many-Pierced-Holes, Does-Not-Take, and Clever-Are-Dead. The name of each musket suggests a quality of the founder king's rule: its power (it easily pierces its subjects), its evenhandedness (it does not unjustly take), and its pervasiveness (it will outwit the clever). The passage is typical of how foreign trade appears in the *Tantara*. Although about weaponry procured through external commerce, the narrative does not mention this trade. Muskets are represented as extensions of domestic politics. (*Source:* François Callet, ed., *Tantara ny Andriana eto Madagascar: Documents historiques d'après les manuscrits malgaches* [Antananarivo, 1981], 796.)

commerce was so socially influential in highland Madagascar?[162] There must be historical reasons for the form, substance, and accent of nineteenth-century highland Malagasy historical memories.

A preliminary explanation: The changing political-cultural context in which *Tantara* narratives were collected more than a century ago fostered social amnesia about enslavement. Callet amassed the texts just when Merina sovereigns had reopened their kingdom to European explorers, merchants, speculators, and Christian missionaries following a period of some twenty-five years of forced exile.[163] By 1873, the year Callet published the first volume of the *Tantara*, more than 20,000 children were enrolled in 498 schools operated by the London Missionary Society (LMS) and the queen and prime minister of the kingdom had converted to Christianity and urged their subjects to do the same (many additional schools were superintended by other Protestant and Catholic mission organizations).[164] The royal baptism, which occurred in early 1869, marked a time of religious transition when a range of highland Malagasy cultural practices came under official disapproval from the royal court. The number of adherents to LMS churches in the central regions of Imerina was more than 225,000 in 1872, possibly half the population.[165] Much to the delight of foreign missionaries, considerable coercion was being employed by Merina administrators during the early 1870s to force highlanders into chapels on Sunday morning.[166] In the face of these developments aimed primarily at shunting highland Madagascar's youth into mission-run schools, Callet's chief informants sought to preserve what they considered venerable and ancient Merina custom. They held up the traditional rulers and practices of yore as examples of cultural integrity in the environment of Europeanization and religious change they found so disappointing. When *Tantara* narratives were being recorded, therefore, highland Malagasy did not have the slave trade foremost in their minds.[167]

This explanation for the local focus of the *Tantara* and the relative silence of its narratives regarding enslavement and the export trade in captives is relevant, but it is only part of the story. It helps to explain why highland Malagasy may have forgotten about enslavement, but not why their memories were so focused on Andrianampoinimerina rather than on other sovereigns. To fully appreciate both the historically produced silences of the *Tantara* and the narratives' preoccupation with memories of Andrianampoinimerina it is important to understand how the once-oral texts compare to contemporary evidence and by what process they were fashioned. Despite extensive *Tantara* texts detailing the domestic policies and speeches of founder king Andrianampoinimerina, there is very little supporting contemporary, foreign-produced evidence with which to reconstruct his domestic politics after about 1790. To a large extent the temporary absence of contemporary data on turn-of-the-century highland Madagascar is a measure of Andrianampoinimerina's success in organizing and regulating the trade in slaves from his dominions. While many Europeans traveled into the slaving frontier of highland Madagascar between about 1770 and 1790, Andrianampoinimerina was loathe to allow foreign merchants into his kingdom after that period.[168] When he did, their movements were scrupulously controlled.[169] As a result, historians have little contemporary evidence for highland Madagascar between about 1790 and 1815, when the slaving frontier moved from the highlands of central Madagascar outward in all directions.[170] Not until king Radama,

Andrianampoinimerina's son and successor, entered into diplomatic conversations with British officials from Mauritius in 1816 did contemporaries again produce documents with eyewitness observations from highland Madagascar. Although *Tantara* narratives are rich for this very period in which contemporary accounts of Andrianampoinimerina's rule are absent, they were collected and printed only after Father Callet's arrival in highland Madagascar in 1864, two generations and more after the events they purport to describe. Thus neither European nor Malagasy sources supply contemporary eyewitness accounts of highland Madagascar during the critical years of the reign of Andrianampoinimerina. This is an obstacle my work shares with all writing about the founder king.[171]

Although it imposes constraints, this obstacle also embodies significant intellectual opportunities. Historians of the slave trade have much advanced knowledge of the demographic, economic, and political dimensions of the transatlantic commerce in human beings—part of its event history—but they have more seldom explored how human experiences related to culture change or what Africans remembered about and thought of enslavement. In particular, most recent work on the slave trade has shunned African-produced narratives and memorial evidence, knowledge critical to writing cultural history, as relevant to interpretation of the past.[172] A principal concern of most work on slavery and the African slave trade has been to reconstruct the past "as it happened" with as little "subjective distortion" from memory as possible. In this respect, recent studies of the slave trade with their emphases on the demography, politics, and economics of slaving (and I do not detract here from their remarkable achievements) tend toward what Gordon Shrimpton calls a correspondence theory of history. Seeing through a "lens" of modernism, he writes, many historians, "believe that something happened or existed 'out there' and that their task is to use every available form of documentation and logic that will produce an account of it that corresponds as closely as possible to the real thing. This is correspondence theory. It proposes that historians can ideally describe what they observe in much the same way as Newton's *Principia* is believed to have described the solar system."[173] Correspondence theory is based on long-standing Western scholarly traditions that separate *logos*, or words whose validity or truth can be argued and supported by data or contemporary observation, with *mythos*, words whose validity lies in their very pronouncement.[174] This separation of "myth" from "history" limits historians to the production of particular sorts of event history that capture only part of human experience. The best way of determining "what really happened in Africa" (*logos*) during the slave trade, the reasoning goes, is to consult contemporary and largely European-produced evidence, which is felt the most reliable. African narratives and memories (*mythos*), which come in a variety of oral and written forms, are suspected of "factual" inaccuracies associated with the malleability of human memory, and hence are rejected.[175]

While concerns about oral and other noncontemporary narratives identify potential problems for establishing chronology or a reliable event history, those concerns may prevent historians from appreciating that such narratives, their silences, and their "distortions"—popular historical memories—are meaningful historical evidence.[176] Memorial evidence, such as oral and written narrative, is potentially useful to professional historians in two different but related ways: as bits of "factual" evidence, like contemporarily compiled observations, and as historical interpretation. While during the 1960s and 1970s some historians of the slave trade employed African narratives in the former way ("oral tradition" as historical evidence for event histories), it is the latter method that is especially useful to cultural historians of Africa, for it demonstrates that knowledge of the past is actively made rather than inherited.[177] "One would greatly misrepresent locally produced historical texts of this genre," writes Wim van Binsbergen of the *Likota lya Bankoya*, a manuscript compilation of Nkoya history (Zambia) similar to the *Tantara*, "if one took them for simple compilations of oral traditions" and therefore simply mined them for nuggets of evidence just as one would with contemporary documents. The "sustained and integrated historical argument" developed in these manuscripts seeks to forward certain ideas while silencing others. This intellectual work and the reasons it was meaningful to particular authors and audiences suggest the issues people considered relevant and important, and why.[178] As memories filtered through the historical consciousness of living generations, popular histories like the *Likota lya Bankoya* and the *Tantara* are not equivalent to contemporary evidence, yet both contemporary and memorial evidence is channeled through cultural and historiographical filters, and each is nevertheless useful in understanding the past.[179] African popular narratives are silent about experiences of enslavement, then, only if scholars sufficiently limit their understanding of that commerce, of human experience, and of the value of African historical consciousness so as to define memorial evidence like the *Tantara* as extraneous to serious historical inquiry.[180]

In recent years social memory has received much attention as scholars seek to understand how imagined communities such as the Merina perceive and commemorate their past. An interest in social memory—defined as the way in which a community understands its history or, more precisely, conceptualizes its experience through a variety of means including narrative, ritual, dance, customs, bodily practices, and other forms of socially meaningful action—requires scholars to temporarily set aside their own historical memories with all their professional techniques and hypotheses. In particular, understanding social memory requires modifying the idea that something verifiable and recoverable happened in the past that can be reconstructed if only factually accurate contemporary accounts can be located in the archives or extracted from "oral traditions" through proper historical procedure, processing, and analysis.[181] Social memory emphasizes "the conceptualization of experience," human agency, and political (rather than technical) processes in the shaping of a meaningful knowledge of the past.[182] "I hold that all human thought and memory operates in the same way everywhere and at all times," writes Jan Vansina, a leading proponent of a universal theory of memory. I cannot agree, for both the object and the processes of social memory are the product of culturally specific and purposeful action in particular circumstances, resulting in a unique consciousness of the past; they are not the end result of retention and transmission of data ("information remembered" in Vansina's terms) through myriad unconscious and individual processes that conform to certain universally applicable principles.

Working with social memory means acknowledging that professional interpretations of the past, no matter how methodologically innovative and attentive to unconventional evidence, no more capture all historical truth nor illuminate human experiences than popular paradigms of history, that both professional and popular historical consciousness are "laminates" of knowledge and understanding derived from experience and present interests.[183] This is not to suggest that contemporary evidence and popular social memories are equivalent registers of the past, nor that they should ever be conflated with each other. Historical interpretation is usually less evident in eyewitness accounts than in memorial ones, and the purposes of texts produced by contemporaries are generally more easily discernable than those of memorial accounts. For establishing chronology and verifying event actions, eyewitness evidence is almost always superior. Although structured by the interpretive biases of its authors, contemporary eyewitness evidence is more easily appropriated in bits and pieces by modern historians, who may fashion several such accounts into a synthetic interpretation, producing a historiography. Social memory imbedded in popular narratives and embodied practices is less serviceable as raw bits of data (although it can be useful as such) than as a digested historical interpretation in itself—a "hypothesis," "historioracy," or historiography in the words of scholars who work with verbal texts.[184] "Cultural readings" of social memory, the Popular Memory Group asserts, come "completely with evaluations, explanations and theories which often constitute a principal value of the account and are intrinsic to its representations of reality."[185] Because social memory is often strong where eyewitness accounts are weak, and the converse, the two sorts of evidence are complementary and each is useful in contextualizing the other. For these reasons I employ both types of historical evidence and interpretation in this synthetic history.

As historical interpretation, social memory becomes meaningful primarily when the intentions of its producers can be ascertained and the history of the narratives uncovered. Whether produced by popular or professional historians, historical consciousness is the outcome of historical process. Just as studies of professional historiography reveal much about the development of the discipline of history and the concerns and intentions of the historians who produced and shaped it, examining the historical development of popular narratives such as the *Tantara* can tell historians a great deal about the concerns and intentions of highland Malagasy during the age of the export slave trade. The social memory embedded in *Tantara* narratives offers modern historians little about the infrastructural organization of enslavement and international commerce; for this they must turn to contemporary European accounts. However, if one accepts the *Tantara* as valuable historical evidence and searches for what the narratives reveal, even implicitly, about the concerns of the highland Malagasy who created and consumed them during the nineteenth century, they unveil much about what rulers and commoners said and did to manage their social relationships and reshape their culture during the time of the slave trade. The value of *Tantara* narratives lies in their historical outlook from the Merina cultural inside and in their insight into the domestic reasons for retention and erasure of historical memories of enslavement. The *Tantara* offer up these lessons, however, only when they are seen as historically produced and transmitted texts, as forms of "social action" in history.[186] Highland Malagasy oral traditions are less a passive "inheritance of the ears" (*lovan-tsofina*) than an actively generated interpretation of the past. In part 2 of this book, I examine when the narratives originated, how they were transformed by highlanders seeking to challenge their king, and why they came to be recorded in their current form. Inasmuch as this history of the origins and transformations of Merina identity and cultural practice examines the generation and uses of *Tantara* narratives through popular politics during the early nineteenth century, it also is a history of the social production and transformation of the narratives themselves, "a story of the story" as David Cohen puts it.[187] If oral tradition is history, this study is a history of oral tradition.

Supplementing the *Tantara* are two additional sets of Malagasy narratives employed in this book. The first is the work of British-educated highland Malagasy historian Raombana, secretary to Queen Ranavalona I (r. 1828–1861). Raombana's study as a youth in London and Manchester was funded by the British government in partial fulfillment of the provisions of a treaty effected in 1820 between the British Governor of Mauritius and King Radama of Imerina (the politics surrounding this treaty are examined in chapter 6). After living and studying for nine years in England, Raombana returned to Antananarivo in 1829 and during the following years wrote an extensive and insightful manuscript history of the Merina kingdom in English.[188] His work never circulated within Madagascar during his lifetime, however, for it developed less than a flattering image of the founder king and subsequent rulers of the Merina kingdom, especially challenging the legitimacy of the queen for whom he served as secretary (this criticism also was probably the reason Raombana chose to compose his work in English rather than in his native tongue). Because the manuscripts developed a censure of Merina royalty, Raombana kept them concealed among his personal effects. If the *Tantara* represents the most publicly approved, widely circulated, and recited of highland Malagasy historical narratives, Raombana's interpretation of Merina royalty was much less reverent and, it has been argued, exemplifies an alternative understanding of highland Malagasy history, a secretive counternarrative.[189]

This interpretation of Raombana's work is convincing when emphasis is placed on the author's lack of esteem for the rulers of the Merina kingdom and on the simmering enmity between them and his family. Raombana's ancestors had been displaced from power by those of the founder king, and hence it is not surprising he considered Andrianampoinimerina an immoral usurper to the kingship in highland Madagascar.[190] A general in the army of king Radama, Raombana's father was shot and burned sometime during the 1820s, accused of lack of resolve during a battle against the Antsihanaka north of Imerina.[191] Raombana also felt that Ranavalona I, his employer upon his return from England, was a tyrant and who illegitimately grabbed the throne of highland Madagascar in cooperation with some unscrupulous and power-hungry men of *hova* status. When one peels away Raombana's antiroyal rhetoric and examines his work for what it reveals about the economic and social policies of Andrianampoinimerina, however, the *Tantara* and Raombana's manuscripts appear extraordinarily congruous. If these two disparate sets of historical narratives advance differing judgments about the legitimacy of Andrianampoinimerina's rise to power, they both affirm the broad social popularity of his domestic policies (see chapter 5). What differs substantively in Raombana's work in comparison to the *Tantara* is that the former speaks more openly of the commercial bases of Andrianampoinimerina's power and demonstrates how popular politics and political violence were mutually reinforcing in the founder king's regime. The *Tantara*, on the other hand, tend to downplay Andrianampoinimerina's applications of violence, emphasizing instead his magnanimity and prudence, seldom detailing the founder king's commercial activities.

Even in the memory of individuals like Raombana who spun "counternarratives" of Andrianampoinimerina, the founder king espoused populist policies, backing them up, if needed, with the application of violence.[192] I am not suggesting that no fundamental rejection of Andrianampoinimerina expressed itself in contemporary narratives; undoubtedly it did. The point is that no such nineteenth-century narratives are today publicly articulated—they have been forgotten, actively or passively suppressed. Highland Malagasy historical memory is today remarkably uniform and positive about the founder king, an interesting contrast to the multiplicity of images of Shaka Zulu that have persisted, even multiplied, from the time of his life to the present.[193] In conversations with highland Malagasy during the 1990s, I found that Andrianampoinimerina was usually seen as a model for achieving national unity in the midst of an ethnically polarized modern politics. Highlanders now tend to emphasize two of the founder king's characteristics: his many wives from different parts of the island, creating national unity through affined ties, and his desire to unite Madagascar under his personal rule (in this connection most people mention his reputed claim that "the sea is the limit of my rice fields"). These views, of course, are not shared by many non-Merina. The historical development of a stereotypical (or metaphorical) image of Andrianampoinimerina in Malagasy narratives of varying authorship and political purpose, such as Raombana's *Histoires* and the *Tantara*, requires explanation. That explanation is an important goal of this book.

Andrianampoinimerina's highland enemies—a minority who numbered among the competing sovereigns of highland Madagascar, the most wealthy individuals and *firenena*, particularly those who drew an income from foreign trade, and the most independent-minded and autonomous kin groups—found little public platform for their grievances, even after his death. Those grievances reflected neither official policy nor popular sentiment. They have been effaced from social memory. Andrianampoinimerina was, and remains, a key heroic "site" of both memory and amnesia for highland Malagasy.[194] Because highland Malagasy historical narratives of varied origins converge in their opinion or social memory of Andrianampoinimerina, I often intersperse observations from the *Tantara* and Raombana's manuscripts in the chapters that follow. The two sets of narratives lead to similar conclusions about how highland Malagasy found certain images of Andrianampoinimerina useful in political struggles.

A third set of Malagasy narratives employed in this book includes 135 recorded interviews I conducted during fieldwork mainly in the Vakinankaratra region of central Madagascar at various times since 1989 (a full list of the interviews can be found in the bibliography). The Vakinankaratra interviews were conducted for a different project—a regional history of the Vakinankaratra during the second half of the nineteenth century—that was not completed because I was obliged for health reasons to depart prematurely from Madagascar during my original research stint. For the most part these interviews pertain to the histories of various *firenena* in the Soanandrariny-Antsirabe-Betafo-Ankazomiriotra axis of the Vakinankaratra

and provide an understanding of how *firenena* were socially formed in political upheaval and migration (most descent groups in the studied area claimed
to have originated in the vicinity of Antananarivo) and how they were differentially structured. Because the narratives are concerned primarily with local
descent groups and their founders, they shed more light on individual *firenena*
identities than they do on what it meant to be Merina, and they are not extensively employed here. What is most interesting about the *firenena* histories
with respect to this project is that the memories developed in them, as in the
Tantara, do not provide any substantive information about international commerce and enslavement for export, even though many of the narratives clearly
refer to population movements in highland Madagascar during the late eighteenth and early nineteenth centuries. These displacements were tied to the
export commerce and its sociopolitical impact on highland societies. What
many of these histories also reveal is that highlanders have made consistent
efforts over the years to link their descent group narratives to more widely
shared narratives of the sort found in the *Tantara*; the two genres did (and
do) not exist separately from each other. What they share is the same fundamental amnesia about the role of enslavement in highland Malagasy history
and, for the descent group histories, the influence of trade on the formation
of *firenena* at the beginning of the nineteenth century. For this project, the
Vakinankaratra interviews are particularly useful in chapter 4, where they
help to describe how some *firenena* were formed and reshaped during the era
of the slave trade.[195]

ORGANIZATION

The cultural impact of the slave trade was a sometimes diffuse and
complex process of cultural renovation mediated by individual decisions,
public opinion, popular rhetoric, and political activity in the age of enslavement and its ensuing decades. To demonstrate this, I have organized
this book into two parts, the first of which explores human strategies in
highland Madagascar's age of enslavement. Part 1 is largely a professional narrative of the traditional sort based primarily upon contemporary documentation rather than highland Malagasy social memory. Chapter 2 details the origins and development of the slave trade from highland
Madagascar to the Mascarenes, examining the organization of the trade
and identifying the various participants to it. The third chapter narrows
the investigation to enslavement itself, analyzing the variety of changing
ways in which export slaves were generated within highland Madagascar
through successive modifications of civic virtue. Chapter 3 closes with a
study of collective resistance to illegitimate enslavement by the
Ravoandriana and offers some reflections on the importance of sliding

African moralities of enslavement. To understand how highland Malagasy reshaped their culture in response to enslavement, I first examine, in chapter 4, how making and trading slaves reshaped economic and social relationships within highland Madagascar. Here I accentuate the differing strategies of highland Malagasy and their rulers in light of the opportunities, challenges, and disasters of the slave trade. The first part of the book, therefore, investigates a variety of ways in which highland Malagasy adjusted their social and economic behaviors to the export commerce in captives.

In the second part of the book, I reflect on how lives transformed by enslavement shifted cultural identities and practices. In part 2 the evidentiary emphasis shifts from contemporary European archived documents to highland Malagasy social memory, for a history of cultural transformation and ethnogenesis in highland Madagascar is impossible without attention to how highland Malagasy both remembered and disremembered their past. I begin in chapter 5 with a study of the domestic politics of founder king Andrianampoinimerina, public opinion concerning those policies, and the origins of a Merina political identity in them. Andrianampoinimerina's popular policies and the response of highlanders to them resulted in intentional and contingent modifications of cultural practice such as transformations in tomb architecture and mortuary ritual. They also shifted class and gender relationships. Chapter 6, which examines the reign of king Radama up to the Avaradrano women's revolt of 1822, is pivotal to the argument. After his rise to power in 1809, Radama reversed many of the popular policies of Andrianampoinimerina and soured his relationship with highland Malagasy rural communities. To advocate royal responsibility, commoners seized Merina political identity and employed it to make demands upon Radama. In the process, they memorialized Andrianampoinimerina and utilized those memories to challenge their new sovereign and to refashion their Merina identity into an ethnicity. Highland Malagasy expressed and sustained their sense of ethnic unity with popularized and moralized historical memories of Andrianampoinimerina. Chapter 6 is about the making of that social memory. In the first part of chapter 7, I reflect on the process by which highland Malagasy silenced histories of enslavement in their historical narratives, obliging scholars to turn to foreign sources for details of the slave trade. This final chapter uses the case study of highland Madagascar to argue that scholars must expand traditional definitions of the African diaspora to encompass all movements of African people, especially those within the Indian Ocean and the African interior. Comparative studies across the diaspora will enhance scholarly understanding of the diverse and ever-protean African identities refashioned through human dispersion in modern times. Highland Madagascar offers important lessons about the African diaspora.

In closing this introductory chapter, I would like to reflect on the intellectual and moral implications of this study. While working on this book I have become acutely aware that the lasting influences of enslavement in highland Malagasy society are so wide-ranging that it is virtually impossible to identify them all. Shaped by my own interests and predilections, this work only scratches the surface of those influences. If the impact of enslavement and the commercial revolution on insular Madagascar was profound and uncountable, historians have only begun to fathom the experiences of the tens of millions of Africans who enslaved and managed the consequences of enslavement on the mother continent. Seeking enrichment and protection, experiencing ineffable pain or the giddiness of newfound wealth and power, Africans refashioned their lives and their cultures in the age of the slave trade. By excavating these experiences now, I intentionally remember them for the future. My purpose is to explore the limits of quantitative history and to honor and memorialize all those who suffered under the intercontinental system of slavery, especially the family and kin who remained behind in the societies from which slaves were drawn. I also seek to demonstrate how Africans have been actively and creatively engaged in transforming their cultures over the last several centuries, even during times of social and economic upheaval resulting from engagement with mercantile capitalism. To accomplish these goals I must exorcise the historical amnesia of professional historiography, modern politics, and highland Malagasy social memory. *Ho fahatsiarovana ny hadino*; in memory of the forgotten.

PART I

ENSLAVEMENT

2

MOVING SLAVES

The wealth and power of Îsle de France is dependent on Madagascar.

—Duc de Praslin[1]

Of all the places where it [Île de France] trades, the only one that is indispensable to its present constitution is Madagascar, because of its slaves and cattle. Madagascar's islanders once contented themselves with bad muskets, but today they want Spanish piasters: everyone perfects themselves.

—Bernardin de Saint-Pierre.[2]

When in 1777 Andrianamboatsimarofy slipped unnoticed into the Andrantsay capital and enticed French merchant Nicolas Mayeur with trading opportunities in the environs of Antananarivo, he acted to draw his landlocked kingdom into the "commercial revolution" of the western Indian Ocean.[3] The primary nature of that connection, which is the subject of this chapter, was an export trade in slaves out of central Madagascar and into the French island colonies of Île de France and Bourbon, collectively known as the Mascarenes.[4] Supplied in exchange for manufactured trade goods and later for silver Spanish piasters, slaves trickled eastward out of central Madagascar well before the last third of the eighteenth century. Highland Malagasy slaves are attested at the east coast in the early 1760s, but were likely present in small numbers for several decades earlier.[5] That eastward trickle of captives became a gush just before 1770 as if a faucet had been suddenly screwed wide open. Sustained by complex and ever-shifting financial and organizational relationships among merchants, kings, chiefs, and commoners, the enslavement and transport of highland Malagasy to the Mascarenes endured for half a century, ending even more brusquely than it began when in 1820 king Radama of the Merina kingdom promulgated an interdiction prohibiting exports of slaves from his dominions.

The eastern-bound commerce in captives arose from a broader food and labor supply trade linking Madagascar and the colonial economies of the Mascarenes. Lacking an indigenous population and therefore a tradition of subsistence agriculture, the Mascarenes and their immigrants were dependent upon Madagascar and eastern Africa for servile labor and life-sustaining supplies of food.[6] The expense of moving bulky and low-value rice from Madagascar's highland interior 200 kilometers to the seaboard was too prohibitive to render a traffic in food of much interest to highland Malagasy merchants. The highlands of central Madagascar were so densely populated by comparison to most other regions of the island that few cattle could find pasture there among the human settlements and farms. For these two reasons most of the rice and beef that Madagascar supplied to the Mascarenes originated along the great island's coasts. The comparative density of population in highland Madagascar, however, meant that labor was a potential export. As in the Lake Nyasa region of east Africa, which emerged as a reservoir of slaves for the western Indian Ocean in the eighteenth century, people were in plentiful supply there and, unlike rice, slaves could move themselves toward the coast.[7] It was the opportunity for opening a profitable commerce in slaves from the Malagasy highlands that attracted merchants like Mayeur into the center of the island in 1777. He was richly rewarded for his efforts; kings like Andrianamboatsimarofy in the region of Antananarivo were prepared to sell him captives for export. Together, merchants and kings—and later the common people of the highlands—pushed the societies of central Madagascar into the mercantile economy of the western Indian Ocean.

DIRECTIONS OF TRADE

Despite the energy with which central Madagascar entered the eastern-bound export trade in captives by 1770, the people of highland Madagascar had long participated in extensive networks of intraisland and oceangoing trade, including an export trade in slaves.[8] Over the last two millennia the Indian Ocean has served as a sea of communication and commerce between Madagascar and the wider world, not an insurmountable barrier. Ancestors of the Malagasy first reached the island in successive migrations from southeast Asia and Africa on ships plying the prevailing trade routes of the Indian Ocean.[9] Archaeological surveys in central Madagascar have revealed Chinese celadon pottery in early seventeenth-century sites.[10] As early as the sixteenth and seventeenth centuries European visitors reported a flourishing commercial exchange between Madagascar's inland and its coasts.[11] Merchants from the interior hawked iron tools and weapons, articles of manufacture in central Madagascar, throughout the coastal areas.[12] "I found they deal

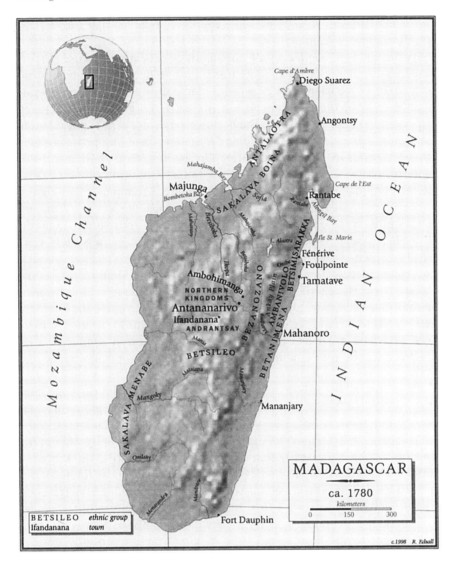

Map 2.1   Madagascar, ca. 1780

very much in metals of all kinds," wrote an English sailor of inland merchants in about 1710.[13] Silk, cotton, and banana bark textiles were a second
notable export of central Madagascar.[14] Highland traders journeyed along the
island's coasts while coastal merchants ventured into the Malagasy highlands.
The Sakalava living along Madagascar's western coast provided cattle to the
people of the interior and received fine silks, cottons, and iron tools in re-

turn.[15] Salt, silkworms, and raw silk were other important items introduced into the highlands from the south.

By the late eighteenth century, communities in central Madagascar participated in circuits of oceangoing trade through both the east and northwest coasts of the islands. The eastward- and northwestward-running trade were based upon discrete networks, histories, and organizations, yet they interacted in significant ways. The northwestern trade was connected into the regional commerce of the Indian Ocean conducted by peoples living around the rim of the sea and stretching back several millennia.[16] For centuries before Europeans entered the Indian Ocean, northwest Madagascar participated in this system as a southeast terminus for the commerce of the east African coast.[17] Seafarers speaking a variety of languages plied trade dhows between east Africa and destinations in northwest Madagascar. Malagasy participants in this commercial system were locally known as the Antalaotra, a Muslim, Malagasy-speaking population who sailed *boutry* (Malagasy dhows) along the Malagasy coastline and about the Mozambique Channel.[18] The eastern trade to the Mascarenes, on the other hand, developed only after Europeans occupied the uninhabited islands in the mid-seventeenth century. Unlike the more ancient trade between Madagascar and the African coast, the eastern commerce with the Mascarenes was conducted exclusively by European vessels, not Malagasy and African ones.

To an extent, central Madagascar's northwestward- and eastward-running systems of overseas commerce were separated through the navigational limitations imposed by wind-powered sailing technologies. Most of Madagascar lies south of the predictable and seasonally alternating rhythms of the northern Indian Ocean monsoons.[19] Still, surface wind patterns and ocean currents in the southwestern Indian Ocean limited when and where sailing vessels could readily navigate around Madagascar's coasts. A vigorous westward-flowing current in the waters north of Madagascar and the prevailing easterly trade winds that bluster there prevented vessels serving the Mascarenes from making timely return voyages between those islands and northwest Madagascar (the primary reason Swahili and Antalaotra settlements were largely limited to Madagascar's northwest coast). Sailing east from the Mozambique Channel across the northern tip of Madagascar and then southeast to the Mascarenes usually required a time-consuming and hence costly diversion nearly a thousand kilometers to the north to circumvent the countercurrents and capture favorable winds blowing in a southerly direction toward the Mascarenes. European vessels based at Île de France and Bourbon before the era of steam were therefore largely restricted by natural forces to voyages along Madagascar's east coast.

Jealously guarded spheres of political influence also served to separate central Madagascar's western trade from its eastern one. Sakalava chiefs ruling along the island's west coast were adamant that French traders who approached their shores did so by sea and not by land. Nicolas Mayeur narrowly escaped with his life at the hands of northern Sakalava king Tsimanompo in 1774 after seeking trade opportunities for the French by crossing the north of Madagascar by land from east to west.[20] French merchants were keenly aware that Muslim traders established along Madagascar's northwest coast, especially those at the primary commercial entrepôt of Bombetoka Bay, were formidable competitors with a sophisticated international network of contacts and generations of business experience in the region.[21] In this respect, European entry into the northwestern trade of Madagascar proved as difficult as similar ventures along the East African coast, where Africans, Arabs, and Indians operated extensively and efficiently.[22] The inhabitants of Madagascar's east coast, by contrast, were not seafarers with transoceanic connections, and Europeans faced significantly less commercial competition when conducting business there.

Despite the natural and political constraints that bifurcated central Madagascar's eastern and western trading systems, there were significant ways in which the two commercial networks intersected. Merchant vessels supplying the French empire in the western Indian Ocean traded from time to time along the west coast of Madagascar during their frequent passages through the Mozambique Channel. Braving contrary winds and currents, these vessels undoubtedly carried a few highland Malagasy slaves to the Mascarenes via Madagascar's northwest coast.[23] Sakalava and Muslim merchants regularly marched cattle from grazing lands along the west coast across the island and into Foulpointe, where they were loaded onto French ships supplying the Mascarenes.[24] Some merchants from the northwest even settled along the eastern littoral, facilitating and financing cattle fetched deep within western Madagascar.[25] This intercoastal commerce crossing the land appears to have been of some antiquity, reported by the early seventeenth century and moving in both directions.[26]

Toward the end of the eighteenth century, merchants from the northwest coast frequently conveyed slaves along the prevailing cattle paths from west to east. These slaves were primarily east Africans, imported into northwest Madagascar and then marched across the northern tip of the island to avoid the contrary winds and currents that obviated easy sailing between Bombetoka Bay and the Mascarenes.[27] At Madagascar's east coast they were transferred into French vessels for the last leg of the voyage to Île de France and Bourbon. Beginning in the late eighteenth century, part of the currency flowing into the highlands of central Madagascar from the east in exchange for exports of slaves was being reexported through the west coast, where it was employed to purchase Indian-manufactured textiles and east African slaves, among other items of commerce.[28]

Reflecting the variety of commercial systems that crisscrossed the island and linked it with surrounding economies in the western Indian Ocean over the last several centuries, Madagascar imported and exported slaves in several directions involving various parts of the island.[29] From central Madagascar itself, slaves traveled outward along the eastward and northwestward axes of trade discussed above. The northwest commerce in slaves was the older of the two, having existed for many centuries prior to the opening of commerce with the Mascarenes, and continuing well after that trade was closed in 1820.[30] As early as 1613 Portuguese missionaries in the Bay of Boeny on Madagascar's northwest coast reported slaves arriving from the Malagasy highlands.[31] Dutch seafarers of the same period noted the ubiquity of highland Malagasy merchants about ports along the northwest coast of the island.[32] During his mission of 1777 Nicolas Mayeur mentioned a northwestern slave trade conducted simultaneously with the eastern one. "The most considerable commerce that is conducted in the center of the island is that of slaves," he noted. "Two-thirds of those who are sold at the east coast come from there, without counting *those that they send to the west* where they sell to the Sakalavas, who themselves sometimes go to trade into the interior with herds of five or six hundred cattle."[33] A herd of 600 cattle in this period might have purchased between thirty and sixty slaves.[34] It is likely that some of these highland Malagasy slaves moved through the northwest coast were loaded onto vessels bound for the Mascarenes rather than conveyed to the east African coast. Jean-Claude Hébert reports that the French vessel *Victoire* took on 80 slaves at Bombetoka Bay in 1784, but it is unclear where those slaves originated.[35] The unknown volume of trade in slaves from highland Madagascar through the northwest coast probably declined during the late eighteenth century.[36] Although studies of the northwestern trade during the nineteenth century have yielded scattered estimates for the annual volume of exports, there is nothing to suggest what percentage of those export slaves originated in highland Madagascar as opposed to other regions of the island.[37]

The northwestern trade, then, accounted for an unknown percentage of captive exports from central Madagascar during the period covered in this book, yet Gwyn Campbell has written that its volume was "much smaller" than the eastern-running trade.[38] At the same time, the northwestern trade brought at least as many African slaves, known in Madagascar as "Mozambiques," into highland Madagascar as were exported from there.[39] These slaves were imported by Arab, Indian, Swahili, and Antalaotra merchants in the opposite direction to the export flow of highland Malagasy captives. Despite its longevity and influence as a conduit of Islamic culture into the Malagasy highlands, the northwestern commerce did not revolutionize highland Madagascar in the way European-carried trade toward the Mascarenes did. When the eastward-running commerce in slaves from central Madagascar gained momentum after 1770, it soon became of greater volume and political significance than the northwestern trade, for unlike the longer-term trade with the northwest, out of it arose a new highland kingdom and collective identity known today as Merina.

FRENCH INDIAN OCEAN EMPIRE

France was a latecomer to European expansion into the Indian Ocean and remained a minor player there into the twentieth century. French ships first rounded the Cape of Good Hope in the early seventeenth century and navigated primarily about Madagascar and the Mascarene islands.[40] Île de France and Bourbon, both of which are considerably smaller than Madagascar itself, lie 900 kilometers due east of central Madagascar in the Indian Ocean. The northern island (Île de France/Mauritius) was first occupied during the mid-seventeenth century by a Dutch East India Company refreshment station. By the early eighteenth century, however, the Dutch Company abandoned its colonization project to the Compagnie Française des Indes (The French Indian Company, hereafter "the Compagnie").[41] The southern island (Bourbon/Réunion) was sporadically occupied by French settlers and their Malagasy slaves during the mid-seventeenth century but it languished economically for nearly a century with only a handful of settlers.[42] During the early years of its presence in the Indian Ocean, the Compagnie was more interested in the economic potential of Madagascar than in the development of Île de France and Bourbon; Rigault, the founder of the monopoly Compagnie, had envisioned French colonies of trade in Madagascar as the Compagnie's primary goal. Pursuing its early vision of lucrative colonization in Madagascar, the Compagnie organized and financed several settlement schemes at Fort Dauphin in southeast Madagascar during the second half of the seventeenth century.[43]

When by the late seventeenth century a welter of violence between irascible French colonists and local Malagasy scuttled grandiose colonial visions of a thriving *France orientale* based at Fort Dauphin, the directors of the Compagnie claimed possession of Île de France in 1715. Given their recent and bitter confrontations with indigenous people in southeast Madagascar, the Compagnie's directors were particularly encouraged by the absence of a native population on the small islands. The Compagnie envisioned turning a profit from tropical agriculture in the Mascarenes, but in the short term it sought to operate refreshment stations for French vessels engaging in the eastern trade, as the Dutch had earlier attempted. When colonists from neighboring Bourbon and the metropole established themselves on Île de France, the Compagnie determined to retain its new Indian Ocean colony.[44] Despite the Compagnie's modest plans for the Mascarenes, however, the islands languished in economic mediocrity well into the eighteenth century. Lying beyond the most heavily sailed sea routes to and from India, the islands were infrequent stopping places for passing ships.[45] By the first third of the eighteenth century the population of Île de France comprised a mere 190 Europeans, 648 slaves, and some slave maroons (escapees).[46] Recognizing the limited potential for economic growth through provisioning passing vessels, the Compagnie dispatched Mahé de Labourdonnais, one of its illustrious captains, to the islands in 1735 with a mandate to explore tropical agriculture. During his tenure as governor (1735–1746) Labourdonnais investigated the prospects for coffee, indigo, and sugar. The governor's experiments with cash crops laid the foundation for later achievements in plantation agriculture. By midcentury a modestly increasing number of Compagnie ships began to call at island ports, and European immigration to the Mascarenes picked up marginally.[47]

Economic development, however, was hindered by the very condition that had attracted the Compagnie to the Mascarenes in the first place: the absence of an indigenous population. Europeans seeking fortune there were aplenty, but who would actually cultivate the envisioned plantations? Without an immigrant population that could be coerced into plantation labor, the colonies would not thrive. These problems once again shifted the Compagnie's attention westward toward Madagascar, the nearest populated land mass where agents of the Compagnie had already been trading for nearly a century. From the early decades of French occupation in the Mascarenes, then, Madagascar came to serve as "a warehouse or general reserve" of food and labor for the two small islands.[48] By the mid-eighteenth century, French economic interest in Madagascar was transformed. From the primary object of colonial desires, the grand island and its people were relegated to playing a support role for colonial development in the Mascarenes.

SUPPLYING THE MASCARENES

Seasonal rhythms of trade between Madagascar and the Mascarenes were largely governed by weather and climatic patterns in the western Indian Ocean. Because both Madagascar and the Mascarenes lie within the hurricane belt of the southwestern Indian Ocean, violent storms there during the austral summer lasting from December to May usually rendered navigation treacherous.[49] Anchoring along Madagascar's east coast also proved difficult during the summer, for in that season the winds shift from the southeast to the northeast and the open roadsteads of the nearly linear seaboard provide inadequate protection for sailing vessels.[50] The austral summer is also the rainiest season in the Malagasy interior. Due to the poor state of passageways along the principal commercial corridors of the island, and especially through the eastern forest, inland travel during the summer was nearly impossible. Because merchants could not move about easily during the summer, inland commerce was restricted to the drier winter months between June and November when passage was comparatively easy.[51] The rains likewise brought malarial fevers with great frequency to unseasoned Europeans and to Malagasy highlanders held at the east coast as captives. Merchants who ventured to remain on Madagascar's east coast and survived several consecutive summers developed a partial immunity to malaria, but they seldom cared to maintain highland Malagasy captives there between November and April lest they perish of fever (like Europeans, transient highlanders possessed little resistance to malaria and their mortality rates were said to be higher than those of newly arrived Europeans, sometimes 50 percent during the first year for highlanders never before resident there).[52] In light of the unpropitious weather and the risk of disease, many foreign merchants temporarily removed to the Mascarenes to sit out the malarial summer. For all these reasons, few Mascarene ships sailed to and from Madagascar between December and May, a period merchants referred to as the "dead season" (*la saison morte*).[53]

Like the trade in slaves from Senegambia to the Americas, the slave trade from central Madagascar to the Mascarenes developed out of a much broader spectrum of commercial relationships.[54] Early Mascarene supply trade along Madagascar's east coast consisted primarily of exports of rice and beef.[55] Export items of secondary importance included pork, timber, raffia cloth, raffia gunny sacks, raffia twine (raffia is the fiber of a palm tree), coffee, and gum copal.[56] The prohibitive cost of transportation by human portage from the interior of Madagascar to the east coast, which could easily double or triple the price of food supplies, meant that rice purchased by Mascarene merchants derived principally from surpluses produced along the coast.[57] Although the amount of rice available at any one coastal location varied dramatically from year to year, the most productive areas were Betanimena just to the south of Tamatave, the Iharana and Onibe rivers near Foulpointe, the region around Fénérive, and Antongil Bay.[58] Little or no rice could be obtained north of Cap de L'Est.[59] Judging by merchants' accounts, supplies of rice for export increased between the late eighteenth and early nineteenth centuries. In 1778 total export supplies of rice along the east coast were estimated at more than 1,250 metric tons; in 1784, 750 tons of rice were obtained from the region between Tamatave and Foulpointe alone.[60] In 1783 *traitants* Guiard and Le Guenne claimed—optimistically—that under the right circumstances the Mascarenes might obtain a combined total of more than 2,800 tons of rice from Tamatave, Foulpointe, Fénérive, Antongil Bay, and Angotsy.[61] In 1807 rice actually purchased by Mascarene merchants amounted to 1,000 tons from Tamatave, 400 tons from Foulpointe, and 600 tons from Fénérive.[62] In 1808 the export potential of the east coast north of Tamatave was evaluated at 2,500 tons annually,[63] and that of Île Ste. Marie and Rantabe at 1,000 tons.[64]

Marketed by men, rice was produced primarily by coastal women and slaves on the sides of hills (*tavy*) and in marshy areas called *horaka*, where soil partitions were raised to control the water.[65] Coastal people generally constructed *horaka* up to several kilometers behind the shore along rivers meandering into the seaboard plain.[66] Rice farmers completed their annual *grande récolte* during April and May at the onset of the drier season.[67] After farmers evaluated their crop, they began selling surpluses to the French in May and June. Europeans purchased all available surplus rice within a few months and little was again available until the next harvest.[68] Rice was priced according to its quality and by means of an elaborate bargaining process. Export rice of two general types—white and *gamella* (a unique Malagasy variety, reddish colored)—were each further divided into several subsidiary qualities.[69] Malagasy farmers and rice merchants negotiated prices for a trade unit called a *gamelle* that could vary with each transaction but usually weighed between five and ten *livres*, although sometimes it could reach as high as thirty (i.e., a *gamelle* could vary from 2.5 to 15 kilos).[70] In an attempt to hedge inflation at the Mascarenes by reducing the costs of imported food, Compagnie officials normally published ceiling prices merchants were authorized to pay their Malagasy suppliers for a *gamelle* of rice. Independent-minded traders, however, resented official intrusions into the market[71] and circumvented them by negotiating trade *gamelle* of different weights.[72] Rice was normally exchanged for manufactured trade goods such as muskets, cotton textiles, gunpowder, mirrors, flints, bullets, knives, and handkerchiefs.[73] Once they purchased rice, merchants had it packed in locally produced raffia gunny sacks for transport to the Mascarenes.

Although cattle supplied to the Mascarenes exited through the east coast, the area of supply spanned the northern and eastern regions of Madagascar. Some cattle intended for the export trade were raised along the east coast itself.[74] A significant minority of export cattle originated from the inland Ankay plain lying between the east coast and the central Malagasy highlands (homeland of the Bezanozano people). The majority, however, hailed from the Sakalava kingdom of Boina on Madagascar's northwest coast.[75] Losses of cattle due to injury during the often treacherous journeys to the east coast could be particularly high, yet the trade remained profitable for the Bezanozano and Sakalava cattle ranchers who earned a living from it.[76] Once they reached the east coast, merchant ranchers grazed their cattle at collection points near major ports and eventually loaded them onto European vessels.[77] Sailing ships normally charged between 200 and 500 cattle each and accomplished between one and three return trips a year, sustaining an average shipboard stock mortality between 25 and 50 percent on each crossing.[78] Malagasy owners bartered their cattle, like rice, for arms, ammunition, European manufactures, and Indian textiles. Merchants reported that live cattle supplies at the coast generally varied from 4,000 to 6,000 head each trading season during the last third of the eighteenth century, but estimates (some of them retrospective) vary considerably.[79] In 1768 officers of the French government estimated the cattle trade at between 4,000 and 5,000 head yearly.[80] In 1792 Dumaine reported that 3,288 live cattle were purchased, of which 1,989 had been exchanged for 130 barrels of gunpowder, 250 muskets, and 200 pieces of blue cloth.[81] During the first decade of the nineteenth century some 2,000 live cattle were annually loaded onto Mascarene-bound ships at Foulpointe alone.[82] Live animals were the most visible form of beef export but salted provisions, termed *salaisons*, consistently prepared from the fattest cattle, were normally taken on in significant proportion to livestock.[83] Mayeur, for example, claimed that just over 6,200 head of live cattle were exported annually from eastern Madagascar between 1770 and 1774 inclusive but, counting *salaisons*, 8,000 to 11,000 from Foulpointe alone.[84] Madagascar was the Mascarenes' butcher shop.

Along with rice and beef, slaves were a primary export from the east coast of Madagascar. The first recorded foreign purchases of eastern Malagasy slaves occurred during the early seventeenth century, effected by Dutch vessels on their way to the newly founded colony of Batavia.[85] Until 1770 the number of slaves purchased in Madagascar by French merchants supplying the Mascarenes was not large, a yearly average of some 500 between 1729 and 1768.[86] During the first two-thirds of the eighteenth century most Malagasy slaves transferred to the Mascarenes, like almost all the rice, originated in the narrow eastern coastal belt. In 1768, for example, Mananjary was said to have supplied a large proportion of export slaves by way of Foulpointe.[87] These early captives entering the Mascarene supply trade were largely victims of conflict among the coastal chiefdoms of eastern Madagascar. Later in the century, many slaves were conducted into the region of Foulpointe along interior trade routes from the northwest coast.[88] In general, however, the low-level Mascarene demand for slaves before 1770 seldom extended far into the interior of Madagascar. All this changed during the last third of the eighteenth century. Economic development at Île de France and Bourbon from 1767 transformed patterns of trade and slave supply in the western Indian Ocean, increasing the demand for slaves from Madagascar. The interplay between elevated Mascarene demand and political developments in Madagascar shifted the source of servile labor far into the Malagasy highlands.

THE SHIFTING GEOGRAPHY OF ENSLAVEMENT

The economic fortune of the Mascarenes brightened considerably when, crippled by ongoing financial losses and unable to properly administer the islands, the Compagnie was forced to cede them to the French crown in 1767. Two years later the French government issued an ordinance abolishing the trade monopoly of the Compagnie at the Mascarenes and allowing all French citizens the right to engage in commerce to and from Mascarene ports.[89] Trade liberalization triggered a sustained period of economic growth in the islands that was seriously interrupted only by periodic English blockades during the revolutionary and Napoleonic wars.[90] The European population of the Mascarenes soared after 1770. Concurrently, the number of privately owned vessels arriving at Mascarene ports more than doubled between 1773 and 1791 from 152 to 361.[91] Although the number of these vessels sailing annually between the islands and Madagascar varied dramatically, yearly arrivals from Madagascar more than tripled, from fewer than ten during the 1770s to thirty, forty, and even fifty or more by the turn of the century.[92]

Mascarene trade with Madagascar not only grew in absolute terms, it became proportionately more important over time. Until about 1785 only some 5 percent of the privately owned vessels arriving in Mascarene ports hailed from Madagascar. After 1785, however, there was an appreciable rise in this proportion to about 15 percent.[93] Mascarene demand for food and slaves from Madagascar expanded significantly in about 1770, rose rapidly from about 1780, declined again for an interim of five years between 1795 and 1800, and then grew dramatically until the end of the second decade of the nineteenth century. The available data confirm contemporary observations that the Mascarenes "flourished with the help of Madagascar."[94] As shipping costs declined and maritime ties between the Mascarenes and Europe became more frequent and reliable, plantation agriculture proved increasingly profitable. Colonists on Île de France and Bourbon expanded export-oriented cultivation of a variety of crops, including coffee, cotton, sugar, indigo, and spices.[95] To expand plantation production colonists increased their purchases of slaves, thereby intensifying European demand for servile labor on the Malagasy coast. In 1810 Britain captured the Mascarenes in its Indian Ocean campaigns of the Napoleonic wars. Although the importation of slaves to British possessions had been prohibited by an act of Parliament in 1807, the slave trade to the Mascarenes continued at even higher levels than during the previous decades as sugar production entered a boom from about 1815.[96] The slave trade reached a higher level than ever before, just as Radama cut the supply from its highland Malagasy sources in 1820.

Most of the Mascarene supply trade was concentrated along the northern portion of Madagascar's east coast, primarily between Tamatave and Antongil Bay (see Map 2.1).[97] Three principal reasons account for this geographical concentration of external commerce. First, as I have already pointed out, winds and currents just north of Madagascar rendered return voyages from the Mascarenes to Madagascar's northwest coast time-consuming and unprofitable; they restricted the supply trade primarily to Madagascar's east coast. Along the virtually bayless east coast, however, only a limited number sites between Tamatave and Antongil Bay offered adequate protection to anchored vessels during the austral winter. The principal locations of these anchorages were Tamatave, Foulpointe, Fénérive, Mahambo, Tintingue, Sainte-Marie, Mananara, and Antongil Bay. Most of the anchorages (the exceptions being Sainte-Marie and Antongil Bay) were created by a partially protective headland projecting outward into the sea, perpendicular to the beach. Outstretched headlands offered a fair defense from the prevailing southeasterly winds of the austral winter on their northern sides but little or no protection during the summer, when winds shifted to the northeast.[98] Thus the geomorphology of the coast played an important role in determining precisely where and when trade could take place. Finally, the differing sociopolitical organizations and predispositions toward enslavement among eastern coastal Malagasy societies served to render certain areas more attractive to European merchants than others. Although the French identified Fort Dauphin in southeast Madagascar as a potential area of supply early in their ventures into the Indian Ocean, the people of that region were loathe to sell many captives across the sea. (This may have stemmed, in part, from a long history of French violence in southeastern Madagascar.)[99] Throughout the eighteenth century and into the first decades of the nineteenth, Fort Dauphin seldom yielded more than 50 to 100 export slaves annually. Its Malagasy merchants, however, continued to supply beef (especially salted preserves, *salaisons*) and rice in significant quantities during this same period at barter prices considerably below those of Foulpointe and Tamatave.[100] Major commercial ports like Tamatave and Foulpointe benefited from their access to productive sources of slaves and food.[101]

Overseas trade afforded people living along Madagascar's northeast coast opportunities to accumulate wealth and profitably dispose of surpluses of rice and beef. As a result, virtually all chiefs in that area welcomed commercial opportunities with seafaring Europeans.[102] Much of the proceeds from the export supply trade were distributed by merchant chiefs among clients to generate and maintain ties of political allegiance.[103] Through this process, external trade emerged as a key force in coastal politics, enabling the amalgamation of chiefdoms into a political confederation—the Betsimisaraka kingdom—during the early eighteenth century.[104] When the Mascarene demand for rice, beef, and slaves began to increase during the mid-eighteenth century, Malagasy control over scarce anchorages between Tamatave and Antongil Bay became even more hotly disputed than it had before. During this period most Mascarene merchants operating in northeastern Madagascar relocated their operations to Foulpointe, the center of Betsimisaraka politics. With a population of some 12,000 in 1783, Foulpointe offered one of the better anchorages along the northeast coast; maturing trade links from the highland interior and the northwest coast terminated there.[105] In 1756 the governor of Île de France dispatched a *régisseur des traites* to Foulpointe.[106] An employee of the Compagnie, the *régisseur des traites* was responsible for maintaining amicable relations with Betsimisaraka chiefs, convincing them to supply slaves and food to Mascarene merchants, setting uniform trading prices and practices, and regulating conflicts between European traders and local communities. The *régisseur* and his successors were remunerated through commissions of between 1 and 10 percent on food and slaves delivered to the Compagnie and the royal government.[107] By 1760 most slaves arriving in the Mascarenes were loaded onto vessels anchored in the Foulpointe roadstead.[108]

Until midcentury Betsimisaraka chiefs administered the food and slave export trade in a relatively coordinated and cooperative fashion. When their leader Ratsimilaho died in 1750, however, the constituent chiefdoms of the confederation began to squabble among one another and the precarious coalition lost its coherence.[109] The problem, as one French observer noted, was that "since these chiefdoms are without any [written] constitution, a king becomes king only by the unanimous agreement of the chiefs."[110] Deprived of their charismatic leader and under the influence of Mascarene merchants who consistently and effectively meddled in Betsimisaraka politics, the chiefs fought among themselves.[111] Ratsimilaho's successors continued to reside at Foulpointe, but their authority waned considerably. Just when Mascarene merchants were being pressed to provide larger quantities of slaves, rice, and beef to Île de France and Bourbon in the years after trade liberalization in 1769, the trading environment at Foulpointe began to deteriorate. French *traitants* resident on Madagascar's coast attempted to increase the number of locally supplied slaves by encouraging disputatious Betsimisaraka chiefs to wage

Photograph 2.1   The erstwhile slaving port of Foulpointe. Like Tamatave and other ports of the east coast, Foulpointe was poorly protected from the open sea by a land spit to its south (seen here with trees). Physical and memorial traces of Foulpointe's slave-trading past have largely disappeared. (*Photo Credit*: Pier M. Larson, 1986.)

war against one another and to sell the prisoners thus captured.[112] The long-term effect of petty wars on the coast, however, was to increase social dislocation and the disruption of the food and slave trade rather than to improve it.

Instead of selling war prisoners to Europeans, Betsimisaraka chiefs retained them as ransom to exchange for members of their own kin who had been captured or might potentially be captured. Almost predictably, rice production plummeted during times of war and there were fewer agricultural surpluses for Europeans to purchase at the coast.[113] Victors in local conflicts routinely destroyed the losers' grain fields and plundered their stores of rice.[114] Mascarene ship captains were sometimes forced to return to the islands with empty vessels.[115] A state of war among eastern chiefdoms also rendered precarious the security of Europeans who traveled away from permanent residences. Both inland and on the coast, merchant caravans were the frequent target of mobile bandits. Markets in the interior remained unreachable.[116] Betsimisaraka chiefs yearned to share in the wealth of trade but found it difficult in their disunion to accumulate the capital necessary to outfit their own trading expeditions. Recalling a pervasive climate of insecurity that had reduced deliveries of rice, beef, and captives after 1760, Mayeur claimed in 1807 that the east coast was "governed by an ant's nest of little despots."[117] By the later decades of the eighteenth century, *traitants*' practice of exploiting Betsimisaraka political tensions to increase the supply of servile labor not only reduced the number of available slaves but cut into exports of rice and beef, generating anxieties in the Mascarenes.[118]

With political insecurity reducing commercial opportunities for Europeans at the coast, Mascarene traders and allied Malagasy merchants searched further afield for fresh sources of slaves. The quest led them into the densely populated highlands of central Madagascar. Why coastal merchants considered the interior a promising source of slaves at a time when supplies were declining at Foulpointe and its immediate hinterland must be sought in the politics of central Madagascar during the mid-eighteenth century, a time when highland Malagasy societies were politically divided much as the Betsimisaraka were. Historical narratives from central Madagascar characterize highland political disunity during the mid-eighteenth century through the metaphor of a magnificent united kingdom torn asunder. According to the story, an astute agricultural innovator named Andriamasinavalona succeeded in creating a single prosperous kingdom in the center of the island during the early eighteenth century. The tradition recounts how, as he approached death, Andriamasinavalona could not determine to whom among his four sons he would bequeath his kingdom. When he expired, therefore, he provided for the equal division of the kingdom among all four of his beloved sons, thereby fracturing the former union into multiple contentious minikingdoms.[119]

When Europeans first entered the Malagasy highlands in the mid-eighteenth century, sovereigns of several minikingdoms there were indeed competing to strengthen and expand their political domains. Political contention in central Madagascar was similar to that obtaining among the Betsimisaraka during the same period, but it led to a strikingly different outcome. Whereas war prisoners among the Betsimisaraka were held locally by groups of kin who hoped to use them to free their own enslaved members, captives in highland Madagascar were controlled by powerful kings without such concerns. Like their coastal counterparts, highland Malagasy sovereigns sought opportunities for accumulating trade wealth. A rapidly increasing demand for slaves at the Mascarenes dovetailed with political conflict in central Madagascar. In a quest for new sources of wealth to distribute along networks of political clients, some highland Malagasy leaders began to sell war captives toward the coast (more on this in the next chapter). By 1777, when Mayeur traveled to Antananarivo, highland Madagascar supplied a full two-thirds of the slaves shipped to the Mascarenes through Madagascar's east coast.

THE PARTIES TO COMMERCE

Pirates lingering about Madagascar's coasts during the late seventeenth century were among the earliest brokers of Malagasy slaves to European settlers at the Mascarenes.[120] Ejected from the Caribbean, some pirates married into Malagasy chiefly families and insinuated themselves and their descendants into powerful political positions along the east coast (there being no competition along that coast from Muslim traders). Pirates and their descendants (locally known as the *zanamalata*, from *zanaka*, child, and *malata*, mulatto) arranged sales of slaves from coastal suppliers to European merchants serving most destinations in the Western Hemisphere. Much of the Mascarene demand for food and labor during the late seventeenth century was channeled through such European outlaws.[121] After the second decade of the eighteenth century, when Mascarene economies experienced their first successes in tropical agriculture, the French regained an interest in Madagascar as a granary and labor reserve. They attempted to displace the pirates and control the trade through a Compagnie des Indes monopoly and direct colonization schemes on the Malagasy coast. Nearly every large-scale French attempt at colonization in Madagascar, however, foundered in violence.[122] When the trade monopoly of the Compagnie des Indes was abolished in 1769, the royal government assumed the exclusive right to conduct the supply trade in Madagascar. In practice, contracts for the royal monopoly in food and slaves were frequently signed with private firms, and Mascarene authorities allowed many private traders, or *traitants*, to negotiate for slaves, cattle, and rice and ready them for shippers. Although "free" trade was opened to all French citizens only after 1796, both the Compagnie and the royal administration that followed it in 1769 protected and even promoted private commerce. Individual Mascarene merchants long played a vital role in the Madagascar trade.[123] By 1787 there were ten *traitants* resident at Foulpointe; by 1792, twenty.[124] The number increased even further after the 1796 liberalization. In 1807 the French *agent commercial* (who had replaced the *régisseur des traites*) enumerated six *traitants* living permanently and six seasonally at Foulpointe, and seven permanently and ten seasonally at Tamatave, for a total of twenty-nine.[125]

Because many of the documents they generated found their way into colonial archives in Mauritius, France, and England, French *traitants* are the most visible actors in the complex mercantile systems that moved slaves from the Malagasy interior to the coast. Yet they were but one set of persons with interests in the Malagasy slave trade. Sovereigns in the highland Malagasy

interior attempted to control the drift of slaves from their dominions. Like
Andrianamboatsimarofy at Antananarivo, many of these rulers were keen to
attract slave merchants into their realms. Between the Malagasy highlands
and the east coast, various chiefs and big men also sought to manage the
movement of captives through their dominions and derive an income from
the commerce as it passed in both directions. Then, of course, there were the
merchants themselves who moved slaves between the interior and the coast.
Contrary to the dominant pattern in most of the African continent where
Africans or *métis* populations specialized in the movement of slaves to the
coast, some of these merchants were Europeans. Mascarene *traitants* organized and led some caravans into the interior of Madagascar and purchased
slaves directly from highland suppliers. Malagasy suppliers actively promoted
such European caravans because they found that itinerant merchants from
the coast were willing to pay premium prices for slaves in the highlands,
having already assumed the risks of conducting an expedition into the interior. For a *traitant* to return to the coast with expensive slaves purchased in
large measure with silver was less financially ruinous than returning with
none at all.[126] *Traitant*-led caravans were composed primarily of Malagasy
porters and associated merchants from the east coast of the island.[127] While
some Malagasy merchants operated under the supervision of *traitants*, many
participated independently in the trade and probably moved the majority of
slaves eastward toward the coast. Among the Malagasy merchants, most until
about 1800 were Betsimisaraka from the east coast who maintained alliances
with Mascarene traders, accessing French mercantile credit by right of their
homeland's proximity to the coast. Over time, however, an increasing number of merchants from highland Madagascar itself, often acting on behalf of
or sponsored by kings from the interior, created a commercial niche for themselves in the export trade. Highland merchants came to significantly displace
coastal traders during the early nineteenth century. Along the sinuous trade
routes linking the Malagasy coast with its interior, a variety of individuals
with interests in the slave trade hovered, some of them stationary, others on
the move. Let me consider each of these participants in turn.

Highland Malagasy who entered the Mascarene trade as captives were
enslaved by kings, social elites, and later by more common people through
methods to be investigated in the next chapter. For the most part these slaves
were exchanged by highland Malagasy suppliers to itinerant merchants who
moved them eastward, but under conditions that highland kings sought to
control so as to tax the revenue that flowed into their kingdoms as a result.
Traitants who ventured into the Malagasy highlands to purchase slaves directly from local suppliers usually did so with the permission and cooperation of the rulers through whose realms they traveled. Whether or not they
personally owned the slaves sold to merchants, Malagasy sovereigns attempted

to control the trade by decreeing exchange values and requiring merchants to request trading permission through presentation of gifts, sometimes exceedingly lavish ones.[128] Rights to purchase slaves and transport them out of the kingdom were then normally granted in exchange for the payment of a "taxe des noirs" for each captive taken westward.[129]

British missionaries explained the fate of highland Malagasy export slaves in the following terms.

> When the traders had obtained a sufficient number of slaves at the capital [i.e., Antananarivo], or any part of the interior, by purchase or exchange of goods, they were conveyed in parties varying from fifty to two thousand, down to the sea-coast for exportation. On commencing the journey, their wrists were usually fastened by means of an iron band. They were then corded one slave to another, and through the whole distance compelled to carry provisions on their heads. Thus driven like cattle to the sea-side, they no sooner arrived there, than they were stowed away in ships, and conveyed to their final and fatal scene of misery and toil, unless their sufferings terminated in death during the passage.[130]

The journey eastward was not as simple as this passage suggests, for the geography and ecology of eastern Madagascar facilitated local control over the movement of people and goods. As they trekked eastward from the highlands to the coast, merchants and slaves traversed two distinct ecological zones. Just beyond the modern town of Manjakandriana in Madagascar's eastern highlands, a steep escarpment plunges several hundred meters over the distance of a few kilometers. Beyond that escarpment lies a narrow plain oriented north–south extending some thirty kilometers wide and several hundred long. Called the Ankay, the southern part of this expansive plain is replete with hills that rise from the surrounding level. Through the Ankay runs the Mangoro River, flowing first southward, then eastward through the mountains, emptying into the Indian Ocean near Mahanoro. Persons moving across the Ankay plain could easily be monitored from the promontories that dot it. Employing the unique topography of their homeland, Bezanozano chiefs who ruled this fertile zone attempted to establish control over commerce passing between central Madagascar and the east coast.[131] In 1790 French trader Dumaine reported considerable difficulty passing with his slave caravans through the Bezanozano chiefdoms of the Ankay plain.[132] To protect their role as intermediaries, Bezanozano chiefs attempted to prohibit coastal merchants from venturing any further than the eastern edge of the Ankay plain, and highland Malagasy suppliers, who lay on the western side of the Ankay, any further than their western border.[133] When Mayeur traveled into central Madagascar in 1777, he chose to march far south of the Ankay to circumvent

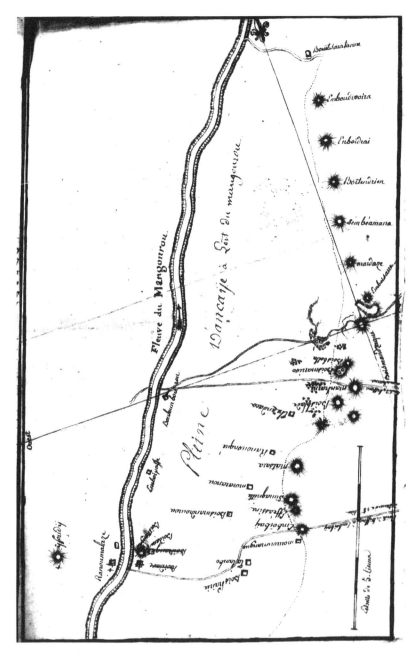

Map 2.2 The Ankay plain, ca. 1807, sketched by Chardenoux. From their hilltop locations, Bezanozano chiefs of the Ankay sought to control the east-west flow of commerce through their homeland. Chardenoux lost several female slaves from his caravans to raiders from these villages in 1807. This map was enclosed in a report Chardenoux delivered to Sylvain Roux, the French *agent commercial* at Tamatave. (*Source*: ADC/FD/101/178v.)

the Bezanozano altogether (he exited the highlands through the very southern tip of Bezanozanoland).[134] Caravans that attempted to break through Bezanozano territory without securing permission and paying transit tolls were often attacked.[135] In 1807 Bezanozano bandits attacked *traitant* Chardenoux's caravan and seized twenty captive women and five men.[136] As strategically located intermediaries to the trade between the highlands and the coast, Bezanozano chiefs employed the geography of the Ankay to derive an income from the slave trade (see Map 2.2).

East of the Ankay lay a tropical forest that blanketed the mountainous transition between the high Ankay plain and the low coastal areas. Different from the open flat Ankay, forest ecology was equally suited to regulating the movement of trade. Surreptitious travel by slave caravans, even under cover of thick rain forest, was practically impossible. Individuals carrying loads, herding cattle, or moving coffles of slaves were constrained by the density of vegetation to employ established passageways. Because of this constraint on free movement, the Ambanivolo people (literally, "those beneath the bamboo") who inhabited the mountainous forest and derived their livelihood from it were able to exert significant control over the movement of trade through their homeland.[137] Unlike the Bezanozano, who preferred to function as trading intermediaries by holding slaves between transactions, Ambanivolo allowed merchants and their caravans to pass through the forest but charged tolls, collected gifts, served as porters, and embraced opportunities to sell food and supplies to transiting trade caravans.[138] In 1808 *traitant* Lagardère reported that caravans normally halted for two days at the largest Ambanivolo town of Beforona, allowing porters to rest and servants to prepare ropes of vegetal matter for fastening slaves together on the return trip. The chief of Beforona routinely collected a trade tax of one piaster per slave exiting eastward through his territories.[139] During the era of the slave trade, Ambanivolo villages crystallized along primary forest pathways. The openness and ease of sight offered by the Ankay plain and the necessity for employing defined paths in the forest offered people inhabiting each ecological zone a degree of ease in establishing control over and taking economic advantage of trade pulsing through their homelands.

At the coast, Betsimisaraka chiefs also sought to derive a revenue from the slave trade by assessing tolls on merchants conveying captives through their realms. Sylvain Roux, the French *agent commercial* in 1807, noted that a certain coastal chief named Maroubé had established himself at an important crossing on the Ivondro river at a place called Bocarine, just kilometers south of the trade entrepôt of Tamatave. In his strategic position at a water crossing, Maroube appropriated communications between Tamatave and the Ambanivolo, obliging all passing merchants to reward him with tolls and gifts.[140] Roux and other *traitants* often noted that Betsimisaraka chiefs did

not directly tax their own people. Instead, they relied for their principal income upon trade and a variety of payments from merchants residing in and
passing through their domains. In this way, they quickly became dependent
on the Indian Ocean trade for both their livelihood and the reproduction of
their power.

Because individuals with competing commercial interests battled for control over various segments of the land-based trade, some slaves traveling
eastward changed hands at ecological, ethnic, and political transitions.[141]
During the first years of the trade, highland merchants marched their slaves
to the western edge of Bezanozanoland. There slaves were purchased by
Bezanozano intermediaries who held them until Ambanivolo, Betsimisaraka,
and European merchants arrived to make purchases of slaves and locally raised
cattle. Slaves and cattle were then marched to east coast ports and delivered
to French merchants.[142] Because Bezanozano and Ambanivolo chiefs benefited from their advantageous position between inland and coastal traders,
and particularly because Bezanozano merely held slaves between transactions instead of moving them toward the coast, they were deeply resented by
inland kings and itinerant coastal merchants alike. On occasion before 1780,
merchants like Mayeur found their way directly into the highland Malagasy
interior. Because they were forced to dodge Bezanozano and Ambanivolo
middlemen along the way, however, foreign merchants seldom encountered
suppliers before 1780. French merchants who successfully reached highland
kings were keen to determine the potential of inland societies to supply slaves,
and they communicated their desire for slaves directly to those able to supply them.[143]

In an effort to enhance their mobility and security along the commercial
routes into the interior, itinerant European *traitants* were quick to enlist
Malagasy allies. Because success in the Madagascar trade required persistence and an ability to forge trusting relationships with potential Malagasy
suppliers and merchant allies, most *traitants* learned enough of the Malagasy
language to obviate a need for interpreters.[144] In their private journals they
sometimes freely exchanged Malagasy and French words.[145] The *Grand
dictionnaire de Madagascar*, a manuscript Malagasy–French dictionary drawn
up by Barthélémy Huet de Froberville early in the nineteenth century, was
based primarily on French merchants' knowledge of the Malagasy dialects
of the eastern coast and interior.[146] Blood brotherhood, the Malagasy practice
of *fatidra*, was also a favorite strategy merchants and their Malagasy suppliers employed to cement commercial relationships with strangers.[147] Despite
(or because of) their competence in Malagasy cultures, *traitants* soon discovered that Malagasy women proved highly reliable and efficient trade associates in addition to cherished companions and sexual partners. The wives
of Malagasy chiefs living along the trade routes, for example, often accepted

advances of trade goods and readied supplies of food for slave-laden caravans on their return to the coast.[148] *Traitants* obtained some of their most valuable intelligence, including reports that local men were planning to plunder caravans, from women along the primary trade corridors.[149] Local women commonly took up European merchants in temporary sexual unions. Daniel Lescallier, who visited the east coast in August 1792, noted the following about these "wives of European traders," or *vadinebazaha* as they were called in Malagasy.

> A white arrives in Madagascar; he chooses himself a woman, who, from that moment, regards herself as attached to him, and this engagement lasts generally with fidelity until the departure of the foreigner from the country. It is she who looks after his interests and directs his business. It is by her as well that all commercial transactions with the natives are conducted. A European would have many difficulties concluding his business without the intervention of his faithful companion, who follows him everywhere. This type of contract, the only marriage they know, is terminated at the departure of the foreigner, with the same facility that it was concluded at his arrival.[150]

In exchange for tying foreigners into local communities, providing them access to land, smoothing difficult relationships with local leaders, and furnishing caravans with needed supplies and food along the way, female trade partners generated personal income and a network of friends and associates for themselves.[151] Such women were the primary retailers of imported arrack rum in Malagasy communities.[152] These *femmes de traite*, as the francophone community termed them, were also key players in the slave trade.[153] Although nearly invisible in most of the documentation historians employ to reconstruct this period, *vadinebazaha* were "very useful for our interests," noted Mayeur, essential allies to the profitable success of the Mascarene trade.[154] Well-known traders like Barthélémy Hugon never ventured anywhere without their Malagasy female business associates.[155] In the final decade of the trade (1810–1820), some *traitants* even engaged women to lead their caravans into the highland Malagasy interior.[156] The importance of female business companions to the success of the Mascarene supply trade was later recognized by French colonial officials, who during the early nineteenth century consistently encouraged unions between European traders and local Malagasy women.[157] While the majority of captives were male, as will be examined in chapter 4, Malagasy women from the coast and from the hinterland areas that slaves transited on their dreary march from the highlands to the east coast all eagerly sought the opportunities participation in slaving might bring.

Like women slavers in the coastal areas of certain parts of west Africa, female slavers in Madagascar advanced their business interests and social status through alliance with foreign merchants.[158]

Employing a variety of social strategies, much as their Muslim counterparts did from the Swahili coast in the early nineteenth century, *traitants* secured the right to make direct slave-purchasing expeditions into the Malagasy interior by about 1780.[159] Yet they continued to suffer periodic setbacks and endemic insecurity along trade routes until the very end of the trade in the second decade of the nineteenth century. In Bezanozanoland six separate slave caravans conducted by European *traitants* were attacked between 1803 and 1807, resulting in the loss of 46 captives, most of them women (although most captives were men, Bezanozano specifically removed women from the caravans).[160] "Our commerce at Tamatave is absolutely destroyed if the roads to Ancove are not free," complained Sylvain Roux in late 1807.[161]

While they were solving passage problems through the interior, *traitants* faced challenges at the coast. In Foulpointe the French establishment and its associates came under pressure from Zakavola, who had risen to the local chiefship in 1791. "Rich in rice and eminently defiant," one French merchant complained, coastal Malagasy jealously guarded their role as brokers between inland suppliers and the French at the east coast.[162] Following several acrimonious disagreements between himself and Mascarene *traitants*, Zakavola attacked the residence of the French *agent commercial* and attempted to assassinate several resident European traders.[163] At about this time Mascarene merchants began to flee southward from Foulpointe to escape Zakavola's depredations, establishing themselves at Tamatave. The demise of Foulpointe as the externally recognized center of export trade was sealed when in 1796 British warships appeared off the town and pummeled the French *palissade* (walled fort) with cannon.[164] What the British navy left of the fortress, local Betsimisaraka burnt to the ground.[165] Insecurity at Foulpointe led to declining use of a passage for slaves from highland Madagascar through Antsihanaka and the northern Bezanozano to the east coast.[166] Together with the destruction of the French establishment at Foulpointe in 1796, the closing of the Antsihanaka route, and the flight of traders southward, the preference of highland merchants for the new export center at Tamatave insured that by 1800 it emerged as the new commercial entrepôt on the east coast to which most Mascarene vessels seeking slaves and food ventured. In 1807 the French government accorded Tamatave official recognition by making it the new seat of its *agent commercial*.[167] Although Foulpointe's new king Sasse and French *traitants* carried their mutual animosities well into the nineteenth century,[168] Tamatave remained the premier port through which highland slaves were channeled toward the Mascarenes until the end of the eastward trade from highland Madagascar in 1820.[169]

Credit provided a necessary lubricant for the movement of highland Malagasy slaves eastward toward the coast. Lines of credit ran like pipelines into the Malagasy interior, tying both participants and victims into the imperial economy of the western Indian Ocean. While some French *traitants* resident at the coast employed their own capital, many borrowed funds at interest from the shipping firms to which they delivered slaves or from the French government trade representative and a variety of other sources.[170] Merchant creditors tended to remain at the Malagasy coast while those who incurred debts during the course of the trading season were most likely to itinerate in search of captives. Sylvain Roux reported this mercantile hierarchy, noting in 1807 that six or seven *traitants peu fortunés* (*traitants* of little wealth) routinely traveled into the Malagasy highlands on commission for those who, because of their greater wealth, were not obliged to undertake the physical rigors of a several weeks' expedition.[171] Betsimisaraka merchants also traveled on commission for French *traitants*, who backed them with operating capital.[172] In this system of movers and stayers, the majority of merchants who purchased, transported, and sold captives eastward—those who assumed the risks and potential profits of holding slaves—were Betsimisaraka operating on a relatively small scale, obtaining credit advances in silver piasters and trade goods from their European associates at the beginning of the winter trading season and returning with deliveries of slaves at the end.[173] When French *traitants* themselves set out on caravan expeditions into the interior, they normally returned to the coast with between fifty and one hundred captives.[174] Although few data exist to estimate the average size of Betsimisaraka-operated caravans, they were probably of smaller scale than these, reflecting a more modest operating capital. On the other hand, coastal Malagasy merchants tended to cooperate with one another, aggregating their resources and traveling in groups to offer mutual assistance and consult with friends on financial matters.[175]

From the opposite end of the land route and acting with the permission and assistance of kings in central Madagascar, highland Malagasy merchants also wedged their way into the commerce in captives. Limited by available capital and lines of credit from hinterland kings, highland merchants clearly operated on a more limited scale than French *traitants* did. Over the years, however, they moved ever larger numbers of slaves toward the east coast.[176] Two of the chief obstacles facing highland merchants were lack of familiarity with trading procedures at the east coast, where slaves entered European vessels, and concerted attempts by their coastal Malagasy competitors to impede their business. Highlanders overcame these difficulties through a variety of strategies. To insure continuity and contacts on both ends of the system, some highland merchants created a trade diaspora by settling in Tamatave with their families to coordinate transfers of captives onto European vessels.[177] In 1808 at least 10 percent of the slaves boarded at Tamatave were conveyed to the coast by highland Malagasy merchants acting for king Andrianampoinimerina.[178] Direct cooperation with French *traitants*, who shared a general interest with highlanders in bypassing Bezanozano, Ambanivolo, and Betsimisaraka intermediaries, was another way in which highland merchants sought to carve out a role for themselves in the trade. The benefits of this cooperation were reciprocal; often highland agents with whom *traitants* left piasters and trade goods in the Malagasy interior acquired slaves for their French allies.[179] Andrianambo, a local representative of Andrianampoinimerina in the Ankay plain, assisted Chardenoux in recovering some of the slaves stolen from his caravan there in 1807. When a few of the plundered captives were not returned, Andrianambo threatened to crush Bezanozano chiefs with a simultaneous assault by French and highland armies converging from opposite directions.[180] Andrianampoinimerina, the rising king of the Malagasy interior, often made war on Bezanozano middlemen, claiming (with some justification) that they were but escaped and recalcitrant cattle herders of highland Malagasy royalty.[181] A highly successful merchant monarch as will be explored in chapter 4, Andrianampoinimerina alternately negotiated and waged war with Bezanozano for safe passage of his itinerant merchants.[182] In 1808 the French *agent commercial*, Sylvain Roux, reported that highland Malagasy merchants routinely paid a local chief 1,000 piasters each year for the right to pass through his territory with their slaves.[183] When in the early nineteenth century British missionaries observed that "it is obvious that many different parties felt an interest in the continuance of the trade," they understood the local complexities of the commerce in slaves.[184] Slaves were moved from highland Madagascar to the east coast through an intricate maze of competing actors, interests, and strategies.

SILVER AND COMMERCIAL STRATEGIES

While textiles of various colors and qualities, muskets, gunpowder, flints, lead bullets, knives, mirrors, brandy, arrack (rum), and other manufactures were frequently exchanged for slaves along the east coast well into the nineteenth century,[185] Malagasy suppliers who entered the Mascarene trade demanded silver from at least the middle of the eighteenth century.[186] From the late 1760s, Malagasy merchants and suppliers required purchasers to pay for significant proportions of their captives in European currency, the silver Spanish piaster (called *ariary* or *farantsa* in Madagascar, see Photograph 2.2).[187] Authorities in France forbade cir-

Photograph 2.2   The two faces of the Spanish piaster. The piaster was an 8 *reales* piece with the portrait of Charles III (king of Spain) on one side and columns on the opposite face. This particular coin, minted in 1776 in the Spanish Americas, is made of South American silver. The "magnificent" coin and others like it with columns on the face opposite the portrait were among those most favored by highland Malagasy in payment for delivery of slaves during the late eighteenth and early nineteenth centuries. (*Source*: J. et S. Chauvincourt, *Les premières monnaies introduites à Madagascar* [Tananarive, 1968], 31.)

culation of French minted currencies outside the metropole, so the Spanish piaster emerged as the most commonly utilized medium of exchange at the Mascarenes.[188] The Compagnie did not begin to employ silver piasters in the Indian Ocean until the 1740s.[189] With no island sources of silver, highland Malagasy turned to external supplies. The first piasters to reach central Madagascar were probably supplied into the interior by Sakalava and Antalaotra merchants who participated in the trading system of the western Indian Ocean through Madagascar's northwest coast, acquired silver from Arab, Swahili, and European merchants, and then exchanged it for slaves, iron, or textiles from the interior.[190] As late as midcentury silver was valued in the Malagasy highlands primarily for the production of jewelry rather than as a currency of exchange.[191] But when Mascarene merchants projected a fresh demand for slaves into central Madagascar around 1770, highlanders were already familiar with silver coins. Because Malagasy valued silver and employed it in a variety of ways, and because the piaster was an important currency of exchange in the western Indian Ocean, the coin emerged by the middle of the eighteenth century as a convenient medium of comparison (or money of account) for commercial transactions in the Mascarene supply trade.[192] This meant that the values of slaves and European trade goods were usually set in piasters to determine what proportions of various trade goods would be acceptable in payment for delivery of captives.[193]

As suppliers of slaves in the Malagasy interior and merchants along the way refused to accept payment entirely in kind—demanding quantities of silver among the bundle of goods exchanged for captives—they converted the piaster from a medium of comparison into a currency of exchange. Slaves in the Malagasy interior were routinely exchanged for a basket of goods including gunpowder, muskets, textiles, and significant amounts of silver piasters.[194] By 1807 one trader reported that slaves were trading for forty-five piasters and two pieces of blue cloth in the highland interior, suggesting that silver currency had come to constitute more than 80 percent of the exchange value of captives (valued at five piasters each piece, the two *pièces toile bleue* in this transaction would have comprised 18 percent of the transaction by value).[195] In 1808 Rondeaux indicated that highlanders generally purchased slaves in exchange for varying quantities of piasters, gunpowder, textiles, and muskets—in that order.[196] Rondeaux's generalization is confirmed by an inventory of *traitant* Lagardère's exchange items established just after his arrival in Antananarivo in 1808. Lagardère's list of trade supplies shows 5,390 piasters and 193 pieces of blue cloth (the latter having a value of 965 piasters at the price of five piasters per piece), and thus his inventory showed a piaster-to-textile ratio of 85 to 15 percent by value.[197] For some reason Lagardère omitted twenty barrels of gunpowder from this inventory but reported having exchanged all twenty barrels for thirty-one slaves, or a value of approximately eighty-five piasters per barrel.[198] Figuring the value of the gunpowder into Lagardère's stock of cloth and piasters produces a value ratio of 67 percent piasters, 12 percent textiles, and 21 percent gunpowder. *Traitants* frequently noted that highland slave suppliers insisted they be paid with "magnificent" silver piasters rather than with trade-quality European manufactures.[199] The negotiating acumen of highland suppliers is captured in the following anti-Semitic journal entry penned by Barthélémy Hugon on May 3, 1808.

> Still good weather without clouds. Continued to purchase male and female slaves with great difficulty because one has to speak at great length with these people, who are merchants to the last point. They are so adroit, they insinuate, knowing very well how to engage you, caressing their merchandise. Even though you tell them that their slaves do not suit you, they are not at all discouraged. They remain with you, speaking to you mysteriously and often they succeed in seducing you, and you purchase. I believe that I can call them the Jews of Madagascar.[200]

The exchange of slaves for overwhelming proportions of silver in the export trade from highland Madagascar contrasts sharply with payment practices in the transatlantic slave trades from Africa, where European currency imports represented on average only about 10 to 15 percent of the basket of goods exchanged for slaves.[201]

The movement toward piasters as a medium of exchange considerably increased the cost of Malagasy slaves at the Mascarenes and contravened the French mercantile principle that captive labor should never be exchanged for hard currency. Yet shippers and merchants who desired to excel in the business of supplying slaves to the Mascarenes were constrained to part with silver coins in Madagascar. Liberalization of trade at the Mascarenes in 1769 and the full opening of the Madagascar trade to French citizens in 1796 sent private traders to Madagascar in increasing numbers. During the months of the dry austral winter European merchants who had earlier remained along the coast began to fan out through the Malagasy interior seeking new trade partners. "They have established isolated posts where the natives of the country bring them their slaves, their rice, and their cattle," reported one informant to the governor of the Mascarenes in about 1807. He proceeded to note that "they occasion by this means a commerce of great prejudice to those *traitants* who do not leave the coast."[202] The intense competition that resulted from new commercial practices beyond the regulation of Mascarene authorities both increased prices and persuaded competing slave traders to pay for slaves with piasters rather than insist on barter and risk forfeiting the sale to a competitor who offered to settle in silver.[203] A successful Mascarene merchant operating along the east African coast scoffed at his *traitant* colleagues in Madagascar who made "cash payments in piasters . . . in haste to be off on their return voyage."[204] Acquiring captives for minted silver rather than for a bundle of assorted trade goods increased costs to Mascarene purchasers between 25 and 50 percent (depending upon precisely what mix of trade goods is employed in the comparison), since the prices European manufactures fetched in Madagascar were considerably higher than those for the same products purchased with silver at the Mascarenes.[205] Malagasy merchants of slave labor commanded a commodity in meager supply in the western Indian Ocean, and they knew they could successfully demand payment in silver from their European clients.[206] The great island's suppliers knew how to "put circumstances to their profit," Nicolas Mayeur opined.[207]

If we shift focus to consider the interests of the highland Malagasy suppliers of slaves, it becomes clear that the increasing demand for and exchange value of slaves over the half-century before 1820 served as incentives for continued participation in the commerce. One of the ways to judge the steadily rising value of slaves in the Mascarene trade is to compare, over time, the relative prices of captives and cattle, the two primary Malagasy stores of wealth during the eighteenth and nineteenth centuries.[208] In 1769 Mayeur noted that the price of slaves in east Madagascar was near twenty-five piasters and that of cattle between three and five, depending upon size and condition.[209]

Thus, when captives first began to leave central Madagascar for the east coast, slaves were normally exchanging for between five and eight times the value of cattle. In 1807, in contrast, slaves were commonly exchanging for eighty piasters, and cattle for between four and six, making slaves thirteen to twenty times the value of cattle during the first decade of the nineteenth century.[210] While substantial increases in the value of slaves relative to cattle insured that highland suppliers continued to participate in the slave trade, the price differential between slaves offered for sale in the Malagasy highlands and at the coast provided incentives for Malagasy and European merchants to hold and transport them eastward. Mayeur reported in 1787 that slaves could be purchased for some fifty piasters in central Madagascar but were being ex-changed for seventy-two at the coast, a markup of some 30 percent.[211] In a remarkable document produced for the governor of the Mascarenes in 1807, Mayeur described the cycle of trade in greater detail. Because it explains the economic logic of the slave trade by attention to the strategies of its Mala-gasy participants, it is worth quoting at length.

> Those of the natives who regularly conduct the commerce in slaves in the interior set out on their first voyage in March taking with them trade goods [purchased or advanced on credit from French *traitants*] appropriate to the area they are heading for. Because they do not have to return until June they have two entire months to sell their goods and to realize their gains in silver. They will certainly find nobody who will agree to sell them slaves for trade goods only, and if they have not carried silver into the interior there is nothing else that can take its place. These merchants of slaves arrive at Foulpointe and sell their captives entirely in piasters and leave again, in order to have the time to make two more voyages before the departure of the vessels; well assured that with silver they will not have to wait [i.e., they would find enthusiastic suppliers in the interior]. But the piasters that come from this last sale, they employ in large part to purchase trade goods [again from *traitants*] that appeal to them. And this is their policy. With our piasters they say, we will go past all the *traitants* and examine at our pleasure all their trade goods, and after having made a choice we will take a musket at one, a stone of cloth at another and likewise at the rest, because all do not have the same trade goods nor the same quality and what's more, with my money, I am considerably freer about the choice of the things that I have need of.[212]

Here in a nutshell was the strategy of coastal Malagasy merchants. They turned credit advances of trade goods into silver through successive return journeys into the interior. Mayeur's summary of trading strategies demon-strates how silver flowed in the direction opposite to slaves. Some silver remained at the east coast, where itinerant Malagasy suppliers demanded silver in payment for deliveries of captives and who in turn employed that silver to purchase items of consumption at the end of the trade year. The entire commercial system was predicated upon a delicate balance of competing strategies among the various strata of French and Malagasy merchants for obtaining and retaining as much silver as possible. Among the European *traitants*, those who possessed sufficient operating capital preferred to remain at the coast, putting their trade goods and silver out on credit to men and women who would itinerate in the Malagasy hinterland. In turn, mobile merchants sought to turn a profit in their businesses so as to become moneylenders and owners of silver themselves. Ideally, *traitants* would sell their trade goods to Betsimisaraka merchants in exchange for piasters at the opening of the trade season. More realistically, when they parted with quantities of silver early in the trading season in exchange for the first delivery of slaves, *traitants* hoped to recoup some of their piasters at the end of the season by selling European manufactured items of local consumption back to their Malagasy slave suppliers. Betsimisaraka merchants, on the other hand, attempted (usually, but not always, unsuccessfully) to exchange their cattle or rice at harvest time for silver with which to purchase slaves in the interior.[213] In turn *traitants* sought to indebt Betsimisaraka merchants during the agricultural season (the commercial off-season) with advances of arrack payable in rice at harvest time.[214]

Silver flowing through the hands of *traitants* and Malagasy merchants that did not remain along the east coast coursed back up the trade routes into the Malagasy highlands. *Traitants* at the east coast purchased slaves from Malagasy merchants for the highest proportions of silver to trade goods; suppliers in highland Madagascar sold them for the least. The increasing number of *traitant*-led caravans heading directly into the interior by the end of the eighteenth century represented an attempt by French traders to reduce the real costs in silver to their commercial enterprises. The strategy had contradictory consequences, however, for *traitants* who attempted to reduce the costs of slaves by venturing themselves into the highland Malagasy interior also assumed "the costs and the risks" of holding slaves who might sicken, die, desert, or be stolen by intermediary residents as they were marched toward the coast.[215]

For the variety of individuals who participated in the enslavement and delivery of captives along the trails linking the eastern seaboard of Madagascar with its highland hinterland, then, the value to be earned in the trade stemmed from two interrelated processes: first, the general rise in the value of slaves relative to other commodities over the course of the half-century of trade, and second, the increasing proportions of silver that astute Malagasy merchants could negotiate in exchange for deliveries of captives. Each of these benefits accruing to Madagascar-based suppliers and merchants of slaves passed new costs on to the end consumers of those slaves in the Mascarenes. Slaveowners in Île de France and Bourbon paid steadily higher prices for their servants over the course of the half-century of trade.[216]

Authorities in the Mascarenes complained bitterly about the hemorrhage of silver into Madagascar and about the rising real costs of slaves it occasioned, yet their concerns were insufficient to reshape the economic and political realities of supply and demand in the western Indian Ocean. As early as 1768 Mayeur noted that traders for the Compagnie would ceremoniously conform to company policy by exchanging trade goods for slaves by day, but then contravene it by allowing their Malagasy suppliers to return to the ship by night and reexchange the merchandise for piasters![217] In 1807 the governor of the Mascarenes suspected *traitants* had begun to pay for supplies of rice with silver and demanded that his new *agent commercial* investigate the matter.[218] That French merchants often purchased rice with piasters in order "to have it promptly and to satisfy the natives" was common knowledge on the east coast of Madagascar.[219] Time and again Sylvain Roux, who served as *agent commercial* at Tamatave between 1807 and 1811, cooked up plans to restrict the trade in piasters and the peregrinations of "cupid and unrestrained" *traitants* about the Malagasy interior.[220] One scheme he submitted to the Mascarene governor called for grounding itinerant and highly competitive *traitants* at their coastal residences and turning the entire land-based marketing system over to Malagasy merchants whose bargaining advantage, he calculated, would wither away as they attempted to divest themselves of their mortal investments in human property. In addition to these measures, he reasonably suggested, the only way to terminate the flow of piasters westward from the Mascarenes to Madagascar was for French authorities in the Mascarenes to make vessel captains declare their shipboard supply of piasters upon embarkation for Madagascar.[221] His elaborate plans were adopted by Governor Decaen of the Mascarenes but never effectively implemented.[222] Roux became so exasperated by the free competition among *traitants* and between *traitants* and Malagasy merchants that he proposed not trading in Madagascar for an entire season to "make them see that we can do without them and their commerce."[223] It was a fantasy. To administratively lower the price of slaves in Madagascar when the Mascarene market was demanding them in greater quantities than ever before would have reduced the flow of captives from the great island and placed Mascarene economies in crisis (not to mention the serious consequences for the Mascarenes of an end to the commerce in food from Madagascar). Henri Prentout, historian of Général Decaen's tenure as governor of the Mascarenes (1803–1810), confirmed that "this commerce was conducted almost always in piasters, sometimes accompanied by trade goods."[224] Despite Mascarene opposition, Malagasy merchants continued to successfully demand payment in ever-higher proportions of silver until the end of the trade in 1820.[225]

Between the opening of the eastward-running export trade from highland Madagascar and its abrupt conclusion in 1820, some 70,000 individuals were sent away into bondage in the Mascarenes. Given a highland population of between one-half and one million during this period, total demographic depletion represented, at most, between 7 and 14 percent over half a century, or well under 0.5 percent annually (less than 5 per 1,000 each year).[226] While epidemic disease could periodically send mortality rates to much higher levels in particular years, this endemic level of enslavement was comparable to that in the export trade of west central Africa (2.5 to 6 per 1,000 each year). As Joseph Miller has illustratively argued for that region, such a rate of enslavement approximates the incidence of endemic violence in modern industrial cities.[227] Because most of the captives marched out of highland Madagascar were men (chapter 4), it is unlikely that the slave trade actually led to a decline in the total population of highland Madagascar.

To conclude that because its demographic impact was moderate the slave trade was of little import in the Malagasy highlands, however, is to err fundamentally. As a broad-ranging social and cultural phenomenon, the slave trade cannot be assessed with quantitative instruments alone. Largely invisible in quantitative assessments, qualitative transformations in everyday life and cultural practice (changes that David Eltis calls "negative externalities") demonstrate that the impact of the slave trade ran far deeper than numbers can suggest.[228] Although highland Madagascar is landlocked, it was not a backwater nor simply a hinterland to distant ports, isolated from the main currents of trade in the western Indian Ocean during the late eighteenth and early nineteenth centuries. Because its merchants and citizens played a direct role in producing and transporting captives—the primary category of external trade by value—central Madagascar entered the regional economy of the western Indian Ocean by 1770. Participation in that regional economy restructured the local economy and everyday life in dramatic ways. Like east Africa, highland Madagascar became a principal source of slaves for the Mascarenes and other destinations from the late eighteenth century; its societies experienced economic, social, and political transformations similar to those of the east African interior during the same period.[229] Everyday life as well as cultural identities and practices were all remade by the export trade in slaves. To identify and probe these transformations, let me now turn to the ways in which slaves were created and contested in the interior of the island.

3

ENSLAVEMENT AND ITS MORALITY

For a long time they have known the continuous need of our colonies for slaves; the methods they put into practice to procure them for us are almost always repugnant.
                                    —Julien Pierre Dumaine de la Josserie[1]

To the victims and the participants in the Mascarene slave trade, commercial capitalism was neither a theoretical concept nor a disembodied experience. To have had a hand in the export commerce as a merchant or a maker of slaves, or to have become the object of attempts at enslavement, was to come face to face with real people, to engage in specific behaviors, and to become involved in a variety of discursive practices that broadened or curtailed the legitimacy of enslavement. The proliferation of enslavements in late-eighteenth-century highland Madagascar left little room for passivity concerning the practices by which new slaves were created. In an economy characterized by multiple levels of opportunity and coercion, however, responses to the trade could be complex and contradictory. Scholars cannot, as a result, reduce human actions in an economy of enslavement to the polar terms of collaboration and resistance, words that presuppose two opposing parties rather than a range of interested persons, actions, and positions. "The slave trade" and "enslavement" collapse a multitude of actors, strategies, motivations, and experiences into shallow and broadly descriptive terms. This chapter seeks to deepen the meaning of these terms by investigating the process of enslavement in highland Madagascar and contests there over its legitimacy in specific circumstances.

Here, therefore, I narrow analytical focus onto the highlands of central Madagascar and onto the practices, relationships, and people that generated slaves of certain individuals and contested the enslavement of others. My purpose is not to recount the experiences of the slaves themselves—a valuable and different project altogether—but to inquire into how the creation of slaves within highland Madagascar, through particular methods of enslavement, transformed civil relationships among those left behind, creating a domestic political crisis at the end of the eighteenth century. By slaving and acting to protect themselves from enslavement and its manifold social consequences, highland Malagasy transformed their way of life and their collective identities. They did so not because "Europe imposed the slave trade" upon them but because foreign merchants together with some highland Malagasy introduced a new set of political and economic circumstances into the highlands.[2] Once they embarked down the path of enslavement, the people of central Madagascar could not individually modify the structural location of their homeland within the seaborne economy of French imperialism, but they could and did, by the range of activities they engaged in, substantially shape how they participated in the slave trade and mediate what effects that participation imparted to their society and culture. How the slave trade "affected" highland Malagasy societies, then, was not a foregone conclusion of enslavement or of European expansion into the Indian Ocean. It was contingent upon how highland Malagasy themselves responded to the opportunities and tragedies of merchant capitalism.[3] To explore the influences of enslavement on highland Malagasy society, I turn first to the notion of legitimacy, or morality, in the making of slaves.

MORALITIES OF ENSLAVEMENT

In a major synthesis of the secondary literature on slavery in Africa, Paul Lovejoy argues that the transatlantic slave trade dramatically increased the use of slaves within Africa itself. Not only did the proportion of slaves within African societies increase over the 400 years of the export trade, he argues, the nature of slavery itself was transformed. From a social practice of marginal economic importance to African societies, slavery and slave labor became key components in many African economies. They did so, as has become clear through research in widely dispersed parts of the Africas, because the export trade in captives generated at least as many new slaves internal to Africa as it carried westward across the Atlantic.[4] In the vocabulary of Moses Finley, many regions of Africa were transformed into "slave societies" whose economies and social structures became dependent upon and organized around slaves and their labor.[5] Lovejoy calls this sea change in the position and importance of slavery within African societies—a change he sees fundamentally tied to the transatlantic slave trade—a "transformation in slavery."[6]

Lovejoy's transformation thesis provokes an important and related question. If Africans transformed slavery as they created and delivered millions of new slaves to the Atlantic coast, did they at the same time transform the *means* by which new slaves were generated within the African interior? Lovejoy suggests, for example, that the escalation of inter-African hostilities that produced a majority of new slaves for the Atlantic and Indian ocean systems was accompanied by qualitative transformations in the process of enslaving captives. Innovations in slavemaking required departures from established and communally accepted practices. For this reason enslavement was sometimes considered illegitimate and subject to dispute.[7] Historians of the impact of the Atlantic slave trade on Senegambia have long argued in a generalizing way that many Islamic reform movements from the seventeenth through the nineteenth centuries rested partially on popular discontent with leaders' complicity in enslavement and the export slave trade.[8] In a similar manner, John Thornton has recently found that disillusionment with leaders' personal greed, warmaking, and participation in enslavement led many persons in the Angolan hinterland to support the Antonian movement of Beatrice Kimpa Vita in the early eighteenth century. Eventually burned alive, Kimpa Vita won popular support for her grassroots challenge to established secular and religious authorities in the kingdom of Kongo.[9]

For another region of the continent, the Shambaa kingdom of east Africa, Steven Feierman offers a specific example of popular discontent with leaders who violated local moralities of enslavement. The courts of chiefs of the Kilindi dynasty in Shambaai (located in the highlands of what is now northern Tanzania) were generally considered places of refuge. Individuals might become dependents of the court in exchange for food and protection in times of crisis. Sometimes kinspeople left human pawns at the court as security against debt or social obligations due a chief. The rules of dependency maintained a clear distinction between a chief's dependents, citizens who could not be sold, and slaves with few rights, who could be alienated from the court in exchange for trade goods or money. In the late nineteenth century, however, some Kilindi chiefs began to disregard the rules of dependency and protection by selling their pawns and other dependents as slaves. Many people resisted this "breakdown of the separation between peasants and slaves." The Bondei in the eastern regions of the kingdom broke away from the Kilindi after 1868 in protest of these transformations in chiefly prerogative.[10]

Tales of the perversion of social custom through the generation of new slaves push scholars to rethink the process of enslavement. Behind their identification of armed conflict as the principal means by which slaves were created within Africa, historians of west Africa have implicitly assumed that war captives could legitimately be sold away into bondage.[11] This assumption has been globally and temporally generalized by Orlando Patterson, who writes in *Slavery and Social Death* that enslavement of war captives was justified in that it represented a merciful commutation of death sentences normally imposed upon prisoners of war.[12] An intrinsic problem with this formulation is that it fails to distinguish among the many varieties of "war"—from political conflicts to economic raids launched for the sole purpose of culling slaves—and varying African attitudes toward them. Another is that it assumes most slaves commenced their bondage as war captives, a problematic proposition explored in chapter 1. Finally, it substitutes a certain and inelastic ideological justification of enslavement for the messy ethical issues and complicated social relationships Africans as moral beings confronted and fudged when they enslaved or themselves faced victimization by capture.

Discussions about African enslavement during the era of the slave trade frequently pointed to the salience of debates about legitimacy and morality in the making of slaves. African suppliers of export slaves, for example, often played upon both local and European notions of justice by claiming that their bondpeople were legitimately obtained when in fact they were not. Writing in 1612, for instance, a petitioner to King Philip III of Spain decried Portuguese slaving in the following terms: "And the blacks themselves falsely assert that the persons whom they bring to be sold are captured in a just war, or they say that they will butcher and eat them if they are not purchased. So that, of every thousand slaves who are captured, scarcely one-tenth will be justly enslaved, which is a notorious fact confirmed by all God-fearing men who reside or have resided in those places."[13] Writing at roughly the same time about the upper Guinea coast, Baltasar Barreira noted that the slave trade rested on multiple levels of complicity and self-interested disregard for local ethical codes.

> What can in general be said about the blacks that are bought and sold in this (part of) Guinea called the (*Guiné de*) *Cabo Verde* is that no examination into the legality of their captivity is made, and no inquiries about it are made either. There are two main reasons for this. One is that the masters of ships, in order to hasten their loading, take all the blacks that are brought to them. . . . The other is that the kings and lords of these parts, in order to buy and possess the goods that the shippers bring from Europe, very commonly enslave blacks that were born and have always been free. . . . [It] . . . cannot be denied that there exist in this Guinea reasons for genuine and legal captivity, such as those of just war and capital crimes. And . . . it is not right to blame them if some of the blacks they buy have been made captives unjustly; adding to this that it is not they themselves who usually buy the slaves for the ships from the natives, but Portuguese men who can speak the language and live in the land and who go further inland taking the goods with which they buy them; and that the fact that the legitimacy of captivity is not inquired into, if it is a fault, should be blamed on these persons and not on the ship owners, and that they follow

the usage that they found in the land, and that has always been practiced since its discovery.[14]

Some centuries later Hope Masterton Waddell, a missionary in the Bight of Biafra, similarly noted in his journal that the people of Calabar "pretend that the slaves they purchase are sold in payment of the debts they have contracted, or for crime or as prisoners of war. . . . At the same time they don't deny the fact that they buy very many children who cannot have been sold for such causes."[15] Even early European opposition to the slave trade, which emerged in theological debates, crystallized around perceived illegitimate enslavement rather than opposition to slavery as such.[16] Despite the distance of some of these commentaries from vernacular discourses in African societies, struggles over the meaning and legitimacy of capturing humans raged close to sites of enslavement, challenging scholars' blanket notions about a stable morality that legitimized the making of new captives. If many Africans, Europeans, and others involved in making, trading, and purchasing Africans regarded slavery as "an inescapable fact of life," they nevertheless differed over and debated who might be legitimately enslaved.[17]

Accepting the notion that prisoners of war or even other categories of individuals such as criminals or debtors necessarily made legitimate slaves, as the statements evinced in the previous paragraph seem to suggest, historians fail to account for how the expansion and transformation of enslavement within Africa shifted African moral systems, transforming rights in persons and metamorphosing civil relationships.[18] Assuming a fixed and unchanging morality of enslavement, most scholars find the sale of captives and others legitimate over a period of profound social transformation. But were prisoners of war and other captives *always* considered legitimately enslaveable? Insufficient research has been conducted into moral conflicts over enslavements within Africa, a significant lacuna, since the great majority of export slaves were freshly "created" through new enslavements; they were not born slaves.[19] Specific examples of enslavement reveal that even when different individuals were captured under similar circumstances, the legitimacy of the enslavements and the course of action taken by kin to retrieve them could vary substantially. In late-nineteenth-century Hausaland, for example, kidnapping was generally considered an illegitimate way to take a slave. Yet when a kidnapped person was subsequently sold by her initial captors, that enslavement became more legitimate, for the purchaser laid a firmer claim to rights in an individual he had purchased than in one he had kidnapped.[20] In relating her life story to Mary Smith, Baba of Karo described how several individuals who had been kidnapped and then sold were ransomed by their kin with payments of cowry shells. In another case, however, that of her mother's sister, Rabi, a daring kinsman fortified with charms procured from the local *malams* (Islamic religious leaders) stole into the household of Rabi's enslavement and boldly carried her away in the dark of night.[21] To take such differing stories of emancipation and the notions of legitimacy that differently underlie each of them seriously, is to destabilize the notion of universal or temporally inflexible concepts of morality in African enslavement. Enslavement and responses to it were ever contingent and fluid.

If local concepts of the legitimacy of enslavement were impermanent and malleable, violated concepts of morality could nevertheless precipitate domestic crises. In a thought-provoking and lengthy study of the transatlantic slave trade from Angola, for example, Joseph Miller describes a chronological progression in kings' strategies for obtaining new slaves. Commencing with the sale of superfluous and marginalized individuals such as witches and other criminals, and progressing through the procurement of political outsiders in raids and war on the external borders of their realms, kings eventually resolved to enslave subjects from within the core of their own domains. They did so, Miller argues, because local people were more independent than outsiders and therefore made less pliable subjects (hence it was in kings' interests to rid themselves of them) and because the resistance offered by communities of plundered outsiders—with whom kings maintained no moral relationships—fostered "potential domestic strains." West central Africa was sent into "a paroxysm of social and political revolution" akin to civil war as kings sought to create slaves from within their own dominions to liquidate debts owed merchants from the coast. Selling dependents posed a "deep dilemma" for kings, Miller writes, especially when royals eroded their own power by doing so. The problem was not popular resistance among kings' subjects to enslavements perceived as illegitimate, he indicates, but kings' self-defeating action that undercut the very wealth in people they sought to amass through distribution of imported goods. But was it not, one might ask by way of extending Miller's fruitful line of inquiry, precisely the relative independence of kings' *own dependents*, not merely the irascibility of outsiders, that fostered this domestic violence? Exactly what sorts of local strains and commentaries on enslavement generated civil war among subjects to whom the king was morally obligated? These are questions of fundamental importance to deciphering elite and commoner strategies in an economy of enslavement and I intend to explore them in the pages that follow.[22]

In the Malagasy highlands of the late eighteenth century, exchanging war captives, pawns, and nonslave persons into export slavery entailed stripping them of communally asserted rights and reducing them to rightless chattel, transforming their social status with a single transaction of sale to someone who would lead them far away from home. To study enslavement in highland Madagascar, then, it is helpful to adopt "a processual approach to the problem" of enslavement, placing changing practices of capture in historical perspective.[23] While at first enslavement for export was innovative and con-sidered illegitimate, with time and the expansion of the export commerce some types of enslavement became more widely accepted than others. The proliferation of conflict, social debt, and kidnapping for the purpose of cre-ating new slaves resulted in slavers arrogating to themselves a new set of privileges in making dependents and slaves. Creating slaves, even by wag-ing war on political outsiders, but especially by plundering from among one's own dependents, spawned conflicts over local moralities of enslavement that eventually shifted how common people perceived particular kinds of cap-ture, as well as the legitimacy of their leaders and neighbors who engaged in the practice.

By moralities of enslavement I mean the degree to which communities from which slaves were removed (and not the enslaved themselves) con-sidered certain methods of enslavement, or the enslavement of individuals in particular circumstances, to be legitimate. Because slavers and the com-munities targeted for enslavement rarely agreed upon precisely which en-slavements were legitimate, moralities of enslavement were seldom clearly defined and almost always contested. By noting that moralities of enslave-ment were contested and transformed over time I do not mean to suggest that Malagasy and continental Africans during the era of the export slave trade considered slavery as a general idea or category to be illegitimate. (Most studies of African resistance to enslavement fail to make the critical distinction between a general acceptance of slavery, on the one hand, and the contestation of particular enslavements as illegitimate, on the other. These studies focus primarily on resistance by the enslaved themselves—individuals who rarely ever found their condition justifiable whatever the method of capture—rather than opinion within the "free" communities from which they originated.)[24] Malagasy commonly recognized a variety of so-cial statuses and rights in persons that set individuals into hierarchical rela-tionships. Yet because nonslave Malagasy, like their American and African counterparts, recognized slavery within their societies and accepted it as a legitimate social station, they did not at the same time consider it legiti-mate for anyone to be made a slave. The same was true of any slaveholding society and underpinned the critical social distinction between slave and citizen. The individual circumstances by which communities accepted en-slavement had to be present and certain procedures and ceremonies fol-lowed for enslavements to be considered socially acceptable or moral.[25] By creating export slaves, slavers often transgressed these communally defined moralities of enslavement to illegitimately transform nonslave persons into exportable captives.

As the volume of enslavements increased over the era of the slave trade, the morality of enslavement tended to shift in favor of slavers. Slavemaking activities once considered illegitimate became generally more acceptable as the ability of rural communities to set the terms of legitimate activity waned and individuals concentrated on contesting the legitimacy of specific enslavements that threatened them with greater immediacy. Pliable and changing, African moralities of enslavement shifted continually with the ebb and flow of local participation in slaving. But concepts of legitimacy and immorality there surely were, for Africans, like all their contemporaries, were human beings whose social organization and interpersonal relationships rested on cultural notions of decency and legitimacy. This may seem obvious, but the volume of scholarly research on European and Islamic moralities of enslavement that led to serious ethical debates and even emancipation movements in the nineteenth century stands in stark contrast to the near absence of serious work on Africans and their varying opinions about enslavement. That Africans came to different conclusions about the general moral acceptability of slavery than their contemporaries in other parts of the nineteenth-century world does not mean that enslavement did not pose serious ethical dilemmas with wide-ranging social consequences for them. The certainty with which moderns argue the total illegitimacy of slavery under any circumstances has unfortunately tended to efface this fact. In the remainder of this chapter I consider enslavement in highland Madagascar and the complex and changing moralities of enslavement that shaped human responses to it.

SOCIAL HIERARCHY AND THE MORAL COMMUNITY

Together with the increasing external demand for captive labor at Île de France and Bourbon, domestic social inequalities facilitated transformation of highland Madagascar's societies into slave-generating and slave-exporting economies.[26] Social equality was neither a reality nor a cultural ideal in central Madagascar. Hierarchies of kingdoms and chiefdoms, social rank, descent, judicial and ritual office, debt, gender, and generation formed dense and crosscutting networks of patronage, obligation, and deference within highland Malagasy societies. Hierarchy was a fundamental principle of human interaction, experienced, negotiated, and recreated through the course of daily encounters. Most individuals were at once superiors and inferiors within an array of human relationships that composed the warp and weft of highland social fabric. In some of these relationships individuals advanced from inferiors to superiors through the course of their lives, in others they could not.

Let me begin with political organization. At 1770 there were several minikingdoms within the Malagasy highlands, each composed of a "mother town" or capital (*renivohitra*) and surrounding "offspring towns," attached villages (*zanabohitra*). According to nineteenth-century historical narratives, four kingdoms predominated in highland Madagascar.[27] In reality the Malagasy highlands were considerably more fragmented than is suggested by popular narratives, and rural communities—especially those on the margins of the minikingdoms but even within them—exercised much autonomy in determining where to place their political loyalties.[28] Ruling the minikingdoms were sovereigns of a privileged social status called *andriana*, a rank roughly analogous to European nobility. *Andriana* were descendants and associates of those who had held political power in highland Madagascar during preceding centuries.[29] A second social status, and one encompassing the vast majority of highlanders, was *hova*. To be *hova* was to be neither of *andriana* extraction nor of servant-slave descent. *Hova* status is thus loosely glossed in English by the concept "commoner" and indeed, like commoners, *hova* occupied an intermediate social position between royalty and servants-slaves. Then there were various categories of what I termed servants-slaves. These included groups that traditionally provided services to sovereigns (cooks, bodyguards, personal attendants) and who were generally considered *mainty*, black.[30] Further, a variety of specific terms designated social dependents of many sorts. In this chapter I am particularly interested in the *zazahova* (literally, "children of *hova*") who can best be described as pawns, individuals provided to creditors as security for financial and social debts.[31] *Zazahova* served specific creditor-masters but nevertheless retained a variety of rights, including the right not to be exchanged away from their homelands in central Madagascar.[32] *Zazahova* were not considered property in the common sense of the term but social dependents over whose labor creditors could exercise certain rights. Finally there was a category of persons designated *andevo*, a status most closely equivalent to that of the English-language concept of a slave: someone who could be bought and sold from the highlands, usually a cultural outsider. Like social categories elsewhere, highland Malagasy statuses of *andriana*, *hova*, *mainty*, *zazahova*, and *andevo* profoundly influenced their members' opportunities in everyday life, but the boundaries among many of these statuses were considerably more porous than prevailing ideology suggested. Individuals could and did slide from one category to another, often in situations of social conflict.

The primary constituent social units of highland Malagasy kingdoms were descent groups, communities that employed languages of kinship to designate social cohesion. These descent groups were known by the term *firenena*, which derives from the noun root *reny*, mother.[33] Considered persons of shared descent, members of a single *firenena*—or "motherhood" in its literal rendering—theoretically shared the same social status. An ideology of endogamy that encouraged marriages among close kin, and especially within *firenena*, served to reinforce the notion of social homogeneity among these "motherhood" members. In reality, the social compositions and histories of *firenena* varied dramatically. *Firenena* histories suggest that descent groups were capable of absorbing individuals from a variety of social and descent backgrounds, recognizing them over time as kin.[34] Although some narratives of *firenena* history and highland Malagasy ideologies of endogamous marriage would suggest otherwise, a single *firenena* might include both *hova* and *andriana* members enjoying the services of *mainty*, *zazahova*, and *andevo* attendants, and, ideology to the contrary, it was often ambiguous whether such servants-slaves could be defined as belonging inside or outside the *firenena*.[35] *Firenena* varied considerably in the size of their populations and in the nature of their links with the ancestral homelands (*tanindrazana*) to which they laid claim.[36] Because most *firenena* varied in size between several hundred and thousands of persons, more restricted ancestries I shall call *teraky* (assuming the form *teraky* x or *teraky* y, literally meaning "descendants of x" or "descendants of y," where x and y were named apical ancestors) crystallized, dissolved, and recrystallized within the *firenena*.[37] During the nineteenth century the bonds linking members of *teraky* were usually both a shared near ancestor and an anticipated common place of burial. Because in highland Madagascar descent is reckoned cognatically (through both mother's and father's line), affiliations with particular apical ancestors entailed considerable exercise of choice. The flexible and shifting politics of kinship in highland Madagascar insured that both *firenena* and *teraky* ebbed and flowed with changing circumstances and personal interests.[38]

Kings and independent chiefs were known in the vernacular as *mpanjaka*, a generic Malagasy term of leadership that designates a person of (or having) *fanjakana*, governance, authority, privilege, dignity.[39] Here I rely on convention: because scholars have chosen to call the multiple polities of central Madagascar "kingdoms" and "minikingdoms," I here call the heads of those polities "kings." For the purposes of this narrative, on the other hand, I shall call the leaders of *teraky* and *firenena* "chiefs" since the scale of their authority was normally more restricted than that of the sovereigns of kingdoms. Both kings and chiefs oversaw their own *fanjakana*, each building authority by securing the allegiance of smaller *fanjakana* or *teraky* (different levels of *fanjakana*, or personal authority, were not exclusive of each other).[40] Conceived of in this manner, *firenena* were usually confederations of *teraky*; kingdoms, federations of *firenena*. Of course, kingdoms, *firenena,* and *teraky* were each crosscut by hierarchies of age, gender, and office, all of which assumed distinctive highland Malagasy forms explored later in this chapter.

If hierarchy was a fundamental principle of social life, highland Malagasy often disagreed about what constituted proper behavior within hierarchical relationships. Debates over such behavior lay at the heart of the constitution of moral communities in central Madagascar.[41] A moral community is a group of people who, for whatever reason, acknowledge responsibilities and obligations toward one another. Manifested in the form of *teraky*, *firenena*, kingdoms, and ultimately Merina identity, highland Malagasy moral communities overlapped and varied in size and purpose. Individuals could belong to several moral communities simultaneously. Within them, individuals of various social statuses sought to define community ideals and moral relationships. Practical matters relating to communal life and human relationships were transacted within highland Madagascar's moral communities. Among the most important for this study are relationships between men and women, creditors and debtors, patrons and clients, sovereigns and citizen-subjects.

Debates over enslavement and proper relationships among highland Malagasy and their rulers tended to pivot around struggles over civic virtue, what the proper, legitimate, and moral relationships between common people and their rulers ought to be.[42] Concepts of civic virtue within moral communities served as standards against which members gauged the social acceptability of human behavior. Commoners, chiefs, and kings each strove to transform ideals of civic virtue and the moral community in ways favorable to their particular interests. Implicit in the practice of moral communities, then, was both a shared recognition of the existence and legitimacy of certain forms of social inequality and the reality that members of the community did not always agree upon what constituted proper behavior within and across those hierarchies. Moral communities were not commonwealths of consensus in central Madagascar but shifting alliances always characterized by social conflict.[43]

By twisting legitimately unequal relationships with their subjects to personal gain, a small elite within central Madagascar shifted the definition of civic virtue as it applied to leadership and opened the highlands to participation in the Mascarene slave trade. Enslavement for export entailed a self-interested reinterpretation of civic virtue by the socially powerful. This reinterpretation was effected through purposeful circumvention of the conventions structuring patron-client, subject-king, captor-prisoner relationships. In turn, these circumventions undermined communal institutions and collective ethos. The practices that generated slaves represented both a quantitative and qualitative heightening of existing systems of inequality. Rather than occurring through a communal consensus over the making of slaves, enslavements promoted a social climate of distrust and fear, fraying the moral community to which both slavemakers and their victims belonged.

ENSLAVING PRISONERS

The first export slaves were generated in the years before 1770 through choices exercised by individual highland kings. These choices represented an innovation in social convention structuring interkingdom political competition, prisoner-taking, and economic rivalry. As was common in many precolonial African societies, military engagements in eighteenth-century highland Madagascar were artful wars—a matching of tactics, ruse, and cunning.[44] The most popular and effective offensive means by which kingdoms and *firenena* forced recognition of their sovereignty upon neighboring hilltop towns and ancestries, for example, was through the practice of *fahirano*, the siege. During a siege, water and food supplies to an elevated enemy settlement were cut, starving the inhabitants into submission.[45] The purpose of encounters between opposing armies, when they actually occurred,[46] was to collect the political submission of unsuccessful competitors or, failing that, to capture prisoners and thereby expand the human wealth of the victorious kingdom or *firenena*.[47] That prisoners were the expected outcome of military encounters is suggested in *Tantara* narratives, which speak of eighteenth-century military engagements primarily in terms of strategies for securing captives.[48] The salience of prisoner-taking in highland Malagasy warfare is further confirmed in the contemporary testimony of French merchants. During his tour through the Andrantsay in 1777, for example, Mayeur noted that few slaves were available because Andrantsay kings had not recently launched any military campaigns.[49]

Whether rulers captured prisoners or collected political loyalties, they expanded the geographic and human reach of their realms while reducing those of their competitors. Political competition among rulers for followers assumed the characteristics of a zero-sum game.[50] As the primary agricultural laborers during the eighteenth century, men considerably enhanced the economic and political viability of the capturing polity while sapping its rivals of precious human resources.[51] (The gender division of labor in eighteenth-century Malagasy agriculture differs substantially from that in most of Africa during the period. I discuss the gender division of labor in agriculture in the next chapter). In some cases, prisoners were incorporated permanently into the society of their capture. In others—and this was the ideal—captors returned prisoners to their home kingdoms and to their kin in exchange for a ransom.[52] Captured men were customarily released to kin in exchange for a significant sum, remembered in the *Tantara* as three piasters.[53] Family members could sometimes redeem captured relatives at highland markets. "In the past," notes one passage from the *Tantara*,

> people did not kill each other when they fought. Instead they captured one another. And if a relative was lost [captured], his family brought their own captives which they exchanged as ransom for him. If they found relatives at the market, they ransomed them there; others ransomed them at their captors' houses, and still others sent friends to deliver the ransom for them. That was the custom in earlier times.[54]

Prisoner ransoming in the late eighteenth century was such a common practice that competing kingdoms institutionalized the ransom market and integrated it into their conduct of war. A passage in the *Tantara* describes how ransoming was conducted in the conflict between king Andrianampoinimerina of Ambohimanga and Andrianamboatsimarofy of Antananarivo (early 1780s) on days of proclaimed respite from military engagements.

> A market was arranged there at Morarano (at Thursday west of Amboniloha); that's where the market was. On the day of the market, there was no fighting; on the days with no market, fighting was resumed. A bonfire was lit at Amboniloha to demonstrate that the day was a market day. And people went there to meet, each seeking their captured relatives and ransoming them. When little was left of the day, people returned home. They did not wait for the evening lest they be captured if caught out at night.[55]

At one time highlanders exchanged their captives primarily for other prisoners, rice, cloth, metal implements and other highland manufactures. By the late eighteenth century, however, as silver become an increasingly important medium of exchange within the Malagasy highlands, ransoms were normally required in significant proportions of silver piasters. Even the bodies of soldiers killed in military engagements were commonly offered by their vanquishers for ransom. Mayeur once witnessed cadavers being ransomed for twenty piasters each. For lesser sums, the main bones of expired kin (probably the *taolambalo* or eight principal bones necessary for proper interment) could be obtained from their captors for a dignified burial.[56] The *Tantara* corroborate these practices but indicate that cadavers were normally ransomed for significantly lower prices, usually between one and two piasters each.[57]

Newly confronted with opportunities offered by the French mercantile economy and its exchange market for human beings, several rulers departed from customary practice and exchanged their captured prisoners of war with slave merchants rather than ransoming them back to family or incorporating them within their subject populations as dependent farmers. This practice could not have been entirely novel, for highland Malagasy slaves had been exported in low volumes toward the northwest coast of the island for centuries (see chapter 2). The high volume of captives traded into the eastward-bound export commerce beginning before 1770, however, was a new departure. A full century later, the historical memory of these enslavements, crystallizing around the names of marketplaces, broke fleetingly through an overwhelming amnesia about export enslavement. One of the few *Tantara* passages that vividly recalls the export slave trade describes the psychological dimensions of insecurity it inflicted upon common people. "There were also markets," the passage reads, "where suppliers [of captives] encountered the Europeans who were offering muskets and gunpowder and European things. Ampamoizankova in the northeast, where captives were sold away from here; Angavokely also to the east, where captives were exchanged for muskets and gunpowder; and Alarobian'Ambohitrambo, to the west, where there were also encounters and exportation."[58] By selling prisoners of war, kings reinterpreted civic virtue to their own ends, ignoring a communally defined morality of enslavement that limited how a victorious leader might dispose of captured prisoners.

It is not known precisely which rulers first sold captives eastward out of the Malagasy highlands nor exactly how their people responded to the new practice. La Bigorne, a longtime French military officer and trader on the eastern coast of Madagascar, offered his military services between 1768 and 1771 to Andrianjafy, then king at Ambohimanga in highland Madagascar. La Bigorne's involvement in enslavements and the commerce in captives enabled him to purchase substantial property in the Mascarenes shortly thereafter.[59] The testimony of Madagascar-born slave Narcisse before the Compensation Committee for the district of Flacq, Mauritius, in 1833, offered an example of enslavement of a prisoner of war during the time of Andrianampoinimerina (before 1809). Narcisse informed the Committee that he was

> a native of a part of Malgache [Madagascar] called Ambouhiméne and that he was seized by the soldiers of King Anglien Nampoin [Andrianampoinimerina], father of King Radame, he was sold at Tananerivo [Antananarivo] to a white named Le Sieur Jacques Fromlou who led the informant with many slaves to the coast at Tomassin [Toamasina, or Tamatave] where he was detained three months and finally embarked aboard a ship with three masts that carried three hundred blacks and fifty negresses.[60]

Although others were undoubtedly involved in early enslavements, La Bigorne, Andrianjafy, and Andrianampoinimerina were among those who supplied slaves to the Mascarenes during the early years of that commerce. That the first muskets in central Madagascar entered circuits of prestige goods and were employed by kings as ritual emblems of power, as Gerald Berg has demonstrated, suggests that competing rulers were the first to generate export slaves from captives of war.[61] Additional evidence is provided by European *traitants*. The first contemporary account of the slave trade in central Madagascar (1777) indicates that most slaves were prisoners of war, implicating militarily victorious kings as the source.[62] "It is rare that a prisoner taken in battle from an enemy reaches our hands if his kin know of his captivity," wrote Mayeur. "It is custom for prisoners to be ransomed by their kin, and the ransom is always higher than the ordinary price of slaves."[63]

These statements, along with the evidence on ransoming practices from the *Tantara*, require careful consideration for they suggest the assertion of a communally defined morality of enslavement. Kings were first required to offer prisoners to their kinspeople for ransoming ("it is custom for prisoners to be ransomed by their kin"). An intensifying Mascarene demand for slaves offered kings a way out of the communally asserted civic virtues that limited the way they handled prisoners of war. With itinerant merchants eager to relieve them of slaves, rulers exchanged captives in return for muskets, ammunition, trade goods, and silver piasters. Given the interest of eighteenth-century sovereigns in acquiring European muskets as insignia of sovereignty, the enticement to sell captives must have been considerable.[64] Prestigious muskets could be obtained only by exchanging captives with merchants from the coast. Social elites soon learned that exchanging slaves with merchants intending to convey them away from Madagascar could not only acquire them foreign muskets, ammunition, trade goods, and piasters, but that these items could be distributed to potential highland allies to generate political dependency and strengthen those that already existed, a process one scholar of the slave trade has aptly termed a "game of people and products."[65]

In affirmation of the illegitimacy with which they sold captives outside the moral community, rulers offered prisoners to merchants surreptitiously.[66] Families sometimes located enslaved relations within merchant caravans and sought to ransom their loved ones in exchange for silver or replacement slaves. Yet even when kin learned of a captive relative, kings turned the situation to their advantage by squeezing higher ransoms for captured prisoners out of their relatives than they could hope to obtain by selling those same individuals directly to itinerant merchants.[67] Most households and *teraky* could ill afford the enormous sums of silver that slavers demanded as ransom for a captive. Prohibitive ransoms were a technique by which slavers sought to make highlanders complicit in their innovative practices, for they encouraged common people to kidnap for their own slaves, captives who could be exchanged in lieu of a seized kinsperson. As kings shifted their slave-generating activities away from capturing the subjects of other rulers to making slaves from within their own political domains, highland Malagasy came in large part to accept the sale of war prisoners, outsiders to the moral community, and focused their protective efforts instead on dangers closer to home.

THE PERILS OF PAWNSHIP

Once leaders breached the customary rights of prisoners acquired from *other* kingdoms by selling them as slaves and allowing others likewise to sell them, they began to target social institutions within *their own* kingdoms to create slaves. Coming in the wake of transformations in the practice of prisoner ransoming, these new social transgressions became more difficult for kings and chiefs to resist and, perhaps, easier to self-justify. Only years after the first captives were sold from central Madagascar, elites in various positions of social power began to create wealth for themselves by converting social institutions within their own dominions into generators of slaves. The geographical source of new slaves after 1770, therefore, shifted from areas external to highland slavers' own moral communities to within those very communities themselves. This inward shift of the slaving "frontier" coincided with a dramatic increase in the volume of captives offered for export to the Mascarenes. Together, conversions of communal social institutions and an increase in the volume of the slave trade after 1770 transformed highland politics. In the short run, kings who sold slaves enhanced their power and wealth; in the long run, they undermined authority from within by incurring the displeasure of their own subjects. The tension between an elite search for wealth, on the one hand, and communally enforced limits to such accumulation, on the other, lay at the heart of late eighteenth-century highland Malagasy politics. The tensions and social transformations flowing from enslavement examined here and in the next chapter created a multifaceted domestic crisis that set the political stage for the rise of Andrianampoinimerina and the making of a new collective identity in highland Madagascar.

Traitants reported that highland chiefs often subjected their people to trials by poison and fire ordeal, condemning to death some who were found guilty of various offenses and selling the others off into slavery. By this means, commented Lebel just at the beginning of the nineteenth century, "the powerful chiefs, especially the Owes [Hova], make an object of speculation out of this ordeal."[68] But principal among the social transformations generating new slaves were innovations in wealth-lending and the disposition of pawns. Wealth lending was considered a legitimate activity within highland communities before 1800. Wealth was culturally conceptualized as a blessing from the ancestors.[69] The mystical power of wealth generation was linked to the notion of agricultural and human fertility and metaphorically expressed through the active verb *miteraka*, to give birth. With ancestral blessing, everyday activities reproduced wealth in all its forms—children, rice, cattle, social dependents, and, by the last decades of the eighteenth century, European-minted silver coins. Within this conceptual system, human activity that

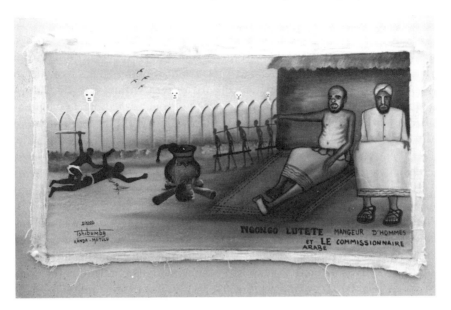

Figure 3.1 "Ngongo Lutete, Man-eater, and the Arab Trader." Painted in Lubumbashi, Zaire, in 1974 by Tshibumba Kanda Matulu, this tableau memorializes chief Ngongo Lutete (ca. 1856–1893), a onetime associate of Tippu-Tip. The painting testifies to a lingering social memory of the slaving chief as a violent and unpopular consumer of humanity. Kanda Matulu's work illustrates the long-term political risks slaving rulers might incur by pursuing short-term goals of enrichment and power through participation in the slave trade. (*Source*: Johannes Fabian, *Remembering the Present: Painting and Popular History in Zaire* [Berkeley, 1996], 32. Reprinted with permission.)

generated profits and worldly wealth (*vola aman-karena*) was not only virtuous but actively encouraged.[70]

 Highland Malagasy were fully aware that to generate wealth one needed not only ancestral blessing but a sufficient supply of operating capital. Entrepreneurs charged interest on loaned capital because wealth in all its forms should "give birth" to benefits for both creditor and debtor. Culturally, highland Malagasy conceptualized wealth generation through flows of credit as a sort of communal sharing. In reality, however, wealth-lending was seldom transacted between social equals and resources were rarely transferred for economic reasons alone. Providing security to dependent households during hungry seasons in the agricultural cycle and at times of life crisis was one of the most commonly accepted means by which wealthy persons attracted valuable political and social dependents. Social inferiors accepted wealth from their social superiors for a variety of purposes: to purchase food during the hungry period before harvests, to ransom captured kin, or to undertake a costly ritual. Although in most cases wealth was repaid in kind, political support and labor service were expected nonmonetary parts of the "interest." Creditors therefore exerted substantial social leverage over their debtors and indeed were often their direct social superiors. When the Mascarene demand for slaves reached into the Malagasy highlands and leaders first set the precedent by selling captives as export slaves, some creditors dared turn their positions of social privilege into new forms of personal advantage.[71]

This process is best illustrated by the making and transformation of social dependents known as *zazahova*, a kind of pawn. Persons appear to have become *zazahova* in three primary ways. The first, as security pledged against a loan, most closely approximates the classical notion of human pawnship operable in many African societies during the era of the slave trade (not all loans obligated debtors to post human security, however.)[72] Unable to fulfill the terms of their financial obligations, debtors could be pursued before kings, chiefs, or their appointed judicial officials.[73] If a solution could not be reached, a debtor might be declared *zazahova* by a competent judicial or political authority.[74] Finally, the dependants of persons condemned or executed by royal justice normally fell into *zazahova* status until relatives redeemed them. Whatever the process of induction, to become *zazahova* was to have financial, material, or social obligation transformed into personal dependence and labor service. *Zazahova* became attached to creditor households as minor members (they were considered among that wide and slippery category of household dependents commonly referred to as *ankizy*, such as children, slaves, and hangers-on). Highland Malagasy symbolically contrasted *zazahova* with adult persons who were entitled to all the gendered privileges of majority in highland society. A specific legal and social category, *zazahova* represented a dishonored social status in which a debtor performed labor service for a creditor or patron as interest on an obligation until that obligation, usually but not always a loan, was repaid. According to communal ethos at 1770, *zazahova* was generally an accepted social station, however disliked by those who filled it.

Was *zazahova* a state of slavery? In his comparative study of slavery, Orlando Patterson defines slaves as kinless, generally dishonored, and natally alienated individuals.[75] Measured by this widely accepted definition of slavery, *zazahova* can only partially be described as slaves. Like slaves, *zazahova* were generally dishonored persons but they were neither kinless nor removed from their homelands. Far from it. A dictionary compiled by British missionaries and published in Antananarivo in 1835 defines *zazahova* as "a slave who is a descendant of a Hova [i.e., highlander]."[76] *Zazahova* seldom lived distant from kin and some even negotiated to eat and sleep within their own households. In some cases *zazahova* women could maintain separate households with their children while serving their new patron; in others, individuals were attached directly to their social superior's household and resided there.[77] According to communal ethos, *zazahova* could not be sold.[78] A common ancestral proverb captured this communal ethic: "As poor as debtors might be, they cannot be sold into slavery."[79] Evidence concerning the duration of *zazahova* status is ambiguous. While some texts claim the status could be passed to children if mothers were not redeemed, most *zazahova* who remained in Madagascar were probably eventually redeemed by kinfolk.[80] *Zazahova* occupied a social status distinct from a second category of household dependents known as *andevo*. *Andevo* more closely match Patterson's definition of slaves. Like slaves, *andevo* were natally alienated outsiders normally drawn from beyond the Malagasy highlands. Before 1770 there were relatively few *andevo* in central Madagascar (this is why most export slaves had to be generated through new enslavements).[81] Those *andevo* in highland Malagasy societies by the mid-eighteenth century were probably captured during engagements with surrounding peoples, especially the Sakalava, or had been imported from east Africa across the Mozambique Channel and through the northwest coast.

Andevo differed from *zazahova* in a range of ways. *Zazahova* spoke highland dialects, *andevo* did not. *Zazahova* shared a homeland and close ancestry with their masters, *andevo* did not. *Zazahova* and their masters participated in the same highland rituals from birth, *andevo* were new to highland society and culture. *Andevo* were outsiders while *zazahova* originated from the Malagasy highlands. It was the kinlessness of *andevo* first entering highland society that distinguished them from *zazahova*.[82] Although the status of *andevo* was probably well known in highland Madagascar by 1770, the sources of such slaves were few. Selling *zazahova* to merchants intending to export them to the Mascarenes, removing them from kin and homeland, and depriving them of their communally secured rights as insider social inferiors made *andevo* out of *zazahova*. Such novel actions of the late eighteenth century breached the expectation that *zazahova* and *andevo* constituted separate social statuses with differing rights. The sale of *zazahova* to itinerant merchants blurred the distinctions between categories of social dependents and represented an attempt by the wealthy to reshape legitimate patronage behavior to their own benefit. As on the African continent, highland Malagasy socially demarcated pawns from slaves, but creditors often disregarded those communally asserted rights by sliding pawns over into the category of salable commodities.[83]

The erosion of moral safeguards surrounding *zazahova* status was socially revolutionary in that it subjected many common people to the perils of export enslavement at the hands of their wealthier neighbors. Disregarding the rights invested in *zazahova* considerably increased the power of patrons, creditors, and masters in their relationships with social inferiors and debtors. High-landers' memories of the ever-present threat of sale to European traders during the era of the slave trade demonstrate the degree to which commoners were concerned by breaches in this morality of enslavement. In a rare passage of the *Tantara* running counter to the general social amnesia of export enslavement, Malagasy conceived the new dangers to which they were subjected through colorful metaphors of cannibalism and consumption, identifying European merchants rather than their Malagasy slavers as the parties most responsible for the unjustified "eating" of the poor.

Andrianampoinimerina did not allow Europeans to come up here [into the heart of Imerina]. From ancient times, among those who ruled in the past, there were none who had seen Europeans. They used to say "Europeans eat people." This was a terrible curse in the past: "We will sell you at Ampamoizan-kova" [a place along the route from highland Madagascar to the east coast where the Indian Ocean is first seen], and "We will sell you to the Europeans." During the time of Andrianampoinimerina if someone said "I am going to send you to Tamatave," it was considered the worst imaginable curse. Those two meeting places, Ampamoizan-kova and Angavokely, were places where people were sold to the Europeans.[84]

Captives sometimes committed suicide thinking that they had fallen into the hands of cannibals. Nineteenth-century Malagasy historian Raombana explains.

The Hova or people of Imerina, had the idea that the Europeans are Cannibals, and that it is the above which compels them to come up to Imerina, for to buy slaves that they may eat them in their own Countries. These ideas are so strong in their minds, that a great number of slaves who were to be sold to them, committed suicides, thereby preferring to kill themselves suddenly, than to be taken across the seas there to be fattened for to be feasted upon by greedy and voracious Europeans. The above was at the above time, the opinions of the generality of the people of Imerina.[85]

Because of the hazardous relationship between wealth lending and enslavement in the highland Malagasy economy of the late eighteenth century, farmers nurtured circumspect attitudes toward wealth lending.[86] A passage in the *Tantara* bemoans the social inequality inherent in moneylending and pawnship: "The people are now tired of what was once common practice—people crying out, 'Give me money and I will live with you and be your slave.'"[87] If the sale of *zazahova* into the Mascarene trade significantly increased the number of highland Malagasy at risk of enslavement, the prolif-

eration of kidnapping that soon followed intensified the social crisis and broadened insecurity within the maturing economy of enslavement.

KIDNAPPING: THE DEMOCRATIZATION OF ENSLAVEMENT

From its origins in the marketing of war prisoners and the sale of *zazahova,*
slavemaking moved beyond the abuse of legitimately unequal social relationships into simple kidnapping, available to everyone and nearly always
considered an act of complete injustice.[88] Common people sometimes kidnapped out of sheer greed but mostly they did so because of the heavy economic and social pressures impinging upon them. These pressures in turn
stemmed from the rapid intrusion of the European slave trade into highland
Madagascar. If someone from within a close network of kin fell victim to
enslavement, she might be saved if relatives exchanged her for a kidnapped
captive of their own or repurchased her. Soon after highland elites sold the
first slaves into export enslavement, then, commoners learned that retrieving
victimized members required either silver coins or replacement slaves. If
highland Malagasy located kin within the slave caravans of itinerant merchants, traders usually required, one merchant wrote, that the enslaved individual be replaced by another slave rather than redeemed for money.[89] Such
demands cut into the fabric of moral communities, pushing highlanders to
engage in slaving themselves to save their "lost" (*very*) kinspeople.[90] By increasing demand for exportable individuals, kings and creditors drew their
subordinates involuntarily into the trading system and thereby reduced local
resistance to it, undercutting communal solidarity. The time frame within
which these incremental erosions of social relationships began to generate
slaves was exceedingly short—little more than a decade or two before 1780
as the slaving frontier passed swiftly throughout highland Madagascar. Originating as a precocious act by kings, slavemaking quickly progressed into a
covert, competitive, and violent business as individuals were surreptitiously
captured and delivered through complex local trading networks to merchants
supplying the Mascarene trade. Kidnapping was a measure of the acuteness
of the crisis of enslavement in central Madagascar, for it signaled that making slaves was no longer confined to the wealthy with privileged access to
institutions that managed large numbers of people.

Kidnapping was symbolic of the tragedy and irony of a maturing slaving
economy: to save themselves from enslavement, common people turned to
enslaving others.[91] In doing so they further damaged the morality of enslavement that served to protect them all from the potentially arbitrary actions of
their social superiors. Herein lies the error of strictly market-oriented interpretations of slave supply that portray slavers as economic free agents who
set aside their moral compunctions over enslavement when the offering price

for captives became too tempting to pass up.[92] In central Madagascar, as elsewhere in Africa, slaves were often created at the end of a long chain of coercion and debt, sometimes reaching back to European banks. While the economy of enslavement disproportionately benefited the wealthy who could generate slaves along self-fashioned networks of credit and patronage, the proliferation of kidnapping implicated a much wider and more popular circle of individuals who enslaved under the duress of various forms of social coercion or to enjoy the fruits of the economy of enslavement along with the wealthy and socially powerful. Slaving in highland Madagascar expanded as if a snowball on a hill, broadening as it rolled along, attracting ever wider networks of people into the sordid business of making slaves and selling human beings off into perpetual oblivion from kin.[93]

Kidnapping fostered a chronically insecure political climate as kings, chiefs, judicial officials, merchants, and desperate commoners alternately sparred with one another and cooperated to acquire silver or to save themselves from misfortune. Although the social and political insecurity of a slavemaking economy characterized by kidnapping adversely affected the highland trading environment, European merchants actively encouraged the practice.[94] Secluded, sparsely populated rural areas were the most likely regions in which kidnappers lurked. A particularly dangerous time to walk alone was in the evening, returning from a regional market or a far-lying field. A passage in the *Tantara* associates kidnapping with travel to and from rural markets.

> Markets were places where people sold things to each other during the day. But when evening came people began to shoot at each other. They would again come together to sell when they entered the markets. People were not bold enough to travel at night so they returned home during the day: They were afraid they would be stolen by the powerful and sold for export. People were afraid of being grabbed by others if they returned home at night.[95]

Kidnapping of herders, farmers working their fields, travelers, and residents of small and isolated villages were both frequent and seldom punished.[96] A young highland girl who served as a domestic slave in the home of Eugène de Froberville, a Creole of Île de France, recounted (in Mauritius) the story of her kidnapping shortly after the beginning of the nineteenth century. "Our parents," she remarked,

> told us that we should flee every time we saw whites or other strangers. I was with other children of the village playing in the fields when several travelers appeared on the path and advanced toward us. Our first thought was to save ourselves, but the strangers did not pursue us and we stopped,

ready to resume our flight if they came closer. We saw them set a sack on
the ground and then leave. When we lost sight of them, we carefully approached the sack which, to our great joy, contained salt, so precious and
good. We immediately set about emptying it and dividing it among our-
selves. But we had hardly finished satisfying our greed when the slave
traders (for that is what these travelers were) came running, captured us
and carried us away despite all our cries and our resistance.[97]

In this story, kidnapping is interpreted as clever entrapment by means of
valued commodities. Merchant Nicolas Mayeur described kidnapping and
highland rural insecurity during 1777 in even more florid terms.

These people are kidnappers far more than one can imagine. People kidnap others and sell them to the first stranger whom they see. According to
the ancient laws of the land, the kidnapping of a man or a woman is punishable by execution. But there are perpetrators who escape. And because
these highland people are very keen to benefit, the lure of wealth and the
hope of impunity triumph over fear. When a kidnapper is actually appre-
hended, this same interest also works upon the spirit of the judge, who
pardons the criminal for a fine of fifteen or twenty slaves, or of the same
value in cattle or silver. The wealth of kidnappers is loved greater than
their lives, which are sacrificed only if they have nothing to pay.[98]

Despite the self-righteousness of Mayeur's account (he must have frequently purchased kidnapped highlanders), its characterization of the underlying mixture of desperation and self-interest that sustained kidnapping vividly depicts the moral and practical dilemmas that faced highland Malagasy
at the end of the eighteenth century. Dumaine, another *traitant*, described
this climate of rampant insecurity and social crisis in 1790.

The methods that they employ to procure slaves for us are nearly all repugnant. A man powerful because of his wealth or his credit does not hesitate at all to seek a quarrel with his weaker neighbor to unjustly deprive
him of his personal liberty. A father sells his children; a child traffics in the
authors of his life. Others take travelers along roads or goat herders and
sell them in the markets held each week in different parts of the highlands.
Several will assemble with weapons and surprise villages during the night
to kidnap the poor inhabitants. Finally, others employ a perfidious ruse
against strange travelers who are too credulous. Some Hovas, I am told,
have put a very deep pit in their house that they have covered with mats.
They ordinarily put an old woman at the door of the house to invite unsuspecting strangers passing by to take some refreshments or food; and if the
man is surprised by the persuasive manners of the woman, he enters and

falls down the hole, from which he cannot escape without help. When night arrives, people come to take him from the hole, pass a cord around his neck, and then go and sell the innocent victim. Many slaves in Hancove are also procured as prisoners of war; these are more rightly acquired.[99]

Dumaine's and Mayeur's descriptions of kidnapping do not entirely speak for themselves. The indignant language *traitants* employed—"repugnant" procedures for creating slaves, "unjustly" deprived personal liberty, disregard for "the ancient laws of the land"—is curious, to say the least, for men who earned their living through the commerce in slaves! Together, Mayeur and Dumaine were responsible for transporting thousands of humans out of the Malagasy highlands. These accounts suggest that the two traders, one of whom spoke the Malagasy language (Mayeur) and both of whom possessed considerable Malagasy cultural knowledge, were acutely conscious that many slaves were created through perversions of a generally accepted morality of enslavement. The image of a duplicitous old woman inviting unsuspecting male passers-by to refresh themselves at her doorstep only to plunge them into a concealed pit encodes a moral vision of enslavement as unjust entrapment leading to a shocking breakdown of virtuous social relations.[100] It may also express a perceived inversion of normal gender roles. In the story, female hospitality, which under normal circumstances served to strengthen social relationships, was the very means by which men were treacherously captured. The tale's emphasis on female agency matches women's key role in the slave trade as associates and informants of foreign merchants (chapter 2). Although cultural outsiders, *traitants* recognized the brazenness with which highlanders twisted social relationships and eroded civic virtue to acquire wealth in silver or to stave off familial disaster. "The king obtains a tax of five piasters from the seller of these poor slaves," wrote one contemporary European visitor, "and therefore tolerates these atrocities which contribute to his wealth."[101] The *traitants* were complicit in these very actions themselves, of course, although the wording of their journals shifts responsibility onto their Malagasy colleagues.

Despite their self-serving renditions of responsibility for slaving, European merchants described pliable local moralities of enslavement. Prisoners of war, Dumaine reasoned, "were more rightly acquired" than the kidnapped. While prisoners of war made generally more acceptable slaves than the kidnapped, enslavement of war captives itself was not seen as categorically legitimate, only more so than kidnapping. Measured by communally formulated moralities of enslavement acknowledged even by foreign merchants, many of the highland slaves created for export were unjustly enslaved. Because of this perception and through the stories highlanders told of enslavement (like that of the duplicitous old woman sitting at the door of her house or the children enticed by a bag of salt), the slave trade came to be widely understood as immoral entrapment, for it thrived on successive perversions of civic virtue with regard to enslavement.[102] And yet despite the generally perceived immorality of the economy of enslavement, many highland Malagasy continued to enslave. Walter Rodney reported a similar situation in which European and African merchants passed the hot potato of responsibility. He wrote that Capuchin missionaries at Cacheu asked African rulers why they participated in enslavement and found "that African slavers recognized their profession for the evil it was, but contended that they indulged in man-stealing because the whites would purchase no other goods." Rodney concluded his discussion of enslavement by noting that if Africans limited exports to those who were "justly" enslaved by their own reckoning, they would, in effect, "call for the abolition of the slave trade."[103] Popular African commentary on enslavement and the trade as manifestations of witchcraft and cannibalism tends to confirm these conclusions, as do modern discourses about slavery that employ local moral codes to criticize enslavement.[104] Like Africans and Europeans in the Atlantic, highland Malagasy were capable of violating their own moralities of enslavement. Communally defined evil lurked behind the making of slaves.

If highland Madagascar's economy of enslavement was initiated through the actions of a social elite, it spread rapidly as some common people, for a variety of reasons, began to participate in slaving. Because they captured and sold human beings, highlanders contributed to an acceleration of social and political disintegration in central Madagascar. The outcome of enslavement that most profoundly animated highland Malagasy politics in the late eighteenth century was a violation of trust in social relationships, both those between rulers and their subjects and among common highlanders themselves. Breaches of civic virtue were evident in each of the many social transformations that characterized central Madagascar during the last quarter of the eighteenth century. The era of the slave trade was a period of rapid change in highland social practices, one that deepened the cleavages and experiences of inequality and violated social arrangements among highlanders and between *firenena* and their kings. First elites, then commoners, sought to progressively collapse, each time with greater brazenness, the distinctions among several separate social categories of humans to enslave. Rural communities did not passively accept this process. Contradictory though highlanders' resistance to enslavement could be (because many participated in enslaving others), opposition was nevertheless present. Resistance did not crystallize around the idea of a universal immunity from enslavement but around specific breaches of civic virtue that resulted in the enslavement of particular individuals with whom highlanders sustained moral relationships they were willing to defend. *Firenena* were not simply defensive players in this game of people and products, attempting to restore pristine customs of the past in a nefarious economy of enslavement. They were key players in Malagasy politics who actively sought to reshape the future of highland society to the benefit of kin and *firenena*. The strategies, triumphs, and limitations of local politics in the era of the slave trade are remarkably illustrated through an instance of *firenena* protest against royal practices of enslavement deemed illegitimate.

CONTESTING ENSLAVEMENT

In 1785 members of *firenena* Ravoandriana boldly challenged their king for selling free persons to a European trader as *andevo* slaves. Our knowledge of the Ravoandriana uprising, one of the three stories offered in the first chapter of this book, does not stem from any of the major parties to the conflict—king Andrianamboatsimarofy or members of the Ravoandriana—but from the observations and experiences of a peripheral participant, *traitant* Nicolas Mayeur. Both extant accounts of the conflict were edited by Barthélémy Huet de Froberville, a contemporary of Mayeur who collected information about Madagascar for British governor Robert Farquhar of Mauritius, and are part of Farquhar's personal collection of Madagascar-related manuscripts now held in the British Library, London. One of the accounts takes the form of a Malagasy–French dictionary entry under the noun *Ravouandriène* (I call this the "*dictionnaire*" account, see Photograph 3.1); the other, a journal of travels and trade in highland Madagascar during 1785 (the "*voyage*" account).[105] The two accounts are so structurally similar that it is reasonable to assume they both stem from a single text originally produced by Nicolas Mayeur.[106] They do not contradict each other in the main, although there are some significant variations between them. With these two documents historians are twice removed from the Ravoandriana protest. Mayeur did participate in some of the incidents described, as shall presently be seen, but he was not party to transactions between the Ravoandriana and their king. Presumably Mayeur gleaned this information from colleagues in the Malagasy highlands. The stories were additionally filtered through the interests and redactions of Barthélémy Huet de Froberville, who prepared the manuscripts in their final form in Mauritius. The story conveyed in the two narratives is a convoluted tale of intrigue and political fluidity, key characteristics of highland Malagasy society during the era of the slave trade. The principal players in the drama are members of the Ravoandriana *firenena* and three highland rulers: Andrianjafy, king at Ilafy; Andrianampoinimerina, king at Ambohimanga and opponent of Andrianjafy; and Andrianamboatsimarofy, king at Antananarivo (see Map 1.2). Peripheral characters are *traitants* Mayeur and Savoureux. The Ravoandriana were free subjects of

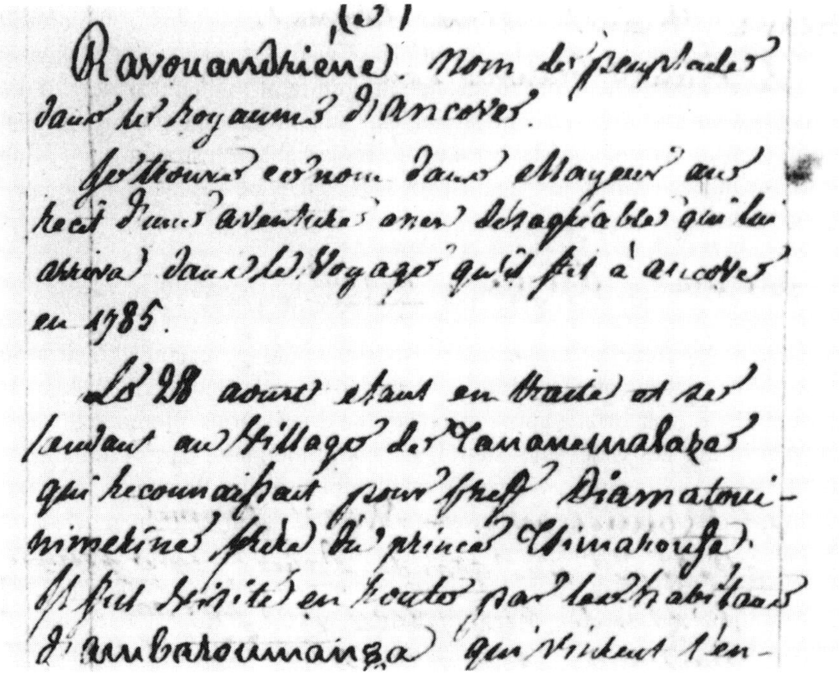
Ravouandriène. Nom des peuplades dans les royaumes d'ancoves.
Je trouve ce nom dans Mayeur aux recit d'une aventure assez désagréable qui lui arriva dans le voyage qu'il fit à ancoves en 1785.
Le 28 aoust étant en route et se rendant au village de Tananemalaza qui reconnaissait pour chef Diamatoui-nimerine frère du prince Dimahoufa. Il fut visité en route par les habitants d'ambatoumanga qui vivent l'en-

Photograph 3.1 Beginning of the entry for "Ravouandriène," in Barthélémy Huet de Froberville's manuscript *Grand dictionnaire de Madagascar*. A Malagasy-French dictionary completed in about 1816, the *Grand dictionnaire* was based largely on information provided by *traitants* who operated in eastern and highland Madagascar. This entry is one of two historical sources for the Ravoandriana revolt of 1785 and probably stemmed from a manuscript originally composed by Nicolas Mayeur in the late eighteenth century. (*Source*: Barthélémy Huet de Froberville, ed., *Le grand dictionnaire de Madagascar*, vol. 4, BL/MD/Add.Mss./18124/141r.)

Andrianjafy, king of Ilafy. They inhabited several villages in the environs of Antanamalaza and Ambatomanga on the eastern fringes of the Malagasy highlands. Both towns exist today, although inquiries there and in the town of Iravoandriana in 1996 and 1997 did not yield a historical memory of either the export commerce or the Ravoandriana revolt.[107]

Competing for political supremacy over Avaradrano (the district to which Ambohimanga, Ilafy, and the Ravoandriana all belonged, see Map 5.1), kings Andrianjafy and Andrianampoinimerina enlisted the support of rural *firenena*. *Tantara* versions of the struggles between Andrianjafy and Andrianampoinimerina are replete with similar royal bids for communal support, and so the resort to wooing descent groups as a political strategy for building a kingdom as portrayed in this struggle are altogether believable.[108] The Ravoandriana flexed autonomous political muscle by withdrawing their support from Andrianjafy and offering it to his rival, Andrianampoinimerina. This was not an exceptional act for *firenena*. In numerous *Tantara* narratives, shifts of rural support for royalty usually occurred secretly, the new alignment being revealed only when "devious" subjects refused to fight for their king, or when they purposely forfeited an important battle.[109] The Ravoandriana must have anticipated a swift victory for Andrianampoinimerina, who they reasonably believed would then protect them as defectors from their erstwhile king. But as it turned out Andrianampoinimerina was unable to deliver protection or to fulfill his bid to unseat Andrianjafy at Ilafy (he was successful at a later time). For his part Andrianjafy was exasperated with the Ravoandriana and, no longer able to trust in their support, abandoned his rights over them to a third ruler, king Andrianamboatsimarofy at Antananarivo. The condition of this transfer of sovereignty was revenge: Andrianjafy stipulated as a requirement of the transfer that Andrianamboatsimarofy enslave and sell at least a portion of the Ravoandriana as *andevo* slaves eastward into the export trade. The "*voyage*" account explains what happened next.

> This prince [Andrianamboatsimarofy] could not refuse an arrangement through which his insatiable cupidity might profit. In consequence, he invited the Ravoandriana of both sexes to come in person on a day he indicated to present their homage to him. Without anticipating the fate that awaited them, and filled with confidence in the great generosity of the prince [Andrianamboatsimarofy], the Ravoandriana set out with the customary gifts. But on the road they were assaulted and most of them arrested by agents of Andrianamboatsimarofy dispatched especially for that purpose. The next day 25 or 30 were sold to Mr. Savoureux.[110]

Despite the Ravoandriana's earlier resolution to support Andrianampoinimerina against Andrianjafy, they agreed to the new transaction for the transfer of their sovereignty to Andrianamboatsimarofy. Two reasons for their compliance with the transfer present themselves. First, Andrianampoinimerina's bid to dispossess Andrianjafy of his kingdom at Ilafy was unsuccessful, hence the Ravoandriana could not as yet count upon Andrianampoinimerina for protection. Second, perhaps the Ravoandriana were eager to be finished with Andrianjafy, for he was otherwise reputed to be highly unpopular.[111] Finally, given the Ravoandriana's acceptance of the transfer and their keen sense of their own potential for collective autonomous action, they must have felt it was within the "rules" of highland Malagasy politics for Andrianjafy to transfer a treacherous *firenena* into the domain of a nearby king. They accordingly set out with "the customary gifts" to swear allegiance to their new protector-king at Antananarivo. The *"dictionnaire"* version claims that the Ravoandriana accomplished that ritual act of submission before they were fallen upon by toughs of their new patron king and enslaved; the *"voyage"* account, on the other hand, claims they were ambushed while en route to Antananarivo. Both narratives concur, however, that between twenty-five and thirty of the captured Ravoandriana were sold to Savoureux the next day.

The Ravoandriana reacted swiftly and with determination to the news that their representatives had been insultingly treated like kinless, rightless *andevo*, captured, and summarily sold to a passing merchant. Both accounts claim that 6,000 of them immediately searched the countryside for their captured kinspeople and converged on Antananarivo. Caught off his guard (probably because he did not anticipate an active and immediate resistance) Andrianamboatsimarofy abandoned his capital and fled in the company of Savoureux, the very *traitant* to whom he had just sold some twenty-five or thirty of the Ravoandriana! His flight is a puissant reminder of the strategic alliances highland kings and foreign slave merchants forged at the end of the eighteenth century. Ravoandriana anger was eventually calmed by their "deference to kings," one narrative suggests, and through performance of the blood brotherhood ritual of *fatidra* (between whom is not specified, but one surmises between key leaders of the Ravoandriana and king Andrianamboatsimarofy), and, the *"dictionnaire"* narrative claims, the release of some of those enslaved.

The confidence and the vehemence with which the Ravoandriana immediately challenged their new king are remarkable, as is the rapidity with which they sought to repair, at least on the surface, their damaged relationship with him. Having considerable experience in the high-stakes game of highland politics, the Ravoandriana were aware of the dangers that a full and prolonged breach in social relationships with a patron king could visit upon them. Collective security required highlanders to maintain a veneer of normalcy with their untrustworthy political leaders. Common highlanders without patrons were unprotected, awash in the dangerous seas of a society in which the powerful often abused their relationships with social inferiors. Yet their need for a patron king and protector did not at the same time prevent the Ravoandriana from invoking their own vision of proper royal behavior. They assembled together to consider how to deal with the problematic Andrianamboatsimarofy, highland kings in general, and their enslaved kinspeople in particular. The *"dictionnaire"* account explains the deliberations at this poignant meeting.

The result of the deliberation was that Andrianjafy having voluntarily renounced his rights over them and having freely transmitted them to
Andrianamboatsimarofy, the latter had thereby become their real sovereign. In consequence they would affirm the allegiance they had already
placed in his hands. It was realized that an act so monstrous had only been
committed at the solicitation of chief Andrianjafy and resolved that the
abuse would be denounced both to Andrianamboatsimarofy himself and to
all the other princes so that it might stop entirely. Finally the Ravoandriana
did solemnly and in the form of an oath make the resolution not to allow
any Ravoandriana under whatever condition or to whomever they had been
sold to leave the province.[112]

The substance of the deliberations suggests that while the Ravoandriana
considered their transfer from Andrianjafy to Andrianamboatsimarofy legitimate (hence implying an admission of the illegitimacy with which they
had first supported Andrianampoinimerina), they found Andrianamboatsimarofy's subsequent capture and sale of some thirty of their nonslave
number to be preposterous in the extreme. Hence the resolution to recognize Andrianamboatsimarofy and to absolve him of blame, claiming that
he had been "solicited" and led astray by the devious request of
Andrianjafy. The course of action elected by the assembly is telling. The
Ravoandriana were quick to absolve their new patron king of personal
responsibility for the sale, laying accountability at the feet of their erstwhile sovereign who had hatched the underhanded plot in the first place.
Collective security and deference to their new king despite Andrianamboatsimarofy's deep and real culpability in the perceived injustice (by
enslaving the Ravoandriana Andrianamboatsimarofy may have been sending a calculated warning to the *firenena* against secretly abandoning him
as they recently had Andrianjafy) required that the Ravoandriana displace
blame toward the party with whom they had already severed their political relationship, Andrianjafy. Yet at the same time they directed a warning toward highland kings in general, making it known that they would
accept no such "abuse" from any of them. In the "*voyage*" narrative, the
assembly named some 300 *firenena* members recently—and, they felt,
illegitimately—captured and sold for export. The Ravoandriana had suffered serious losses to the export trade over recent years and were seeking to impress upon their rulers a communal understanding of civic virtue as it applied to royal behavior, one consistent with preservation of the
domestic citizenship rights of nonslave persons. The public enumeration
of 300 "lost" was a powerful evocation of memory in a political struggle.
The sense of pragmatic and carefully considered action that emanates from
these deliberations demonstrates the creative capacity of highland Mala-

gasy to navigate the constraints of highland politics in an imaginative and sometimes effective manner.

Mayeur first learned of all these events on his way into Imerina, where he planned to purchase slaves. The *"dictionnaire"* account explains:

> On August 28 Mayeur was purchasing slaves and heading toward the village of Antanamalaza which recognized Andrianampoinimerina, brother of Andrianamboatsimarofy, as its chief. He was visited en route by the inhabitants of Ambatomanga who wanted him to engage in commerce with them. They told Mayeur, however, that they did not anticipate the king of Ancove [Andrianamboatsimarofy] would grant them that favor because he had become displeased with them: not because of insubordination—they recognized him as their sovereign—nor because he had any complaints about their loyalty, but because he knew they were justified in making representations to him on an unhappy affair of which they were the victims. Mayeur asked them what the affair was and offered them his services as mediator with the prince. They thanked him, but contented themselves by telling him that because purchasing slaves was the object of his voyage they engaged him strongly not to purchase any Ravoandriana of free caste. He would certainly lose them, resolved as they were to wrest them from whomever held them. The inhabitants of Ambatomanga additionally told Mayeur that Mr. Savoureux had just purchased several Ravoandriana from prince Andrianamboatsimarofy and that quite certainly Savoureux would not get them out of the country. Mayeur was very thankful for this opening and promised these good people to not purchase anyone who was known to be free.[113]

Ravoandriana living at Ambatomanga confronted Mayeur, delivering him a threat. They warned him not to purchase any illegitimately enslaved kin, whom they resolved to remove from trade caravans by force if necessary. At the same time they indicated to Mayeur that they had slaves of their own to sell ("wanted him to engage in commerce with them"). The account embodies, then, the chief contradiction facing rural highland Malagasy during the era of the slave trade: protection of one's own kin sometimes required enslaving others, effectively undercutting the possibility of inter-*firenena* alliances against enslavement. Mayeur could not purchase slaves from the Ravoandriana without the permission of their king ("they did not anticipate that the king of Ancove would grant them that favor"), but that Mayeur communicated directly with potential rural suppliers of slaves away from the "mother town" and its rulers reveals that kings could not entirely hope to control the trade nor suppress the flow of information between merchants and common Malagasy.

Unlike in west central Africa, where kings sought to insulate their subjects from the merchants who moved humans off to the coast or along the Guinea coast where Europeans "dealt with Africans through the ruling class," *traitants* in highland Madagascar mingled among the common people.[114] Highlanders used their frequent encounters with itinerant foreigners to monitor their activities and to promote their self-defined interests. While they remained subjects of particular rulers who legislated the rules of commerce, commoners might also pursue independent political strategies with passing merchants. Indeed, what the Ravoandriana revealed to Mayeur was the soreness of their relationship with their king resulting from his recent sale of Ravoandriana to Savoureux. Mayeur offered to mediate the dispute for them with Andrianamboatsimarofy. That Mayeur felt he might effectively intercede with Andrianamboatsimarofy for the *firenena* suggests that *firenena* sometimes employed foreign intermediaries on political errands and that *traitants* could be politically intimate with highland Malagasy rural communities as well as with their kings.[115] The *"dictionnaire"* account here challenges a stereotype of slave merchants and the communities from which they wrenched slaves as implacable enemies unconcerned with mutual social relationships and public perceptions of the legitimacy of their actions. (More cynically, or perhaps more realistically, it reveals the depth of their mutual complicity in making slaves.) Slaving societies like those of highland Madagascar were structured by complex and contradictory relationships, confounding simple formulations of complicity and resistance. Yet opposition to particular kinds of enslavements there was, even if that opposition in many instances was disregarded by rulers, merchants, and others.

One month later, when Mayeur and his Malagasy associates were leaving Imerina with caravans of plodding slaves, they were again accosted by members of the Ravoandriana. The *"voyage"* narrative continues.

At one *lieue* of distance from Antanamalaza, Mayeur learned that the inhabitants of Ambatomanga had seized six slaves from some of his people who had preceded him [on their way eastward out of the highlands], under the pretext that they were of free extraction. The people of Ambatomanga stopped Mayeur himself by their village and threatened to pillage his caravan. He owed his health, on this occasion, to the prudence of some elders of the place, who employed all their influence on the multitude to make them back off. Acutely alarmed by this catastrophe, which he had not anticipated because of the precautions he had taken not to have any Ravoandriana among his slaves, he got away from that dangerous countryside very promptly. He managed to arrive, by about four o'clock in the afternoon, at the town of Ambatoitany.[116]

Despite their warning to Mayeur on his way into the country, the Ravoandriana at Ambatomanga accused the *traitant* of purchasing unjustly enslaved members of their *firenena*. Because of their strategic location along the eastern confines of Imerina—which *traitants* were obliged to traverse with their captives on their way to the coast—they were in a position to enforce their opinions. The contested captives were returned to freedom.[117] While *traitants* and common highland Malagasy sometimes engaged each other in mutually beneficial relationships, underlying tensions frequently broke to the surface. Mayeur and his caravan were nearly assaulted near Ambatomanga by an angry crowd. The *traitant* and his entourage escaped only because of determined intervention on their behalf by some of the village elders. Mayeur's strategy was to flee from Ambatomanga as fast as he could to put himself away from that "dangerous countryside." To what extent Mayeur had heeded the Ravoandriana's warning not to purchase their kinspeople and actively inquired into the origins of his slaves cannot be known. That he dispatched Malagasy merchant deputies to precede him with coffles of slaves (as many *traitants* did) suggests that his Malagasy agents traveled independently about the highlands purchasing and conveying captives for him, perhaps in the effort to prevent the concentration of bondpeople lest they easily sicken or combine in revolt. Mayeur could not have directly supervised the transactions of all his associates, who may well have purchased slaves also on their own account.[118]

The "*dictionnaire*" version portrays a more diplomatic and nuanced confrontation between Mayeur and the Ravoandriana. While the Ravoandriana followed through with threats to release illegitimately enslaved members from both Mayeur's and Savoureux's caravans, they absolved Mayeur of any responsibility for having purchased some Ravoandriana, saying he must have been "tricked" into doing so. Not only did *firenena* seek to maintain stable relationships with untrustworthy patron kings who might potentially protect them and with whom they could deal in a moment of difficulty, they carefully cultivated their contacts with the very merchants who carried so many highland Malagasy off into bondage at the Mascarenes! Perhaps sometime in the future the Ravoandriana might need to bargain with a *traitant* for release of a kinsperson, to obtain another favor, or to sell him captives of their own (this may have been the gist of the message delivered by the elders who interceded with the angry crowd at Ambatomanga). The irony of these contradictory but carefully cultivated relationships between *traitants* and highland *firenena* illustrates the dilemma of the economy of enslavement with great poignancy: rarely did rural communities possess either the will or the power to challenge the commerce itself and its merchants as immoral. Rather, they concentrated on battles closer to home, specific incidents pertaining to their own kin and *firenena* that conflicted with their sense of civic virtue and moral enslavement. In such contests they could sometimes be highly successful. Yet at the same time their focus on local struggles for *firenena* preservation prevented an effective front against the many tragedies and atomizing social consequences of the slave trade as a larger system. While they protested the sale of their own kin, some of them continued to sell others.

AUTONOMY AND ITS LIMITS

Whether generated through war, a disregard for *zazahova*'s rights, or by kidnapping, export slaves were produced through intense social conflict. Slavemaking within the highland frontier of enslavement did not integrate the societies of central Madagascar; it tore them apart. Conflict reinforced a sense of local belonging as kin strove to save their own yet remained complicit in the enslavement of others. The moral communities to which individuals might turn for protection were shrinking. Common highlanders actively sought alliances with kings for refuge, but kings were unlikely, in return, to ransom individual subjects from slave caravans should their luck take a turn for the worse. When Walter Rodney remarked of rulers along the upper Guinea coast that "their responsibilities for the security of their subjects had been almost entirely jettisoned," he might have described many of the late eighteenth-century leaders of central Madagascar.[119] Individuals were left to seek their own means of security. Creating dense ties of kinship and moral obligation was one of the strategies pursued by highland Malagasy to protect themselves from the slaving elite and from one another. Doing so was often extremely difficult and did not always yield the desired result. In an economy of enslavement, the bonds of kinship functioned like a double-edged sword. While they might protect individuals from the depredations of outsiders, they could equally become the means by which dependents were yielded up to enslavement (witness most processes by which *zazahova* were created and subsequently sold into *andevo* slavery). Because of the pervasive social climate of conflict and distrust during the late eighteenth century, slaves were generated in a fluid political field rather than in a fixed and unchanging one. There were no "traditional" social structures in late eighteenth-century highland Madagascar. The first European descriptions of central Madagascar reflect a society already linked into an expanding international economy of commercial capitalism, not an isolated backwater.[120] Highlanders' responses to the local crises of enslavement fostered significant social transformations.

In a time of crisis, kings, merchants, individuals, and kin-based communities each pursued their own interests. Political alliances were broken and reformed. Leaders and subjects exercised considerable autonomy over the political choices they faced. *Firenena* evaluated the options before them and carefully deliberated their rhetorical and political responses to the actions of sometimes unpredictable sovereigns. Kings attempted to erode the social practices and distinctions that served to protect their subjects from enslavement. Both kings and *firenena* articulated their own concepts of civic virtue but did not always abide by them. When they abandoned Andrianjafy, the Ravoandriana, for example, must have felt they could enhance collective security by joining Andrianampoinimerina. That they supported Andrianampoinimerina but were later forced to admit the illegitimacy with which they had done so demonstrates how *firenena* felt themselves no more bound to kings' concepts of civic virtue than their rulers were to communally defined moralities of enslavement. Andrianamboatsimarofy succeeded in his plan to capture and sell thirty Ravoandriana to a French trader, yet when faced with the wrath of some 6,000 Ravoandriana he quickly admitted his "error."

If kings and rural communities negotiated their interests with skill, each nevertheless faced practical constraints in their inevitable mutual dependence. Once they started to enslave, neither kings nor commoners could single-handedly take central Madagascar out of its structural position in the French imperial economy as a supplier of slave labor to the Mascarene islands. Despite their daring bid to switch political allegiance from one king to the next, their physical and verbal protests against a violated morality of enslavement, and their partial victories (such as the Ravoandriana's collective success at releasing enslaved kinspeople), highlanders were unable to arrest the socially corrosive process of enslavement. Indeed, to save themselves from bondage they participated in making slaves of others. Rural folk remained exceedingly vulnerable in the economy of enslavement. Although sensitive to kin-based protests of a violated morality of enslavement, adept rulers usually captured the last moves by turning a politically complicated situation to their own advantage. As a result, rural resistance to the presumptions of powerful men to breach social precedent and sell war captives, then *zazahova*, and finally "free" political dependents to slave traders was sincerely offered but largely ineffective at preventing enslavements over the long run. Rural communities were usually the losers. Despite their determined liberation of some thirty enslaved members in 1785, the Ravoandriana had lost 300 of their number during preceding years. The export slave trade from highland Madagascar endured thirty-five years beyond the Ravoandriana revolt.

On the other hand, kings faced their own constraints. The story of the Ravoandriana's protest illustrates the political perils that awaited kings who chose to engage in the risky business of disregarding the popular opinion embodied in *firenena* theories of moral enslavement to generate export slaves.[121] While distribution of trade wealth generated clients for patron kings, it did not necessarily purchase them greater independence from those same clients. It provided them with a potentially more efficient—and riskier—strategy for accumulating power. Far from "rendering the kings relatively autonomous of domestic political opposition," making slaves from subject dependents enmeshed kings ever deeper in a quagmire of popular resentment, producing a "dangerous countryside."[122] When they engaged in behavior that transgressed a communally asserted morality of enslavement, kings gambled away their public popularity for short-term financial gains. By selling his newly acquired political dependents, king Andrianamboatsimarofy soured his popularity with the Ravoandriana. When 6,000 of his nonslave subjects chased him unceremoniously from Antananarivo, they testified to this political reality. The infamous reputation of Andrianamboatsimarofy for selling his subjects to the Mascarenes was still enshrined in social memory and narrated in verbal traditions some forty years later.[123]

Highland *firenena* played high-stakes politics with limited options, as the story of the Ravoandriana illustrates, but they held one trump card in their depleted hands: they could and did switch political loyalties when it suited their interests. While circumscribed by the limited range of choices available to them, highlanders elected political affiliations that influenced patterns of state formation in highland Madagascar. The Merina kingdom emerged out of such complex games of people and products in the age of the slave trade. In the following chapter I turn to the economic and social impact of the slave trade on highland Malagasy communities and to the strategies commoners and kings each deployed to navigate the social perils and political opportunities of a society in the throes of enslavement.

4

STRATEGIES IN A
SLAVING ECONOMY

> This metal is the spirit that enlivens the commerce of the country.
> —Nicolas Mayeur[1]

An accumulation of enslavements over highland Madagascar's half-century of export trade insured that nearly everyone who escaped personal capture experienced the slaving economy firsthand through some connection to victimized friends and kin. In any one year only a small minority of households could have been directly affected by the loss of kin to the Mascarene trade. Enslavement for export directly visited 1 to 2 percent of highland households each year, at most.[2] But at this rate, between 1770 and 1820 as many as 70 percent of households might have experienced the loss of a member to the export trade. To be sure, this figure overrepresents the reach of the slave trade, for it fails to account for either multiple enslavements afflicting a single household or for individuals captured beyond central Madagascar but funneled through it, which became increasingly common after 1800 (this did not include east African slaves, who transited north of Imerina). Because networks of kinship and acquaintance were much wider than coresidential groups, though, it was considerably more likely for individuals to know someone beyond their immediate coresidents who had been enslaved than to experience enslavement firsthand. Far from everyone was at risk of enslavement or personally visited by the misfortune of capture, but slaving over the half-century of export trade directly touched a significant and ever-expanding proportion of the residents of highland Madagascar with the bitter experience of involuntary separation from enslaved kith and kin.

If the risks of enslavement were pervasive, they were structured by demand for unfree labor at the Mascarenes as well as in highland Madagascar. European colonists in the Indian Ocean islands preferred young male captives, most of whom they put to work at hard labor in agriculture and domestic service. The gendered structure of demand on the Mascarene side of the commercial system preferentially targeted men for enslavement in highland Madagascar and nurtured transformations there in the gender division of labor. These changes in the gendered economy of labor were also promoted by the preference of highland Malagasy for female and youthful dependents/slaves, such as the *zazahova* discussed in the previous chapter. Despite a broadening social participation in enslavement in the Malagasy highlands, silver that flowed into central Madagascar after 1770 was not evenly distributed. The structures of a slaving economy channeled new resources along carefully designed social trajectories that funneled centripetally toward commercially adept kings, then spun back outward along intricate networks of social patronage. By this means the new wealth in trade goods and piasters emerged as a key tool in highland Malagasy domestic political strategies. The most astute kings learned to acquire wealth through participation in the slave trade while maintaining relationships of trust with the *firenena* owing them allegiance. Mastery of this potentially unstable and tension-filled strategy underwrote Andrianampoinimerina's political success. In the late eighteenth century, Andrianampoinimerina achieved control over the eastward flow of slaves to the Mascarenes while at the same time mustering significant political support from the people of his kingdom. This chapter explores the diverse strategies of commoners and sovereigns in highland Madagascar's complex slaving economy.

GENDERED ENSLAVEMENT

Those who created export slaves within central Madagascar carefully selected their victims by age and gender. The first highlanders to dispatch captives into the eastward-bound export commerce were kings who traded men almost exclusively, individuals seized from the realms of opposing leaders (chapter 3). When kidnapping and pawn selling emerged shortly thereafter as consequential methods of enslavement, those who created slaves were no longer constrained by potential supplies of warriors to sell only men, yet for the most part they continued to do so. The demographic structure of Malagasy populations in the Mascarenes provides a first approximation of the significance of gender on enslavement in highland Madagascar. The percentage of women within the Mascarene slave population was always well below that of men. In a study of slavery in Mauritius, Moses Nwulia found that between two-thirds and three-quarters of the Malagasy slaves landed at the Mascarenes were young men.[3] Commenting on an 1812 census that enumerated 59,734 slaves in Mauritius, Mascarene governor Farquhar noted that "The slave popula-

tion of Mauritius and Bourbon consists of Creoles, Caffres, Malays, Hindoos and natives of Madagascar, of which about two-thirds are males."[4] Indeed, from 1740 and until the end of the highland Malagasy slave trade to the Mascarenes in 1820, the proportion of females in Mauritius's slave population hovered at around one-third. Even seven years after the ending of the slave trade from central Madagascar (1827), the slave population of Mauritius consisted of nearly twice as many men as women. Of these slaves, the Madagascar-born comprised 64% men, 34% women, and only 2% children aged sixteen and younger, who were nearly evenly split between boys and girls.[5] On the eve of slave emancipation in 1832, the proportion of females among all the slaves had risen to an all-time high of 40%, no doubt due to the nearly even gender balance among the creole slaves who by then composed more than half the servile population.[6] A similar gender imbalance characterized the slave population of Bourbon in the late eighteenth and early nineteenth centuries.[7]

The demographic composition of slave populations in the Mascarenes approximates the gender distribution of those captured for export in the center of Madagascar, but Mascarene censuses were notoriously inaccurate and may overestimate the proportion of women and girls in the slave trade from Madagascar. *Traitant* Lagardère, for example, arrived in Tamatave from central Madagascar in May 1808 with 157 slaves, 21 of whom were female, or just over 13 percent of the entire caravan.[8] Petitioning for his freedom before the Compensation Committee for the district of Flacq at Mauritius in 1833, one Madagascar-born slave named Narcisse related that during the reign of Andrianampoinimerina (i.e., before 1809) he had been transported to Mauritius aboard a vessel bearing some 350 slaves, of whom 50 were women, or 14 percent.[9] If Lagardère's slave caravan and Narcisse's oceanic passage are representative of the mix of men and women in the Malagasy slave trade, female slaves comprised less than one-fifth of the captives exported from the highlands and loaded onto ships at the coast. Taking the census figures in the preceding paragraph into consideration, however, it is likely that the average proportion of women in the trade over the years was closer to one-third, contrary to what narrative data suggests. Indeed, there is ample evidence of women among highland Malagasy export captives. In August 1762 LeGentil affirmed that women were among the slaves loaded onto ships bound for the Mascarenes.[10] When in the early nineteenth century Bezanozano plundered slave caravans heading toward the coast, they usually removed female captives from them.[11] The French *agent commercial* at Madagascar's east coast noted in 1807 that Mascarene householders prized Malagasy women and girls as maids.[12] At the same time, the practice of favoring female slaves with manumissions in the islands would have skewed Mascarene servile populations toward a higher proportion of men than among new arrivals from Madagascar. Emancipated women often became the mistresses and wives of French settlers.[13] Yet the rate of manumissions during the early nineteenth century suggests that the impact of selective emancipation upon the ratio of male to female slaves was minimal. In a little over two years (1804–1807) only 244 manumissions were recorded at Île de France out of a total slave population of some 60,000.[14] Into the mid-1820s, enfranchisements remained steady at an even lower level of between 50 and 100 each year despite continued growth in the servile population.[15]

The intersection of domestic and international demand for servile labor sustained these gendered patterns of enslavement. Mascarene planters preferred men for field work; Malagasy suppliers chose to sell their male captives to foreigners bound for the islands where the demand for them was greatest and prices highest. Women and children enslaved or pawned in central Madagascar, by contrast, were in high demand there and fewer of them than men were marched eastward to the coast for export. Because they were in higher demand and shorter supply at the east coast, where slaves were loaded onto Mascarene-bound vessels, adult male captives at Tamatave and Foulpointe usually cost 25 percent more than bondwomen.[16] The combination of Mascarene census data and contemporary narrative observations suggests, then, that slave cargoes leaving the Malagasy coast after 1770 consisted of about two-thirds or more men, one-third or fewer women, and an unknown number of children.[17]

This demographic pattern of enslavement dovetails with the political geography of Malagasy captive supply. In the early period of this study, until the last years of Andrianampoinimerina's reign, most slaves sold eastward hailed from within the societies of highland Madagascar itself (within what is now known as Imerina). Although Mascarene owners preferred men, the proliferation and popularization of slavemaking in the late eighteenth century allowed for larger numbers of women to enter the trade than had been the case when most slaves were war prisoners. Promising protection from capture to those who would join him, Andrianampoinimerina threatened to enslave those who refused to submit to his sovereignty.[18] When Andrianampoinimerina died in 1809, his son Radama adopted much the same procedure, but on a much vaster geographical scale, marching huge armies outside the highlands to collect new allegiances and to capture those who resisted.[19] From the center of highland Madagascar, the slaving frontier pushed outward to the coasts after the first decade of the nineteenth century. Highland armies expanding beyond Imerina normally retained female captives of external military expeditions while selling male prisoners to the Mascarenes.[20] This transition in the source of slaves from highland Madagascar to its periphery also marked a dramatic increase in the number of slaves held domestically, most of whom were women and children. From 1770 to 1820, then, the process of making slaves came full circle. Beginning with the early vending of war prisoners controlled largely by kings, it underwent a transitional period (about 1770–1810) when slaves were produced by a variety of individuals largely within the Malagasy highlands. It terminated with the enslavement of war captives outside the highlands by Radama's expanding armies. Throughout this period, enslavement for export was disproportionately the experience of young men in their late teens and twenties.

Highland Malagasy, who during the early and transitional periods outlined in the previous paragraph managed to avoid the tragedy of enslavement, faced a new set of social challenges stemming from the loss of kin into the export commerce. Adjustments to the loss of kin produced far-reaching consequences for household structures, the gendered balance of social power, and the organization of labor, the sort of domestic developments Joseph Miller recently termed the "great transformation."[21] Because of slaving's gendered demography, the many immediate consequences of enslavement all implied a shift in the relationships of men and women in marriage, households, and society. For example, acts of enslavement that generated male export *andevo* slaves produced households of dependent *zazahova* women and children. In judicial proceedings most women were considered dependents of their husbands and, as a result, most debt was incurred by men.[22] Unlike women, men could liquidate debts by pawning their spouses and children to creditors as *zazahova*. Nicolas Mayeur explained: "Men who are in debt or who have committed robbery surrender their wealth as payment. If their wealth is not sufficient to reimburse the theft, nor to pay the debt or the fine, they surrender their wife. It is up to the relatives of the woman to redeem her. If the wife is not enough, they surrender one or several of their children. In the end, they can become slaves themselves."[23] Children and women, especially junior partners within polygynous unions, were among the most vulnerable within interlaced networks of debt that bound men together in patron-client relationships.[24] Wives and children of condemned and indebted men sold as export slaves were usually acquired by the man's creditors or his sovereign as *zazahova*. A *Tantara* passage explains this process as it applied to men condemned by royal justice.

> The people called *zazahova*, they are *hova* but also dependents [*ankizy n'olona*, or literally, "children of people"]. They are not like the majority of *hova*, they are dependents. And this is what makes them *zazahova*: their father commits a fault against royal edict and is enslaved or executed. The

man's wives and children are then appraised and purchased by someone, and they too become dependents. If they do not have relatives to redeem them then their offspring also become dependents. Even *andriana* from across the highlands have been "lost" and became servants of people [*mpanompo n'olona*] when they could not redeem themselves, and they became *zazahova*.[25]

The efforts of highland slavers to increase the number of male captives for export, therefore, correspondingly augmented the number of female and juvenile *zazahova* who remained within the Malagasy highlands (some of these persons, as explained in the previous chapter, were later exported). If there had been a gender balance in *zazahova* held in highland Madagascar before the late eighteenth century, the equilibrium was decidedly shifted toward a preponderance of women and children by 1800. In this respect highland central Madagascar exhibited a gendered pattern of slave creation similar to that obtaining on the African continent, where native consumers retained the majority of new female slaves while male captives were exported across the Atlantic in higher percentages than were originally captured in the African interior.[26] Directly linked as the increase of *zazahova* was to the Mascarene trade, the highland Malagasy case of slave creation does not conform to John Thornton's argument for west Africa that slavery was "widespread" before the external slave trade.[27] In central Madagascar enslavement, pawnship, and the oceanic slave trade were all fundamentally interlinked.

The trend toward a preponderance of women and children among the *zazahova* population was mirrored, although to a lesser degree, in the gender composition of *hova* and *andriana*, or nonslave persons. As slavers removed cumulatively larger numbers of "free" men from highland societies over the decades of slaving activity, adult women began to predominate numerically in the nonservile population as well. By the early decades of the nineteenth century this adult gender imbalance, exacerbated by induction of men into a new army, had reached alarming proportions.[28] For the women who remained at home in highland Madagascar, the social and economic consequences of absent fathers, fathers-in-law, uncles, husbands, brothers, sons, and other adult male relatives are not so easily determined. Did the women in households that lost male members to the export trade enjoy greater social privilege in the absence of their men or were such households left more socially vulnerable? An answer to this question is complex and contradictory, if not somewhat speculative given the sparseness of contemporary documentation. Formulating it requires investigating transformations in the division of labor by gender within highland central Madagascar.

TRANSFORMING WOMEN'S LABOR

The demographic composition of slave caravans leaving highland Madagascar embodied significant consequences for the division of household labor by gender.[29] Differentiated by activity, men's and women's labor was complementary to the economic reproduction of households. In contrast to mainland African societies, in eighteenth-century highland Madagascar men conducted most agricultural production, insuring household food security. Women, on the other hand, were intensively engaged in cottage weaving industries that produced a wide range of textiles in silk, cotton, and other vegetal fibers (see Photograph 4.1).[30] While agriculture provided households with necessary subsistence and exchange foodstuffs, weaving furnished them with critical sources of extra-household income. Consider Mayeur's observations about the highland gender division of labor in 1777: "It is a custom in the country that the women do not perform any heavy labor. They are uniquely occupied with their silk, with their cotton, with working banana and raffia leaves, and with making woven mats. They do not even perform tasks inside the house because it is the men who pound the rice, who cook, etc."[31] Several years later Mayeur reaffirmed this characterization, insisting that

> Highland women are exempt from all fatiguing labor, even that of the household. Their principal occupation is to spin their silk, cotton, and hemp; to prepare strings of banana and raffia bark in order to make loincloths; to weave the mats used in the household; and finally, to manufacture clay pottery for the use of their own domestic group. The husband goes to the fields and works the land, digs irrigation canals, plants rice and other food plants. He goes to the markets established throughout the province to sell the works of his wives and to bring back, in return, objects of taste and utility that might please his family.[32]

These are fantastic reports for anyone who is familiar with modern highland Malagasy society, where most women do not weave, men seldom cook in the presence of women, and women perform a significant share of day-to-day agricultural labor. Can Mayeur's accounts be accurate? Like nearly all slave merchants, Mayeur traveled about the Malagasy highlands primarily during the agricultural off-season when arid weather facilitated displacement. Could he have been describing a seasonal pattern of female economic activity particular to the dry winter? It is possible, yet Mayeur was sometimes delayed in his departure from the highlands until November, well after the rains recommenced and rice transplanting was under way.[33] Furthermore, while highlanders conducted the bulk of rice cultivation during the rainy season (the crop called *vary*

Photograph 4.1 Woman weaving a silk toga (*lamba*). During the late eighteenth century, women's cottage textile industries were the primary source of extra-household income. These industries, especially weaving in banana bark and cotton, entered decline during the era of the slave trade as women became more heavily involved in agriculture. (*Photo Credit*: Thomas Jørgensen, courtesy of the Norwegian Missionary Society, Stavanger, Madagascar Photograph number 0050.)

vakiambiaty), they commonly cultivated areas with sufficient water supply during the austral winter in a process called "first rice" (*varialoha*).[34] Vegetables and other hillside crops have always been cultivated during the dry months of the highland winter. Mayeur was not only fluent in the Malagasy language, by the time he wrote these accounts he had lived on the island some twenty years (since 1762) and had traveled extensively in its interior and along its coasts. He was an avid collector of Malagasy historical narratives and a careful reading of his accounts demonstrates a scrupulous attention to detail and interpretation.[35] These considerations suggest that Mayeur was a meticulous observer. Even if it is hypothesized that he reproduced a highland *ideal* of labor differentiation by gender based upon conversations with highlanders (versus an eyewitness account of that labor), that ideal had been reversed by the mid-nineteenth century.[36] If Mayeur was correct, the significant presence of highland women in agricultural production today was not true of the eighteenth century. The origins of highland Madagascar's modern gender division of labor in agriculture, Mayeur's observations suggest, should be sought in the demography of slaving. Demographic transformations in highland Madagascar issuing from enslavements for the export trade did not reinforce existing patterns of labor organization by gender, as they tended to do in many regions of Africa, but modified them.[37]

The gender and age structure of slave caravans did not in and of itself transform the working lives of those left behind. Men and women's creative adjustments to familial tragedy animated the reorganization of labor and social relations in the Malagasy highlands. A fundamental decision facing highland Malagasy was reallocation of household labor to compensate for the absence of enslaved kin. Because very few of the export slaves were children, the removal of adults increased the ratio of children and elderly dependent upon the remaining active agricultural laborers. Men remaining in households from which male and some female members had been captured probably intensified their agricultural labor in the effort to sustain food production. If household decision-makers could access human and capital resources from networks of extended kin, they might support existing levels of agricultural production without disturbing the female-centered economy of textile manufacture and, with it, the prevailing gender division of labor. In practice, both agricultural and textile production probably suffered through reductions in the amount of labor time that men and women could devote to them. Without sufficient quantitative or narrative data it is difficult to gauge the degree to which agricultural production was curtailed through human losses to the slave trade. Merchants along Madagascar's east coast were certain that the insecure environment of enslavement reduced agricultural productivity there, and there is no reason to assume the same did not hold true for central Madagascar.[38] Highland Malagasy historical narratives, for example, characterize the late eighteenth century as a time of hunger and recurring famine.[39] While famine serves as a metaphor for social dislocation and interkingdom political rivalry during this period, the relevance of idioms for hunger to highland Malagasy of the time suggests that there was an experiential basis for such language.[40] At the beginning of the nineteenth century, for example, Andrianampoinimerina identified increasing agricultural productivity among his key priorities, and the measure rallied considerable popular support.[41]

Although intensification of male labor would have offered households one means to cope with the loss of members to enslavement, decisions about labor reallocation ran contrary to the cultural norms governing gender-specific economic activity. However creative their range of responses, household decision makers inevitably deployed female labor into

Photograph 4.2 Women weeding a rice field in the Vakinankaratra, southwestern Imerina. Much transplantation and weeding of rice, the staple food in highland Madagascar, is now conducted by women. Women's labor became increasingly important in agriculture from the end of the eighteenth century when the export slave trade and then the drafting of men into Radama's army (see chapter 6) drained men from the rural areas. (*Photo Credit*: Pier M. Larson, 1990.)

agricultural production and away from textile manufacture.[42] The early nineteenth-century gender division of labor in which women toiled in the fields leaves little room for alternative explanations.[43] Households that experienced the loss of kin to the Mascarene slave trade were likely the first in central Madagascar in which women consistently participated in rice agriculture (see Photograph 4.2).[44]

The eastward-running trade in captives was not the only international economic force impinging upon the gender division of labor in highland central Madagascar. Muslim and Sakalava merchants from Madagascar's northwest coast began to retail Indian-manufactured cotton textiles within the highland Malagasy interior as income from the slave trade flowing into the center of the island increased demand there for consumer items from abroad. From about 1780 Gujarati-produced fabrics exported from Surat in northwestern India were the most common foreign textiles offered at weekly highland markets.[45] (Cottons of external manufacture were also being exchanged for captives in the Mascarene trade, arriving in the highlands from the east.) While during his journey through central Madagascar in 1777 Mayeur never once mentioned Indian textiles for sale in highland markets, he noted in 1785 that "one finds in these markets all the productions of the great island, and even many products from India that Europeans and Indians import from Surate."[46] Purchasing imported fabric rather than manufacturing it domestically offered household managers a new choice; Indian textiles began to significantly cut into the market for vegetal-fiber fabrics. In central Madagascar, cloth, clothing, and prestige were intertwined in complex ways.[47] Homespun styles of cotton and banana bark colored with locally available natural dyes served as everyday clothing.[48] Malagasy considered locally woven silks particularly prestigious for ritual purposes, especially when used as burial shrouds (*lambamena*). When they donned luxurious silk shawls dyed indigo blue with borders of inwoven tin and glass beads, highlanders displayed a wealth and prestige that only the most affluent could afford.[49] On the other hand, wearing imported cloth could suggest one's prosperity in trade wealth, connections to a wider world, and an innovative interest in new patterns and colors. Dressing in imported cloth and European apparel, including top hats, some highlanders expressed their social privilege and displayed wealth gained through the system of international trade.[50] Highland culture and demand structures for cloth were complex and interwoven.

Combined with an accelerating movement of women out of household textile manufacture, the rise in demand for imported cloth weakened the domestic weaving industry. This process proceeded slowly at first but after 1800 it gained momentum. While foreign textiles faced expanding consumer markets in the Malagasy highlands, female-managed industries that supplied local fabrics (especially of cotton and banana bark) at first suffered, then entered decline. Imported cottons appear to have supplanted local banana-bark fabrics by the turn of the century, when they were no longer noted.[51] Production of locally woven cotton textiles was more resilient. In 1820 when the export slave trade from the Malagasy highlands came to an abrupt end, cotton was still cultivated with frequency about Antananarivo, suggesting that local industry continued to supply a significant percentage of the textile market.[52] A British weaver reported in 1826 that

> Every woman in the country from the kings wives to the slaves are weavers. They will sit upon their heels weaving from morning till night a month together for 1/8 of a spanish dollar. Most families spin and weave the whole of their own clothing. The markets are stacked with home made goods. No cloth meets with a rapid sale though their partiality for foreign manufac-

tures is excessive, if it be not superior to their own in whiteness fineness, brilliancy of colours &c.[53]

This portrait of household cotton industries may have been exaggerated, for it was offered in defense of the missionary artisan's inability to turn a profit at an industrial weaving scheme. Nevertheless, it reveals that the cotton clothing industry of highland Madagascar had by no means vanished by the early nineteenth century. While cotton weaving for the production of clothes did not disappear from central Madagascar until much later, the domestic textile economy was weakened at the end of the eighteenth century. The most resilient sector of the textile industry remained production of silk fabrics for ritual purposes and for fine, occasional, or ceremonial clothing.[54] Silk weaving, however, was increasingly performed by complex associations in geographically circumscribed territories, not by most highlanders as once was the case.[55]

As women reduced production of banana-bark and cotton fabric for everyday clothing and devoted more of their time to agricultural labor, they and their closest kin forfeited a key source of extra-household income. Through household textile industries, women had produced cloth with important use and exchange values. Surplus domestically woven cloth employed neither to clothe household members nor consumed in domestic ritual entered circuits of exchange.[56] There were two means by which cloth brought income into households. In the first, through circulation among kin in exchange for labor, food, seeds, or agricultural implements, cloth generated social capital. In the second, textiles were sold and exchanged in the marketplace, fetching exchange goods and silver currency. In an increasingly monetized highland economy, locally manufactured cloth, especially the prized silks, could sell for unbelievably high prices. In 1777, for instance, some complete outfits in silk varied between 15 and 150 silver piasters—the higher price considerably more expensive than a slave! Well-woven cotton *lamba* and *totorano* (cloth pieces of approximately 2 by 2.5 meters) sold for between 1.5 and 2 piasters each in about 1810.[57] Returns on labor in agriculture could not compare. As domestic units forfeited income through reductions in textile production, more and more households in highland Madagascar purchased clothing in the markets rather than producing it at home.

What were the implications of these transformations for women's social and economic status? In households that lost young men to the export trade, women assumed greater responsibility for making everyday economic decisions and for performing necessary labor. Household structures were beginning a process of transformation in which women became decision makers and laborers in *both* textile and agricultural production. Such developments undoubtedly increased the independence of women who managed to steer their way clear of debt and pawnship, bringing some social acceptance of their capacity to manage local economic resources. In a similar vein, women's access to and publicly recognized rights over agricultural resources must have increased during this period. Since data for patterns of eighteenth-century land tenure in central Madagascar are virtually nonexistent, this assumption cannot be demonstrated with authority. It is known, however, that during the nineteenth century both men and women held agricultural property and independently transferred it to their descendants, a process compromised through French law and administrative practice during the colonial period.[58] Perhaps women who assumed the responsibilities of agricultural production from men after 1770 acquired new access to agricultural property and the right to manage and transfer it independently of their male partners. While this proposition merits further research, European observers of the mid and late eighteenth century noted a gender equality (economic and social) in highland Madagascar that they contrasted with a perceived social subordination of women on the coasts.[59]

Women's forays into cultivation may have enhanced their access to and control over valuable agricultural resources, but the loss of male kin expanded social and economic vulnerability within increasingly feminized households. Generally considered legal dependents within highland society, female managers may have found themselves in a weaker position than their male kin to effectively bargain with household creditors. Their ability to mobilize male labor for rice production was probably also diminished (men being absent or reluctant to work under the direction of women). As home textile industries languished, women lost access to a valuable source of exchange income that brought items from the outside into the household economy. They may also have faced difficulty in finding the time and resources to weave or to purchase the fabric necessary to clothe their families. Reinforcing an erosion of the eighteenth-century division of labor, some men began to participate in weaving activity, a process that gained momentum into the twentieth century.[60]

As has been noted by other scholars of the slave trade, gender imbalances generated through export trades in slaves facilitated shifts in African marriage patterns.[61] In central Madagascar the swelling proportion of women in the adult population favored an intensification of polygyny, a practice that no doubt increased during the era of the slave trade.[62] The effects of polygynous unions on women's status are also generally ambiguous. While polygyny is often associated with the waxing power and privilege of men, the more extensive domestic networks into which polygynous marriages anchored women in an era of feminized poverty could offer substantial advantages over nuclear households in protection, dense kinship ties, and access to resources. Increasingly common among the wealthy during the late eighteenth century, polygyny was a focus of royal policy during the reign of Andrianampoinimerina (see chapter 5).

On balance, the commerce that deprived some 70,000 highlanders of their lives with family in the land of their birth feminized agricultural labor and impoverished households within the highlands of central Madagascar. Slaving and the decline in textile production that accompanied it initiated a shift in the capacity to generate extra-household income away from rural women to a minority of increasingly wealthy men, well-placed persons who found innovative ways to capture the silver flowing into the Malagasy highlands. This process probably offset the economic gains that women derived through their newfound acquisition and management of agricultural resources. Agriculture was necessary to household subsistence, but not a dependable source of liquid extra-household income. As wealth in silver played an ever more important role in the highland economy, women became progressively separated from opportunities to accumulate it. Few highland women earned an income from the slave trade; the opportunities of human commerce went mainly to their counterparts on the coast and along the eastward route of the slaves. Slaving initiated a process of domestic economic transition in the Malagasy highlands from an economy in which extra-household income was generated by women through weaving industries to one in which women were income poor. In the process, a wealthy elite of slavemaking and slavetrading men sought to monopolize control over and access to silver coins, a new currency of power.

SILVER AND POWER

Among the best-documented domestic economic ramifications of Africa's export trade in slaves are the introduction of new currencies and the increase in local money supplies fostered by international commercial activity.[63] While studies of the expansion of African money supplies as a result of the external slave trades have assisted scholars in understanding the potential of commerce to transform African economies, *how* foreign currencies were employed in the nitty-gritty of African social relationships remains inadequately explored.[64] In a recent essay, Miller argues that distribution of imported textile currencies in west central Africa enhanced social divisions and enabled kings to expand their political identities.[65] But what specific consequences did the circulation of currencies have for the lives of common people and their relationships with their rulers? That wealthy slave merchants and the African political elite largely benefited from the importation of foreign currencies is well established, but precisely how they did so and what its consequences for the cohesiveness of local communities were merits further inquiry. Exploring the question of currency imports at greater length requires special attention to the impact of money on social relationships.

The increase in foreign silver circulating about central Madagascar during the last third of the eighteenth century derived from both the cumulative volume of silver coins entering the highlands and the creative political strategies to which some highlanders began to employ the new currency. The purposes to which the *nouveaux riches* deployed silver and the increasing necessity for households to acquire the precious metal to discharge economic and social obligations transformed human relationships in highland Madagascar far beyond silver's minimal significance as a new medium of exchange. Those who accumulated silver sought to increase their social power by distributing the trade currency among clients, friends, and allies, yet in turn they demanded prestations, often in silver, labor, and political affiliation, as a counterpart to such currency distributions. As a key tool in new strategies of elite dominance at the end of the eighteenth century, silver became a means by which kings and chiefs sought to undercut the self-sufficiency of household economies and increase the dependence of highlanders on their rulers for physical and social security.

In their introduction to *Money and the Morality of Exchange*, Jonathan Parry and Maurice Bloch contest the commonly disseminated idea that money embodies an "intrinsic power to revolutionise society and culture."[66] Arguing that the idea of the immorality of money is deeply rooted in Western culture, Bloch writes in his contribution on central Madagascar that money is considered morally neutral there but that its acquisition and use can become objectionable if they contradict certain fundamental cultural principles.[67] Bloch appropriately cautions the historian of highland Madagascar that it is *what* highlanders *chose to do* with silver rather than the metal itself that unleashed socially transformative forces.[68] The same idea is expressed in a popular Malagasy proverb: "Money, like stone and iron, does not give birth [i.e., provide interest]; the mouth and words of agreement alone cause it to increase."[69] As I pointed out in chapter 2, the exchange of slaves for Spanish piasters vastly expanded the circulation of silver as money within central Madagascar, displacing earlier currencies such as beads, cloth, rings, and firearms.[70] Writing in 1807, Mayeur was impressed by the degree to which silver functioned as a currency. "This metal is," he remarked, "the spirit that enlivens the commerce of the country."[71] Yet while the highlands and the east coast of Madagascar were probably among the most intensely monetized economies of the island during the late eighteenth century, silver still mediated few everyday exchanges.[72]

To illustrate this, I have estimated in Tables 4.1 and 4.2 the average annual influx of silver into central Madagascar, a calculation dependent upon two additional variables: the average annual number of slaves exported from highland Madagascar and the average amount of silver exchanged in each transaction. Data for slave exports from central Madagascar employed in Table 4.1 are based upon a retrospective census of Malagasy slave exports published elsewhere.[73] Estimates for the average amount of silver exchanged for slaves from highland Madagascar over the years are based upon contemporary observations. For a number of reasons, contemporary writers did not provide clear and consistent figures for the prices of export slaves. In the first place, sale price differentials between highland and coastal Madagascar differed by at least 30 percent and not all contemporary observers indicated whether the prices they cited were applicable to the coast or to the inland.[74] Second, slave prices fluctuated significantly from one year to the next and from the beginning to the end of the trading season, often increasing by 20 percent or more between the opening of the slaving season in June and its closing in October.[75] Third, the value of children was fixed significantly above that for young men, although relatively few children probably entered the trade.[76] Fourth, prices varied by gender, men fetching higher prices at the coast than women.[77] Fifth, purchasers seldom paid for slaves entirely in silver, although the trend over the era of the export trade was for greater proportions of slaves' exchange values to be settled in piasters. Accepting these qualifications, I have tried to match the general rise in the total price of slaves between 1770 and 1820 with information about the percentage of those prices actually settled in silver rather than with manufactured goods. Through 1801 I have employed the average silver price of 40 piasters per slave; from 1802 to 1810, 50 piasters; and from 1811 to 1820, 60 piasters.[78] These figures are utilized in Tables 4.1 and 4.2 to estimate the influx of piasters into central Madagascar.

When compared to contemporary observations, the estimated figures in Table 4.1 appear to understate currency inflows. In 1785, for example, Mayeur reported that the French slave trade annually placed some 120,000 piasters into the hands of highland suppliers, while Table 4.1 provides a substantially more modest figure of 47,560 piasters for that year.[79] In 1807 Sylvain Roux estimated the influx of piasters in exchange for slaves at 120 to 140 thousand, more than double the figure calculated for that year by the methods used in constructing Table 4.1.[80] Four considerations help reconcile the disparity in these figures. The first is that the figures provided here are *very rough estimates* and are useful only for establishing

Table 4.1 Influx of Silver into Highland Madagascar, 1769–1820: Estimated from a Retrospective Census of Slave Exports

Years	Average Annual Slave Exports[1]	Average Piasters per Transaction[2]	Average Annual Pisaster Influx
1729–1768	0	na	0
1769–1793	1,189	40	47,560
1794–1801	530	40	21,100
1802–1810	1,032	50	51,600
1811–1820	2,414	60	144,840
Total	66,861	—	3,271,400

1. From highland Madagascar. Source: Larson, 1997b: table 2, 142.

2. Source: Chapter 4, note 78. A portion of transactions was also paid in kind.

Table 4.2 Influx of Silver into Highland Madagascar, 1787–1819: Estimated from Contemporary Observations of Slave Exports

Source	Year	Estimated Slave Exports[1]	Average Piasters per Transaction[2]	Piaster Influx
Dumaine	1787	1,340	40	53,600
Fressange	1803	650	50	32,500
Chardenoux	1806	1,340	50	67,00
Roux	1807	2,000	50	100,000
Mayeur	1807	2,345	50	117,250
Mariette	1807	1,005	50	50,250
Hugon	1808	1,105	50	55,250
Hugon	1808	1,550	50	77,500
Roux	1808	1,950	50	97,500
Rondeaux	1808?	1,700	50	85,00
Roux	1810–11	2,000	60	120,000
Colin	1811	1,550	60	93,000
Hastie	1816	2,345	60	140,700
Bojer	1819	2,345	60	140,700

1. From highland Madagascar. Source: Larson, 1997b: table 3, 143. Where high and low export figures were provided in the source table I have substituted a single midrange figure (e.g., 1,550 for 1,500–1,600).

2. Source: Chapter 4, note 78. A portion of transactions was also paid in kind.

broad orders of magnitude. They are starting points from which future research may establish more reliable estimates. Second, Roux's estimate provided earlier in this paragraph applied to the east coast and not to highland Madagascar. Not all the piasters arriving at the east coast were conveyed into the Malagasy highlands. Third, payment for slaves was not the only means by which silver found its way into highland Madagascar. And fourth, contemporary observers reported that a significant proportion of the currency flowing into central Madagascar was being exported westward out of the highlands in exchange for textiles and other trade goods supplied by merchants hailing from the region of Bombetoka Bay.[81] The remaining discrepancy between these contemporary estimates and those derived in Tables 4.1 and 4.2 may suggest that significantly more than 70,000 slaves were exported from highland Madagascar between 1769 and 1820, the silver prices paid for them were higher than those assumed above, or the contemporary estimates of currency inflows were too high. Future research should consider these problems and establish more reliable figures for currency inflows into highland Madagascar.

Subject to very significant error, both the retrospective and the contemporary estimates of currency flows into highland Madagascar in Tables 4.1 and 4.2 make the same fundamental point: the Malagasy highlands were not awash in silver during the era of the slave trade. With a highland population of some half million at 1800 (or even one as low as 250,000 or less, which is unlikely), these influxes of silver averaged below half a piaster per capita annually.[82] The same picture emerges even if the annual influx of piasters is doubled or halved from that estimated in Tables 4.1 and 4.2. The point is that most exchanges among kin and certainly the majority of transactions for individual households were conducted by barter and according to in-kind prestations that characterized the communal ritual and economic cycle.[83] Even in the age of the slave trade there simply was not enough silver to fully monetize the economy. Mayeur noted in 1785 that most petty market exchanges were transacted by barter rather than in silver.[84] Before 1800 most highland Malagasy acquired food, clothing, and other items of consumption through their own production, from extended kin, or by barter, not through monetized exchanges. Despite the limited reach of monetization, however, as the slave trade annually brought more coins into the Malagasy highlands silver mediated an increasing number of ordinary economic and social transactions. While foreign trade probably accounted for only a small part of domestic income per capita, its consequences far outweighed the relative unimportance of its proportion of that income. Even in its economic dimensions, the impact of the slave trade cannot be adequately measured by its contribution to domestic income per capita, a mistake made by David Eltis for west Africa. Income and influence are not equivalent.[85]

In highland Madagascar's currency-deficient economy, silver fostered socioeconomic inequality. Piasters entering the Malagasy highlands first flowed through the hands of slavers and, exchanged for social debt and market goods, drifted across rural communities and into individual households. Highland Malagasy slave suppliers distributed trade wealth among potential clients to create networks of political power (see the last section of this chapter). Far from generating the economic equality that distribution of trade-derived wealth implies, such "shared" piasters created dependency and transformed receivers into social and economic debtors. Charged by creditors at rates commonly reaching 50 percent per annum or more, interest was termed "offspring of money" (*zana-bola*).[86] But money was fertile only for those able to effectively deploy it to create dependents or to increase their stock of operating capital. Jacques Dez has argued that exchanges of silver in the era of enslavement were based upon the notion of *fanjakana* (government, authority, power) as opposed to *fihavanana* (kinship).[87] This may be a useful way of thinking about the influence of silver on social relationships, but distribution of wealth in exchange for human loyalty was clearly the extension of a political strategy of the highland Malagasy *longue-durée*, not an entirely novel practice. What was new was the form that distributed wealth took—silver.

Whole piasters represented prodigiously large sums for most Malagasy.[88] To create smaller currency denominations people carefully chiseled the minted coins into as many as 720 pieces.[89] Varying in weight and value, these bits of silver were named according to a complex highland scheme of accounting.[90] Highlanders employed locally manufactured balances to measure even the smallest bits of silver (see Photographs 4.3 and 4.5).[91] Most merchants and wealthy persons owned balances, but it is unlikely that the poorest households had access to them and hence remained susceptible to paying and receiving falsely weighed currency.[92] Once silver emerged as a medium of social and economic exchange, highlanders multiplied its influence by counterfeiting piasters.[93] Skillful highland smiths duplicated piasters by mixing or coating more common metals such as iron, tin, and copper with silver derived from melted coins and jewelry. Because many coins reaching central Madagascar were old and worn, duplicating surface patterns was relatively easy.[94] Counterfeit coins probably increased the currency in circulation by only a fraction, but counterfeiting was a significant way in which men with metalworking skills could generate personal income. That nearly a third of highland men knew how to work silver suggests that the potential for counterfeiting was enormous.[95] Highland Malagasy were not the only persons who engaged in counterfeiting or who passed doctored coins in market transactions. In 1786 a Mascarene *traitant* at Foulpointe disbursed 3,000 silver-coated lead piasters before astute merchants in the Malagasy highlands pointed out the

Photograph 4.3 Bamboo money holder and cut piasters. To create smaller currency denominations highland Malagasy cut whole silver piasters into bits of varying weight. Most money transactions involved such bits of silver, which had to be carefully weighed with each transaction to insure accurate payment. (*Source*: J. et S. Chauvincourt, *La monnaie coupée et les poids monétaires de Madagascar* [Tananarive, 1967], 27.)

subterfuge to the Betsimisaraka slave traders who were the victims of the ruse.[96] Other merchants fashioned "silver" jewelry from tin and other metals for their Malagasy trade associates. In the welter of transactions occurring within bustling weekly markets, much counterfeit coin passed through the hands of ordinary people.[97]

Increasingly important as a medium of social and economic exchange, the piaster emerged a paramount symbol of the new wealth of international trade. From the late eighteenth century highland Malagasy no longer spoke of wealth simply as *harena*, or riches in "property," but as *vola aman-karena*, wealth in "money *and* property."[98] The wealthy brandished their economic success by melting piasters into silver plates and spoons.[99] The most fashionable highland women outfitted themselves with ponderous silver chain necklaces, earrings, bracelets, and rings.[100] While sovereigns were once buried in wooden

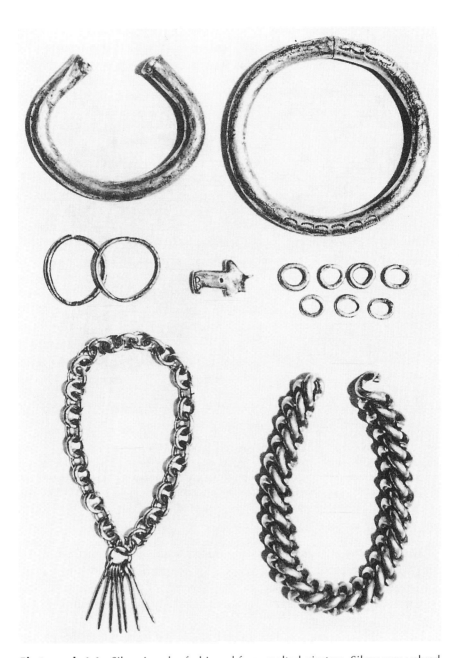

Photograph 4.4 Silver jewelry fashioned from melted piasters. Silver was valued as more than a currency. Highland jewelers melted piasters to fashion jewelry—bracelets, necklaces, earrings, chains, and other pieces—for personal adornment. A significant jewelry-making tradition, in silver as well as in gold, persists into the present. (*Source*: J. et S. Chauvincourt, *Les premières monnaies introduites à Madagascar* [Tananarive, 1968], 5.)

canoes, rulers of the early nineteenth century had themselves interred in elaborate silver sarcophagi constructed from masses of melted piasters.[101] Even royal palaces were decorated with silver roofs and trimmings.[102] Like cattle, rice, textiles, or control over human dependents, silver bestowed considerable social prestige on its proprietors. Unlike these more common and familiar indigenous forms of wealth, however, silver signified success in bridging the external economies of maritime capitalism with those of Madagascar's interior societies. Silver was also the means to fulfill new desires nurtured through participation in external trade. With supplies of silver, wealthy highlanders bought access to the European commodity markets of the Indian Ocean, outfitting themselves with locally rare and hence prestigious manufactured items such as European hats, mirrors, and scissors.[103] Mayeur noted in 1785 that highland men traveled "to the markets established throughout the province to sell the works of their wives and to bring back, in return, objects of taste and utility that might please their families."[104] The distressed, too, longed for such objects of taste and utility that might please their families but could ill afford them. A common nineteenth-century proverb captures this all-too-common angst: "Rafotsibe went to the market, she desired many things but had nothing with which to purchase them."[105] In the era of the slave trade, the piaster and the luxurious foreign goods it purchased became public symbols of wealth and success *par excellence*.

When distributed through political channels, silver traveled complex yet purposefully guided trajectories. Coin could be transformed into social and political capital by astute and well-placed individuals who disbursed money through existing social networks or created new ones. In turn, counterflows of silver and loyalty along those very same networks translated back into political and economic power. The endeavors of some late eighteenth-century highland sovereigns to collect tribute in silver rather than in kind is a paramount example of this process. Unlike their counterparts along the east coast of Madagascar and throughout most of the island, sovereigns in the Malagasy interior customarily supported themselves through regular taxation of their subjects.[106] Highland royal treasuries had usually been supported through in-kind taxes of various kinds. Some rulers began to compel monetization of these contributions in the new economic climate of the late eighteenth century.[107] Like French colonial masters nearly a century later, some highland kings assessed taxes in coin rather than in kind, driving their subjects into the new money economy. Not all highland rulers elected this option. The pace of silver monetization within individual kingdoms varied dramatically, the result of royals' careful manipulation of fiscal policy. In 1777 Mayeur wrote the following about Andrianamboatsimarofy's kingdom at Antananarivo.

All free people, men, women, children, pay the king annually a half piaster each, and a tenth part in nature of all the animals they possess. They
pay in addition for their slaves a quarter piaster per head. They furnish for
each laborer, slave or free, a measure of rice that I evaluate at a weight of
60 pounds [*livres*]. This imposition is reduced by a third when the harvest
has not been abundant, and by half when there was no harvest. In this last
case, those who don't have rice purchase it at whatever price, because the
king does not maintain any plantations and does not receive anything in
place of the rice.[108]

Even by 1777 some highland Malagasy rulers had adopted partial taxation in silver, at least in principle. Considering that the maximum annual
currency inflow to central Madagascar was below one-half piaster per capita
(see earlier in this chapter), an annual tax of one-half piaster for each nonslave
person represented an unusually large amount of silver.[109] With his annual
silver tax, Andrianamboatsimarofy claimed ownership of virtually every new
piaster flowing into his kingdom! Silver taxes embodied both qualitative and
quantitative differences from in-kind taxes. In-kind tribute, Mayeur tells us,
was levied in two categories, animals and rice. Andrianamboatsimarofy assessed livestock at a rate of some 10 percent annually, so payments were
directly dependent upon the size of herds, a flat tax applying to poor and
wealthy alike. He assessed tribute rice only upon laborers, an undefined term
that probably referred to adults who undertook agricultural production (i.e.,
primarily men, but an increasing number of women). Rice prestations, which
were exceedingly regressive because rich and poor owed exactly the same
measure, were calculated in an unspecified unit (probably the *vata*) that
Mayeur evaluated at near sixty pounds.[110] The *vata*, however, was a flexible
measure. Like the *gamelle* employed to measure rice along Madagascar's
east coast, its volume could change with each transaction.[111] On the other
hand, Andrianamboatsimarofy fixed head taxes of one-half piaster upon every nonslave individual in a household and a quarter piaster on each slave.
Unlike in-kind tribute, taxes in silver took account neither of wealth held nor
of the ability to pay. The piaster tax was the first tribute levied on every
single individual, regardless of his or her relationship to the means of production or to kin. In contrast to in-kind payments, levies in silver were highly
regressive and socially atomizing.[112]

Taxes in silver also animated exchange markets for rice, the staple food
in highland Madagascar. Individuals who could not generate sufficient
in-kind tax payments in rice, Mayeur writes, were obliged to purchase
grain with silver and then submit the market produce to the king. If silver-meager households were constrained to purchase rice in order to discharge tribute obligations, their members either did not eat rice or pur-

chased that on the market too. While even into the twentieth century most highland households obtained their food outside of money markets, in times of meager agricultural production a certain number, impossible to quantify, resorted to the market for the Malagasy staple of life.

Because silver taxes were heavy and highly regressive, king Andrianamboatsimarofy of Antananarivo dared not rigorously collect them. Mayeur explains: "The tributes that the king levies are paid quite regularly. On the other hand, in order not to crush his people, this prince does not require their collection until strangers come into his province, because he uses the money to pay for the merchandise that is brought to him and to purchase his gifts."[113] It is not surprising that Andrianamboatsimarofy implemented his scheme for silver taxation in principle only. The impossibility of annually collecting one-half a piaster per capita from an increasingly impoverished peasantry imposed itself upon his pecuniary schemes. It is difficult to see how the silver levy could have been popular with Andrianamboatsimarofy's rural constituencies. Given the willingness of the Ravoandriana to publicly chastise Andrianamboatsimarofy for illegitimate enslavements, it does not take much imagination to consider what the collective response of *firenena* might have been when royalty attempted to harvest such huge amounts of silver from the citizenry. (It is very likely that Andrianamboatsimarofy's taxation policies help to explain his unpopularity with highland Malagasy and his subsequent defeat by Andrianampoinimerina).[114] Despite the fiscal burdens he placed upon his subjects, Andrianamboatsimarofy continued to pursue his strategies for collecting the precious metal currency. During his visit to the region of Antananarivo eight years later (1785), Mayeur encountered a vigorously enforced system of taxes that, he wrote, were "collected from the farmers with great exactitude."[115] Tribute taxes in rice, silk cloth, and silver were paid not only to kings, as examined here, but also to more immediate social superiors, who in turn passed a portion of the tribute on to their patrons.[116] Claims upon common highlanders' wealth in kind and in silver, then, multiplied in proportion to their subordination within a web of social and political relationships. Vigorous collection of silver tributes forced commoners into the growing and externally oriented economy of silver exchange. In the absence of a labor market that could remunerate workers with silver, there were few choices for those desiring to acquire the precious metal necessary for payment of taxes other than to offer agricultural, textile, and craft production for sale on the ubiquitous markets of the highlands, to kidnap and sell slaves, or to borrow it from creditors.

Popular attitudes toward the hazards of borrowing silver manifested themselves in the rise of new vocabularies to speak about credit transactions.

Jacques Dez writes that while loans were once commonly conceived by variations of the morally neutral term *indrana* (movement, transfer), they were
later conceptualized by the charged and metonymic *sambotra* (captured, captive) when they entailed transfers of silver. The raw humor in this semantic
transformation is tempered by the slippery relationship between debt and
capture for export or domestic enslavement.[117] Silver money, argues Dez, came
to be associated with the unpopular strategies of kings who sought to monetize social and credit transactions to generate slaves and personal incomes.[118]

Silver thus became far more than a means of exchange, an object of
popular desire, or an element of social display in late eighteenth-century
highland Madagascar. By 1780 it had become a necessity. Piasters came
to symbolize the international economy that embodied immense risk for
common people. A half piaster a year—impossible for most people to
amass without the assistance of kin or patrons—could not in itself keep
highland kings at bay. Finding themselves with the difficult burden of
servicing debts and managing their financial obligations to a variety of
social and political superiors, those with little access to silver—most highlanders—were exceedingly vulnerable to the loss of self and kin through
enslavement. Families with access to a sufficient number of piasters might
redeem an enslaved kinsperson with silver. At average prices of between
thirty and sixty piasters normally payable at least two-thirds in silver,
however, redemptions meant collecting together an enormous number of
coins. Saving the unfortunates who fell prey to enslavement by redeem-
ing them was a privilege available only to the wealthy and to those having sufficiently developed social networks to guarantee short-term access
to silver in times of crisis. To be without silver in the years following
central Madagascar's entry into the western Indian Ocean's economy of
mercantile capitalism was to be extremely vulnerable and awash and in
the unpredictable seas of an international economy.

THE PRESSURES OF SILVER

Highlanders pursued silver to discharge social and political obligations,
to protect kin from enslavement, and to gain access to prestigious foreign
goods. Each of these activities introduced new tensions into *firenena* and
teraky communities. Pressures for silver emanating from social superiors
drove highlanders to search for the precious metal in a partially monetized exchange economy. Debtors were squeezed between the Scylla of
creditors' demands for silver and the Charybdis of a silver-meager
economy. By these means the silver of external trade came to play an
influential role in the lives of highland Malagasy, even if the precious
metal was relatively scarce and the foreign commerce that supplied it

represented only a fraction of highland Madagascar's total income. The quest for silver led most highland persons ever deeper into relationships of social and economic inequality and into debt. As a result, transactions in silver tended to increase on highland markets, to which common people were both driven and drawn. Unsurprisingly, markets acquired a negative assessment in the popular imagination. Highland Malagasy attitudes toward markets are well known because markets became "sites of memory" around which historical narratives crystallized during the nineteenth century.[119] The purposes to which wealthy Malagasy deployed silver were largely unpopular and that unpopularity was symbolized by the financial abuses highlanders came to associate with weekly markets.

Weekly commercial gatherings, called "meetings" (*tsena*), were foci of trade and centers of cultural exchange.[120] "Individuals of all kingdoms and all countries can be seen coming there to sell and to buy," observed Mayeur. "The crowds of local people and foreigners are phenomenal at these markets."[121] Highlanders attended weekly markets from early in the morning until midafternoon or evening, depending upon the distance of the market from nearby villages and the security of the location. During the chilly winter months people commenced gathering at designated points only in the midmorning after the sun had begun to warm the air.[122] Contributing to the vibrancy and excitement of markets were music makers, healers, and merchants, all assembling together to exchange food, implements, cloth, news, gossip, and ideas. To both Mayeur and Hugon the *tsena* were analogous "to the fairs we have in different provinces of France."[123] *Tsena* were not only vibrant foci of cultural and community life but centers of exchange where silver-needy farmers strove against nearly impossible odds to convert agricultural and manufactured goods into bits of silver, the "small money of the bazaars."[124] Because most market transactions were conducted by barter in 1777, commoners' pursuit of silver must have been largely unsuccessful.[125] Places where commoners might obtain silver, *tsena* were economically insecure locations where foreign and domestic merchants, speculators, creditors, would-be patrons, and moneychangers (offering larger pieces of coin or whole piasters in exchange for bits of cut silver, and vice versa), dazzled, cheated, and even coerced desperately poor women and men.[126] The genre of amusing highland folktales featuring Ikotofetsy and Imahaka, two tricksters who cunningly cheat the unsuspecting out of both money and dignity, may date to this period and resonates with most commoners' experiences.[127] Given such experiences, it is scarcely surprising that markets were negatively assessed in the popular imagination.[128]

If ambivalent attitudes toward markets testified to the hardships farmers incurred in the quest for silver, struggles to exchange local products for sil-

Photograph 4.5   A moneychanger's box. Moneychangers were experts at cutting piasters into smaller denominations and exchanging cut silver for whole coins. This convenient toolbox includes a balance, some bits of cut silver, and weights (bottom center). (*Source*: J. et S. Chauvincourt, *La monnaie coupée et les poids monétaires de Madagascar* [Tananarive, 1967], 45.)

ver are less visible in historical narratives but they were pivotal to social survival. Produced by women, certain silk and cotton textiles could command superior monetary returns on highland markets. Within households that lost male kin to slaving, however, the inevitable shift of women's labor from textile to agricultural production limited the amount of time women could devote to producing fabric for the market. Manufacture of the most valued and luxurious silk cloth required significant inputs of labor, time, and fine materials. Most weavers manufactured less expensive cotton and banana-bark cloth that could not be sold for large amounts of money.[129] To acquire silver by marketing agricultural produce, on the other hand, highlanders would have to intensify farm labor and place marginal lands into production. Doing so entailed risks of its own as rural agricultural laborers, especially those working far-lying fields alone or laboring in small groups, were the most vulnerable to kidnappers who lurked in quiet countrysides.[130]

When intensified household production could not match the need for silver, managers liquidated their assets by releasing cattle, selling pawns (*zazahova*), pawning kin as *zazahova*, and exchanging land—if indeed any of these options were available to them. Few people near Antananarivo owned cattle because high population densities and intensively farmed fields severely restricted available grazing areas, and the zebu cattle of Madagascar did not tolerate cold highland winters very well.[131] Some families maintained cattle within the highlands or delegated someone to graze them on the more sparsely populated grasslands of its western and eastern fringes, as far away as the Ankay plain. Cattle were valuable assets and represented one of the few investments whose successful management was primarily dependent upon local knowledge. In addition to fecund sources of wealth, cattle were important capital and technological inputs in rice production. Highland Malagasy utilized cattle to prepare fields for transplanting rice seedlings. Just before transplanting, farmers drove cattle about flooded rice paddies to create a fine mud in which to embed the young rice plants.[132] If a farmer owned cattle, she would not have to call upon others to access this valuable yet scarce resource during the few weeks each year that most highlanders transplanted rice (*vakiambiaty*). Borrowing cattle for preparing rice fields meant incurring external social debts that required counter exchanges of labor (*valintanana*) or, potentially, silver. On the other hand, households with cattle at their disposal might lend them out and thereby become social creditors, able to call upon a network of associates for help in time of crisis or, if necessary, require silver when in acute need of it. Beyond their utility in the cultivation of rice, cattle provided the manure highlanders employed to fertilize hillside *tanety* fields of beans, corn, and a variety of vegetables (see Photograph 5.3). Despite their importance to successful agriculture, cattle were probably one of the first assets with which households parted in times of financial crisis. Cattle were a chief item of exchange in highland markets.[133] Market butchers also sold meat piecemeal, suggesting that slaughter offered another opportunity for exchanging cattle against silver. Although beef was not an everyday constituent of the highland Malagasy diet during the late eighteenth century, its availability at weekly markets suggests that silver had entered into circuits of exchange for food.[134]

Dependents were a second asset that socially affluent households might exchange for silver. Before 1800, as I pointed out in the previous chapter, few households owned *andevo* slaves, who could legitimately be sold. Desirous for silver to distribute along potential networks of social patronage or under pressure to supply it up a chain of debt, creditors sometimes illegitimately relinquished *zazahova* to raise silver. When they sold or transferred *zazahova* to another master, highlanders participated in the redefinition of civic virtue, transforming individuals entitled to protection from sale into chattellike and salable *andevo*. In desperation for silver to discharge social obligations and to stave off the threat of enslavement for export, some household managers, especially the poorer ones who did not have *zazahova* of their own to release, resorted to pawning subordinate family members as *zazahova* to social creditors.[135] Pawning a kinsperson to a trustworthy creditor who was likely to respect the custom against selling *zazahova* was preferable, of course, to losing one permanently into export enslavement. To be female or a child during the late eighteenth century, however, was to be at risk of becoming *zazahova*; to be *zazahova*, in turn, was to be at serious risk of enslavement for export. *Zazahova* relationships that shielded impecunious households from irreversible losses of kin into the export slave trade further entrenched social inequality within the Malagasy highlands.

When liquidation of human and animal property proved insufficient to acquit social and financial obligations, some households forfeited rice fields. Available only in limited quantities in the valleys where water could be effectively managed, ancestral rice land was sometimes sold outright to raise silver for taxes or to redeem kin.[136] The practical result of a market in land was the rise of a small group of near landless and landless households at the turn of the nineteenth century.[137] Despite the existence of a small market for rice land, most forfeited fields were not sold into permanent alienation but deposited as security against a loan of silver. Highlanders termed pledges of land for financial security the "muzzle" (*fehivava*). When they borrowed money through a "muzzle" agreement, highlanders transferred the land pledged against the loan to the creditor. Theoretically, creditors could charge no interest on the silver lent in exchange for land. Practically, of course, interest was derived from the use of the fields during their alienation from proprietary households. Debtors were "muzzled" and could not recoup their rice fields until they had finished repaying the borrowed silver. While creditors might spare farmers from a permanent alienation of their land by offering an alternative to outright sale, the "muzzle" symbolized the intense desperation of rural households torn between a need for silver on the one hand and the unequal social relationships that might shield them from the dangers and indignities of highland markets on the other.[138]

Rulers' strategies for increasing their share of silver conflicted with highlanders' desires for autonomy and pressed common people into relationships of financial and social debt. The great majority of highland Malagasy were destitute at the turn of the nineteenth century. In 1808 Barthélémy Hugon described Andrianampoinimerina's subjects in the following terms: "His people in general are very poor, inspiring the greatest misery; having to cover themselves with bad pieces of fabric they purchase from our porters, [said pieces of cloth] being half and even three-quarters used, in exchange for knives or spoons of iron."[139] In chapter 3 I explored how the Ravoandriana challenged Andrianamboatsimarofy and his attempt to shift the rules of slavemaking by enslaving the free. Yet collective protests, even when they were stunningly effective in particular cases, could not stay the erosion of personal security and the transformation of social relationships inherent in highland Madagascar's political economy of silver.[140] Social and economic pressures impinging upon common people encouraged kidnapping. Enslaving and selling a single captive for thirty or sixty piasters, for example, might pay a household's taxes for several years. The pressure in many cases was unbearable. With no intrinsic value of its own, silver could not revolutionize highland Malagasy politics. But entrepreneurs who learned to strategically distribute that silver generated social and political power for themselves, employing the semiprecious metal to transform human relationships. Andrianampoinimerina was a premier example of such an entrepreneur. He first mastered the trade, thanks to his predilection for commercial relationships with foreigners, and then thoroughly transformed the political geography of highland Madagascar.[141]

MAKING A POLITICAL IDENTITY: ANDRIANAMPOINIMERINA

Human labor was a prime economic resource in eighteenth-century highland Madagascar, as it was elsewhere in Africa.[142] Irrigated rice fields located primarily in valleys and flood plains were also scarce, yet rice productivity could be multiplied almost proportionately to the amount of labor applied to a given field. Control over people opened avenues to wealth and influence for the sufficiently savvy and well-enough-placed to encircle themselves with tribute-paying and politically supportive commoners. Men and women who could deliver protection and leadership collected a network of dependents around them, eventually forming new *firenena*, or "descent groups," whose posterity would remember them as apical ancestors.[143] When in the late eighteenth century it became possible for highlanders to readily exchange humans for silver, merchants discovered the personal benefits of buying and selling social influence with foreign currency and imported trade goods. Offering a share of trade wealth to silver-poor clients afforded merchants a new means of attracting followers. Successful patrons in the late eighteenth century were usually prosperous entrepreneurs who acquired wealth through international trade and garnered the political submission of dependents to whom they distributed trade wealth and protection from enslavement. While generating bonds of affinity and obligation, offers of food, wealth, and social protection deepened political hierarchies. Like kings in the Angolan interior of west central Africa, highland Malagasy leaders turned their material profits from foreign trade back into people and political power. Givers initiated transactions to confirm the inferiority of receivers; receivers returned political support and repayments of silver in exchange for protection. To assemble a coterie of dependents in the late eighteenth century, then, a potential leader would have to access the wealth of international trade.[144]

Limited human resources in the highlands and a finite demand for slaves in the Mascarenes fostered a hearty competition among potential suppliers in highland Madagascar for a niche in the export slave trade. At the same time, Malagasy participation in the slave trade raised the hazards of highland politics for both commoners and their leaders. By selling their subject-citizens as slaves, kings chipped away at the bedrock of their political stability. The Ravoandriana revolt of 1785 demonstrates how fragile the political affinity between slaving kings and their rural constituents could be. The contradictory and potentially self-destructive process of creating a political identity by slaving propelled kings into heightened competition with one another in this game of people and products. Aspiring rulers contended over a finite number of farmer subjects. "Throughout my travels," noted Jacques de Lasalle about his peregrinations in highland Madagascar during 1797, "I did not encounter one chief who did not bear witness of his friendship, each striving to answer questions about his country, making clear his desire to see a trade establishment placed in his domain and that he would not neglect anything to make it prosper."[145] Retaining and remaking political influence in the economy of enslavement entailed edging potential competitors out of the slave trade and thereby undercutting the flow of wealth with which they could transact relationships of dependency and obtain access to foreign weapons and ammunition.[146] But participation in the export trade also unleashed forces of social atomization, linking the economy of mercantile capitalism to transformations in daily life. The social tension inherent in slaving and its resulting expansion and dissolution of social groups leads to an important question for historians of highland Madagascar: How did Andrianampoinimerina simultaneously manage the socially divisive forces of enslavement and draw highland Malagasy into a cohesive kingdom at the beginning of the nineteenth century?

Answers to this question can be explored by turning from archived European documentation to Malagasy historical narratives. During the mid-nineteenth century, as I noted in the first chapter of this book, Malagasy historian Raombana composed a manuscript history of the Merina kingdom based upon popular narratives circulating within his extended family. According to Raombana, external trade was the means by which aspiring highland Malagasy kings procured both the wealth and the weaponry that propelled them into political power. European traders frequented the court of Andriamasinavalona during the first "golden age" of Merina unity (about 1700), writes Raombana. Muskets, he postulates, were ubiquitous during Andriamasinavalona's reign and were the root cause of "the terrific civil wars which afterward ravaged Imerina."[147] Raombana notes that foreign weaponry acquired through trade supplied the means of destruction that enabled the rulers of highland Madagascar to disrupt the lives of common people.

Andrianampoinimerina's supremacy at Ambohimanga in the years following his usurpation of the kingship, reasons Raombana, rested largely upon his ability to field more musket-yielding highlanders than his competitor, Andrianjafy.[148]

If according to Raombana the importation of European-manufactured muskets and ammunition underlay civil strife and political power during the eighteenth century, trade wealth was the currency of Andrianampoinimerina's successful politics at the beginning of the nineteenth. During the late eighteenth century, notes Raombana, locally resident *hova* in the province of Avaradrano were enriching themselves with cattle, slaves, and silver piasters through trade with itinerant European merchants. This accumulation of trade wealth outside the purview of royal control posed a threat to Andrianjafy, the king of Ambohimanga. As a result, he set out to dispossess his affluent *hova* subjects of their newly acquired fortunes. Andrianjafy desperately attempted to shore up his rapidly dispersing political power by systematically accusing his wealthy *hova* subjects of practicing witchcraft, a pretext for royal confiscation of allegedly ill-gotten gain.[149] Andrianampoinimerina, a pretender to Andrianjafy's rule and an *andriana* skilled in trade, capitalized on this situation by allying himself with the beleaguered *hova* merchants and promising to act favorably toward them. He assured the slave traders that he would respect their wealth if they supported him and further enticed them with promises of economic and political reward if they would help him to obtain the kingship by ruse or outright force. The *hova* traders accepted; in alliance with Andrianampoinimerina they conducted a successful coup d'état at Ambohimanga while Andrianjafy was temporarily absent from the town.[150]

What differentiated Andrianampoinimerina from his contemporaries, according to Raombana, was his successful trade relationships with coastal merchants who ventured into the Malagasy highlands searching for captives. Raombana portrays Andrianampoinimerina as a shrewd bargainer who could calculate economic gain with skill. Once in power at Ambohimanga, Andrianampoinimerina and his *hova* allies redoubled their commercial relationships with itinerant merchants from the east coast. Andrianampoinimerina exchanged slaves for muskets and silver piasters. With some of his piasters Andrianampoinimerina purchased cattle, a prized and long-standing symbol of wealth in the highlands where pasturage was scarce. With deliveries of "whole bag-fulls of dollars" and cattle (Raombana, following his English way of thinking about wealth transfers, characterizes these transactions as "bribes"), Andrianampoinimerina convinced rival kings and their advisers to submit themselves to his political supremacy.[151] This method of proceeding, according to Raombana, was highly successful. It won the headmen of the *firenena* confederations of Tsimahafotsy, Mandiavato, and Tsimiamboholahy to Andrianampoinimerina's camp. If competitors persisted in refusing his offers of wealth, Andrianampoinimerina extended promises of economic gain and gifts of cattle to their courtiers and thereby diminished their core political support.[152] Raombana describes how Andrianampoinimerina triumphed in this process against king Andrianjafy, who after his defeat at Ambohimanga ruled the remainder of his truncated kingdom of Avaradrano from the nearby town of Ilafy.

> Had this simple and unfortunate King, acted like Andrianampoinimerina, by bribing his plebian [i.e., *hova*] Head people, it is probable that He would also have succeeded, and thus not brought to an untimely end; but it seems that He had not much money, whilst His opponent had a great deal, for it is stated that Europeans now and then visited Ambohimanga for the purpose of buying slaves from Him and his people, and thus He obtained enormous sums of money, which He employed for the purpose already mentioned; and for the procuring of good and new muskets, that with them, He may achieve the conquests of Avaradrano, and after that is accomplished, all Imerina.[153]

Distribution of trade wealth could not secure everyone's allegiance, Andrianampoinimerina discovered, and against the Manisotra living south of Antananarivo he employed cannon.[154] Other kings were not unmindful of Andrianampoinimerina's methods, Raombana points out, but they were not as skillful at emulating them. Unable to attract merchants to their courts and having no ongoing external source of war captives, many kings resorted to kidnapping from within their own realms. This political error seriously eroded their popular support and made their subjects even more amenable to Andrianampoinimerina's political overtures.[155]

Raombana's less-than-flattering interpretation of the key role of external trade in Andrianampoinimerina's rise to power was nourished by a resentment of the founder king that simmered within his extended family; his history here reads like the antithesis of *Tantara* narratives, which strongly downplay trade to emphasize Andrianampoinimerina's politically savvy, magical ability, and readiness to apply military force.[156] Nevertheless, Raombana's observations are largely supported by contemporary evidence. The subjugation and incorporation of the Andrantsay (a region in the southwest corner of the Malagasy highlands, see Maps 1.2 and 5.1) into Andrianampoinimerina's expanding kingdom illuminate the direct relationship between management of international trade and state building at the beginning of the nineteenth century. Before Andrianampoinimerina conquered it in about 1808, the Andrantsay was by far the largest and most agriculturally prosperous kingdom within highland Madagascar.[157] A loose political unity, the Andrantsay was composed of several chiefdoms confederated under one sovereign who lived at Ifandanana, some twenty kilometers west of the modern town of Betafo. In contrast to the chronic bellicosity among the politically fractured northern kingdoms surrounding Antananarivo, relationships among Andrantsay chiefdoms were comparatively peaceful. Yet by 1808 when Andrianampoinimerina's armies marched southward, they readily subjugated the once-powerful Andrantsay and incorporated it as the sixth and final district (*toko*) of Imerina. While the *Tantara* and most popular historical narratives circulating within modern highland Madagascar attribute Andrianampoinimerina's success in this endeavor to his consummate wit and magical power, contemporary evidence offers an altogether different perspective.[158]

The Andrantsay had prospered with a peacetime economy after 1750 because of its high density of population and the strength of its agriculture fed by the Andrantsay River. But in the new climate of competitive international trade after 1770 the Andrantsay languished. Its downfall under new circumstances can be attributed to the reasons for its earlier success. As Mayeur discovered during his intelligence-gathering venture of 1777, the confederated kingdoms of the southern highlands generated few war captives. By contrast, the kingdoms in the northern region about Antananarivo were at war and able to offer slaves by the mid-1770s when Mayeur ventured into the Malagasy interior. They quickly gained an economic advantage over their Andrantsay counterparts, attracting most slave merchants and, along with them, most of the silver flowing into the Malagasy highlands.

In the decades following Andrianamboatsimarofy's disguised adventure into the Andrantsay (one of the three stories with which the first chapter of this book opened) rulers in the Antananarivo region began to turn toward the Andrantsay as a source of captives. After he grabbed the kingship of Ambohimanga and subsequently conquered most of the northern region of what is now Imerina, Andrianampoinimerina commenced sending his merchants to purchase slaves and his armies to plunder for them in the Andrantsay.[159] The source of slaves highland merchants supplied into the Mascarene trade after about 1800, then, began to shift toward the southern periphery of Andrianampoinimerina's kingdom. Fewer captives were now generated through kidnapping and the perversion of social institutions within Andrianampoinimerina's own kingdom; they were increasingly the victims of his victorious armies and the activities of his allied merchants beyond the four core districts of Imerina (Imerina *efa-toko*). Because Andrianampoinimerina promised not to enslave from within his own dominions, the more his kingdom expanded, the further from Antananarivo his armies and merchants were obliged to search for their captives.

By the turn of the century, the scale and intensity of northerners' slave raids south into the Andrantsay had increased significantly. Fressange, who traveled in Madagascar just after the turn of the century, commented that "the people of the Andrantsay are a vulgar and cowardly pastoral people, they are the play things of the Hoves who wage war on them to take slaves."[160] "The wars of Andrianampoinimerina have furnished a very large number of slaves for the last several years," noted Nicolas Mayeur in 1807.[161] A design to weaken the internally prosperous and populous Andrantsay may have figured just as importantly in these attacks as Andrianampoinimerina's desire to acquire slaves for sale to French traders at the coast. Despite ongoing hostilities with their northern neighbors, Andrantsay merchants also sold slaves from the south to merchants from the region of Antananarivo. In 1790 *traitant* Dumaine noted that "although the Hova population is immense, they are nevertheless in the necessity of seeking slaves from the Andrantsay, a neighboring country which surrounds Hancove on the south and west forming a quarter circle; the slaves that our commerce derives from that area are preferable to the Hovas or Amboilambs in that they are curly for the most part and of a darker black."[162] Many of these "black and curly-haired" slaves were not from the Andrantsay proper, but hailed from the southwestern coast of Madagascar. Writing soon before Andrianampoinimerina's conquest of the Andrantsay, the French government's surgeon attached to the *agent commercial* at Foulpointe confirmed the importance of the commerce in slaves passing from the southwest coast of Madagascar, through the Andrantsay and Antananarivo, to the French at Madagascar's east coast. "Further South and in the center of the island two days' walk from Ancove," he wrote, "is found the large province of Andrantsay or the Betsileo who trade with Andrianampoinimerina on one side, & in the south all the way to the Bay of St. Augustine, the Betsileos annually sell to Ancove from four to five hundred slaves obtained from markets in the southern part, Ancove sells them cattle and textiles of various sorts."[163] Beyond a source of slaves itself, the Andrantsay emerged as an intermediary of coastal slaves for the Antananarivo area.

Sylvain Roux recognized the Andrantsay as an important source of servile labor after his arrival at the Malagasy coast in 1807. "It is," he wrote of the Andrantsay, "the country that offers us the most resources for this interesting commerce."[164] Direct commerce with the Andrantsay looked especially attractive to Roux when during the 1807 and 1808 trading seasons Andrianampoinimerina unilaterally inflated the prices and terms he was willing to allow his allied merchants to accept for slaves from, and passing through, highland Madagascar. In those two years Andrianampoinimerina raised the exchange equivalent of his captives to 45 piasters and two pieces of white cloth, a real cost to *traitants* of nearly 60 piasters, "which has never been the case before," lamented Roux.[165] Later that year, Andrianampoinimerina resolved to refuse textiles altogether in partial payment for slaves. All future deliveries of captives were to be settled strictly in piasters and gunpowder. In retaliation for these measures, which increased the real cost of highland Malagasy slaves both in Madagascar and at the Mascarenes, Roux threatened to take French commerce to Andrianampoinimerina's enemies. "He will fear himself deprived of the commerce and especially his gunpowder that makes him a referee of all the area to the west [of Madagascar's east coast] and the master of all the people he fights," wrote Roux confidently.[166] In addition to these countermeasures, Roux and the *traitants* agreed in 1808 to boycott the trade with Andrianampoinimerina and to oblige several highland Malagasy merchants arriving in Tamatave with caravans of slaves from the highlands to return with them to Andrianampoinimerina.[167]

Frustrated with Andrianampoinimerina's corner on the supply of slaves from highland Madagascar, the "taxe des noirs" he required *traitants* to pay when they exited his kingdom with captives, and chronic insecurity along the route between Tamatave and Antananarivo, Roux sought to open direct commercial relationships with rulers in the Andrantsay.[168] With justification, Roux felt that the passage of Andrantsay slaves through Antananarivo before their arduous march toward the east coast simply raised their price. According to Roux, the Andrantsay enjoyed human and agricultural prosperity similar to Andrianampoinimerina's expanding state to the north, but Andrianampoinimerina wielded a military advantage predicated upon years of experience in the battlefield and a privileged access to supplies of gunpowder in the Mascarene trade.[169] In an attempt to bypass the Antananarivo middlemen surrounding Andrianampoinimerina and to acquire Andrantsay slaves directly and more cheaply from the southern kingdom, Roux sought in early 1808 to open a direct commerce with Andriamanalinabetsileo, the king of Andrantsay. By exchanging silver and gunpowder directly for Andrantsay slaves, *traitants* could help to militarily strengthen the languishing southern kingdom. Although Roux did not verbalize it in his communications with his superiors at Île de France, this strategy carried a further benefit for French merchants. By pitting the Andrantsay against Andrianampoinimerina's expansionist state to the north, perhaps two slave-producing states in the interior could be competitively positioned against each other to insure a steady flow of captives into the Mascarene islands. In early 1808 Roux dispatched a *traitant* by the name of Duhoulbec along with the representative of another *traitant*, Lagardère, to confer with Andriamanalinabetsileo in his capital and apprise him of French intentions.[170]

Andrianampoinimerina, however, was not to be outfoxed. Before Duhoulbec reached the Andrantsay capital, Andrianampoinimerina's spies learned of the French plan. Andrianampoinimerina immediately fathomed its disastrous implications for his kingdom-building project and dispatched a party of men (probably soldiers) to confront the Andrantsay king. Andriamanalinabetsileo, reports Roux, retreated southwest to escape

Andrianampoinimerina's "envoys." While Andrianampoinimerina employed strongarm tactics against Andriamanalinabetsileo, he intervened directly into Andrantsay slave markets. Employing a classical strategy for cornering markets, Andrianampoinimerina offered twice the prevailing market price for any slaves originating from or passing through the Andrantsay and by this shrewd commercial tactic succeeded in insuring that Andrantsay suppliers would sell their captives northward through Antananarivo rather than directly to the French at the coast. Andrianampoinimerina would temporarily eat the financial loss for purchasing slaves dear from Andrantsay and selling them cheap to the French to retain his long-term control over the supply of slaves from the highland interior to the east coast. Confident in the success of these combined measures to protect his dominant position in the supply market for captives, Andrianampoinimerina informed Roux that he had maneuvered to "ruin and render naught the operation of Duhoulbec."[171] "He complained of us," wrote Roux of Andrianampoinimerina, "knowing the chief of Andrantsay as his enemy: we furnished him [Andriamanalinabetsileo] with gunpowder and muskets: it appears that he wants to absolutely become the master of all the [highland] plain of Madagascar to the south and to the north."[172] *Traitants* would have to continue purchasing their slaves through Antananarivo. "For a savage prince," Roux once opined, Andrianampoinimerina is capable of "extraordinary things."[173]

At length convinced he had no other choice than to concede Andrianampoinimerina's control over the supply of highland Malagasy slaves, Roux eventually resolved to bargain with Andrianampoinimerina for better financial terms. In exchange for his monopoly over the supply of captives from the Malagasy highlands, Roux proposed, Andrianampoinimerina should agree to provide a constant 2,000 to 2,500 slaves annually at prices and payment terms convenient to French *traitants*. In return, Roux and his associated merchants working the Mascarene trade would engage never to exchange gunpowder with anyone in Madagascar but Andrianampoinimerina.[174] Roux even suggested that the east African slaves annually marched by Muslim and Sakalava merchants from the Bay of Bombetoka directly to Foulpointe (see chapter 2) should be funneled through Antananarivo instead, creating advantages for both Andrianampoinimerina and the French while cutting Muslim and Sakalava merchants out of the slave transportation sector altogether.[175] Roux wanted personally to convince Andrianampoinimerina of these proposed terms but failed to effect an anticipated journey to Antananarivo during the 1808 trading season.[176] Like Roux's many plans for controlling commerce at the east coast (see chapter 2), these elaborate schemes remained unimplemented. Without French cooperation, however, Andrianampoinimerina's control over trade in the highlands was already complete and his expansion northward into Antsihanaka would soon cut off Antalaotra and

Sakalava access to the east coast. If no one but Andrianampoinimerina in highland Madagascar could supply the French with captives, no one there but Andrianampoinimerina could receive French shipments of gunpowder in return. With or without Roux's formally negotiated cooperation, Andrianampoinimerina had secured his interests and cornered most silver weaponry, and ammunition flowing from the east coast into the Malagasy highlands.

If muskets and gunpowder served largely symbolic roles in Malagasy warfare during the late eighteenth century, contemporary Malagasy and Europeans were convinced that European military technology played a key role in Andrianampoinimerina's conquests after 1805.[177] Raombana, as I have shown, claimed that muskets and gunpowder undergirded royal power.[178] Several *Tantara* narratives mention the importance of muskets and gunpowder in political conquest but say little about how they were acquired.[179] Archaeologists have suggested that the defensive walls surrounding highland villages were thickened during the late eighteenth century because firearms were becoming important to the conduct of warfare.[180] Coastal Malagasy frequently complained when French *traitants* supplied gunpowder to Andrianampoinimerina.[181] The Bezanozano chiefs who sporadically plundered *traitant* caravans passing through their territory after 1807 cited displeasure at the way French commerce served to arm and privilege Andrianampoinimerina above anyone else.[182] Indeed Andrianampoinimerina developed a formidable military reputation during the last years of his life. Barthélémy Hugon, who knew the highland king well, wrote in his journal of a voyage to Antananarivo in 1808 that Andrianampoinimerina "continues everywhere to be a victor, and it is to his science, his genius, his policies, and especially to his bravery in dangerous circumstances that he owes his supreme luck."[183] "The Oves love to conquer," noted his contemporary Rondeaux in the same vein, "this people cannot exist without war, Andrianampoinimerina in his large expeditions can carry up to twenty thousand men in his army."[184] If neither gunpowder nor trade wealth could substitute for the usefulness of a well-organized and numerous army in the conquest of new territories, each served to tip the military balance in favor of Andrianampoinimerina.

Effectively deprived of trade wealth and therefore the means of self-defense by Andrianampoinimerina and his French partners, Andrantsay chiefdoms fell easily to their expansive neighbor from the north. Within a year of the events described above, Andrianampoinimerina, his son Radama, and a vast northern army marched against the Andrantsay and subjugated its constituent minipolities. Most Andrantsay chiefs submitted without fighting, popular narratives suggest, and those who did were eventually defeated and enslaved.[185] Having secured a near monopoly over the export of slaves and the import of silver and gunpowder, Andrianampoinimerina reigned supreme in the Malagasy highland interior. The fall of the once-prosperous and powerful Andrantsay in the transformed climate of monopolistic foreign trade demonstrates how international commerce had come to play a decisive role in highland Malagasy politics by the beginning of the nineteenth century. Acquiring trade wealth and weaponry while depriving others of the same had become an effective means for securing political supremacy. In about 1809, just before Andrianampoinimerina's death, Epidariste Colin summed it up in one short sentence: "Of all the chiefs of Madagascar," he wrote, Andrianampoinimerina "is without a doubt the richest."[186]

HIGHLAND MADAGASCAR'S *CONJONCTURE*

At the beginning of the nineteenth century highland Madagascar was at what Fernand Braudel once called a *conjoncture*.[187] This *conjoncture* was shaped by a myriad of individual decisions exercised by French and Malagasy in the time of the slave trade, extending mercantile capitalism into the landlocked interior and anchoring it firmly within local communities and social relationships. Slaving offered opportunities to some and brought tragedies and hardships to countless others. Common people fell prey to debt and kidnapping. Women and men could no longer expect erstwhile social institutions to protect them or their kin from enslavement. Within this uncertain environment, the capacity of the institutions and conventions of kinship and citizenship to insure personal security from enslavement waned as many people were pried from their social and political milieux. The result was a socially fluid and geographically mobile society in which local communities and corporate groups, whether domestic units, *teraky*, *firenena,* or entire kingdoms, were in a process of dissolution and recrystallization. Entire communities within the Malagasy highlands were uprooted, dissolved, and reformed during the era of the slave trade.[188] In the Vakinankaratra (or the Andrantsay) of the southwest highlands, for instance, the majority of local descent groups trace their origins to heterogeneous southward migrations of chiefs, their entourages, slaves, hangers-on, and clients from the Antananarivo region during the social upheavals after 1770, losers in wars of trade and political attrition.[189]

The erosion of political, civil, and kinship institutions that might have protected the vulnerable in other circumstances sent highlanders in search of new relationships of trust with their peers and social superiors. The poor pursued companions and patrons who would espouse civic virtue and respect social rights forfeited during the era of the slave trade. For their part kings sought bigger kingdoms and vaster arenas of power. But if rising kings like Andrianampoinimerina could no longer rule without mastering the challenges of an international economy neither could they sustain their political ambitions over the long term without attending to the aching predicaments of commoners and their broken communities. That popular memories of Andrianampoinimerina such as those embedded in the *Tantara* virtually ignore the founder king's commercial practices suggests that highlanders saw far more than an astute and accomplished merchant in him. It is to the domestic politics of Andrianampoinimerina and his successor, the popular bases of their support, memories of their reigns, and the relationship of these to transformations in Merina identity and cultural practice that I turn in part 2 of this book.

PART II

CULTURE

5

POPULAR POLITICS

The Merina are eggs who cannot change their mother. . . . I see the
various *firenena*, they are all mine, I love them all, and I shall mix
hairs as I please.

—Andrianampoinimerina[1]

[L]ong-established usages seem to require the appearance at least of
equity and justice in the proceedings of the ruler, and the exercise of
his power conformably with acknowledged rights of the people. No
sovereign would feel himself safe whose rule was condemned by the
majority of his people; but a sovereign whose rule was wise and just
would be regarded with admiration and veneration, as being almost
more than human.

—William Ellis[2]

Beneath the social fermentation bubbling through highland Malagasy societies during the late eighteenth century rested a deep crisis of collective identity. As in other African communities during the age of enslavement, relationships among highlanders and between them and their leaders had become strained and tinged with distrust as chiefs, kings, and commoners each
implemented a range of strategies for survival and advancement that included
participation in the export commerce.[3] An important dimension of the collective identity crisis was an ebbing in the size of primary social groups as rural
communities folded in upon themselves seeking refuge from the misfortunes
of enslavement (chapter 3). Collective identity entails a shared sense of social unity, but after 1770 highland Malagasy communities were more fractured than they had been over the preceding several decades. Because of
this, the collective identity crisis afflicting highland Malagasy also assumed
political dimensions. By the late eighteenth century highland Malagasy could
not rely upon moral relationships with their leaders, their peers, or their kin
to protect them from bondage. For the Ravoandriana, a key concern in transactions with their king was achieving physical security from illegitimate cap-

ture by reinforcing moralities of enslavement that discouraged sovereigns from capturing and selling their subjects. By pressing leaders they distrusted and pursuing relationships with those they might rely upon, *firenena* acted to expand and redefine their moral communities and hence their collective identities. For his part, by striving to politically appropriate all highland Madagascar for himself, Andrianampoinimerina sought to generate a novel sense of highland political identity, one loyal to his kingdom-building project. As crosscutting royal and popular strategies for the transformation of political relationships confronted one another in highland Madagascar, they shifted identity politics to center stage and nurtured a new, complex, and locally textured political identity in highland Madagascar—being Merina.

Control over international trade was necessary but insufficient to secure for Andrianampoinimerina a stable exercise of power. If he were to unite all highland minikingdoms into one consolidated polity he would have to mitigate the social consequences of the very trade he derived his wealth and weaponry of expansion from. One way in which Andrianampoinimerina sought to resolve this dilemma was to promise those who submitted themselves to his sovereignty exemption from enslavement and to create captives only from *outside* the frontiers of his dominions.[4] Yet Andrianampoinimerina's popular politics could not end there. Building a kingdom required more than a monopolization of trade and promises of protection from enslavement. Andrianampoinimerina sought the political support of highland Malagasy at a time when communal relationships were badly frayed and ill will festered between highlanders and many of their leaders. Simply put, given their experiences with illegitimate enslavement over the preceding decades, *firenena* and their members had little reason to trust each other or their kings. Restoring trust to political relationships and redefining frayed civic virtues in an era of enslavement was probably the most difficult political challenge Andrianampoinimerina faced in uniting highlanders into a single political unity. Because he recognized this challenge and skillfully deployed measures to address it, Andrianampoinimerina emerged as a popular and successful leader.

The creation of the Merina kingdom at the turn of the nineteenth century was both a political and an imaginative process, the physical amalgamation of a state but also the thinking and acting of a new collective identity by highland people. To imagine is to form a mental image of something, to conceptualize intellectually, to interpret, or to creatively describe a tangible reality through symbol, word, or metaphor. While imagining normally implies an individual, nonverbal, and introverted mental exercise, the collective imagination that interests me in this chapter was characterized by its public expression in the form of a political language whose vocabulary resonated with people's historical experience. Imagining a kingdom entailed articulating a culturally based understanding of the political relationships structuring the

realm and deploying a language that evoked the legitimacy of those hierarchical relationships. To collectively imagine the new kingdom implied speaking about that entity as a distinct community of people with common interests and civic responsibilities. Andrianampoinimerina's kingdom was, in the
words of Benedict Anderson, an "imagined community," for its members
sought to articulate an inter-*firenena* ethos of mutual belonging, a new sense
of citizenship in a body politic.[5]

An "imagined" kingdom is also an appropriate paradigm for Andrianampoinimerina's polity in that the polity and Andrianampoinimerina himself
are known more through mid- and late-nineteenth-century social memory than
through contemporary eyewitness documentation (see chapter 1). The Andrianampoinimerina known today was remembered, or imagined, by highland Malagasy in very specific political circumstances after his death (chapters 6 and 7). To know Andrianampoinimerina as a remembered founder king,
however, is not to know him through hazy and unreliable myth as opposed to
hard fact, but to shift historical paradigms and modes of historical interpretation, as if to examine a cut diamond from its multiple facets.[6] It is to experience Andrianampoinimerina, borrowing the expression of Andeanist historian Thomas Abercrombie, through a highland Malagasy history rather than
through a history of highland Madagascar.[7] Each type of history reveals different and complementary truths about highland Madagascar's past. In previous chapters, highland Madagascar and its people's experiences were viewed
primarily through the eyes of non-Malagasy. As the author of this book, I
interpreted (or memorialized) the economic and social effects of the slave
trade—"event truths"—through organization of contemporary eyewitness
evidence and attention to certain principles of chronology and professional
argumentation. In the present chapter I explore mid-nineteenth-century highland Malagasy interpretations of Andrianampoinimerina—"cultural truths"—
sustained through social memory, a collectively produced understanding of
the past. Events reported in social memory (particularly those in the last sec-
tions of this chapter) cannot be substantiated with contemporary eyewitness
accounts, for (as I explained in chapter 1) few foreigners ventured into highland Madagascar during the reign of Andrianampoinimerina. Some dimensions of late nineteenth-century popular histories can be validated by roughly
contemporary accounts, however, and may additionally be checked against
archaeological and ethnographic work. Where disparate lines of evidence
converge, I argue with greater confidence about the literal accuracy of the
events described. This is particularly true with respect to developments in
tomb building and mortuary ritual, where archaeology and historical ethnography can be brought to bear. Where I must rely solely on the *Tantara*, as
with most of Andrianampoinimerina's social legislation, however, I shift interpretive gears to seek the historical-cultural meaning and significance of

social memory, widely spread and collectively held memories of the past. Parsing social memory for the cultural meaning of human experience is both a relevant and a pressing task for professional historians. Just as culture is historically produced, history is culturally expressed, embedded in the things people both say and do in the present.[8]

To place greater interpretive credence in a profile of Andrianampoinimerina that emerges from contemporary evidence than in one which emanates from Malagasy language narratives (or conversely, to accept social memory and contemporary evidence as equivalent registers of history) is to fail to fully appreciate what Andrianampoinimerina *meant* to highland Malagasy as distinct from what he actually did and did not do. Highland Malagasy "historioracy" is less concerned with "what really happened" in the past than with attributing meaning to past events and with creating and transforming the moral communities whose past is being recounted. Although social memory conveys things that happened in the past, it is always and simultaneously about the construction of identity in the present.[9] Once produced, Merina identity was sustained during the nineteenth century in particular historical circumstances through a dynamic process of remembering and interpreting Andrianampoinimerina. Failing to understand the cultural meaning of the Merina founder king, historians cannot fathom how Merina identity was transformed after his death. How highland Malagasy remembered Andrianampoinimerina and his popular administrative policies as cultural facts of enormous political influence and relevance guided both their behavior and their understanding of themselves as an imagined community.[10] Rejecting popular social memories of Andrianampoinimerina as ahistorical and fantastical, while in conformity with a narrow conception of history as verifiable event, is both oxymoronic (social memories are historically formed) and condescending to highland Malagasy historical sensibilities.[11] It is to abjure useful and rich interpretations of the past. Because of the virtual absence of contemporary accounts pertaining to the reign of Andrianampoinimerina, scholars must employ popular narratives creatively and critically or foreswear much insightful comprehension of his reign. Historians ought, Indian Oceanist Hubert Gerbeau reminds us, to "take into account what they hear and not only what they read."[12] Hearing and hearing "deeply," in turn, mean appreciating highland Malagasy historical understanding on its own terms rather than simply appropriating it as bits of historical data to be fitted into professional narratives. Reflecting the heterogeneity of the extant historical sources about Andrianampoinimerina, and consequently the limits of our knowledge about him, this chapter paints a historical canvas from social memory and other forms of historical evidence, shifting among disparate but complementary interpretive paradigms.

Because of the complexity and contentiousness of the methodological issues raised in the two preceding paragraphs, I want to further clarify my argument about the complementary truths of social memory and contemporary evidence. Unlike in other chapters of this book where eyewitness evidence is much denser, I do not claim precise knowledge of Andrianampoinimerina's policies or their actual effectiveness as remembered in popular histories. In a sense, such event history is irrelevant to this inquiry into the origins of Merina identity and highlanders' use of a metaphorical image of Andrianampoinimerina in political struggles after his death (chapter 6). In these struggles, it was not "what actually happened" under Andrianampoinimerina that was relevant, but how highlanders interpreted what had happened. Specifically, social memory informs historians that highlanders favorably compared their founder king to his successors and apprises them of the specific bases upon which they did so. Yet neither do I believe that popular memories of Andrianampoinimerina are simple fabrications with no relationship either to actual experience of his rule or to its event history. If the literal accuracy of specific events and policies described in nineteenth-century social memories cannot be verified, there is, nevertheless, to borrow the words of David Henige, a link between "what happened and evidence of what people subsequently thought had happened."[13] In a study of nineteenth- and twentieth-century images of Shaka Zulu relevant to the methodology I employ here, Carolyn Hamilton writes that "Histories and ideologies that are successful resonate in a body of information known to both their promoters and those whom they seek to persuade." Historical memories do not rise out of thin air; no party to conflicts over historical knowledge can simply invent the past and make it stick, especially when deploying those memories against their opponents. There are material limits to historical invention.[14]

The purpose of this chapter is to delineate the significance of Andrianampoinimerina as a cultural hero, a political resource for highland Malagasy of the early nineteenth century, and to relate that image of Andrianampoinimerina to the historical origins of Merina ethnicity. The narrative in this chapter therefore inhabits the ambiguous intellectual space between the uses of memorial evidence as event fact (history), on the one hand, and historical interpretation (meaning), on the other, a challenge historians of Africa have long struggled with in their use of orally conveyed historical traditions.[15] Because of the paucity of contemporary evidence for domestic policy during Andrianampoinimerina's reign, this tension between what are sometimes considered as mutually exclusive uses of memory and event is unavoidable. Yet the ambiguities and tensions of social memory and event history are also productive in the quest for Merina identity history. I will return to consider the complementary relationship between social memory and professional history in the closing chapter of this work.

Accompanying an inchoate ethos of pan-*firenena* belonging as Merina in Andrianampoinimerina's kingdom was a unique political language, one decidedly populist and decidedly moral. Populist because at the end of the eighteenth century the personal strategy of Andrianampoinimerina and the collective strategies of rural communities converged in fragile alliance. Moral because the political language of state building was a rhetoric of collective identity that rearticulated standards of civic virtue. Morality entails the classification, judgment, and social regulation of human behaviors. A new social morality in turn-of-the-century highland Madagascar was aimed specifically at the popular regulation of three domains of behavior: political behavior, class behavior, and gender behavior. Collective identities are seldom expressions of egalitarianism, for they legitimize complex social arrangements, inevitably hierarchical, and present them as culturally unique. For these reasons, the making of a unified political identity in central Madagascar entailed intervention into the social relationships that created different experiences for kings and commoners, *teraky* and *firenena*, wealthy and poor, men and women.

The first historical traces of a specifically Merina identity emerge from social relationships and struggles over the meaning of mutual responsibility, or citizenship, in the newly unified kingdom of highland Madagascar.[16] To be Merina in Andrianampoinimerina's kingdom was first and foremost to identify oneself as a subject of the new king, to participate in a moralized political identity that implied new rights and responsibilities, and to be an active participant in the expanding *polis* called Imerina. The *polis*, a classical Greek city-state and root of the modern term politics, was ideally a community of citizens with responsibilities toward each other and free from the tyranny of an aristocratic ruler, yet in which there were some noncitizen slaves, as in highland Madagascar. Governed by a monarch rather than a representative assembly, Imerina failed to fulfill all the ideals of the classical *polis*, yet what was so important about Andrianampoinimerina's reign in the memory of highland Malagasy were the moralized rights and responsibilities he articulated for his citizen-subjects. Citizenship, by which I broadly mean political and social obligations among members of a body politic, was key to Andrianampoinimerina's new *polis*, for it implied that individuals were invested with moral rights and responsibilities and that civic virtue ought to regulate human interaction.

The vernacular vocabulary of citizenship in turn-of-the-century highland Madagascar pivoted around a conception of royalty as a source of life and order for commoners. In royal ritual Andrianampoinimerina often portrayed himself as the sun. He designated nonslave citizens of his kingdom by the collective term *ambaniandro*, "those beneath the sun," and *ambanilanitra*, "those beneath the sky."[17] In 1808 Andrianampoinimerina explained this metaphor of royal power to a visiting *traitant*, claiming that "all the people and provinces under his protection are under the sun, which sees everything and enlightens everything."[18] To be Merina was to be an *ambaniandro*, a citizen under the light of Andrianampoinimerina's expanding realm, loyal to the sovereign yet deserving of protection from him and respect from fellow citizens. The moralized sense of citizenship that Andrianampoinimerina articulated for his subjects at the turn of the nineteenth century laid the cultural foundations for a subtle transformation of Merina political identity, after the death of Andrianampoinimerina, into an ethnic identity. Integrally engaged with Andrianampoinimerina in the making of Merina political identity, highland Malagasy retained a political independence they later transformed into an ethnic identity. This chapter explores the making of Merina political identity; the next, its transformation into an ethnicity as highlanders protested their king's attempt to redefine citizenship and royal sovereignty.

THE LANGUAGE OF POLITICAL IDENTITY

A newly imagined community, Andrianampoinimerina's *polis* required a shared ritual and political vocabulary for articulating the responsibilities of the sovereign and his citizen-subjects. That language could not be invented from thin air. It was based upon long-standing discursive and ritual traditions linking highland Malagasy culture back to Austronesian roots.[19] If it is argued that highland Malagasy political language represented a "timeless and transcendental ancestral order" existing beyond the realm of human intention and everyday experience, however, the significance and meaning of that language to highland Malagasy in the age of enslavement cannot be fully understood.[20] Cultural vocabulary takes on emotional and intellectual force when it speaks to people's experiences, rooting itself in the unfolding of their lives. Structuring highland Malagasy political discourse during the reign of Andrianampoinimerina was a paradigm of social experience that drew symbolic contrasts between the old economy of enslavement and the newly constructed civil state. That paradigm articulated metaphoric oppositions of chaos, associated with enslavement and its accompanying destruction of kinship, and order, associated with the redefinition of kinship and citizenship by Andrianampoinimerina and his allies.[21] Metaphor, one variety of trope or figurative use of language, is a common form of human communication by which something—such as an idea, relationship, process, or situation—is illustrated and imbued with emotional force by analogy to something else.[22] Metaphor is the subject of considerable research in the fields of language and literature, where it is conceived as a linguistic and rhetorical device. Metaphor has also become the subject of inquiry in the social sciences and history.[23] My interest in metaphor lies not in its technical characteristics but in its rhetorical and imaginative potential in political discourse. To think of metaphor as a historical-political phenomenon in central Madagascar, it is fruitful to begin with the suggestion of J. Christopher Crocker that tropes offer powerful "programs" and "persuasions" in social relationships.[24]

As recorded in the *Tantara*, Andrianampoinimerina often described the period before his ascent to power as a time of *fanjakana hova*.[25] Literally meaning "authority/government of and by *hova*" (*hova* were not considered legitimate candidates for royalty), the expression evoked notions of decentralized power, shrinking primary social groups, immoral lawlessness, contention, and disorder, and associated them all with *hova*—and therefore illegitimate—rule.[26] In his political rhetoric, Andrianampoinimerina contrasted *fanjakana hova* with *fanjakan'andriana* (authority/government of and by a single *andriana* or sovereign) as a model of orderly, united, moralized, and legitimate government. To construe his violent appropriation of power as a legitimate project beneficial to a populace racked by disorder and contention, Andrianampoinimerina spoke of his rule as orderly *fanjakan'andriana*. While the notion of *fanjakan'andriana* provided a culturally rooted justification for Andrianampoinimerina's political ambitions, it also expressed something rural communities came to expect of their new sovereign: to bring order to the communally and historically experienced chaos, division, insecurity, and illegitimacy of an economy of enslavement. The founder king's metaphoric self-justifications, then, were not simply wool over his subjects' eyes.[27] Royal political language could be of use to *firenena* in their quest for trusting relationships with sovereigns and each other, offering a persuasive rhetoric by which rural communities could press locally formulated programs upon their rulers. Definitions of order and chaos or legitimate and illegitimate behavior could diverge, but sovereigns and subjects, women and men, slaves and free, often fashioned their political rhetoric with explicit reference to the metaphoric language of *fanjakana hova* and *fanjakan'andriana*. Through a dynamic tension between royal self-justification and popular appeals for royal accountability, the key political metaphor of *hova* chaos versus *andriana* order served as a template from which a variety of popular discourses were cast at the beginning of the nineteenth century. Many of these purposely articulated polar images of chaos and order will appear in the pages that follow.

Also crucial to the development of a unified political identity within Andrianampoinimerina's kingdom was the way the founding sovereign chose to represent the expansion of his *polis*: as a territorial expansion (*itatra*, *fahabeazana voho*) or unification (*fivoriana*) of Imerina, the area immediately surrounding the capital at Antananarivo, rather than as a conquest of neighboring territories.[28] As the geographical reach of the *polis* expanded, so

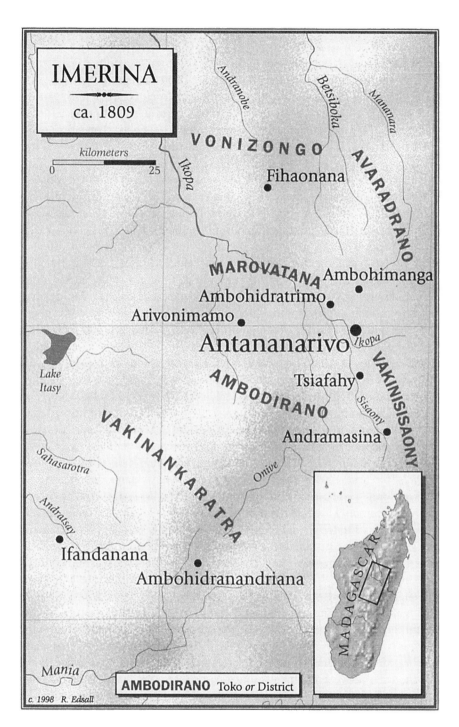

Map 5.1 Imerina, ca. 1809

too did Imerina.[29] A complement to this idea, Andrianampoinimerina elected to define those newly joining the kingdom as citizen *ambaniandro*, as Merina, rather than as conquered subjects or permanent foreigners.[30] These choices were strategic ones that facilitated a geographic expansion of political identity in the Malagasy highlands. Inclusiveness deflected political attention away from the external boundaries of the realm and concentrated it instead on the significance of outward movement from a centripetal point, the capital. The social transactions most productive of highland Malagasy political identity at the beginning of the nineteenth century were not those differentiating Merina from non-Merina, but relationships linking *firenena* and *ambaniandro* to the center of Imerina, the royal court at Antananarivo. This is what highlanders meant when they spoke of Antananarivo as their central or primary place (*foibe*).[31] Taking their cue from Andrianampoinimerina and his subject-citizens, even foreign *traitants* began to call the newly united kingdom "la grande province d'ymirne" (the *large* province of Imerina), distinguishing it from Imerina proper, the region of Antananarivo.[32] Whatever the coercion and material politics of kingdom building on the ground, imagining political conquest as an expansion of Imerina rather than as a confederation of micropolities of which Imerina was but one (the model for the Andrantsay "kingdom," to the south) was among the most influential of forces shaping the rise of a unified Merina identity across the Malagasy highlands.[33]

Andrianampoinimerina based administrative classification of his expanding kingdom of Imerina upon the concept of a lot, division, or district (*toko*). The first phase of identity expansion comprised extension of Imerina to four districts surrounding the capital of Antananarivo (Imerina *efa-toko*, "of four districts"). These four districts—Avaradrano, Marovatana, Vakinisisaony, Ambodirano—were considered remnants of the four divisions of a legendary eighteenth-century kingdom ruled by Andriamasinavalona.[34] The second phase of expansion included the addition of districts further afield, Vakinankaratra and Vonizongo (creating Imerina *enin-toko*, "of six districts").[35] "In the time of Andrianampoinimerina," relates the *Tantara*, "Imerina was enlarged to include six districts."[36] "The land and the government are mine, he [Andrianampoinimerina] said; so I will make all *ambaniandro* part of Imerina. And I will make of Imerina six districts: Avaradrano I will make one-sixth, Vakinikisaony one-sixth; Marovatana one-sixth, Ambodirano one-sixth, Vonizongo one-sixth, Vakinankaratra one-sixth."[37] Embedded within the administrative vocabulary of Andrianampoinimerina's territorial expansion, then, was a tension between the royally expedient notion of highland political unity and the reality of district subdivisions and the individual *firenena* identities within them. Here the analogy of Imerina and the Greek *polis* is particularly apposite in that, like Imerina, the *polis* was composed of constituent descent groups termed *demes* (from whence, ultimately, Maurice Bloch's terminology to gloss *firenena*).[38] Tensions between political unity and regional distinctiveness also manifested themselves in highland Malagasy vocabularies of identity. As Gerald Berg has demonstrated, Andrianampoinimerina often suggested his kingdom was one huge family.[39] The notion of the nation as an integrated network of kin denied a fundamental reality, of course: not all citizens of Imerina were related by descent. Primary allegiances at the turn of the century were to one's *firenena* and *teraky*, not to sovereigns who often betrayed their subjects or to strangers who might seek to enslave. The complex tensions between the newly imagined *polis* as one immense family of *ambaniandro* and a countervailing reality of *firenena*, administrative, kin, class, and gender divisions within that polity informs the balance of this chapter. Merina identity was inchoate during the reign of Andrianampoinimerina, and complexly associated with the identities of *firenena* and other local communities that comprised the kingdom.

FIRENENA AND ROYAL POWER

Because of their discrete identities and potentially autonomous visions of how rulers should rule, *firenena* and their members were of paramount concern to Andrianampoinimerina. From the opening of the export trade in highland Malagasy slaves, *firenena* became increasingly malleable in the hands of wealthy individuals who, as Andrianampoinimerina had, distributed silver to create dependents, assuring rural communities who submitted to them of protection from enslavement. Whereas members of a single *firenena* conceptualized one another through the idiom of kinship, *firenena* could be assembled from coresident strangers.[40] Many *firenena* were clearly the product of social upheavals that brought disparate people together during the eighteenth century.[41] By restricting his rivals' access to silver and other forms of trade wealth, Andrianampoinimerina attempted to prevent chiefs and kings from expanding their influence by building and strengthening loyal *firenena* of their own. Control over trade was Andrianampoinimerina's premier top-down economic strategy for achieving political power (chapter 4). It inhibited competitors, but it did little in itself to attract popular support. Indeed, by positioning himself to control the export trade in slaves from the Malagasy highlands, Andrianampoinimerina potentially exposed himself to the very criticisms the Ravoandriana had unleashed in their revolt against Andrianamboatsimarofy in 1785.

Andrianampoinimerina therefore also sought a complementary, bottom-up political strategy. Instead of attempting to efface *firenena* and their unique identities, he tried to freeze them by "slamming on the brakes" and fostering a more rigid identity consciousness within them. This strategy privileged a communal ethos that restrained the socially manipulative activities of the king's wealthy competitors. Andrianampoinimerina's conservative political strategy entailed regulating kinship transactions at the heart of *firenena*. The founder king sought to solidify kinship fictions of the late eighteenth century into kinship realities by first arresting the process of *firenena* formation and then presenting existing *firenena* as royally authorized, enduring groups of "natural" or biological descent. The cultural/ideological/imaginative work of creating a highland kingdom, then, was one of crystallizing dynamic *firenena* and presenting them as timeless and unchanging entities. By this means, Andrianampoinimerina attempted to harden fluid identity structures and cultural practices at the local level. Kingdom building in highland Madagascar was not, then, a zero-sum identity game in which the power of royalty increased while that of the *firenena* withered away. Merina identity did not efface local identities, it reinforced them. Similar to the making of royal power on Ijwi Island in central Africa, in which "clans grew and took new forms as part of that very context within which kingship itself was conceived, nurtured, and shaped," royal administrative policy and ritual in highland Madagascar reinforced and recreated *firenena* identities at the turn of the nineteenth century.[42] As a corollary, royal power did not flow unidirectionally from the court at Antananarivo toward the countryside; it was fashioned in a conflictual, dialectical process of interaction between sovereign and people. It is counterproductive, therefore, to conceptualize kingdom building in highland Madagascar as primarily a repressive movement, as a complete and mature highland royalty existing apart from the actions and intentions of common people, imposing its will upon them from the outside. As with the Sakalava monarchy of the Analalava region of northwest Madagascar, Merina monarchy "did not emerge full-grown." "It grew," rather, "over time from the efforts of people" seeking security and social order in the age of enslavement.[43] By heeding popular grievances and soliciting popular support, Andrianampoinimerina rooted royal power in his people. Though subject to considerable erosion over time, that royal power endured until it was overthrown by French colonizers in 1895.

This interpretation of state-*firenena* relationships in Andrianampoinimerina's kingdom suggests a modification of most scholarship about the period, which defines state building as the process of royal political, military, and ideological domination of largely passive subjects (and descent groups) by an autonomous royal power coming from the outside.[44] Andrianampoinimerina has been variously represented as a masterful agricultural engineer,[45] a skillful legislator and politician,[46] an efficient warrior,[47] an adept fashioner of political discourses,[48] and an ingenious cultural intermediary between ancestors and living subjects. The most influential theory of state formation in highland Madagascar is the last of these, which accentuates the critical role of royal ideology as a stable

Figure 5.1 Imaginary portrait of Andrianampoinimerina painted by Ramanan-kirahina, 1905. This portrait interprets Andrianampoinimerina as the embodiment of tradition with his white toga (*lamba*), spear, bare feet, plaited hairstyle, and silver amulet (*ody*) attached to his forehead. While the founder king's stature is portrayed as tall and his skin exceedingly fair, a *traitant* who conversed with Andrianampoinimerina in 1808 described him as "black and ugly." (*See*: Françoise Raison-Jourde, *Bible et pouvoir à Madagascar au XIXe siècle: invention d'une identité chrétienne et construction de l'état* [Paris, 1991], illustration between pages 380 and 381.)

"system of obedience" guiding the actions of common people. Building on the work of Alain Delivré and Maurice Bloch, Gerald Berg names this ideological system "*hasina* ideology." *Hasina* is a complex notion denoting efficacious power, sacred life force, and blessing that originates in departed ancestors, is passed along to living rulers, and is in turn channeled to those rulers' living subjects. "Merina saw historical reality as the product not of human agency," Berg writes,

> but of ancestral beneficence, *hasina*, which flowed downwards on obedient Merina from long-dead ancestors in a sacred stream that connected all living Merina. For obedient Merina, politics consisted in nothing more and nothing less than the lifelong quest to position oneself favorably in that sacred stream as close as possible to ancestors and then to reap the material benefits of that cherished association. Ancestors made their pleasure known by bestowing blessings, "superior" *hasina*, on those who honored them. In return, Merina offered "inferior" *hasina*, material goods, to their ancestors *via* a living intermediary. This transaction took place between individuals of unequal status. Members of households presented inferior *hasina* to heads of households who in turn presented inferior *hasina* to heads of kinship groups, and heads of kinship groups presented inferior hasina to heads of other kinship groups of superior status. Presentations of *hasina* occurred many times a year during rites of transition and defined a social hierarchy in which all individuals and groups found their place. The person occupying the central position of authority in each transaction was considered to be a representative of all long-dead ancestors, and he had the power to dispense their goodwill in the form of "superior" *hasina*. While superior *hasina* might be passed on by an intermediary representing ancestors, the ultimate source of superior *hasina* flowed from tombs in which ancestors were buried and from the ancestral lands (*tanin'drazana*) surrounding them.

According to this system of *hasina* ideology, or a "cult of blessing" as Maurice Bloch denotes it, sovereigns legitimized their power by achieving the highest possible position (for the living) within the stream of ancestral blessing. At the same time, they accumulated substantial wealth in the form of inferior *hasina* from their subordinates. Riches obtained outside the *hasina* system, such as from trade or plunder, could also be legitimized by portraying them as a blessing from the ancestors. *Hasina* ideology obtained such a "wide acceptance" and long-term stability among highland Malagasy, note this theory's proponents, that no one—including the sovereign—was able to manipulate its essential meaning. Rulers' *hasina* was enhanced by the sacred royal talismans (*sampy masina*) obtained from the various districts and provinces of the kingdom, becoming key emblems of royal power. *Hasina* ideology and struggles to climb its ladder of ancestral blessing were the basis of an enduring "traditional authority," in the words of Bloch, lasting from olden times to the present. Through *hasina* ideology, its practices, and it objects, sovereigns imposed their rule on the *firenena* of highland Madagascar.[49]

The most sophisticated of extant interpretations for highland Malagasy royal power that take the cultural and vernacular context of sovereignty seriously, emphases on *hasina* ideology fall short of a sufficient and satisfying explanation for the rise of the Merina kingdom. They fail not because royalty did not employ *hasina* ideologies or the royal talismans as strategies of rule—they certainly did—but because the structural formulation of *hasina* ideology as a stable and unchanging system primarily accessible to and benefiting rulers removes ideology from its historical context (when and how, for example, did it originate?) and leaves little meaningful room for the independent agency and intellectual capacity of nonroyals. To accept *hasina* ideology as explained in this literature is to embrace the prejudices of the rulers of highland Madagascar. Studies of *hasina* ideology, a Malagasy version of divine kingship that locates all significant kingdom-building activity and ritual interpretation in the (admittedly limited) cultural work of leaders, have either assumed that commoners' interpretations and use of royal discourse and ritual were nonexistent or that they were unimportant and without influence.[50] While royal charisma and appeals to *hasina* ideology were indispensable to Andrianampoinimerina's personal success, the Merina kingdom was neither singlehandedly assembled by the founder king nor founded under ideological conditions that he entirely controlled or benefited from. The Merina kingdom, Merina identity, and even modern royal power did not originate full-grown; each took shape through political conflict and concrete struggles in the era of the slave trade. Common highland Malagasy were far from docile when faced with the pretensions of royal power. They participated actively in commenting on and shaping their rulers' sovereignty in everyday transactions as well as in extraordinary and violent confrontations. In the process of engaging one another, kings and commoners fashioned and refashioned ideologies of blessing, fertility, and ancestral authority—*hasina* ideologies—each acting in their respective interests. Ritual, ancestral authority, and *hasina* ideologies, the primary constituents of Merina tradition, were practices and languages of political struggle, the basic cultural resources from which highland Malagasy ordered their lives in times of peace and crisis. As a result, those "ideologies" endured as political languages over the years, languages common to rulers and ruled that could be employed to weaken and destabilize royal power as well as to strengthen it.[51]

An underlying reason for the persistence of an intellectually and politically passive peasantry in the historiography and historical anthropology of highland Madagascar is that during the reign of Andrianampoinimerina royalty and commoners entered into a strategic yet brittle alliance, merging their political goals while temporarily muting their class differences. While Andrianampoinimerina's policies toward *firenena* checked the political maneuvering of his rivals through restrictions on their ability to manipulate kinship and draw new *firenena* around them, it resonated with the efforts of rural communities to create a conservative environment of greater social stability and royally respected social identity. Social innovations and fluid *firenena* during the eighteenth century had favored an erosion of personal security, aided in the making of slaves, and built the careers of many "big men"; commoners like the Ravoandriana sought to reverse these troubling developments to protect members of their descent groups. *Tantara* narratives attribute royal policies to Andrianampoinimerina, and the elements of those policies are articulated in the founder king's reported actions and words. *Firenena*, however, were key allies of the new sovereign and, like the Ravoandriana, advocated populist policies with their leaders. Together, royal politics in the era of the slave trade and the political goals highlanders pursued independently in its aftermath helped to shape the political language and social policies of Andrianampoinimerina at the beginning of the nineteenth century. Royal strategies were formulated in the context of public opinion, which in turn was shaped by human experiences in a slaving economy. Highland Malagasy sovereigns were neither omnipotent nor unconcerned about public opinion; some, and especially Andrianampoinimerina, acted responsively toward their constituents while simultaneously pursuing the rewards and vanities of earthly power. In this way, the "effects of the slave trade" were translated into political programs. Let us turn to the founder king's rhetoric and policies as recorded in highland Malagasy social memory.

THE RULE OF KIN AND COURT

Restrengthening the moral bonds of kinship was of paramount concern to highlanders at the end of the eighteenth century. Andrianampoinimerina responded to this concern with a socially conservative rhetoric by frequently emphasizing the unique and inflexible pedigree of each individual. "So whoever we are," he proclaimed, "let us each have our ancestors, whether we be *andriana* or *hova*, *mainty* or *fotsy*."[52] Shortly after unifying the six districts of his kingdom into Imerina, Andrianampoinimerina sought to tie each individual into a distinct kin structure, such as a *firenena*, that could be named and administered.

> Let each now return home to his ancestral land. But if you return to your ancestral land, and when you arrive there you wrest the ancestral land of others away from them, I will find you at night in your bed. And espe-

cially if you gather together and say, "we put him in power" and take advantage of the fact that people are constantly on the move about the kingdom, if you do this on my land I will put you to death. For no one has accomplished this unification but me. And when the speech was finished Andrianampoinimerina asked the people, "Who do you love?" "We love you," said the people. "You liars," said Andrianampoinimerina, "what you would really love is to return to your homes, for it is not me at all that is sweet to you." And the people replied, "How right you are," and they laughed. That is how the people were sent off. And when all had returned home they were happy and contented.[53]

Andrianampoinimerina acknowledged the endemic social fluidity and geographic mobility stemming from a slaving economy, but he would not at the same time admit the role of international trade in fostering it. He contrasted a "return to ancestry" with the socially fragmenting reality of uprooting, movement, and political uncertainty.

"Whoever may have pointed a musket toward me," he is reported to have exclaimed, "whoever moved out across the land like locusts, whoever was like fire spread by lightning, whoever might have acquired some land in the east—all must return to the ways of the ancestors, for I do not cause the loss of ancestry, so return to your ancestry, each to enter his or her kind. . . . The people were then dismissed. Each returned to the name of their ancestors, each returned to their sort."[54]

By revaluing kinship Andrianampoinimerina created a new and socially conservative ancestral order within his kingdom. This new order rested upon a hierarchy of districts, *firenena*, and family (*isan'toko, sy isam-pirenena sy isam-pianakaviana*).[55] The identity pursued by highland *firenena*, exemplified by the actions of the Ravoandriana examined in chapter 3, was not one of internal social equality but rather one in which hierarchical relationships between subjects and leaders were trustworthy and considered orderly, fertile, and legitimate. Andrianampoinimerina's policy of revaluing the social hierarchies of kinship and political dependency, consistent with this vision of moral relationships, attracted highlanders' support.

Despite articulating a conservative theory of kinship, however, Andrianampoinimerina claimed an opposing right for the sovereign to intervene into local affairs and to regulate local kinship politics as he saw fit. One of Andrianampoinimerina's well-remembered statements was a claim to be "master of the ancestors."[56] As master of the ancestors he proceeded to officially authorize *firenena* across the kingdom, ranking them into a new political hierarchy and granting them certain social and economic privileges. Alain Delivré and Gerald Berg have described how Andrianampoinimerina conferred differential status, or *tantara* (with a small "t"), upon the *firenena* of the kingdom, enshrining that status in court-authorized histories (*Tantara*, with a big "T").[57] One *Tantara* narrative suggests that Andrianampoinimerina grouped and named the famous Tsimahafotsy *firenena*, creating it from the core supporters of his coup d'état at Ambohimanga.[58] Rather than setting royal power in direct opposition to *firenena*, then, Andrianampoinimerina both reinforced and transformed *firenena* and their identities at the beginning of the nineteenth century, aligning them with royal power. To speak of his complex policies of unity through strengthening *firenena*, Andrianampoinimerina resorted to metaphors of hair. Because of the individuality of its strands and its resemblance to the tall grass that grows unchecked on the hills of central Madagascar, highlanders likened hair to chaotic and wild natural forces. Highland folklore, for example, is replete with stories about small, antisocial, elflike creatures (*angalampona* and *ikalanoro*) speaking unintelligible tongues and living about the countryside, especially near water courses. These creatures all sport long unbraided hair falling over their shoulders to the ground.[59] Highland Malagasy refer to uncultivated land as "land of long hair" (*tany lava volo*).[60] Conceived as naturally chaotic, hair could only be tamed and ordered and its fertile potential released to human good through the controlled violence of cutting and braiding.[61] For this reason hair served as a useful metaphor for kingdom building, which required violent submission to a new sovereign. Once he had conquered and united the six districts of his kingdom, the *Tantara* report, Andrianampoinimerina exclaimed, "the hair of Imerina is now pacified."[62] By submitting all highland Madagascar to his power, another text indicates, Andrianampoinimerina "pacified the hair of the *ambaniandro*."[63] Just as the potency and wild nature of a newborn child required taming through a ritual cutting of first hair growth (*ala volo* or *fanalabolonjaza*), so too the potentially rebellious structures of the body politic required proper grooming from the royal court.[64] "I see the numerous *firenena* across the land," Andrianampoinimerina exclaimed, "they are all mine, I love them all, but I will mix hairs as I please."[65] Administratively regrouping and restructuring *firenena* was therefore conceptualized as a proper parting and braiding of the political hair of the kingdom. Thus groomed, uncut hair symbolized a complete community; to designate "everyone" highlanders employed the adjective "without-cut-hair" (*tsivakivolo*), as in *ambaniandro tsivakivolo*, or "all of the *ambaniandro*."[66] Those who demurred at the king's politics were said to "cause hair to stand out straight" (i.e., to release it from the braids and plaits fashioned by the sovereign).[67] Andrianampoinimerina repeatedly warned his people not to tamper with his social engineering.[68]

Kingdom building also served to anchor *firenena* identities to particular ancestral territories, or *tanindrazana*. *Firenena*, like the Ravoandriana, had sought exemption from arbitrary capture and alienation of their members as *andevo* slaves far from their natal homelands before the rise of Andrianampoinimerina. Yet it was precisely the realization of such popular aspirations in royal policy during the reign of Andrianampoinimerina that brings a historical dimension to the cultural phenomenon of modern Merina descent groups and territorial attachment so richly described by Maurice Bloch in 1971.[69] Andrianampoinimerina's restrictions on geographical mobility served a dual purpose. For the founder king they represented one component in an interlocking series of effective measures of social control. For rural communities the royally sanctioned linking of *firenena* to specific ancestral homelands respected and reinforced local identities. In its provision for geographical fixing, Andrianampoinimerina's politics of *firenena* reaffirmed commoners' right to protection from arbitrary enslavement, a right severely eroded during the late eighteenth century. When Andrianampoinimerina defined the borders of the six districts of his kingdom, he prohibited *firenena* and their members from moving into different territories of Imerina.[70] If the geographical and social mobility characteristic of the late eighteenth century were neither checked nor centrally controlled, new patrons might still draw commoners seeking security toward them, challenging royal power and splintering *firenena*. With this possibility in mind, Andrianampoinimerina refused his people the right to change the location of their households or the *firenena* to which they belonged.[71] "Each must live among their particular ancestry," he exclaimed. "If, on the other hand, there are those who attempt to move about, I will not allow it, for I alone retain the authority to mix your hairs, O Merina."[72] Andrianampoinimerina was particularly scrupulous in restricting the individual mobility of people from the most privileged *firenena* of *andriana* status, his most likely opponents. Social groups seen as legitimately able to field candidates for the kingship in highland Madagascar were collectively termed the Andrianteloray (a subset of *andriana*). Here are Andrianampoinimerina's words to them at the beginning of the nineteenth century.

And this is what I say to you Andrianteloray: you may not live in lands other than those here within Avaradrano [Andrianampoinimerina's home district]. Lest you move off to Vakinisisaony, to Ambodirano, to Marovatana, to Vonizongo or even to Vakinankaratra. If you move there, I shall not allow it, said Andrianampoinimerina. So remain here within Avaradrano, because here is where I can watch you and can see you. You are not just anyone, for you are the source from which appear all the ruling sovereigns. Thus I will not separate you from my presence and from that of Avaradrano; you are kin and part of me and I do not desire you to be separated. I will join you together as one here in my presence, said Andrianampoinimerina.[73]

Consonant with his self-interested ideology of kinship as something most appropriately fixed at birth or authorized by the royal court, Andrianampoinimerina delighted in speaking of highland social organization through the image of an egg that cannot change its mother, its natural and blood kin—or in the case of highlanders, their mother *firenena* and district.

> And this is what I say to you O Merina of the six districts: I make you eggs that cannot change your mother, you *ambaniandro*. For if eggs change their mothers, there will be no one among you who will willingly approach Ambohimanga and Ilafy and Ambohitrabiby and Antananarivo [the kingdom's capital and the principal towns of Avaradrano, Andrianampoinimerina's home district]. Therefore I make you eggs that cannot change your mother you Merina of the six districts: and I will make everyone to reside in their own district of Imerina.[74]

To mediate local disputes within individual *firenena*, Andrianampoinimerina empowered a local group of male elders called the *fokonolona*. Much has been written about the *fokonolona* and its structures and functions during the time of Andrianampoinimerina and up to the present.[75] Most studies place too much emphasis upon the *fokonolona* as a formal institution of governance and too little on the revaluation of the social power of community elders (called the *loholona*, or "heads of the people") that the reorganization of *fokonolona* represented during the reign of Andrianampoinimerina. In reality, the *fokonolona* tended to denote the collective will of village elders, largely male, and served as a metaphor for local judicial and administrative autonomy.[76] Ideally, each *fokonolona* exercised authority within the jurisdiction of a single *firenena*, if it were relatively small. When a descent group encompassed a large number of people, Andrianampoinimerina created several *fokonolona*, one for each big village or collection of smaller villages. "Each shall judge their own, whether it be a *firenena* or even a single town," proclaimed Andrianampoinimerina.[77] *Fokonolona* were composed of prominent men in a community and charged with managing local conflicts.

> Those who are the eldest people within the village are to become the members of the *fokonolona*. It is forbidden to contradict the elder. In times past people observed mutual respect and consulted among one another. If the

majority said "yes," the matter was finished—that is what was called "agreed by the wives and agreed by the children." Conflicts over rice land, inheritance disputes, disagreements over ancestral land, domestic disputes, divorces, adoptions, disavowing of children, each of these small cases is to be the responsibility of the *fokonolona*.[78]

Andrianampoinimerina charged *fokonolona* with regulating the local politics of kinship. Individuals who intended to perform blood brotherhood, adopt, disown (children), marry, and divorce were required to apply to the *fokonolona* for permission. Those engaging in questionable actions contrary to a conservative understanding of kinship or in opposition to local popular ethos were reported to the royal court.[79] Empowerment of *fokonolona* to decide the most local of disputes represented a significant shift of authority away from merchants, patrons, and big men—who tended to be young upstarts entangled in the new commerce of French empire—to communal male elders as a collective. This populist purpose of the *fokonolona* was explicitly articulated by the founder king. "The *fokonolona* shall have the power to reduce to slavery when agreements are broken, to destroy the influential men when they commit abuses."[80]

Beyond the judicial role of the *fokonolona* in settling local disputes, the collective was instructed to act as an instrument of popular social control. Andrianampoinimerina charged the *fokonolona* with searching about the countryside and "pushing away" criminals and those of "bad spirit."[81] The *fokonolona* thus served as a sort of neighborhood social police. Men who could not "support" their ancestral land and their *firenena* were "driven away" by the *fokonolona* into the presence of the king and their land was allocated to others.[82] A final function of the *fokonolona* entailed intervention into the ritual life of the community to create ceremonies expressive of *firenena* solidarity and identity. Attributed to *fokonolona* in the time of Andrianampoinimerina, "beating the gate" (*mively vavahady*) brought communities together to pledge allegiance to one another and to forswear antisocial activities such as witchcraft. "Beating the gate" ceremonies bore a resemblance to the "beating water" and "spearing cattle" rituals (*mively rano* and *milefon'omby*) by which the representatives of highland communities swore political allegiance to Andrianampoinimerina.[83] The political architecture of Andrianampoinimerina's kingdom shifted power from wealthy and independent individuals to the mature male representatives of local communities (the *loholona*), revaluing the gender and generational hierarchies of yore, and crushing independent and unauthorized political activity by local entrepreneurs and would-be political competitors to the sovereign.

While Andrianampoinimerina delegated much autonomous regulatory power to each of the kingdom's many *firenena*, he also maintained a centralized administrative check on that royally sanctioned autonomy. He delegated representatives of royal power, often *firenena* outsiders, to each kin group.[84] In keeping with his political vocabulary of kinship, Andrianampoinimerina named these rural overseers the "spouses of the land" (*vadintany*). "Spouses of the land" were charged with surveying life in the countryside, conveying intelligence back to the sovereign, regulating disputes the *fokonolona* were unable to resolve, and carrying messages in both directions between the royal court and local communities.[85] While *firenena* enjoyed a certain autonomy and distinct identity, the royal labor service (*fanompoana*) required of all nonslave men symbolized the universal subordination of all *firenena* to the king.[86] "I will make labor service a unifier," claimed Andrianampoinimerina, "everyone shall serve me, but as for ancestors, each has their own."[87]

Andrianampoinimerina's politics of *firenena*, then, was woven from several cultural strands, each of which anchored his power locally and alleviated commoners' anxieties about the slaving economy. At its center stood a conservative ideology that prohibited (illegitimate) enslavement of citizens for export and articulated a restrictive definition of kinship to include only those relationships arising naturally, slowly, from blood or approved and regulated by a watchful, elderly, and male *fokonolona*. Also prominent was a restriction on unofficially authorized physical mobility, anchoring *firenena* and concentrating their members within particular "ancestral homelands" known as *tanindrazana*. Coupled to these was a creative policy that expressed and reinforced local *firenena* identities through collective rituals of belonging. One purpose of these policies was to prevent self-styled big men from building networks of clients outside the purview of royal power.[88] Another was to reinforce local autonomy under the watchful eye of the sovereign, solving people's problems while garnering their political support in exchange. Andrianampoinimerina's vision of an ordered kingdom of kin was the antithesis of the social principles informing state building among the Imbangala of west central Africa or the early nineteenth-century Nguni chiefdoms of southeast Africa. In these two societies, political power was based upon the incorporation of nonkin into age and military groups that could be centrally controlled and on whose success hinged a weakening of kin-based authority and the disempowerment of elders.[89] In highland Madagascar under Andrianampoinimerina, by contrast, royal policy advocated a sophisticated cultural politics* that revalued kinship and its generational and gender hierarchies, nurturing kin-based identities and social practices and securing consent through strategic alliances with rural communities organized according

---

*By cultural politics I mean conscious efforts to reshape culture in ways that transform sociopolitical relationships among members of a community. My understanding of the term is similar to that explicitly set out by Bravman in his recent study of Taita ethnic identity (1998: 8–9).

to principles of kinship. State building may either reinforce or destroy existing systems of kinship; in highland Madagascar it strengthened them under the surveillance of an emergent royal power.

Andrianampoinimerina frequently referred to his policies with respect to *firenena* as a solemn agreement sealed by a stone obelisk (*orimbato*) of the sort highland Malagasy erect to commemorate important people and covenants.[90] "*Orimbato* are stones that make sovereigns rule," relates one *Tantara* narrative, "they are memorializations (*fahatsiarovana*) of the words of the sovereign when she makes an agreement with the people. The sovereign gives her word to the heads of the people and the stone is a remembrance of the words given, and it can never be changed."[91] The king's citizen-subjects, too, considered their political alliances with Andrianampoinimerina through the metaphor of the *orimbato*, a solemn agreement cast in the permanence of stone and nourished in the collective memory for all time.[92] The analogy between a visible *orimbato* of stone and a metaphorical one of memory captures the significance of social memories of Andrianampoinimerina to the people of highland Madagascar and their collective identity. Like a lasting *orimbato* planted firmly in the ground, Andrianampoinimerina and his popular politics lived on after his death in the memories of highland Malagasy, who revived and deployed that memory of a popular king and his populist politics in specific political struggles. While conservative in purpose and linked by analogy to the permanence and stability of stone, the founder king's policies toward *firenena*, his foundations of royal power, were crafted for the political moment and nourished fresh cultural traditions and social practices. Nowhere is this more evident than in highland Malagasy mortuary culture.

RESHAPING TRADITIONS OF DEATH

Now conspicuously present nearly everywhere in highland Madagascar, tombs (*fasana*) link the living to discrete ancestral territories (*tanindrazana*) and provide a physical dwelling for the bodies and spirits of the dead. Highland Malagasy periodically remove ancestral remains from their family tombs and rewrap them with new winding sheets, a ritual called *famadihana*. Malagasy tombs and their accompanying mortuary ritual have attracted much scholarly attention.[93] Because of the importance of tombs and mortuary ritual to modern highland Malagasy identity and cultural practice, both have come to be seen as quintessentially Merina.[94] Most scholars have portrayed Austronesian preoccupations with the dead, family tombs, and proper burial on ancestral lands as a time-honored tradition, part of a wider Austronesian civilization of death.[95] A careful examination of the historical evidence, however, suggests that although highland Malagasy mortuary habits have ancient antecedents in Austronesian culture, the modern social meanings of death and related cultural practices have been in constant flux.[96] Modern highland Malagasy mortuary practices owe much to cultural politics in the era of the slave trade.[97]

Tombs are associated with some of the earliest archaeological sites in highland Madagascar but their absence around many settlements until the nineteenth century suggests that tomb burial was far from normative until recently.[98] Only a small proportion of existing highland Malagasy tombs are datable to the eighteenth century and earlier, and the trend over the last two centuries has been from individual burial in earthen graves and modest tombs constructed entirely of small stones and mortar to collective burial in ever larger, monumental, and more permanent stone slab, brick, and masonry structures.[99] Early nineteenth-century reports from the eastern regions of Imerina surrounding Ambatomanga suggest that individual burial prevailed there.[100] In the Vakiniadiana, also in eastern Imerina, people in certain villages were interred in common burial grounds corresponding to village political moieties. During the nineteenth and twentieth centuries tombs appeared as local ancestries (*teraky*) constructed separate burying places of stone.[101]

Historical memory corroborates archaeological investigation about a progression from diverse burial practices to near universal interment in collective stone tombs.[102] "In earlier times," Andrianampoinimerina is reported to have said, "everyone did as they wished when someone died; they buried their dead wherever they desired."[103] "According to former practice," another *Tantara* passage claims, "every household constructed a small tomb to bury all the members living in one house. These were small individual graves like those in which persons not yet placed in the tomb are buried and that could not be entered. They were constructed from small rock, and stones were erected outside to mark the spot."[104] Although archaeological studies suggest a significant proliferation in tomb building during the reign of Andrianampoinimerina, *traitants* who traveled in central Madagascar during the late eighteenth century reported that tombs were not unknown at that time. During his visit to Antananarivo in 1777, for example, Mayeur noted that "Families have an underground chamber or pit in which the dead are laid on beds of wood elevated from the ground. The monument is marked on the exterior by a work of masonry made with rock and clay which, above the surface of the ground, has the same dimensions as the underground part. Its form is usually a slightly elongated square."[105] In an account of another visit eight years later (1785) Mayeur provided a more detailed description of highland tombs and mortuary practice.

The dead are placed in quite deep pits so that they can be set standing upright.[106] The bodies are usually wrapped in shrouds of silk or cotton according to the means of the family and aligned on trestles at the bottom of the cave. Around them reigns a masonry structure of about eight feet wide and six feet high. The purpose of the masonry is to mark the spot where the body lies. Each family has its own tomb. But this does not mean that a dying person who requests to be buried in a place of his own designation will be summarily denied his final wishes. Some want to be laid close to their rice fields to watch their crops mature; others want to be set on the top of high mountains to enjoy the magnificent scene of the great expanse of their land; and finally others assign their burial place to the center of villages to hear the inhabitants speak amongst themselves and see the strangers who arrive there. It is common to see old people led by a stick toward the tombs of their ancestors and stay there often six or seven hours on end. Like the people of Ancaye [to the east of Imerina], the rich people of Hancove place large stones close to their tombs. These durable markers are more characteristic of the ostentation of the survivors than their veneration of the dead.[107]

The convergence of various lines of evidence relating to tombs and burial practices suggests that considerable variety in burial methods and tomb architecture characterized the Malagasy highlands during the late eighteenth century and that such variation in mortuary culture paralleled fractured social and political identities. According to the *Tantara* and Mayeur, the dead were usually buried individually or by household. Nearly all eighteenth-century tombs surveyed by archaeologists were constructed for individual burial.[108] Many of these tombs could not be entered easily by the living. In 1777 Mayeur observed rectangular tombs measuring eight feet wide by six feet tall. These were clearly for household (i.e., collective) burial. Bodies were commonly placed on wooden trestlelike beds within those tombs. Before the advent of tiered beds, one passage of the *Tantara* claims, bodies were simply piled one atop the other.[109] Both contemporary and memorial sources concur that when highland Malagasy constructed tombs during the eighteenth century, they fashioned them of small stone and clay mortar. Wealthy highlanders generally erected large stone obelisks (*orimbato, tsangambato, vatolahy, vato mitsangana*) in the vicinity of their tombs to mark the location of burial. This may suggest that tombs were not visually prominent ("The purpose of the masonry is to mark the spot where the body lies"). Not everyone was buried in household tombs. Individuals might choose a personal site of interment away from a tomb or collective burial ground. Tombs of the eighteenth century demonstrate greater architectural variety than those of the nineteenth.[110] In some places, extra-tomb burial included mass burial grounds corresponding to village moieties. In the absence of any overarching cultural or administrative code setting out the guidelines for proper burial, *teraky, firenena*, households, and individuals followed local precedent and were free to exercise considerable choice.

If eighteenth-century burial practices demonstrated substantial variation, tombs built after 1800 were more uniform and contrasted significantly with those constructed before the nineteenth century. The tombs Andrianampoinimerina urged his subjects to construct were generally much larger than earlier ones, normally from three to five times the size of late eighteenth-century models. Larger tombs united multiple households in expanded *teraky,* who built and maintained a common place of burial rather than smaller separate ones. "In the time of Andrianampoinimerina the people were urged in speeches to employ their kinship to build huge tombs," relates the *Tantara*. "'Join together to drag the stones [for constructing the tomb], for this is what will make you love one another. Join together to drag the stones that do good.'"[111] Writing after 1820, British missionaries to central Madagascar reported that some of the new rectangular tombs were twenty feet wide and fifty feet long.[112] Many new tombs measured twenty by thirty feet in width and breadth and ten feet from floor to ceiling. As tombs became larger and more conspicuous—monuments in themselves—highland Malagasy discontinued erecting external obelisks to mark the location of burial.[113] Wooden trestles lining the floors of eighteenth-century tombs were replaced in nineteenth-century sepulchers by multitiered beds of granite that were usually placed along the north, east, and south walls.[114] Most important, highland Malagasy shifted their building techniques from small stone-and-mortar constructions of the age of the slave trade toward a preference for massive frameworks of rock exfoliated from granite outcroppings by alternately heating and cooling fissures in the stone. In these new tombs, five massive stone slabs served as the four walls and the ceiling; the floor of the tomb consisted of packed earth (see Photograph 5.1).[115] Transitions in architectural style and method of burial were neither instantaneous nor uniform, but new ideals that highlanders strove to emulate. Often, stone slabs were retained as the primary interior framework of a tomb, which was then embellished with horizontally aligned small stones on the outside, maintaining a stylistic continuity with eighteenth-century models. Soon after British missionaries introduced clay bricks to highland Madagascar, some highlanders constructed tombs from them.[116] Tomb owners moved bodies from old tombs to new ones, rewinding them with fresh shrouds in the process. Transferring bodies from old tombs to newly constructed ones was among the key reasons for a renaissance in *famadihana* ceremonies of secondary burial after midcentury.[117]

Photograph 5.1 Construction of a granite slab tomb near Antsirabe, ca. 1898. Such tombs were constructed of five massive slabs of granite: four for the walls and a final slab for the ceiling (seen in the foreground). The people shown here may be construction laborers engaged by the tomb's owners. (*Source*: Photographer unknown; courtesy of the Norwegian Missionary Society, Stavanger, Madagascar Photograph number 1278.)

Constructed with an interior framework of huge granite slabs, most nineteenth-century tombs were more permanent and considerably more expensive to build than earlier models. They consumed more cooperative labor than previous tombs had. "The site having been chosen," wrote British missionaries about the construction of tombs in the early nineteenth century,

> a large excavation is made in the earth, and the sides and roof of the vault are formed of immense slabs of stone. Incredible labour is often employed in bringing these slabs from a distance to the spot where the grave is to be constructed. When they are fixed in their appointed positions, each side or wall of a vault or tomb, six or seven feet high, and ten or twelve feet square, is often formed of a single stone of the above dimensions. A sort of subterranean room is thus built; which, in some parts of the country, is lined with rough pieces of timber. The stones are covered with earth to the height of from fifteen to eighteen inches. This mound of earth is surrounded by a

curb of stone-work, and a second and third parapet of earth is formed within the lower curb or coping, generally from twelve to eighteen inches in height, each diminishing in extent as they rise one above another, forming a flat pyramidal mound of earth, composed of successive terraces with stone-facing and border, and resembling, in appearance, the former heathen temples of the South Sea islanders, or the pyramidal structures of the ab-origines of South America: the summit of the grave is ornamented with large pieces of rose or white quartz. The stone-work exhibits, in many in-stances, very good workmanship, and reflects great credit on the skill of the native masons. Some of these rude structures are stated to be twenty feet in width, and fifty feet long.[118]

The durability of nineteenth-century tombs and the outlay of collective labor required to construct them were precisely the reasons they emerged as an object of royal policy. Building tombs brought extended kin together to finance construction and transport the cumbersome sheets of granite, some weighing more than a ton (see Photograph 5.2).[119] Quarrying and construc-tion required skills best left to specialists, but transporting the granite from quarry to construction site occupied the entire community. The first British missionaries to Madagascar described the communal significance of "drag-ging the stone" (*mitari-bato*).

> Sometimes five or six hundred men are employed in dragging a single stone. A man usually stands on the stone, acting as director or pioneer. He holds a cloth in his hand, and waves it, with loud and incessant shouts, to animate those who are dragging the ponderous block. At his shout they pull in concert, and so far his shouting is of real service. Holy water is also sprinkled on the stone as a means of facilitating its progress, till at length, after immense shouting, sprinkling, and pulling, it reaches its destination.[120]

A passage from the *Tantara* describes this collective labor with greater cul-tural insight.

> As for the practice called dragging the stone: rope is made by braiding *fandrotrarana* grass and twisting *horom-potsy* grass. These ropes are grasped by many people and pulled out taught [the rock at one end]. Men take their position at the front of the rope [closest to stone], and women and children theirs at the end of the rope. That is called dragging the stone. And the people pull. And the person called flag holder, or lead singer, or cloth waver, or order giver, stands on top of the rock giving orders to the people. He dances and guides the people who are pulling the stone saying [and the pullers responding]:

Dislodging this stone.	Let's dislodge it.
It's but thin!	It's but thin!
Dragging!	Dragging!
Oh my!	Oh my!
Eha!	Eha!
Or can't you do it?	We can!
Is there some?	Yes there is some!
Astounding!	Astounding!
When a man dies.	That's why such a "march"!

The lead singer and the stone pullers sing responsive songs like this. Before he leads them in song again, the lead singer makes funny faces to cause the people to laugh and to rest. And the people work together to pull. Made to sing, the rock moves along until its weight is lessened.[121]

The dramatic collective energy invested in tomb construction during the early nineteenth century can be fully appreciated only when set against life experiences within highland Madagascar's economy of enslavement. "[S]igns and techniques often come to be potent precisely because of the historical circumstances in which they acquire their meanings," Jean and John Comaroff write in the preface to a recent compendium of articles on local cultures in global interaction. Indeed, transformations in highland Malagasy mortuary culture reflected "the global processes that hitch local cultures and communities to the increasingly global forces that encompass them."[122] Tomb building brought highlanders together in communal, multiple-household expressions of social solidarity with potent symbolic value in an era of social fragmentation and an external commerce in slaves. Seldom directly expressed as such, tomb construction and burial on ancestral land was a practical guarantee and moral statement against enslavement for export expressed through a royally advocated cultural policy. Andrianampoinimerina's tomb-building policy was popular in that it recognized and legitimized communal yearnings for social solidarity, physical security, and geographical attachment at a time when highland Malagasy communities had been rent apart in unprecedented ways. Constructing permanent stone tombs within which ever wider networks of kin buried their dead was a means of symbolically reemphasizing the importance and indivisibility of kin and reversing a social atomization manifested by the more individualized households and nuclear family burial of the slaving economy. Addressing Andrianampoinimerina, a representative of the *ambaniandro* expressed the significance of these transformations to highland Malagasy in one succinct phrase: "You do not cause us to

Photograph 5.2 *Mitari-bato,* pulling the ponderous granite slab for a new tomb. *Mitari-bato* united kin and their neighbors in communal labor that emphasized commitment to ancestors and attachment to homeland. Note the man (at left) standing on the slab and encouraging the laborers by waving his hand in the air. Note also the gender order of the laborers, with men near the granite and women at the opposite end of the rope. (*Photo Credit*: Johannes Einrem, 1901, courtesy of the Norwegian Missionary Society, Stavanger, Madagascar Photograph number 0665.)

lose our ancestors" (losing one's ancestors was a euphemism for slavery).[123] By the early nineteenth century, burial in multiple-household tombs had become the norm in most regions of highland Madagascar.[124] "Many of the Malagasy begin to erect their tombs in early life," noted British missionaries, "And make their completion through a series of years one of the most important objects of their existence, deeming a splendid or costly depository for their mouldering bodies, the most effectual means of being held in honourable remembrance by posterity."[125] Only in extremely rare circumstances (excommunication from kin) would persons be individually and permanently buried outside a tomb. Parallel to Andrianampoinimerina's restrictions on physical mobility, tombs bound individuals to their homelands in a way that houses did not. As Maurice Bloch has shown, this was symbolically enacted in rituals that contrasted the permanence of stone tombs (order) with the evanescence of mud and wooden houses (chaos).[126]

In addition to its popular political value, tomb building and tomb burial dovetailed with the founder king's economic strategies to control wealth in silver coursing into the Malagasy highlands. By encouraging tomb building, Andrianampoinimerina motivated his subjects to direct their fortunes into existing, royally recognized *firenena* rather than to employ them to generate new communities outside the purview of royal power.

> "If you use all your wealth, if it was employed to build a tomb, it is not wasted at all—wealth is visible in tombs," said Andrianampoinimerina. "You will be buried forever in a tomb. You only pass by here above but your flesh remains forever in the tomb." To begin with, Andrianampoinimerina required the people to fetch stones, and each built good, well-made tombs, beginning with the twelve hills where the royal ancestors lay. "My tombs where my ancestors rest are finished, so finish your tombs well that your ancestors may rest. This is what I do to make you love one another. And here is what I say to you *ambaniandro*, you will construct tombs; tombs will be the visible sign of your wealth, and your wealth will be consumed in your tomb. I do not deceive the people."[127]

Archaeologists Kus and Wright conclude their investigation of early nineteenth-century archaeological sites in the Avaradrano district of Imerina by noting that "Even if we don't use the accounts of oral tradition, we can know from only the archaeology that an essential sociopolitical transformation took place in Avaradrano."[128] Changes in tomb building and mortuary practice were a key component of that sociopolitical transformation. The cultural politics of kingdom building at the beginning of the nineteenth century reinvented death in highland Madagascar and invested it with new cultural significance and practices relevant to people's contemporary experiences. Far from practicing an unbroken and unchanging culture of death, highland Malagasy found in tomb building and the new forms of mortuary ritual that accompanied it—such as the renaissance of *famadihana*, or secondary burial, whose history I explore elsewhere—a practical solution to their predicaments of social atomization and insecurity in an economy of enslavement.[129] Tombs were key locations for performance of ritual and important sites for the enactment, interpretation, and manipulation of ancestral and royal authority, idioms of power in highland Madagascar.[130] Tombs and funerary ritual became fundamental cultural expressions of Merina political identity and symbols of the alliance between a powerful king and his citizen-subjects. Upon the death of Andrianampoinimerina, the local social solidarity evoked by the new stone tombs and their associated practices proved useful cultural resources for highlanders. Tombs and their rituals emerged as physical and emotional foci for popular *firenena* theories of civic virtue and good government. They remain so into the present.

MORALIZING THE ECONOMY

If a renaissance of mortuary culture reemphasized the civic virtues of communal solidarity, Andrianampoinimerina offered hope to the miserable and impecunious.[131] Compassion for the highland Malagasy poor featured prominently in the founder king's political rhetoric. One of Andrianampoinimerina's favorite statements expressed his philosophy of social justice: "Let the small have their share, and the big have theirs, lest people struggle with each other and the small and the unfortunate become poor; so let everyone have their share."[132] Social reform in the early nineteenth century aimed to lessen the "struggle" of emergent class tensions, to revive flagging economic productivity, and to allocate an economic "share" proportional to one's social station—not to generate a social equality that had never existed. "The first measures of King Andrianampoinimerina after all the District of Avaradrano had acknowledged his sovereignty," wrote Raombana, were

> very good, for he encouraged agriculture very much, which in some measure had languished during the civil contest of seven years there—He also encouraged very much the home manufactures of cotton Garments that the people may be well clothed; and he encouraged the visitations of Europeans in His Dominion that He may obtain arms and other things from them—Thus by the above measures, He secured the affections of His subjects, for it was soon perceived by them, that their real interests was uppermost in his mind.[133]

By pursuing populist policies, protecting his subjects with European weaponry, and endowing his kingdom with an organization generally perceived as socially just, Andrianampoinimerina sought to win the admiration and loyalty of his subjects. The founder king assumed a long-term political vision. Lasting power did not rest upon squeezing commoners while favoring the rich but in reviving the economy and allowing even the poor to enjoy a humble lot.

Promises of land reform extended hope to those at the bottom of the economic ladder and appealed especially to families most adversely affected by the slave trade. As I indicated in chapter 4, the poorest households often parted with both cattle and land to obtain silver with which to requite money taxes and to protect themselves from enslavement. A small proportion of highlanders were landless at the end of the eighteenth century, particularly women with few or weak kinship ties.[134] The frequency of Andrianampoinimerina's pleas that the poorest highlanders be allocated rice fields suggests that landlessness was a significant concern, but also that there were practical limits to the redistribution of landed property. Ideally, rice land in areas where water could be controlled was to be redistributed such that each productive household held resources commensurate with its needs. Land sufficient for feeding one household was termed a *hetra,* and each household was theoretically to receive such a parcel. Andrianampoinimerina's appeals for universal distribution of *hetra*, however, were probably more a moral and political recognition of the right of highlanders to subsistence than an actual realization of significant reform in tenure.[135] The size of *hetra* could vary by a factor of ten, and some households therefore enjoyed access to much larger surfaces than others.[136] Those with sufficient rice land were encouraged to supply some of it to poorer households.[137] In addition to his injunction that all households should possess at least one *hetra* of rice paddy, Andrianampoinimerina discouraged private accumulation of hillside, nonrice land (*tanety*) by prohibiting tree planting there (planting trees established personal ownership).[138]

A cornerstone of the highland economy, agriculture suffered through declining productivity, less extensive cultivation, and a reduction of household labor power during the era of the slave trade (chapter 4). When agriculture languished, as it did during the closing decades of the eighteenth century, so too did the economic strength of the entire region.[139] Much of Andrianampoinimerina's moral rhetoric therefore concerned insuring favorable conditions for the promotion of agriculture.[140]

Andrianampoinimerina identified uncontrolled water and famine, its result, as the foremost enemies of his people. He employed famine as a metaphor for social injustice and considered the construction and maintenance of river levees a means for combating it.[141] Hydrological projects emerged as major foci of labor service during the early nineteenth century.[142] Labor demanded by the royal court was conceptualized as a direct benefit to agrarian communities rather than as a method of rural exploitation. "Levees are the food that satisfies you," Andrianampoinimerina proclaimed.[143] Andrianampoinimerina's discourse of labor service articulated a new highland work ethic. One of the mandates given to royal "spouses of the land" emissaries sent among the *firenena* was to insure that everyone labored diligently.[144] Even orphans and widowed women who appealed to Andrianampoinimerina seeking support were supplied with spades.[145] Andrianampoinimerina considered labor as a means for preventing social injustice and famine.[146] During times of famine "the big look for opportunities to consume the poor and the poor search for opportunities to steal."[147] The use of cattle by the wealthy to generate the mud necessary for rice transplanting was interpreted as a socially unacceptable display of wealth. Promulgated to reduce the destruction of rice by unattended cattle, restrictions on pasturing cattle in central Imerina implemented by the founder king curbed ostentatious displays of wealth, "for the wealthy have many cattle, and the poor are aggrieved; the wealthy act pretentiously and release their cattle in people's fields: I shall put an end to it."[148]

Andrianampoinimerina repeatedly condemned the use of force and strong-armed tactics by the rich against the poor and reminded the wealthy that they must work as diligently as the destitute.[149] Public castigation of the wealthy crystallized around images of communal and economic irresponsibility, showy finery, and ostentatious display of silver that assumed especial meaning in the generalized poverty of the era of the slave trade.

> If there are people who refuse to work, who refuse to expend the extra effort to fertilize their fields—whether men or women—who say "I am a wealthy person," who act haughtily, who refuse to carry fertilizer because they are well dressed, who wear many [silver] ankle bangles, who dress themselves up and wear silver bracelets, who think only of all the fine things they have in their house, what will they dress themselves with if there is no rice for them to eat? That kind of behavior brings enemies into my land, said Andrianampoinimerina, so if there are people who will not work or employ fertilizer, who worry only about their finery, if they do that to my land, I will find them guilty.[150]

To further promote agricultural prosperity, Andrianampoinimerina actively encouraged charm makers, especially those who created the famous hail charms (*ody havandra*) that protected against crop devastation in the months before the rice harvest. He exempted specialists who produced hail charms from obligatory labor service.[151] Farmers whose rice had escaped damage during the critical weeks before the harvest were encouraged to support charm makers with significant in-kind gifts. Likewise, Andrianampoinimerina ex-horted charm makers to be exacting in their instruction of clients in proper use of the charms and in observance of their taboos (*fady*), lest they prove ineffective or lead to destruction of precious crops rather than preservation of them.[152]

In popular memory, the farmer-armies of Merina expansion were another area of significant reform. Andrianampoinimerina organized military cam-paigns to respect highland agricultural rhythms and to insure rural food se-curity. Andrianampoinimerina announced his military campaigns well in advance of their departure, and he temporarily drafted his subjects only dur-ing the winter agricultural off-season. For significant campaigns, only part of the male population participated at any one time while the balance re-mained at home. After a specified period, farmer-soldiers on active duty were allowed to venture back to their households, replaced by others in turn. Ro-tated in this way, Andrianampoinimerina's farmer-soldiers and their kin shared the burdens of military duty. No single set of households absorbed all the social costs of military campaigns at one time and the sovereign recognized the competing claims of kin and royalty to the labor of men.[153] Ideally, officers distributed war booty among the ranks. Andrianampoinimerina countenanced booty remuneration for military service because recruits were never compensated in any other manner. The king claimed the largest proportion of booty in slaves and cattle (generally two-thirds), but he allowed soldiers to retain cloth, cooking pots, money, and furnishings of various kinds.[154] Highland Malagasy remembered Andrianampoinimerina's military policies with fondness during the mid-nineteenth century. Raombana, the Malagasy historian, captured the popular esteem of Andrianampoinimerina's soldiers for their king in a captivating passage about toothaches, divination, and pregnant wives.

> There is a peculiar character of King Andrianampoinimerina which I cannot help relating here, in-as-much as it shews his real characteristic characters, and the characters of his rude warriors. At the commencement of his rebellion against King Andrianjafinandriamanitra, and his war with the Tsimiemboholahy people, he had made it a rule, and which rule he always adhered to, which is, not to allow to go to the wars, those who has the toothache; those whose wives, are in a state of pregnancy; and those whom the sikidy or Divinitions says, will die if they go to the wars. It is stated that the King has been severely troubled with the toothache, which he often pronounced to be the worst sickness that ever afflicted the human race, and therefore he would not allow to go to the wars those who are afflicted with it—for He knows by experience the dreadful effect of the Tooth-ache—from which He often suffers very badly—As the not allowing to go to the wars, those whose wives are in a state of pregnancy, it is founded upon the good ideas, that they may cherish and keep in good spirits their wives, who would be low spirited if their husbands were to go to the wars, and may produce abortions on account of their anxieties for them—The above is also a good rule of the King —And as the not allowing to go to the wars, those whom the Divinations, says, will die if they go to the wars. The above rule originated from extreme superstitions, as well as the notions of preserving the lives of his men; and the three above rules which were strictly adhered to, completely won for him, the sincere attachments and affections of the people for Him, and made them fight bravely for him, which in concurrence with some other circumstances afterward made Him the sole sovereign of Imerina.[155]

Andrianampoinimerina is also remembered to have transformed tax collection within his realm to lessen the financial burdens weighing upon the poor. During the late eighteenth century, as I wrote in the previous chapter, some kings began to demand taxes in silver rather than in kind.

Andrianampoinimerina softened that system by providing penurious households with in-kind alternatives to payment in silver. The founder king conceptualized his taxation system as a "cow hump that unites" (*tongoa mihonkona*).[156] The symbolism of this image is drawn from the zebu cattle of Madagascar, blessed with considerable humps of fat atop their backs that serve as reserves of energy for the winter when dry grasses offer poor nutrition. While tax revenues spiraled toward the royal court at Antananarivo, the language Andrianampoinimerina employed to conceptualize the system envisioned taxation as a form of collective security rather than as a means of impoverishing the citizenry. The primary base of royal revenue was the "single spade" (*isam-pangady*) paid by individual cultivators for each *hetra* of rice land they cultivated.[157] The "single spade" normally consisted of rice contributions but could be demanded in money. However, the destitute with little rice land were permitted to pay their tribute in manioc. Unlike rice, which was cultivated in terraces on the valley bottoms, manioc could be readily grown on plentiful rain-fed hill (*tanety*) land and required less labor per caloric output than rice (see Photograph 5.3).[158] Permitting less prestigious and far less well enjoyed manioc to substitute for rice as tribute, Andrianampoinimerina eased the tax burden on households squeezed by labor and land shortages. "Manioc is the support of rice," Andrianampoinimerina asserted in promotion of his popular tax policy.[159]

Markets and marketing were a final significant domain of remembered economic policy reform. The list of royal measures promulgated to remedy exploitation in the markets of Imerina reads like the antithesis of most highlanders' experience at the market fairs of central Madagascar during the late eighteenth century (chapter 4). Weekly markets where highlanders exchanged raw materials, crops, livestock, manufactured items, and silver were strictly regulated in an effort to alleviate commoners' experiences of exploitation. Andrianampoinimerina granted permission for market goers to summarily execute thieves, a practice of popular justice observed in central Madagascar until today.[160] He noisily condemned those who speculated in rice during times of hunger.[161] He enjoined the wealthy to practice social responsibility, exhorting them to purchase market goods liberally from humble vendors, thereby distributing their wealth among the poor.[162] "Spouses of the land" spied for the royal court on local markets throughout the highlands to insure that prices remained reasonably low by community standards.[163] Unsurprisingly, the wealthy voiced opposition to Andrianampoinimerina's market initiatives, for they impinged on cherished profit-making practices.[164] In turn, Andrianampoinimerina often rebuked the haughtiness (*avonavona*) of the wealthy. They were enjoined to obey the local regulations of the *fokonolona* and not to scorn

Photograph 5.3 The landscape of highland Madagascar. This photograph, taken during the dry agricultural off-season, shows terraced rice fields in the valley, where water can be controlled, and food gardens on the sloping hillside *tanety*, where manioc and vegetables are cultivated. (*Photo Credit*: Pier M. Larson, 1986.)

the community elders who composed them.[165] Alcohol and gambling, instruments historically employed by the highland rich to exploit the poor, were outlawed.[166] When Andrianampoinimerina learned that a disproportionate number of wealthy persons were dying in trials by poison ordeal as a result of popular accusation, however, he was obliged to retrench on his rhetoric against them.[167] There were practical limits to populist policy, for some of the wealthiest men of the kingdom served in the king's political entourage or as officers in his army, and they held his ear (see chapter 6).

To regulate behavior in the popular interest was to modify it. Memory of Andrianampoinimerina's moralized economy is significant because moral policies, by definition, transform human behavior. New moral codes defined ideal civic behavior and structured experiences within the emerging community of Merina identity. Just as economic behavior in the economy of enslavement had differently affected wealthy and poor, so too did the new standards of civic virtue articulated by the founder king. Easing the intensifying class tensions of highland Malagasy society by revaluing kinship, promoting collective labor, and refashioning social justice through the elaboration of new social hierarchies, kingdom building also intervened in relationships between the genders. Regulating kinship, of course, meant controlling the most fundamental of social transactions between men and women. While individual decisions in the politically fractured economy of enslavement had shaped the nature and direction of transformations in gender before the rise of Andrianampoinimerina (chapter 4), a coordinated royal policy did so at the beginning of the nineteenth century. From its origins, Merina identity entailed new gender relationships and hierarchies.

ENGENDERING THE IDENTITY

A young man became a citizen, or *ambaniandro*, when with a female partner he formed a separate household (*tokantrano* or *ankohonana*).[168] As citizens of Imerina, men were required to attend royal proclamations (*kabary*).[169] In the time of Andrianampoinimerina, women were normally not counted as *ambaniandro* nor subject to citizen responsibilities (e.g., royal labor service) unless they managed *hetra* and paid taxes on them.[170] A significant minority of women who managed households in which no adult male was present (usually between 5 and 10 percent of households) were recognized as *ambaniandro*. These women were variously called "women supporting themselves" (*vehivavy mitondra tena*)[171] or "women carrying *hetra*" (*vehivavy mitondra hetra*).[172] The significant number of female-managed households by the mid-nineteenth century probably also existed in earlier years and was primarily a combined result of the slave trade and high mortality among Merina armies of expansion.

While royal administrators recognized a significant minority of adult women as autonomous taxpaying *ambaniandro*, most women remained in a legal standing subordinate to men. In most instances women could not press accusations against their partners in the kingdom's judicial apparatuses.[173] Curtailment of women's rights was justified in royal discourse through a depreciation of the way in which they were said to express themselves. Andrianampoinimerina caricatured women's speech as "gossip" and "rumor" (*kitsanitsany*). Likening *kitsanitsany* to disorderly speech that ruined the order of kinship, Andrianampoinimerina warned his subjects, "Do not employ the *kitsanitsany* of women, because the *kitsanitsany* of women kills the land; I do not like it, it is kinship I prefer."[174] It is not surprising that Andrianampoinimerina justified an administrative subordination of women by reference to female modes of communication. As Elinor Keenan has demonstrated, people from central Madagascar consider women's speech more direct and confrontational than the ceremonial public *kabary* of men.[175] During the early years of the kingdom, challenges to authority structures were conceptualized through the idiom of direct female speech that ought to be muffled to stave off chaos and promote unity. "Do not bother spouses of the land with long-winded, embarrassing *kabary*," Andrianampoinimerina declared. "If there are women who drive the spouses of the land crazy with such speech I shall sell them [into slavery]."[176] The royal definition of women and their modes of expression as antikinship and antistate placed women at odds with Andrianampoinimerina's politics of revaluing family and community, the cornerstones of his social reconstruction of highland Malagasy society in the age of enslavement. Culturally defined female qualities were seen as injurious to the structure and functioning of the new state.

Andrianampoinimerina intervened directly into the formation of new households by restricting the range of royally sanctioned domestic associations (*fanambadiana*) into which men and women could enter and by appreciably shifting the balance of gender privilege within such associations in favor of men. Usually glossed "marriage," *fanambadiana* derives from the noun root *vady*, "spouse, companion, associate, mate." Polygyny was on the rise during the late eighteenth century because of the gender imbalances generated by the slave trade (chapter 4). As highlanders remembered it, Andrianampoinimerina's domestic legislation, however, discouraged polygyny, possibly because wealthy men tended to accumulate several wives, depriving younger men of spouses and building themselves large networks of kin potentially injurious to royal power.[177] If polygyny was officially discouraged, it was nevertheless practiced. Divorces, or "thanking a spouse" (*fisao-bady*), also came under royal regulation as the nineteenth century opened. "Andrianampoinimerina did not give only one speech concerning marriage [*fanambadiana*], but he always continued to speak upon the subject to bring good to his people," report the *Tantara*.[178] Intervention into marriage relationships assumed several forms. One of the king's primary concerns was to reiterate the principle of respecting social rank in sexual relationships. Marriages contracted across *andriana*, *hova*, and *mainty* lines were metaphorically characterized as the flooding of rice paddies, the water rising to a common level and obscuring the different heights of the respective fields and the purposely raised earthen partitions between them (*valabe*). Such marriages were to be punished by enslavement of the offending spouses, depriving them of the protection accorded to properly behaved citizen *ambaniandro*.[179] To this injunction Rahagamainty, an adviser to Andrianampoinimerina positioned as an advocate for the citizenry, responded in affirmation, "so let everyone have their ancestry, whether *andriana* or *hova* or *mainty* or *fotsy*, for we will kill whoever defrauds ancestry."[180]

Royal intervention into household formation sought to limit marriage relationships to ones sealed by the transfer of a "sheep's rump" (*vodiondry*), a wealth exchange passing from the groom's to the bride's family.[181] Reinforcing sheep's-rump unions at a time when enhanced social and physical mobility in the economy of enslavement allowed men and women to enter new kinds of unions clearly operated to the disadvantage of women. There were two reasons for this. First, a husband and his extended family in a sheep's-rump marriage gained certain custodial rights in the children resulting from that union. Second, Andrianampoinimerina conceived of the husband in such relationships as the "lord of the spouses" (*tompombady*) and invested in him most rights relating to the severance of the relationship while removing them from the two spouses' respective kin and, some passages assert, even the local *fokonolona*. The purpose was to recognize the initiation of divorces as the sole prerogative of a husband.

> Andrianampoinimerina made divorces difficult [for women to obtain]. If divorces were to be granted, they could not be granted by the *fokonolona*, they could not be granted by the parents of the two individuals. No, it was the man alone who could grant a divorce; this was called "hidden divorce." . . . I do not make marriages like joint property; only the lord of the spouse is her lord. Even I who am lord of the government am not able to grant a divorce to a man's spouse, even more so that no one else may do so! And this is also what I say to you *ambanilanitra*: not even those who are *andriana* in their father's line or *andriana* in their mother's line may grant divorces, not even those who are of good father or good mother may grant divorces to a third party [i.e., declare a wife free from her husband]; whoever might dare to do it, I shall find them guilty."[182]

This passage is telling, for it suggests that women commonly drew upon a variety of social resources to initiate complaints against their husbands and to win divorces from them. To this Andrianampoinimerina was opposed. The effect must have been significant for the ways a woman and her advocates could negotiate marriage relationships. Because husbands under such an unregulated system of divorce could send their wives away without much reflection, Andrianampoinimerina provided for a period of twelve days during which a husband could "regret" his action, change his mind about the divorce, and resume the relationship by fetching his wife back to his place of residence.[183]

The growing imbalance in officially sanctioned gender privilege extended to the division of properties at divorce. In a practice called the "third of a hand" (*fahatelontanana*), household property was to be divided upon divorce such that two-thirds went to the husband and one-third to the wife.[184] It is difficult to assess whether and how this mandate may have modified existing practices since how spousal property was typically apportioned at the conclusion of unions during the eighteenth century is unknown. Andrianam-poinimerina represented the "third of a hand" as a protection for wives whose husbands refused to allocate them any property at divorce, but he also spoke of it as a reward to men who served in royal armies, sacrificing their lives for the expansion of the kingdom while their women engaged in less dangerous domestic duties: "The man gathers the land, gathers the government, travels far, does all in his power to strengthen the kingdom; and you women guard the house and live there, you don't go anywhere, and that is why I divide the wealth in thirds if there is a separation; two-thirds to go to the man and one-third to the woman."[185] Andrianampoinimerina also granted an extraordinary right to soldiers who served him: to lynch the man (and possibly the plaintiff's wife too; the wording is ambiguous) who, in a soldier's absence on government duty, became sexually intimate with the soldier's wife. If, on the other hand, members of the local community seized a soldier's wife and her lover in adultery, both were to be sold into slavery and two-thirds of the proceeds offered to the injured husband. This practice may evoke the sexual anxiety that military service elicited for men who were called to serve for longer periods and at greater distances in Andrianampoinimerina's armies than in those of sovereigns who preceded him. Power over human life was a significant concession that Andrianampoinimerina granted his combatants, and one he revoked once much of highland Madagascar had been submitted to his authority. Toward the end of his reign, Andrianampoinimerina is remembered to have levied stiff fines in silver and cattle on both parties to adultery, when the case involved a soldier's wife.[186] When it did not involve the wife of a soldier, adultery itself was subject to little royal legislation, except where the status of any resulting children was concerned. And in such cases officials placed the onus of having committed adultery on the woman rather than on her male lover. Thus Andrianampoinimerina required women to apologize to their husbands by means of a ritualized formula termed the "may I die" (*matesaniaho*) when caught in adultery, but he did not suggest additional sanctions.[187]

Andrianampoinimerina's marital regulations provided husbands with significant and far-reaching gender privileges with respect to their wives' sexuality as well as their physical and marital mobility. Wives whose husbands considered them "cantankerous" (*maditra*) were empowered with a variety of officially sanctioned methods to enforce their wills on the women. The social meanings of a "cantankerous" wife are ambiguous at best and could refer to several situations: a woman seeking assistance from family in a marital dispute, including divorce; a woman asserting independence of physical mobility by "not staying put" at home (*tsy mety hitoetra,*[188] *malain-kitoetra*[189]); a wife seeking sexual partners outside the marriage (consonant with the previous situation); or simply an "unsatisfactory" wife.[190] When their wives became "cantankerous," the king suggested that men present them with the customary notification that they intended to marry an additional woman (the *taha*, a payment generally of lesser value than a "sheep's rump"), leaving the "stubborn" partner as a second or third, less secure, and financially ignored wife.[191] Such a practice, he urged them, should be "employed to break her when she is stubborn."[192] Another form of marriage punishment, in which a wife was effectively abandoned but not allowed to remarry, was known as the "hanging spouse" (*vady ahantona*) and prevented a woman from entering a new officially recognized association with the rights it might bring.[193] Bound by the "hanging spouse," a woman could not claim custody of children she bore through sexual relationships with other men.[194]

Finally, highlanders remember that Andrianampoinimerina charged men with surveying and enforcing the labor of their wives, seeing that they performed either agricultural labor or "women's handicrafts" (*taozava-bavy*).[195] The founder king repeatedly reminded the *ambaniandro* they were to become the "kings of their own households" (*samy manjaka eran'ny varavarany*).[196] As most *ambaniandro* were men, the king's domestic regulations modified the economic complementarity of men's and women's labor that characterized eighteenth-century highland Madagascar (chapter 4). Although women benefited along with their men through many of Andrianampoinimerina's social policies for reconstructing highland Malagasy society in the era of slave trade, not all such policies offered them the same advantages they offered men. If the economy of enslavement had intensified women's labor and shifted access to and control over extra-household income from women to men (chapter 4), Andrianampoinimerina's moralized economy institutionalized that power in new administrative structures and legal practices. Official rhetoric and royal legislation reflected the gender tensions emerging from sociocultural transformation in the time of Andrianampoinimerina.[197] Succeeding sovereigns built upon the founder king's foundation of marital legislation, embedding royal power and Merina identity in the transformation and regulation of intimate and gendered relationships.

A FRAGILE ALLIANCE

With its emphasis upon a social organization regulated through local channels of kinship and elder male authority yet manipulated and enforced through a central administration, Andrianampoinimerina's cultural politics foreshadowed the twentieth-century practice of indirect colonial rule. Colonial administrators, like Andrianampoinimerina, promoted local social identities to deepen central political control. And like the "creation of tribes" by European colonial policy during the twentieth century, Andrianampoinimerina's social policy produced contradictory results. The multiple *firenena* identities that crisscrossed Merina unity not only lent sophistication and emotional power to that unity, they provided descent groups with a means of exercising autonomy and resisting royal legislation. Both Andrianampoinimerina's politics and that of indirect rule promoted new social traditions such as tomb building and conceived of them as long-enduring practices. Seen in this perspective, colonial administrative strategies and their outcomes in "invented" traditions and customs were not new to African experience. "Invented" to solve practical problems in a time of crisis, administratively nourished traditions provided a cultural cornerstone for Merina political identity and became associated with the popular memory of Andrianampoinimerina in succeeding generations.[198]

For Andrianampoinimerina, forging a common political identity from the communally fractured societies of central Madagascar was the surest way to create a stable and enduring power. It was a challenge in which he largely succeeded. When the founder king died in 1809, the people of Imerina—especially those of the four central districts of Avaradrano, Marovatana, Ambodirano, and Vakinisisaony—considered themselves a political community.[199] Like his contemporary George Washington on the opposite side of the globe, Andrianampoinimerina was a "symbolic leader," the embodiment of a useful and popular political union. Through both Washington and Andrianampoinimerina, citizens of newly created polities "expressed their sense of moral harmony, their common attachment to a new political unity." Symbolic leaders, wrote Barry Schwartz of Washington, "incarnate the highest moral principles of a nation, embodying them in a form that can be understood and loved."[200] This was true of the public image of Andrianampoinimerina. Although both North Americans and highland Malagasy celebrated a newfound unity in their founder leaders, the "highest moral principles" of their respective unities—the civic virtues embodied by their respective leaders—were different. Whereas Americans celebrated Washington as an embodiment of their civilian and democratic principles, highland Malagasy adored Andrianampoinimerina for his reinforcement of kinship and his policies of moralized economy.

The founder king emerged as a cultural hero in popular memory, as the preceding pages exploring that popular memory amply demonstrate. He was a key symbol of highland Malagasy identity, unity, and good government. The prime author of a common political identity who set rhetorical and material limits on the behavior of slavers and the wealthy, and who articulated a conservative philosophy of kinship and inalienable attachment to rural homeland, Andrianampoinimerina offered tangible benefits to most highland Malagasy who affiliated with him. Royal alliance with rural communities supported mutually beneficial goals for both king and commoners. What for Andrianampoinimerina was the making of a more expansive and stable royal power was for highlanders a solution to gnawing anxieties about the insecurities of enslavement, the manipulation of kinship to the benefit of the wealthy, the importance of connection to place, and the desire for trustworthy relationships with rulers. Remaking royal power and generating security for commoners in the late eighteenth century unleashed powerful crosscurrents in highland Malagasy identity politics. The sense of a common Merina political identity emerging from populist politics at the turn of the nineteenth century dovetailed with the personal goals of Andrianampoinimerina.

As in Mao's China, policies that curbed the prerogatives of the wealthy momentarily united the interests of a leader and his humble subjects.[201] It was a fragile alliance across a considerable social divide, however, for while rooting and broadening royal power it fostered social autonomy among restrengthened *firenena*, producing and legitimizing a popular power that could—and eventually did—turn against royal prerogative. By establishing themselves in the imagination of their subjects, royals provided commoners with powerful and effective political vocabularies and sowed the seeds for popular challenges to their newfound power. The frail alliance linking *firenena* and the Merina sovereign snapped upon the founder king's death, retransforming Merina identity in the process. I now turn to that key moment in the early reign of King Radama, a crucible of Merina ethnicity.

6

MEMORY IN THE TENSION OF CITIZENSHIP AND SOVEREIGNTY

The code of laws is in the King's own mind.
—Charles Hilsenberg and Wenceslaus Bojer[1]

The veneration of the Malagasy for the customs derived from tradition, or any accounts of their ancestors, is one of the most striking features of their national character. This feeling influences both their public and private habits; and upon no individual is it more imperative than upon their monarch, who, absolute as he is in other respects, wants either the will or the power to break through the long-established regulations of a superstitious people.
—Missionaries of the London Missionary Society[2]

A culturally productive tension between the "king's own mind" and "the veneration of the Malagasy for the customs derived from tradition" nurtured Merina ethnic identity during the early decades of the nineteenth century. Like his father, Radama was an ambitious and resourceful sovereign. By forging a diplomatic alliance with Britain he transformed his father's landlocked kingdom into an islandwide polity stretching to the sea. With the assistance of British training, arms, and logistical support Radama created a professional army that marched in all directions from Antananarivo collecting political allegiances from inland and coastal rulers. Simultaneously with his politics of British alliance, Radama invited evangelists of the London Missionary Society to Antananarivo and supported them at his court. In doing so, he appropriated the technology of writing in Latin script and put it to use in the construction of a more centrally controlled administrative bureaucracy that curtailed the autonomy of *firenena* and *fokonolona*. When Radama terminated the export trade in slaves from highland Madagascar in 1820, he deprived the old counselors and friends of Andrianampoinimerina of their primary income of foreign silver, eliminating them as serious political competitors. Men of influence among the *firenena* who were associated in the public mind with the popular policies of the founder king, Andrianampoinimerina's former counselors were lasting representatives of his populist agenda. With European collaborators and technologies, Radama replaced the powerful counselors of his father with an entourage of politically marginal foreign advisers and governors from the periphery of Imerina. While eliminating the allies of his father, Radama sought to distance himself from the social policies and popular discourses of Andrianampoinimerina. By 1822 when the women of his home district rose to protest his European-style haircut, Radama had—in a manner very different from his father's—transformed politics and administrative structures in highland Madagascar.

The social costs of Radama's expansion fell heavily upon Imerina's rural communities. By 1820 when Radama terminated the export trade in slaves from Imerina, most captives sold toward the Mascarenes did not originate from highland Madagascar; they were victims of Radama's outwardly expanding armies. Ending the slave trade was not, therefore, the popular act it might have been had the caravans of export slaves consisted primarily of highlanders themselves. In fact, abolition of the export slave trade, linked as it was to the simultaneous development of a professional army that permanently drained young highland men from their *firenena* and associated them with recruits from other regions of Imerina under the direct command of the sovereign, helped to galvanize popular opposition against Radama. Like the social transformations that accompanied the slave trade, changes in rural life that followed Radama's mortiferous military expeditions necessitated adjustments to the gender division of labor and thrust highlanders into a new crisis of subsistence. The economy of export enslavement at an end, Radama drafted larger numbers of young highland men from their countryside households into his permanent armies and corps of labor service (*fanompoana*) than the export trade had ever removed as bondpeople over previous decades. The domestic ramifications of Radama's military expansion evoked those of late eighteenth-century experiences of enslavement. Yet while the slave trade had included some women among its victims, Radama's human prestations were aimed almost exclusively at men in their physical prime. As in the late eighteenth century, highland women and the poor (not altogether separate categories of people) were left to manage the multiple and generally unhappy consequences of a profoundly gendered rural depopulation.

With memories of the unpopular economy of enslavement still fresh in their minds, highland Malagasy soon came to oppose the actions of their new king and to associate them with the "civil war and virtual anarchy" of the late eighteenth century, the erstwhile chaos of *fanjakana hova*.[3] Radama's innovations at the royal court, including his close association with foreign Christian missionaries, fostered a widespread perception throughout the kingdom that he was abandoning his ritual responsibilities toward his people.[4] Unlike his father, Radama was not a populist nor a man of the people but a ruler who preferred to remain physically and culturally aloof from his subjects yet ever jealous of their support. He did not relish consulting *firenena* or clothing his political discourse in a language of justice and moralized social relationships. As adept as Andrianampoinimerina at conducting diplomatic relationships with foreigners, Radama appropriated personally and politically more from European material and social culture than his father had. Disapproving of their new king's fondness for things foreign, his recruitment of young men into the standing army, and his centralized administrative style, highlanders chose to characterize their opposition as the sacred preservation of "long-established regulations." Newly rearticulated at the beginning of the nineteenth century, traditions of Merina identity and citizenship became the object of contention and popular attempts at protection during the reign of Radama and his successors. Rather than fulfilling his royal obligations by keeping social order within the kingdom and upholding the administrative, military, and cultural traditions of his father, Radama was, his citizen-subjects began to charge, taking them back into the chaos characteristic of the late economy of enslavement.

By claiming to preserve Andrianampoinimerina's many traditions in the face of Radama's innovations, highland Malagasy transformed Merina identity from a political extension of royal power into a cultural resource for contesting that power. During the reign of Radama, Merina identity came to embody a culture of protest against innovations in royal power that impinged upon self-defined *firenena* interests. This pattern of social protest endured through the French invasion of Madagascar in 1895 and into the twentieth century. At the core of that resistance rested a popular historical memory of Andrianampoinimerina as the virtuous defender of "long-established tradition." A political culture of considerable popularity among the kingdom's rural communities, as explored in the previous chapter, Andrianampoinimerina's moralized society and its associated administrative politics that simultaneously emphasized *firenena* and Merina identities were celebrated throughout the nineteenth century in popular historical memory and performative ritual. This process commenced soon after the death of Andrianampoinimerina in 1809 when Radama implemented profound transformations in the rural areas of Imerina. Confronting their first collective crisis as a unified political community—as Merina citizens—highlanders deployed historical memories of Andrianampoinimerina and his moralized cultural politics in defense of their self-defined communal interests. In so doing they appropriated Merina political identity and its popular rhetoric of civic virtue from the royal court and turned it back on Radama as an incisive discursive weapon of dissent.[5] Who could refute the political wisdom and social vision of the celebrated founding father? By claiming the rights of Merina citizenship once promised by Andrianampoinimerina in defense of subsistence and cultural conservatism in the face of Radama's policies they found so threatening, highland Malagasy transformed Merina political identity into Merina ethnic identity.

Ethnic identities do not inevitably issue from shared genetic characteristics, cultural practices, or historical experiences. They are the result of *processes* of purposeful interpretation and politicization of human characteristics, relationships, and experiences that foster an imagined community of citizens claiming a shared origin, history, and culture. In highland central Madagascar the human transactions most relevant to the formation of Merina identity, as I have argued throughout this book, transpired within the emerging ethnic community itself. When highlanders claimed the rights of citizenship and respect for rural self-sufficiency once popularized by Andrianampoinimerina, they decoupled Merina identity, or citizenship, from its erstwhile political moorings to the royal court. After the death of Andrianampoinimerina, Merina sovereigns no longer dispensed Merina identity to those who accepted their power; commoners in Imerina seized their existing political identity as Merina with its accompanying historical narratives and demanded their "traditional" civic rights as citizen-subjects in a new era of militarized social crisis. To be Merina after 1809 was to participate in a collective project of remembering Andrianampoinimerina as a popular sovereign and to deploy those historical memories in the preservation of traditions of political discourse and moralized economy articulated by the founder king at the beginning of the nineteenth century. If highland Malagasy had accepted flattering historical narratives of Andrianampoinimerina when they united politically under the founder king, they found that unity as Merina both true and useful when they employed positive historical images of Andrianampoinimerina in political struggles. After his death, Andrianampoinimerina emerged as a "site of memory" or a useful "metaphor" whose heroic image served to perpetuate Merina identity through successive generations.[6] It is primarily through this social memory in the form of *Tantara* narratives that Andrianampoinimerina is known today. Popular historical memory underpinned Merina ethnicity and simultaneously informs modern scholars of its origins.

There was nothing magical in the transformation of Merina political identity into a nascent ethnic identity during the reign of Radama. To describe that transformation is to enrich the notion of ethnicity, which emerges differently within each community. At the same time, there was no single moment at which Merina identity shifted from political to ethnic. The transformation occurred over time as common highland Malagasy employed ideologies of shared culture and origin to foster mutual responsibility. Highland Malagasy experienced their collective identity in a more continuous way than scholarly categorization of it as political or ethnic would suggest, yet very significant changes in that identity did occur over the years. From signifying political allegiance to Andrianampoinimerina to empowering highlanders with the cultural and moral vocabulary for collectively making demands on their new sovereign, being Merina matured over the course of the early nineteenth century.

Ethnicity is currently the source of much intellectual confusion. At the most general level, what we call ethnicity is a human perception of intragroup similarity and/or intergroup difference usually attributed to descent. Like gender, race, and national identities, ethnic identities are socially constructed rather than inherent, but unlike these identities they are not cultural expressions of some palpable physical reality (i.e., sex for gender, phenotype for race, nation for nationality) called ethnicity. Ethnicity as scholars have tended to employ the term since its invention in the post–World War II period is a politicized category of collective identity that may rest upon any one or a combination of an extremely wide mélange of physical, cultural, and economic bases (skin color, religion, language, descent, dress, occupation, adaptation to ecological niche, and the like). Originating from this heterogeneous and confounding intellectual soup, ethnicity is an imprecise and slippery category (and, I think, not as analytically significant as is generally assumed); it is expressed differently in each case and must be understood as historically fashioned in culturally unique circumstances. There are no universal rules or conditions for ethnogenesis and ethnic identity. For this reason, most existing theories of ethnicity and ethnogenesis inadequately account for the wide variety of specific and historically grounded processes by which ethnic communities come into their own. Inasmuch as ethnogenesis is culturally and politically embedded in local experiences, perceptions, and languages, a general theory of ethnicity is an oxymoron.

Today, ethnicities are frequently conceptualized as units or categories of collective identity within a multiethnic or subnational field, whence scholars' modern preoccupation with ethnicity as emerging through transethnic interaction (see chapter 1).[7] In highland central Madagascar, by contrast, Merina ethnicity emerged in a political field in which other ethnic categories were not particularly significant. Highland Malagasy first claimed Merina identity not to differentiate themselves from cultural "others" but to extract concessions from their rulers. The principal difference between Merina as a political identity and Merina as an ethnic identity, then, was who employed that identity, how they articulated it, and for what purposes they did so. When Andrianampoinimerina extended Merina identity to his political dependents he made of it a political affiliation. When highlanders claimed Merina identity after Andrianampoinimerina's death to impress their vision of proper royal behavior on their sovereigns they ethnicized it, expressing popular interests through it. Because it emerged in specific historical experiences and addressed particular problems faced by real people, Merina ethnicity was not mysterious, inscrutable, nor "Janus-like" during the early nineteenth century, although highlanders were skilled at bending it to various needs and uses.[8] It did not function as.Merina ethnicity does today in altogether different political circumstances.[9] During the early nineteenth century, specific political activities and human experiences linked Merina identity to the histories and lives of highland Malagasy over the previous half-century. Merina ethnicity was the product of historical experience and an ongoing process of transformation. Let us now turn to the origins of that transformation during the early years of Radama's reign.

MEMORY AS POPULAR POWER

Although Andrianampoinimerina expired at Antananarivo in 1809, nearly every professional history of his successor's incumbency commences some six years later with the arrival of British emissaries in Antananarivo. The first several years of Radama's reign, however, are crucial to understanding the divergence of royal and popular political strategies—and hence the origins of Merina ethnicity—during the early nineteenth century. Still a "beardless boy" in his mid to late teens when his father died, Radama was guided by ritual experts (*mpitaiza*) during the burial of Andrianampoinimerina and the year of mourning that followed.[10] The *Tantara* suggest Radama was residing at Ambohimanga when his father died at Antananarivo.[11] This is contradicted by accounts of Andrianampoinimerina's death in *History of Madagascar*, Raombana's *Histoires*, and elsewhere, which claim Radama was at Antananarivo.[12] The British missionaries' account specifies that on the evening Andrianampoinimerina felt his death near, he issued orders for Radama to be confined in the royal house called Masoandro, the "sun," inside the court at Antananarivo, there to be guarded by the king's corps of bodyguards (*Tsiarondahy*).[13] There is culturally meaningful symbolism to Radama's confinement that night in the "sun-house." Highland Malagasy associated night with death and with the passage of the living into the mystical world of the ancestors.[14] Night was (and remains) a dangerous time when witches and sorcerers engaged in their socially injurious activities.[15] According to early nineteenth-century cultural practice, the death of an individual was not to be acknowledged until sundown. If someone in a household expired during the day, family members maintained their composure and normal routine, notifying others at sunset. Mourning could commence only when the sun "died" (*maty masoandro*).[16] While Andrianampoinimerina lay on his deathbed, the new king was confined in the "sun-house." In the morning, he would rise over the kingdom and its citizen *ambaniandro*, those "beneath the sun."

Before court officials publicly announced Andrianampoinimerina's death, they undertook preparations to proclaim Radama as the new king. Criers enjoined the *ambanilanitra* to assemble, probably at Andohalo (a speech ground in Antananarivo), where it was announced that "Radama is now made king, for he is the successor of Andrianampoinimerina as lord of the land and the government."[17] The *ambanilanitra* responded to the announcement with a speech rich in memory and metaphor welcoming Radama as sovereign, but also warning him not to stray from the "words" of Andrianampoinimerina. The power of the speech lies in its ambiguity. Ostensibly a popular expression of support for Radama, it repeatedly warns the new king not to abandon the political traditions of his father.

> We give you our trust, Radama, even now that Andrianampoinimerina is gone. Andrianampoinimerina gathered this government, and you have been put in his place, Radama, so we *ambanilanitra* give you our trust indeed. And if there is someone who overturns the words given by Andrianampoinimerina, we will consume him, Radama. You will not have to consume him, for we will do so ourselves. We preserve the word of Andrianampoinimerina. That which we did in the time of your father we will continue to do now. If the words of Andrianampoinimerina are overturned, let those who must be enslaved be enslaved and those who must die, die! We will not mitigate our devotion to you for the love of our wives or for that of our children. We will attempt neither to aggrandize ourselves nor to curry the favor of big men, for we are the substitutes of Andrianampoinimerina, we are the stones inscribed with a message [*orimbato*]. We keep Andrianampoinimerina's words like money we gather, like pearls. The words of Andrianampoinimerina are like an inheritance from the ancestors; if their weight is not sufficient, we will increase it; if they go astray, they shall be beaten. For if the word of Andrianampoinimerina is not accomplished let those who must be enslaved be enslaved![18]

Politely submerged under the *ambanilanitra*'s collective offer of loyalty runs a not-so-subtle message that Radama should live up to the responsibilities of his office as defined by his father. "We are the commemorative stones," claims the speaker, "raised to preserve a message." The imagery of this assertion is key, for it referred to Andrianampoinimerina's frequent memorialization of his alliance with *firenena* as a towering stone obelisk (*orimbato*) raised to commemorate the new relationship between royalty and rural communities (chapter 5). Radama's citizen-subjects were saying, in effect, that "We the *ambanilanitra* are living stone obelisks etched with the memory of Andrianampoinimerina, his words, his traditions, his moralized society and economy." The people offer their contingent support to the new king if he, in return, will govern in the ways of his father. Demanding that the new king behave like the old one is here more than a formulaic utterance. Popular responses to Radama's kingship led to a public articulation of a moralized memory of Andrianampoinimerina, suggesting proper royal be-havior to the new sovereign. Radama replied in kind with a rhetoric of memory.

> If you remember the words of Andrianampoinimerina, O *ambanilanitra*, you are not orphans, for you have me; I am the orphan. Because I dwell here among you, Andrianampoinimerina lives, for you are his replacement. So take heart, O *ambanilanitra,* I am here to replace Andrianampoinimerina; for I am a commemorative stone inscribed with a message. That which you brought to the rule of Andrianampoinimerina I ask you to complete now, for he has now turned his back [died]. That is my message to you, *ambanilanitra*. I give you courage, *ambanilanitra*, for courage and trust that is reciprocally given is like masses of silver. I dwell with you and you dwell with me, though I am the father and I am the mother.[19]

Matching the popular rhetoric of his people, Radama recognized the role of his subjects as guardians of Andrianampoinimerina's memory ("An-drianampoinimerina lives, for you are his replacement"; "that which you brought to the rule of Andrianampoinimerina I ask you to complete now"). It was a dramatic transfer of historical memory from the new sovereign to his people, for Radama is never again reported to have spoken with such conciliatory and populist rhetoric. The new king's courtiers seldom sang the praises of Andrianampoinimerina; that role passed to the *firenena*. The *Tantara* do not specify at which capital Radama's first public ap-pearance took place. Most likely the above-reported speeches were of-fered at Antananarivo (Andohalo), where Raombana and the British mis-sionaries indicate Radama was residing when his father died. After Radama had been presented to the people, he was conveyed to Ambohimanga for a week while his father's body lay in state in his favorite Antananarivo house named Besakana. Separation of Radama from participation in all events surrounding the preparation and burial of his father's body was stipulated by highland ideas concerning ritual pollution: "If a prince is to become sovereign, the living and the dead must not be mixed."[20] At the end of one week, Andrianampoinimerina's body was conveyed to Ambohimanga to be laid in the king's ceremonial house of Mahandrihono, a symbolic parallel of Besakana at Antananarivo. Simultaneously, and by a different route so as not to cross the procession carrying his father's body, Radama traveled in the opposite direction, from Ambohimanga to Antananarivo. The parallel symbolism of the deceased sovereign and the new one exchanging residences in the twin royal capitals is significant. Although Radama had been proclaimed king at the same time as Andrianampoinimerina's death was first made public, that he was absent from the burial proceedings of his father and that his movements mirrored those of Andrianampoinimerina's body confirmed for the population that he would indeed ascend as the new sovereign.[21]

Radama's first public act after the burial (*afenina*, literally "hiding") of his father in the royal tomb at Ambohimanga was to depart from Antananarivo and venture back to Ambohimanga, where he mounted the sacred rock called Ambatomasina to announce a full year of mourning (*fisaonana*) for the departed founder king.[22] At Ambatomasina Radama offered up an abbreviated invocation (*vavaka*) calling upon Andrianampoinimerina. He then moved to the sacred rock called Ampamoloana and uttered the following words: "I invoke you, Andrianampoinimerina, here at your rock called Ampamoloana, that you placed here, for you have showered me with the good blessings of your government, that I may rise up and grow old together with my people. Andriamanitra Andriananahary! Andrianampoinimerina!"[23] Radama next proceeded to the third sacred rock called Ambatomenaloha near Ambohimanga and offered a similar invocation.

In his invocations from the sacred rocks, Radama is reported to have appealed neither to his ancestors (*razana*) nor to the royal talismans (*sampy*), but simply to Andrianampoinimerina specifically and to *andriamanitra andriananahary*, a form of deity.[24] Both the king's neglected invocations had been enjoined upon the people by Andrianampoinimerina during his life and were also expected of a new sovereign.[25] The royal ancestors and talismans, after all, were key sources of *hasina*, the sacred efficacy that rendered the sovereign powerful according to the royal ideology of Andrianampoinimerina. Andrianampoinimerina had been but an intermediary of their *hasina*.[26] During his first public appearances, then, Radama neglected and devalued both the royal talismans and his ancestors by refusing to invoke them in his public prayers. In a second narrative of Radama's first appearance in public, the new king is reported to have announced the duration and rules for the mourning of his father but not to have offered any invocations at all.[27] One *Tantara* narrative even alleges that Radama did not believe in the royal talismans, boasting of his personal power over them and claiming himself, not the talismans and their ritual experts, as *andriamanitra* (an embodiment of numinous power).[28] Radama's omissions were noted by his people and enshrined decades after his death in social memory.

Speechgivers from the court (*mpikabarin'andriana*) traveled across the kingdom to inform the people of their duties during the period of mourning. They called upon highlanders to observe a number of prohibitions, including an interdiction against singing, playing instruments, and clapping hands, all of which produced an eerie, palpable quiet across the land.[29] In addition, the king's criers enjoined the *ambaniandro* to sleep on the floor instead of in their beds, to not wash their feet, and to use only cold water for bathing other parts of the body. While mourning for a departed sovereign, highland Malagasy also customarily eschewed most forms of creative labor, especially ironworking.[30] The court's criers indicated that Radama had set the period of mourning to a full year and that the king's subjects were to clip their hair (*mibory*) four times, once every three months.[31] Precluding coiffure, the exhortation to clip hair left men's and women's heads in visible disarray. Hair cutting inscribed mourning visually upon *ambaniandro* bodies, reinvoking the metaphorical parallel between hair and the kingdom so often articulated by Andrianampoinimerina. Together with the founder king expired his ordered realm, symbolized by the shearing of the neatly parted, braided, and plaited hair of his subjects.

At the end of the year of mourning Radama was presented for a second time to his people in the "showing" ceremony (*fisehoana*). The "showing" was conducted twice, once each in the twin capitals of the kingdom, Antananarivo and Ambohimanga. During the year of mourning, Radama resided at Antananarivo, and that is where he first presented himself. The two "showing" ceremonies are described in the *Tantara* as having been conducted quite differently, with an abbreviated and simple ritual at Antananarivo and a significantly more elaborate one at Ambohimanga. In Antananarivo, Radama descended from the royal court to the speech ground called Andohalo and stepped up upon the sacred rock, there to receive the *hasina* of his subjects (*hasina* was, in the sense relevant here, a symbolic submission through offerings of silver piasters from each district and *firenena*). When the presentation of *hasina* was complete, Radama spoke in simple words to the assembled people telling them to take courage, that Andrianampoinimerina had given him the government, and that they had no need to fear. He presented gift cattle to be shared among his subjects.

When he completed the "showing" at Antananarivo, Radama turned north to Ambohimanga, where, it is reported, he revisited the sacred rocks of Ambatomasina and Ambatomenaloha and there "performed customs" (*naka fomba*). He then entered the house of Rabefiraisana, the civilian head of

Avaradrano district appointed by Andrianampoinimerina, to eat rice porridge. While they were eating, a throng of local people arrived at the house speaking vociferously, invoking Andriamanitra, Andriananahary, the royal ancestors, and the royal talismans. The enthusiastic "traditional" prayers of the common people crowding about the new king were the first invocations reported in the *Tantara* that called upon either the royal ancestors or the royal talismans during the entire ceremonial year following Andrianampoinimerina's death. By surrounding their new king and offering elaborate invocations naming both the ancestors and the talismans, as Andrianampoinimerina had once done but as his successor repeatedly neglected, the people of Ambohimanga instructed Radama in proper ritual comportment.[32] The clamorous and complete prayers of Ambohimanga farmers that contrasted with the new king's cursory invocations point to an emerging pattern of popular protest against the perceived failure of Radama to live up to the popularly remembered "traditions" of Andrianampoinimerina. Commoners would push Radama to pursue his "traditionally" defined royal responsibilities during the remainder of his reign.

When invocations at the house of Rabefiraisana were concluded, Radama returned to Ampamoloana rock, mounted upon it, and addressed his people. Several royal talismans were displayed prominently there, the first reported public display of them during the whole first year of Radama's reign. Their reported conspicuousness at Ampamoloana so soon after his subjects showered Radama with "traditionally" proper invocations citing the talismans may have been a concession to popular pressure. Of this incident the *Tantara* report that "the people approached the king and sang: Our king, e e e, great king. The royal talismans were there surrounding him: Manjakatsiroa, which was close to him and in front of him, and Kelimalaza, and Fantàka, and Behaza, and Tsimahalahy, and Vatamena &; and Mahavaly [all names of royal talismans] was carried by itself ahead of everyone to search the road and rid it of all witchcraft."[33] When the events were completed, Radama repaired to the royal court and spent the night in Mahandrihono house.

Events resumed the next morning at Fidasiana near Ambohimanga. Radama mounted the sacred rock and received tribute from *firenena* across Avaradrano. The royal talismans were displayed there as well, and the people of Avaradrano presented *hasina* to the keepers of the talismans. At the conclusion of the *hasina* presentation, Radama issued orders for representatives from *firenena* across the kingdom to come to Amboara (a place close to Ambohimanga) for a grand royal *kabary* in two weeks' time. Over the next two weeks, people assembled at Amboara, encamped in tents in the surrounding fields. On the appointed day, Radama appeared before his people outfitted in a culturally eclectic costume. About his waist the king supported a ceremonial *lambotapaka* loincloth made of fine silk and often worn by men during ritual occasions such as the circumcision ceremony.[34] In contrast to the *salaka fohy* or *salaka fohy rambo* (loincloth of short tail), which were worn on an everyday basis and did not interfere with productive activities, the *lambotapaka* was long, flowing, white, and clean. On his head Radama wore a two-cornered European hat (French, *bicorne*), an elongated hat coming to two points or horns, one in front and one behind the head.[35] The *satro-dava*, as it was locally called, was commonly worn by European military officers in ceremonial style; Radama, aware of its value as an elite good, had probably procured it from merchants engaged in the slave trade. The young king then addressed his people with the following words.

> I am your father, O *ambanilanitra*; I have been placed among you by Andrianampoinimerina, for he has left you to me. The mourning is now finished, the fog is lifted, and fat shall be rubbed on our hair. And this is what I reveal to you, O *ambanilanitra*: have true courage, for I am your father, I am your mother. Redouble your work efforts. For of the desires of Andrianampoinimerina there is not one that I shall not fulfill, not even one as small as a grain of rice. He has left this land and this government to me, and I shall not neglect any of it.[36]

Radama's statement that the people could now anoint their hair with fat lifted the prohibitions of mourning. Highland Malagasy used fats and oils to condition their hair, especially when plaiting and braiding.[37] During the year of mourning, using fats to condition hair was prohibited and it was left dry, stiff, and ungroomed like the windswept and crackling grass on highland hillsides during the rainless winter. Fat (especially the fat of a zebu hump) symbolized fertility, wealth, and ancestral blessing. It was rubbed into hair at the end of the mourning to demonstrate that royal blessing was again granted for normal activities to resume, for shorn hair to grow back long, and for unbraided and unplaited hair to be rebraided and replaited. Metaphorically, the *firenena* of the kingdom, like separate strands of hair, were to be rebraided under the new sovereign.

Randrianimanana of the Andriantompokoindrindra (a rank of *andriana*) then stood to respond to Radama. He offered *hasina* to the king from his people, asking the king's blessing in return. This is what he said:

> Here at Amboara-the-sacred is where Andriantsimitoviaminandriana and Andriambelomasina [ancient kings] ruled, and where Andrianampoinimerina also ruled. And if you have now come to this sacred land, Radama, we Andriantompokoindrindra, the eldest sibling of the Merina, present

hasina to you. Here is the *hasina* we present to you, and we invoke Andriamanitra! Andriananahary! the twelve sacred mountains! and the royal talismans that have made the twelve kings sacred! With this *hasina* we give you thanks, we offer you our devotion, and we desire that you might grow old among the people.[38]

Following Randrianimanana's speech, representatives of each *firenena* in the kingdom presented *hasina* to Radama in the descending order of social rank established during the reign of Andrianampoinimerina.[39] "Radama was happy," report the *Tantara*. The king took up his shield and spear and wished courage upon the people with a short and unceremonious exhortation: "Take courage, O *ambanilanitra*, for the presentation of the *hasina* that makes me sacred is now complete. Lie completely still, O Merina: for I am the father and I am the mother. So return home and work, O *ambanilanitra*." The author of this passage in the *Tantara* then adds parenthetically—and no doubt sarcastically—"No additional advice (*hevi-panjakana*) was given, but the call to work was his only word."[40] Unlike his father, Radama felt ill inclined or unequipped to fulfill the royal role of oratorical master. *Tantara* narratives that contrast Andrianampoinimerina's elaborate speeches and invocations with Radama's curt and abbreviated ones suggest that the new king's behavior was interpreted as inappropriate. First subtly articulated during the early months of the new king's reign, that popular disapproval with royal policy expanded over the years of Radama's rule to encompass military and cultural practices.

THE SOCIAL COSTS OF WAR, 1809–1815

Radama's determination to conquer more territory for his kingdom preoccupies memories of his reign. The new king's early vow to fulfill all the desires of Andrianampoinimerina, even "to the last grain of rice," was a manifest reference to the famed yet unfulfilled statement of his father that "The sea shall be the limit of my rice fields" (*ny riaka no valampariako*).[41] "Radama girded himself with a *salaka fohy*" (a loincloth for manual laborers), report the *Tantara*, "to accomplish the desires of Andrianampoinimerina."[42] Judging by the content of the *Tantara* concerning the time between Radama's ascent to kingship and the arrival of British envoys at Antananarivo, the most notable development in the lives of highland Malagasy before 1816 was the repeated war-making of their king. Although there must have been more than war on the minds of the *ambaniandro* during this time, the focus of collective memory on Radama's military designs suggests the far-reaching impact of military campaigns on highland Malagasy lives during the early reign of Radama. Huge armies of highland men accompanied by kinspeople marched eastward toward the Bezanozano, southward among the Betsileo, and southwestward to the Sakalava (see Map 2.1).[43]

The *Tantara* describe these early military campaigns in a language suggesting a departure from the war-making traditions of Andrianampoinimerina. Most notable is the continuous nature of Radama's military activity, with a significant expedition departing Antananarivo each winter. People living in the highland capital later explained to British missionaries that because of the ongoing heavy loss of young men's lives in Radama's early military expeditions, those remaining at home struggled to maintain agricultural production and insure subsistence.[44] The *Tantara* corroborate these contemporary observations, noting that food security during Radama's reign was compromised, especially as a result of the hemorrhage of labor from cultivation when men abandoned Imerina to fight in the distant reaches of Madagascar.[45] Concerns for the tremendous loss of soldiers' lives and the impact of war making on the rural economy during these early years of Radama's rule suggest why social memory focuses on the military. Radama set new precedents for military service that threatened the physical and social integrity of local kin groups and households.

Radama's farmer-soldiers on temporary duty, like those of Andrianampoinimerina, were responsible for their own subsistence and were required to carry, purchase, or plunder for their own provisions.[46] *Tantara* narratives assume that highland armies seized much booty in slaves and movable property in Betsileo during Radama's early campaigns, and it is likely that some of these goods reached individual soldiers through patronage distribution networks at whose apex stood commanders of the army.[47] Yet despite comparatively low casualty rates among soldiers in the Betsileo wars, military action exacted its toll on recruits and on their kin back home. Illness was the primary killer of armies in Madagascar during the nineteenth century, a fact the French learned in 1895 when most of the casualties within armies of colonial conquest were produced by fevers and dysentery.[48] Reports from the early nineteenth century indicated that mortality in Radama's armies reached as much as 50 percent per annum.[49] In addition to illness, soldiers' inconsistent access to plundered food imposed significant hardships, as such nourishment rarely offered sufficient nutrition, much less satisfaction. Because Radama never implemented a centralized plan for feeding his farmer-soldiers, many men were accompanied by female family members or servants who cooked for them, bore their supplies of food, and returned to Imerina with their remains for proper burial should they expire far from home. Because the wealthy could normally exempt themselves from military service with payments of as high as ten piasters, Radama's temporary armies were generally drawn from among the poorer highland households (the majority), those who could not afford to excuse themselves from its onerous demands.[50]

Figure 6.1 Portrait of Radama by French painter André Coppalle, 1825. Radama posed for Coppalle, an amateur painter from Mauritius, several times during the latter's stay in highland Madagascar (1825–26). Radama was not happy with the results. In dismissing Coppalle from his service in 1826, the king complained that the Mauritian painter was "not very capable." The European military uniform in which Radama is shown suggests how the young sovereign wished to be remembered. (*See*: Françoise Raison-Jourde, *Bible et pouvoir à Madagascar au XIXᵉ siècle: invention d'une identité chrétienne et construction de l'état* [Paris, 1991], illustration between pages 380 and 381.)

Soldiers and the kin who moved with them sometimes suffered severe physical deprivation.

Among Radama's early military expeditions, those conducted westward against the Sakalava are most remembered for the misery they brought upon farmer-soldiers, slaves, and kin accompanying them, as well as on the women, children, and aged remaining at home. In popular memory, Radama launched three expeditions against the southern Sakalava (Menabe) and their king, Ramitraho. These expeditions were probably conducted in successive years before 1815. The *Tantara* indicate the first of the expeditions was launched only after the circumcision ceremony had been observed.[51] Circumcision (*famorana*) was normally practiced during the early months of the austral winter (May and June), so it is likely the expedition departed during the winter months, as was also custom under Andrianampoinimerina (according to Andrianampoinimerina's precept of assured rural subsistence, farmers serving in the army were guaranteed to be home in the austral spring as rain began to fall and crops required attention). The second campaign marched from Antananarivo exactly a year later, "when the year returned again"—also in the winter. The *Tantara* state explicitly that the third and most disastrous campaign departed Imerina during the *ririnina*, the winter.[52]

Although each of the expeditions to the Sakalava Menabe was conducted according to Andrianampoinimerina's timetable favoring the agricultural calendar (i.e., during the agricultural off-season), they are all remembered for the tremendous toll on human life they exacted. The death of so many men without any meaningful gain in territory, political authority, or booty during the first two campaigns confronted Radama with questioning rural households as he arranged the third. When the king announced his intention to launch a third attack against the Sakalava, he found it necessary to justify himself and claim he was not misusing his authority. "I shall wage war at Maharivo and at Ranomainty," the *Tantara* report Radama as saying, "So I inform you *ambaniandro*, for I do not abuse my authority. You *ambaniandro* have been given to me by Andrianampoinimerina; He has given you to serve me forever here in this land. So I am going to go and wage war, and I inform you now."[53] Radama allowed the *ambaniandro* one month during which to prepare their provisions and to present themselves at camp. When all the men were assembled at the end of one month, it was the women and the children who spoke, addressing Radama: "We wish you courage, sir, in your government here in this place. Do not be afraid and do not be apprehensive, sir, for we children and women give courage to the *ambaniandro*; so travel safely and may your coming and your going be equally successful."[54] Radama called upon nearly the entire population of fighting-age men in Imerina to participate in his third expedition against the Sakalava; having twice failed even to see Ramitraho, Radama and his generals were very eager to effect their purpose. British missionaries later reported that the army consisted of 100,000 people, including accompanying servants and slaves, many of whom were women.[55]

Tantara narratives vividly recall the winter of the massive Menabe campaign as a time when only women and children remained at home: "And when the king and the *ambaniandro* left Imerina, the children and the women were not afraid of the frost; they guarded each village. This is what the contribution of the children and the women was to the government of the king. For children who reached the height of an adult's neck and older were the ones who were unafraid of the frost and guarded each village."[56] The reference to frost in the preceding passage invokes more than the physical coldness of the wintertime (highland winters are indeed chilly, although it seldom freezes), when the campaign was conducted. In highland Madagascar coldness is associated with states of chaos and disorder, the opposite of proper *fanjakan'andriana*, or royal political order.[57] A metaphoric reading of this passage suggests that the absence of so many men from highland villages made them cold, chaotic, and disordered, transforming social relations and chilling those remaining at home. Like the plundering of young men for the export slave trade, enlistment into Radama's armies "cooled the land."[58]

Merina soldiers did not actually engage Sakalava in any of these three expeditions. Along with their king, Ramitraho, the Sakalava abandoned their capital (Mahabo) and scorched the earth as Radama and his farmers approached. The mass army of highlanders was left with nothing to feed itself. Highland farmer-soldiers faced horrendous starvation, wandering about the western Malagasy desert (*efitra*) searching for the elusive Sakalava king and his warriors. As he had been forced to do during the two previous campaigns, Radama turned back empty-handed. The defeat of Radama's soldiers in the third campaign was total; starving and emaciated, they straggled homeward across the barren desert. Having faced nothing but scorched earth, they did not partake in the booty of war, the only compensation rural armies might hope for. Individuals who recounted these events to Father François Callet in the mid-nineteenth century could still remember that when famished men returned to the western frontiers of Imerina and first encountered cultivated fields, many perished after greedily stuffing themselves with taro root.[59]

Each set of military campaigns in the first several years of Radama's reign—beginning with the Bezanozano, then the Betsileo, and finally the Sakalava—carried highland armies farther from their homeland in the center of the island. Each inflicted higher levels of mortality on the ranks and was accompanied by greater social costs. The hunger and starvation that accompanied Radama's early campaigns, reports Raombana, "made the people murmur and grumble very much."[60] The parallels between Radama's economy of expansion and highland Madagascar's late eighteenth-century economy of enslavement were immediate and striking. Both exerted similarly structured demographic and gendered transformations in the highland countryside and both were policies of fundamental contradiction, expanding the political geography and economy of the kingdom, on the one hand, yet shoving the social costs of that expansion onto rural households, on the other. Like Andrianampoinimerina several decades earlier, Radama stood at a political crossroads in 1815. And like Andrianampoinimerina, Radama opted for a sociopolitical restructuring, but one of an entirely different character than his father had. Spurred by his desire to create an island-wide kingdom and by the rural resistance that mortiferous military campaigns generated, Radama sought an external rather than an internal alliance: an association with Britain rather than with the *firenena* of his realm. While Andrianampoinimerina secured royal power by finding self-interested solutions to the plight of rural communities in an economy of enslavement, Radama did so by restructuring his temporary armies into a professional force independent of *firenena* control and by adopting a range of foreign technologies of power, none of which fundamentally addressed the detrimental impact of his politics of expansion on the people of his kingdom. Because in fundamental respects his personal political ambitions recreated the eighteenth-century economy of enslavement and because he refused to rhetorically or socially align himself with his people, Radama soon became an unpopular sovereign.

THE DOMESTIC ORIGINS OF FOREIGN ALLIANCE

If Radama based territorial expansion upon the army, he sought to remove its long established military commanders from their power. Known as the "friends" (*namana*), these individuals were the former counselors and advisers of Andrianampoinimerina. Their influence was based upon positions of command in the army and control over the material wealth and the patronage networks it fed. The ascendancy of the friends within Andrianampoinimerina's armies secured for them significant monetary benefits resulting from the export of war captives from highland Madagascar. Testimony to their intimacy with the founder king, some friends attended upon Andrianampoinimerina at his deathbed.[61] When Andrianampoinimerina expired, the friends continued to rule over the founder king's networks of trade and political patronage, managed the army for Radama, and instructed the teenage sovereign in royal etiquette.[62] During his first several years as king, Radama struggled with the friends to wedge himself into the supply market for export slaves and to establish a degree of political independence from them. Contemporary reports confirm that Radama was far from capable of meaningfully regulating the sale of slaves from the center of the island, primarily because the friends personally controlled and benefited from the sale of victims captured during military expeditions.[63] As many as 70 percent of the slaves passing along the primary routes from the inland to the east coast were not personally owned by Radama.[64] Andrianampoinimerina had managed to regulate the trade by imposing a *tax de noirs* on export activity, by stipulating the times and places where his subjects could sell slaves to European traders, and by gathering the wealthiest and most influential slave traders around him at the royal court.[65] Radama's influence as a teenager over the actions of his father's experienced adult advisers, on the other hand, was tenuous at best, and it is unlikely that royal taxes officially due Radama's treasury on the export of slaves were evenly collected. By 1816, too, potential sources of war captives were shrinking fast. "I think that Radama's opportunities for procuring slaves are nearly exhausted by the submission of people to whom he could bring war; this commerce is not far from extinguishing itself," commented an envoy of the British government in late 1816.[66] In any case, if Radama were to base his power on wealth derived from the slave trade, as his father originally had, he could ill prevent the friends from enriching themselves at the same time. Realizing that trying to increase his political independence through an intensification of the slave trade would merely reproduce his subordination to the friends, Radama began to entertain thoughts of ridding himself of his father's advisers by other means.

Displacing the friends would not be easy. They commanded the instrument of Radama's emergent power—the army—and were strategically located at the very center of the kingdom, living immediately about the royal court. Andrianampoinimerina had allocated ground to the west of the court (*andrefandrova*) to his friends among the *firenena* Tsimahafotsy, while he allowed those from the *firenena* Tsimiamboholahy to build residences north of the court (*andafiavaratra*).[67] British missionaries later explained this spatial arrangement: "In the immediate neighbourhood of the palace are the houses of several of the judges, the nobles, and the principal officers in the army, constituting this part of the town . . . the Westminster of Tananarivo."[68] The friends surveyed Radama's actions and threatened to frustrate any royal measure that might reduce their influence at the court. While he could not budge them from their proximity to the royal court, Radama sought to displace the friends from their military command and appoint them to civilian duties, thereby sidelining them from the highest levels of decision making and curbing their access to exportable war captives and the wealth in silver they fetched. Radama accomplished this by appointing friends as superior judges, or *andriambaventy*, a new and civilian branch of service to the kingdom he created especially for this purpose.[69] It is unknown precisely when Radama initiated this strategy, but it is clear he implemented it with the goal of removing friends from military command.[70] One of the social enticements for friends to become *andriambaventy* was that nomination elevated *hova* men (the social status of most friends and military commanders) to *andriana*. Despite the social privileges accorded by civilian judgeships, the friends were not pleased with Radama's scheme to relegate them to hearing cases of contention over ancestral property, witchcraft, and divorce—the customary domains of such judges and the principal legal passions of highland Malagasy until today.[71] Radama maintained a keen watch over the men he appointed *andriambaventy*, and he sought opportunities to publicly humiliate them.[72] If Radama spared the lives of the friends, he plotted to assassinate their children, even to exile them from Madagascar.[73]

But sidelining *namana* into judicial duties was not effective in itself. The political conjuncture in which Radama found himself sovereign of Imerina pushed the youthful king to adopt strategies of rule that departed significantly from those of his father and to seek new associates from the margins of the kingdom who would necessarily become dependent on him. As he approached adulthood and sought the means to assert political independence from the friends, Radama calculated that his best chance of undermining the power of his inherited advisers lay not in shifting them into his judiciary but in cutting off their access to external supplies of silver and in balancing their influence against a new set of foreign royal allies. Radama's alliance with the British, who by the end of the Napoleonic Wars had emerged as the premier naval power in the Indian Ocean, displacing the French at Île de France and Bourbon, should be read in light of the young king's emerging strategies of domestic rule.[74]

Most scholars writing about this period have assumed that the impetus for the Anglo-Merina alliance of the early nineteenth century originated with the governor of Mauritius. The alliance, they write, unfolded to the tune of British policy implemented by Governor Robert Farquhar and represented the culmination of a grand British scheme to limit French influence in Madagascar and to put an end to the slave trade between eastern Madagascar and the Mascarenes.[75] Whether they place emphasis on Farquhar's desire to limit French influence or to end the slave trade, scholars have invariably understood the relationship between Radama and Governor Farquhar through the eyes of Farquhar rather than through those of Radama. Jean Valette, for example, described the Anglo-Merina alliance of 1817 as the "the cornerstone of English policy" and assumed that through the alliance "Farquhar was magnificently able to effect the plan that he had laid out."[76] When the politics of the alliance are viewed from Antananarivo and the available documents read carefully for what they reveal about Radama's timing and mo-tives, however, a different picture emerges. Radama initiated the alliance and pursued it for his own strategic and personal interests; Farquhar was at first reluctant to take Radama's bait, but faced with political pressures of his own eventually came to see the alliance as in his best interests. Along with the friends, most highland Malagasy opposed Radama's unfolding affiliation with Britain.

In early 1815 Radama dispatched one of his personal servants, a man named Rampola, to visit John Thompson, the agent of the British government charged with surveying and organizing the trade in Tamatave. Rampola sought gun-powder from Thompson, offering to exchange it for slaves, and desired to open relations with the British. But Rampola was poorly treated by Thomp-son, who insisted that Radama purchase the powder with silver. At that time he had no instructions from Mauritius to cultivate the friendship and good-will of the Merina court.[77] Following Thompson's rebuff of Rampola, Radama determined to wait for the governor of Mauritius to change his mind. No one was more aware than Radama that a friendly relationship with the British would be cause for political disaffection among the friends—men upon whom Radama was politically dependent and whom he constantly watched, afraid of a possible move to unseat him. If Radama were to pursue an alliance with Britain and end the export trade in slaves, he would need a determined ally in the governor of Mauritius. Until Farquhar had decided to enforce a ban on the slave trade, Radama dared not act. It wasn't until 1816 that Governor Farquhar began to seek an alliance with Radama in earnest.

Although the trade in slaves into Mauritius had been illegal (according to British law) since the British acquired the island from France in 1810, im-portation of servile labor from Madagascar and east Africa continued clan-destinely at higher levels than previously.[78] During the first decades of the nineteenth century Mauritius was experiencing growth in sugar production and this economic expansion would be jeopardized by an end to the impor-tation of slave labor. No wonder Governor Farquhar was uninterested in ac-tively pursuing an end to the slave trade from Madagascar until the gross illegalities in Mauritius were brought to the attention of the British public.[79] If Farquhar dragged his feet about ending the illegal trade into Mauritius, he was nevertheless interested in stemming the flow of slaves into neighboring Bourbon, returned to France in 1814 at the settlement of the Napoleonic Wars. France had not yet effectively ended the slave trade to its possessions (this happened only with the abolition of slavery in 1848) and the British navy was powerless to arrest the flow of slaves from eastern Madagascar into Bourbon, just as they were incapable of ending the illegal trade to Mauritius. By international convention British warships cruising the Indian Ocean were not permitted to prevent vessels flying the French flag from carrying slaves and could not board them to examine their cargoes.[80] What the British navy could not achieve for Farquhar, perhaps Radama could.

In 1816 Farquhar responded to Radama's overtures by dispatching Chardenoux, a longtime *traitant* in the Indian Ocean trade, to Antananarivo to communicate his interest in pursuing an alliance.[81] Chardenoux's mission was followed shortly thereafter by another delegation from the Mauritian governor led by Captain Lesage, who concluded a formal treaty of friendship and alliance and performed blood brotherhood (*fatidra*) with Radama.[82] In early 1817 Farquhar dispatched James Hastie as ambassador to Radama's court with instructions to enter into an agreement with Radama to end the export trade in slaves from his dominions.[83] The "negotiation" of a treaty to end the foreign sale of slaves from central Madagascar represented one of the single most politically transformative moments in Radama's reign. First drafted in 1817 and finally implemented three years later, the treaty created an alliance between Radama and the British at Mauritius, enabling Radama to thrust aside the friends and to replace them with a new entourage of Malagasy and European counselors. Unlike the friends, Radama's new courtiers (with the exception of close members of his family like Ramananolona and Ramanetaka who he sent to govern faraway provinces) were all men without prominence in the influential *firenena* of Imerina. They originated from the social and geographical periphery of the realm and relied directly upon Radama for their power and advancement.[84] These new retainers came to be known as the *maroseranina*, "the many who are passed by" but also, possibly, "the many sea ports," an expression that captured their peripherality and multiplicity of origins.[85] The culmination of a long-nourished desire, the treaty to abolish the export slave trade also was a domestic political revolution.

While implementing his revolution, however, Radama faced a broad-based resistance. The precautions he exercised to appear deferential to the influential opinions of the popular friends of Andrianampoinimerina while "negotiating" the treaty of 1817 have been widely and incorrectly interpreted by modern historians as evidence of the king's irresolution in the matter of banning the export slave trade.[86] Radama navigated an exceedingly precarious political course during August, September, and October of 1817, the three months during which he and Hastie hammered out the text of the original treaty in Antananarivo. These were crucial days for Radama when his authority teetered in an uneasy balance. It was unclear whether he would gain the upper hand against the friends, who benefited most from the slave trade and who were entirely opposed to ending it. During his residence in Antananarivo, Hastie repeatedly played on Radama's hunger for ascendancy over his political rivals, suggesting that if he did not seize the moment and sign the treaty his inaction would be tantamount to recognizing that he was commanded by his subjects rather than governor of them.[87] Late one evening as Radama complained of his political difficulties to the British ambassador, Hastie quipped that if the sovereign could only cause his will to prevail over his old counselors, he would emerge "a king before tomorrow."[88] Seen from within the kingdom, the lengthy negotiations leading to the signing of the treaty in Tamatave on October 23, 1817, represented a triumph for Radama in an internal political struggle. The powers and prerogatives of the Merina kingship were being reinvented in late 1817.

While the treaty to end the export trade in slaves was being negotiated, Radama met frequently with both the friends (some of whom, recall, were now in the office of *andriambaventy*) and members of the *maroseranina*, while during his spare moments he visited the British ambassador's personal quarters to engage in intense moments of whist and chess.[89] But Radama's arguments with the friends could not convince them to agree with his proposed politics of foreign alliance and an end to the export slave trade. Although adduced to safeguard their means of accumulating wealth, the arguments produced by Andrianampoinimerina's old advisers against ending the slave trade did in fact raise serious administrative dilemmas for the king. For example, highland armies had been accustomed to dispose of male war prisoners by selling them as slaves out of Madagascar. What could be done with these potentially rebellious men, claimed the friends, when they could no longer be exported from the island? How could Merina armies effect retribution upon rebellious villages and provinces if men could not be threatened with enslavement and sale across the seas?[90] And without the royal revenues resulting from taxes on the sale of slaves to European merchants, how would the army procure the arms and ammunition it required to achieve its ambitious military objectives? This was the question that most seriously preoccupied Radama.[91] Finally, asked the friends, where would the silver money that circulates in Imerina come from if its source—payment for exportation of slaves—were abruptly terminated?[92]

Taking these arguments to Hastie, Radama and his new ministers secured a clause in the treaty providing for an annual British payment to Radama of what was called the "equivalent." The equivalent consisted of an assortment of money, arms, ammunition, and trade goods for the king's military and personal consumption. It was ostensibly inserted into the treaty as compensation to Radama for financial losses resulting from the cessation of the slave trade.[93] Radama thought the equivalent important, but not for financial reasons (other than its part in ending his old advisers' access to imported silver).[94] One provision of the equivalent called for instruction in England of several of Radama's young subjects at the British government's expense (this was the provision under which Raombana, the highland Malagasy historian, studied in London and Manchester during the 1820s). Missionary David Jones noted in 1820 that "Radama values this article for the instruction of his people more than any other part of the equivalent."[95] In fact, the king indicated at one point that his desire for the equivalent represented more a matter of pragmatic politics to placate the friends' opposition than a real desire for financial compensation. Radama needed to demonstrate to his people that they would receive something valuable in exchange for eschewing the slave trade, a clever attempt at diffusing the friends' opposition to termination of their financial perquisites. While arranging with Hastie for the transportation of the equivalent from Tamatave into the highlands, Radama remarked that "as the Slave Traffic was prohibited he was very desirous his people should see the equivalent arrive."[96]

During the first two weeks of October, when Radama faced a nearly universal challenge from the friends, Ratefy, one of Radama's new advisers who hailed from the western fringes of the kingdom and was also the king's brother-in-law, worked in concert with Hastie to try to convince the adamant old men to consent to Radama's course of action.[97] Yet the royal court encountered protest from a more popular source, the *firenena*. On the morning of October 9, Radama dispatched Ratefy to address a gathering of 5,000 *firenena* "heads of the people" (*loholona*) from across the kingdom at the royal speech ground of Andohalo. "They remained there until noon," reports Hastie. "When Radama sent for me to apprise me of the result of the *kabary* (speeches), he was very violently agitated and told me that his subjects had had the impudence to ask whether he had become the slave of the English and that they claimed they would fight with sticks and stones rather than suffer their subordination."[98] As guardians of their respective *firenena*, the "heads of the people" opposed the treaty as likely to intensify the expansion of the army and continue to undermine the ability of rural households to feed themselves. In addition, an end to the slave trade would remove the financial benefits to common highland Malagasy of commerce in export slaves, some revenue of which trickled down to the *firenena*. Even common farmer-soldiers could gain indirectly from this wealth by seeking patrons among the higher army officers who derived a livelihood from the trade. By the night of October 9, the tension between Radama, the friends, the "heads of the people," and the *firenena* mounted to a tipping point. Not only did the *firenena* and the friends disagree with the king, they threatened to withhold cooperation in calling up armies and in supporting the king's military adventures.[99]

But Radama was adamant. On the night of October 9 he determined to conclude the treaty over the objections of his many opponents, although he doubted his orders to cease the slave trade would be obeyed to the letter.[100]

"He cried out with a loud voice that he was English," reports Hastie of his conversation with a headstrong king that evening, "and that he would force his people to obey him."[101] Now resolved to negotiate the details of the treaty of alliance and to push through with an end to the slave trade, Radama and his new *maroseranina* counselors moved quickly. Radama and Hastie agreed upon the terms of the treaty in Antananarivo during the days following October 9. A week later, on October 17, special envoys of governor Farquhar and *maroseranina* counselors of Radama signed the completed document at Tamatave. Radama immediately issued public instructions throughout his kingdom that no more slaves should be exported from the island. The orders were implemented with remarkable effectiveness; the supply of slaves to French traders slowed to a clandestine trickle. By the middle of 1818, however, the treaty lapsed. In the absence of Governor Farquhar (who had returned on temporary furlough to London), the interim governor Hall of Mauritius refused to deliver the stipulated equivalent to Radama. Radama and Hastie worked desperately to encourage Hall to implement British obligations under the treaty, but to no avail.[102]

The equivalent, as I have indicated, was of little financial concern to Radama. He desired a publicly visible compensation for his losses in the trade, but he had negotiated the treaty primarily for political reasons, not monetary ones. The equivalent represented but a fraction of his former revenues and Radama had promised to distribute the equivalent among his political opponents rather than keep it for the royal treasury (another concession aimed at winning the support of the friends).[103] But when the equivalent failed to arrive in Antananarivo, Radama was obliged to retreat from the alliance he so passionately desired. The king's political position was exceedingly tenuous in the face of general public disapproval with the British failure to uphold its treaty commitment and he dared not continue the ban on slave exports. By the middle of 1818 Radama removed the export ban with little disruption to that year's normal flow of slaves toward the east coast. Most of these unfortunates were landed surreptitiously at Mauritius and Bourbon. Publicly, Radama repudiated the English in the strongest terms. Hastie was informed that "Radama has in some measure apologized to his People for having entered into any agreement, against their wishes which the treaty of 1817 was and has now made a solemn covenant that he will not again do so or hold any friendship with those who have deceived them."[104] Despite his necessary public backtracking, Radama remained personally committed to the treaty and the alliance. When Governor Farquhar returned to Mauritius after a three-year absence and dispatched Hastie back to Antananarivo, the old treaty was re-signed and reimplemented on October 11, 1820, but again over the concerted opposition of the friends and the *firenena*.[105] Radama acted swiftly to enforce the treaty, and within weeks the trade in slaves from areas of eastern Madagascar under his control ground to a halt. As in 1817, export slaves awaiting embarkation onto Mascarene vessels at Tamatave and Foulpointe were returned to the Malagasy highlands.[106] After nearly five decades, the export trade in slaves from Madagascar's highlands was at an end. Widely opposed by the populace which now benefited from slaving beyond the borders of Imerina, the end to the slave trade only increased Radama's mounting unpopularity.

THE BITTER FRUIT OF MISSION AND STANDING ARMY

Conceived against the popular will, Radama's British alliance bore bitter fruit for the people of highland Madagascar. Between implementation of the export ban on slaves in late 1820 and the Avaradrano women's revolt in early 1822, Radama spearheaded two sets of significant social transformations within his kingdom. In each of them, Europeans played a visible and critical role. The first and least influential of these was the introduction of Christianity and Christian literacy into the kingdom. When Hastie returned to Antananarivo in late 1820 he brought with him a Welsh missionary named David Jones, an emissary of the London Missionary Society who desired to evangelize in Radama's realm.[107] Joined in May 1821 by fellow countryman David Griffiths, Jones sought to obtain children from Radama to whom he could teach English and set to scriptural translations.[108] Jones was accommodated by Radama *within* the enclosure of the royal court (*rova*) and there formed a school where he taught the English language and led students placed with him by orders of Radama in memorizing Christian hymns and catechisms in English.[109] Favored by Radama and highly visible at the royal court, Jones and Griffiths mixed uncomfortably with the court intellectuals surrounding the king—diviners, astrologers, and keepers of the royal talismans. When Hastie claimed that Jones was installed "at the court of Radama to the entire exclusion of the teachers of horrid superstition & idolatry," he overstated the degree to which Radama had thrust aside the court intellectuals once so valued by Andrianampoinimerina, but he accurately reflected what would have been perceived across the kingdom as royal favoritism for foreign religious specialists.[110] The coercion Radama exercised to bring children into the mission schools (attending the schools became an extension of *fanompoana* labor service once reserved for adult men only) and the foreign nature of the instruction young students received there soon garnered opposition. If the schoolchildren themselves were sometimes enthusiastic about their apprenticeship with the missionaries, their parents were not. Many justly feared the missionaries were in league with Radama to retain their children in government service (most of the early students were drafted by Radama as scribes for his far-flung bureaucracy, subjecting them to privations and deadly disease, the lot of slaves and soldiers).[111] In a remarkable display of parental displeasure with the missionaries in January 1822, the schoolchildren's parents accused them of being "great liars and deceivers," and "worse than beasts, dogs, pigs and cats (the most despicable animals in their sight)."[112] "It is true we have the patronage of the king," wrote newly arrived missionary John Jeffreys in mid-1822, "but there are many watching us with jealous eye."[113]

The earliest encounters between adult Malagasy and missionaries during the first two years of the London Missionary Society's presence in Antananarivo can only be described as an experience of profound discontinuity. By embracing the missionaries as intimate members of his new *maroseranina* advisers, Radama introduced a set of foreign ritual experts at the royal court, individuals who both the Malagasy and the missionaries themselves interpreted as displacing those set there by Andrianampoinimerina. A creative and fascinating intellectual "middle ground" between European mission Christianity and Malagasy ideas and practices, something I explore elsewhere, had not yet materialized.[114] The first Malagasy would not be baptized for nearly fifteen years. But in 1822 the social structure of the expanding Christian religious community composed of missionaries and their schoolchildren foreshadowed a generational pattern of conversion that would characterize central Madagascar for the entire nineteenth century. Most converts would come to the Christian community through mission schools and the majority of them would be youths, even infants.[115] The basis of social protest against Christianity from early on was profoundly generational (adults) and at its center lay struggles over the socialization and education of children.[116] Radama's plans for employing foreign missionaries to strengthen his civil administration and including them among his *maroseranina* intimates insured that protest over innovations in royal prerogative would crystallize around Christian schools and royal favoritism for foreign clerics. Missionaries, as will be seen, felt themselves a primary target of the women who confidently protested Radama's haircut in May 1822.

While missionaries emerged as conspicuous and unpopular symbols of Radama's politics of foreign alliance, the king's plans for transforming the highland army into a permanent fighting force intensified a gender-structured depopulation of the countryside commenced by enslavements during the late eighteenth century.[117] More than the rising influence of British missionaries in the socialization of Malagasy children, transformations in the army during the years before 1822 help to explain the women's displeasure with Radama and his new hairstyle in April of that year. In late 1816, little more than a year after the last and fatal Sakalava campaign described in an earlier section of this chapter, governor Farquhar's envoy, Lesage, arrived in Antananarivo with two British sergeants.[118] Lesage and the sergeants carried instructions from Farquhar to impress Radama with the fighting potential of a modest squad of European-trained and equipped men. When Lesage departed Antananarivo in March 1817 he left the two sergeants with the young king. Over the next several months these two men worked with Radama and his commanders to train small groups of soldiers in British military drills. Because the sergeants offered training during the primary agricultural season (October to May), Radama enlisted the recruits with whom they worked from among the sons of the wealthiest families of the kingdom. Wealthy households could better absorb a loss of male labor to the domestic economy and Radama felt obligated to offer the first new opportunities in his army to the sons of those who had so strenuously opposed his European alliance (many were later favored with promotions). The soldiers were trained in small groups of 50 until nearly 400 were capable of performing drills to English military commands.[119]

From mid-1817 Radama retained an English and a French officer to train his armies. Both were appointed to military leadership, displacing friends, and both joined Radama's entourage of *maroseranina*. The English officer, James Brady, was one of the two sergeants offered to Radama by Lesage as discussed in the previous paragraph. The French officer, Robin, a fugitive from colonial authorities at Bourbon, sought employment from Radama independently.[120] As members of the *maroseranina*, Brady and Robin assisted Radama in removing the last friends from military command. By 1820, the foreign commanders had succeeded in training a few thousand of Radama's soldiers in European combat techniques.[121] In October that year missionary David Jones, newly arriving in Antananarivo, rejoiced at the achievement in his diary: "I confess that I cannot describe in writing the order among such a number of soldiers under arms, (all going through their exercise by english commands) the music, the dancing, the crowds of spectators looking at us ascending all around."[122] Despite the delight expressed by foreign observers over the regularization and Europeanization of Radama's military, only a small portion of the army had been trained in new combat techniques by late 1820. A paucity of foreign training personnel was one reason for this. Radama's refusal to remunerate his soldiers was another. Finally, the extremely high silver costs required to properly outfit thousands of men with muskets at a time when Radama's commercial revenues suffered from the end of the export slave trade was a third. Opting for European technology and military training precisely when he was most ill equipped to supply soldiers with the appropriate imported technology, Radama was unable to financially support his ambitious goals. Rather, the new army in 1820 was still "more like an armed mob, running wild," than a disciplined corps of warriors.[123] It relied upon strength in numbers as well as the psychological capital of the foreign-trained elite brigade and the logistical support provided by British naval vessels for campaigns along the coast. When Radama's army marched westward in a new search for the Sakalava king in 1820, for example, it did not rely primarily on the new European-trained recruits. It moved, as it had before, with a temporarily amassed army nearly 100,000 strong.[124]

Radama's mass armies and their extended absences from highland Madagascar even during the rains are remembered in the *Tantara* as having contributed to famine during his reign.[125] In addition to the major campaigns about which many have written, every year at least ten separate operations composed of 500 to 2,000 soldiers each departed from Antananarivo into the peripheries of the expanding kingdom. The details of most of these smaller campaigns remain unknown, but Raombana, who informs us of them, estimated that total mortality averaged 25 percent by the time the men returned home (several months).[126] Discontent with the mortiferous conditions of military service became particularly acute after early 1821, when Radama announced that his officers would be recruiting a new set of men to undergo European-style training and serve in the military as permanent rather than temporary soldiers. The creation of a professional and permanent army after 1820 was Radama's military innovation of greatest social impact upon highland Malagasy society. Ever since his return to Antananarivo in 1820, Hastie had advised Radama "against any occurrence to the levy en masse for the purposes of warfare, & the substitution of a regular standing force, capable of enforcing the internal tranquillity of the Country."[127] This was finally accomplished when the treaty of alliance with Britain was reimplemented in late 1820.

With the aid of the literacy afforded by British missionaries and their students (scribes to create and manage lists and enumerations), Radama conducted a series of censuses throughout the kingdom.[128] In the process, census takers classified men as either soldiers (*miaramila*) or civilians (*borijano*, from the French term *bourgeois*) liable for royal labor service.[129] Considered occupational men of war, soldiers could be called upon to assemble at any time of the year, including the prime agricultural season. Not all soldiers stood an equal chance of serving in the life-consuming military campaigns of the 1820s, however. Some men classified as soldiers were more effectively defended from recruitment by their *firenena* and their individual patrons than others. Intimate connections between high officials in the military and their home *firenena*, for example, could spare some soldiers from actually being mobilized. Some communities were more proficient at falsifying ages, hiding their young men, or obtaining civilian classifications than others. Local recruiters could be convinced by various means, usually material, to pass up particular individuals. In addition, wealthy soldiers could normally

Figure 6.2 Graphite sketch of Radama reviewing his troops, "Vobouaze," east coast, 1823. Note the order in the ranks, muskets with bayonets, cannon, horses, and European attire of the soldiers and officers, especially their hats. (*Source*: B.-F. Leguével de Lacombe, *Voyage à Madagascar et aux îles Comores, 1823 à 1830* [Paris, 1840], vol. 1, frontispiece.)

purchase an exemption from service by paying fees in silver directly into the king's treasury.[130] Radama's foot soldiers, therefore, were among the poorest and most miserable men in the land. Access to more prestigious and lucrative positions as officers was restricted to men from wealthy families in celebrated and powerful *firenena* or to foreigners.

Recruitment into the standing army commenced in 1821. Early in that year, missionary Jones wrote,

> about 50,000 assembled together; the greatest number of them were the King's generals, Captains and heads of villages under Radama's dominion in Ova, not including other outward provinces who are in subjection to him also. He intends to take the field against the Sakalaves in the southwest in two months longer with an immense army of above 100,000 men to reduce them to subjection and quietness, and at the same time leaves an immense number at home to keep his territories from any outward enemies.[131]

The target of 100,000 professional soldiers suggested by Radama was very large and more a symbol of the king's determination to defeat the southern Sakalava than a seriously projected goal. Radama called his army "the 100,000 men" (*foloalindahy*), but his largest expeditions, which may have approached that number of people, were composed of significant proportions of civilians accompanying soldier kin. Radama was planning two major royal campaigns for 1822: a military expedition westward to secure the submission of the southern Sakalava (Menabe) king Ramitraho and a permanent military colony at Foulpointe on the east coast. Recruiting for these operations commenced in November 1821, just as the rains began to fall. Radama timed his draft and accompanying training exercises to coincide with the peak austral spring labor bottleneck when farmers normally prepared their fields and planted their crops. For several months over the primary agricultural season, collective attention focused on the preparations for war unfolding at Antananarivo. Soldiers were enlisted with the reluctant cooperation of the "heads of villages" (probably the *amboninjato*, heads of hundreds, and the *loholona*, "heads of the people"). Missionary David Griffiths reported the activity. "Though preparation for war is as repugnant to our private feelings as to our avowed principles," he noted, "we can not but admire His Majesty's proceedings in raising up such a mighty host since last Novembr, viz. Above 11,000 volunteered youth, well disciplined."[132] "Volunteered," that is, by the local "heads" on the orders of Radama. In late December Radama dispatched an official report of new recruits to James Hastie listing 11,100 freshly mustered soldiers distributed among the districts of Imerina as follows:[133]

Avaradrano	2,100
Vakinisisaony	2,100
Ambodirano	2,100
Marovatana	2,100
Voromahery	500
Vonizongo	1,500
Vakinankaratra[134]	350
Vakiniombifotsy[135]	250
Ny Mainty[136]	100

Barnsley, the temporary British envoy to Antananarivo during Hastie's absence in early 1822, reported that Radama continued recruiting throughout the rainy season. "Radama is daily increasing his Army," Barnsley wrote to Hastie on March 6, 1822, "and learning them their exercise."[137] By the end of March the number of recruits to the new European-trained core of the army numbered a full 13,000.[138] Radama devoted most of his time to overseeing the training and organization of these new soldiers.[139] The ambitious king announced he would depart Antananarivo with the new army just after celebration of the *fandroana* ceremonies of the Malagasy (lunar) new year that fell in mid-May 1822.[140]

RECRUITMENT AS ENSLAVEMENT

When judged solely by the number of households directly affected by the loss of young men, the creation of a permanently standing army was far more profound in its social impact than the export slave trade had ever been. During the half-century that some 70,000 captives were exchanged out of central Madagascar, the highlands sustained an average annual loss of about 1,300 individuals (some 3 per 1,000), most but not all of whom were adult men. Beginning in 1822, Radama marched from one end of Madagascar to another with armies and accompanying kin and servants sometimes numbering close to 100,000 people. Training or at war, often absent from home during the growing season, men no longer played the prominent role in domestic agriculture they once had. And many never returned home. Mortality within Radama's army was truly astounding.[141] Combat casualties were least responsible for deaths. Inadequate nutrition, starvation, and disease killed most of those who perished. With a minimal immunity to malaria, people from highland Madagascar quickly succumbed to malarial fevers (*tazo*) along the island's coasts. Mortality due to disease among coastal regiments was reported to reach as high as 50 percent per annum.[142] In 1822 alone, out of an expeditionary force of some 70,000 soldiers and their attendants who marched westward into the Sakalava land, some 25,000 to 30,000 never returned home; they died of starvation and disease.[143] Although no precise statistics are available, the annual mortality within Radama's armies suggested by these figures meant that, at the very least, military expansion removed men equal to several times the average annual number of slaves exported from the center of the island between 1770 and 1820.

In Radama's scheme of expansion, Imerina became a domestic labor reserve for military regiments and for vast corps of royal labor service.[144] "The formation of a regular National Army on the same discipline as the European soldiers has in great measure depopulated the province of Imerina, and indeed of all Madagascar," opined Merina historian Raombana at midcentury. The continual recruitment of new soldiers to replace those who had died during previous years "much annoyed" the people of highland Madagascar, he noted.[145] Paradoxically, the very instrument of Merina territorial expansion—the army—served to train highland attentions on the unpopular actions of the royal court at Antananarivo rather than to focus them on differentiating Merina identity from that of the conquered people of the kingdom. The army that made Merina political hegemony after 1809 weakened highland Malagasy *firenena* by siphoning men away from them. At the same time, it cut into the authority of *fokonolona* elders, the *loholona* whose participation in local governance Andrianampoinimerina had once sought to increase, by wresting control of the young men forming Radama's regiments from them. Uniting soldiers from across the kingdom together into his standing army, Radama nurtured a professional military identity independent of individual *firenena* and the affective ties of kinship. The standing army, unlike Andrianampoinimerina's temporarily mobilized farmer-soldiers, was fundamentally anti-kinship, despite the organization of regiments by *firenena*. Subject to the king's personal command, soldiers from particular *firenena* could be turned against their own, as happened in 1822 when women rose to challenge the king only to be repressed by their own sons.

If the early nineteenth century brought death and misery to thousands of men recruited and marched toward the periphery of Radama's expansive kingdom, it feminized households and experiences of poverty on the "home front" in Imerina. The demographic consequences produced by massive male conscription and mortality required women remaining in Imerina to implement far-reaching economic adaptations. Having performed distinct but equally valuable labor for the reproduction of households during the eighteenth century, the men and women of central Madagascar were being pushed and pulled into separate economic and social worlds by the early nineteenth. This process commenced during highland Madagascar's economy of enslavement (chapter 4), but it dramatically accelerated through Radama's regime of military expansion. During the early nineteenth century, British missionaries reported that the ratio of women to men in villages across Imerina commonly approached three, four, and sometimes even five to one![146] An influx into Imerina of female slaves captured beyond the highlands by Radama's expanding armies reinforced the feminization of the countryside.[147] Economically, culturally, and demographically the highland Malagasy countryside was becoming a women's world.[148]

A transformation in women's economic roles from textile producers to farmers that commenced during the late eighteenth century under the demographic pressure of the slave trade continued and accelerated after 1809. Their labor time increasingly consumed by agriculture and matters of nutritional survival, women did not weave with the regularity they once had. The history of women's cotton textile industries in nineteenth-century highland Madagascar has yet to be fully explored.[149] Cotton was still being cultivated and woven in central Madagascar during the early 1820s, as I noted in chapter 4, but the availability of Indian-manufactured fabrics imported through Mauritius and the northwest coast of the island—

together with the increasing demands of farming—kept women from spinning and weaving cotton for clothing as they formerly had. With food security foremost in their minds, highlanders began to reduce production of cotton, a labor-intensive crop.[150]

Parallels in economic transformation between the era of the slave trade and Radama's economy of expansion multiply when one considers the role of silver in highland Malagasy households. As did some highland Malagasy kings during the early era of the slave trade, Radama levied new fees and taxes payable in silver in 1821 to help support his expenditures for imported equipment and foreign officers in his new standing army.[151] Individuals could also exempt themselves from serving in the ranks if they paid a fee of ten piasters.[152] Not coincidentally, Radama imposed the new silver taxes and fees just when the export slave trade ended in 1820 and the flow of new silver into central Madagascar slowed to a trickle. The years after 1820 were silver-poor ones for most highland Malagasy as well as for Radama's treasury.[153] Significant reduction in the supply of silver just as Radama sought to increase the monetary tax burden on his citizen-subjects put highland households in a very difficult position, analogous to experiences in the era of the slave trade. Taxation in silver, which Andrianampoinimerina had sought to abolish, was being reinstated by his successor.

The household monetary crisis was exacerbated by the price of rice, which skyrocketed with each of Radama's military campaigns. Production suffered as a result of the absence of men and accompanying kin during the growing season and harvest. The market demand for rice with which to feed agriculturally unproductive soldiers also increased. Both these processes served to raise domestic prices.[154] While his people struggled to insure subsistence, Radama eschewed the rhetoric of agricultural progress that Andrianampoinimerina had so ardently and repeatedly articulated. In fact, through his strategies of expansion the king negated his father's promises of highlanders' right to subsistence. Once again facing a food crisis and an impending demographic catastrophe, highlanders began to vociferously claim Andrianampoinimerina's erstwhile populist promises and policies as "long-established regulation."

"The king's own mind" thus opened a breach in the fragile political alliance between rural communities and royalty established during the era of Andrianampoinimerina. Gone were the exhortations to *firenena* solidarity and identity, the policies that reinforced them, the rhetoric of assistance to the poor, the affirmations of a right to subsistence, the popular interventions in the market, and especially the promises of protection from alienation and death beyond *firenena* homeland. The standing army, like the age-grade regiments of king Shaka Zulu, a southern African contemporary of Radama, increased state authority by disempowering descent group elders. Radama was far more unpopular with his people than his enthusiastic British allies wished to believe.[155] Amid the divergences between the politics of Radama and those of Andrianampoinimerina there were also important convergences in the effects of their differing strategies of power on the relationship of the genders. Although it consumed the lives of so many highland men, the new army concentrated power in the hands of a small group of men who rose to the apex of the new regiments.[156] This did not represent a break with Andrianampoinimerina's tradition, but an extension of the differential experiences that his project of kingdom building had secured for men and women. The structure of the army and its system of military rank and honors was an exclusively male domain, built upon the further transformation of women into farmers and a disempowerment of increasingly feminized households. The pattern of economic and gender asymmetries that Radama accelerated through his ambitious military conquests were fundamentally similar to those pursued by Andrianampoinimerina: the institutionalization and professionalization of male power in new structures of administration and military, on the one hand, and the socioeconomic neglect and marginalization of women managing the agricultural economy, on the other. While the new military structure offered a novel domain for advancing male power within the societies of highland Madagascar, it also provided the context for increased control over the sexuality of soldiers' wives. Like Andrianampoinimerina, Radama imposed several sexual restrictions on the female partners of his male recruits.[157]

Radama not only faced opposition from among the friends of Andrianampoinimerina who stood to lose control of the political apparatus from which they derived their prestige and wealth, then, he encountered an increasingly disgruntled public, especially the *firenena* elders, or *loholona*. Fundamentally in question was the right and ability of the king to ignore Andrianampoinimerina's erstwhile promises and to arrogate to himself the prerogative of taking the kingdom in the direction of a personal ambition, whatever the consequences for the *firenena*, the men, and the women from whom he ultimately required support and consent. Those who observed Radama in his daily business commented on the inordinate number of bodyguards that surrounded him as he moved in public and on his frequent promenades about Antananarivo in disguise to secretly ascertain the disposition of his people toward their sovereign.[158] By April of 1822 the collective attention of the kingdom centered on developments at the royal court and their practical influence on the daily lives and livelihoods of people across the kingdom. Open protest of Radama's exigent policies burst forth in a cultural idiom whose import was scarcely understood by contemporary foreigners in Antananarivo and seldom explored by modern scholars of central Madagascar. When women demanded that Radama observe a "traditional" hairstyle in April 1822, they were one of the many local groups then acting to ethnicize Merina identity, drawing strength from the memory and populist political rhetoric of Andrianampoinimerina.

THE CONTENTIOUS LANGUAGE OF HAIR

On April 3, 1822, Radama cut his hair, severing the customary plaits from his head.[159] Some accounts suggest that before cropping his own hair the king observed and contemplated the shearing of his brother's plaits, a carefully braided hairstyle sported by both men and women.[160] "The hair is divided into a great number of small tresses, varying according to fancy," reported two contemporary observers of Malagasy hairdos, "and a great deal of time is spent in keeping it in order" (see Photograph 6.1).[161] British missionaries described highland Malagasy hairstyles in greater detail.

> The Hovas dress it in numerous plaits one over another, on each side; the women placing gold and silver pins in one or two particular plaits in front, above the forehead. . . . Those of rank and property amongst the Malagasy frequently have their hair braided, and arranged in such a manner as to present a beautiful and elegant appearance, being formed into a large number of knots and ringlets, which are tastefully arranged in rows, circles, or sections, and richly supplied with valuable unguents. There are ten or twelve different modes of plaiting, and of arranging the plaits, having their distinctive names. A difference is sometimes, though very rarely, observed between married and unmarried women, in this part of their personal ornament; the former wearing their hair twisted up, and secured on the top of the head, while the latter allow it to flow negligently over the shoulders.[162]

Highlanders employed nearly thirty terms to describe their "fantastically plaited" hairstyles, some ten of which referred to men's hairdos.[163] Visiting highland Madagascar in 1825, Englishman Henry Singer Keating assessed some of these hairdos in critical terms but through an analogy readily accessible to his compatriots. "Their heads," he wrote, "were dressed in the Ovah fashion, viz., made into a great number of small plaits or cords, knotted at the ends and hanging down about their ears, presenting an appearance very like the mops they wash the carriages with in England." Not all styles were so aesthetically displeasing to him, though. "They had it beautifully plaited and frizzed out, according to the Malgache

Photograph 6.1 Malagasy woman with plaited hairstyle. This photograph, probably of a Bara woman from the region of Ihosy (not part of Imerina), was taken near the beginning of the twentieth century. Her plaits are similar to those sported by men and women in highland Madagascar during the early nineteenth century. (*Photo Credit*: Ole Jensenius, courtesy of the Norwegian Missionary Society, Stavanger, Madagascar Photograph number 0839.)

fashion," he noted later of another set of coiffures, "and I am certain that the head dress of half-a-dozen Paris belles would not take up the time that theirs must have done."[164]

Finding his brother's new crewcut to his taste, Radama promptly eliminated his plaits, too, trimming his hair close to his head. When the king appeared in public, his hairdo astounded both Malagasy and foreigners. Unexpected, its multivalent symbolism was electric. Highlanders cut their hair short (*mibory*) only when in mourning for the loss of a sovereign.[165] To effect his change in hairstyle, Radama requisitioned one of the foreign workmen sponsored by British missionaries to the royal court. Missionary David Griffiths explained.

> His Majesty employed one of the Artizans to cut his hair at his country seat. When his Majesty returned, came an announcement to us Missionaries that he has cut his hair and now looks one of us. The pride of these people consisted not in cleanliness and dress, but in plaiting their long black hair, neatly and curiously. Of this they thought a great deal, and I am certain that if a person would offer any of them a thousand pounds for cutting his hair, he would not accept of it.[166]

For Griffiths, the king's haircut was remarkable in that it represented a rupture with folk traditions of personal grooming, a negation of cultural pride. Plaited hairstyles were such an integral part of highland culture, Griffiths reasoned, that they even lay beyond the influence of market forces. Gerald Berg writes that highland Malagasy women were offended by Radama's haircut because they considered grooming men's hair to be their own prerogative. That custom was negated by the king's turn to foreign barbers and, of course, by parting with his own plaits.[167] Reflecting the primary concerns of the *ambaniandro*, on the other hand, *Tantara* narratives link Radama's haircut to military recruitment into the new standing army during the austral summer of 1821–1822. Like civilians, highland soldiers regularly plaited their hair. "In 1817," reported Lewis Locke, "as I passed through Radama's encampment, I observed a female taking great pains in plaiting a man's hair, and I was told that this was a regular custom among them."[168] Ratefy—Radama's military commander-in-chief, his sister's husband, and member of the *maroseranina*—returned to Antananarivo from a short visit to London early in 1822. While in England he had observed military inductees having their heads shaved and recommended the practice to Radama for his newest recruits. Radama concurred. As supreme commander of his regiments, he set an example by first shaving his own head and then commanding his newly recruited soldiers to do the same. Raombana also links hair cutting to the military, suggesting that James

Hastie urged Radama to shave his recruits so their plaits would no longer "grease his military Hats and uniforms." The king's haircut could speak in multiple ways.[169]

The meanings of hair in highland Madagascar, as I have emphasized throughout this work, were rich, varied, and closely associated with notions of social well-being and political order. To have one's hair cut short by the hand of another was to socially subordinate oneself to that person and to have the transition from an independent to a dependent social status marked visually upon the body.[170] When highland armies marched war captives back to Imerina as slaves, for example, they shaved the individuals' heads as a badge of dishonor and a symbol of their newfound servitude and subordination. The hair of condemned criminals was likewise sheared.[171] When in the late eighteenth century the king of Marovatana (see Map 5.1) developed a reputation for illegitimately enslaving his own subjects, highlanders renamed him Rabehety, "Mr. big scissors," a reference to his penchant for cutting the hair of ill-gotten captives.[172] For Andrianampoinimerina to claim the right to "mix hairs," to braid the many *firenena* of the kingdom into a complex social coiffure, and to cut the hair of his recruits was to assert his sovereignty. Symbolically, then, by shaving his head at the hands of foreigners, Radama marked himself as a subordinate, even a prisoner, of his British allies.[173] It was powerfully emotional symbolism. Recall that during the "negotiations" for an end to the slave trade, the heads of local communities had accused Radama of being a slave to the English (page 228). This popular perception was now visibly fulfilled before the collective eyes of the kingdom.

Many civilian men interpreted Radama's haircut as a prescription for them similarly to shave off their plaits. Mission schoolboys and men directly surrounding Radama sought the king's approval (or, perhaps, escape from his wrath) by avidly responding to his message. "Their attachment to the King and their high regard for his character and notions," reported David Griffiths

> are such that they thought nothing of their plaited hair & would not rest satisfied till the King was pleased to give them his consent to cut theirs also. On the following morning the children of the school and the principal folks in town would give us no rest either tormenting us to cut their hair or to lend them combs & scissors, saying that they become like the whites whom they call vazaa.[174]

By cutting his hair in the European military fashion, Radama inscribed royal policy upon his body. Visually symbolized by the rapid spread of hair cutting among soldiers, court officers, and schoolboys, the new ideas introduced by European counselors at the court were being embraced as useful tools of royal politics. Specifically, hair cutting served as a potent symbol for the ascendancy of the standing army and for transformations in the experiences of men and women that that it entailed. In many cultures, including those of highland Madagascar, hair symbolizes adulthood, fertility, and sexuality. In the ceremony of *ala volo*, or child's first hair cutting, women eagerly ingested clipped remnants of children's first hair growth to enhance their fertility.[175] Hair cutting is a common practice in rites of passage around the world and, in the context of hair's multivalent symbolism, is often understood as a metaphor for emasculation.[176] We cannot be certain that highlanders understood the king's haircut in precisely this way, but stories of hair cutting were one of the languages in which the people of central Madagascar talked about political relationships. According to a popular historical narrative from the nineteenth century, Andriamanalinabetsileo, king of the Andrantsay confederation, forced Andrianampoinimerina to negotiate with him on important political matters by secretly shaving off his (Andrianampoinimerina's) beard and the hair on one side of his head, sapping him of his power.[177] The *ambaniandro* had shaved their own heads four times in mourning for Andrianampoinimerina, cutting away symbols of their vitality and fertility, expressing the painful loss of a popular sovereign through practices of personal grooming.

Hair cutting in April 1822 coincided with important transitions in men's and women's experiences within Radama's expanding kingdom. Shearing men's heads of their hairdos brought recruits through an emotional rite of passage into the new masculine world of the standing army where royal power imposed on personal autonomy and *firenena* communities in new and menacing ways, with all its practical consequences for men's and women's lives. As elsewhere, hair cutting in highland Madagascar signified relationships of social constraint and power. This was most immediately manifest in the cutting of slaves' hair, as we have seen, but it applied more broadly. More than symbolically, the autonomy men lost as their plaited hair fell to the ground Radama appropriated for himself. The standing army, as I have demonstrated, was no longer based upon the traditions of Andrianampoinimerina that guaranteed a right to subsistence, nor even on a European model that provided remuneration for services rendered—it rested on a ruinously extortionate system in which Radama provided little in return but occasional war booty for the sacrifices of his people and the lives of his men. By having their plaits cut away, highland men passed into a new form of subordination to royal power.

A sovereign's head shorn of its plaits spoke in additional ways. Dispossessed of its patterns, plaits, and groomed divisions, Radama's hair could no longer symbolize the kingdom as parted and ordered into its proper or legitimate social and political subunits. An undifferentiated chaos of hair now replaced the careful partitions and rankings of districts, *firenena*, and status groups once enacted by Andrianampoinimerina and symbolically displayed every day upon the king's head and those of his men and women. Given highlanders' experiences with the new king since the death of Andrianampoinimerina, Radama's haircut assumed especial meaning, for personal grooming spoke directly to political intentions. Was Radama intimating he would no longer respect the social hierarchies of Andrianampoinimerina's "traditional" political order and its protections for *firenena* and common households? Having created a standing army by disregarding the military practices of his father that promised to only temporarily call upon the men of the kingdom, was Radama now seeking to transform the social and administrative structure of the kingdom to his personal benefit? While Radama's haircut raised questions about the appropriateness and legitimacy of his political intentions, he simultaneously advocated sartorial innovations, deepening highlanders' experiences of cultural transformation. "Ever since this time," wrote David Griffiths of Radama's haircut, "the King dressed himself every day in an European dress, and many of the people have put on hats and caps and have paid greater attention to cleanliness and dress. The greatest part of the caps they wear, were made by themselves, a good imitation of our caps."[178] Radama intended his subjects to adopt elements of European clothing and personal grooming; apparently, many men had awaited just this moment to sport publicly the innovative imitations of European style they had privately fashioned from local products. Also disturbing was Radama's failure to consult with his people about the royally sanctioned cultural changes. Unlike Andrianampoinimerina, Radama seldom conferred with his citizen-subjects in grand assemblies (*kabary*). "After the formation of the army," wrote British missionaries perceptively, "these councils of the nation became less frequent and are now mere matters of form."[179] One of the most striking contrasts between *Tantara* narratives of Andrianampoinimerina and of Radama is the relative paucity of *kabary* the latter king is reported to have delivered in comparison to the former. Maintaining legitimately "ordered" social divisions within the kingdom by consulting with the *ambaniandro* about royal intentions and innovations was one of the fundamental bases of royal power and ritual; it was popularly seen as a primary responsibility of the sovereign. Social order produced through consultation insured blessing, which in turn brought agricultural and human fertility.[180] In highland Madagascar, as elsewhere, hair also served as a metaphor for fertility.[181]

Of concern to everyone, human fertility most directly affected women's lives. Highland Malagasy recognized the awesome procreative power of women and, as in many cultures, viewed women as the sole genitors of children.[182] This capacity was recognized in social vocabulary: highland Malagasy conceptualized *firenena* as "motherhoods" (recall that the root of *firenena* is *reny*, mother), suggesting that all kinspeople ultimately issued from the same womb. While the king and male elders claimed to channel ancestral blessings and fertility to women through public ritual, women actively pursued their own fertility through a variety of practices including and excluding men.[183] Take, for example, women's practice of *vaky volo* ("parting hair"), a ritual hair grooming in preparation for a boy's circumcision ceremony.[184] On the appointed day for the *vaky volo*, hairdressers parted and braided women's hair so it was divided into four fields representing the four districts at the center of Imerina. The social cohesiveness of the kingdom was symbolically insured by inscribing royally sanctioned social divisions on women's heads. Each section of the hairdo, neatly parted and separated from the others, represented the political order that Andrianampoinimerina imposed on his kingdom, a precondition, according to royal ideology, of agricultural and human fertility.

Because of the connections between body symbolism and the body politic, when women's cultures of fertility burst out into the open they could provoke dramatic political transformations. Both the women's revolt of 1822 and the *ramanenjana* spirit possession movements of 1863, for example, challenged kings to observe rituals that represented sovereigns as the source of fertility. In 1822 the women of Avaradrano district were defeated, as will presently be seen, but in 1863 country women possessed by *ramanenjana* spirits enacted rituals of fertility and clothed themselves with symbols of fertility to demand that their king (Radama II, r. 1861–1863) observe his ritual responsibilities. Their protest ultimately toppled the reigning sovereign and led to a revolution in political leadership.[185] By cutting his hair in April 1822 and requiring his male soldiers and civilians to do the same, Radama eliminated a premier body symbol of royal responsibility that insured the fertility and well-being of his people. As anthropologist Jeannette Marie Mageo recently argued with reference to female sexuality in Samoa, body symbols such as hair assume especial public moral significance in moments of profound social transformation.[186] Grooming the "symbolic body" emblazoned visible moral messages on the person. As "moral codes written on the body," transformed hairdos signified the passing of Andrianampoinimerina's moralized economy. Hair cutting coincided with a shifting balance between local autonomy and royal power in which, to the members of *firenena*, the king symbolically eschewed his moral obligation to insure social order or to honor Andrianampoinimerina's "long-established tradition." To Radama and his subjects, hair cutting embodied manifold and interconnected meanings. All these varied meanings, however, led many highland Malagasy to the same conclusion: shearing off the king's plaits and those of his male subjects were negligent and dangerous acts in a moment of political crisis. Hair cutting was an unjustified constraint on the autonomy of the common people and threatened to produce a new sociopolitical chaos in which established traditions structuring the relationship between *firenena* and the sovereign were dishonored by the new king. Most poignantly and pertinently, these menacing developments smacked of the untrustworthy relationships that festered between leaders and their subjects during the age of the slave trade.

Royal hair shorn of its plaits spoke in manifold ways, yet it was the women of Avaradrano district, Radama's homeland (see Map 5.1), who openly challenged the king in April 1822. The practical hardships imposed upon women by the absence of their men in the army, the loss of a valued cultural privilege (plaiting the hair of their menfolk), and the especial personal and emotional importance of rituals of fertility to them explains, in part, why it was women and not men who challenged the king. Narratives of the rebellion suggest additional reasons. Interpretive differences in the extant narratives of hair cutting during 1822 confirm that both gender and social position shaped experiences in Radama's expansionist kingdom. The women who joined together in protest were from "a district to the North," wrote the missionaries, almost certainly Avaradrano. *Tantara* narratives confirm this.[187] Of all six districts, Avaradrano retained premier status in Andrianampoinimerina's social hierarchy.[188] Avaradrano was the homeland of Andrianampoinimerina, Radama, and of most of the founder king's "friends" whom the new sovereign had removed from positions of command in the army.

The women of Avaradrano, therefore, represented a politically influential region of the kingdom whose erstwhile leaders had experienced significant disenfranchisement over the preceding decade. Radama's symbolic disregard for differentially ranked social and political divisions through both hair cutting (which applied to all soldiers, regardless of status) and the alienation of the "friends" would thus have been seen as a particular insult by the privileged *hova* and *andriana* of Avaradrano. Most of the children attending the two mission schools in Antananarivo hailed from well-placed Avaradrano families. As primary household and agricultural managers in the absence of their men who served in the king's armies, women were more immediately affected by the extension of royal labor service to children through European education, a process that removed youngsters from the household economy and socialized them in a setting far from parental control.

If women took the rhetoric and political implications of hair cutting seriously, so too did the king. The manner in which Radama viewed the women's challenge is conveyed by missionaries in their *History of Madagascar.* The foreigners' narrative suggests that Radama was uncertain of the fidelity of his new military recruits.

> Against the public innovations, a spirit of daring opposition was evinced by a number of females in a neighbouring district, and a large meeting was held, to which the discontented repaired. Information of these proceedings soon reached the capital. About two thousand soldiers were immediately summoned; they renewed their oaths of allegiance, promising that whoever should be found guilty of creating a disturbance, *even if their own parents should be implicated*, they required but the king's order or permission to put them to death: after these assurances of fidelity, the soldiers were ordered to guard the capital.[189]

What was striking about the oath Radama administered to his new standing troops was its antifilial, anti*firenena* rhetoric ("even if their own parents should be implicated, they required but the king's order or permission to put them to death"). Many of Radama's elite troops, it is known, were sons of Avaradrano. The contrast between Andrianampoinimerina, who is remembered to have aligned royal power with a reemphasis on kinship and community, and Radama, who required his soldiers of diverse *firenena* to forswear the affinities of kin, suggests that highland Malagasy perceived the young king's actions as fundamentally antikinship.[190] The following day, April 16, between 4,000 and 5,000 women gathered at Ambatoroka, a village immediately to the east of Antananarivo. United in their resolve, reports David Griffiths in his journal for that day, they dispatched messengers to the royal court to protest Radama's innovations,

> saying that they came hither to inform his Majesty that they were not satisfied with all his proceedings. The King sent to them back to demand what were their grievances. Whether they were vexed because their friends and relations were made soldiers and employed in his service, or because they were too heavily taxed. To these questions they gave negative answers. But the ladies and the principal ones came forward & said that they came hither to testify that they were dissatisfied with His Majesty's proceedings, and to request Him to change his conduct, and put an end to or deliver the whites in town to them. His Majesty sent them a second message to ask them, Was he not King and could not he do as he pleased in these things without consulting them.[191]

The Avaradrano women emphasized they were not questioning Radama's right to tax them or to take soldiers from among their male kin, but that they

were disturbed by his departure from tradition through hair cutting and favoritism for foreigners, and, by association, with his neglect of royal responsibilities. Although the women denied the relevance of recent taxation initiatives and military recruitment to their revolt, Radama's mention of these two
potential grievances suggests both of them were not only plausible but weighing heavily upon his and his subjects' minds. Instead of confronting the king
over material matters, however, the women chose to dispute Radama by reference to a rhetoric of tradition that implied a breach in royal responsibility
("they were dissatisfied with His Majesty's proceedings . . . conduct").

History of Madagascar provides a longer, more detailed, and slightly altered account of what transpired between Radama and the women from
Avaradrano on April 16.

> In reply, Radama sent to ask them what were their grievances; if they were
> too heavily taxed, or if they were displeased at having their sons employed
> in the army; whether he were their king or not, and whether they had cho-
> sen some other king in his stead? They replied to these questions in the
> negative; but said, they were the caretakers [probably *mpitaiza*, a word
> suggesting the relationship between nurse and child] of the king, and com-
> plained because he had adopted the customs of the foreigners; had allowed
> them to teach him and his people; had changed the customs of his ances-
> tors; and, finally, he had cut off his hair, and drank spirituous liquors.
> Radama sent back a message to ask, if, being king, he had not a right to do
> as he pleased with his hair without consulting women; reminding them, it
> was the inalienable right of the twelve monarchs [an allusion to traditions
> of royal rule] to do as they pleased, and added, that he would presently
> give them proof of this, by taking care that their own hair should never
> grow again.[192]

The terms in which Radama and the women debated hair cutting are
captured in this fascinating portion of the British missionaries' account.
Radama suggested that perhaps the women were displeased because of
taxation and military recruitment, the legitimacy of which he attributed
to royal prerogative ("whether he were their king or not"). But however
much military recruitment and the recently imposed monetary tax weighed
upon his subjects, they were not the grounds upon which the Avaradrano
women chose to found their grievances. There were more powerful and
legitimate bases, they believed, for complaint. While they did not feel
empowered to directly challenge taxation and recruitment, which it is
known they in fact resented (see earlier in this chapter), they boldly
claimed Radama "had adopted the customs of the foreigners" and "had
changed the customs of his ancestors." Radama was flouting his ritual
responsibilities as provided in "tradition," which during the reign of An-

drianampoinimerina and in the myth of the "twelve sovereigns" he al-
luded to in the above account, had assumed popular dimensions through
alignment with *firenena* and the reaffirmation of kinship. Radama answered the women in kind with a rhetoric of tradition, but one adjusted
to his own interests. Was it not tradition, he inquired, for kings to act as
they wished ("the inalienable right of the twelve monarchs to do as they
pleased")? The king's ultimate responsibility, he claimed, was to himself,
not to his people. As does the missionaries' account, the *Tantara* suggests
that Radama emphasized his "traditional" prerogative as king to make
his own decisions without consulting his people. "Whoever has brought
these words to me," Radama is reported to have retorted, "whoever, whoever, let them be executed. Whether women or children were the source
of this speech, they have forbidden me to carry out my desire. What they
have done prevents me from being king, so I shall execute whoever for-
bids me to carry out my will. So I appeal to you *ambaniandro* not to
forbid me from the accomplishment of my desire."[193]

If Radama interpreted the revolt as an unjustified and insolent popular
challenge to royal authority, British missionaries felt they were the primary
target of the women's grievances. ("But the ladies and the principal ones
came forward & said that they came hither to testify that they were dissatisfied with His Majesty's proceedings, and to request Him to change his conduct, and put an end to or deliver the whites in town to them," wrote David
Griffiths.) *Tantara* accounts, on the other hand, while not exonerating foreigners of responsibility for the king's actions, emphasize why it was the
Avaradrano women who stepped forward to challenge their king. All three
versions of the revolt in the compendium of popular narratives stress people's
disbelief and shock over Radama's haircut and his desire to extend hair cutting to the military. Because of Avaradrano's seniority among the districts,
relates one narrative, the *ambaniandro* of the entire kingdom appointed men
from that particular district to confront Radama. Unlike contemporary European accounts, *Tantara* narratives further suggest that the men of Avaradrano
put their womenfolk up to the task of confronting the king instead of doing
it themselves.

> The *ambaniandro* gathered and delivered speeches saying: "What shall
> we do about this, *ambaniandro*? Radama has shaved his head. Even
> among the twelve kings who reigned none ever shaved his head! But
> Radama now cuts his hair, shaves it off. So what shall we do about
> this, *ambaniandro*? Let us go and advise him (*hananatra azy*)." And so
> they discussed among themselves. And when the *ambaniandro* spoke
> they said: "You people of Avaradrano go first and advise him, and if
> you do not succeed in teaching him, then we shall all unite, for you

Avaradrano are the fathers of the *ambaniandro*." And then Avaradrano also spoke and said, "You go first, you children and women to advise Radama, telling him in your kind of talk (*ny fiteninareo*), we have come to advise you. Sir: do not cut your hair for this is not a custom observed by kings, sir, say we children and women from Avaradrano. King Andriantsimitoviaminandriana did not cut his hair, Andriambelomasina ruled and never cut his hair; Andrianampoinimerina also ruled and never clipped his hair. Now we have you, Radama, and you create a military, and you cut your hair. Sir, this hair cutting is not a custom of kings."[194]

Tantara texts thus claim that the women who confronted the king were merely a front for men displeased about the formation of the standing army and Radama's breach of royal custom in clipping his hair. Unlike the missionaries' narrative, which was from the cultural outside but nevertheless contemporary, the *Tantara* account, recorded more than two generations later, and probably from male informants, transforms a contemporary version of the revolt in which men were peripheral to the protest—indeed, many of them were even complicit in hair cutting—into one in which they appear as the prime movers, inciting the Avaradrano women into action. What is particularly revealing about this passage is the reason it adduces for why the men sent their women and children to confront Radama: their "kind of talk." The reasoning is not explicit here, but the narrative likely refers to a common highland Malagasy perception that women's speech is more publicly and acceptably direct and confrontational than men's.[195] Narratives composed by men during the mid-nineteenth century cite the efficacy of women's speech as the reason for sending them to confront Radama.

Having assured himself the allegiance of the 2,000 soldiers who guarded Antananarivo on the night of April 15, Radama resolved to act with force. When the next day more than 4,000 women gathered at Ambatoroka, just east of Antananarivo, and dispatched messengers to him, the king, Griffiths reports, replied with orders of his own.

The next orders issued, were to select the principal people out of the crowd, & ask all who were the first instigators of this mutiny. Were there any men that excited them to this, or was it merely their own inventions &c &c. They boldly replied they and they alone were the only instigators of it, and said that every woman of note, even the King's own mother, should be fined a spanish dollar [a silver piaster] that would refuse to join them. The next orders delivered were to set 4 of the principal ones apart and as soon as the gun fired, the soldiers *of the very same district* ran with great speed and put these four women to death with the point of their bayonets.[196]

In a potent rejection of *firenena* loyalty, Radama commanded soldiers from Avaradrano to execute women of their own district. As in the *Tantara* narrative, where men claimed to have put women up to the revolt, Griffiths reports that Radama questioned the protesters about whether men were behind their action or whether they were acting on their own. Although Griffiths does not answer this question explicitly, his version of the events suggests that the women acted on their own initiative, just as they had claimed to Radama. Accepting this information, Radama proceeded with executions of key female leaders. The missionaries' account elaborates upon Radama's strategy of repression in greater and slightly different detail.

> Having ascertained who were the ringleaders, five of them were selected, and orders were given to *the soldiers of their districts and families* so to cut off their hair that it should never grow again. The order was mournfully obeyed, and they perished under the bayonets of the soldiers in sight of the multitudes of females, and a vast concourse of people from the town. . . . The bodies of the five women who were put to death, remained upon the spot until they were devoured by dogs and birds. The company of rebellious females were detained where they had assembled during the space of three days, guarded by troops, and without food or shelter. They entreated to be released, and said, that unless the king should exercise mercy, they must all perish. He then sent word that they might return to their respective homes, and attend to their domestic duties, but must leave the business of government to himself, and not interfere again in the affairs of the kingdom.[197]

In his account, Raombana alleges Radama was drunk, executing three elderly women of very high rank (*zanakambony*) and severely flogging the rest before releasing them. Having ordered execution of the women's leaders at the hands of their own sons, reports Griffiths, Radama assured the missionaries of his protection.

> These women (said He) were disaffected, because they wished to remain for ever in ignorance, be like beasts, and fools, and because I would have them instructed, and become wise, and like Europeans, because they were displeased with Him for cutting his hair or the consulting them [i.e., foreigners] and also adopting European customs. That he had put four of the principal ones to death and that we need not fear nor apprehend any evil on account of that, for I (said he) will arrange all these things as to put an end at once to such wicked tricks as these. We thanked Him, for his gracious promises of regard and protection.[198]

The Avaradrano women's revolt of April 1822, the single most overt popular challenge to royal power in nineteenth-century highland Madagascar, ended in ostensible defeat. It was a bitter failure, for the women were unable to impose their version of royal responsibility upon the king. In turn, Radama renounced his political and administrative alliance with *firenena* by commanding his soldiers to repress their own kin. In their fateful challenge to Radama on the grounds of violated tradition, however, the women of Avaradrano had claimed certain rights as citizens and taken a step toward ethnicizing Merina political identity and reminding their king that there *were* popular limits to the exercise of his power, even when he claimed the upper hand through mobilization of his new instrument of repression, the standing army.

ETHNICITY AND THE RHETORIC OF TRADITION

Each of the preceding narratives reporting Radama's haircut and women's opposition to it places a rhetoric of tradition and royal responsibility at the core of highlanders' concerns. The king and his citizen-subjects both accepted that "ancestral tradition" (*fomban-drazana*) should guide the actions of the sovereign, but each understood that tradition differently and did so for specific reasons. As Andrianampoinimerina had in his day, Radama claimed royal innovation as tradition to justify his social reforms. Clinging to their memory of the popular political traditions of Andrianampoinimerina (which they also attributed to the founder king's ancestors), on the other hand, the women of Avaradrano challenged Radama to steer his behavior toward a popular or civic vision of royal virtue that placed constraints on the sovereign's power. In so doing, the Avaradrano women drew from the toolbox of Merina political identity that assumed a moral bond and alliance between highlanders and their ruler. The women acted to position that new political identity in opposition to royal power, which had promoted it in the first place. When highland Malagasy claimed tradition to press their citizenship interests at the royal court, as they did during Radama's rule and throughout the reigns of his successors, they acted to transform their political identity into an ethnicity.

A politicized collective identity grounded in a claimed common origin, cultural unity, shared history, and sense of mutual moral obligation, an ethnicity is established through purposeful action, through attempts to place cultural sentiments and practices in the service of particular interests. Andrianampoinimerina had made Merina identity a condition of submission to royal power. Highlanders claimed Merina identity for themselves after the death of Andrianampoinimerina and defended its traditions, as they knew and desired them, to achieve specific political goals of local autonomy, a right to subsistence, and modestly responsible government in the particular historical circumstances of Radama's reign. While Andrianampoinimerina and his successors sought to promote being Merina as a political identity to expand their power and the number of their subjects, commoners asserted it differently, using that same identity to define proper behavior for themselves and royalty and to protect *firenena* from the excesses of royal power. Merina identity and its traditions were useful cultural resources for both sovereign and citizen-subject; because of this dual utility, highlanders and their rulers came into conflict over Merina identity, its practices, and behaviors. While Radama sought to confirm his power through a royal vision of civic virtue as unquestioned obedience by highlanders to the personal will of the sovereign, commoners defined civic virtue as the preservation of *firenena* and their constituent households through adherence to the key principles of Andrianampoinimerina's erstwhile government—by emphasizing the sovereign's alliance with *firenena*. Before and after the Avaradrano women's revolt, highlanders repeatedly challenged royalty to live up to the excellent example of Andrianampoinimerina (more on this in chapter 7). While they, too, attempted to appropriate the memory of Andrianampoinimerina to legitimize changes in royal policy, rulers were decidedly less enthusiastic about the memory of the founder king than were their subjects.[199] No one recited Andrianampoinimerina's praises more vigorously than the commoners of highland Madagascar, from whom François Callet collected historical narratives after 1864.[200]

Throughout the nineteenth century and even into the twentieth, discourses of tradition and memories of Andrianampoinimerina remained cultural resources for highlanders and underpinned an ever-changing Merina identity. When highland Malagasy contested ancestral tradition, they actively sought to appropriate the rhetoric of royal power, or "ancestral authority" and "*hasina* ideology" as scholars of highland Madagascar have variously termed it (see chapter 5), to popular interests. Tradition, ancestral authority, and *hasina* ideologies were the stuff of everyday political struggles, cultural idioms through which highland Malagasy contested fundamental social-political relationships and expressed their citizenship responsibilities to one another.[201] Through their traditions, highland Malagasy mobilized "the power of knowledge concerning proper conduct" to influence the behavior of their sovereigns and to shape their life circumstances.[202] If a political discourse of ancestral tradition remained visible and popular in highland Malagasy public affairs over the years, the varying and specific purposes to which highlanders deployed it challenges Maurice Bloch's proposition that royal ideology and its rituals are formalized and separated from the realm of everyday life and experience in highland Madagascar.

In a succession of publications, Bloch has argued that highland Madagascar presents a paradox of dramatic sociopolitical transformation over the last two centuries while ritual symbolism, the source of a "traditional ideology" empowering sovereigns, has remained remarkably stable. "The Merina case is a case where ideology is strongly developed by ritual although it is vague as ideology always is," he writes. The unvarying and "vague" ideology of Merina ritual serves the interests of an equally vague "traditional authority," or "*hasina* ideology" in the words of Gerald Berg, embodied in those rituals and benefiting elders and sovereigns. The fundamental ideology of highland Malagasy ritual seldom changes, Bloch explains, because ritual language and gestures, including types of ritualized dance, are fixed and highly formalized, largely resistant to innovation. Kings and chiefs (much less commoners) cannot fundamentally manipulate or transform that ideology of traditional authority, but rulers can benefit from it by strategically positioning themselves as mediators of ancestral blessing, or the power of *hasina*, to their retainers and subjects. For Bloch, the meanings of ritual, traditional authority, and ideologies of ancestral blessing are fixed and rigid, passing through the centuries largely unchanged even when specific ritual actions are themselves modified in particular historical circumstances. If the ritual practices that articulated royal ideology have a history, royal ideology itself does not. Ritual communication, Bloch writes, is "a system of communication which has largely given up the power of creativity." He continues: "The effect of formalization and the impossibility of linguistic creativity means that ritual is a kind of tunnel into which one plunges, and where, since there is no possibility of turning either to right or left, the only thing to do is to follow." In highland Madagascar, an enduring traditional ideology stems from this "dualism of knowledge [ritual] and mind [everyday consciousness]."[203]

With this study, I suggest a different way of understanding royal power in highland Madagascar, one rooted in a history of enslavement, social conflict, and political struggle. Inasmuch as ideology issues from the things people say and do, it is helpful to think of the making and reshaping of royal power through peoples' reflective choices of political strategies and rhetorical languages rather than to postulate a stable, unchanging, and vague "ideology." The cultural resources highland Malagasy employed in their political encounters were drawn from the practices of everyday life and the knowledge derived from experience; these resources were available to both rulers and ruled. The cultural idiom rulers employed to articulate and rationalize their power in highland Madagascar, for example, was the same idiom in which commoners ordered local politics. The language, practices, and objects of royal power derived from the mundane and from the populace; they did not exist in a separate or privileged domain of reality and experience. The Malagasy language and its meanings, of course, were the common heritage of all highlanders. Royal rituals, such as the circumcision explored by Bloch in a book-length monograph, or even the royal bath, developed from long-standing practices within the *firenena* taken up instrumentally by the rulers of highland Madagascar.[204] Even the royal talismans were procured from local intellectuals in the countryside, brought to Antananarivo, and set to the work of legitimizing rulers' sovereignty.[205] In highland Madagascar, royal power founded itself on intensely familiar languages, practices, and objects. The reproduction of certain ways of speaking about royal power and sovereignty was not the inevitable outcome of a lack of choice, innovation, or original interpretation of formalized ritual. It was the cumulative result of many specific and individual elections to employ an intimate and influential rhetoric of tradition to pursue disparate interests, especially in times of crisis characterized by enslavement and recruitment into a standing army. The reason for certain continuities in political language, ritual symbolism, and historical memory in highland Madagascar lay not in formalized and unreflective repetition but in the renaissance and renovation of familiar and powerful words and practices in new circumstances.

If common highlanders reinforced royal power by resisting it with a cultural-political vocabulary shared by royalty, they nevertheless employed the most effective rhetorical strategy available to them when they claimed that Radama was violating tradition and taking them back into the chaos of *fanjakana hova*. By appropriating the languages of royal power and images of Andrianampoinimerina as their own, commoners defended their interests most effectively, and sovereigns were forced to directly confront them or to adjust their behavior (or both simultaneously). Ritual was a source of social power and ideology in highland Madagascar, but it was not the sole source nor one unavailable to the innovations of leaders or their citizen-subjects. When they claimed that Radama was failing to live up to Merina tradition by clipping his plaits, the women of Avaradrano dared directly challenge their king. Appropriating royal languages to popular interests was not to relinquish autonomy to a traditional authority, but to pragmatically reassert it for a populist one. Abandoning powerful languages to the sovereign, if even to espouse a counternarrative, would have been to abdicate an effective strategy.[206]

These reflections suggest that an interpretive paradigm of popular politics that separates political expression into public and private (or mundane and "transcendent") domains cannot satisfactorily account for either the making of Merina identity or royal power; the two being inextricably intertwined. To employ terms popularized by James Scott, highland Malagasy did not differentiate between public and private transcripts, reciting royal ideology in public while rejecting it when out of the earshot of their social superiors.[207] The ideas and conversations that underpinned Merina identity did not operate on separate social stages; they were imbricated in one another. Because commoners and their rulers spoke the same language, highland Malagasy could effectively imagine themselves as an ethnic community, employing their common language and moralized claims to advocate mutual responsibility with the intention of influencing each other's behavior.[208] The very words and symbols that articulated Merina identity, then, served to mask, albeit weakly, internal conflicts and varying political strategies. Merina identity was forged in and through the lingering social tensions and political divisions of the age of enslavement. Neither Merina identity nor its rituals, traditions, and ideologies were rigidly fixed and formalized; they ebbed and flowed as highlanders lived their lives and fought their political battles.

7

LESSONS FROM THE AFRICAN DIASPORA

[I]t is in society that people normally acquire their memories. It is also in society that they recall, recognize, and localize their memories.

—Maurice Halbwachs[1]

Voluntary and involuntary elisions of memory and the partial perspective of witnesses require us to view matters from a variety of angles. The researcher cannot neglect the archives, but to apprehend the dimensions of memory and the diversity of its facets he is necessarily driven to other sources.

—Hubert Gerbeau[2]

MEMORY AS POWER AND SILENCE

In preceding chapters I explored popular histories from the *Tantara* and historical evidence from nineteenth- and twentieth-century sources to plumb the significance of Andrianampoinimerina as contemporary politician and modern symbol. In the process I uncovered a "secret" history of *Tantara* narratives, a history that sets the documents within the dynamic and tension-filled highland Malagasy response to mercantile capitalism in the Indian Ocean.[3] Popular historical memories of Andrianampoinimerina did not and do not exist independently of human experience in highland Madagascar; they are integrally tied to experiences of a slaving economy, state formation, political struggles, and Merina ethnogenesis. Yet as suggested in the first chapter of this book, while Merina identity grew from highlanders' responses to enslavement, *Tantara* texts, the key shared narratives of that identity, contain little explicit mention of enslavement, the export slave trade, and the sociopolitical predicaments these brought to the lives of highland Malagasy.[4] The explanation for this seem-ing paradox I have developed in the preceding chapters proposes that the cultural politics highland Malagasy and their sovereigns pursued at the dawn of the nineteenth century served to erase an explicit memory of that trade. While commemorating the noble deeds of their founder king to employ his memory as a political weapon, highlanders largely, although not completely, effaced narratives of slaving, its organization, and imme-diate consequences. This process of social amnesia required several de-cades to mature, propelled along by sovereigns' and citizen-subjects' struggles over mutual rights and responsibilities in a changing political economy.[5] This first section of the concluding chapter traces "the social organization of forgetting" in highland Malagasy history.[6]

Narratives in praise of Andrianampoinimerina issued at the beginning of the nineteenth century from court historians surrounding the founder king and justifying his ascent to power.[7] Typical of royal praise litera-ture, these verbal legends celebrated the king by recounting the excel-lence and popularity of his politics and by announcing his prophesied right to rule. They seldom referred to the material bases of his power, participation in international trade. Such information might suggest An-drianampoinimerina was more worldly and politically calculating, less mystical and sacred (*masina*) than royal ideology would have it. Court historians preferred not to mention Andrianampoinimerina's slaving ac-tivities lest they raise questions about his civic virtue or distract from his popularity. For their part, highland Malagasy were willing to overlook enslavement among Andrianampoinimerina's commercial activities as long as he delivered on his promises to protect *them* from the misfortunes of capture and exile across the seas. Andrianampoinimerina's praise narra-tives were popular in their time in that they articulated a new sense of order and populist economic morality that benefited the majority of high-land poor while censuring the wealthy and powerful amidst the glaring inequities of the slave trade. Highlanders embraced the narratives, mak-ing of them a shared Merina history superimposed over their many and varied descent group chronicles, sometimes integrated with them in cre-ative ways.[8] During the lifetime of Andrianampoinimerina, highland Malagasy warmed to the praises of their king.

The stories that first expressed highlanders' unity as Merina, then, did not memorialize a shared or bitter experience of vulnerability to enslave-ment and forced exile. They were tales recounted by survivors, the men and women who had been at risk of enslavement but had themselves es-caped direct victimization. From a desire to influence the behavior of their sovereigns, highlanders emphasized the noble deeds and promises of their founder king who successfully, if temporarily, mitigated many of the in-

Photograph 7.1 Statue of Andrianampoinimerina, Imerimandroso. The statue is modeled after Ramanankirahina's imaginary painting of 1905 (see Figure 5.1). Modern inhabitants of Imerimandroso, a town some 15 km north of Antananarivo, remember Andrianampoinimerina as a unifier, a sentiment they capture in a proverb several townspeople repeated to me in explanation of the statue: "strife in the morning, peace in the evening" (*miady maraina, tsara hariva*). The origin of the proverb in the town's history is related in *Tantara*, 493–94. (*Photo Credit*: Pier M. Larson, 1986.)

jurious social effects of the economy of enslavement. If praise narratives spun by Andrianampoinimerina's courtiers to legitimize his conquest of central Madagascar selectively disremembered the king's participation in the slave trade, highland Malagasy during the reign of Andrianampoinimerina's unpopular successors further expunged enslavement from their historical memories by presenting the founder king as a paragon of just and legitimate royal behavior. Radama's courtiers dared not wholeheartedly espouse the narratives, for they promised social justice, a moralized economy in which rural subsistence and promotion of agriculture figured centrally, and an end to the royal plunder of labor from rural communities, all of which ran directly counter to Radama's plans for highland Malagasy soldiers and laborers within his expanding kingdom. Formerly the pride of the royal court, the narratives became decentralized following Andrianampoinimerina's death, moving outward from Antananarivo to the *firenena*. When Father Callet collected *Tantara* narratives during the mid-nineteenth century, he found them scattered across the highland countryside, not concentrated at the royal court, as they once had been.[9] By the mid-nineteenth century, the *Tantara* were less royal histories than popular histories of royalty.

Grafted by local historians onto their repertories of *firenena* history, narratives in praise of Andrianampoinimerina were redirected against the royal court as incisive rhetorical weapons of criticism.[10] If they dared not challenge Radama and his successors directly and in plain language, highland Malagasy could applaud the policies and traditions of Andrianampoinimerina, which embodied an implicit criticism of royal politics after 1809. Even in extraordinarily direct challenges to the sovereign, such as the Avaradrano women's revolt, highlanders resorted to public memories of Andrianampoinimerina as a model of tradition. When they employed historical memory to invoke the promises of personal security and subsistence once conferred upon Merina citizen-subjects by Andrianampoinimerina, highland Malagasy appropriated Merina identity from the sovereign, using it to curb the actions of their king and those who would literally or metaphorically enslave them.

During the reigns of Radama and his successors, highland Malagasy claimed the praise narratives of Andrianampoinimerina to imagine themselves as a community of interest independent of their sovereigns and thereby to ethnicize their collective political identity. This was true even during the reign of Ranavalona I (1828–61), who, rising to power upon the death of Radama, understood the magnitude of the swelling rift between *firenena* and the royal court. Although she attempted to recapture the admiration of her subjects through symbolic realignment with the memory of Andrianampoinimerina in a way that her predecessor and successors did not, her excesses in military recruitment, war making, labor service, and summary justice pushed many of her subjects into starvation and banditry.[11] It was narratives of tacit protest against such experiences and invoking a popularized memory of Andrianampoinimerina that Callet collected into the *Tantara* soon after Ranavalona's death.

Photograph 7.2 Relief portrait of Radama by Nirina, ca. 1997. The author purchased this wood, paper maché, and oil color tableau, based on Coppalle's famous 1825 painting (see Figure 6.1), at a stand of craft souvenirs at Ambohimanga (Andrianampoinimerina's first seat of government). The ubiquity and popularity of this martial image of Radama attest to a continuing memory of Andrianampoinimerina's son and successor as a man of war.

True to their legacy as effective political speech, *Tantara* narratives ran afoul of the kingdom's rulers as soon as they were authorized in print. When Callet published the first volume of the *Tantara* on the presses of the Catholic mission in 1872, Prime Minister Rainilaiarivony banned the texts from public circulation.[12] Jean Valette, director of the Malagasy National Archives during the first decade of national independence (the 1960s), could not have known of Rainilaiarivony's act of historical suppression. Offering a mistaken interpretation of the *Tantara* still widely accepted by modern scholars of Madagascar, he counseled historians to employ the narratives with care, for they proffered, he argued, an elite and official history of the Merina kingdom that had been fashioned to further the political claims of Prime Minister Rainilaiarivony and his family.[13] Ten years later Alain Delivré refuted Valette's assertion. Delivré found the reason for Rainilaiarivony's opposition to the *Tantara* in the economic, political, and ritual privileges the narratives accorded certain descent groups within the kingdom. Ignoring the privileges granted to particular *firenena* by Andrianampoinimerina, or not wishing to provide published voice for contradictory claims, Rainilaiarivony suppressed the compendium.[14]

Françoise Raison-Jourde reaffirmed Delivré's conclusion and nuanced it with further reasons why the prime minister might have prevented the *Tantara* from circulating among his subjects. She writes that since the Bible had replaced the royal talismans in 1869 as the primary symbol of royal power, a volume dedicated to the religious and cultural traditions of the past, including the history of the now-destroyed royal talismans, would have operated at cross-purpose to royal power (the royal talismans, considered by many as the principal opponents of Christianity, were publicly burned on orders of Queen Ranavalona II in 1869, several months after she and Rainilaiarivony were baptized into Protestantism). In addition, Raison-Jourde argues, the publication and circulation of manuscripts represented an act of identity definition beyond control of the royal court. In the context of the official censorship of the period, printing historical narratives constituted an act of defiance.[15] Drawing as they do on identity politics and the tension-filled relationships between *firenena* and kingdom authorities, Delivré's and Raison-Jourde's explanations for Rainilaiarivony's act of narrative suppression are convincing. Since the reign of Radama in the early nineteenth century, rulers of the Merina kingdom looked skeptically upon praises for Andrianampoinimerina, opposing the independent programs in support of which commoners recited them. This was particularly true during the last decades of the nineteenth century, when royal labor service and massive military recruitment pushed many common highland Malagasy into abject poverty and lives in the margins of Merina administration and beyond.[16]

By turning Andrianampoinimerina into a symbol of all that was desirable in a sovereign, highlanders participated in effacing evidence of the founder-king's role in the slave trade and in reinforcing, in their own way, the "*hasina* ideology" that justified royal power. Commoners did, therefore, play a key role in reproducing royal power, but they did so in their own fashion by independently pursuing self-defined interests. This was the irony of their success. Because a majority of highland Malagasy became owners of slaves during the reign of Radama and his successors, their elision from historical narratives of painful experiences related to enslavement and slaving during the era of export trade may have served to ease their brusque transition from potential victims of enslavement into slaveholders. Highlanders suppressed fundamental historical experiences in their collectively held memories, but those suppressions were necessary if narratives of Andrianampoinimerina were to be pressed into the service of *firenena* interests and autonomy. Since most modern histories of the early Merina kingdom have relied heavily and for the most part uncritically upon popular Merina historical narratives, elision of the presence and influence of international commerce and enslavement on highland Malagasy society at the beginning of the nineteenth century has been reproduced in secondary literature. Even British missionaries, who were so opposed to the slave trade on principle when they first arrived in central Madagascar during the 1820s, retold the history of Andrianampoinimerina from popular narratives by ignoring the founder king's commercial activities. Reflecting popular opinion when they composed their impressive *History of Madagascar* during the first decade and a half of their presence in the highlands (the compendium was actually published in 1838), they acknowledged the prevalence of slaving during Andrianampoinimerina's reign but attributed the activity to the king's immoral opponents, leaving the founding hero and wealthiest and most powerful of slaving kings unsullied.[17]

One of the missionaries' chief sources about the character and government of Andrianampoinimerina was a former *maroseranina* counselor of Radama, one Prince Aristide Coroller. His account of the founder king resembled those prevailing at the time, yet was tempered with criticisms that were rarely voiced publicly.

> His [Andrianampoinimerina's] views were extensive and ambitious; so much so, that nearly the whole of his life was spent in making wars and conquests, though, at the same time, he encouraged his people in commerce and agriculture, and would occasionally work with his own hands for the sake of exercise, as well as to set an example of industry to others. . . . He respected hoary hairs, loved justice, and presided fre-

quently in person on the judgment-seat, to watch over the rights of his people, rewarding those who administered justice impartially, and severely punishing every instance of the contrary. He was very eloquent, and liberal and generous to his own people. Yet notwithstanding these home virtues, his political interests induced him to commit many acts of gross injustice towards his rivals and the chieftains whom he conquered.[18]

Consistent with the politics of historical memory laid out in the previous chapter, some of the most negative assessments of the founder king, however mild and qualified, were voiced by the courtiers and associates of Radama and his successors. If Andrianampoinimerina had acted with gross injustice, went those stories, it was toward ethnic outsiders and his wealthy and powerful domestic opponents, individuals with interests in the local slave trade. That Prince Coroller was among the few of his contemporaries to have reproached Andrianampoinimerina for his treatment of those who were not "his own people" is understandable, for he hailed from Madagascar's east coast.[19] Over the years, it was the admirable image of Andrianampoinimerina and his "home virtues" that prevailed in the social memory of highland Malagasy, shaping elite narratives like those of Prince Coroller and Raombana as well as popular ones such as the *Tantara*.

When *Tantara* accounts were being set in print in the late nineteenth century, people in the Vakinankaratra (the southwestern district of the Merina kingdom) looked fondly back on earlier sovereigns, particularly Andrianampoinimerina, as having presided over "good and golden old times" characterized by "peace and quiet."[20] Highlanders who rallied to the *menalamba* anti-colonial resistance after the French conquered Imerina in late 1895 embraced Andrianampoinimerina as a symbol of legitimate political sovereignty and good government. This image was employed as a criticism of both the conquering French and the *hova* rulers of the island who, they felt, had neglected both the traditions and political order of the founder king.[21] At the end of the century, Anthony Tacchi published an article about Andrianampoinimerina's rise to power in the mission-sponsored journal *Antananarivo Annual and Madagascar Magazine*, never once mentioning enslavement or external trade. Instead he reiterated the vision of popular narratives that the responsibility of a king was to produce *fanjakan'andriana* (social order) out of *fanjakana hova* (insecurity and chaos). "He is undoubtedly the most important king of Madagascar history," wrote Tacchi of Andrianampoinimerina, "forming the link between the chaos of the last century and the order of the present one."[22] Both highland Malagasy popular vocabularies and historical narratives informed the accounts fashioned by resident foreigners, and each of these in turn served as primary reference material for nineteenth- and twentieth-century historians of Andrianampoinimerina. The Malagasy editors of the *Firaketana*, a historical dictionary published in the mid-twentieth century in the Malagasy language, hardly mentioned enslavement in their entry for Andrianampoinimerina. The few passages in that *Firaketana* entry referring to slaves—all in passing—are limited to the mention of captives retained within Madagascar, whom Andrianampoinimerina "treated well if they did not rebel"; export slaves and international trade are entirely absent from the narrative.[23] The same is true of the entry for Andrianampoinimerina in Raolison's *Dictionnaire historique et géographique de Madagascar* published in 1966.[24] Based on the *Tantara* and European accounts that drew from popular memory, most twentieth-century histories of Andrianampoinimerina either neglect or downplay the considerable role of external trade and enslavement in the rise of the founder king.[25] Profoundly shaped by popular historiography, professional research on the Merina kingdom reproduces the silences of nineteenth-century social memory.[26]

Among popular historians and in the popular culture of modern highland Madagascar, Andrianampoinimerina remains a vibrant and relevant political symbol today. The founder king and his practical wisdom are frequent themes in the speeches delivered during ceremonies (such as the *famadihana*, circumcision, and marriage), in the performances of *hira gasy* singing troupes, in the media, and in popular culture generally.[27] A pamphlet of sixteen pages published in Antananarivo for local distribution shortly after the independence of Madagascar (1960) offers a typical example of the continuing utility of Andrianampoinimerina in modern political rhetoric. In the pamphlet, one Joseph Rakotonirainy makes of Andrianampoinimerina and his policies a model for postindependence leaders. "Before the year of 1787," Rakotonirainy writes at length,

> the arrival of King-democrat Andrianampoinimerina, all Madagascar was in anarchy. Imerina was in chaos. Misery was everywhere. Justice was corrupted. Civil war was in a latent state. The population lived in insecurity; crops were cultivated but insufficiently, from which sprang sporadic famines. Armed bands were formed almost everywhere to engage in rapine and theft. Before such a state of things, it was necessary for Andrianampoinimerina to make a rapid and total reconstruction of the country. If he wanted to avoid its impending disorganization, he had to find a means to end this national degradation. He established a precise plan that conformed to the usages and customs of the country, and it was, as if by miracle, that he succeeded in reorganizing

it in only a few years. . . . Like the times that preceded the arrival of Andrianampoinimerina, we now live in a similar era, a cycle of disorder and public misery. My goal is to attract the attention of men of good will in Madagascar and to show them the road to follow. It is for this reason that I contend we should not hesitate to modernize the principle of the fokonolona of 1787 in the common interest of all the inhabitants of Madagascar. . . . From the time of his arrival, Andrianampoinimerina purified his kingdom. The unjust and tyrannical chiefs were punished and their [ill-gotten] goods confiscated. Justice reestablished, the people were happy in work and abundance. Imerina lived in Peace. In that time there were no beggars because the mutual aid of the fokonolona had as its goal the interest of the Community and the rehabilitation of each person by work in Union. Order reigned everywhere because everyone was aware of the advantages of Peace and brotherly Union. . . . This was the past. It shows us the possibilities and the way to follow in the Future of Madagascar.[28]

Published in 1962, Rakotonirainy's idealistic exposé bears all the key elements of nineteenth-century memories of the Merina cultural hero. Andrianampoinimerina restored order to chaos, justice to injustice, unity to disunity. He infused an immoral and demoralized society with a sense of purpose and virtue. His wise rule is a prudent and exemplary path for modern leaders to tread. Despite dramatic political transformations in highland Madagascar since 1822, this popular image of Andrianampoinimerina, and the political uses to which it has been applied, has persisted into the present.

The reproduction through the generations of a metaphorical image of Andrianampoinimerina as a cultural hero who brought order and social justice to chaos and insecurity exemplifies the tendency of social memory to conventionalize the past into what is frequently termed myth or metaphor. As Gordon Shrimpton argues with reference to ancient Greek historians, such conventionalized renditions of historical experience "orchestrate the society's forgetting of traumatic or uncomfortable details." In the case of highland Madagascar, the uncomfortable details of Andrianampoinimerina's slaving and that of his citizen-subjects were forgotten in the process of turning Andrianampoinimerina into a useful symbol. "Myth," Shrimpton concludes, "is the wastebasket of the collective memory."[29] If the founder king and his policies were popular in their own time, a positive image of Andrianampoinimerina enabled highlanders to discard memories of trauma in the effort to protect themselves from the excesses of royal power during the nineteenth century. It is ironic that the nefarious consequences of a world economy and the abuses of royalty aided highland Malagasy in the long-term retention of a vibrant memory of their founder king and an enduring sense of their ethnic unity.[30] Yet these, in turn, were the product of an historical amnesia that persists into the present. Tied as it was to present political struggles, the production of a historical memory in highland Madagascar was a form of social action, a "dimension of political practice."[31] By acting to shape their life experiences, highland Malagasy forged both their history and their historiography.

THE FORGOTTEN DIASPORA

I have argued throughout this book that enslavement and its aftermath in societies of the African continent are integral parts of the African diaspora. Yet literature searches for subjects and titles containing *African diaspora* return an overwhelming majority of works on the experiences of Africans and their descendants in the Atlantic, particularly in Europe and the Americas. To understand why, in practice, the African diaspora has become restricted to its transatlantic component it is useful to undertake an intellectual history of the concept. The term *diaspora* originates from related Greek words used to describe Greek colonization of Asia Minor and the Mediterranean; like "ethnicity" (see chapter 1), it first entered Western European languages through the medium of biblical translation into European vernaculars. In its first modern applications to human dispersion (dating to the late nineteenth century), "the Diaspora" referred to the traumatic experiences of Jews in exile since Babylonian times, a classical "victim diaspora."[32] Although historians have spoken of human "dispersions" since at least the fifteenth century, the term *diaspora* as applied beyond Jewish experiences is a very new academic and popular concept dating to the mid-1960s.[33] Traditionally diasporas have been defined, following the Jewish example, as traumatically dispersed ethnic or racial minorities who maintained some physical or emotional connection to real or imagined homelands of origin. As an increasing number of populations have claimed diasporic experiences and identities since the mid-1960s, however, the meanings of *diaspora* have become more capacious, slipping from the control of scholars' pens. Attempts to set out the characteristics of a diaspora now inevitably fail to match the experiences of large populations which view themselves in a "diasporic condition."[34] The practical difficulty with diaspora as an intellectual concept, then, lies both in its malleability and in its association with post-1960 identity politics in dispersed and socially displaced communities.

While founded in the work of nineteenth- and twentieth-century American scholars, intellectuals, and activists like Alexander Crummell, Edward W. Blyden, Marcus Garvey, W.E.B. Du Bois, Melville Herskovits, and others, the concept of an African diaspora was first explicitly articulated in print by George Shepperson, professor of history at the University of Edinburgh, in a paper delivered at the University of Dar es Salaam in 1965 and subsequently published in a compendium of articles edited by Terence Ranger in 1968.[35] Fostered in the intellectual context of African history, the African diaspora was soon claimed by scholars working on the plight of Africans and their descendants in the Americas. Under the twin assumptions (both of which are registered in the title of Shepperson's pioneering article of 1968) that diaspora meant "Africans abroad" and that "abroad" meant outside the African continent, the African diaspora as articulated in the literature has always privileged the experiences of Africans in the Americas over those on the continent and elsewhere. The origin of forced African migrations, Africa became in this literature a "mythologized" or "imagined" homeland to which few descendants of those forced migrants actually desired to return.[36]

Flush with energy and a fierce sense of intellectual independence in this same period (post-1960), the (mainly white) scholars working in the newly burgeoning field of African history eschewed the concept of an African diaspora as applying to Africa itself and distanced themselves from mythmaking about Africa emerging from the western side of the Atlantic. At the same time, they considered the study of Africans and their descendants in the Americas as lying beyond the conceptual boundaries of African history.[37] In the Americas, persons of African descent seldom sought a physical return to Africa—they fought, rather, for full and equal integration into American societies—but sought a positive affirmation of identity as sons and daughters of Africa by reimagining an African homeland of origin.[38] Because through creolization, economic exploitation, and racial denigration the descendants of Africans in the Americas lost their attachment to and memories of specific continental African homelands, languages, and cultures, that African "homeland" came to correspond over time with Africa's continental borders, homogenizing diverse societies into an imagined continental identity that first emerged in the thought of creolized Americans. (Recently, historians have recognized this as an intellectual problem and are successfully seeking to recover the human and cultural links between specific African ethnic homelands and American destinations.)[39] The formation of African-American identities, based as they were on the idea of a unitary Africa and African identity, entailed a simultaneous and profound amnesia, not only of Africa's diversity, but of continental traumas, forced migrations, and other displacements associated with enslavement there. The formative African-American experiences of slavery and racial exploitation, it was assumed, commenced with direct European exploitation at the African coast.

Figure 7.1 "Sirboko's Slaves carrying Fuel and cutting Rice," central Africa. A fundamental principle of Africa's internal slave trades was to move slaves as far away from kin as possible, preventing them from escaping home. The experiences of Africans living and laboring in exile within Africa challenge us to rethink our notion that slaves within the continent were not "abroad" and therefore not to be counted as part of the African diaspora. (*Source:* John Hanning Speke, *Journal of the Discovery of the Source of the Nile* [Edinburgh and London: William Blackwood and Sons, 1863], between pages 102 and 103.)

If these partial memories of Africa underpinned African-American identities in the context of new world racism, they remained unconvincing intellectual paradigms for scholars of the African continent. Yet while working on slavery and the slave trade, Africanists continued for the most part to accept Americanist formulations of the African diaspora—they simply refused to view that diaspora as applying in any meaningful way to the experiences of Africans within Africa. Nor did they understand African history as encompassing the experiences of Africans outside the continent. The Americocentric African diaspora as currently formulated, then, makes for highly problematic intellectual paradigms of continental African experiences of enslavement and dispersion. Yet historians of Africa have been reluctant to challenge it, in part because they implicitly participated in its making. While many definitions of the African diaspora pay lip service to the movement of Africans in both the Atlantic and Indian oceans as well as across the "sea" of the Sahara and, sometimes, even within Africa itself, it is the dispersal of Africans about the Atlantic, especially in the Americas, that captures a near monopoly of modern studies under the banner of the African diaspora.[40] There are compelling practical and intellectual reasons for enlarging the spatial and analytical scope of the African diaspora to encompass all the movements and displacements of African peoples during the early modern and modern eras and to permit greater cross-fertilization of research and perspective. The core assumption informing most conceptualizations of the African diaspora—that dispersion commenced at the African coastline, or possibly its interior but only involved people who moved westward, eventually crossing the Atlantic—is one of these reasons. The "route of the slave" did not, of course, begin at the coast as UNESCO's slave route project now so rightly recognizes. But more important, certain intellectual filters have been responsible for placing intra-African forced migrations (about which the UNESCO slave route project is largely silent) as lying beyond the pale of the African diaspora. Africans, though displaced within the African continent, are still considered as having dwelt within their homeland—"Africa"—and thus did not experience exile. Conceptualization of a common Black or "Black Atlantic" identity, as Paul Gilroy termed it, tends to place all persons born in Africa and residing there at "home" wherever they were and in whatever condition they may have lived. Both these propositions, implicit in most formulations of the African diaspora, ultimately stem from the process of amalgamation of multiple African ethnic identities into a single black racial identity in the vicious climate of chattel slavery and racism in the Americas.[41] Yet they each fail to faithfully account for continental Africans' own experiences and consciousness and cannot be substituted for them.

The sheer magnitude of human displacements within Africa provides a further reason for rethinking traditional formulations of the African diaspora and for viewing that dispersion, as Philip Curtin once suggested, as a key dimension of world history with Africa at its center.[42] Although the transatlantic slave trade remains the single largest extracontinental forced migration of Africans occurring over the half-millennium between 1400 and 1900 (some 12 million leaving Africa), the trans-Saharan trade (nearly 8 million) and the Indian Ocean and Red Sea trades (more than 4 million), while operating over longer time spans than the transatlantic commerce, together approximated the volume of forced African migrations to the Americas.[43] Linked to each of these forced migrations from Africa were the internal African slave trades serving domestic markets, probably equal to or greater in magnitude than all three of the external movements combined.[44] The cultural significance of intracontinental movements of Africans as a result of the slave trade has been largely ignored in diaspora studies, in part because the race-based definitions of minorities in host societies that Americanist scholars commonly employ

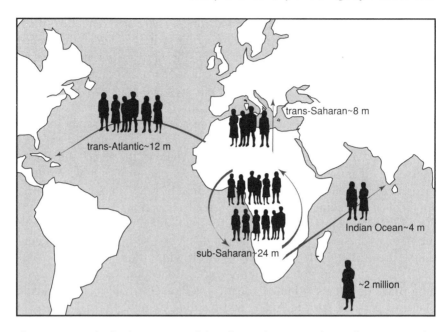

Figure 7.2 Multiple destinations of the African diaspora. African dispersion in the era of slaving was of significantly higher volume than is suggested by transatlantic movements alone. Together, trans-Saharan and Indian Ocean dispersions roughly equaled in volume the transatlantic flow of bonded Africans. This figure, based on the most empirically grounded estimates available (see text), depicts the multiple destinations of enslaved Africans. Of those destinations, sub-Saharan African societies were the single most significant as measured by the volume of coerced dispersion. Most scholars of the slave trade have concluded that probably as many or more slaves were retained within Africa as were sent across the Atlantic, the Sahara Desert, and into the Indian Ocean. (*Credit*: Office of Design and Publications, The Johns Hopkins University.)

to define diaspora communities are inadequate in most African societies. In Africa, language and ethnic differences loom greater than race. Seen in its broader context, the transatlantic slave trade represented about one-half of the external forced migration of Africans and only about one-quarter, and probably less, of the entire African diaspora resulting from enslavement. Responsible scholars must account for these human experiences, largely forgotten in studies of the African diaspora (see Figure 7.2).

If raw numbers of forced migrants testify to the necessity for broadening the spatial scope of the diaspora and placing the African continent at its center, the potential comparisons across that global dispersion offer intellectual incentives for pursuing comparative studies. Opening investigation of the diaspora to the full range of African experiences in early encounters with expanding Europe and its economies as well as with other world systems will illuminate rather than obscure Africans as both historical agents and victims in global history. Traditionally, the societies or homelands from which diasporic migrants hailed have not been included in diasporas because the idea of diaspora neatly separated homelands from areas of dispersion. Separating source, destination, and transit societies in the African portion of the African diaspora, however, is difficult in practice. Most African societies that exported slaves were themselves consumers of servile labor. This was true of highland Madagascar, too, which imported slaves from east Africa and other regions of the island while simultaneously exporting them into the Indian Ocean. Source societies for some were destinations for others; understanding cultural transformations in the context of the slave trade will require attention to both these human movements. Lands of origin have been excluded from diasporas in part because definitions of human dispersion operated solely with a spatial-linear model of physical displacement. Those left behind in source societies, like highland Madagascar in the slave trade to the Mascarenes, however, transformed their ways of life in response to the very forces that drove kith and kin from their midst. Individuals who remained behind frequently reconstructed kinship relations, rescaled political loyalties, moved their places of residence, transformed divisions of labor, and shifted social organization and cultural practices. These real and material social displacements were integrally linked to the export trade—as again demonstrated in the case of highland Madagascar—and created an "internal social and cultural dispersion" comparable in many respects to the "external migratory dispersion" characterized by experiences of the enslaved in exile from their places of birth. Including source societies for slaves within the African diaspora—a major argument of this book—means broadening our understanding of that dispersion to include both long-distance involuntary population movements and the demographic, economic, social, and cultural displacements in "homelands" integrally linked to them.

The impact of the slave trade on the African societies that supplied slaves to other regions of the continent and intercontinentally, as I argued in chapter 1 of this book, is the least known among the many cultural transformations associated with slavery. Yet it is potentially one of the most consequential in terms of the absolute number of persons affected. Herbert Klein has written that the African population exposed to the Atlantic slave trade in 1700 was some 25 million, or one-half of the entire population of the continent south of the Sahara. When those domestically affected by Africa's other external and internal trades are taken into account, the numbers become extremely large.[45] What is needed to unlock these many experiences is not only greater synergy among scholars working on opposite sides of the Atlantic portion of the African diaspora, following Africans as they move westward across the ocean (a welcome development of recent years spearheaded by UNESCO's slave route project), or similar projects in the Indian Ocean and Islamic world, but increased cooperation among all scholars investigating the worldwide dispersion of Africans moving in multiple directions and remaining within the African continent.[46] The African diaspora, then, consists of several closely interlinked dispersions that created related yet distinct human experiences: transatlantic, trans-Saharan, trans–Indian Ocean, and internal African forced migrations, and the various social and cultural displacements of Africans living in source societies from which forced migrants were wrenched. In terms of population dispersals, the center of gravity in the African diaspora is (and was) Africa rather than the Atlantic, and scholars working on the diaspora should either specify the particular portion of that massive and compound dispersion they are working on or consider it in its entirety. Lack of specificity leads to ignorance of the diversity of experiences in the African diaspora. Because of its size and complexity, the great African dispersion might best be considered as a set of related diasporas with unique histories, identities, and memories of trauma, each of which originates within Africa but is differently connected to both its African origins and the intercontinental forces that coercively pried persons lose from kith, kin, and routines of everyday life.

Let me briefly consider two long-neglected African diasporas this study directly engages: intracontinental forced migrations and the Indian Ocean dispersion. Long neglected in diaspora studies (although not in African history), intracontinental African population movements and transformations in source societies for slaves accent the similarities and differences of human experience across the global dispersion of African people. To be sure, Africans forced to cross the ocean and adapt to life in the Americas and in the Indian Ocean underwent different experiences from those internally exiled among foreign peoples or remaining in source societies on the African continent. Yet there are sufficient similarities across the diaspora, as Alpers has cogently argued in a recent study on African dispersion in the Indian Ocean, to merit fruitful comparisons.[47] How did slavery in Africa compare to bondage elsewhere in the diaspora? How did local economies and ideologies shape master–slave relationships? Did slaves in Africa form distinct cultures in the societies of their enslavement or did they become thoroughly integrated into their masters' cultures? What is distinctive about race as a means of labor control in the

Americas when set alongside African systems of servile subordination based upon ethnicity, language, and other social markers? How were ethnic identities formed and reshaped in the internal African diasporas as, say, compared to those of North America or the Indian Ocean? How were continental African cultures (both sources of slaves and their destinations) remade as a result of slaving activity? By whose actions were these changes effected? And, what light do sociocultural changes in Africa shed on the rise of African-American cultures in the western Atlantic? Such comparisons across the diaspora will undoubtedly offer much insight into African slavery as a global phenomenon differently experienced in its many regions, much as recent comparative work in the Americas has served to stress the similarities and differences among slave societies there.[48]

Opening the diaspora beyond the Americas and the African interior to the Indian Ocean will further enrich understanding of the dispersion of African people.[49] Slaving in the Indian Ocean brought captives in various numbers to destinations in the Americas, to the length of the East African coast and some hinterland societies, to the Cape of Good Hope, to the Red Sea and Persian Gulf, to the Arabian Peninsula, to the Indian subcontinent, to far eastern destinations in China, Japan, and Indonesia, and to the Indian Ocean islands, including most notably Zanzibar and Pemba, the Comoros, the Seychelles, Madagascar, Mauritius, and Réunion (see Photograph 7.3).[50] Sources of slaves destined for most societies of the Indian Ocean and beyond spanned the entire sub-Saharan coastline of Africa, though the overwhelming majority of captives exited through the east coast of the continent proper or from Madagascar and were generally drawn from its eastern and central hinterlands. Transatlantic, trans-Saharan, and Indian Ocean trade economies intersected both in the interior of Africa as merchants and markets encountered each other from opposite directions and in the frequent movement of seaborne commerce between Africa's two flanking oceans and the Mediterranean Sea. With distinct economic and trade patterns, both the Atlantic and the Indian oceans became integrated into the same world economy after Vasco da Gama rounded the Cape of Good Hope in 1498. Africans of the Indian Ocean diaspora were therefore subject to an array of experiences comparable to those of Africans in the Atlantic: enslavement, disruption of source societies, forced labor, and political, cultural, and identity transformations in both source and destination regions.

While enabling insightful comparisons, Indian Ocean diaspora experiences and the varied contexts in which they took place offer fruitful contrasts to the Atlantic diaspora. Most of the slave societies and economies of the Indian Ocean were organized differently from those of the Ameri-

Photograph 7.3 "Abyssinian Slave Children" in Aden, southern Arabian Peninsula, Indian Ocean. The Indian Ocean and Red Sea trades together accounted for some 4 million Africans removed from the continent. Many of these persons were children. Understanding their experiences will enrich histories of the African diaspora. (*Source*: M. French-Sheldon, *Sultan to Sultan: Adventures among the Masai and other Tribes of East Africa* [London: Saxon & Co., 1892], 44.)

cas, and the flourishing trade that predated the arrival of Europeans was conducted by Arabs, Asians, and Africans.[51] That ancient commerce continued to operate alongside and interact with European trade and colonial economies into the modern era.[52] Islam was an important influence on many slaveholders of the Indian Ocean, and local ideologies of slavery emerged from a heterogeneous set of agricultural and commercial cultures. In his treatise on slavery in Zanzibar, Frederick Cooper demonstrated that setting Indian Ocean plantations beside those in the Americas problematized much about the roles of labor organization, race, and religion for Americanist scholars who mistakenly believed American experiences of slavery to be normative.[53] Indian Ocean studies less well circulated among or celebrated by scholars of the Atlantic likewise offer fresh perspectives on diaspora, economy, society, and culture in the intercommunicating zone of a long- and well-traveled ocean.[54] Despite offering new insights to historians thinking about the African diaspora in terms of the Atlantic, Indian Ocean studies nevertheless share some fundamental conceptual kinship with works on the Atlantic. In a pioneering article on the African diaspora of the northwestern Indian Ocean, for example, Edward Alpers identifies a still-diffuse literature on African influences there and lays out directions for future research on the dispersion of African cultural forms about Arabia, the Persian Gulf, and western India.[55] Valuable and stimulating in itself, Alpers's work replicates the vision of Alanticists, whose diaspora begins at the African coast. Placing Africa at the center of a global dispersion with people spiraling outward in all directions both intra- and intercontinentally will facilitate useful comparison and cross-fertilization of scholarship across the diaspora, pushing appreciation of African experiences and the interconnections between Atlantic and Indian oceans to new dimensions.

DIASPORIC IDENTITIES

By probing diverse experiences across the vast and varied African diaspora, scholars will shed new light on the uniqueness of enslavement, memory, and identity in particular areas. Full appreciation for the rich and varied identities in the African diaspora must be based upon culturally specific investigations of historical memory as manifested in the stories African peoples tell about the past and on the language and cultural logic in which they tell them. Paul Gilroy's concept of a Black Atlantic is unsatisfactory in this respect. In his work, Gilroy subordinates transatlantic "communities of interpretation and sentiment" to the cultural logic and languages of Africans in North America and the Caribbean. "I want to develop the suggestion," he writes, "that cultural historians could take the Atlantic as one single, complex unit of analysis in their discussions of the modern world and use it to produce an explicitly transnational and intercultural perspective."[56] For Gilroy, however, "vernacular culture" in the Black Atlantic is Anglophone, North American, and Caribbean.[57] Yet self-identification as Black in Anglophone speech communities is but one thin slice of the African Atlantic (much less the diaspora proper), ringed as it is by a variety of African cultures. The Black Atlantic is significantly more complex, multidimensional, and multilingual than Gilroy allows. By mistakenly conflating the Anglophone Americas with the "Black Atlantic," Gilroy explores but one subset of the many African cultural experiences in the vast and varied diaspora, virtually ignoring its African and non-Anglophone portions. Gilroy's interest in "mutation, hybridity, and intermixture" works well in examining the cultural interactions within an Anglophone world, but it is less useful for understanding the multivernacled Black Atlantic (and notably Africa) with its varied modes of narration and memory.[58] "Transnational and intercultural" approaches to the Black Atlantic must recognize the profound cultural discontinuities that have characterized and continue to characterize cultural diversity in the Atlantic world, despite persistent intercommunication. Vessels crossing the Atlantic and Indian oceans linked disparate societies, languages, and cultural worlds; African, European, Middle Eastern, and Asian cultures were never unified, despite intensive intercommunication and integration into a single world economy.

Memorialization of enslavement has proved a powerful means of identity formation for Africans in the Americas.[59] Among others, Gilroy characterizes how slavery has recently served as a cultural resource for Black identity formation. "It is thus the relationship between masters and slaves that supplies the key to comprehending the position of blacks in the modern world," he writes. "The desire to return to slavery and to explore it in imaginative writing has offered Morrison and a number of other contemporary black writers a means to restage confrontations between national, scientific, and enlightened Euro-American thought and the supposedly primitive outlook of prehistorical, cultureless, and bestial African slaves."[60] But experiences of enslavement, as in the case of highland Madagascar, are not universal sites for historical memory and identity formation in the diaspora. The relationships between continental African identities and the slave trade are far more complex and contradictory than those between African-American identities and the commerce in human beings, if only because Africans were both masters and slaves in large numbers. In highland Madagascar, for example, well over half of all nonslave persons owned slaves in the middle of the nineteenth century.[61] This pattern was repeated widely, though unevenly, across Africa during the nineteenth century.[62] If experiences and memories of enslavement and racial oppression are key to African identities in the Americas, similar trauma has been purposefully forgotten or differently remembered by many Africans in other parts of the diaspora. Although remembering and commemorating enslavement is characteristic of some Africans, particularly the descendants of slaves, countervailing forces of social amnesia are particularly robust in many parts of the continent, especially among the descendants of slaveowners.[63] Coming to a unified understanding of what might more properly be called "the African Atlantics" or, in its expanded version, "the African diasporas" will require seriously complicating Gilroy's Black Atlantic and the politics of memory lying behind it. In this sense the philosophies of the North American Afrocentric movements (which largely reject memorialization of enslavement as a means of identity formation) act as an important intellectual force demonstrating that memorialization of trauma is not universal to the African diaspora, even in its Western manifestations.

If memorialization of victimization by enslavement cannot serve as the basis for a common African identity across the diaspora, the slave trade and its multiple effects, including experiences of enslavement, forced migration, masterhood, and economic-cultural transformation in host and destination societies do offer powerful lenses through which varied experiences can be appreciated as a whole. "Slavery," writes Paul Lovejoy, "provides a key to understanding African history, however varied the relationships of exploitation were."[64] The challenge for scholars of African dispersion is not to generalize from one specific set of African experiences, modes of popular memory, or types of identity formation to the whole of the African diaspora, but to ask of the various African diasporas— including persons of different culture and language, of distinct historical relationships to the slave trade as descendants of slavers, victims, near victims, slaveholders, and the like—how they fashion narratives about the historical experiences of their ancestors. This approach to a period of profound economic, political, and cultural transformation for many African peoples at home as well as across the seas recognizes the centrality of human bondage to modern diaspora identities. At the same time it allows for a diversity of remembering and forgetting—of modes of memory—to characterize African cultures and modern identities.

Researching the varied experiences of African slavery through the lens of memory, memorialization, and amnesia—through the historical representations of the African diaspora's diverse peoples—adds a cultural and humanistic component to the often dry and disembodied business of historical reconstruction from contemporary European sources. Unfortunately, unlike their colleagues working on slavery in North America, historians of the slave trade and slavery in Africa have been narrowing rather than broadening their field of historical evidence and their professional methodologies in recent years.[65] Although some of the earliest studies of the slave trade emerging from the renaissance of African history during the 1960s and 1970s were partially based upon popular and elite African narratives (formalized "oral traditions" for the most part), most major studies of the slave trade published during the last twenty years are based exclusively or nearly exclusively upon contemporary written documents produced by Europeans.[66] The reluctance of historians of African slavery and the slave trade to meaningfully engage African memories is a serious shortcoming that returns African historiography to colonial patterns. Jean-Pierre Chrétien's observations about colonial historians' attitudes toward African narratives regrettably describes much work on the slave trade today.

> Such a lack of respect for oral testimony is shown by the absence of pub-
> lished texts [of oral testimonies or oral traditions] in almost all scholarly
> works appearing between 1890 and 1950. Quotes were diminished to sum-
> maries or hidden in the analysis. In the end, it was the foreign observers
> themselves who were quoted, as if they were the authors and witnesses of
> an entire culture. When confronted with the written words of European
> visitors the spoken words of African actors were effaced.[67]

Studies in the history of slaving, slavery, and diaspora must break with this "growing new orthodoxy against oral tradition" to employ a greater diversity of historical evidence and to listen more attentively to what Africans have to say about their ancestors' experiences.[68] Innovative approaches to African history will entail not only finding new traces of the past and new ways of employing that evidence of the past, but appreciating the ways in which the people being studied ordered, understood, and brought meaning to their traumatic experiences.[69]

Taking historical memory seriously entails moving beyond the comfortable territory of European languages and tempering numbers and economic projections with serious work in vernacular languages and cultures.[70] It means allowing interpretations and reconstructions of contemporary data to be shaped by African worldviews, narratives, vocabularies, artistic expressions, ritual action and symbolism, organizations of space, and embodied memories (such as spirit possession, dress, coiffure).[71] Following such "poetical" clues to the African past also will require moving away from overly formal definitions of African narratives as "oral tradition" serviceable primarily as evidence in the same way as the archives, the manner in which earlier studies of the slave trade conceptualized them.[72] Rather, where African narratives exist, whether spoken or written, they should be considered as memorial evidence, stories with their own histories whose evidence often lies subtly embedded in language, genre, emphasis, and historically developed silences. To access these memories of the past, historians will need to renew attention to "the appearance of historical knowledge in unexpected locations."[73]

Figure 7.3 "Negress Attendant Going to the Bath," Algiers, Algeria. "The baths are great places of rendezvous for the Arab women. . . . They are seen with their children in the streets going to the bath, accompanied by a gorgeous negress carrying a bronze vessel filled with necessary articles, and other baskets and bundles, containing a complete change of linen; also several strings of orange blossoms." Some 8 million sub-Saharan Africans crossed the Sahara desert as slaves. What kinds of lives did they and their descendants live in the lands of their dispersion? (*Source*: Frederick Arthur Bridgman, *Winters in Algeria* [London: Chapman and Hall, 1890], 107.)

Histories of enslavement attentive to memory will move from a focus on markets, prices, organization, demography, and the social and political impact of the slave trade—important themes that competent scholars have advanced markedly in the last years and indeed continue to refine—to transformations in culture and identity. It is time to cross-fertilize quantitative assessments of the slave trade with qualitative work deeply imbedded in African historical consciousness. This sort of paradigm shift has already characterized studies of industrialization and its related social and cultural transformations in Europe, and it is now occurring in a plethora of studies on cultural transformation in the African diaspora of the Americas.[74] As highland Madagascar's confrontation with the external slave trade suggests, African cultural transformations run much broader and deeper than recent studies of the demographic and economic impact of the trade demonstrate. Much work remains to be conducted on the refashioning of African cultures through the actions of slavemakers and merchants, adjustments by communities targeted by enslavement, and contributions of slaves to the societies of their capture. This work will advance only through a constructive engagement with both contemporary and memorial evidence.

African memories bring historians closer to how the subjects of historical studies experienced, considered, and managed the slave trade and its multiple effects on their lives. Because memory is about interpretation as well as retention and elision of data, memories and their absence challenge historians to reconcile their own interpretations of contemporary data (professional memories) with those of Africans over the years (elite and popular memories). Rather than "distorting" professional histories of enslavement, African narratives will enrich and modify them, enabling scholars to unlock and appreciate the diverse patterns of identity formation in the African diaspora. Most of all, listening closely enough to African memories of trauma and enslavement to identify elisions and silences will assist scholars in understanding the diversity of diaspora experiences, setting the transformation of African identities in particular places within the wider comparative context of the full African diaspora.

HISTORY AND MEMORY

What do highland Malagasy experiences of enslavement and social memory suggest about the relationship between history and memory in a more general sense? Fostering ambiguity, *history* denotes at least two separate notions: things that happened in the past (history as experience) and the representation of those past happenings in the present (historical reflection).[75] It is the second meaning of history, representation of the past, that characterizes both the historical profession and social memory.

Because it has passed in time, the past no longer exists and cannot be relived; it can only be reflected upon or reconstructed from the various traces it leaves in the present. Representation and recovery of the past through consultation and interpretation of its surviving traces are an imperfect, partial, and always subjective exercise dependent upon what traces of the past are found and consulted, how they are interpreted, and what political or historiographical purposes that interpretation serves in the present.[76] Because the foregoing characteristics of historical reflection hold true for both guild history and popular social memory, these two ways of understanding the past have more in common than most definitions of them admit.

Most scholars have tended to set history (by which they mean the profession of history) and memory at opposite ends of a spectrum of knowledge of the past, differentiating history as a professional activity governed by rules, procedures, and precedent from memory expressed through such diverse and "undisciplined" popular genres as myth, verbal narrative, imagery, ritual, tradition, song, dance, and identity.[77] This conceptual dichotomization of history and memory has served over the last several generations to delimit the acceptable methodological and evidentiary boundaries of the historical guild. The frontier between professional history and its "others," considered as "memory," has long been contended within the academy. The struggle of oral historians to promote their innovative methods and data ("oral tradition as history") within the historical guild is but one example of an ongoing contention over memory and history.[78] Today, many historians working with nontraditional sources are interested in both the "integral relationship as well as the tension" between history and memory, expanding their interests in memorial sources well beyond oral narratives.[79] My intent in these closing remarks and in this work more broadly is to argue that the traditionally conceived opposition between history and memory fails to acknowledge the fundamental similarities between them as *complementary*—not equivalent—representations of the past, denying their interdependence. More specifically, setting history and memory into opposition appropriately highlights the methods and attention to precedent in evidence and historiography that set the professional historian's discipline apart from social memory, but it inhibits fruitful inquiry into the relationships between enslavement and African culture change. Historians interested in how the slave trade transformed African identities and cultural practices will need to work seriously with memory as well as with contemporary narratives and other forms of historical evidence and human consciousness.

To demonstrate the methodological and theoretical problems of setting memory and history into opposition, let me examine the work of Pierre

Nora, a French historian who adheres to the traditional understanding of history and memory and whose influence on anglophone and francophone scholarship has been significant in recent years. Adopting the words of Nora, we might understand Andrianampoinimerina as a *lieu de mémoire*, a site "where memory crystallizes and secretes itself." Nora argues that memory is an almost ineffable state of equilibrium, tradition, myth, and meaningful ritual broken by the "acceleration" of history and modernity, its opposite. Modernity and its historians generate critical discourses of this static memory and thereby destroy it, he argues. "Memory and history, far from being synonymous, appear now to be in fundamental opposition." In the modern era, sites of memory are but mere remainders of the "pure consciousness" of the past, "monuments of history torn away from the movement of history."[80] Memory, writes Nora, tends to give way when subjected to the individualizing forces of modernity, producing a multiplicity of private or individual memories. This atomization of memory is possible only where there is a certain will to remember, he notes, and because sites of memory are endowed with a "capacity for metamorphosis, an endless recycling of their meaning and an unpredictable proliferation of their ramifications."[81] It is this illusive yet persistent quality of sites of memory that might assist us in conceptualizing how memories of Andrianampoinimerina have functioned over the changing political and economic circumstances of the last two centuries as symbols of legitimate rule and good government. Nora elaborates:

> One simple but decisive trait of sites of memory sets them apart from every type of history to which we have become accustomed, ancient or modern. Every previous historical or scientific approach to memory, whether national or social, has concerned itself with *realia*, with things in themselves and in their immediate reality. Contrary to historical objects, however, *lieux de mémoire* have no referent in reality; or, rather, they are their own referent: pure, exclusively self-referential signs. This is not to say that they are without content, physical presence, or history; it is to suggest that what makes them sites of memory is precisely that by which they escape from history. In this sense, the site of memory is double: a site of excess closed upon itself, concentrated in its own name, but also forever open to the full range of its possible significations.[82]

At first inspection, the heroic image of Andrianampoinimerina seems to qualify well for Nora's notion of memory as something stable, primordial, antihistory, without historical referent. Such a conclusion is reinforced by modern visions of Andrianampoinimerina that bear a striking resemblance to nineteenth-century historical narratives such as those of

Raombana and the *Tantara*. But to consider Andrianampoinimerina in his numerous contemporary and modern manifestations, as I have in these pages, is to acknowledge a complex but unmistakably connected relationship between Andrianampoinimerina as *lieu de mémoire* (or *mythos*) and Andrianampoinimerina as *realia* (or *logos*), a man of flesh and blood who commerced in slaves and forged a kingdom together with his people at the dawn of the nineteenth century. To engage seriously Nora's proposition that human beings must express a *will* to establish sites of memory, however, is to set history (in both of its meanings) and memory back into a more dialectical interaction and to suggest conclusions about their qualities contrary to those he and his professional colleagues usually offer. Human memories are informed and shaped by changing but concrete social and historical circumstances; they are not "pure, exclusively self-referential signs." The Andrianampoinimerina of *realia* was popular even in his own time, for example; Andrianampoinimerina the acclaimed *lieu de mémoire* was not a fanciful invention.[83] By *willing* to embrace Andrianampoinimerina and make him relevant to their lives, their aspirations, and their changing historical circumstances over the last two centuries, highland Malagasy have placed social memory in the service of transforming their society and their collective identity—key elements of their history. In making their history, highland Malagasy have likewise shaped their social memory.

History (as things that happen) and memory, therefore, do not stand apart in highland Madagascar. They reproduce each other. Andrianampoinimerina remains a site of memory today because he has been politically useful and pertinent to highland Malagasy over the generations.[84] The continuing utility of Andrianampoinimerina to real people nearly two centuries after his death underscores how important it is for scholars to excavate the social and emotional meanings of political symbols in historical context. Symbols do not exist hermetically of themselves; they acquire meaning only through human interpretation. Interpretation, in turn, is influenced by social relationships and consciousness of experience. If the core meaning of Andrianampoinimerina as a moral and just leader has remained stable over nearly two hundred years, it has done so because people find such symbolism a meaningful "resource to deploy" in shaping their present and in producing their past, their history. Andrianampoinimerina lives but through the memories of the living; with his memory, highland Malagasy forge their history.

If social memory and history as the lived past are interdependent, what is the relationship between history and memory as registers, reflections, or representations of experience? To answer this question let me take three concrete illustrative examples encountered in this study. Memories of slavery tend to crystallize around different historical experiences and interpretations (Nora's "sites" of memory) according to who is remembering and in what circumstances they do so. The professional "memory" I have developed in this book (especially in Part 1) utilizing contemporary European sources emphasizes the organization of enslavement, the operation of transportation networks, and the demographic, economic, and social impact of enslavement on daily life. These professional reflections are guided by intellectual engagement with existing paradigms of historical scholarship and attention to professional standards of evidence. By collectively imagining themselves as Merina, on the other hand, highland Malagasy organized their historical memories around their founder king Andrianampoinimerina and elided many details of enslavement that are of such interest to professional historians like myself. In contrast to the foreign professional historian, highland Malagasy produced social memories concerning the era of the slave trade relevant to their historical experiences, cultural predispositions, and present political needs. The discrepancies between these two differing registers of the past become the professional historian's "problem" for exploration.[85] Finally, memories of victimization by enslavement become meaningful to cultural theorists like Paul Gilroy, who see in such common victimization and African movements about the Atlantic the making of an intercommunicating Black Atlantic culture.

In their varying contexts, each of these distinctive representations of the past offers their memorializers meaningful interpretations of historical experience. History as professional reflection on the past, therefore, is not fundamentally different in social purpose from memory nor distanced from the social and historiographical influences that shape remembering and forgetting. Professional historiography is a particular form of memory, and social memory is a specific form of history. Like Peter Burke, I see the historian as a "remembrancer," a custodian and shaper of public memory who may remind people what they would rather forget.[86]

But popular memory performs the same function. Common highland Malagasy were custodians of the public memory and pushed their sovereigns to remember and act on images of Andrianampoinimerina they (the rulers) would rather have forgotten or ignored. In political struggles, professional, official, and popular memories are often pitted against one another, strategically forgetting while causing others to remember what they would rather not or what they abjure. We have frequently seen such struggles over memory erupt in modern contentions over museum displays and public ceremonies of commemoration.[87] For this reason, I do not share the pervasive professional separation of history and memory as fundamentally differing modes of apprehending the past. "Memory," writes

Jacques Le Goff, emphasizing a notion common well beyond French historiography, "is the raw material of history. Whether mental, oral, or written, it is the living source from which historians draw. . . . To privilege memory excessively is to sink into the unconquerable flow of time." "In fact," he continues in a later passage, "there is no such thing as history without *scholarship*."[88] To the contrary, memory and history (as reflections on the past) are deeply and inevitably imbricated together, as this history of Andrianampoinimerina and his continuing narrative legacy richly demonstrates. To grant Le Goff his conceit that history is exclusively the fruit of scholarship is to deny nonprofessionals their historical consciousness and to eschew the complex and fruitful interconnections among professional history and social memory. Le Goff's proposition is false; it would weaken professional understandings of the past if observed by historians, for it reduces social memory to the "raw material" of historical reconstruction. As I have argued throughout this work, social memory embodies its own interpretations and meanings—it constitutes an historiography (or "historioracy" in the case of oral narratives) that historians must take seriously in their professional reconstructions. Mining social memory for nuggets of evidentiary "raw material," once proposed as the proper treatment of oral tradition, is fraught with problems and contradictions.

In contrast to Halbwachs, Nora, Le Goff, and others, I see memory—which is fundamentally an ongoing interpretation of the past through an incessant selection, elision, and organization of data—as an activity common to both professional and popular historians, to individuals as well as to collective groups. This is not to suggest that the methods and conclusions of guild history and popular memory are or should ever be equivalent registers of the past. Professional historians must always seek to employ, reconcile, layer, and situate variant strands of evidence and retain an explicitly critical distance from each of them; social memory adheres to no such rules. Although differently structured and "purposed" memorializations of the past, guild history and social memory lead to parallel historical truths, though those truths may be very different, and both offer useful insights into human experience. History and memory are forever in productive tension, and in a variety of ways. Popular memories (Nora's and Le Goff's "memory" or "lived history") are far more resilient in the face of professional ones (Nora's and Le Goff's "history" or "the science of history") than either of these scholars admits.[89] In Madagascar, popular memories have profoundly shaped the writing of professional histories. In turn, popular historians have creatively engaged professional histories; their narratives have not been destroyed by them.[90]

Each unique, history and memory are inseparable. For this reason, popular and professional memories of the slave trade, differing modes of historical reflection, can be set into productive tension. Both are essential components, in the words of Hubert Gerbeau, of a total "geography of memories."[91] For historians of culture change in the African diaspora, encounters among different registers of historical memory and forms of historical evidence will lead to cross-fertilization of understanding, fresh intellectual discoveries, and renewed awe at the tremendous creativity of the human spirit in the face of the spectacular and mundane inhumanities of enslavement.

NOTES

PREFACE

1. I employ the term *early modern* with respect to highland Madagascar with the thematic emphases Roberts develops in a recent essay (1997) on early modern India.

2. Law and Lovejoy, 1997, have moved part way toward this conceptualization of the African diaspora, urging scholars of African history to include the movement of Africans to the Americas as part of their intellectual responsibilities. Their focus, however, is on the "two-way movement between Africa and the diaspora" (diaspora conceived as the western Atlantic) and does not include Africa and other destination regions for slaves as lying within that diaspora (195). See also Lovejoy, 1997b: 3–4, 9, which acknowledges that many new slaves remained in Africa (as does all of Lovejoy's work) but conceptualizes the diaspora as synonymous with the transatlantic "Slave Route" (12: "in West Africa and in the diaspora").

3. The "Black Atlantic" is a concept developed in Gilroy, 1993.

4. The increasingly voluminous body of historiography on maritime and commercial history in the Indian Ocean is still poorly conceived as linked to economic, social, and cultural transformations in the interior, even in such key manufacturing regions supplying the Indian Ocean as Gujarat, India. See esp. Chaudhuri, 1985: 228; Arasaratnam, 1990. See also Steensgaard, 1974; Pearson, 1976, 1988, 1991; Brenning, 1977; Arasaratnam, 1978; Kling and Pearson, 1979; Prakash, 1979; Rothermund, 1981; Boxer, 1985; Das Gupta, 1984, 1986; Palat et. al., 1986; Subrahmanyam, 1986, 1990; Panikkar, 1996. Wallerstein (1987) more satisfactorily sets Indian economic history within the context of the Indian Ocean.

5. Arasaratnam, 1990: 226.

6. Arasaratnam, 1990: 234.

7. For colonialism and sovereignty, see Feierman, 1990: chap. 5; Mamdani, 1996.

8. For slaving within a stateless society, which does not conform to this general pattern, see Hawthorne, 1998, 1999.

9. Corrigan and Sayer, 1985; Joseph and Nugent, 1994.

10. Vérin, 1979, 1990: 31–50; Domenichini, 1981; Dewar, 1996.

11. See Morgan's essay (1997) on the perils of assuming a prior and fixed African ethnicity carried by slaves to the Americas.

12. See Ellis, 1869: 9. The inclusiveness of the social category *mainty* has shifted over the years. During the early nineteenth century it did not refer to the slaves of private individuals or to their descendants but only to the personal servant corps of royalty. By the late nineteenth century, though, and into the twentieth, individual slaves and their descendants came to be included among the *mainty*.

13. For shorter, specialized works on the history of slavery in highland Madagascar, see Larson, 1987; Campbell, 1988b; Graeber, 1996c; Rakoto, 1997.

14. See Hastie (1903b: 251); Graeber (1996c: 67–68, 268–70).

15. Complementing my own focus on *fotsy* experiences and memories of enslavement, Graeber (1997) explores those of the *mainty*, the descendants of slaves.

16. These are but convenient glosses for the Malagasy language terms, which, of course, are not equivalent to their English counterparts.

17. See Bloch (1978: 315–18) for a similar argument.

18. For highland Madagascar, Berg (1996: 49–51) has argued for the fundamental similarity in the status of slaves and free. To sustain this argument, however, one must ignore the fundamental distictions that Malagasy themselves made between *olompotsy* ("white" people) and various categories of "slaves," such as *andevo* and *zazahova*. Indeed, Berg's reservations about a distinction between slave and free are based primarily upon the observations of foreigners, who tended to see all Malagasy as "enslaved" to some higher despotic authority.

19. This is a debated proposition, generally referred to as the "transformation thesis." See Rodney, 1970: 260–70; Lovejoy, 1983: 274–76. The transformation thesis have been questioned by Fage (1989: 108–12), Thornton (1992: 72–97, esp. note 64), and Inikori (1996). The transformation thesis is retained in this work because it conforms to the case of highland Madagascar (see chap. 4) and accurately represents transformations in African slavery during the eighteenth and nineteenth centuries.

20. There is no Indian Ocean or Mediterranean equivalent, for example, to Law and Mann's excellent essay (1999) on Atlantic-oriented communities of Slave Coast Africans.

CHAPTER 1

1. Fabian, 1996: 230.

2. Rodney, 1970: 259.

3. Probably Andrianoninasandratra, who ruled previous to the more popularly known Andriamanalinabetsileo. See Dez, 1967: 664–65. Ifandanana is now abandoned and lies north of the highway about four kilometers west of Soavina and east of Antohobe (some 20 kilometers west from Betafo) on National Route 34.

4. Mayeur, 1913b.

5. Ramboasalama was the future Andrianampoinimerina, the founder of the Merina kingdom.

6. *Le grand dictionnaire de Madagascar*, vol. 4, BL/MD/Add.Mss./18124/141r–143r; Mayeur, 1913a: 29–30.

7. The long quotation is from David Griffiths, entry for 16/04/22 in his journal from 18/01/22 to 19/07/22, LMS/J/1. Principal accounts of the women's revolt of

April 1822: *Tantara*, 1078–80; Griffiths, journal entries for 3/04, 15/04, and 16/04, in his journal from 18/01/22 to 19/07/22, LMS/J/1; Jeffreys to Arundel, Tamatave, 8/05/22, LMS/1/3/C; Jeffreys, 1827: 37–38; Hilsenberg and Bojer, 1833: 254; *HOM*, vol. 1, 287–89; *RH*, II, 798–810.

8. For a list of works pertaining to the impact of the slave trade on Africa, see Miller, 1993: 470–74.

9. See Anstey, 1975: 83–88; Inikori and Engerman, 1992b, for winner/loser formulations of the impact of the slave trade.

10. Curtin, 1974: I, 154. See also Klein, 1999: 55, 72.

11. Becker and Martin, 1982; Inikori, 1982c; Roberts, 1987; Barry, 1998: 107–25.

12. Curtin, 1974: vol. 1, 197–342; Harms, 1981: 48–108; Eltis, 1991; Law, 1991: 219–21.

13. Alpers, 1973; Gemery and Hogendorn, 1979b; Rodney, 1982: 95–103; Inikori, 1982b; Inikori, 1992.

14. Jones, 1963; Horton, 1969; Martin, 1972: 16874; Northrup, 1978: 86–89; Becker and Martin, 1982.

15. Lovejoy, 1983: 66–87; Thornton, 1992: 98–125.

16. Harms, 1981: 175–215; Lovejoy, 1983: 107; Manning, 1990: 16–17, 99–102, 133; Law, 1991: 221.

17. Curtin, 1969; Anstey, 1975: 58–82; Thornton, 1980, 1981a, 1981b, 1983; Becker, 1988; Manning, 1990: 38–85, 1992; Law, 1991: 219–24.

18. Rodney, 1966; Inikori, 1982b: 38–45; Lovejoy, 1983; Eltis, 1987: 223–29.

19. Fage, 1969, 1980; Lovejoy, 1983; Klein and Lovejoy, 1979; Eltis, 1987: 223–29; Thornton, 1992.

20. Alpers, 1973, 1975: 264–67; Curtin, 1974: vol. 1, 309–42; Northrup, 1978: 146–230; Rodney, 1982: 95–103; Inikori, 1982b: 13–60, 1994; Eltis, 1987; Eltis and Jennings, 1988.

21. Lovejoy, 1989: 386.

22. This literature of prodigious volume is identified in Miller, 1993: 39–275.

23. Miller, 1993: 419–70. Some of the most important of these works are Mannix, 1962: 40–45; Thomas and Bean, 1974; Bean, 1975; Klein, 1978; Palmer, 1981; Rawley, 1981; Villiers, 1982; Conrad, 1983, 1986: 15–52; Miller, 1988: 314–633; Postma, 1990; Eltis and Engerman, 1990, 1992, 1993; Thomas, 1997; Blackburn, 1997: 97–108; and Eltis, 1997, 2000.

24. Miller, 1993: 275–310. Influential works include Meillassoux, 1975; Grace, 1975; Cooper, 1977; Miers and Kopytoff, 1977; Lovejoy, 1983; Ross, 1983; Robertson and Klein, 1983a; Worden, 1985; Searing, 1993; Shell, 1994; Eldredge and Morton, 1994; Glassman, 1995; Sundiata, 1996; Scully, 1997.

25. Most scholars of the slave trade estimate that the African external trades produced more slaves displaced and held internally within Africa than were exported to non-African destinations. For domestic commerce linked to the transatlantic slave trade, see Lovejoy, 1983: 60–65; Miller, 1988: 140–69, 379–442 (esp. 440–41, 153); Manning, 1990: 38–59; Klein, 1992: 39–41; Searing, 1993: 44–58 (esp. 53); Klein, 1998: 1, 39–41. The African counterpart trades to the Indian Ocean and Red Sea slave trades are quantified in Lovejoy, 1983: 153; Clarence-Smith, 1989b: 3; Austen, 1989, 1992; Manning, 1990: 38–59 (esp. 47). For linkage of domestic African commerce to the transsaharan slave trade, see Austen, 1979, 1992; Lovejoy, 1983: 60–65; Manning, 1990: 38–59; Mack,

1992: 97. Of 18 million slaves exported from Africa between 1500 and 1900, writes H. Klein in a synthesis of work on the many external slave trades, only 11 million had crossed the Atlantic, or slightly over 60 percent of the total. The external trades to nonatlantic destinations comprise more than 40 percent of this total when the several centuries prior to 1500 are taken into account (the transsaharan and Indian Ocean trades were of lower annual volume but endured over a much longer period than the transatlantic trade.) At the same time, writes Klein, as many slaves were held internally within the Africas as were living in the Americas during the late eighteenth and nineteenth centuries (H. Klein, 1999: 129, 165).

26. I borrow my words from Miller, 1988.

27. This phrase derives from UNESCO's Slave Route Project. See Diène, 1994. For literature on African routes (as personal narratives of enslavement and exile) see Miller, 1993: 474–77; Kilekwa, 1937: 9–17; Baldock, 1963; Curtin, 1967; Alpers, 1983; Conrad, 1983: 3–52; Wright, 1993; Equiano, 1995: 46–61. See also the many articles in Gemery and Hogendorn, 1979a; Miller, 1988: 173–442.

28. Postma, 1990: 106.

29. Symbolic of this fact, Joseph Miller's comprehensive bibliography of the literature on slavery and the slave trade contains no bibliographic category for enslavement or its equivalent. The few works which tangentially treat this fundamental dimension of slaving and slavery are subsumed under other categories. New scholarship is beginning to acknowledge the importance of enslavement and the centrality of Africa to the African diaspora (Lovejoy, 1997a; Diouf, 1998: 19; Larson, 1999).

30. Daaku, 1968: 134.

31. Davidson, 1961: 102–7; Verger, 1968; Stein, 1970: 83–84; Deschamps, 1972b: 68–71, 100–13; Craton, 1974: 25–26; Klein, 1978; Palmer, 1981: 24–28; Rawley, 1981: 271–72; Villiers, 1982; Reynolds, 1985: 6, 33–37; Conrad, 1986: 39–40; Galenson, 1986; Daget, 1990: 123–26; Walvin, 1992: 25–31; Gaston-Martin, 1993; Walvin, 1996: 35; Blackburn, 1997; Thomas, 1997: 370–80, 713–15.

32. Austen and Derrick, 1999; Dike, 1956: 40–1; Newbury, 1961: 26; Davidson, 1961; Daaku, 1970: 28–32; Isaacman, 1972: 52–53, 89–91; Martin, 1972: 117–18; Curtin, 1974: vol. 1, 110, 153–96; Alpers, 1975: 226–30, 240–41; Patterson, 1975: 76–78; Beachey, 1976; Kopytoff and Miers, 1977: 12–14; Northrup, 1978: 65–80; Kea, 1982: 105–6, 197–201; Lovejoy, 1983: 66–87; Meillassoux, 1986: 45–78; Boulègue, 1987: vol. 1, 134–37; Roberts, 1987: 17–19, 36–39, 94–95, 114; Miller, 1988: 115–26; Manning, 1990; Postma, 1990: 106; Law, 1991: 182–85; Thornton, 1992: 98–125; Searing, 1993: 33–38; Page, 1997: xxvi–xxvii; Gomez, 1998: 154–58; Barry, 1998: 61, 107, 114; Klein, 1998: 4–5. One of the most convincing and culturally situated discussions of enslavement is Harms, 1981: 24, 32–37. Enslavement is seldom listed in book indexes, including those of major works in the field. Miller, 1988, 1993; Thornton, 1992 (chap. 4 is entitled "The Process of Enslavement and the Slave Trade"); Klein, 1998. Manning, 1990: 229, supports entries for "enslavement," while Lovejoy, 1983: 340 requests the reader to "see criminals; debtors; prisoners of war; raids."

33. Daaku, 1968: 135.

34. Larson, 1999: 336–37. See also the following paragraphs (in the text) and chap. 7.

35. Klein, 1999: 115.

36. See Larson, 1999.

37. For the notion of a dynamic slaving frontier see Lovejoy, 1983: 80, 83–87; Miller, 1988, 140–53; Law, 1991: 188; Feierman, 1995: 358–59. Davidson (1961: 197) calls this zone a "slaving watershed." See Hawthorne (1998: 171–76) for analysis of changes in a specific slaving frontier similar to those argued here for highland Madagascar.

38. One notices, for example, that Miller (1988: 40–139), who has written extensively about a particular slaving frontier, proposes an interpretation of what happens in and around such areas primarily through an elegant reading of secondary materials rather than through a richly documented study of primary sources. On the sparseness of information concerning slaving frontiers, see also Martin, 1972: 122, 125; Alpers, 1975: 194, 226–27; Thomas, 1997: 713.

39. Curtin, 1974: vol. 1, 154. See also Barry, 1998: 3–125.

40. See references in notes 31 and 32; Bazin, 1974, 1982; various articles in Meillassoux, 1975; Bathily, 1986; Becker, 1986; Manning, 1990: 89, 130; Klein, 1998: 4–5; Diouf, 1998: 8–15, 18–34; Klein, 1999: 57–59, 71, 117. For the trans-Saharan and Red Sea trades into the Ottoman Empire, see Toledano, 1982: 15–19, which speaks primarily of prisoners of war and kidnappees, and secondarily of persons "sold" by their kin in a variety of ways; Cordell, 1985; Ewald, 1990.

41. Meillassoux, 1971: 54. See also Meillassoux, 1986: 45–78.

42. Barry, 1998: 96.

43. Thornton, 1992: 99.

44. Lovejoy, 1983: 66–78, 135–58 (quotation, 68).

45. Thomas, 1997: 376, 792. For an emphasis on warfare as the primary producer of African slaves in a broad synthesis of the literature, see Blackburn, 1997: 102–7.

46. Miller, 1988: 115–22, 126–59, 665 (violent slaving), 122–26, 667 (mercantilistic slaving).

47. Alpers, 1975: 230–32, 239–42 (quotation, 242); Beachey, 1976: 181–219. See also Lovejoy, 1983: 158; Isaacman, 1986.

48. Despite this observation, Manning (1990: 110) also characterizes enslavement in generalized terms.

49. See also Lovejoy, 1997c.

50. Cordell, 1985; Ewald, 1990; Mahadi, 1992: 121–22.

51. Rawley, 1981: 272 (50% of slaves are prisoners of war); Fage, 1989: 113 (one-third of slaves are prisoners of war); Walvin, 1992: 26 (upwards of 70% of slaves are kidnapped). The difference between war captives and the kidnapped invokes a distinction Curtin once drew (1974: vol. 1, 156–58) between political and economic enslavement. See also Daaku, 1968: 136.

52. Koelle, 1854.

53. Hair, 1965: 193–203.

54. These proportions are retained by Fage, 1989: 113.

55. These are the two broad categories of enslavement employed by Harms, 1981: 33.

56. Northrup, 1978: 65–84.

57. Barber, 1840: 9–15.

58. See, for example, Thornton, 1998: 100; Klein, 1999, 71.

59. Lovejoy, 1994a (quotation 164); Lovejoy, 1994b.

60. Diouf, 1998: 40, 48.

61. Thornton, 1998: 100.

62. Indeed Lovejoy and Richardson assume (1995: 269) that individuals enslaved in the central Sudan were exported, either to the Atlantic or across the Sahara; they mention internal markets only briefly (270, 286).

63. Klein, 1998: 53–57.

64. Mahadi, 1992: esp. 122–24; Diouf, 1998: 34–41.

65. See, as an example of these points, Hawthorne's recent study (1998: 130–36, 153–56, 162–64) of enslavement in Guinea-Bissau.

66. Curtin, 1974: vol. 1, 175–77; Kopytoff and Miers, 1977: 14–15, 72; Thornton, 1980: 426–27; Robertson and Klein, 1983b; M. Klein, 1983; Lovejoy, 1983: 16, 34, 62–65, 109, 118–19, 139, 182, 216, 230, 240, 273, 277; Miller, 1988: 130, 159–69; Manning, 1990: 22, 41–45, 89–90, 97–99, 130; Mahadi, 1992; Wright, 1993: 26, 34–35; Searing, 1993: 44–58; Lovejoy and Richardson, 1995; Klein, 1998: 1, 39–41.

67. The data are from Eltis and Engerman, 1992: Table 1, 241. See also H. Klein, 1983: 29–38; Eltis and Engerman, 1993; Eltis, 1997: Table 3, 31.

68. Lovejoy, 1983: 25, 59–60; Manning, 1990: 22–23, 45–46, 52–54, 128, 137; Wright, 1992: 181; Schroeter, 1992: 200–201; Klein, 1992: 39-41; Lovejoy and Richardson, 1995: 269; Klein, 1999: 9, 165–66. If one separates the Indian Ocean trade into northern (Red Sea, Horn of Africa) and southern (Swahili coast, Mozambique) components, there is more of a gender balance among southern slave exports while northern ones are predominantly female. See Manning, 1990: 52.

69. See esp. Robertson and Klein, 1983b; Mack, 1992. Manning (1990: 22–23, 47) postulates that in the Sahelian Savanna and the Horn of Africa "the remaining population became dominantly male" because the corresponding trans-Saharan and Indian Ocean external trades that drew primarily on these two areas were composed primarily of females. These assumptions, unfortunately, fail to distinguish between free and slave in the "remaining population" because it appears that women tended to predominate among slaves even in those areas that supplied the trans-Saharan and Indian Ocean trades. For women predominating among slaves where Manning's model would project a predominance of men, see Klein, 1992: 39–41.

70. Although a consensus has formed with respect to the predominance of women as slaves in Africa, there is less agreement about the different ways in which men, women, and children were captured. See, for example, the lack of gender specificity regarding means of enslavement in Manning, 1990: 51, 54–55, 90. Indeed, few scholars of the slave trade explicitly address this question in their work, but the different fates of the genders and generations can be deduced from much of the data on enslavement. More research is required on this issue.

71. Robertson and Klein, 1983b: 5, 11. For the capture of women and children during war, see Crowther and Wright's narratives of enslavement in Curtin, 1967: 289–316 (esp. 300–304) and 317–33 (esp. 324–27); Mack, 1992: 94–97. For the ejection of women and children from within lineages see Wright, 1993: 31–32, and below in the text. For the semisurreptitious sale of high-value female slaves in West Africa, see Mack, 1992: 98.

72. Eltis and Engerman, 1992: Fig. 4, 252.

73. Eltis, 1987: 256.

74. Wright, 1993: 7; see also 10.

75. Miller, 1988: 130–35 (quotation 130).

76. Nwachukwu-Ogedengbe, 1977: 139.

77. Thomas and Bean, 1974.

78. Rodney, 1970: 113, 117, 253, 257.

79. Martin, 1972: 166.

80. MacCormack, 1977: 194.

81. Alpers, 1975: 266.

82. Northrup, 1978: 70, 71.

83. Miller, 1988: 122.

84. Diouf, 1998: 34.

85. Wright, 1993: 43.

86. Dike, 1956: 37–41; Lovejoy, 1983: 82–84. Northrup (1978: 114–45) minimizes the importance of the Aro oracle in producing slaves.

87. Miller, 1988: 132; Wright, 1993: 7, 10.

88. Alpers, 1983; quotation from 192.

89. Lovejoy, 1997a. An increasing number of new studies are doing just this.

90. See note 27 for narratives of enslavement. For a description of the social conflict surrounding enslavements in east Africa see Feierman, 1995: 364–70. For the perversion of civil relationships in cases of kidnapping in nineteenth-century Hausaland see Hiskett, 1985: 114.

91. Lovejoy's excellent work (1997b, 1997c) on the biographies of slaves and the effects of enslavement on daily life are an important contribution to this effort. While Lovejoy's emphasis (especially in 1997b) is on a broad understanding of the transformation in the lives of people in West Africa, in this book I focus on a single society.

92. Wright, 1993: 59–62.

93. Curtin, 1967: 40.

94. Kilekwa, 1937: 9–10.

95. Curtin, 1967: 198.

96. Hiskett, 1985: 113.

97. On this point see also Hawthorne, 1998: esp. 156, 180–97.

98. John Thornton, (1988), has made an important contribution with his study of the role of discontent with enslavement and popular support for religious change in the eighteenth-century kingdom of Kongo.

99. Influential works on slave culture in the Americas and the Africas include Genovese, 1974; Wood, 1974; Levine, 1977; Blassingame, 1979; Littlefield, 1981; Stuckey, 1987, 1994; Sobel, 1987; Creel, 1988; Piersen, 1988; Mintz and Price, 1992; Mullin, 1992; Hall, 1992; Gomez, 1998; Morgan, 1998; Berlin, 1998; Miers and Kopytoff, 1977; Strobel, 1979: 8–21, 156–81, 196–217; Janzen, 1982; Robertson and Klein, 1983; Eastman, 1988, 1994; Mason, 1990; Glassman, 1991, 1995; Worden and Crais, 1994.

100. Lovejoy, 1997a. For exemplary studies of this sort, see Thornton, 1991, 1993; Gomez, 1998. See also Palmer's (1996) criticism of recent Americanist histories of slavery.

101. This is as true of the earliest statements of the African diaspora (Shepperson, 1968) as it is the most recent (Law and Lovejoy, 1997; Alpers, 1997).

102. A much broader set of issues emerge if one identifies the ways in which Atlantic cultures were transformed in ways not directly associated with slavery. For example, a fascinating theme of emerging work is the cultural feedback of extracontinental African diaspora peoples, identities, and practices on continental African ones. See, for example, Verger, 1968: 599–635; Turner, 1975; Harris, 1977a, 1977b, 1982; Lindsay, 1994; Law,

1997; Lovejoy, 1997a; Law and Lovejoy, 1997, Law and Mann, 1999. See also Gilroy, 1993, and a variety of other works on Africans and their descendants in the Atlantic.

103. By "secret" history I do not mean a history hidden from all but the few. A secret history of the slave trade is one which has been socially effaced but subsequently remembered. I owe my terminology to Stern, 1995: esp. x.

104. Ministère de l'Economie, 1993: 21.

105. The death of Andrianampoinimerina is conventionally dated to early 1810, an error. On the dating of Andrianampoinimerina's death to 1809 see Roux to Decaen, Tamatave, 15/07/09, ADC/FD/102/288v; *HOM*, vol. 2, 128; Delivré, 1974: 214–27.

106. General histories of the Merina kingdom include Deschamps, 1972a; Mutibwa, 1974; Prou, 1987; Vérin, 1990; Brown, 1995.

107. Although he failed to elaborate, by contrast, geographer J.-P. Raison (1976: 193, 195) suggested that Malagasy ethnicities were historically formed.

108. At the extreme, some modern scholars and Merina ethnic activists ascribe Merina identity to the Austronesian-speaking immigrants to Madagascar and not to the African ones, melding a disingenuous scheme of race classification that ranks Indonesians over Africans to a mistaken history of highland Malagasy ethnicity.

109. Testimony of La Case, who reported a region named "Himaire" in 1667, cited in Delivré, 1974: 12, 341, n. 4. The definition for *erinerina* is derived from Richardson, 1885: 139. For *Antaimerina* see Grandidier, 1895.

110. Many Indian Ocean merchants were Muslim, and most Malagasy cultures, though not Islamic in religion, were profoundly influenced by historical contacts across the ocean with the Islamic world. Highlanders never adopted the pejorative term *Amboalambo* suggested by their island neighbors.

111. For the earliest recorded examples, see Mariano, 1904: 13; Ellis, 1979: 157–58.

112. See, for example, the discussion about *hova* in La Vaissière (1885: 52–53) and A. Grandidier (1895: 49), two of the few culturally sensitive readings of the term in nineteenth- and early twentieth-century European writing on highland Madagascar.

113. This refusal is best illustrated through discourse at the cultural interface between Malagasy and European usage. See Raombana's usage of *hova* to mean "plebian" (*RH*, I, 52, 92). When referring to all the highland Malagasy, Raombana writes "people of Imerina" (*RH*, I, 86, 102, 186, 308), but when denoting the *hova* in particular he qualifies this statement, writing, "the Hova people of Imerina" (*RH*, I, 199). For a lengthy discussion of these issues, see Larson, 1996; *Firaketana*, no. 178 (Avril 1955), 2d. ed., entry for "Hova," 295–96. For additional examples of how European nomenclature of kin, clan, and tribe were never adopted by Malagasy, see Domenichini, 1989.

114. *Oxford English Dictionary*, 1989: vol. 5, 423–24; *Larousse du XXᵉ siècle*, 1930: vol. 3, 316; Bloch and van Wartburg, 1964: 240; *Trésor de la langue française*, 1980: vol. 8, 246.

115. Tonkin, McDonald, and Chapman, 1989: 12.

116. Liddell and Scott, 1925–1940: I, 480.

117. Warner and Lunt, 1941: 220; Riesman, 1953–54: 15; Glazer and Moynihan, 1963, 1975: 1–26; Novak, 1971.

118. Wallerstein, 1960: 133. "I had the impression that I had literally invented the word," Wallerstein recalls of *ethnicity* (Wallerstein, letter to the author, 03/03/97).

119. For work on polyculturalism in African cities which commenced under the rubric of "tribalism" but ended under that of "ethnicity," see Bascom, 1955; Balandier, 1955; Richards, 1956; Mitchell, 1956, 1957, 1960, 1987; Epstein, 1958; Kuper, Watts, and Davies, 1958; Little, 1959; Banton, 1960; Southall, 1961; Powdermaker, 1962; Mayer, 1962; Wilson and Mafeje, 1963; Gluckman, 1965; Kuper and Smith, 1969; Enloe, 1973; Cohen, 1974; Young, 1976, 1986; Rothchild and Olorunsola, 1983; Wilmsen with Dubow and Sharp, 1994; La Gorgendière, King, and Vaughan, 1996.

120. For classical treatments of ethnicity or tribalism in historical context, see Leys, 1975: 199–200; Young, 1976; Iliffe, 1979: 318–41; Ranger, 1983; Chanock, 1985; Amselle and M'Bokolo, 1985; Newbury, 1988; Vail, 1989; Chrétien and Prunier, 1989; Amselle, 1990; Mamdani, 1996.

121. See esp. Barth, 1969: 9–38; Horowitz, 1985; Thompson, 1989; Eriksen, 1993; Alonso, 1994. For an explicit criticism of the predominant approach to ethnicity similar to the one developed here, see Bravman, 1998.

122. See, for example, Jourdain, 1839: 14.

123. *Tantara*, 616, 890, 892.

124. Dubois, 1938: 10–27 (Betsileo); Valette, 1966b: 1006–9 (Betsileo); Huntington, 1973a: 12, 26 (Bara); Esoavelomandroso, 1979: 285–356 (Betsimisaraka); Kottak, 1980: 4–5, 45–49, 88–109 (Betsileo); Wilson, 1992: 17, 25 (Tsimihety).

125. David Johns's dictionary (1835: 234) defines *tanindrana* as "a stranger, those from a distant district."

126. For an explicitly contrary interpretation applied to the period after 1828, one that conforms to the dominant paradigm, see Esoavelomandroso, 1989. See also Alvarez, 1995.

127. The work of Epstein (1978) and Bentley (1987) has been particularly influential to my thinking about an internal paradigm of ethnicity. See also Larson, forthcoming, d.

128. For an example, see the speeches of founder king Andrianampoinimerina reproduced in *Tantara*, 705–55.

129. See, for example, "Kabary nataon'Ilehimijila tany Manerinerina fony izy nihaona tamin'dRadama raha nanatitra taratasy," in Rainandriamampandry, 1972: 107, 108.

130. For some examples of Merina as a community of people, see *Tantara*, 290 (*veloma ry Merina*), 297 (*ray Merina*), 298 (*mandehana re Merina*), 299 (*izany no ambara'ko amy nareo, ry Merina*), 310 (*Mandre va hianareo, ley Merina?*), 375 (*izay no ambara ko amy nareo Merina*), 709 (*izao no angaroa'ko volo anareo ry Merina*), 728 (*ary izany no lazai'ko amy nareo ry Merina*); Rainandriamampandry, 1972: 109, 117 (*Veloma, ray Imerina ambanilanitra*); Domenichini, 1985: 92 (*ary nony efa nanaiky ho an-dRamboasalama avokoa Imerina*), 78 (*ary nony inona, dia niady antrano Imerina*). For examples of Merina as a toponym, see *Tantara*, 656 (*lohasakalava, ao Antsiriry, an-tsisiny Merina any andrefana*), 667 (*Betatao, farany Merina amoron'ala*); Rainandriamampandry, 1972: 110 (*hahabe voho an'Imerina*); Domenichini, 1985: 348 (*dia tonga taty Imerina*), 328 (*nitondra an-dRafaroratra hiakatra Imerina*), 294 (*ka 15 andro dia tonga aty Imerina izy*).

131. *Tantara*, 12 (*Ary Andrianampoinimerina nahefa any Merina*), 287 (*Dia azo ny avokoa i Merina*), 301 (*Dia niady i Merina nony niamboho Andriamasinavalona*), 311 (*Raha tsy maty eto hianao, tsy avelako raha tsy ome'nao ahy i Merina*), 421 (*Izy no tompo ny fahatelo ny Merina, fony niady an-trano*), 707 (*Fa mandry volo i Merina;*

nampandry volo any Merina hianao), 707 (*Atao ko akanga tsy roa volo i Merina. . . . fa ahy izao Merina tafa kambana izao*); Rainandriamampandry, 1972: 108 (*mifanantera amin'Imerina ambanilanitra*), 110 (*izay nofinari-bavan'Andrianampoinimerina nahary fenitra an'Imerina*), 116 (*fa Imerina tsy iaraha-mitondra*).

132. See *Tantara*, 252 (*anaty ny Vakinisisaony*), 253 (*Ambohiniazy, any Tasy—ao Andriambahoaka*; *Ambohitrondrana anaty ny Mamo—ao Andriamary*), 420 (*fa nampakatra any Sakalava*).

133. *Tantara*, 728. I discuss this at length in Larson, 1996.

134. Rainandriamampandry, 1972: 117; Domenichini, 1985: 144, 298, 354.

135. *Tantara*, 8 (*Ary koa misy izay firenen-gasy aty Merina, izay taranaky ny Vazimba, hono: ny Antehiroka no isa ny*), 8 (*Izany tantara izany dia voa soratra amy ny teni-gasy*), 17 (*Hoy ny hira malagasy*), 18 (*oha-bolana ny Gasy koa izany*).

136. For some recent approaches to ethnicity as performance, with which this study is closely aligned, see Sharp and Boonzaier, 1994; Astuti, 1995; Lambek and Walsh, 1997; Bravman, 1998. For ethnicity as aimed at producing and constraining behavior see also Harms, 1981: 141–42.

137. Lonsdale, 1992: 466, 350. For recent developments of Lonsdale's concept of "moral ethnicity," see the essays by Geschiere and Ranger in La Gorgendière, King, and Vaughan, 1996. One could equally speak about a "moral community," the term preferred by Glassman (1995: 20). I borrow "imagined community" from Anderson, 1983.

138. For two examples, one drawing on Western intellectual traditions and the other on moralizing discourses of gender and sexuality in colonial Zimbabwe, see Taylor, 1989: 3–107; Jeater, 1993.

139. Breen, 1997: 73, 93.

140. For a comparable relationship between historical narrative and identity among an east African people, see Willis, 1992.

141. Rappaport, 1990: 183–86.

142. For examples of the approach criticized here, consult the citations in note 120. For a criticism similar to the one I develop here, see Bravman, 1998: 9–15.

143. Harms, 1981; Curtin, 1984: 38–59; Isaacman, 1986; Willis, 1993; Spear and Waller, 1993; Atkinson, 1994; Glassman, 1995; Greene, 1996.

144. The classic example is Harms's study (1981: 126–42) of the expansion of Bobangi identity along the Congo River.

145. Hobsbawm and Ranger, 1983.

146. Harms, 1982: 197–215; Austen, 1993: 89–110.

147. Shaw, 1997, forthcoming.

148. Janzen, 1982.

149. Baum, 1997, 1999.

150. Drury, 1969: 277; Dumaine, 1810b: 184; Hilsenberg and Bojer, 1833: 254; *HOM*, vol. 1, 285.

151. See Berlin, Favreau and Miller, 1988: xiii–xxii, xliii–xlvii.

152. Examples of secretive memory of enslavement within African societies include Klein, 1989, 1998: 238–39, 245, 251; Johnson, 1992: 162; Rasmussen, 1999: esp. 74–77; Baum, 1999.

153. Graeber, 1996b: esp. 428–29, 1996c: 55–56. See also Rasmussen, 1999: 87.

154. See Munthe, 1982; Berg, 1996: 43–46.

155. For a discussion of *firenena* groups in eighteenth- and nineteenth-century highland Madagascar, see Domenichini, 1989: 24–25; Larson, 1995, forthcoming, b. Today *firenena* means "nation" and no longer refers to descent groups; the semantic shift occurred during the late nineteenth century when missionaries appropriated *firenena* to gloss the English concept of "nation" in their elementary and secondary school curricula.

156. Giddens, 1979: 9–95; Williams, 1985: entry for "individual," 161–65; Csordas, 1994.

157. Guyer, 1981. For highland Madagascar, see Graeber, 1996c.

158. Desan, 1989; Glassman, 1995: 12–25. For highland Madagascar, see Graeber, 1996c. While I share Bravman's (1998: 5) clearly and expertly developed criticism of approaches to community as "shorthand for a harmonious group effect," I don't agree that a "romanticizing haze" surrounds the concept. For at least two decades scholars have been disaggregating and elaborating simplistic ideas about mutuality in communities.

159. Larson, 1995, forthcoming, b; Graeber, 1996c: 240–308. The same is true elsewhere in Madagascar (Cole, 1996: 101–5).

160. For similar observations, see Ratsivalaka, 1979: 114; Berg, 1988: 203; Raison-Jourde, 1991: 20. This problem is true of other collections of oral traditions, such as the famous *Ta'rikh es-Sudan* and the *Ta'rikh al-Fatash* of the central Niger River (Hunwick, 1985: 21).

161. The version employed here is Callet, 1981. For studies of the *Tantara*, see Delivré, 1974; Larson, 1995. See also the entry for "Callet" in *Firaketana*, no. 107 (Février 1947), 409–10.

162. While the *Tantara* say little about Andrianampoinimerina and enslavement, they do not neglect enslavement altogether. However, enslavement and slavery are seen primarily in domestic terms, with prisoners of war becoming slaves to their conquerors or ransomed back to their kin. See *Tantara*, 495, 508, 537, 543, 549, 605, 854. Several *Tantara* narratives mention the importance of muskets and gunpowder for political conquest but say little about how they were acquired through external trade (*Tantara*, 384, 488, 912–16). Two passages (*Tantara*, 854, 668) mention the names of markets where highland captives were offered for export sale.

163. Colin and Suau, 1895: vol. 1, 21–29; Gow, 1979: 1–77; Raison-Jourde, 1991: 167–237.

164. London Missionary Society, Imerina District Committee, Statistics for the Year 1872, LMS/10/5/B. For an introduction to the Madagascar mission of the LMS, consult Gow, 1979.

165. London Missionary Society, Imerina District Committee, Statistics for the Year 1872, LMS/10/5/B.

166. Cousins to Mullens, Antananarivo, 22/10/69, LMS/8/6/C; Barker to Mullens, Antananarivo, 16/01/71, LMS/9/3/A; Cousins to Mullens, Antananarivo, 03/08/71, LMS/9/4/A; Brockway to Mullens, Amparibe, 18/10/71, LMS/9/4/B; Cousins to Mullens, Antananarivo, 29/01/72, LMS/10/1/A; Cameron to Mullens, Antananarivo, 20/02/73, LMS/10/4/C; Nielson to Hovedbestyrelsen, Masinandraina, 05/01/70, I-32, NMS/132/3; Rosaas to Hovedbestyrelsen, Loharano, 08/08/71, I-64, NMS/132/7; Egnæs to Hovedbestyrelsen, Ambohimasina, 17/06/71, I-74, NMS/132/7; Rosaas to Hovedbestyrelsen, Antsirabe, 31/07/72, I-105, NMS/132/9; Stueland to Hovedbestyrelsen, Fandriana, 28/02/73, I-130, NMS/133/1.

167. For a similar interpretation, see Delivré, 1974: 119–38; Raison-Jourde, 1991: 99, 625–26.

168. *Tantara*, 1074.

169. *Tantara*, 854; Roux to Decaen, "Réflexions en forme de rapport à son Excellence le capitaine général par l'agent commercial à Madagascar, 1re avril 1808," 01/04/08, ADC/FD/101/241r–242v; *HOM*, vol. 2, 130; Ratsivalaka, 1979: 113–35.

170. An interesting contrast to the African continent, where frontiers tended to move from the coast into the interior.

171. On this point, see also Valette, 1965: 277–85.

172. See esp. Inikori, 1982a; Lovejoy, 1983; Eltis, 1987; Miller, 1988; Manning, 1990; Law, 1991; Thornton, 1992; Inikori and Engerman, 1992a; Searing, 1993; Klein, 1998 (Klein makes a minimal use of African narratives in a study that is otherwise based primarily upon secondary literature and some archival work). A similar skepticism about memorial interviews with ex-slaves in North America characterized historical work on the western side of the Atlantic (Berlin, Favreau, and Miller, 1998: xiii–xxii).

173. Shrimpton, 1997: 8, 80.

174. Hees, 1994: 3. For a classical statement of the difference between *mythos* as unreliable myth and *logos* as provable and factual history, see Finley, 1965.

175. See esp. Law, 1991: 5.

176. Fields, 1994.

177. For histories of slavery and the slave trade based partially or largely on "oral tradition," see Isaacman, 1972; Alpers, 1975; the essays by Isaacman and Isaacman, Dunbar, Miller, Hartwig, Holsoe, Tlou, Baier and Lovejoy, and Baldus in Miers and Kopytoff, 1977; Northrup, 1978; Harms, 1981; Strobel, 1983; Robertson, 1983; Roberts, 1987. A recent study of enslavement in what is now Guinea-Bissau (Hawthorne 1998, forthcoming) is the only serious work on oral tradition and slavery to come out of the academy since Roberts, 1987. For the use of "oral tradition" as historical evidence, see Vansina, 1985. I owe the distinction between a constructed and an inherited past to Abercrombie, 1998: 21.

178. Van Binsbergen, 1992: 59. For discussion about the problems and opportunities of "contamination" in such sources, see 103–5.

179. Burke, 1989: 99.

180. Cohen's criticism (1989) of formalized approaches to oral tradition as defining oral evidence in an overly restrictive manner is of relevance to this question. See also Tonkin, 1992.

181. See how Thompson (1994) rethought the issues of methodology and evidence in autobiographical interviews while producing the second edition of his influential book, *The Voice of the Past*.

182. Thompson, 1994: 4.

183. Cohen, 1994: xiv, xxii, 21, 24; Ochs and Capps, 1996.

184. Tonkin, 1992: 4 (historioracy). Vansina (1985: 196) writes of a "historiology (one dare not write historiography!) of the past, an account of how people have interpreted it. As such oral tradition is not only a raw source. It is a hypothesis, similar to the historian's own interpretation of the past." Unfortunately, Vansina does not expand on these remarks, for they run against the grain of his extensive work on oral tradition as historical evidence, messages of the past preserved through generations and accessible

to historians once they have mastered certain techniques. On this point, see also Connerton, 1989: 13–14.

185. Popular Memory Group, 1982: 228.

186. Tonkin, 1992: 96–97.

187. Cohen, 1994: 1–23.

188. Ayache, 1976a, 1976b. Part of Raombana's manuscript has been published by Ayache as Raombana, 1980, 1994. Hereafter these works are designated in the notes as *RH* I and *RH* II, respectively.

189. "Neither in its texture nor form, and even less in its spirit," writes Ayache (1979: 198) of Raombana's work, "does [it] have anything in common with recitations of legends on which the collective Malagasy memory had been weaned." On this point, see also Ayache, 1976a: 14–19, 133–34, 183–89.

190. Ayache, 1976a: 33–38.

191. This execution is described in Tyerman and Bennet, 1831: vol. 2, 519.

192. See, for example, Raombana's description (*RH* I, 348–51) of Andrianampoinimerina's rise to power at Ambohimanga. For the parallel *Tantara* narratives that also report violence but do not emphasize popular discourse to the same degree as Raombana, see 422–27.

193. For images of Shaka Zulu, see Hamilton, 1998: esp. 48–70.

194. Nora, 1989.

195. These interviews are described at greater length in Larson, 1995. For the dynamic relationship between *firenena* histories and those of the *Tantara*, see Larson, forthcoming, b.

CHAPTER 2

1. Saint-Yves, 1901: 8 (Duc de Praslin, ministre de la marine, "Projet d'un établissement à Madagascar," 21/11/67).

2. Saint-Pierre, 1983, 175.

3. McPherson, 1993: 208.

4. The principal islands in the Mascarenes were Île de France and Bourbon (now Mauritius and Réunion), but the group included many smaller dependencies, most notably the Seychelles. During the period covered in this book the Seychelles were administratively attached to Île de France. Statistics for Île de France, therefore, incorporate trade between Madagascar and the Seychelles.

5. Le Gentil de La Galaisière, vol. 2, 498–99. See also Hébert, no date: 6. I would like to thank J.-C. Hébert for sharing his unpublished manuscript with me. The Spanish piaster was the primary currency of European trade in the Indian Ocean during the eighteenth century. See Chauvincourt, 1968.

6. For Mascarene trade with east Africa, which focused on servile labor rather than food, see Freeman-Grenville, 1965; Graham, 1967: 110–29; Stein, 1970: 119–26; Filliot, 1974a: 163–74; Alpers, 1975: 94–98, 126–27, 150–66, 185–91, 214; Beachey, 1976: 11–66; Sheriff, 1987: 41–48; Capela and Medeiros, 1989.

7. Alpers, 1975: 243.

8. Campbell, 1993; Ratsivalaka, 1995: vol. 1, 49–35.

9. Deschamps, 1972a: 13–60; Vérin, 1979, 1990: 31–50; Domenichini, 1981; Dewar, 1996.

10. Wright and Kus, 1979: 7.

11. Kent, 1970: 217–18.

12. Rondeaux to Decaen, no place, no date [probably 1808], ADC/FD/101/252r.

13. Drury, 1969: 278.

14. Jacques de Lasalle, "Notes sur Madagascar prises sous la dictée de Monsieur de la Salle par Monsieur d'Unienville en 1816," BL/MD/Add.Mss./18135/123r; Rondeaux to Decaen, no place, no date [probably 1808], ADC/FD/101/252r; Dumaine, 1810a: 45.

15. Dumaine, 1810a: 37, 42.

16. Toussaint, 1966, 1974; Chaudhuri, 1985, 1990; McPherson, 1993.

17. Vérin, 1975; Domenichini-Ramiaramanana, 1988.

18. For a description of this trading system, see Rantoandro, 1983–1984; Campbell, 1981: 214–20, 1993: 130–33; Larson, 1992: 166–69.

19. Even so, successful sailing from Madagascar to particular destinations in the northern Indian Ocean (where the monsoon regime was active) required departures at certain unvarying times of the year. See Dubois, 1674: 61.

20. "Rapport du baron de Benyowsky au ministre sur l'ouverture d'un passage par terre, de Louisbourg à Bombetock, situé à la côte occidentale de Ile," no date [01/09/74], AN/P/COL/C^{5A}/4/34; Nicolas Mayeur, "Mémoire historique, politique et commercial sur les parties de l'isle de Madagascar qui me sont connues, pour servir de base aux projects que le Gouvernement Français peut former dans cette grande isle pour des établissements fixes, tant agricoles que commerciaux," Trois Ilôts, Canton de Flacq, 01/11/07, ADC/FD/101/32r; Mayeur, 1912a. Ratsivalaka (1995: vol. 1, 97–112, 186–210) explores Sakalava trading interests.

21. "Extrait de la correspondance de M. de Modave exprimant son avis et ceux de MM. Dumas et Poivre sur l'opportunité d'un établissement à Madagascar," (lettres des 5, 6, 7, et 30 août 1768), AN/P/COL/C^{5A}/3/20; Sylvain Roux, "Rapport de l'agent commercial de Madagascar à Monsieur le Commandant et Administrateur pour le Roy à l'isle de Bourbon, de ses observations dans l'exploration de la partie N.E. de la côte de Madagascar," St. Denis de Bourbon, 20/01/19, in Valette, 1962b: 39; Dumaine, 1810a.

22. Isaacman, 1972: 83–85; Alpers, 1975; Pearson, 1998.

23. Hébert, 1983–1984.

24. Mémoire de messieux Guiard et LeGuenne sur la traite qui se peut faire à Madagascar, 10/83, BL/MD/Add.Mss./18135/194r; Mayeur, 1912a: 64, 70–71, 75, 79.

25. Jacques de Lasalle, "Notes sur Madagascar," BL/MD/Add.Mss./18135/125r–125v.

26. Armstrong, 1984: 214, 223.

27. Roux to Decaen, "Réflexions en forme de rapport," ADC/FD/101/240r–241r; Rondeaux to Decaen, no place, no date [probably 1808], ADC/FD/101/251r; Alpers, 1975: 214–15.

28. Mémoire de messieux Guiard et LeGuenne sur la traite qui se peut faire à Madagascar, 10/83, BL/MD/Add.Mss./18135/193v; Anonymous, "Mémoire sur Madagascar" [ca. 1785], BL/MD/Add.Mss./18126/95; Rondeaux to Decaen, no place, no date [probably 1808], ADC/FD/101/251r; Roux to Decaen, Foulpointe, 27/08/07, ADC/FD/102/26v; Dumaine, 1810a: 28; Freeman-Grenville, 1965: 125, 148, 182, 190; Hébert, 1983–1984: 237, 246.

29. For work on other slave trades to and from Madagascar, see Hardyman, 1963; Platt, 1969; Campbell, 1981, 1989; Armstrong, 1984; Armstrong and Worden, 1988; Allibert, 1995; Barendse, 1995; Rantoandro, 1995.

30. *HOM*, vol. 1, 94; *RH* I, 553–55; Vérin, 1975; Hébert, 1989–1990: 74–78; Campbell, 1993: 140.

31. Mariano, 1904: 12–13.

32. Ellis, 1979: 157–58.

33. Mayeur, 1913b: 163; the emphasis is mine. See also anonymous, "Mémoire sur Madagascar," BL/MD/Add.Mss./18126/56; Mayeur, 1913a.

34. The value ratio of cattle to slaves varied between ten and twenty cattle per slave between 1770 and the first decade of the nineteenth century. See Mayeur, "Mémoire historique, politique et commercial," ADC/FD/101/57r [1769 ratios]; Mariette to Decaen, Quartier de Flacq, 25/02/07, ADC/FD/101/291v [1807 ratios].

35. Hébert, 1983–1984: 244.

36. Hébert, no date: 13.

37. Campbell, 1981: 214–20, 1989: 185, 1993: 140; Ratsivalaka, 1995: vol. 1, 390.

38. Campbell, 1993: 140.

39. Mayeur, "Mémoire historique, politique et commercial," ADC/FD/101/57r.

40. Toussaint, 1966: 125–27; McPherson, 1993: 181, 192, 209–16. Several French ships had rounded into the Indian Ocean during the early sixteenth century, but the Compagnie des Indes, which initiated the first sustained French contact with the Indian Ocean, was created only in the early seventeenth century (Hall, 1996: 284).

41. Toussaint, 1972: 20–29. The Compagnie Française des Indes was not one company but six, each of which replaced a failed forerunner. Because the French government granted each company a trade monopoly in the Indian Ocean, historians refer to the collective as "La Compagnie." See Weber, 1904; Haudrère, 1989: vol. 1, 9–38.

42. Lougnon, 1958; Toussaint, 1972: 29–32.

43. Weber, 1904: 68–187; Froidevaux, 1934: 3–85.

44. Toussaint, 1972: 44–47.

45. Toussaint, 1967: 65; Chaudhuri, 1985: 131.

46. Bowman, 1991: 12.

47. Toussaint, 1972: 47–50.

48. Prentout, 1901: 299.

49. Chaudhuri, 1985: 127–28.

50. Le Gentil de La Galaisière, 1781: vol. 2, 430.

51. Mayeur, "Mémoire historique, politique et commercial," ADC/FD/101/35v.

52. Chouette, untitled document, Port Louis, 01/06/06, BL/MD/Add.Mss./18135/157v; Rondeaux to Decaen, no place, no date [probably 1808], ADC/FD/101/252v.

53. Tellor to Léger, Port-Nord-Ouest [Île de France], 26 brumaire an 12ᵉ, BL/MD/Add.Mss./18134/132r; Roux, "Rapport de l'Agent commercial," in Valette, 1962b: 34; Le Gentil de La Galaisière, 1781: vol. 2, 424–27, 430; d'Unienville, 1838b: 234–35; Petit de la Rhodière to Gouverneur Milius, Saint-Denis, 10/02/19, in Valette, 1962b: 53, 55; Donque, 1972.

54. Curtin, 1974: vol. 1, 197–232.

55. Anonymous, "Mémoire sur Madagascar," BL/MD/Add.Mss./18126/87; Toussaint, 1967: 486–523.

56. Toussaint, 1967: 519. For raffia products (locally called *rabanes*), see Lescallier, 1803: 17–18. Lescallier traveled during 1792.

57. Roux, "Rapport de l'agent commercial," in Valette, 1962b: 21.

58. "Etat des postes de la côte de l'este de Madagascard," Port du Nord-Ouest, Île de France, 27 ventose an 4e, BL/MD/Add.Mss./18134/33r-v; Houssaye to Léger, Tamatave, 09/06/07, BL/MD/Add.Mss./18134/116r; Mayeur, Louisbourg, 06/07/78, MNA/HB/6/19/51r; Mayeur, "Mémoire historique, politique et commercial," ADC/FD/101/35r; Roux, "Rapport de l'agent commercial," in Valette, 1962b: 25–26.

59. Mariette to Decaen, Quartier de Flacq, 25/02/07, ADC/FD/101/291r.

60. Valette, 1966a: 44 (1778, Mayeur), 45 (1784, Dumaine). All figures in this paragraph are reported in *livres* and converted by the author to metric tons at the rate 2,000 *livres* per ton.

61. "Mémoire de messieurs Guiard et le Guenne sur la traite qui se peut faire à Madagascar en Octobre 1783," in BL/MD/Add.Mss./18135/186–93.

62. Mariette to Decaen, Quartier de Flacq, 25/02/07, ADC/FD/101/290r; In 1815 Fénérive exported 400 tons of rice. Chochot to Telfair, Port Louis, 03/03/15, BL/MD/Add.Mss./18134/40v.

63. Rondeaux to Decaen, no place, no date [probably 1808], ADC/FD/101/250v.

64. Mariette to Decaen, Quartier de Flacq, 25/02/07, ADC/FD/101/290v.

65. Chevalier de la Serre, "Journal du voyage fait à Madagascar (1777)," AN/P/COL/C^{5A}/9/3/51r; Roux to Decaen, Tamatave, 16/10/07, ADC/FD/102/69v–70r; Lescallier, 1803: 10–11.

66. De la Serre, "Journal du voyage fait à Madagascar," AN/P/COL/C^{5A}/9/3/20r; Baron de Mackau to Gouverneur Milius, on board the Golo in Saint-Denis harbor, 19/12/18, in Valette, 1962b: 109.

67. Mayeur, Louisbourg, 25/11/78, MNA/HB/6/20/56r; Roux to Decaen, Tamatave, 16/10/07, ADC/FD/102/70v.

68. De la Houssaye to Léger, Tamatave, 05/07 and 05/06/07, BL/MD/Add.Mss./18134/110r, 120v; Brain to Gouverneur Milius, Saint-Denis, 10/01/19, in Valette, 1962b: 84; Petit de la Rhodière to Gouverneur Milius, Saint-Denis, 10/02/19, in Valette, 1962b: 65.

69. "Renseignemens statistiques sur la Colonie de Ste. Marie de Madagascar," AN/CAOM/AGGM/1Z/26; Rochon, 1971: 345.

70. "Déclarations de Quelques Traitans de Foulpointe," received by the Lucie on 27/06/07, BL/MD/Add.Mss./18134/39r; Mayeur, Louisbourg, 25/11/78, MNA/HB/6/20/55r; "Mémoire sur les établissements français," no date [1774], AN/P/COL/C^{5A}/4/6; Mariette to Decaen, Quartier de Flacq, 25/02/07, ADC/FD/101/291v.

71. De la Serre, "Journal du voyage fait à Madagascar," AN/P/COL/C^{5A}/9/3/22r and 31r.

72. De la Houssaye to Léger, Tamatave, 00/05/07, BL/MD/Add.Mss./18134/110v; de la Houssaye to Léger, Foulpointe, 11/06/07, BL/MD/Add.Mss./18134/118v; Roux to Decaen, Tamatave, 14/11/07, ADC/FD/102/123r; Roux to Decaen, Tamatave, 28/11/07, ADC/FD/102/147r.

73. Mayeur, Louisbourg, 06/07/78, MNA/HB/6/19/51r; de la Serre, "Journal du voyage fait à Madagascar," AN/P/COL/C^{5A}/IX/3/8r, 43r–44r, 52r.

74. Lescallier, 1803: 17.

75. Mayeur, "Mémoire historique, politique et commercial," ADC/FD/101/23r, 64r; Mayeur, 1912a: 64, 67, 70–71, 79.

76. Dumaine, 1810b: 165, 168–70, 176–77, 211. For cattle mortality on land and sea, see Mayeur, "Mémoire historique, politique et commercial," ADC/FD/101/62v–63v.

77. De la Houssaye to Léger, Tamatave, 09/06/07, BL/MD/Add.Mss./18134/115v.

78. Mayeur, "Mémoire historique, politique et commercial," ADC/FD/101/63r; Saint-Yves, 1901: 6, 16 (cattle losses). Mayeur claims that three return trips a year was common for Mascarene vessels. This number is also suggested in Morice, "Plan of Operations for the Trade of the Coast of East Africa," n.d., in Freeman-Grenville, 1965: 191. In 1770 the *Africain*, trading on account of the royal government, planned five return trips between Port Louis and Madagascar. Desroches and Poivre to Laval, Port Louis, 07/05/70, BL/MD/Add.Mss./18134/63r. Statistics compiled by Toussaint (1967: 490) suggest three trips annually was rare (being too many), but this may reflect the incompleteness of his data.

79. Mayeur, Louisbourg, 06/07/78, MNA/HB/6/19/51r; Toussaint, 1967: 492–93.

80. Untitled document, AN/P/COL/C^{5A}/3/8bis.

81. Valette, 1966a: 46. For cattle prices, see also Bouton to Léger, Port Nord, Île de France, 11 brumaire an 12e, BL/MD/Add.Mss./18134/34v; Tellor to Léger, Port Nord-Ouest [Île de France], 26 brumaire an 12e, BL/MD/Add.Mss./18134/135v; Tellor to Léger, Fort Dauphin, 15 ventose an 12e, BL/MD/Add.Mss./18134/145r.

82. Mariette to Decaen, Île de France, 25/02/07, ADC/FD/101/290r.

83. Desroches and Poivre to Laval, Port Louis, 07/05/70, BL/MD/Add.Mss./18134/62v; Chevreau to Robinet de la Serre, Port Louis, 30/06/84, BL/MD/Add.Mss./18134/67r; Untitled document, AN/P/COL/C^{5A}/3/8b; Mayeur, "Mémoire historique, politique et commercial," ADC/FD/101/58r, 64r–66r. See also Roux to Decaen, Foulpointe, 27/08/07, ADC/FD/102/33r. Toussaint's census (1967: 519) of maritime cargoes arriving in the Mascarenes from Madagascar listed 104 cargoes of cattle and 32 of *salaisons*.

84. Mayeur, "Mémoire historique, politique et commercial," ADC/FD/101. The earlier figure is from 58r; the later from 34v.

85. *Trois voyages à Madagascar de Van der Stel, deuxième gouverneur Holondais de l'île Maurice en 1641–1642, 1644 et 1645*, in Grandidier, 1903–1920: vol. 3 (1905), 30–41; Filliot, 1974a: 18; Armstrong, 1984: 222–23.

86. Larson, 1997b: 142.

87. Dumaine? to Glément, Réduit [Île de France], 31/10/68, BL/MD/Add.Mss./18140/24v.

88. These interior trade routes are said to have been pioneered during Ratsimilaho's tenure as Betsimisaraka king (Mayeur, "Mémoire historique, politique et commercial," ADC/FD/101/23r).

89. Toussaint, 1967: 124–28, 167–74. See also Toussaint, 1954, 1972: 53–69; Fuma, 1992: 20–21.

90. Toussaint, 1972: 70–88.

91. Toussaint, 1967: 167, 169, 183.

92. Toussaint, 1967: 499.

93. Calculated from figures in Toussaint, 1967: 167–73, 183–84, 499.

94. M. Aug. Billiard, "Vues sur Madagascar," 15/03/21, AN/CAOM/SG/MAD/12/20r.

95. Prentout, 1901: 190–95, 289–95; Wanquet, 1980: vol. 1, 35–40.

96. Beachey, 1976: 25–36; Teelock, 1998: 21–129.

97. See Mayeur, "État des postes de la côte l'este de madagascard," Port du Nord-Ouest, Îsle de France, 27 ventose an 4ᵉᵐᵉ, BL/MD/Add.Mss./18134/33r-v; Lamie, "Notes," BL/MD/Add.Mss./18135/64r–79v; Chouette, untitled document, Port Louis, 01/06/06, BL/MD/Add.Mss./18135/159r.

98. Le Gentil de La Galaisière, 1781: vol. 2, 424–27, 430; d'Unienville, 1838b: 234–35; de la Rhodière to Milius, Saint-Denis, 10/02/19, in Valette, 1962b: 53, 55; Roux, "Rapport de l'Agent commercial," in Valette, 1962b: 34; "Answers to questions by Morice," dated 30/06/77, in Freeman-Grenville, 1965: 164–65; Donque, 1972: 87–144.

99. Saint-Yves, 1901: 16.

100. Saint-Yves, 1901: 16. "Tableau Approximatif de la Traite dans le Sud de Madagascar," ADC/FD/101/315r–316v (100 annually); Mayeur, "Mémoire historique, politique et commercial," ADC/FD/101/34v–35r (40–50 annually). See also Mécusson to Decaen, Fort Dauphin, 27 Pluviose an 12ᵉ, ADC/FD/101/327; Desroches and Poivre to Laval, Port Louis, 07/05/70, BL/MD/Add.Mss./18134/62r–63v; Bouton to Léger, Port Nord, Îsle de France, 11 Brumaire, an 12ᵉ, BL/MD/Add.Mss./18134/34r–v; Prefet Colonial [Léger] to Tellor and Jekell, Île de France, 15 nivoise an 12ᵉ, BL/MD/Add.Mss./18134/141v–144v; Jekell and Tellor to Léger, Fort Dauphin, 26 Germinal an 12ᵉ, BL/MD/Add.Mss./18134/153r; "Mémoire de messieux Guiard et Le Guenne sur la traite qui se peut faire à Madagascar," BL/MD/Add.Mss./18135/187r.

101. The rise of port cities closest to productive interiors was also a pattern on the Indian subcontinent (Arasaratnam, 1994: 10–32).

102. De la Serre, "Journal du Voyage fait à Madagascar," AN/P/COL/C⁵ᴬ/9/3/10r.

103. De la Houssaye to Léger, Tamatave, 00/05/07, BL/MD/Add.Mss./18134/111r.

104. The single best source for Betsimisaraka history remains Mayeur's unpublished "Histoire de Ratsimila-hoe, Roi de Foule-pointe et des Bé-tsi-miçaracs," BL/MD/18129/ff.82–144. Other sources include Grandidier, 1898; Aujas, 1905–1906, 1907; Petit, 1967; Esoavelomandroso, 1979: 32–48; Brown, 1995: 75–90.

105. "Mémoire de messieux Guiard et LeGuenne sur la traite qui se peut faire à Madagascar," 10/83, BL/MD/Add.Mss./18135/189v.

106. Filliot, 1974a: 133–34. For background information on the *régisseur des traites*, later called the *agent de commerce*, see Chouette, untitled document, Port Louis, 0l/06/06, BL/MD/Add.Mss./18135/157r–160v.

107. Desroches and Poivre to Laval, Port Louis, 07/05/70, BL/MD/Add.Mss./18134/63v; Préfet colonial to Tellor and Jekell, Île de France, 15 nivose an 12ᵉ, BL/MD/Add.Mss./18134/69v–70r; Roux to le Préfet, Tamatave, 28/07/07, BL/MD/Add.Mss./18134/76v; Roux to le Préfet, Tamatave, 01/05/08, BL/MD/Add.Mss./18134/106v.

108. LeGentil de la Glaisière, 1781: Vol. 2, 429–30; Saint-Yves, 1901: 5.

109. Mayeur, "Mémoire historique, politique et commercial," ADC/FD/101/23v and following folios.

110. Le Gentil de La Galaisière, 1781: vol. 2, 529–30.

111. For the role of French merchants in fomenting political disunion among the Betsimisaraka, see Mayeur to Citoyen gouverneur Général, Canton des Trois Ilôts [Île de France], 22 ventose an 10ᵉ, BL/MD/Add.Mss./18136/47r–49v; Ratsivalaka, 1995: vol. 1, 119–361.

112. Mayeur blamed this policy specifically on La Bigorne, an interpreter employed by the Compagnie des Indes, who led Betsimisaraka chiefs in a revolt. Mayeur, "Mémoire historique, politique et commercial," ADC/FD/101/24r; Mayeur, "Dialogue qui eut lieu entre moi et plusieurs naturelles," no place, no date [probably 1807], ADC/FD/101/78v; Copland, 1822: 38–39.

113. Mayeur, Louisbourg, 06/07/78, MNA/HB/6/19/52r–53r; Rondeaux to Decaen, no place, no date [probably 1808], ADC/FD/101/250v; Mayeur, "Des variations dans les prix des objets de traite et de leurs causes (ca. 1790)," in Valette, 1966c: 275–78; d'Unienville, "Questions sur Madagascar," BL/MD/Add.Mss./18134/21r; Copland, 1822: 40.

114. Anonymous, "Réflexions sur l'isle de Madagascar," no place, no date, ADC/FD/101/193v.

115. Mayeur, "Mémoire historique, politique et commercial," ADC/FD/101/24; Saint-Yves, 1901: 3.

116. "Tableau comparatif des notes et instructions données par la capitaine général aux différentes personnes envoyés par lui à Madagascar avec les résumés de leurs rapports," no place, 1808, ADC/FD/101/220v.

117. Mayeur, "Mémoire historique, politique et commercial," ADC/FD/101/42r. See also Mayeur, "Dialogue," ADC/FD/101/78r.

118. Dutch traders on the west African coast faced a similar dilemma; the conflicts they encouraged to produce export slaves impeded the smooth operation of trade (Postma, 1990: 89–91).

119. *Tantara*, 293–360; *RH* I, 207–71. Although the existence of this historical tradition is attested as early as 1807 by Mayeur ("Mémoire historique, politique et commercial," ADC/FD/101/57v), there is no contemporary documentary evidence of such a unified kingdom in the early eighteenth century.

120. Le Gentil de La Galaisière, 1781: vol. 2, 526; Pridham, 1849: 151–54; Grandidier, 1942: 35; Deschamps, 1949; Rochon, 1971: 198–214.

121. Rochon, 1971: 195–96; Filliot, 1974a: 32–33, 119–20. A significant number of pirates living about Malagasy shores settled at Bourbon when an amnesty was offered. Most pirates were gone from Malagasy shores by 1725. See Barrasin, 1953; Ratsivalaka, 1995: vol. 1, 121–26.

122. See Benyowsky, 1791; *Précis sur les établissements*, 1836; d'Unienville, 1838b: 307; Carayon, 1845; Sainte-André, 1886; Cultru, 1906; Foury, 1956; Deschamps, 1972a: 80–81; Filliot, 1974a: 130, 132.

123. For some of the earliest French traders in eastern Madagascar and their active promotion by trade authorities, see Martin, 1990: 168, 174–75; Desroches and Poivre to Laval, Port Louis, 07/05/70, BL/MD/Add.Mss./18134/65r–v. For the ever-changing official organization of the trade, consult Mayeur, "Mémoire historique, politique et commercial," ADC/FD/101/46r, 58v; Valette, 1966a: 36–39; Filliot, 1974a: 120–28; Ratsivalaka, 1995: vol. 1, 148–72, 253–75, 326–57. Slave trading monopolies seldom worked anywhere in Africa. Klein, 1999: 77–82.

124. Filliot, 1974b; Valette, 1966d: 897.

125. Mariette to Decaen, Quartier de Flacq, 25/02/07, ADC/FD/101/290r–290v.

126. Chouette, untitled document, Port Louis, 01/06/07, BL/MD/Add.Mss./18135/157v.

127. Hébert, 1979: 101.

128. Chardenoux to Roux, no place, no date [probably 1807], ADC/FD/102/113r.

129. Chardenoux to Roux, no place, no date [probably 1807], ADC/FD/102/114r.

130. *HOM*, vol. 2, 152 (quotation), 222.

131. Mayeur, 1913a: 34; de la Houssaye to Leger, Tamatave, 09/06/07, BL/MD/Add.Mss./18134/116v–117v.

132. Dumaine, 1810b: 153.

133. Filliot, 1974a: 159.

134. Mayeur, 1913b: 145–47, 171.

135. Fressange, 1808: 22.

136. Chardenoux to Roux, no place, no date [probably 1807], ADC/FD/102/115r.

137. Roux to Decaen, Foulpointe, 27/08/07, ADC/FD/102/23r.

138. Lagardère, journal, 12/07/08 to 29/07/08, in Hébert, 1996: 235–36.

139. Lagardère, journal, 13/05/08 and 14/05/08, in Hébert, 1996: 230.

140. Roux to Decaen, Tamatave, 28/07/07, ADC/FD/102/15v.

141. Filliot, 1974a: 159; Ratsivalaka, 1995: vol. 1, 267. The same pattern prevailed in the early slave trade of east Africa (Alpers, 1975: 194, 241).

142. Dumaine, 1810b: 146–218; Filliot, 1974a: 159; Hébert, no date: 35–36.

143. Mayeur, 1913b.

144. Mayeur, "Mémoire historique, politique et commercial," ADC/FD/101/61r.

145. A typical example: "5 9bre. Parti de Marmandia, fait *sacaf* à Vouitsara" (*sacaf*, or *sakafo*, is the Malagasy word for food or meal). Chardenoux, journal, late 1807, ADC/FD/102/164v.

146. Barthélémy Huet de Froberville, *Le grand dictionnaire de Madagascar*, ca. 1816, BL/MD/Add.Mss/18121–18132.

147. Lescallier, 1803: 8.

148. Barthélémy Hugon, "Aperçu de mon dernier voyage à Ancova de l'an 1808," 20/04/08, BL/MD/Add.Mss./18129/9v; Lebel, "Exposé sur Madagascar présenté à Son Eminence le Gouverneur Farquhar par M. Lebel [1801–1803]," BL/MD/Add.Mss./18125/210r–210v.

149. The importance of merchants' alliances with women along the trade routes is best illustrated in the journal of Chardenoux, late 1807, ADC/FD/102/163r–177v.

150. Lescallier, 1803: 22.

151. Tellor to Decaen, Fort Dauphin, 28 Nivose an 12e, ADC/FD/101/313v; Mayeur, "Mémoire historique, politique et commercial," ADC/FD/101/53v–54v; Roux to Decaen, Foulpointe, 27/08/07, ADC/FD/102/30r.

152. Chardenoux to de la Houssaye, Tamatave, 21/06/07, BL/MD/Add.Mss./18134/131r.

153. Barthélémy Huet de Froberville, *Le grand dictionnaire de Madagascar*, ca. 1816, BL/MD/Add.Mss/18125/68v–69; Mayeur, 1913b: 168; Valette, 1967. See also Ratsivalaka, 1995: vol. 1, 170–72.

154. Mayeur, "Mémoire historique, politique et commercial," ADC/FD/101/54v.

155. Ratsivalaka, 1979: 129–30.

156. *HOM*, vol. 2, 233.

157. Milius to le Ministre de la Marine & des Colonies, Ste. Suzanne, 16/07/20, AN/CAOM/SG/MAD/12; "Rapport sur l'expédition de Madagascar," Paris, 28/12/20, AN/CAOM/SG/MAD/12; De Frappaz to Forestier, no place, 00/07/20, AN/CAOM/SG/MAD/12; Frappaz to Ministre de la Marine, Paris, 31/05/20, AN/CAOM/SG/MAD/12/26;

Unknown to Forestier, Paris, 26/06/20, AN/CAOM/SG/MAD/12/26; d'Unienville, "Questions sur Madagascar," BL/MD/Add.Mss./18134/22r.

158. Brooks, 1976, 1983; Mouser, 1983.

159. In this respect the caravans of Madagascar resembled those of west central Africa where coastal merchants pushed their way into the interior (Martin, 1972: 119–22; Miller, 1988: 173–313), but contrast with those of east Africa where inland merchants speaking Yao, Nyamwezi, and Kamba pushed their way toward the coast, linking the inland with the commerce of the Indian Ocean (Lamphear, 1970; Roberts, 1970; Isaacman, 1972: 72–94; Alpers, 1975: 58–64).

160. Boyd to Roux, Tamatave, 25/08/07, ADC/FD/102/177v; Roux to Decaen, Tamatave, 28/07/07, ADC/FD/102/15v. See Chardenoux, journal, late 1807, ADC/FD/102/163r–177v for a description of the measures taken to retrieve stolen slaves.

161. Roux to Decaen, Tamatave, 14/11/07, ADC/FD/102/122r. For continuing problems with "liberté de passage" on the inland routes, see Roux to Decaen, Tamatave, 21/11/07, ADC/FD/102/128r.

162. Lasalle, 1898: 573.

163. Chapelier, 1811: 73–75.

164. This engagement was part of the Indian Ocean battles of the revolutionary and Napoleonic Wars (Graham, 1967: 24–57; Toussaint, 1974: 66–71). For a description of the *palissade* in 1792, see Lescallier, 1803: 3–4.

165. Fressange, 1808: 14.

166. Lamie, "Notes," Port Louis, 01/06/16, BL/MD/Add.Mss./18135/70v.

167. Decaen to Mariette, no place [Île de France], 06/04/07, ADC/FD/101/96v.

168. Roux to Decaen, Tamatave, 23/11/07, ADC/FD/102/134r–139v.

169. Despite problems with the anchorage there ("Reflexions sur l'isle de Madagascar," author unknown, no place, no date, ADC/FD/101/195v; "Tableau comparatif des notes," no place, 1808, ADC/FD/101/224r). For more on the shift of trade from Foulpointe to Tamatave, see Lamie, "Notes," Port Louis, 01/06/16, BL/MD/Add.Mss./18135/70v; Ratsivalaka, 1995: vol. 1, 392–99.

170. Mayeur, "Mémoire historique, politique et commercial," ADC/FD/101/58v.

171. Roux to Decaen, "Réflexions en forme de rapport," 01/04/08, ADC/FD/101/241v. Roux himself probably employed *traitant* Lagardère to purchase slaves for him in the highland interior during the 1808 trading season (Hébert, 1996: 217, 238–44). A similar system of stationary creditors and itinerant debtors operated in French Gorée and St. Louis of Sénégal (Klein, 1998: 22).

172. Chardenoux, journal, late 1807, ADC/FD/102/170r.

173. Mayeur, "Mémoire historique, politique et commercial," ADC/FD/101/2r, 25v, 45v, 47r, 48v–49r, 58v; Mayeur, "Dialogue," no place, no date [probably 1807], ADC/FD/101/75v, 81v, 82r; Roux to Decaen, "Réflexions en forme de rapport," 01/04/08, ADC/FD/101/237v–238v.

174. Hugon, "Aperçu de mon dernier voyage," 21/04/08, BL/MD/Add.Mss./18129/9v.

175. Mayeur, "Mémoire historique, politique et commercial," ADC/FD/101/61v. For the aggregation of independent merchants into larger caravans elsewhere in Africa, see Alpers, 1975: 230; Miller, 1988: 101, 191.

176. After 1800 highland merchants are regularly mentioned in *traitant* documents. French and highland Malagasy merchants generally treated each other as comrades and

shared important information of mutual interest. For a typical example of "ovas venant de vendre leurs noirs à Tamatave," see Chardenoux, journal, late 1807, ADC/FD/102/167r.

177. Roux to Decaen, "Réflexions en forme de rapport," 01/04/08, ADC/FD/101/242v; Roux to Decaen, no place, no date, [probably 1808], ADC/FD/101/252r.

178. Roux to Decaen, "Réflexions en forme de rapport," 01/04/08, ADC/FD/101/241r–241v. For caravans led by highlanders, see also Hugon, "Aperçu de mon dernier voyage," 21/04/08, BL/MD/Add.Mss./18129/9v.

179. Hugon, "Aperçu de mon dernier voyage," 24/04/08, BL/MD/Add.Mss./18129/12r; Lagardère, journal, 11/08/08, in Hébert, 1996: 237.

180. Chardenoux journal, late 1807, ADC/FD/102/171r. See also Chardenoux to Roux, Woitsara, 12/11/07, ADC/FD/102/161v.

181. Rondeaux to Decaen, no place, no date [probably 1808], ADC/FD/101/252v. See also *RH*, I, 198–99.

182. Chardenoux to Roux, no place, no date [probably 1807], ADC/FD/102/114r; "Notes remises par M. Chocal en 1816," BL/MD/Add.Mss./18135/24r.

183. Roux to Decaen, "Réflexions en forme de rapport," 01/04/08, ADC/FD/101/242r.

184. *HOM*, vol. 2, 150–51.

185. "Tableau comparatif des notes," no place, 1808, ADC/FD/101/213v; Roux, "Réflexions en forme de rapport," 01/04/08, ADC/FD/101/238v; Toussaint, 1967: 494–95.

186. Dumaine? to Glément, Réduit [Île de France], 31/10/68, BL/MD/Add.Mss./18140/721r; Desroches and Poivre to Laval, Port Louis, 07/05/70, BL/MD/Add.Mss./18134/63r–v.

187. "Etat de l'approvisionnement de marchandises de France," no date [1769], AN/P/COL/C^{5A}/3/8; "Assortiment de marchandises proposés pour la traite de Madagascar," no date [00/05/69], AN/P/COL/C^{5A}/3/9; "Assortiment pour 50 Mff. de marchandises ordonnés par Monseigneur pour la traite des Nègres," AN/P/COL/C^{5A}/3/9bis; "Mémoire sur Madagascar par M. Chevillard," no date [1773–1776], AN/P/COL/C^{5A}/3/14/209; Roux, "Rapport de l'Agent Commercial," in Valette, 1962b: 46. For a description of these coins, see Campbell, 1993: 128. Most of the coins Malagasy called *ariary* were made of silver from Spanish America, although there were several kinds of coins in circulation, including some of French mint (Molet, 1962: 27–30; Chauvincourt and Chauvincourt, 1968).

188. Prentout, 1901: 208. French merchants also employed the piaster to procure slaves in Mozambique (Alpers, 1975: 96).

189. Filliot, 1974a: 210.

190. Chauvincourt and Chauvincourt, 1968: 16–22, 25–6.

191. Anonymous, "Mémoire sur Madagascar," BL/MD/Add.Mss./18126/58; Lescallier, 1803: 19; Chauvincourt and Chauvincourt, 1968: 4–5; Drury, 1969: 277; *Tantara*, 71; Hébert, 1989–1990: 72; Graeber, 1996a: 14–15.

192. It was also the primary money of account in the Mascarenes (Prentout, 1901: 208–9). During the seventeenth century, Spanish *reales* had served as a money of account in the Dutch trade of northwest Madagascar (Barendse, 1995: 153).

193. Mariette to Decaen, Quartier de Flacq, 25/02/07, ADC/FD/101/291r.

194. Roux to Decaen, "Réflexions en forme de rapport," 01/04/08, ADC/FD/101/240r.

195. Boyd to Roux, Tamatave, 25/08/07, ADC/FD/102/143r. The piaster price of blue cloth is established in Lagardère, journal, 27/05/08, in Hébert, 1996: 231. This journal

entry also indicates that Andrianampoinimerina set the same exchange price for slaves (45 piasters and 2 pieces of blue cloth) during the 1808 trading season.

196. Rondeaux to Decaen, no place, no date [probably 1808], ADC/FD/101/252r.

197. Lagardère, journal, 13/08/08, in Hébert, 1996: 237. The exchange ratio of pieces of blue cloth and piasters (5 piasters per piece of cloth) is from the entry for 27/05/08, p. 231.

198. The transaction is reported on 17/08/08, in Hébert, 1996: 237. The value of a barrel of gunpowder in piasters is calculated in the following manner: Slaves were exchanging for a value of 55 piasters (45 piasters and 2 pieces of blue cloth). The exchange value of 31 slaves was thus 1,705 piasters, and the approximate exchange value of each barrel of gunpowder 1,705 ÷ 20, or 85.25 piasters. The direct piaster exchange value of gunpowder was substantially cheaper than suggested by this calculation, indicating why barter was so much more advantageous for *traitants* than purchasing slaves with currency.

199. Mayeur, Louisbourg, 25/11/78, MNA/HB/6/19/52r; Lasalle, 1898: 581; Saint-Pierre, 1983: 175.

200. Hugon, "Aperçu de mon dernier voyage," 03/05/08, BL/MD/Add.Mss./18129/15v.

201. Lovejoy, 1983: chap. 3 and 5; Manning, 1990: chap. 5, esp. 100.

202. "Réflexions sur l'isle de Madagascar," no place, no date, ADC/FD/101. The first quotation is from 192v; the second from 193r.

203. Roux to Decaen, "Réflexions en forme de rapport," 01/04/08, ADC/FD/101/240r; Mayeur, "Mémoire historique, politique et commercial," ADC/FD/101/68v.

204. Morice, "Plan for a Trading Centre on the East Coast of Africa," Île de France, 24/09/77, in Freeman-Grenville, 1965: 196.

205. Tellor to Decaen, Fort Dauphin, 28 Nivose an 12e, ADC/FD/101/312v; Mayeur, "Mémoire historique, politique et commercial," ADC/FD/101/66v–67r; "Réflexions sur l'isle de Madagascar," no place, no date, ADC/FD/101/193v; Roux to Decaen, "Réflexions en forme de rapport," 01/04/08, ADC/FD/101/238r. See also Molet, 1962: 12; Valette, 1966a: 43.

206. Mayeur, 1912a: 60; 1912b: 100, 107.

207. Mayeur, "Mémoire historique, politique et commercial," ADC/FD/101/57v.

208. "Questions sur Madagascar," réponses d'Unienville, Port Louis, 09/10/15, BL/MD/Add.Mss./18134/22v.

209. Mayeur, "Mémoire historique, politique et commercial," ADC/FD/101/57r.

210. Mayeur, "Mémoire historique, politique et commercial," ADC/FD/101/59r.

211. Mayeur, "Mémoire historique, politique et commercial," ADC/FD/101/59r.

212. Mayeur, "Mémoire historique, politique et commercial," ADC/FD/101/67v.

213. Mayeur, "Mémoire historique, politique et commercial," ADC/FD/101/58v, 59v, 69r.

214. Roux to Decaen, "Réflexions en forme de rapport," 01/04/08, ADC/FD/101/238v.

215. Mayeur, "Mémoire historique, politique et commercial," ADC/FD/101/59r.

216. While prices of slaves in the Mascarenes could vary dramatically with their personal characteristics and skills, they increased considerably between 1760 and 1804 for a series provided to me by Richard B. Allen. I would like to thank Richard for his assistance in researching these prices from among his personal notes. See also Filliot, 1974a: 217–19.

217. Mayeur, "Mémoire historique, politique et commercial," ADC/FD/101/67r.

218. Decaen to Roux, no place [Île de France], 07/07/07, ADC/FD/101/103v–104r. During 1807 a certain M. D'huile came from Isle Bonaparte (Bourbon) with four or five thousand piasters and purchased rice at three piasters and a half for each 100 *livres* (Roux to Decaen, Tamatave, 28/11/07, ADC/FD/102/146v).

219. Chardenoux to de la Houssaye, Tamatave, 21/06/07, BL/MD/Add.Mss./18134/131v.

220. Roux to Decaen, Foulpointe, 27/08/07, ADC/FD/102/26r.

221. Roux to Decaen, Foulpointe, 27/08/07, ADC/FD/102/26v.

222. For Roux's plans to control the commercial practices of French merchants, consult the correspondence from Roux to Decaen in ADC/FD/102. This correspondence is summarized briefly in Prentout, 1901: 314–23. See also "Copie d'un pétition de messieux les traitans de Foulpointe à Monsieur Frère, Foulpointe," 26/05/07, BL/MD/Add.Mss./18134/72r; orders issued by DeCaen, Îsle de France, 07/04/08 and 17/10/08, BL/MD/Add.Mss./18134/130r–134v. Roux's letters from 1809 and 1810 make it clear that his schemes were never implemented. See, for example, Roux to Decaen, Tamatave, 15/07/09, ADC/FD/102/292r–292v.

223. Mayeur, "Mémoire historique, politique et commercial," ADC/FD/101/47r.

224. Prentout, 1901: 124.

225. "Mémoire sur les établissements français," no date, [1774], AN/P/COL/C⁵ᴬ/4/6/9v; "Répertoire de la correspondance du baron de Benyowsky (1773–1777)," AN/P/COL/C⁵ᴬ/4/16/8v; "Note résumant le rapport de M. de Kerguelen sur Madagascar," no date [1790s], AN/P/COL/C⁵ᴬ/5/5/2r.

226. Larson, 1997b.

227. Miller, 1988: 153–54. See also Thornton, 1992: 117.

228. Eltis, 1991: 118.

229. Alpers, 1975; Cooper, 1977; Sheriff, 1987; Feierman, 1995; Ratsivalaka, 1995: vol. 1, 137–361.

CHAPTER 3

1. Dumaine, 1810b: 180.

2. Barry, 1998: 61.

3. For similar arguments, see Curtin, 1974: vol. 1, 153; Northrup, 1978: 146; Miller, 1988: 105; Thornton, 1992: 74. This study considers how highland Malagasy shaped their own experience of global capitalism and contributes to an existing literature on local engagements with international economies. For a Latin American comparison, see Stern, 1988.

4. Lovejoy, 1983: 60–65, 1989: 387–93; Inikori, 1982b: 38–45; Miller, 1988: 153–67, 380; Manning, 1990: 47, 92, 104, 130; Klein, 1990: 239–40, 1998: 1, 39–41; Searing, 1993: 53; Klein, 1999: 56–57, 126, 129, 165.

5. Finley, 1968.

6. Lovejoy, 1983: 274–76. See Preface note 19 for debates about the transformation thesis.

7. Lovejoy, 1983: 83–87, 119–21, 126.

8. Barry, 1972, 1998: 50–54, 57–59, 94–106, 306–14; Klein, 1972, 1990: 241–44, 1998: 44–53 (esp. 44–45); Robinson, 1975; Hilliard, 1985: 161; Fisher, 1988; Bathily,

1989. For the ethical debate over enslavement in Islamic Africa, see Willis, 1985b, 1985c; Hiskett, 1985; Barbour and Jacobs, 1985; Diouf, 1998: 20–30, 41.

9. Thornton, 1998.

10. Feierman, 1990: 145–67. For descriptions of similar processes elsewhere, see Isaacman, 1972: 114–23; Glassman, 1995: 89.

11. Davidson, 1961: 138, 211–12, 225–26, 233; Curtin, 1974: vol. 1, 154–55; Beachey, 1976: 182–83; Adamu, 1979: 166–67; Lovejoy, 1983: 85; Roberts, 1987: 18; Miller, 1988: 51–52; Postma, 1990: 89; Law, 1991: 182–84, 345–50; Thornton, 1992: 99–109; Searing, 1993: 129–62; Diouf, 1998: 8–15. For Madagascar, see Ratsivalaka, 1995: vol. 1, 274.

12. Patterson, 1982: 5. Ratsivalaka (1995: vol. 1, 274) makes this assumption for enslavement in Madagascar.

13. Anonymous, in Conrad, 1983: 12.

14. Baltasar Barreira, "Concerning the slaves that come from the parts of Guinea which are called Cape Verde," in *Jesuit Documents on the Guinea of Cape Verde and the Cape Verde Islands, 1587–1617*, trans. P.E.H. Hair, assembled by Avelelino Teixeira da Mota (issued for the use of scholars by the Department of History, University of Liverpool, 1989), doc. 16, quoted in Hawthorne, 1998: 106.

15. Waddell, "Journal," 9 (1852), folio 120, cited in Northrup, 1978: 78, n. 92.

16. Blackburn, 1997: 177–80.

17. Hiskett, 1985: 124.

18. For the concept of "rights in persons" as it relates to African slavery, see Kopytoff and Miers, 1977: 7–11.

19. Lovejoy, 1983: 274–76.

20. This principle is frequently evinced in African narratives of enslavement. The moment of greatest desperation in a victim's experience was frequently not initial capture, when the victim held out the hope of freeing herself by appealing the illegitimacy of the enslavement to others, but the moment of subsequent sale, when rights in the captive were more firmly established by the transfer of payment, and hopes of emancipation faded. See esp. Wright, 1993: 76, 84.

21. Smith, 1981: 68–73, 105–86.

22. Miller, 1988: 115–35, 676, quotations from 122, 127, 105. That the legitimacy of enslavements in Angola was a potentially significant problem is suggested by the fact that slaves leaving port in Luanda might claim their freedom by presenting themselves before the governor of Angola and asserting they had been unjustly enslaved (Miller, 1988: 390, 403).

23. The phrase is borrowed from Kopytoff and Miers, whose early interpretive essay on African slavery (1977: esp. 61) appropriately argued the importance of transformations in "rights in persons" to the study of servitude in Africa. Similarly, historians of enslavement need to remain attentive to transformations in "rights in persons" as it relates to the legitimacy of enslavements.

24. Roberts and Klein, 1980; Rathbone, 1985; Klein, 1988, 1998: 159–77, 197–205; Roberts, 1988; McGowan, 1990; Forbes, 1992; Lovejoy and Hogendorn, 1993: 31–63. An exception is Hawthorne, 1998: 136–39.

25. One of the best examples of "rules" of enslavement comes from a historical study of Diola religion (Baum, 1999). For ceremonies of enslavement, see Harms, 1981: 33–34.

26. This chapter is a development of Rodney's observation (1970: 257) that the domestic stratification of west African societies at the time of European contact "was what primarily determined the way in which external forces were received."

27. *Tantara*, 293–360; *RH* I, 207–71.

28. On this point, see also Cabanes, 1974: 50.

29. Raison, 1984: vol. 1, 96–97.

30. Some servants-slaves, such as the group called *Tandonaka*, were considered to be of *hova* extraction and not classed among the *mainty*. Generally, however, all the servants of the sovereigns were *mainty*. See *RH* I, 91–92 for a description of these categories. By the late nineteenth century and especially into the twentieth, the category of *mainty* became more broadly inclusive, including slaves, former slaves, and their descendants. Consult the Preface for a further discussion of the *mainty*.

31. Falola and Lovejoy, 1994.

32. *Tantara*, 915.

33. Bloch (1971: 37–72) calls these groups "demes." It is a curious testimony to scholars' lack of attention to nineteenth-century Malagasy language usage that *firenena* have been variously termed "demes," "*tanin'drazana* land groups," "clans," "*foko*," "*karazana*," and other questionable Malagasy and non-Malagasy terms. For more about *firenena,* see Larson, 1995.

34. Larson, 1995: 309–16. See also Bloch, 1967: 127; Berg, 1988: 202.

35. Scholars of highland Madagascar usually err in considering *firenena* as either purely *hova* or purely *andriana* (see, for example, Bloch, 1978: 316), when in practice they are often composed of individuals brought together from two or more status groups.

36. For a discussion of the link between *firenena* and their *tanindrazana,* consult Bloch, 1971: 35–36, 105-37; Larson, 1995: 309–16.

37. Raison, 1984: vol. 1, 90, calls these groups *taranaka*; Graeber, 1996c: 214, calls them families or *fianakaviana.*

38. Augustins, 1973; Vogel, 1982; Graeber, 1995.

39. Delivré, 1974: 159–63.

40. This was simply a larger-scale process of building a reputation and posthumous memory that Graeber (1995: 266–68) has described for tomb groups.

41. This term is suggested by Glassman, 1995: 12–25.

42. See Lonsdale, 1992.

43. See esp. Bravman, 1998: 4–9, 15–17.

44. Berg, 1985; Martin, 1972: 23–24; Peires, 1982: 135–60; Miller, 1988: 85–94; Thornton, 1988.

45. *Tantara*, 564, 606.

46. *Tantara*, 495, 508, 525, 528, 537, 564.

47. Exceptions to the rule of nonviolent encounters are relatively few and far between. See *Tantara*, 564, 605, 609, for examples of military encounters that are remembered to have produced significant casualties.

48. *Tantara*, 495, 508, 537, 543, 605. For similar strategies in west central Africa, see Martin, 1972: 117.

49. Mayeur, 1913b: 154.

50. For a similar process elsewhere in Africa, see Harms, 1987; Miller, 1988: 73.

51. The eighteenth-century division of labor is discussed in chap. 4.

52. Hébert, 1989-1990: 83–85. Ransoming on the east coast operated in much the same way. See Nicolas Mayeur, cited in Valette, 1970: 538.

53. *Tantara*, 543, 549.

54. *Tantara*, 854. Personal pronouns are not gender-specific in the Malagasy language; I have employed the masculine pronoun here because most captives were men.

55. *Tantara*, 508.

56. Mayeur, 1913a: 33.

57. *Tantara*, 541, 544.

58. *Tantara*, 854.

59. Ratsivalaka, 1995: vol. 1, 150–52.

60. MNA/IG/44/Claim #3591, 02/08/33. I would like to thank Ned Alpers for sharing this reference with me.

61. Berg, 1985.

62. Mayeur, 1913b: 154.

63. Mayeur, 1913a: 45.

64. Berg, 1985.

65. Miller, 1988: 71.

66. Mayeur, 1913a: 45.

67. Mayeur, 1913b: 169.

68. Lebel, "Exposé sur Madagascar," BL/MD/Add.Mss./18135/208v.

69. For perspectives on the conceptual relationships among wealth, blessings, and ancestors, see Bloch, 1986; Berg, 1988.

70. *Tantara*, 938–99; Bloch, 1989d: 178–79.

71. *HOM*, vol. 2, 148–49.

72. *Tantara*, 779. For case studies of pawnship in Africa, see Falola and Lovejoy, 1994.

73. *RH* I, 93.

74. European observers usually described *zazahova* as slaves, failing to make the linguistic and social distinctions between them and *andevo*. See, for example, Anonymous, "Mémoire sur Madagascar," BL/MD/Add.Mss./18126/67, which describes the process of "enslavement" for debt.

75. Patterson, 1982: 1–101. These themes are echoed by Meillassoux, 1991: 23–40, 67–77, 99–115.

76. Johns, 1835: entry for *zazahova*, 280.

77. Larson, 1987: chap. 6.

78. Larson, 1987: 49–55; *Tantara*, 323, 915.

79. Domenichini-Ramiaramanana, 1972: 72, 389.

80. For generational transmission of *zazahova* status, see *Tantara*, 323. As a rule, social status in highland Madagascar was derived through the mother, not the father (*Tantara*, 322). For redemptions by family, see Anonymous, "Mémoire sur Madagascar," BL/MD/Add.Mss./18126/67.

81. Larson, 1987: chap. 3.

82. For a more detailed discussion of the differences between *zazahova* and *andevo*, consult Larson, 1987: chap. 4.

83. Falola and Lovejoy, 1994: 4–5, 14, 64–67, 72–73, 86–89, 187, 218; and especially the essay by Morton (1994); Lovejoy and Richardson, 1999.

84. *Tantara*, 854. For Ampamoizankova, see *Tantara*, 668; *HOM*, vol. 2, 152. For rumors of Europeans as cannibals, see *HOM*, vol. 2, 151.

85. *RH* I, 552–53.

86. Everywhere in eastern and highland Madagascar debt could easily lead to en-slavement. Anonymous undated document, BL/MD/Add.Mss./18135/59r.

87. *Tantara*, 779. The term translated "slave" here is *andevo* rather than *zazahova*, and was probably used to give the statement greater force.

88. *Tantara*, 321.

89. Dumaine, 1810b: 191. For a case of redemption (the story of Andriantsimanazy), see *Tantara*, 503.

90. *Tantara*, 854.

91. *Tantara*, 854. See also Hawthorne, 1998: 137–39, 147.

92. Rodney, 1970: 121; Manning, 1990: 33–37, 99–102, esp. 101.

93. My moralized language ("sordid business") reflects both my own ideas and the prevailing opinion of highland Malagasy at the time.

94. Mayeur, 1913a: 14–49.

95. *Tantara*, 854.

96. Mayeur, 1913a: 45.

97. Eugène de Froberville in Leguével de Lacombe, 1840: vol. 2, 246, n. 1.

98. Mayeur, 1913b: 169. See also 166, in which the king of Antananarivo comments on rampant kidnapping within his dominions.

99. Dumaine, 1810b: 180–81. The same story can be found in *HOM*, vol. 2, 148; Leguével de Lacombe, 1840: vol. 2, 31–32.

100. For similar stories along the Guinea coast, see Hawthorne, 1998: 155.

101. Leguével de Lacombe, 1840: vol. 2, 32.

102. For African-American stories with similar moral conclusions—suggesting the culpability of Europeans and Africans in the Atlantic slave trade—see Gomez, 1998: 199–214.

103. Rodney (1970: 118–19). See also the comments of Baltasar Barreira, "Concerning the Slaves That Come from the Parts of Guinea Which are Called Cape Verde," (1606) cited in Hawthorne, 1998: 106.

104. Austen, 1993; Shaw, 1997; Rasmussen, 1999; Baum, 1999.

105. De Froberville, *Le grand dictionnaire de Madagascar*, vol. 4, BL/MD/Add.Mss./18124/141r–143r; Mayeur, 1913a: 29–30, 34.

106. In his *Grand dictionnaire* entry (BL/MD/Add.Mss./18124/141r), de Froberville writes that his information comes from "Mayeur's account." We can assume the account was written because de Froberville claims he "found" the name Ravoundriène there.

107. LFC/SR 129, 130, 135.

108. *Tantara*, 420–33.

109. For examples, see *Tantara*, 423, 425–26, 428–29, 484–85, 505–6. See also how the Tsimiamboholahy and the Zanamanarefo are remembered to have secretly switched allegiances from their king to Andrianampoinimerina (Tacchi, 1892: 481–82).

110. Mayeur, 1913a: 29.

111. *Tantara*, 760–61; *RH* I, 328–31, 462–67.

112. De Froberville, *Le grand dictionnaire de Madagascar*, vol. 4, BL/MD/Add.Mss./18124/42r–43r.

113. De Froberville, *Le grand dictionnaire de Madagascar*, vol. 4, BL/MD/Add.Mss./18124/41r.

114. Rodney, 1970: 114; Martin, 1972: 24, 97–101, 114–15; Miller, 1988: 3, 177, 183.

115. For another example, see Hugon, "Aperçu de mon dernier voyage," BL/MD/Add.Mss./18129/14v.

116. Mayeur, 1913a: 34.

117. For a similar incident further east, in Bezanozanoland, see Chardenoux to Roux, no place, no date [probably 1807], ADC/FD/102/113r.

118. Many itinerant *traitants* employed Malagasy agents to purchase slaves for them in the highlands and along the route to the coast. See Hugon, "Aperçu de mon dernier voyage," 02/04/08, BL/MD/Add.Mss./18129/12r.

119. Rodney, 1970: 258–59.

120. This point is effectively argued in Ratsivalaka, 1995: vol. 1, 137–361.

121. This principle also operated elsewhere on the island (Mécusson to Decaen, Fort Dauphin, 27 Pluviose an 12e, ADC/FD/101/327r).

122. Miller, 1988: 134. Two especially well-documented examples of this in east Africa are the Bondei rebellion in the Shambaa kingdom (Feierman, 1990: 53–56, 112–19) discussed earlier in this chapter, and the revolts of commoners and slave armies on the Mozambican prazos (Isaacman, 1972: 114–23).

123. *HOM*, vol. 2, 124.

CHAPTER 4

1. Mayeur, "Mémoire historique, politique et commercial," ADC/FD/101/59v and 68v.

2. This estimate is based on an average household size of five (*HOM*, vol. 1, 113), the assumption that no more than one individual per household was enslaved, a stable highland population of one-half million (see Larson 1997b: 141), and an average annual export of 1,000 to 2,000 persons. Basing himself on census records from the 1880s, Graeber (1996c: 268, n. 32) suggests that mean household size (adults only) was exactly 2.5, which, if true, suggests that total household size would have been near five. The 1993 Malagasy national census (Ministère de l'Economie, 1993) indicates that mean modern household sizes in highland Madagascar are between four and five.

3. Nwulia, 1981: 42.

4. Farquhar to Earl of Liverpool, Port Louis, 28/07/12, in House of Commons, 1826: no. 8, 21.

5. An observation supported by the higher price of children than of adults in Madagascar (Roux to Decaen, "Réflexions en form de rapport," 01/04/08, ADC/FD/101/240r).

6. Figures in this and the preceding several sentences are derived from the text and tables in Kuczynski, 1949: vol. 2, 755–74.

7. Azéma, 1859: 336; Scherer, 1974: 26–27; Gamaleya, 1984: 19–20; Gérard, 1984: 327; Payet, 1990: 17; Fuma, 1992: 35.

8. Lagardère, journal, 05/09/08, in Hébert, 1996: 238.

9. MNA/IG/44/Claim #3591, August 2, 1833. I would like to thank Ned Alpers for sharing this reference with me.

10. Le Gentil de La Galaisière, 1781: vol. 2, 381.

11. Chardenoux to Roux, no place, no date [probably 1807], ADC/FD/102/115r; Boyd to Roux, Tamatave, 25/08/07, ADC/FD/102/177v; Roux to Decaen, Tamatave, 28/07/07,

ADC/FD/102/15v. Hugon reports purchasing "*noirs et négresses*" ("Aperçu de mon dernier voyage," 02/05/08, BL/MD/Add.Mss./18129/15v; see also his entry for 03/05/08, 17r, and 05/05/08, 19v).

12. Roux to Decaen, Tamatave, 16/10/07, ADC/FD/102/75v. See also Leguével de Lacombe, 1840: vol. 2, 245, n. 1.

13. Bowman, 1991: 16.

14. Prentout, 1901: 140. Richard B. Allen informs me that on average, 0.2 percent or less of the Mauritian slave population could hope to be manumitted each year during the late eighteenth and early nineteenth centuries (personal communication). See also Allen, 1999.

15. Kuczynski, 1949: vol. 2, 763. See also Teelock, 1998: 98–99, 220–21.

16. In 1807, for example, male captives at the Malagasy coast generally cost 80 piasters and female captives 60. Mariette to Decaen, Quartier de Flacq, 25/02/07, ADC/FD/101/291v; Decaen to Mariette, no place [Mauritius], 06/04/07, ADC/FD/101/97v. See also Leguével de Lacombe, 1840: vol. 2, 246–47. This pattern of slave prices, in which female slaves were more highly valued than men in the interior, but comparatively less valued at the coast, held also for nineteenth-century west Africa (Lovejoy and Richardson, 1995: 281–83).

17. The sexual imbalance in slave cargoes landed at Mauritius continued well past the end of the trade from Madagascar (Beachey, 1976: 30).

18. *Tantara*, 321, 912–16, 779; Mayeur, "Mémoire historique, politique et commercial," ADC/FD/101/57v; Ratsivalaka, 1995: vol. 1, 408.

19. Valette, 1962a, 1979; Decary, 1966.

20. Larson, 1987: chap. 5. After 1820 men captured by Merina armies were routinely executed because there was no market for them (Freeman to Palmerston, Dublin, 16/01/38, PRO/FO/48/1, 234; *Tantara*, 322, 609; *HOM*, vol. 2, 520; Little, 1970: 52).

21. Miller, 1988: 135. Unlike Miller, who sees this transformation primarily in terms of elite political strategies (40–139) and changing demographic structures (140–169) on both sides of a moving frontier of enslavement, this chapter investigates changes in the everyday lives of those left behind in an economy of enslavement. For a generalized study of export slaves' daily lives along the route to the coast, see Lovejoy, 1997b.

22. *Tantara*, 815, 823, 827.

23. Mayeur, 1913b: 169.

24. For sale and pawning of wives, termed "men eating women," see *Tantara*, 794.

25. *Tantara*, 323.

26. Robertson and Klein, 1983b: 4–10.

27. Thornton, 1992: 72–97. See also Klein, 1998: 1.

28. See *HOM*, vol. 1, 114, 152.

29. See also Thornton, 1983: 40–41, 44.

30. Anonymous, "Mémoire sur Madagascar," BL/MD/Add.Mss./18126/61–64, 76; Lescallier, 1803: 19–20; d'Unienville, "Questions sur Madagascar," Port Louis, 09/10/15, BL/MD/Add.Mss./18134/20v.

31. Mayeur, 1913b: 168.

32. Mayeur, 1913a: 37.

33. Mayeur, 1913a: 36, 1913b: 171.

34. *Tantara*, 277.

35. Ratsivalaka, 1977: 81, 84; Berg, 1985: 265, n. 7.

36. For the ideal gender division of labor during the mid-nineteenth century see *Tantara*, 277, 323; Larson, 1987: chap. 6, 7.

37. See Lovejoy, 1983: 129, and the essays by Robertson and Klein, Meillassoux, Harms, Strobel, Olivier de Sardan, and Keim in Robertson and Klein, 1983a.

38. Mayeur, Louisbourg, 06/07/78, MNA/HB/6/19/52r–53r; Rondeaux to Decaen, no place, no date [probably 1808], ADC/FD/101/250v; Mayeur in Valette, 1966c.

39. Several named famines are mentioned in the *Tantara*: 296 (Tsimiofy), 395 (*mosary be*), 404 (*mavovava zoky, mavovava zandry*).

40. Explicitly so in the case of *Tantara*, 395, which attributes the "great famine" (*mosary be*) to political discord among highland kings. For famine as a metaphor of social strife, see also Kus, 1997: 203–4.

41. *Tantara*, 728–55; *RH* I, 417–18; Raison, 1984: vol. 1, 111–17.

42. For a similar process in Angola, where women also predominated in the population as a result of the transatlantic slave trade, see Thornton, 1980: 424.

43. *Tantara*, 277, 323–24; *HOM*, vol. 1, 294.

44. See also Manning, 1990: 132.

45. Morice, "Plan of Operations for the Trade of the Coast of East Africa," n.d., in Freeman-Grenville, 1965: 190. For the movement of Indians and Indian commerce into the western Indian Ocean more generally, see Alpers, 1975: 85–94, 159.

46. Mayeur, 1913a: 43.

47. Feeley-Harnik, 1989.

48. Mayeur, 1913a: 37.

49. Mayeur, 1913b: 160–61.

50. *Tantara*, 926.

51. Leguével de Lacombe, 1840: vol. 2, 33–34. Martin (1972: 106, 165) reports a similar substitution of palm cloth by cotton imports in west central Africa. In the Niger river delta, by contrast, Northrup (1978: 169–71) reports that textile imports did not appreciably affect the local textile industry. This is also the position taken by Thornton (1992: 48–53) for Africa more generally.

52. Jones to Bogue, Tananarive, 3/11/20, LMS/1/2/B; Hastie to Griffiths, Port Louis, 18/02/21, LMS/1/2/B, 38; Hastie to Griffiths, Port Louis, 18/02/21, LMS/1/2/B, 39. Leguével de Lacombe (1840: vol. 2, 34) reports that homespun cotton *totorano*, finely woven textiles with borders in red and blue, were available on highland markets in 1824. For a slightly later period (ca. 1829) see also Jourdain, 1839: 15.

53. Rowland to Burder, Antsahadinta, 13/06/26, LMS/2/3/A. See also Griffiths, Journal, 01/08/22 through 10/04/23, entry for 17/09/22, LMS/J/1.

54. Silk weaving is the only textile industry mentioned in the *Tantara*, 933–35.

55. Today, for example, the silk industry of central Madagascar is concentrated in and around the towns of Isandrandahy and Arivonimamo (Green, 1996: 16–21).

56. Mayeur, 1913a: 37.

57. Mayeur, 1913b: 153; "Notes remises par M. Chocal en 1816," BL/MD/Add.Mss./ 18135/26r, 34v. Fressange (1808: 23–24) reported that silks could sell for the price of a slave, about 60 piasters. Hugon ("Aperçu de mon dernier voyage," BL/MD/Add.Mss./ 18129/19r) reported in 1808 that pieces of *landimena* cloth sold for at least 50 piasters. *Tantara* accounts claim that the prices of some *lamba*, or pieces of cloth, had once been as high as 100 piasters.

58. Bartholemé, "La propriété à Madagascar avant la conquête," Tananarive, 21/02/ 99, AN/CAOM/AGGM/5(4)D/1; Larson, 1992: 107–9.

59. Anonymous, "Mémoire sur Madagascar," BL/MD/Add.Mss./18126/79–80.

60. Green, 1996: 16–17.

61. Thornton, 1980: 425, 1983: 42–46; Lovejoy, 1983: 20, 118-19, 161, 174–75, 177; Manning, 1990: 132–23, 142; Thornton, 1992: 86.

62. "Extract of Report by James Hastie," Antananarivo, 17/03/25, LMS/2/2/A; Griffiths to Arundel, Antananarivo, 20/12/25, LMS/2/2/D, 13. During the eighteenth century, by contrast, polygyny was restricted to the "*grands chefs.*" However, concubinage, or informal relationships not formalized by the transfer of *vodiondry* from groom's to bride's kin, were widespread. See Anonymous, "Mémoire sur Madagascar," BL/MD/Add.Mss./ 18126/68.

63. Jones, 1958; Johnson, 1970; Lovejoy, 1974; Curtin, 1974: vol. 1, 260–70; Hogendorn and Gemery, 1981; Hogendorn and Johnson, 1986; Law, 1991: 45–58.

64. In his study of the Atlantic slave trade to 1680, for example, Thornton (1992: 43– 53) fails to examine the local social uses of imported goods and currencies, arguing the marginality of their impact because of their inferior quality by comparison with African manufactured goods. See also Klein's generalized discussion of imported currencies (1999: 125).

65. Miller, 1988: 71–104.

66. Parry and Bloch, 1989b.

67. Bloch, 1989d. See also Graeber, 1996c: 178.

68. The following analysis suggests, however, a revision of Bloch's conclusions about the long-standing moral neutrality of money and markets in highland Madagascar.

69. *Tantara*, 919.

70. Molet, 1962: 7–48; Chauvincourt and Chauvincourt, 1968: 3–4; Dez, 1970b: 69; Martin, 1990: 186; Barendse, 1995: 151–53; Graeber, 1996a: 14.

71. Mayeur, "Mémoire historique, politique et commercial," ADC/FD/101/59v and 68v.

72. Historians of Africa have often overstated the degree to which currency imports were evenly distributed or to which they mediated everyday exchanges. Lovejoy (1983: 104), for example, writes that an estimated per capita money supply of 1 pound sterling in an area covering eighteenth-century Dahomey, Oyo, Nupe, the Bariba states, and Hausaland "indicates a thoroughly monetized economy over this vast region."

73. Larson, 1997b.

74. For example, Mayeur ("Mémoire historique, politique et commercial," ADC/FD/ 101/59r) reported that in 1787 the price of slaves was 50 piasters in the highlands and 73 piasters at Foulpointe.

75. Roux to Decaen, "Réflexions en form de rapport," 01/04/08, ADC/FD/101/240r.

76. During the 1807 trading season, for example, adult slaves generally sold for 60 piasters and children for 75 to 80 (Roux to Decaen, "Réflexions en form de rapport," 01/ 04/08, ADC/FD/101/240r).

77. Mariette to Decaen, Quartier de Flacq, 25/02/07, ADC/FD/101/291v; Decaen to Mariette, no place [Mauritius], 06/04/07, ADC/FD/101/97r–97v. This same gendered price structure applied to the seventeenth-century Dutch trade in northwest Madagascar (Barendse, 1995: 153).

78. Mayeur, "Mémoire historique, politique et commercial," ADC/FD/101/57r (25– 30 piasters in 1769); Mayeur in Valette, 1966a: 42 (25 piasters in 1774); "Répertoire de

la correspondance du baron de Benyowsky," AN/P/COL/C^{5A}/4/16/8v (65 piasters at the east coast during the 1770s); "Mémoire de messieux Guiard et Le Guenne sur la traite qui se peut faire à Madagascar," 10/83, BL/MD/Add.Mss./18135/189r (52 piasters in 1783); Dumaine, MNA/HB/1/51/92–98 (52 piasters in 1784); Mayeur, "Mémoire historique, politique et commercial," ADC/FD/101/59r (50 piasters in the highlands and 73 piasters at Foulpointe in 1787); Dumaine, MNA/HB/16/3/18r (600 livres or about 115 piasters in 1787); de Froberville in Valette, 1966c: 276 (90 piasters in 1806); Hugon, "Aperçu de mon dernier voyage," BL/MD/Add.Mss./18137/14v–15v (60 piasters in 1808); Mayeur, 1966c: 276 (between 20 and 62 piasters in 1807–1808); Roux to Decaen, "Réflexions en form de rapport," 01/04/08, ADC/FD/101/240r, (38–40 piasters in about 1803); ibid., (90 piasters and 2 pieces of cloth in 1807); ibid., (60 piasters in 1808); ibid., (price fluctuations over the course of the trading season); Roux to Decaen, Tamatave, 14/11/07, ADC/FD/102/121r–121v (paid 320 piasters for 4 *"beaux noirs ovas,"* or 80 piasters each); Lagardère, journal, 27/05/08, in Hébert, 1996: 231 (45 piasters); Lagardère, journal, 08/08/08, in Hébert, 1996: 237 (paid "Diambavola," 40 piasters and 2 pieces of *toile bleue* for a slave, or about 50 piasters total).

79. Mayeur, 1913a: 43.

80. Roux to Decaen, Tamatave, 28/11/07, ADC/FD/102/147v.

81. "Mémoire de messieux Guiard et Le Guenne sur la traite qui se peut faire à Madagascar," 10/83, BL/MD/Add.Mss./18135/193v; Anonymous, "Mémoire sur Madagascar," BL/MD/Add.Mss./18126/95; Rondeaux to Decaen, no place, no date [probably 1808], ADC/FD/101/251r; Roux to Decaen, Foulpointe, 27/08/07, ADC/FD/102/26v; Dumaine, 1810a: 28; Hébert, 1983–1984: 237, 246.

82. Population estimates are based on the following mid-nineteenth century censuses: "Fikiambanany ny isany ny Borozoany amy ny sasakady atsimo," Mahamasina, 23 Alohotsy 1842, ARDM/AR/IIICC/392/18/1r–2v; Untitled document, Antananarivo, 15 Adimizana 1843, ARDM/AR/IIICC/392/432/430v, 431v; "Ny fikiambanany Borozoany sy isany vola naloany tamy ny Merina enintoko tao Andohalo," Antananarivo, 26 Asorotany 1844, ARDM/AR/IIICC/386/11/1v; "Ary Isany Borozoany," Ambohimanga, 13 Adijady 1846, ARDM/AR/IIICC/395/14/11v.

83. Dez, 1970b: 42–51, 69.

84. Mayeur, 1913a: 43. See also Dez, 1970b: 63.

85. Eltis, 1987, 1991; Eltis and Jennings, 1988.

86. *Tantara*, 918; *HOM*, vol. 2, 149; Molet, 1962: 33–35.

87. Dez, 1970b: 52, 1970c.

88. Dez (1970c: 176) has demonstrated the tremendous deflation of the value of the piaster over the course of the nineteenth century.

89. Hugon, "Aperçu de mon dernier voyage," BL/MD/Add.Mss./18129/18v.

90. *Tantara*, 916–20; Mayeur, 1913a: 44, 1913b: 163; Molet, 1962: 13–26; Chauvincourt and Chauvincourt, 1967.

91. Mayeur, 1913a: 44, 1913b: 163.

92. Counterfeited money, false weights, and tampered currency scales were all in circulation within the highland economy (Mayeur, 1913b: 166). Measurement of silver was complicated by the absence of standard weights in these eighteenth-century markets (*Tantara*, 884).

93. Dumaine, 1810b: 179; Lasalle, 1898: 575; Molet, 1962: 30–32.

94. *Tantara*, 72.

95. Mayeur, 1913b: 163.

96. Mayeur, "Dialogue," 01/11/07, ADC/FD/101/83v; Saint-Yves, 1901: 3–4.

97. Mayeur, 1913b: 43.

98. Molet, 1962: 32.

99. *Tantara*, 924; *HOM*, vol. 2, 130.

100. Anonymous, "Mémoire sur Madagascar," BL/MD/Add.Mss./18126/77–78; Lescallier, 1803: 19, 21; *HOM*, vol. 2, 134–35.

101. Andrianampoinimerina was buried in a silver canoe along with some 300,000 piasters (*Tantara*, 1058; Jourdain, 1839: 8). Radama, also placed in a silver coffin, is reported to have been buried along with 10,000 piasters (Tyerman and Bennet, 1831: vol. 2, 558; *HOM*, vol. 1, 254).

102. *Tantara*, 1109.

103. Among these products the *Tantara* mention muskets and gunpowder (924), hats (926), mirrors (927), soap (927), and tobacco (928).

104. Mayeur, 1913a: 37.

105. *Tantara*, 919–20.

106. Mayeur, "Mémoire historique, politique et commercial," ADC/FD/101/49v; Rondeaux to Decaen, no place, no date [probably 1808], ADC/FD/101/252r. A *traitant* with apparent experience in highland Madagascar before the late eighteenth century claims, to the contrary, that highlanders (whom he calls northerners) paid few taxes (Anonymous, "Mémoire sur Madagascar," BL/MD/Add.Mss./18126/44). Although he composed his manuscript in about 1785, this anonymous *traitant* drew upon his experiences of the last 30 or 40 years in Madagascar. It is thus possible that taxation itself was relatively new to the highlands during the era of the export slave trade.

107. Dez, 1962: 188; Dez, 1970b: 52–59.

108. Mayeur, 1913b: 163.

109. The high rate of taxation in and around Antananarivo can be explained partially by the region's greater integration into the slave trade in comparison to other areas of the highlands, bringing a higher proportion of silver within its borders.

110. For information on the *vata*, see *Tantara,* 729, 885–86.

111. "Déclarations de Quelques Traitans," 27/06/07, BL/MD/Add.Mss./18134/39r; Mayeur, Louisbourg, 25/11/78, MNA/HB/6/20/55r; "Mémoire sur les établissements français," no date [1774], AN/P/COL/C⁵ᴬ/4/6.

112. Dez, 1970c: 192.

113. Mayeur, 1913b: 163–64.

114. The *Tantara* (760–61) attribute Andrianamboatsimarofy's unpopularity to his and his courtiers' indulgences in liquor, cannabis, and tobacco. This view is adopted by Berg, 1988: 197; Ratsivalaka, 1995: vol. 1, 499–501.

115. Mayeur, 1913a: 47.

116. Mayeur, 1913b: 163–65.

117. Dez, 1979c: 199.

118. See also Dez, 1970b: 70.

119. Nora, 1989.

120. *Tantara* narratives (854–58) name these markets *fihaonana* and contrast them to markets during the time of Andrianampoinimerina, which are termed *tsena*. Contemporaries, however (Mayeur, 1913a: 43), confirm that eighteenth-century markets were called *tsena*.

121. Mayeur, 1913b: 163.

122. Mayeur, 1913a: 42–43.

123. Mayeur, 1913a: 44–45; Hébert, 1979: 110.

124. Rondeaux to Decaen, no place, no date [probably 1808], ADC/FD/101/252r.

125. Mayeur, 1913a: 43; Dez, 1979b: 63.

126. For the role of moneychangers, who were also experts at cutting whole piasters into smaller denominations, see Locke, 1835: 238; Molet, 1962: 27; Chauvincourt and Chauvincourt, 1967.

127. Rainandriamampandry, 1972: 32–54; Dahle, 1984: 39–53.

128. *Tantara*, 854–84.

129. For textile prices, see Mayeur, 1913b: 153, 160–61.

130. *Tantara*, 854; Mayeur, 1913a: 45, 1913b: 169.

131. Mayeur, 1913a: 42, 1913b: 154. See also Hugon, "Aperçu de mon dernier voyage," BL/MD/Add.Mss./18129/17v.

132. Mayeur, 1913b: 159, 161.

133. Mayeur, 1913b: 159, 161.

134. Mayeur, 1913b: 162.

135. Dumaine, 1810b: 180–81.

136. *Tantara*, 503, 590, 776, 808; Cabanes, 1974: 50. Boiteau (1974: 152, 166) claims, erroneously, that land was not salable before the rise of Andrianampoinimerina.

137. Esoavelomandroso (1982) has reached the same conclusion, although by other means.

138. Dez, 1970a: 30; Esoavelomandroso, 1982: 24–25.

139. Hugon, "Aperçu de mon dernier voyage," BL/MD/Add.Mss./18129/17v.

140. Dez, 1970b: 63.

141. Ratsivalaka (1995: vol. 1, 153–55) claims to have found a document proving Andrianampoinimerina spent part of his childhood gaining an education at Île de France. Such an experience would have predisposed him to involvement in the Indian Ocean trade and may help explain his competence at mastering it.

142. My interpretation of elite political strategies in this section of the chapter is heavily influenced by the work of scholars of trade and elite politics in east and central Africa (Gray and Birmingham, 1970; Jackson, 1976; Miller, 1988: 40–139; Feierman, 1995).

143. Larson, 1995: 309–16. For an example of how this process functioned on the scale of individual tomb groups, see Graeber, 1995: 266–68.

144. Miller, 1988.

145. Lasalle, 1898: 577.

146. For a similar interpretation, but with respect to differently read evidence, see Ratsivalaka, 1995: vol. 1, 434–37.

147. *RH* I, 274–75, 291. Raombana claims (*RH* I, 146) that the first muskets reached the inland during the reign of Andrianjaka.

148. *RH* I, 342–55.

149. *RH* I, 328–31. The property of convicted witches, by custom, belonged to the king and their accusers.

150. *RH* I, 342-55.

151. *RH* I, 365. Incidents of kings offering money to potential supporters are also found in the *Tantara*. See, for example, Andrianampoinimerina's offer of money to the

Tantsaha peasants (*Tantara*, 484–85); Andrianamboatsimarofy's unsuccessful attempt to win the support of Andriantsidiso by offering him 100 piasters, *Tantara*, 506.

152. For Ambohidratrimo, *RH* I, 475–78; for Imerinatsimo, *RH* I, 479–87. See also *Tantara*, 485, which describes a similar process with reference to the Tantsaha peasants.

153. *RH* I, 373–74.

154. *RH* I, 489–503. The *Tantara* version of this confrontation does not include cannon (563–65), but other passages concerning Andrianampoinimerina mention them (507, 658).

155. *RH* I, 462–67.

156. Ayache, 1976a: 32–38.

157. Dez, 1967: 657–77.

158. For versions of the popular narratives, see *Tantara*, 614–27; "Teny Nampitondrain'Andrianampoinimerina hankany Amin'Andriamanaliny Betsileo," in Cousins, 1873: 4–6; Jouannetaud, 1900; Baron, 1903; Stefany, 1912; Fontoynont and Raomandahy, 1940; Savron, 1940. I collected several oral renditions of this story west of Betafo in 1989 and 1990 (LFC/SR/17, 42, 60, 67, 71, 80, 83, 84, 88). While details vary, all accounts portray the confrontation as a magic duel.

159. *Tantara*, 321, 632–33.

160. Fressange, 1808: 24–25. Orthography: les Andrantsaïes, Antancoves.

161. Mayeur, "Mémoire historique, politique et commercial," ADC/FD/101/57v. Orthography: Dieu=Empouine.

162. Dumaine, 1810b: 179–80.

163. Rondeaux to Decaen, no place, no date [probably 1808], ADC/FD/101/252v. Orthography: andransaillé, bésiléo, Dianampoeen.

164. Roux to Decaen, Tamatave, 26/05/08, ADC/FD/102/227r–227v.

165. Royal to Decaen, Tamatave, 23/08/07, ADC/FD/102/143r; Boyd to Roux, Tamatave, 25/08/07, ADC/FD/102/143r; Roux to Decaen, Tamatave, 18/05/08, ADC/FD/102/198r.

166. Roux to Decaen, Tamatave, 24/05/08, ADC/FD/102/225v.

167. Roux to Decaen, Tamatave, 24/05/08, ADC/FD/102/225r–225v.

168. For the "taxe des noirs," see Roux to Decaen, Tamatave, 29/07/08, ADC/FD/102/247r; Chardenoux, journal, late 1807, ADC/FD/102/114r.

169. For the equivalent economic prosperities of Andrianampoinimerina's and Andriamanalinabetsileo's kingdoms, see Roux to Decaen, Tamatave, 21/06/08, ADC/FD/102/229r. For Andrianampoinimerina and his monopoly over imports of French gunpowder, see Roux to Decaen, Tamatave, 18/12/07, ADC/FD/102/158r; Chardenoux, journal, late 1807, ADC/FD/102/168v.

170. Details of this mission are revealed in Roux to Decaen, Tamatave, 26/05/08, ADC/FD/102/227r and following.

171. Roux to Decaen, Tamatave, 21/06/08, ADC/FD/102/229r.

172. Roux to Decaen, Tamatave, 26/05/08, ADC/FD/102/227r–227v.

173. Roux to Decaen, Tamatave, 17/10/07, cited in Delivré, 1974: 226.

174. Roux to Decaen, Tamatave, 26/05/08, ADC/FD/102/227v.

175. Roux to Decaen, Tamatave, 22/08/08, ADC/FD/102/253r.

176. Roux to Decaen, Tamatave, 29/06/08, ADC/FD/102/231r.

177. For the ceremonial role of muskets, see Mayeur, 1913a: 33, 1913b: 149; Berg, 1985. Thompson (1974), by contrast, argues for the importance of muskets to Andrianampoinimerina's conquests.

178. *RH* I, 353, 417.

179. *Tantara*, 384, 488, 912–16.

180. Kus and Wright, 1986: 60.

181. Roux to Decaen, Tamatave, 04/12/07, ADC/FD/102/158r–158v.

182. Chardenoux, journal, late 1807, ADC/FD/102/168v, 170r.

183. Hugon, "Le Journal de B. Hugon," entry for 03/05/08, in Ratsivalaka, 1979: 16.

184. Rondeaux to Decaen, no place, no date [probably 1808], ADC/FD/101/252v. Orthography: Dianampoeen.

185. *Tantara*, 614–27, 656 (for peaceful submission), 632–34 (for military confrontations and enslavements).

186. Colin, 1811: 89.

187. Braudel, 1982.

188. *HOM*, vol. 1, 118–19; Ratsivalaka, 1995: vol. 1, 221–23, 411–12.

189. LFC/SR/18, 39, 82, 95, 120, 122, 124. See also Larson, forthcoming, b.

CHAPTER 5

1. *Tantara*, 808, 707.

2. Ellis, 1857: 793.

3. John Thornton has described this process for the kingdom of Kongo in the late seventeenth and early eighteenth centuries (1998: 1, 26, 43–44, 104, 137–38, 162, 165, 206, 214).

4. *Tantara*, 321, 678, 912–16, 779; Mayeur, "Mémoire historique, politique et commercial," ADC/FD/101/57v; Ratsivalaka, 1995: vol. 1, 408.

5. Anderson, 1983: 5–7.

6. An understanding of these various historical "facets" of Andrianampoinimerina is made possible only by shifting the historical metaphor through which one views the founder king. My methodological approach is best explained by White 1978: 27–50, 121–34, esp. 47.

7. Abercrombie, 1998: 14, 317, 408. See also Rappaport, 1990: 25.

8. For history as culturally expressed, see Lambek, 1998; for the notion of popular memory as similar to social memory, see Popular Memory Group, 1982: 205–52, esp. 206–11.

9. For a general discussion of these observations, see Tonkin, 1992: 121, 126, 132–36.

10. I borrow the term "social fact" from Moore (1986), although I employ it in a different way than she does. I differentiate social fact from what might be called event fact; the truths imparted by each kind of fact are equally valid yet refer to different domains of human experience.

11. The development and limitations of the modern Western historical methodology that I criticize here are examined in White, 1978; Novick, 1988; Young, 1990; Shapin, 1994.

12. Gerbeau, 1989, 7.

13. Henige, 1986: 97.

14. Hamilton, 1998: quotation from 71.

15. See Miller, 1980b: esp. 20–21, 31, 50; Feierman, 1974: esp. 40–90.

16. For struggles over citizenship and inclusion in another east African context, see Glassman, 1995.

17. For the analogy between the king and the sun see *Tantara*, 261. For definitions of *ambaniandro* and *ambanilanitra* see *Tantara*, 366, n. 1. Probably the work of Callet, this note suggests that *ambanilanitra* was a more inclusive term than *ambaniandro*, meaning all nonslaves, while *ambaniandro* referred to all *ambanilanitra* excepting near kin of the sovereign. This definition contrasts with *Tantara*, 709, which explicitly defines *ambaniandro* as everyone living in highland Madagascar, including slaves. Confusion over the status of slaves suggests that *ambaniandro* and *ambanilanitra* were porous categories of citizenship whose meanings drifted according to social context and individual usage.

18. Hugon, "Aperçu de mon dernier voyage," 29/04/08, BL/MD/Add.Mss./18129/14v.

19. For the Austronesian roots of Malagasy peoples and cultures, see Bellwood, 1985: 102–58.

20. Bloch, 1982, 1986: 157–95, 1989c.

21. Metaphoric oppositions of chaos and order are a common way in which leaders justify their power. The point here is not that this type of political language was unique to highland Madagascar, but why and how it was meaningful to highland Malagasy at the beginning of the nineteenth century, given their historical experiences over previous decades.

22. Black, 1962; Sapir, 1977; Soskice, 1985: esp. chap. 1–4; Fernandez, 1991.

23. For example, Sahlins, 1981.

24. Crocker, 1977: 60.

25. *Tantara*, 784, 854–55, 861, 873, 878, 884, 888.

26. *Firaketana*, No. 178 (Avril 1955), entry for *Hova*, 296–97.

27. On this point, see also Kus, 1997: esp. 209.

28. *Tantara*, 432–33 (*vory*); Rainandriamampandry, 1972: 110 (*hahabe voho an'Imerina*).

29. Jourdain, 1839: 7; Leguével de Lacombe, 1840: vol. 2, 29; Mille, 1970: 9, 11, 56–59; Ratsivalaka, 1995: vol. 1, 214–15; Larson, 1996: 553.

30. This contrasts with the strategies of the Zulu leadership during the time of Shaka and Dingane, who "sought to maintain a clear distinction between a cluster of 'insider' chiefdoms in the state's heartland, and various clusters of 'outsider' chiefdoms in its geographical peripheries" (Wright and Hamilton, 1996: 26).

31. *Tantara*, 300. *Foibe* today means "headquarters."

32. Roux to Decaen, Tamatave, 29/07/08, ADC/FD/102/246r (emphasis is mine). For Imerina as the immediate environs of Antananarivo, see Ratsivalaka, 1995: vol. 1, 214–15; Larson, 1996: 553.

33. For an excellent eyewitness account of Andrianampoinimerina's politics of violence, see Lebel, "Exposé sur Madagascar," BL/MD/Add.Mss./18125/210r–210v and the discussion of this document in Hébert, 1979.

34. *Tantara*, 293–360; *RH* I, 207–71.

35. *Tantara*, 985–1002.

36. *Tantara*, 672.

37. *Tantara*, 709.

38. Bloch, 1971: 41–58.

39. Berg, 1988: 205. See also Bloch, 1987: esp. 296.

40. Bloch, 1967: 127; Berg, 1988: 202; Larson, 1995: 309–16.

41. Larson, 1995: 309–16.

42. Newbury, 1991: 4, 7, 165, 178 (quotation), 196, 198, 209, 211–12, 227–35.

43. Feeley-Harnik, 1991a: 399.

44. Bloch, 1967: 122–28, 1981: 140, 1983; Cabanes, 1974: 51; Raison, 1984: vol. 1, 96–99; Berg, 1985, 1988.

45. Isnard, 1953; Cabanes, 1974; Bloch, 1978.

46. Julien, 1908; Lanois, 1932; Rabemananjara, 1952: 31; Deschamps, 1972a: 121–27, 1977.

47. Ralaimihoatra, 1965: esp. 112–16; Deschamps, 1976: esp. 398–99.

48. Raison-Jourde, 1984.

49. Berg, 1996: 29–30 (long quotation). For the intellectual development of *hasina* ideology and its relationship to the royal talismans, see Delivré, 1974: 140–71, 192–98; Bloch, 1978: 310–29, 1986, 1989b, 1989c; Berg, 1995, 1996. For the role of the *sampy*, or royal talismans, in royal power, see *HOM*, vol. 1, 395–410; Freeman and Johns, 1840: 53–56; Rainandriamampandry, 1972: 151–58; Domenichini, 1985; Berg, 1986, 1998: 71–85.

50. See, in particular, the interpretations of *hasina* ideology in Bloch, 1986: esp. 175–95, 1989c: esp. 131–32; Berg, 1995: esp. 77, 1996. Bloch (1986: 11) warns scholars not to attempt "to grasp what, in the end, it is impossible to grasp: what rituals mean to the participants and the onlookers. This type of search for meaning, although not pointless, has no end." On this point, see also Bloch, 1986: 183. Berg (1996: 31) acknowledges the possibility of alternative interpretations of *hasina* but limits such interpretation to elite competitors of royalty. Modifying his earlier emphasis on the unchallenged authority of *hasina* ideology as a "system of obedience," Berg considers "domestic challenges to royal ideology" in his most recent publication (1998: esp. 69, 88, 91). Despite this recent modification of his position, his central premise about the lasting stability of *hasina* ideology remains unchanged.

51. For similar approaches to Malagasy culture history, see Feeley-Harnik, 1984; Middleton, 1997.

52. *Tantara*, 790.

53. *Tantara*, 705.

54. *Tantara*, 705–6.

55. *Tantara*, 796.

56. *Tantara*, 737.

57. Delivré, 1974: 163–65; Berg, 1977: 2, 1988: 197. See also *Tantara*, 732–42; Larson, 1995: 301–3.

58. *Tantara*, 427.

59. Dubois, 1938: 1112; Vig, 1973: 17–18; Domenichini, 1985.

60. This metaphor was also used by Andrianampoinimerina (*Tantara*, 807).

61. See Bloch, 1986, for the interrelationships among violence, blessing, and fertility in highland Malagasy history.

62. *Tantara*, 707.

63. Rainandriamampandry, 1972: 110 (*hampandry volo ny ambaniandro*).

64. *Tantara*, 413; Rainandriamampandry, 1972: 139–40.

65. *Tantara*, 707.

66. See Domenichini, 1985: 266 (*Andriandranando tsivakivolo*).

67. *Tantara*, 708.

68. *Tantara*, 718, 724.
69. Bloch, 1971: esp. 105–37.
70. *Tantara*, 709–19.
71. Raison, 1984: vol. 1, 103–10.
72. *Tantara*, 709.
73. *Tantara*, 713.
74. *Tantara*, 709. See also *Tantara*, 808.
75. Delteil, 1931; Arbousset, 1950; Condominas, 1961.
76. See also Graeber, 1996c: 112–13.
77. *Tantara*, 823.
78. *Tantara*, 823. See also the list of disputes placed under the jurisdiction of the *fokonolona* in *Tantara*, 775–82.
79. *Tantara*, 835.
80. *Tantara*, 823.
81. *Tantara*, 815.
82. *Tantara*, 808.
83. For *mively vavahady*, see *Tantara*, 835, 841; for *mively rano* and *milefon'omby*, *Tantara*, 706. It is likely that Andrianampoinimerina borrowed his rituals of political allegiance from communal practices and that the *mively vavahady* was based upon prior local rituals of the same or a similar sort rather than invented anew at the beginning of the nineteenth century.
84. *Tantara*, 816.
85. *Tantara*, 809, 825–27.
86. *Tantara*, 718. I am in agreement with Campbell (1988b: 463–68), who argues that *fanompoana* was not of great economic significance until the reign of Radama. See also *RH* I, 520–21.
87. *Tantara*, 708.
88. Among the Sakalava of northwest Madagascar, Feeley-Harnik reports (1991a: 340), sovereigns typically enslaved individuals who sought to enlarge their wealth and power by "expanding their own networks of kin, clients and slaves." Andrianampoinimerina found a creative and prophylactic solution to this perennial problem of politics in an economy of merchant capitalism by empowering local communities to police their own.
89. Miller, 1976: 161–67, 225–51; Wright and Hamilton, 1989: 57–74.
90. *Tantara*, 543, 546, 712, 714, 745, 776–77. See also *HOM*, vol. 1, 256.
91. *Tantara*, 387.
92. See *Tantara*, 1056–57; and below in text.
93. A. Grandidier, 1886; G. Grandidier, 1912; Decary, 1962; Althabe, 1969; Bloch, 1971; Huntington, 1973b; Barré, 1977; Rabedimy, 1979; Rajaonarimanana, 1979; Kottak, 1980: 228–59; Feeley-Harnik, 1991a; Graeber, 1995; Middleton, 1995.
94. Rajaoson, 1969; Bloch, 1971: 145–71; Molet, 1979: vol. 2, 295-8; Raison-Jourde, 1991: 705–38; Graeber, 1995.
95. Hertz, 1907; Miles, 1965; Hudson, 1966; Metcalf, 1982; Metcalf and Huntington, 1991.
96. See, for example, Larson, forthcoming, a.
97. Similar modifications in mortuary practices, including tomb architecture, have taken place elsewhere on Madagascar. Among the Hazohandatse of the south, for ex-

ample, modern practices of monumental stone tomb building can scarcely be traced back two hundred years (Middleton, 1995: 224).

98. Kus and Wright, 1986: esp. 53, 55, 57, 60; Raharijaona, 1986: 85–86.

99. Decary, 1962: 44–66; LeBras, 1971; Molet, 1979: vol. 2, 271; Kus and Wright, 1986: 54, 56, 57, 60–61; Raharijaona, 1986: 85–88; Raison-Jourde, 1991: 723–25.

100. A careful reading of Jeffreys's description of mortuary ritual in and around Ambatomanga (1827: 132–33) leads to this conclusion.

101. Vogel, 1982: 121–29, 170–75.

102. *Tantara*, 258–59.

103. *Tantara*, 784.

104. *Tantara*, 800.

105. Mayeur, 1913b: 169. For confirmation of the use of wood inside eighteenth-century tombs, see LeBras, 1971: 38–40.

106. This seems both improbable and at variance with the following sentence.

107. Mayeur, 1913a: 48–49.

108. Decary, 1962: 59–62; LeBras, 1971: 10–43; Molet, 1979: vol. 2, 271; Kus and Wright, 1986; Raharijaona, 1986; Rakotovololona, 1986.

109. *Tantara*, 259.

110. LeBras, 1971: 11.

111. *Tantara*, 800.

112. *HOM*, vol. 1, 245.

113. In the nineteenth century burial obelisks were erected only for individuals whose bodies were never recovered for proper tomb burial (*Tantara*, 268–69). LeBras (1971: 63–64) suggests that *tsangambato* were replaced by columns in nineteenth-century Labordian-style tombs.

114. LeBras, 1971: 40, 64.

115. *HOM*, vol. 1, 245; Kus and Wright, 1986: 60–61. For a description of these tombs during the late nineteenth century, see Dahle, 1878: vol. 2, 64–68; Sibree, 1880: 227–30, 1896: 300–301; Abinal and de la Vaissière, 1885: 197–98; Grandidier, 1886: 228.

116. Coppalle, 1970: 55.

117. *HOM*, vol. 1, 246; Molet, 1979: vol. 2, 276–308; Raison-Jourde, 1991: 717–25; Graeber, 1995: 259; Larson, forthcoming, a.

118. *HOM*, vol. 1, 244–45.

119. *Tantara*, 269–71.

120. *HOM*, vol. 1, 246.

121. *Tantara*, 269–70. See also Dahle, 1878: vol. 2, 64–66 for a similar description, and the photograph of *mitari-bato* in Mager, 1898: 200.

122. Comaroff and Comaroff, 1993: xxii.

123. *Tantara*, 813.

124. *HOM*, vol. 1, 243–56. For variations in nineteenth-century tomb building and mortuary ritual, see Larson, forthcoming, a, c.

125. *HOM*, vol. 1, 248.

126. See Bloch, 1971: 130–31, 1986: 38, 92–93.

127. *Tantara*, 800.

128. Kus and Wright, 1986: 61.

129. Larson, forthcoming, a, c.

130. See also Graeber, 1986c; Feeley-Harnik, 1984, 1991a.

131. See Raison-Jourde, 1984.

132. *Tantara*, 731. See also *Tantara* 782, 802; *Firaketana*, no. 41 (Mai 1940), entry for Andrianampoinimerina, 118.

133. *RH* I, 417–18.

134. Esoavelomandroso, 1982.

135. See also Dez, 1970a: 35; Boiteau, 1974: 156.

136. Raison, 1972: 111; Douessin, 1974: 57–58.

137. *Tantara*, 729.

138. *Tantara*, 730–31.

139. Isnard, 1953; Cabanes, 1974; Bloch, 1978.

140. *RH* I, 417–18; Dez, 1970a.

141. *Tantara*, 803–9.

142. *Tantara*, 745–53; Isnard, 1953.

143. *Tantara*, 746. See also Campbell, 1988b: 467.

144. *Tantara*, 809.

145. *Tantara*, 806.

146. A good example is *Tantara*, 803.

147. *Tantara*, 802.

148. *Tantara*, 746.

149. *Tantara*, 731.

150. *Tantara*, 803.

151. *Tantara*, 802.

152. For *ody havandra,* see *Tantara*, 802; Rainandriamampandry, 1972: 159–60.

153. For the practice of rotating warriors and allowing them rest breaks from battle, see also *RH* I, 434.

154. *Tantara*, 679–86.

155. *RH* I, 427–30.

156. *Tantara*, 728.

157. *Tantara*, 730.

158. *Tantara*, 729.

159. *Tantara*, 730.

160. *Tantara*, 767.

161. *Tantara*, 802.

162. *Tantara*, 857.

163. *Tantara*, 807.

164. *Tantara*, 872–75.

165. *Tantara*, 798, 799.

166. *Tantara*, 779.

167. *Tantara*, 765–66.

168. *HOM*, vol. 1, 163.

169. Hilsenberg and Bojer, 1833: 270.

170. For information on the legal positions of wife and husband in highland society, see Hilsenberg and Bojer, 1833: 259.

171. *Tantara*, 729, 805–6.

172. Most kingdom censuses classified households in which there was no productive-age male as *vehivavy mitondra hetra*. I have calculated the figure of 5–10 percent fe-

male-headed households from the census of 1843, dated Antananarivo, 15 Adimizana (ARDM/AR/IIICC/392/432/430v and 431v).

173. *Tantara*, 815, 823, 827. By the late nineteenth century this situation had changed and women brought cases of their own to royal courts (see ARDM/AR/IIICC/362–77).

174. *Tantara*, 708.

175. Keenan, 1974a: 207–16, 1974b. See also Larson, 1995: 322–25.

176. *Tantara*, 827.

177. *Tantara*, 328, 792–93.

178. *Tantara*, 790.

179. *Tantara*, 790.

180. *Tantara*, 790.

181. *Tantara*, 790–91; *RH* I, 49.

182. *Tantara*, 791. See also *Tantara*, 327–28.

183. *Tantara*, 328, 793.

184. *Tantara*, 328, 792; *RH* I, 52–53.

185. *Tantara*, 328, 792 (quotation).

186. *Tantara*, 329, 794.

187. *Tantara*, 329.

188. *Tantara*, 328, 791.

189. *Tantara*, 328.

190. *Tantara*, 328, 791–92.

191. *Tantara*, 328. See also *Tantara*, 327.

192. *Tantara*, 328.

193. *Tantara*, 791–92. See also *RH* I, 53–54.

194. This was called *mananton-jaza* (to "suspend children").

195. *Tantara*, 807.

196. *Tantara*, 782–83.

197. Compare with Golan, 1990.

198. Hobsbawm and Ranger, 1983.

199. True to its legacy, the eastern section of *firenena* Ravoandriana, including the town of Ambatomanga, rebelled against Radama soon after Andrianampoinimerina's death. The rebels were crushed by Radama's armies; Ambatomanga was evacuated as a consequence. See *Tantara*, 1060–61, 1067; Ratsivalaka, 1995: vol. 1, 505–7.

200. Schwartz, 1987: 20, 107. See also Longmore, 1988.

201. Meisner, 1977: 31–51.

CHAPTER 6

1. Hilsenberg and Bojer, 1833: 269.

2. *HOM*, vol. 1, 359.

3. These are the words of Tacchi (1892: 479), whose history of Andrianampoinimerina was based upon popular narratives and will be revisited in chapter 7.

4. On this point see also Larson, 1997c.

5. My inspiration here is Scott, 1985, 1990.

6. Nora, 1989 (site of memory); Hamilton, 1998: 32–35 (metaphor).

7. Bravman, 1998; Larson, forthcoming, d.

8. Vail, 1989: 6.

9. In highland Madagascar today there appears to be a growing bifurcation in the expression of Merina identity, in which urban dwellers generally have a much keener sense of their ethnic identity as Merina than rural people. The relationships that sustain Merina identity today conform more closely to the dominant paradigm of ethnic identity formation as occurring within a multiethnic field. See Graeber, 1996b: 429.

10. For issues of succession to Andrianampoinimerina, see *Firaketana*, no. 41 (Mai 1940), entry for "Andrianampoinimerina," 117; Valette, 1972; Delivré, 1974: 270–74; Deschamps, 1977: 94–96. The "beardless boy" insult is that of Fisatra, the Betsimisaraka chief of Ivondro, south of Tamatave (*HOM*, vol. 2, 160). Contemporary estimates of Radama's age in 1809 vary between 9 and 18: Hugon, "Aperçu de mon dernier voyage," BL/MD/18137/14v; Jones to Burder, Antananarivo, 18/10/20, LMS/1/2/B; Hilsenberg, 1829: 153; Hilsenberg and Bojer, 1833: 268; *HOM*, vol. 2, 128; *RH* II, 563. Basing himself on a tradition in the *Tantara*, Ratsivalaka (1995: vol. 1, 499) claims Radama was born in August 1793, making him 16 years old by late 1809 (the above-cited passage in *HOM* claims Radama was born in 1792).

11. *Tantara*, 1059.

12. See, for example, Coroller's account in Jourdain, 1839: 19–23.

13. *HOM*, vol. 1, 100. For Raombana's version, see *RH* II, 563–68.

14. *Tantara*, 259–62.

15. Molet, 1979: vol. 1, 338; Graeber, 1996c: 158-64.

16. *HOM*, vol. 1, 233. The *Tantara* ascribe night mourning and burial only to sovereigns (*Tantara*, 784).

17. *Tantara*, 1056.

18. *Tantara*, 1056–57.

19. *Tantara*, 1057.

20. *Tantara*, 1059.

21. For the parallel symbolic significance of Antananarivo and Ambohimanga more generally, see Kus and Raharijaona, 1994. I would like to thank Kus and Raharijaona for sharing their article with me prior to publication.

22. For the significance of the *vatomasina*, sacred stones on which sovereigns delivered their speeches and on which new sovereigns were supposed to appear, see *Tantara*, 355–87, 433; Molet, 1979: vol. 1, 222–26. For the broader significance of stone in highland Madagascar, see Kus and Raharijaona, 1998.

23. *Tantara*, 1059.

24. Today *Andriamanitra* means "God." *Andriamanitra* was claimed by missionaries in the early nineteenth century to name their God, Jehovah. *Andriamanitra* or *andriamanitra andriananahary* did not have the meaning of "supreme" deity in 1810 that it later acquired through Christian evangelization and biblical translation. The best essay on the meanings of Andriamanitra to highland Malagasy in the early nineteenth century (at the time Christian missionaries arrived in the area) is Freeman and Johns, 1840: 51–56.

25. *Tantara*, 809–14. See also *Tantara*, 677–78, 680–81, 809–14. For a history of the royal talismans, see Delivré, 1974: 185–98; Domenichini, 1985; Berg, 1986.

26. Berg, 1985, 1988.

27. *Tantara*, 1062.

28. *Tantara*, 1104–5.

29. See David Griffiths, journal entry for 22/01/22, LMS/J/1, for a description of the impact of mourning for Radama's mother's eldest sister.

30. See also *Tantara*, 259. These prohibitions were similar to those of the "funeral sequence" in the *fandroana* or new year ritual of highland Malagasy (Bloch, 1987: 277–79; Larson, 1997c).

31. Various *Tantara* narratives suggest the *ambaniandro* cut their hair from three to six times (*Tantara*, 1060, 1062).

32. *Tantara*, 1047–49. See also the examples of complete invocations in *Tantara*, 58–59, 102.

33. *Tantara*, 1065.

34. Abinal and Malzac, 1987: entry for *Lambotapaka*, 380.

35. *Tantara*, 1065. Narratives of Andrianampoinimerina's "showing" (*fisehoana*) indicate that he, too, wore such a hat (*Tantara*, 432).

36. *Tantara*, 1065.

37. *Tantara*, 694.

38. *Tantara*, 1065.

39. *Tantara*, 1065–66.

40. *Tantara*, 1066.

41. *Tantara*, 433, 803.

42. *Tantara*, 1068.

43. *Tantara*, 1060–63, 1067–73; Ratsivalaka, 1995: vol. 1, 504–13.

44. *HOM*, vol. 1, 355. See also *HOM*, vol. 1, 140; Thompson, 1974: 433.

45. *Tantara*, 804.

46. Berg, 1996: 37–39.

47. *Tantara*, 1067, 1072.

48. Jacob, 1996.

49. "Extract of Report by James Hastie," Antananarivo, 17/03/25, LMS/2/2/A; Griffiths to Arundel, Antananarivo, 20/12/25, LMS/2/2/D, 13.

50. *HOM*, vol. 2, 252.

51. In principle, the circumcision was conducted once every seven years though in reality the number of years between circumcisions could vary considerably. British missionaries witnessed a kingdomwide circumcision in 1825. The circumcision referred to in the *Tantara* was probably the second previous circumcision to 1825—or counting back fourteen years, that of approximately 1811. For the timing of circumcision ceremonies during the early nineteenth century, see Bloch, 1986: 113–22.

52. *Tantara*, 1068.

53. *Tantara*, 1069.

54. *Tantara*, 1069.

55. *HOM*, vol. 1, 128. This estimate of Radama's army outstrips the missionaries' representation of the highland population two pages earlier (126), which was 80 to 100 thousand. A likely explanation for this discrepancy is that the 80 to 100 thousand figure provided by the missionaries was the population of taxpaying adult men (almost the size of the army) and not the total highland population. If this were true, nearly all taxpaying adult men were called to participate in the third Sakalava campaign.

56. *Tantara*, 1069.

57. For the symbolism of coldness and heat in relationship to mortuary ritual, see Bloch, 1971: 162, 1986: 38–39, 58.

58. *Tantara*, 1074.

59. *Tantara*, 1069. For starvation and the Sakalava campaigns, see also *RH*, II, 596, 699–700.

60. *RH* II, 700.

61. *Tantara*, 1053; "Teny nataon Andrianampoinimerina, A.D. 1810," in Cousins, 1873: 7–13; Cousins, 1885.

62. Contemporaries usually identified and named nine to ten of the most influential of the *namana*. Chardenoux (journal, BL/MD/18129/157-76), for example, mentioned Ralala and "nine principles" of Radama, naming seven of these ten (all of whom witnessed the blood brotherhood between himself and the king in 1816): Ralala, Andriamambavola, Rainitsiroba, Rampola, Manohy, Ratsalika, and Andriamandrosomanana. To these should be added the names of Andriankotonavalona and Andriantsoanandriana, famous military commanders of Andrianampoinimerina. Hastie always observed the *namana* from afar. See Hastie, journal, 9/09/17, 1903a: 176; Hastie, journal, 9/10/17, 1903b: 264–65. He reports, on a typical occasion (journal, 9/10/17, 1903b: 264), that the king was surrounded by twenty-four of his "old counsellors," certainly members of the *namana*.

63. Hastie, journal, 15/08/17, 1903a: 178; 21/08/17, 1903a: 184; 03/09/17, 1903b: 243; 05/09/17, 1903b: 245; 06/10/17, 1903b: 259; 20/02/18, MNA/HB/10/2/30; Hastie to Farquhar, Tamatave, 11/09/20, MNA/HB/13/25/14.

64. Jones, journal entry for 05/10/20, LMS/J/1/12; *HOM*, vol. 2, 229 ("few belonged to him"). Hilsenberg and Bojer (1833: 264–65) noted that between 30 and 40 percent of slaves exported from Imerina belonged to Radama. Berg's assertion (1996: 51) that "no source of wealth lay beyond the king's control" is therefore unsupported.

65. Ratsivalaka, 1979.

66. "Rapport de Mr. Chardenoux," Port Louis, 13/09/16, MNA/HB/7/3/380.

67. Andrefandrova: *Firaketana*, no. 37 (Jan. 1940), 21; Andafiavaratra: *Firaketana*, no. 35 (Nov. 1939), 551–54.

68. *HOM*, vol. 1, 101.

69. Some *namana* retained influential positions in the civilian administration. Coppalle reported in 1825 (1970: 10/10/25, 47) that Ralala (Rahalala) was Radama's "prime minister" and sat in his stead as commander-in-chief during Radama's temporary absence from the capital hunting wild cattle.

70. *Tantara*, 1094.

71. Witness Rainitsimindrana's proverb-laden lecture to Radama when he learned of his "appointment" as *andriambaventy* (*Tantara*, 1098–99; Cousins, 1873: 14–17).

72. For a typical example, see *HOM*, vol. 1, 101–2.

73. Of the four sons of Andriamamba, for example, Radama executed one, two fell in his armies, and the fourth, named Ratsitatane, the king banished to a Mauritius jail with the collusion of the British administration there. From the prison in Port Louis Ratsitatane masterminded a slave revolt that gripped Europeans in the Mauritian capital with fear (Leguével de Lacombe, 1840: vol. 2, 12–22; Coppalle, 1970: 28/01/26, 59).

74. On this point, see Hastie's comments in his journal (6/10/17, 1903b: 259). Ratsivalaka (1995: vol. 1, 495, 520) also makes this point but finds that Radama desired British diplomatic recognition for the Merina kingdom as an independent state.

75. This interpretation stems in part from an overreliance on European perspectives and was originally based upon statements Farquhar himself made in explaining the purpose of the alliance (R.T. Farquhar, Minute, Port Louis, 03/09/22, MNA/HB/7/110/1v–

2r). British missionaries at Radama's court further popularized Farquhar's interpretation (*HOM*, vol. 2, chap. 6 and 7). For perpetuation of this idea, see also Valette, 1962a: 7–12, 1979: 169–71; *RH* II, 601ff, esp. 700–14; Munthe, Ravoajanahary and Ayache 1976: 20–27; Prou, 1987: 43–45; Ratsivalaka, 1995: vol. 1, 439–597.

76. Valette, 1962a: 12.

77. Chardenoux, journal, 14/07/16, BL/MD/18129/169r.

78. Gerbeau, 1980; Wanquet, 1988; Daget, 1996; Larson, 1997b: 134–35.

79. Barker, 1996: chap. 3 and 4. I would like to thank Professor Barker for sharing proofs of his book with me before its appearance in print. See also Teelock, 1998: 46–53.

80. Hastie to Farquhar, Tamatave, 11/09/20, MNA/HB/13/25/19; Beachey, 1976: 232–41; Klein, 1998: 19–25.

81. Valette, 1963. See also Ratsivalaka, 1995: vol. 1, 516–22.

82. Lesage, journal, PRO/CO/167/34.

83. One of the best biographies of Hastie is, interestingly, *Tantara*, 1081–82. See also Toussaint, 1941: 46–47; *Firaketana*, no. 41 (Mai 1940), entry for Hastie, 123–26.

84. I thus disagree with Berg's conclusion (1996: esp. 33, 51) that there was a fundamental continuity in the careers of royal advisers during the reigns of Andrian-ampoinimerina and Radama. Virtually all the men whose careers Berg considers in the article hailed from the periphery of Imerina or from Radama's own family rather than from Andrianampoinimerina's core base of support in Avaradrano; what is continuous in careers is elite origins, not service under Andrianampoinimerina. Rainitsiroba was the only *namana* I know to have survived in a military position in Radama's regime, serving as general of the Mainty, or "blacks," a less than fully prestigious and influential position. By the time of Radama's death in 1828, though, Rainitsiroba had achieved the tenth honor (*Tantara*, 1108; *"Teny navalin-dRainitsiroba, 10 vtra, an-dRadama I,"* in Cousins, 1873: 26).

85. A port (where customs were paid) was known as a *seranana*. On the other hand, *seranina* was a verb in passive voice, "to be passed by" (Richardson, 1885: entry for *serana*, 567). The *maroseranina* date to the reign of Radama, not that of Ranavalona, as Berg has written (1996: 54).

86. Munthe, Ravoajanahary and Ayache, 1976: 26–27, 40–41; Ratsivalaka, 1995: vol. 1, 574–96. Hastie, however, clearly understood Radama's predicament (journal, 1903b: 260–68).

87. Hastie, journal, 06/10/17, 1903b: 260.

88. Hastie, journal, 09/10/17, 1903b: 264.

89. Hastie, journal, 16/08/17, 1903a: 181; 18/08/17, 1903a: 182; 02/09/17, 1903b: 241; 04/09/17, 1903b: 244.

90. Hastie, journal, 3/09/17, 1903b: 243; 11/10/17, 1903b: 266.

91. Hastie, journal, 05/09/17, 1903b: 245.

92. Hastie, journal, 12/10/17, 1903b: 267.

93. Munthe, Ravoajanahary, and Ayache, 1976: 38–43; Campbell, 1987: 398–99.

94. If we are to believe Raombana (*RH* II, 1030–38), Radama was negligent and relatively unconcerned about his finances, seldom counted his money, and routinely allowed his subordinates to siphon off his rightful share of war booty. These observations are supported by *Tantara*, 1105–8, 1117–19; Pfeiffer, 1981: 146.

95. Jones to Telfair, Antananarivo, 14/10/20, LMS/1/2/A.

96. Hastie, journal, 20/02/18, MNA/HB/10/2/30.

97. For Ratefy's background, see *Tantara*, 518–22.

98. Hastie, journal, 09/10/17, 1903b: 264. See also *HOM*, vol. 2, 187.

99. Hastie, journal, 07/10/17, 1903b: 261. For another statement of *namana* opposition to the treaty, see *HOM*, vol. 2, 185.

100. Something the king admitted to Hastie (Hastie, journal, 12/10/17, 1903b: 268) only after promising to sign the treaty.

101. Hastie, journal, 09/10/17, 1903b: 264.

102. *HOM*, vol. 2, 200–201; Barker, 1996: 25–29.

103. For distribution of the equivalent, see *HOM*, vol. 2, 228. For the equivalent as a fraction of slave trade revenues, see Thompson, 1974: 424–25.

104. Hastie to Farquhar, Tamatave, 11/09/20, MNA/HB/13/25/8.

105. *HOM*, vol. 2, 220–43.

106. *HOM*, vol. 2, 245–46, 249.

107. For a history of the origins of the LMS mission to Antananarivo, see *HOM*, vol. 2, 201–24; Gow, 1979; Raison-Jourde, 1991. For a history of the LMS itself, see Lovett, 1899; Goodall, 1954.

108. Jones to Burder, Antananarivo, 20/07/22, LMS/1/4/A. Virtually all translation work to 1822, including the first portions of scripture, was conducted by the young Malagasy students. On the translation work of Malagasy students, see also *RH* II, 996.

109. Jones to Burder, Antananarivo, 29/03/22, LMS/1/3/B; Jones to Burder, Antananarivo, 03/05/21, LMS/1/2/C; Jones to Darby, Antananarivo, 14/03/22, LMS/1/3/C.

110. Hastie to Griffiths, Port Louis (Mauritius), 18/02/21, LMS/1/2/B.

111. *HOM*, vol. 2, 289–90; *RH* II, 998.

112. Griffiths, journal entry for 01/04/22, LMS/J/1.

113. Jeffreys to Burder, Antananarivo, 22/06/22, LMS/1/4/A.

114. Larson, 1997a.

115. Within the Vakinankaratra, for example, whereas the first 300 individuals baptized into the Lutheran churches of the Norwegian Missionary Society were predominantly middle-aged and adult men, the next 30,000, baptized between about 1875 and 1900, were mostly teenagers. Baptismal registers of the Norwegian Missionary Society, NMS archives, Isoraka, Antananarivo.

116. See Campbell, 1988a.

117. The best study of the formation of Radama's professional army is Berg, 1996: 35–40.

118. For clarification of common misperceptions about this mission, see Ratsivalaka, 1995: vol. 1, 526–40.

119. *Tantara*, 1095–96; *RH* II, 629–41, 660–62; Valette, 1962a: 18–19; Berg, 1996: 35–9.

120. *RH* II, 715–17; Decary, 1966: vol. 2, 10–11.

121. Valette, 1962a: 19.

122. Jones, journal entry for 3/10/20, LMS/J/1. See also *HOM*, vol. 2, 223–25.

123. Locke, 1835: 239.

124. Robin, "Copie exacte de la relation de la guerre faite contre Ramitra Chef des Séclaves par sa Majesté Radama et Envoyée par lui à son frère Jean-René, Commandant

en Chef à Tamatave," PRO/CO/167/51; Decary, 1966: vol. 2, 10. See also *RH* II, 697–98, 597–98.

125. *Tantara*, 804.

126. *RH* II, 994–95.

127. Farquhar to Hastie, Mauritius, 30/04/22, MNA/HB/7/72.

128. *Tantara*, 1110–13.

129. See Campbell, 1988b: 468, n. 15; Berg, 1996: 35–36.

130. *HOM*, vol. 2, 252.

131. Jones to Burder, Antananarivo, 03/05/21, LMS/1/2/C.

132. Griffiths, journal entry for 25/04/22, LMS/J/1.

133. Radama to Hastie, Tananarivoux, 23/12/21, MNA/HB/13/45. Berg has written (1996: 35–40) that Radama's soldiers, drawn from the various *firenena* ("*tanin'drazana* ancestral land groups") of the kingdom as demonstrated by this list, were "shorn of household ties" to become Voromahery.

134. The note following this figure suggests that the recruits were from Valalafotsy (a far western territory) rather than from the Vakinankaratra proper.

135. Not a *toko*, the Vakiniombifotsy comprised the territory along the Ombifotsy River to the southwest of Antananarivo, normally reckoned a part of Ambodirano.

136. "The blacks" (*mainty*), not a *toko* but a social category of persons considered servants of the sovereign, and their descendants.

137. Barnsley to Hastie, Tananarivo, 06/03/22, MNA/HB/7/42.

138. The *Tantara* reports 14,000 (1876–77); Raombana, 12,000 (*RH* II, 784, 839); *HOM*, 13,000 (*HOM*, vol. 2, 258). The *HOM* passage cited above suggests the recruits volunteered themselves during a single royal speech (*kabary*) in December 1821.

139. Jones to Darby, Antananarivo, 14/03/22, LMS/1/3/C; Jones to Burder, Antananarivo, 29/03/22, LMS/1/3/B.

140. Before the *fandroana* Radama dispatched part of his older army, the Rainiolona division, with James Brady; he would follow with the new recruits (Barnsby to Hastie, Indrinsoamourn, 18/05/22, MNA/HB/7/75).

141. Thompson, 1974: 433.

142. This number represents an upper limit. Radama argued with Hastie in 1817 (*HOM*, vol. 2, 188) that if he took an army of 20,000 men to the coast during the rainy season (when mosquitoes were most prevalent) he was sure at least one-third of them would die.

143. *HOM*, vol. 2, 254.

144. Campbell, 1988b.

145. *RH* I, 95–96; *RH* II, 995.

146. *HOM*, vol. 1, 114, 152. See also *RH* II, 973–77.

147. *RH* I, 432; *RH* II, 810–16; Larson, 1987: chap. 5 and 6; Campbell, 1988b: 474.

148. Thornton (1980: 423) reaches the same conclusion for eighteenth-century (colonial) Angola, a destination for female slaves and a source of men for the Atlantic commerce.

149. Unfortunately, recent work on textiles (Green, 1996) has focused primarily on silk, not cotton.

150. For comparable dilemmas pitting food security against cotton production in colonial Africa, see Isaacman and Roberts, 1995: 23, 34–36, and accompanying articles in that compendium.

151. *Tantara*, 1080; *HOM*, vol. 2, 257.

152. *HOM*, vol. 2, 252.

153. Campbell, 1986.

154. *Tantara*, 804.

155. Compare, for example, *RH* II, 981–82 with the rosy reports from Hastie, the British ambassador in Antananarivo, or the letters of the LMS missionaries teaching at the royal court (LMS, incoming letters).

156. Berg, 1996.

157. *Tantara*, 333.

158. For bodyguards, see Jones, journal entry of 4/10/20, LMS/J/1; Griffiths, journal entry for 23/02/22, LMS/J/1. For Radama in disguise, see *HOM*, vol. 1, 199, 377.

159. Principal accounts of this incident, which occurred at the king's countryside residence of Mahazoarivo, and the ensuing revolt are found in Griffiths, journal entries for 3, 15, and 16/04/22, LMS/J/1; Jeffreys to Arundel, Tamatave, 8/05/22, LMS/1/3/C; *Tantara*, 1078-80; *HOM*, vol. 1, 287–89; Jeffreys, 1827: 37–38; Hilsenberg and Bojer, 1833: 254; Tyerman and Bennet, 1831: vol. 2, 502-3; *RH* II, 798–810.

160. Decary, 1965: 286–90.

161. Hilsenberg and Bojer, 1833: 255.

162. *HOM*, vol. 1, 286–87. See also Chapman, 1943: 35.

163. Jeffreys, 1827: 133. Decary (1965: 286–90) lists some of the most common male hairstyles: *rorasoa, randrana vonkalana, ampanga, rikiriky, randran'ketsa, randrantsarihina, sori-bilana, tsy tongatonga, lambo miditra.*

164. Henry Singer Keating, typescript produced by his heirs of an original journal, entitled "Narrative, &c.," Bodleian Library, Oxford, MS.Eng.misc.c.29, 38, 101.

165. One tradition (*Tantara*, 310ff; Hébert, 1989–1990: 79) relates that king Andriantomponimerina of Ambohidratrimo (son of Andriamasinavalona) required his subjects to crop their hair and wear only a long lock on the front of their heads (*sanga kely*). The injunction, which may have indicated a cultural borrowing from the Islamic tradition linking highland Madagascar to the northwest coast and Indian Ocean, was remembered as having been opposed by the rest of highland Malagasy, who fought successfully to depose Andriantomponimerina for the innovation.

166. Griffiths, journal entry for 3/04/22, LMS/J/1.

167. Berg, 1998: 88–89.

168. Locke, 1835: 232.

169. *Tantara*, 1078–79; *RH* II, 798–99.

170. Thus the Tsimihety ("those who do not cut their hair") of northwestern Madagascar derived their name from a refusal to subordinate themselves to Merina overrule (Wilson, 1992: 16–26).

171. *Tantara*, 768, 781.

172. *RH* I, 462, 477.

173. Nearly a century later French colonists shaved the heads of Malagasy recruits for the First World War and of men forced into hard labor for the colonial government (SMOTIG). Desertions increased dramatically at haircutting time (Decary, 1965: 284).

174. Griffiths, journal entry for 3/04/22, LMS/J/1.

175. *Tantara*, 413.

176. Berg, 1951; Leach, 1958; Hallpike, 1969; Cooper, 1971; Kilmer, 1982; Mageo, 1994.

177. *Tantara*, 619, n. 1.

178. Griffiths, journal entry for 03/04/22, LMS/J/1. For later changes, see also the passage from Robert Lyall's journal (1827) in Berg, 1998: 87. For changes in dress among highland women, which lagged behind those of men, see Jourdain, 1839: 15.

179. *HOM*, vol. 1, 379.

180. Bloch, 1986.

181. Leach, 1958; Mageo, 1994.

182. Molet, 1979: vol. 2, 19–22, 170–73. Theoretically employing a cognatic system of reckoning descent in which ancestry was traced through both mother's and father's side, nineteenth-century highland Malagasy usually tended to emphasize their mother's line over their father's because of the difficulty of ascertaining paternity. Tacchi reported (1892: 480) how Andrianampoinimerina traced his ancestry primarily through his mother's line, through which he had a claim to royal power, adducing the common nineteenth-century proverb that "Cows calve; not the bulls."

183. For public ritual, consult the works of Bloch and Molet in the Bibliography; for private rituals of fertility, see Domenichini, 1985: 300–304; Larson, 1992: 101–15, 130–33.

184. *Tantara*, 73–74, 80–81; Bloch, 1986: 56.

185. For the *ramanenjana,* see Davidson, 1889; F. Raison, 1976. Bloch (1986: 145–46) shows how the *ramanenjana*-possessed women enacted elements of the circumcision ritual.

186. Mageo, 1994: 422, 426.

187. *Tantara*, 1079. An alternative narrative of these events also published in the *Tantara* claims that the women were more broadly drawn from central Imerina, representing Avaradrano, Marovatana, Ambodirano, Vakinisisaony, and Voromahery (the direct environs of Antananarivo). The Avaradrano origin of the women is retained here because it is confirmed in contemporary accounts. The broadening of the women's origin to all central Imerina in one of the several memorial accounts, however, may suggest how widespread the opposition to Radama's haircut was among highland Malagasy.

188. *Tantara*, 710–12.

189. *HOM*, vol. 1, 287–88. The emphasis is mine.

190. For more on Radama's policies of weakening and manipulating the kinship ties of his soldiers, see Berg, 1996: 36–37.

191. Griffiths, journal for 16/04/22, LMS/J/1.

192. *HOM*, vol. 1, 288.

193. *Tantara*, 1080.

194. *Tantara*, 1079.

195. Keenan, 1974a, 1974b; Larson, 1995: 322–25; Graeber, 1996b: 433–35.

196. *RH* II, 802–805; Griffiths, journal entry for 16/04/22, LMS/J/1. The emphasis is mine.

197. *HOM*, vol. 1, 288–89. Another narrative (*Tantara*, 1079) suggests that only two female leaders were executed. The emphasis is mine.

198. *RH* II, 802–805; Griffiths, journal entry for 16/04/22, LMS/J/1.

199. Witness the paucity of references to Andrianampoinimerina in narratives of royal speeches during the reign of Queen Ranavalona I (*Tantara*, 1120–75) and her successors (*Tantara*, 1180–90).

200. Delivré, 1974: 27–68.

201. In her study of cattle sacrifice among the southern Betsimisaraka of eastern Madagascar, Cole (1996: 84–108, 1997) provides a richly documented ethnographic description of the individual manipulations of "*hasina* ideology" that I am discussing here.

202. Feeley-Harnik, 1991a: 441. For an interpretation of struggles over traditions and rituals of citizenship in a context very different from the one I describe here, see Glassman, 1995: esp. 1–25.

203. Bloch, 1986: 157–95; 1989b: esp. 21, 27, 40 (quotation), 41 (quotation); 1989c: esp. 123 (quotation); 1996: 227 (quotation). In many respects Berg's formulation of *hasina* ideology (1985, 1988, 1995, 1996, 1998) is similar to Bloch's concept of royal power as developed in this paragraph. For both scholars, royal ideology is enduring and stable and clearly beneficial only to rulers. Berg departs from Bloch, however, in that he does not see royal ideology as articulated only through ritual and, in a recent publication (1998), even allows for a certain measure of challenge to royal ideology from below.

204. Bloch, 1986: esp. 105, 117–19; 198: esp. 271–72.

205. Domenichini, 1985; Berg, 1986, 1998: 71–73; Graeber, 1996b.

206. Stern, 1982.

207. This is the thesis in Scott, 1990.

208. Rasmussen, who has written about the memory of slavery among the Tuareg (1999), suggests in Scott's language that certain narrative commentaries on slavery are "hidden transcripts" or "weapons of the weak." Nevertheless, what is significant about the commentaries on slavery by both former slaves and noble slaveholders is that they all play on the "noble cultural values" of patronage, generosity, dignity, reserve, and speech by indirect allusion to make their points. On the nineteenth-century eastern coast of Africa (Glassman, 1995), slaves and masters both engaged the same languages and rituals to further their social position in Swahili society. If slaves and masters commonly employed the same languages in their social struggles and interactions, how much more so among various strata of the "free" population?

CHAPTER 7

1. Halbwachs, 1992: 38.

2. Gerbeau, 1989: 10.

3. This "secret" history only becomes apparent once *Tantara* narratives are viewed as the product of a particular historical and political process. For my use of *secret*, see Stern, 1995: esp. x.

4. The slave trade is not entirely absent from the compendium, as a careful reading of part I of this book will reveal (esp. chapter 3), but information is fleeting and fragmentary, perhaps one full page of text at most in a 1,200-page compendium. Most important, the relationship between Andrianampoinimerina and foreign commerce is undeveloped. The slave trade leaves its mark on the texts in powerful yet indirect ways, as argued in this and the two previous chapters.

5. For the notion of social amnesia, a counterpart to social memory, see Burke, 1989: 106, 108–10.

6. Burke, 1989: 108.

7. Larson, 1995: 299–309.

8. Larson, 1995: 316–22.

9. See the map in Delivré, 1974: 66, which shows the locations from which *Tantara* narratives were collected. My interpretation of the popular nature of *Tantara* narratives runs counter to the work of most historians of Madagascar, who assume that these are elite texts. For an explanation of my position, see Larson, 1999: 353, n. 42. One example of the colloquial narrative use of *particules locatives* discussed in that note is *Tantara*, 623: *Lehidama mampaneky an'Ambohimitsara, dia nahazo taty andrefan'Ankaratra; ary ny tafika nenti'ny ray ny nahazo taty atsinanan'Ankaratra nahazo any Mahavikia.* See also Berg, 1980: 237, n. 32, for problems with Delivré's method of determining the origins of narratives.

10. For examples of the melding of *Tantara* and *firenena* narratives, see Larson, forthcoming, b.

11. *HOM*, vol. 2, 517–19, 521–22; Robert Lyall to Charles Colville, Tananarivou, 06/11/28 (entry for Oct. 22), MNA/HB/19/8. On this basis (but not on continuity of leadership) I agree with Berg (1995: esp. 73–74) about a fundamental continuity between the reigns of Radama and Ranavalona.

12. Tacchi, 1892: 496; *Firaketana*, no. 107 (Fév. 1947), entry for "Callet," 410.

13. Valette, 1965: 280–83. In a similar vein, Ellis (1985: 60) writes of "official" and "unofficial" versions of oral history during the nineteenth century; unofficial versions, he writes, were actively suppressed.

14. Delivré, 1974: 64.

15. Raison-Jourde, 1991: 626.

16. See Campbell, 1988a, 1988b, 1991, 1992.

17. *HOM*, vol. 2, 122–29, esp. 124, 127.

18. *HOM*, vol. 2, 125.

19. For a biography of Coroller, see Berg, 1996: 58–59.

20. Wilhelmsen to Hovedbestyrelsen, Soavina, 18/04/76, NMS/134/2 (printed in *NMT*, no. 8, Aug. 1876, 363); Lars Dahle to Hovedbestyrelsen, Antananarivo, 11/09/84, NMS/136/4 (printed in *NMT*, no. 23, Dec. 1884, 446).

21. Ellis, 1985: 66–67, 96–97, 107, 129, 154.

22. Tacchi, 1892: 481, 474–96.

23. *Firaketana*, no. 41 (Mai 1940), entry for Andrianampoinimerina, 106–19 (quotation, 118).

24. Raolison, 1966: 55–59.

25. The following works treat Andrianampoinimerina's rise to power primarily in domestic terms, seldom, and in some cases not at all, mentioning the export slave trade: Malzac, 1930: 83–162; Grandidier, 1942: 85–152; Heseltine, 1971: 97–99; Deschamps, 1972a: 121–27, 1976: 399–402, 1977: 77–97; Ralaimihoatra, 1982: 111–28; Bloch, 1986: 13–15; Prou, 1987: 11–36; Mutibwa with Esoavelomandroso, 1989: 413–16; Vérin, 1990: 77–90; Brown, 1995: 104–10. A Marxist, Boiteau (1958: 62–82) was among the few historians writing before Malagasy independence who saw external trade as significant to Merina state formation. In his study of the development of kingdoms in highland Madagascar, Bloch (1978: esp. 109–115) finds international trade important to highland rulers, but only as a source of weapons. Berg (1985: esp. 273–74, 1988: esp. 201–2) writes about Imerina and external trade, though he does so not to accentuate its importance but to argue that—*pace* Bloch—its influ-

ence was not particularly significant, especially with respect to Andrianam-poinimerina's acquisition of firearms and the impact of those firearms on state building. Hébert (1979, 1983–1984, 1989–1990, 1996, no date) and Ratsivalaka (1995) are the principal exceptions to the historiographical tradition of viewing Andrianampoinimerina's rise in strictly or primarily domestic terms and without reference to the management of trade wealth.

26. Several similar studies of the social production of amnesia are presented in Cohen, 1994.

27. See also Vérin, 1990: 89.

28. Rakotonirainy, 1962: 1, 15, 16.

29. Shrimpton, 1997: 91.

30. Although enduring, that ethnic identity is sustained in the modern era by means other than those explored here for the early nineteenth century.

31. Popular Memory Group, 1982: 205.

32. Cohen, 1997: 1–29; *Oxford English Dictionary*, 1989: vol. 4, 613 (entry for *diaspora*). Before the late nineteenth century, Jewish experiences were understood as a dispersion, not a diaspora.

33. *Oxford English Dictionary*, 1989: vol. 4, 813 (entry for dispersion); Tölölyan, 1996: esp. 3–16; Shepperson, 1976: 2, 1993: 41; Harris, 1993c: 4. "This is, I believe," wrote Shepperson in 1976 of *The African Diaspora: Interpretive Essays*, "the first book, academic or otherwise, to contain the words 'African diaspora' in its title" (1976: 9). Shepperson was himself sometimes credited with originating the term "African diaspora" (Kilson and Rotberg, 1976: 487).

34. Safran, 1991; Tölölyan, 1996; Cohen, 1997: 177–96; Clifford, 1997: 24–77.

35. Shepperson, 1968. For definitions of the African diaspora, see Harris, 1968, 1992, 1996, 1997; Rodney, 1975; Shepperson, 1968, 1976, 1993; Curtin, 1979; Knight with Talib and Curtin, 1989; Skinner, 1993. Few Indian Ocean studies are specifically framed in terms of African dispersion. The primary exception is the work of Harris (see list of works cited). See also Chittick and Rotberg, 1975; Popovic, 1976; Talib, 1988; Kohli, 1990; Alpers 1997, 1999. An increasing number of scholarly studies about the experiences of slaves and other Africans around the Indian Ocean and its islands, although not explicitly developed with the concept of diaspora in mind, join these works (Filliot, 1974a, 1974b; Alpers, 1975, 1983; Cooper, 1977; Wanquet, 1980, 1988, 1996; Nwulia, 1981; Bisoondoyal and Servansing, 1989; Clarence-Smith, 1989a; Wright, 1993; Glassman, 1995; Teelock, 1998; Allen, 1999).

36. A fact seldom admitted in studies of return to Africa. This feature of the African (-American) diaspora runs up against many definitions of a diaspora as a dispersed population that fervently desires a return to homeland (e.g. Safran, 1991: 83–84).

37. Law and Lovejoy (1997) review this development.

38. Safran, 1991; Cohen, 1997: 31–42.

39. Thornton, 1991, 1992, 1993; Lovejoy 1994a, 1994b, 1997a; Gomez, 1998; Morgan, 1998.

40. Even Africanists Law and Lovejoy, who acknowledge trans-Saharan and intra-African movements of slaves from the central Sudan in a paragraph of their recent attempt to "reappropriate the diaspora" (1997: 182), then proceed in the remainder of their collective work to assimilate the diaspora to the Americas.

41. The best single description of this process is Gomez, 1998.

42. Curtin, 1979: esp. 4.

43. Austen, 1979, 1989, 1992; Lovejoy, 1983: 19, 25, 45, 137; Hunwick, 1992: 5; Klein, 1992: 39; Toledano, 1998: 9; Klein, 1999: 56, 126, 129, 165. The trans-Saharan and Red Sea trades probably well exceeded the figures adduced in the preceding works because of the high mortality rates during capture and in transit across the desert, which are not accounted for, and because forced African migrations to Asian regions have never been counted. See Hiskett, 1985: 117; Mahadi, 1992: 125; Mack, 1992: 97, 100–101; Collins, 1992: 141; Wright, 1992: 181–82; Alpers, 1997: 64. Inikori, who has also published estimates for the various slave trades (1992: 82–83), dissents from these widely accepted figures. He places the transatlantic trade at 15.4 million and the trans-Saharan trade at nearly 4 million.

44. For domestic commerce linked to the transatlantic slave trade see Lovejoy, 1983: 60–65; Miller, 1988: 140–69, 379–42 (esp. 440–41, 153); Manning, 1990: 38–59; Klein, 1992: 39–41, 1998: 1, 39–41; Searing, 1993: 44–58 (esp. 53). The African counterpart trades to the Indian Ocean and Red Sea slave trades are quantified in Lovejoy, 1983: 153; Clarence-Smith, 1989b: 3; Austen, 1989: 21-44; Manning, 1990: 38-59, 47. For the linking of domestic African commerce to the trans-Saharan slave trade, see Austen, 1979: 23–76; Lovejoy, 1983: 60–65; Manning, 1990: 38–59. See also Klein, 1999: 126, 129, 165.

45. Klein, 1999: 126.

46. For examples of recent and stimulating research in the Atlantic and Indian oceans that nevertheless are focused primarily on extracontinental or coastal movements as "the diaspora," see Law and Lovejoy, 1997; Law and Mann, 1999; Alpers 1997.

47. Alpers, 1997: esp. 67.

48. See esp. Morgan, 1998; Berlin, 1998.

49. I leave aside the trans-Saharan slave trade in this discussion of the diaspora in order to emphasize how Atlantic and Indian ocean histories (with which I am most familiar and with which this book deals) can inform each other.

50. Austen, 1982; Toledano, 1982: esp. 21–28; Sheriff, 1987; Clarence-Smith, 1989a; McPherson, 1993: 247–50.

51. Hourani, 1963; Toussaint, 1966, 1974; Chaudhuri, 1985, 1990; Das Gupta and Pearson, 1987; McPherson, 1993; Das Gupta, 1994; Risso, 1995.

52. Kling and Pearson, 1979; McPherson, 1993: 137–97; Pearson, 1998.

53. Cooper, 1977.

54. Alpers, 1975, 1997, 1999; Sheriff, 1987; Bissoondoyal and Servansing, 1989; Wanquet and Jullien, 1996; Rakoto, 1997; Teelock, 1998; Allen, 1999.

55. Alpers, 1997.

56. Gilroy, 1993: 15.

57. Gilroy centers his narrative on (male) Anglophone writers, scholars and music makers such as W.E.B. Du Bois, Frederick Douglass, Richard Wright, Martin Delaney, Edward Wilmot Blyden, James Baldwin, and Alexander Crummell.

58. Gilroy, 1993: 223.

59. See esp. the standardization of stories about enslavement among nineteenth-century African Americans as explored in Gomez, 1998: 199–214.

60. Gilroy, 1993: 219–20.

61. Graeber, 1996c: 67–68, 268–70.

62. Lovejoy, 1983: 159–282.

63. Olivier de Sardan, 1976; Cooper, 1977: 274–75; Graeber, 1997; Klein, 1998: 243–51; Rasmussen, 1999.

64. Lovejoy, 1983: 34.

65. See the discussion about the historiography of slavery in North America and the uses of memorial evidence in Berlin, Favreau, and Miller, 1998: esp. xiii–xlvii.

66. The former genre includes Isaacman, 1972; Alpers, 1975; the essays by Isaacman and Isaacman, Dunbar, Miller, Hartwig, Holsoe, Tlou, Baier and Lovejoy, and Baldus in Miers and Kopytoff, 1977; Northrup, 1978; Harms, 1981; Strobel, 1983; Robertson, 1983; Alagoa, 1986; Roberts, 1987; Wright, 1993; Hawthorne, 1998, forthcoming. Examples of the latter genre include Rodney, 1970; Martin, 1972; Inikori, 1982a; Lovejoy, 1983; Eltis, 1987; Miller, 1988; Manning, 1990; Law, 1991; Thornton, 1992; Inikori and Engerman, 1992a; Searing, 1993; Klein, 1998. (Klein makes a minimal use of African narratives in a study that is otherwise based primarily upon secondary literature and some archival work; see chap. 14 in his work for discussion of African narratives.)

67. Chrétien, 1986: 77.

68. Newbury, 1986: 161.

69. See Abercrombie, 1998: 409.

70. See Hawthorne, 1998: 46–47.

71. Most work on historical memory embedded in African cultural practices has been conducted by anthropologists, and anglophone scholars of Madagascar are prominent among them (Feeley-Harnik, 1991b; Lambek, 1992, 1998; Stoler, 1995; Middleton, 1997; Cole, 1998). See also Connerton, 1989: 41–104. For ritual and the slave trade, see Hawthorne, 1998: 187; Baum, 1999; Shaw, forthcoming.

72. See Isaacman, 1972; Alpers, 1975; Northrup, 1978; Harms, 1981; Roberts, 1987. For a criticism of these literal approaches to oral tradition, consult Tonkin, 1992: esp. 83–96. I borrow "poetical" from Lambek, 1998.

73. Cohen, 1994: 112. See also Cohen, 1989.

74. Indeed, this shift is already under way, as evidenced in Lovejoy, 1997a; Law, 1997; Baum, 1999; Shaw, forthcoming. See also Janzen, 1982.

75. Tonkin, 1992: 2.

76. See, for example, Rappaport's study (1990) of the development of Páez historical thought in highland Columbia from the late eighteenth to the twentieth century.

77. Finley, 1965.

78. Thompson, 1978; Miller, 1980; Henige, 1982; Vansina, 1985; Samuel and Thompson, 1990; Tonkin, 1992.

79. Hamilton, 1994: 9.

80. Nora, 1989: quotations from 7–8. For history and memory as fundamentally opposed, see also Le Goff, 1992.

81. Nora, 1989: 19.

82. Nora, 1989: 23–24.

83. Hamilton's revisionist study (1998) of popular narratives of Shaka reaches a similar conclusion: while plastic, popular narratives of Shaka, both African and European, were based on actual events and previous narratives. They were not pure inventions.

84. Abercrombie (1998) reaches similar conclusions with respect to the continuing importance of Andean "pathways of memory" to everyday and ritual life in highland

Bolivia, despite systematic campaigns by colonial authorities seeking to erase such registers of historical memory.

85. See also Abercrombie (1998), which takes the variance and interaction of Andean and Spanish ways of remembering as its organizing theme.

86. Burke, 1989: 97, 110.

87. Karp and Lavine, 1991; Karp, Kreamer, and Lavine, 1992; Coombes, 1994; Cohen, 1994; Simpson, 1996; Kurin, 1997.

88. Le Goff, 1992: xi–xii, xvii (emphasis in original). See also Carr, 1964; Finley, 1965; Fischer, 1970; Halbwachs, 1980; Nora, 1989; Connerton, 1989: 13–21; Gillis, 1992: 92. A notable exception is Lukacs, 1968.

89. "Lived history" and "the science of history" are Le Goff's terms (1992: xv).

90. Most histories of the Merina kingdom rely heavily on the *Tantara*. At the same time, highland Malagasy popular historians often draw on material from professional histories in the construction of historical narratives about their descent groups. See Larson, forthcoming, b.

91. Gerbeau, 1989: 29

BIBLIOGRAPHY

BOOKS AND ARTICLES

Abercrombie, Thomas. 1998. *Pathways of Memory and Power: Ethnography and History Among an Andean People*. Madison, Wis.

Abinal, Antoine, and Camille de la Vaissière. 1885. *Vingt ans à Madagascar: colonisation, traditions historiques, moeurs et croyances*. Paris.

Abinal, Antoine, and Victorien Malzac. 1987. *Dictionnaire malgache-français*. Fianarantsoa, Madagascar [first published in 1888].

Adamu, Mahdi. 1979. "The Delivery of Slaves from the Central Sudan to the Bight of Benin in the Eighteenth and Nineteenth Centuries." In Gemery and Hogendorn, *Uncommon Market*, 163–80.

Ajayi, J.F. Ade, ed. 1989. *General History of Africa*, vol. 6, *Africa in the Nineteenth Century Until the 1880s*. Berkeley, Calif.

Alagoa, E.J. 1986. "The Slave Trade in Niger Delta Oral Tradition and History." In Lovejoy, *Africans in Bondage*, 125–35.

Allen, Richard. 1999. *Slaves, Freedmen and Indentured Laborers in Colonial Mauritius*. Cambridge, England.

Allibert, Claude. 1995. "Les hollandais et Madagascar." In Evers and Spindler, *Cultures of Madagascar*, 87–99.

Alonso, Ana María. 1994. "The Politics of Space, Time and Substance: State Formation, Nationalism and Ethnicity." *Annual Review of Anthropology* 23: 379–405.

Alpers, Edward A. 1973. "Re-thinking African Economic History: A Contribution to the Discussion of the Roots of Underdevelopment." *Ufahamu* 3, 3: 97–129.

——. 1975. *Ivory and Slaves: Changing Patterns of Trade in East Central Africa to the Later Nineteenth Century*. Berkeley, Calif.

——. 1983. "The Story of Swema: Female Vulnerability in Nineteenth-Century East Africa." In Robertson and Klein, *Women and Slavery in Africa*, 185–219.

——. 1997. "The African Diaspora in the Northwestern Indian Ocean: Reconsideration of an Old Problem, New Directions for Research." *Comparative Studies of South Asia, Africa and the Middle East* 17, 2: 62–81.

————. 1999. "A Complex Relationship: Mozambique and the Comoro Islands in the Nineteenth and Twentieth Centuries." Paper presented to the Colloque International "La Problématique de la Recherche au Service du Développement dans les Pays Insulaires: le cas des Comores vingt ans après la création du CNDRS." Moroni, Comores, Jan. 27–28.

Althabe, Gérard. 1969. *Oppression et libération dans l'imaginaire: les communautés villageoises de la côte orientale de Madagascar*. Paris.

Alvarez, Albert Roca. 1995. "Ethnicity and Nation in Madagascar." In Evers and Spindler, *Cultures of Madagascar*, 67-83.

Amselle, Jean-Loup. 1990. *Logiques métises: anthropologie de l'identité en Afrique et ailleurs*. Paris.

Amselle, Jean-Loup, and Elikia M'Bokolo, eds. 1985. *Au coeur de l'ethnie: ethnies, tribalisme et état en Afrique*. Paris.

Anderson, Benedict. 1983. *Imagined Communities: Reflections on the Origin and Spread of Nationalism*. London.

Anstey, Roger. 1975. *The Atlantic Slave Trade and British Abolition, 1760–1810*. London.

Antze, Paul, and Michael Lambek, eds. 1996. *Tense Past: Cultural Essays in Trauma and Memory*. London.

Arasaratnam, Sinnappah. 1978. "Indian Commercial Groups and European Traders, 1600-1800: Changing Relationships in Southern India." *South Asia* 1, 2: 42–53.

————. 1990. "Recent Trends in the Historiography of the Indian Ocean, 1500 to 1800." *Journal of World History* 1, 2: 225–48.

————. 1994. *Maritime India in the Seventeenth Century*. Delhi, India.

Arbousset, Francis. 1950. *Le fokon'olona à Madagascar*. Paris.

Armstrong, James C. 1984. "Madagascar and the Slave Trade in the Seventeenth Century." *Omaly sy Anio* 17–19: 211–33.

Armstrong, James C. and Nigel A. Worden. 1988. "The Slaves, 1652–1834." In Elphick and Giliomee, *The Shaping of South African Society*, 109–83.

Astuti, Rita. 1995. *People of the Sea: Identity and Descent Among the Vezo of Madagascar*. Cambridge, England.

Atkinson, Ronald Raymond. 1994. *The Roots of Ethnicity: The Origins of the Acholi of Uganda Before 1800*. Philadelphia.

Augustins, Georges. 1973. "Parenté, résidence et régime foncier dans un village d'Imamo (hauts plateaux de Madagascar)." Thèse de troisième cycle, Université de Paris X.

Aujas, L. 1905–1906. "Notes sur l'histoire des Betsimisaraka." *Bulletin de l'Académie Malgache* 4: 104–15.

————. 1907. "Essai sur l'histoire et les coutumes des Betsimisaraka." *Revue de Madagascar* 9: 501–15.

Austen, Ralph A. 1979. "The Transsaharan Slave Trade: A Tentative Census." In Gemery and Hogendorn, *Uncommon Market*, 23–76.

————. 1981. "From the Atlantic to the Indian Ocean: European Abolition, the African Slave Trade, and Asian Economic Structures." In Eltis and Walvin, *The Abolition of the Atlantic Slave Trade*, 117–39.

————. 1989. "The 19th Century Islamic Slave Trade from East Africa (Swahili and Red Sea Coasts): A Tentative Census." In Clarence-Smith, *The Economics of the Indian Ocean Slave Trade*, 21–44.

———. 1992. "The Mediterranean Islamic Slave Trade out of Africa: A Tentative Census." *Slavery and Abolition* 13, 1: 214–48.

———. 1993. "The Moral Economy of Witchcraft: An Essay in Comparative History." In Comaroff and Comaroff, *Modernity and Its Malcontents*, 89–110.

Austen, Ralph A., and Jonathan Derrick. 1999. *Middlemen of the Cameroons Rivers: The Duala and Their Hinterland, c. 1600– c.1960.* Cambridge, England.

Ayache, Simon. 1976a. *Raombana l'historien (1809–1855): introduction à l'édition critique de son oeuvre.* Fianarantsoa, Madagascar.

———. 1976b. "Un intellectuel malgache devant la culture européene: l'historien Raombana." *Archipel* 12: 95–119.

———. 1979. "Beyond Oral Tradition and into Written History: The Work of Raombana (1809–1855)." In Kent, *Madagascar in History*, 197–227.

Azéma, Georges. 1859. *Histoire de l'Île Bourbon depuis 1643 jusqu'au 20 décembre 1848.* Paris.

Baier, Stephen, and Paul E. Lovejoy. 1977. "The Tuareg of the Central Sudan: Gradations in Servility at the Desert Edge (Niger and Nigeria)." In Miers and Kopytoff, *Slavery in Africa*, 391–411.

Balandier, Georges. 1955. *Sociologie des Brazzavilles Noires.* Paris.

Baldock, W.F. 1963. "The Story of Rashid Bin Hassani of the Bisa Tribe, Northern Rhodesia." In Perham, *Ten Africans*, 81–119.

Baldus, Bernd. 1977. "Responses to Dependence in a Servile Group: The Machube of Northern Benin." In Miers and Kopytoff, *Slavery in Africa*, 435–58.

Banton, Michael. 1960. *West African City: A Study of Tribal Life in Freetown.* London.

Barber, John W., ed. 1840. *A History of the Amistad Captives.* New Haven, Conn.

Barbour, Bernard, and Michelle Jacobs. 1985. "The Mi`raj: a Legal Treatise on Slavery by Ahmad Baba." In Willis, *Slaves and Slavery in Muslim Africa*, vol. 1, 125–59.

Barendse, R.J. 1995. "Slaving on the Malagasy Coast, 1640–1700." In Evers and Spindler, *Cultures of Madagascar*, 137–55.

Barker, Anthony J. 1996. *Slavery and Anti-Slavery in Mauritius, 1810–33: The Conflict Between Economic Expansion and Humanitarian Reform Under British Rule.* London.

Baron, R. 1903. "Kabary Malgache: Kabary II. Teny nampitondrain'Andrianampoinimerina tamin'Andriamanalina Betsileo." *Bulletin de l'Académie Malgache* 2, 3: 169–71.

Barrasin, Jean. 1953. *Bourbon, des origines jusqu'en 1714.* Paris.

Barré, J.-F. 1977. *Pouvoir des vivants, langage des morts: idéo-logiques Sakalava.* Paris.

Barry, Boubacar. 1972. *Le royaume de Waalo.* Paris.

———. 1998. *Senegambia and the Atlantic Slave Trade.* Cambridge, England.

Barth, Frederik, ed. 1969. *Ethnic Groups and Boundaries: The Social Organization of Culture Difference.* Bergen, Norway.

Bartlett, F.C. 1995. *Remembering: A Study in Experimental and Social Psychology.* Cambridge, England.

Bascom, William. 1955. "Urbanization Among the Yoruba." *American Journal of Sociology* 60: 446–54.

Bates, Robert H., V.Y. Mudimbe, and Jean O'Barr. 1993. *Africa and the Disciplines: The Contributions of Research in Africa to the Social Sciences and Humanities.* Chicago.

Bathily, Abdoulaye. 1986. "La traite atlantique des esclaves et ses effets économiques et sociaux en Afrique: le cas de Galam, royaume de l'hinterland sénégambien au dix-huitième siècle." *Journal of African History* 27: 269–93.

———. 1989. *Les portes de l'or: le royaume de Galam (Sénégal) de l'ère musulmane au temps de négriers huitième–dix-huitième siècle.* Paris.

Battistini, René, and G. Richard-Vindard, eds. 1972. *Biogeography and Ecology in Madagascar.* The Hague, Netherlands.

Baum, Robert. 1997. "The Slave Trade in Diola (Senegal) Oral Tradition." Paper presented at the Conference on The Atlantic Slave Trade in African and African American Memory. University of Chicago, Program on African and African American Studies, May 24, 1997.

———. 1999. *Shrines of the Slave Trade: Diola Religion and Society in Precolonial Senegambia.* Oxford.

Bauman, Richard, and Joel Sherzer, eds. 1974. *Explorations in the Ethnography of Speaking.* London.

Bazin, Jean. 1974. "War and Servitude in Segou." *Economy and Society* 3: 107–43.

———. 1982. "Etat guerrier et guerres d'état." In Bazin and Terray, *Guerres de lignages*, 319–74.

Bazin, Jean, and Emmanuel Terray, eds. 1982. *Guerres de lignages et guerres d'états en Afrique.* Paris.

Beachey, R.W. 1976. *The Slave Trade of Eastern Africa.* London.

Bean, Richard. 1975. *The British Trans-Atlantic Slave Trade, 1650–1775.* New York.

Becker, Charles. 1986. "Conditions écologiques, crises de subsistance et histoire de la population à l'époque de la traite des esclaves en Sénégambie (dix-septième–dix-huitième siècles)." *Canadian Journal of African Studies* 20: 357–76.

——. 1988. "Les effects démographiques de la traite des esclaves en Sénégambie: esquisse d'une histoire des peuplements du XVIIe à la fin du XIXe siècle." In Daget, *De la traite à l'esclavage*, vol. 2, 71–110.

Becker, Charles and Victor Martin. 1982. "Kayor and Baol: Senegalese Kingdoms and the Slave Trade in the 18th century." In Inikori, *Forced Migration*, 100–125.

Beidelman, T.O. 1986. *Moral Imagination in Kaguru Modes of Thought.* Bloomington, Ind.

Bellwood, Peter. 1985. *Prehistory of the Indo-Malaysian Archipelago.* Orlando, Fla.

Bentley, G. Carter. 1987. "Ethnicity and Practice." *Comparative Studies in Society and History* 29, 1: 24–55.

Benyowsky, Maurice Auguste. 1792. *Voyages et mémoires.* Paris.

Berg, Charles. 1951. *The Unconscious Significance of Hair.* London.

Berg, Gerald M. 1977. "The Myth of Racial Strife and Merina Kinglists: The Transformation of Texts." *History in Africa* 4: 1–30.

———. 1980. "Some Words about Merina Historical Literature." In Miller, *The African Past Speaks*, 221–39.

———. 1985. "The Sacred Musket: Tactics, Technology, and Power in Eighteenth-Century Madagascar." *Comparative Studies in Society and History* 27, 2: 261–79.

———. 1986. "Royal Authority and the Protector System in Nineteenth-Century Imerina." In Kottak, et. al., *Madagascar: Society and History*, 175–92.

———. 1988. "Sacred Acquisition: Andrianampoinimerina at Ambohimanga, 1777–1790." *Journal of African History* 29, 2: 191–211.

———. 1995. "Writing Ideology: Ranavalona, the Ancestral Bureaucrat." *History in Africa* 22: 73–92.

———. 1996. "*Virtù*, and *Fortuna* in Radama's Nascent Bureaucracy, 1816–1828." *History in Africa* 23: 29–73.

———. 1998. "Radama's Smile: Domestic Challenges to Royal Ideology in Early Nineteenth-Century Imerina." *History in Africa* 25: 69–92.

Berlin, Ira. 1998. *Many Thousands Gone: The First Two Centuries of Slavery in North America.* Cambridge, Mass.

Berlin, Ira, Marc Favreau, and Steven F. Miller, eds. 1998. *Remembering Slavery: African Americans Talk About Their Personal Experiences of Slavery and Freedom.* New York.

Berman, Bruce, and John Lonsdale. 1992. *Unhappy Valley: Conflict in Kenya and Africa.* London.

Bissoondoyal, U., and S.B.C. Servansing, eds. 1989. *Slavery in South West Indian Ocean.* Moka, Mauritius.

Black, Max. 1962. *Models and Metaphors: Studies in Language and Philosophy.* Ithaca, N.Y.

Blackburn, Robin. 1997. *The Making of New World Slavery: From the Baroque to the Modern, 1492–1800.* London.

Blassingame, John W. 1979. *The Slave Community: Plantation Life in the Antebellum South.* New York.

Bloch, Maurice. 1967. "Notes sur l'organisation sociale de l'Imerina avant le règne de Radama Ier." *Annales de l'Université de Madagascar, Série Sciences Humaines* 7: 199–232.

———. 1971. *Placing the Dead: Tombs, Ancestral Villages, and Kinship Organization in Madagascar.* London.

———. 1978. "The Disconnection Between Power and Rank As a Process: An Outline of the Development of Kingdoms in Central Madagascar." In Friedman and Rowlands, *The Evolution of Social Systems,* 303–40.

———. 1981. "Tombs and States." In Humphreys and King, *Mortality and Immortality,* 137–47.

———. 1982. "Death, Women and Power." In Bloch and Parry, *Death and the Regeneration of Life,* 211–30.

———. 1983. "The Changing Relationship Between Rural Communities and the State in Central Madagascar during the 19th and 20th Centuries." In *Les communautés rurales: recueils de la Société Jean Bodin* 40: 233–47.

———. 1986. *From Blessing to Violence: History and Ideology in the Circumcision Ritual of the Merina of Madagascar.* Cambridge, England.

———. 1987. "The Ritual of the Royal Bath in Madagascar: The Dissolution of Death, Birth and Fertility into Authority." In Cannadine and Price, *Rituals of Royalty,* 271–97.

———. 1989a. *Ritual, History and Power: Selected Papers in Anthropology.* London.

———. 1989b. "Symbols, Song, Dance and Features of Articulation: Is Religion an Extreme Form of Traditional Authority?" In Bloch, *Ritual, History and Power,* 19–45.

———. 1989c. "From Cognition to Ideology." In Bloch, *Ritual, History and Power,* 106–36.

———. 1989d. "The Symbolism of Money in Imerina." In Parry and Bloch, *Money and the Morality of Exchange*, 165–90.

———. 1996. "Internal and External Memory: Different Ways of Being in History." In Antze and Lambek, *Tense Past*, 215–33.

Bloch, Maurice, and Jonathan Parry, eds. 1982. *Death and the Regeneration of Life*. Cambridge, England.

Bloch, Oscar, and W. van Wartburg, eds. 1964. *Dictionnaire étymologique de la langue française*. Paris.

Bock, Philip K., ed. 1994. *Handbook of Psychological Anthropology*. Westport, Conn.

Boiteau, Pierre. 1958. *Madagascar: contribution à l'histoire de la nation malgache*. Paris.

———. 1974. "Les droits sur la terre dans la société malgache précoloniale." In *Sur le mode de production asiatique*, 135–68. Paris.

Boulègue, Jean. 1987. *Le Grand Jolof (XIIIe–XVIe siècle)*. 2 vols. Paris.

Bowman, Larry. 1991. *Mauritius: Democracy and Development in the Indian Ocean*. Boulder, Colo.

Boxer, C.R. 1985. *Portuguese Conquest and Commerce in Southern Asia, 1500–1750*. London.

Braudel, Fernand. 1982. *La Méditerranée et le monde méditerranéen à l'époque de Philippe II*. Paris.

Bravman, Bill. 1998. *Making Ethnic Ways: Communities and Their Transformations in Taita, Kenya, 1800–1950*. Portsmouth, N.H.

Breen, T.H. 1997. "Making History: The Force of Public Opinion and the Last Years of Slavery in Revolutionary Massachusetts." In Hoffman, Sobel, and Teute, *Through a Glass Darkly*, 67–95.

Brenning, J.J. 1977. "Chief Merchants and the European Enclaves of Seventeenth Century Coromandel." *Modern Asian Studies* 11, 3: 321–46.

Brooks, George E. 1976. "The Signares of Saint-Louis and Gorée: Women Entrepreneurs in Eighteenth-Century Senegal." In Hafkin and Bay, *Women in Africa*, 19–44.

———. 1983. "A Nhara of the Guinea-Bissau Region: Mãe Aurélia Correia." In Robertson and Klein, *Women and Slavery in Africa*, 295–319.

Brown, Mervyn. 1995. *A History of Madagascar*. London.

Burke, Peter. 1989. "History as Social Memory." In Butler, *Memory*, 97–113.

Butler, Thomas, ed. 1989. *Memory: History, Culture and the Mind*. Oxford.

Cabanes, Robert. 1974. "Evolution des formes sociales de la production agricole dans la plaine de Tananarive." *Cahiers du Centre d'Etudes des Coutumes* 10: 47–60.

Callet, François, ed. 1981. *Tantara ny Andriana eto Madagascar: documents historiques d'après les manuscrits malgaches*. 2 vols. Antananarivo, Madagascar.

Cameron, James. 1874. *Recollections of Mission Life in Madagascar During the Early Days of the L.M.S. Mission*. Antananarivo, Madagascar.

Campbell, Gwyn. 1981. "Madagascar and the Slave Trade, 1810–1895." *Journal of African History* 22: 203–27.

———. 1986. "The Monetary and Financial Crisis of the Merina Empire, 1810–1826." *South African Journal of Economic History* 1, 1: 99–118.

———. 1987. "The Adoption of Autarky in Imperial Madagascar, 1820–1835." *Journal of African History* 28, 3: 395–411.

———. 1988a. "Missionaries, Fanompoana and the Menalamba Revolt in Late Nineteenth Century Madagascar." *Journal of Southern African Studies* 15, 1: 54–73.

———. 1988b. "Slavery and Fanompoana: The Structure of Forced Labour in Imerina (Madagascar), 1790–1861." *Journal of African History* 29, 3: 463–86.

———. 1989. "Madagascar and Mozambique in the Slave Trade of the Western Indian Ocean, 1800–1861." In Clarence-Smith, *The Economics of the Indian Ocean Slave Trade*, 166–93.

———. 1991. "The Menalamba Revolt and Brigandry in Imperial Madagascar, 1820–1897." *International Journal of African Historical Studies* 24, 2: 259–92.

———. 1992. "Crises of Faith and Colonial Conquest: The Impact of Famine and Disease in Late Nineteenth-Century Madagascar." *Cahiers d'Etudes Africaines* 32: 409–53.

———. 1993. "The Structure of Trade in Madagascar, 1750–1810." *International Journal of African Historical Studies* 26, 1: 111–48.

Cannadine, David, and Simon Price, eds. 1987. *Rituals of Royalty: Power and Ceremonial in Traditional Societies.* Cambridge, England.

Capela, José, and Eduardo Medeiros. 1989. "La traite au départ du Mozambique vers les îles françaises de l'Océan Indien, 1720–1904." In Bissoondoyal and Servansing, *Slavery in South West Indian Ocean*, 247–309.

Carayon, Jean-Louis. 1845. *Histoire de l'établissement français de Madagascar pendant la Restauration.* Paris.

Carr, Edward Hallett. 1964. *What Is History?* New York.

Cartier, Michel, ed. 1984. *Le travail et ses représentations.* Paris.

Chandra, Satish, ed. 1987. *The Indian Ocean: Explorations in History, Commerce and Politics.* New Delhi, India.

Chanock, Martin. 1985. *Law, Custom and Social Order: The Colonial Experience in Malawi and Zambia.* Cambridge, England.

Chapelier, M. 1811. "Fragmens sur Madagascar." *Annales des Voyages, de la Géographie, et de l'Histoire* 14: 59–101.

Chapman, Olive Murray. 1943. *Across Madagascar.* London.

Chaudhuri, K.N. 1985. *Trade and Civilisation in the Indian Ocean.* Cambridge, England.

———. 1990. *Asia before Europe: Economy and Civilisation of the Indian Ocean from the Rise of Islam to 1750.* Cambridge, England.

Chauvincourt, Jean, and S. Chauvincourt. 1967. *La monnaie coupée et les poids monétaires de Madagascar.* Tananarive, Madagascar.

———. 1968. *Les premières monnaies introduites à Madagascar.* Tananarive, Madagascar.

Chittick, H. Neville, and Robert J. Rotberg, eds. 1975. *East Africa and the Orient: Cultural Syntheses in Pre-Colonial Times.* New York.

Chrétien, Jean-Pierre. 1986. "Confronting the Unequal Exchange of the Oral and the Written." In Jewsiewicki and Newbury, *African Historiographies*, 75–90.

Chrétien, Jean-Pierre, and Gérard Prunier, eds. 1989. *Les ethnies ont une histoire.* Paris.

Clarence-Smith, William Gervase, ed. 1989a. *The Economics of the Indian Ocean Slave Trade in the Nineteenth Century.* London.

———. 1989b. "The Economics of the Indian Ocean and Red Sea Slave Trades." In Clarence-Smith, *The Economics of the Indian Ocean Slave Trade*, 1–20.

Clifford, James. 1997. *Routes: Travel and Translation in the Late Twentieth Century.* Cambridge, Mass.

Cohen, Abner, ed. 1974. *Urban Ethnicity.* London.

Cohen, David William. 1989. "The Undefining of Oral Tradition." *Ethnohistory* 36, 1: 9–18.

———. 1994. *The Combing of History.* Chicago.

Cohen, Robin. 1997. *Global Diasporas: An Introduction.* London.

Cole, Jennifer. 1996. "The Necessity of Forgetting: Ancestral and Colonial Memories in East Madagascar." Ph.D. diss., University of California, Berkeley.

———. 1997. "Sacrifice, Narratives and Experience in East Madagascar." *Journal of Religion in Africa* 27, 4: 401–25.

———. 1998. "The Work of Memory in Madagascar." *American Ethnologist* 25, 4: 610–33.

Colin, Élie, and Pierre Suau. 1895. *Madagascar et la mission catholique.* 2 vols. Paris.

Colin, Epidariste. 1811. "Notes de M. E. Colin (ca. 1809)." *Annales des Voyages, de la Géographie, et de l'Histoire* 14: 89–91.

Collins, Robert O. 1992. "The Nilotic Slave Trade: Past and Present." *Slavery and Abolition* 13, 1: 140–61.

Comaroff, Jean, and John Comaroff, eds. 1993. *Modernity and Its Malcontents: Ritual and Power in Postcolonial Africa.* Chicago.

Condominas, Georges. 1961. *Fokon'olona et collectivités rurales en Imerina.* Paris.

Connerton, Paul. 1989. *How Societies Remember.* Cambridge, England.

Conrad, Robert Edgar. 1983. *Children of God's Fire: A Documentary History of Black Slavery in Brazil.* Princeton, N.J.

———. 1986. *World of Sorrow: The African Slave Trade to Brazil.* Baton Rouge, La.

Coombes, Annie E. 1994. *Reinventing Africa: Museums, Material Culture, and Popular Imagination in Late Victorian and Edwardian England.* New Haven, Conn.

Cooper, Frederick. 1977. *Plantation Slavery on the East Coast of Africa.* New Haven, Conn.

———. 1979. "The Problem of Slavery in African Studies." *Journal of African History* 20, 1: 103–25.

Cooper, Wendy. 1971. *Hair, Sex, Society, Symbolism.* New York.

Copland, Samuel. 1822. *History of the Island of Madagascar.* London.

Coppalle, André. 1970. *Voyage à la capitale du roi Radama, 1825–1826.* Tananarive, Madagascar.

Cordell, Dennis. 1985. *Dar al-Kuti and the Last Years of the Trans-Saharan Slave Trade.* Madison, Wis.

Corrigan, Philip, and Derek Sayer. 1985. *The Great Arch: English State Formation as Cultural Revolution.* Oxford.

Cousins, William E., ed. 1873. *Malagasy Kabary from the Time of Andrianampoinimerina.* Antananarivo, Madagascar.

Cousins, William E. 1885. "Translation of the Farewell Speech of Andrianampoinimerina." *Antananarivo Annual and Madagascar Magazine* 15: 44–51.

Craton, Michael. 1974. *Sinews of Empire: A Short History of British Slavery.* Garden City, N.Y.

Craton, Michael, ed. 1979. *Roots and Branches: Current Directions in Slave Studies.* Toronto.

Creel, Margaret Washington. 1988. *"A Peculiar People": Slave Religion and Commu-nity-Culture Among the Gullahs.* New York.

Crocker, J. Christopher. 1977. "The Social Functions of Rhetorical Forms." In Sapir and Crocker, *The Social Use of Metaphor*, 33–66.

Csordas, Thomas J. 1994. "Self and Person." In Bock, *Handbook of Psychological An-thropology*, 331–50.

Cultru, Prosper. 1906. *Un empereur de Madagascar au XVIIIe siècle, Benyowszky.* Paris.

Curtin, Philip D., ed. 1967. *Africa Remembered: Narratives by West Africans from the Era of the Slave Trade.* Madison, Wis.

Curtin, Philip D. 1969. *The Slave Trade: A Census.* Madison, Wis.

———. 1974. *Economic Change in Precolonial Africa: Senegambia in the Era of the Slave Trade.* 2 vols. Madison, Wis.

———. 1979. "The African Diaspora." In Craton, *Roots and Branches*, 1–17.

———. 1984. *Cross-Cultural Trade in World History.* Cambridge, England.

Curtin, Philip D., Steven Feierman, Leonard Thompson, and Jan Vansina. 1995. *African History: From Earliest Times to Independence*, 2d ed. London.

Daaku, Kwame Yeboa. 1968. "The Slave Trade and African Society." In Ranger, *Emerg-ing Themes*, 134–40.

———. 1970. *Trade and Politics on the Gold Coast, 1600–1720: A Study of the African Reaction to European Trade.* Oxford.

Daget, Serge, ed. 1988. *De la traite à l'esclavage: actes du colloque international sur la traite des noirs, Nantes 1985.* 3 vols. Paris.

———. 1990. *La traite des noirs: Bastilles négrières et velléités abolitionnistes.* Paris.

———. 1996. "Révolution ajournée: Bourbon et la traite illégale française, 1815–1832." In Wanquet and Jullien, *Révolution française et Océan Indien*, 333–46.

Dahle, Lars, ed. 1878. *Madagaskar og dets Beboere.* 2 vols. Christiania [Oslo], Nor-way.

———. 1984. *Anganon'ny Ntaolo.* Antananarivo, Madagascar [first published in 1962].

Darian-Smith, Kate, and Paula Hamilton, eds. 1994. *Memory and History in Twentieth-Century Australia.* Melbourne, Australia.

Das Gupta, Ashin. 1984. "Indian Merchants in the Age of Partnership, 1500–1800." In D. Tripathi, *Business Communities of India*, 27–39.

———. 1986. "The Maritime Merchant and Indian History." *South Asia* 7, 1: 27–33.

———. 1994. *Merchants of Maritime India, 1500–1800.* Brookfield, Vt.

Das Gupta, Ashin, and Michael N. Pearson, eds. 1987. *India and the Indian Ocean, 1500–1800.* Calcutta, India.

Davidson, Andrew. 1889. "The Ramanenjana or Dancing Mania of Madagascar." *Antananarivo Annual and Madagascar Magazine* 13: 19–27.

Davidson, Basil. 1961. *Black Mother: The Years of the African Slave Trade.* Boston.

Davis, David Brion. 1975. *The Problem of Slavery in the Age of Revolution, 1770–1823.* Ithaca, N.Y.

Decary, Raymond. 1962. *La mort et les coutumes funéraires à Madagascar.* Paris.

———. 1965. "Les anciennes coiffures masculines à Madagascar." *Journal de la Société des Africanistes* 35, 2: 283–316.

———. 1966. *Coutumes guerrières et organisation militaire chez les anciens malgaches*, 2: *l'histoire militaire des Merina.* Paris.

Delivré, Alain. 1974. *L'histoire des rois d'Imerina: interprétation d'une tradition orale.* Paris.

Delteil, Pierre. 1931. *Le fokon'olona (commune malgache) et les conventions de fokon'olona.* Paris.

Desan, Suzanne. 1989. "Crowds, Community, and Ritual in the Work of E.P. Thompson and Natalie Davis." In Hunt, *The New Cultural History*, 47–71.

Deschamps, Hubert. 1949. *Les pirates à Madagascar.* Paris.

———. 1972a. *Histoire de Madagascar.* 4th ed. Paris.

———. 1972b. *Histoire de la traite des noirs de l'antiquité à nos jours.* Paris.

———. 1976. "Tradition and Change in Madagascar, 1790–1870." In Flint, *The Cambridge History of Africa*, vol. 5, 393–417.

———. 1977. "Andrianampoinimerina, ou la raison d'état au service de l'unité malgache." In Julien, *Les Africains*, vol. 2, 77–97.

Dewar, Robert E. 1996. "The Archaeology of the Early Settlement of Madagascar." In Reade, *The Indian Ocean in Antiquity*, 471–86.

Dez, Jacques. 1967. "Le Vakinankaratra: esquisse d'une histoire régionale." *Bulletin de Madagascar* 256: 657–701.

———. 1970a. "Eléments pour une étude de l'économie agro-sylvo-pastorale de l'Imerina ancienne." *Terre Malgache, Tany Malagasy* 8: 9–60.

———. 1970b. "Eléments pour une étude sur les prix et les échanges de biens dans l'économie Merina ancienne." *Bulletin de l'Académie Malgache* 48, 1–2: 41–90.

———. 1970c. "Monnaie et structures traditionnelles à Madagascar." *Cahiers Vilfredo Pareto: Revue Européenne des Sciences Sociales* 21: 175–202.

Diène, Here Doudou. 1994. "A New International Project: The Slave Route." *The UNESCO Courrier* (Oct.): 29.

Dike, K. Onwuka. 1956. *Trade and Politics in the Niger Delta, 1830–1885.* Oxford.

Diouf, Sylviane A. 1998. *Servants of Allah: African Muslims Enslaved in the Americas.* New York.

Domenichini, Jean-Pierre. 1981. "La plus belle 'énigme du monde' ou l'historiographie coloniale en question." *Omaly sy Anio* 13–14: 57–76.

———. 1985. *Les dieux aux service des rois: histoire orale des sampin'andriana ou palladiums royaux de Madagascar.* Paris.

———. 1989. "Tribu, ethnie, nation à Madagascar: peut-on corriger les dénominations?" In Chrétien and Prunier, *Les ethnies ont une histoire*, 15–31.

Domenichini-Ramiaramanana, Bakoly. 1972. *Ohabolan'ny ntaolo: exemples et proverbes des anciens, recueillis par W.E. Cousins et J. Parrett avec la collaboration de T.T. Matthews.* Tananarive, Madagascar.

———. 1988. "Madagascar." In Elfasi, *General History of Africa* vol.3, 681–703.

Donque, Gerald. 1972. "The Climatology of Madagascar." In Battistini and Richard-Vindard, *Biogeography and Ecology in Madagascar*, 87–144.

Douessin, R. 1974. "Géographie agraire des plaines de Tananarive." *Madagascar Revue de Géographie* 25: 12–154.

Douglas, Mary, and Phyllis M. Kaberry, eds. 1969. *Man in Africa.* London.

Drescher, Seymour. 1986. *Capitalism and Antislavery: British Mobilization in Comparative Perspective.* New York.

Drury, Robert. 1969. *Madagascar: or, Robert Drury's Journal, During Fifteen Years' Captivity on that Island, and a Further Description of Madagascar by the Abbé Alexis Rochon.* New York [first published in 1792].

Dubois. 1674. *Les voyages faits par le Sier D.B. aux Isles Dauphine ou Madagascar & Bourbon, ou Mascarenne, les années 1669.70.71 & .72.* Paris.

Dubois, H.M. 1938. *Monographie des Betsileo.* Paris.

Dumaine, J.P. [Julien Pierre Dumaine de la Josserie]. 1810a. "Idée de la côte occidentale de Madagascar." *Annales des Voyages, de la Géographie, et de l'Histoire* 11: 20–52.

———. 1810b. "Voyage fait au pays d'Ancaye dans l'île de Madagascar, en 1790." *Annales des Voyages, de la Géographie, et de l'Histoire* 11: 146–218.

Duminy, Andrew, and Bill Guest, eds. 1989. *Natal and Zululand: From Earliest Times to 1910.* Pietermaritzburg, South Africa.

Dunbar, Roberta Ann. 1977. "Slavery and the Evolution of Nineteenth-Century Damagaram (Zinder, Niger)." In Miers and Kopytoff, *Slavery in Africa,* 155–77.

d'Unienville, Baron. 1838a. *Statistique de l'Île Maurice et ses dépendances.* Paris.

———. 1838b. "Essai sur Madagascar." In d'Unienville, *Statistique de l'Ile Maurice et ses dépendances,* 223–344.

Eastman, Carol M. 1988. "Women, Slaves and Foreigners: African Cultural Influences and Group Processes in the Formation of Northern Swahili Coastal Society." *International Journal of African Historical Studies* 21, 1: 1–20.

———. 1994. "Expressive Culture and Oral Tradition: Clues to African Influences on Swahili History." In Harms, et al., *Paths Toward the Past,* 27–37.

Eldredge, Elizabeth A., and Fred Morton, eds. 1994. *Slavery in South Africa: Captive Labor on the Dutch Frontier.* Boulder, Colo.

Elfasi, M., ed. 1988. *General History of Africa* vol. 3, *Africa from the Seventh to the Eleventh Century.* Berkeley, Calif.

Ellis, Stephen. 1979. "Un texte du XVIIème siècle sur Madagascar." *Omaly sy Anio* 9: 151–66.

———. 1985. *The Rising of the Red Shawls: A Revolt in Madagascar, 1895–1899.* Cambridge, England.

Ellis, William, ed. 1838. *History of Madagascar: Comprising also the Progress of the Christian Mission Established in 1818; and an Authentic Account of the Persecution and Recent Martyrdom of the Native Christians.* 2 vols. London.

———. 1857. "Madagascar." In *Encyclopaedia Britannica,* 8th ed., vol. 8, 790–96. Boston.

———. 1869. *The Martyr Church: A Narrative of the Introduction, Progress, and Triumph of Christianity in Madagascar.* Boston.

Elphick, Richard, and Hermann Giliomee, eds. 1988. *The Shaping of South African Society, 1652–1840.* Middletown, Conn.

Eltis, David. 1987. *Economic Growth and the Ending of the Transatlantic Slave Trade.* Oxford.

———. 1991. "Precolonial Western Africa and the Atlantic Economy." In Solow, *Slavery and the Rise of the Atlantic System,* 97–119.

———. 1997. "West Africa and the Transatlantic Slave Trade: New Evidence of Long-Run Trends." *Slavery and Abolition* 18, 1: 16–35.

———. 2000. *The Rise of African Slavery in the Americas.* Cambridge, England.

Eltis, David, and Stanley L. Engerman. 1990. "The Volume, Age/Sex Ratio, and African Impact of the Slave Trade: Some Refinements of Paul Lovejoy's Review of the Literature." *Journal of African History* 31, 3: 485–92.

————. 1992. "Was the Slave Trade Dominated by Men?" *Journal of Interdisciplinary History* 23, 2: 237–57.

————. 1993. "Fluctuations in Age and Sex Ratios in the Transatlantic Slave Trade, 1663–1864." *Economic History Review* 46, 2: 308–23.

Eltis, David, and Lawrence Jennings. 1988. "Trade between Western Africa and the Atlantic World in the Pre-Colonial Era." *American Historical Review* 93: 936–59.

Eltis, David, and James Walvin, eds. 1981. *The Abolition of the Atlantic Slave Trade: Origins and Effects in Europe, Africa, and the Americas*. Madison, Wis.

Enloe, Cynthia. 1973. *Ethnic Conflict and Political Development*. Boston.

Epstein, A.L. 1958. *Politics in an Urban African Community*. Manchester, England.

————. 1978. *Ethos and Identity: Three Studies in Ethnicity*. London.

Equiano, Olaudah. 1995. *The Interesting Narrative and Other Writings*. New York.

Eriksen, Thomas Hylland. 1993. *Ethnicity and Nationalism: Anthropological Perspectives*. London.

Esoavelomandroso, Manassé. 1979. *La province maritime orientale du "Royaume de Madagascar" à la fin du XIXᵉ siècle (1882–1895)*. Antananarivo, Madagascar.

————. 1982. "A propos des groupes paysans en Imerina (1794–1810)." *Omaly sy Anio* 15: 19–30.

————. 1989. "Une arme de domination: le 'tribalisme' à Madagascar (XIXᵉ–milieu du XXᵉ siècle)." In Chrétien and Prunier, *Les ethnies ont une histoire*, 259–66.

Evers, Sandra, and Marc Spindler, eds. 1995. *Cultures of Madagascar: Ebb and Flow of Influences*. Leiden, Netherlands.

Ewald, Janet. 1990. *Soldiers, Traders, and Slaves: State Formation and Economic Transformation in the Greater Nile Valley, 1700–1885*. Madison, Wis.

Fabian, Johannes. 1996. *Remembering the Present: Painting and Popular History in Zaire*. Berkeley, Calif.

Fabre, Geneviève, and Robert O'Meally, eds. 1994. *History and Memory in African-American Culture*. New York.

Fage, J.D. 1969. "Slavery and the Slave Trade in the Context of West African History." *Journal of African History* 10, 3: 393–404.

————. 1980. "Slaves and Society in Western Africa, c.1445–c.1700." *Journal of African History* 21, 3: 289–310.

————. 1989. "African Societies and the Atlantic Slave Trade." *Past and Present* 125: 97–115.

Falola, Toyin, and Paul E. Lovejoy, eds. 1994. *Pawnship in Africa: Debt Bondage in Historical Perspective*. Boulder, Colo.

Feeley-Harnik, Gillian. 1984. "The Political Economy of Death: Communication and Change in Malagasy Colonial History." *American Ethnologist* 11, 1: 1–19.

————. 1989. "Cloth and the Creation of Ancestors in Madagascar." In Weiner and Schneider, *Cloth and Human Experience*, 73–117.

————. 1991a. *A Green Estate: Restoring Independence in Madagascar*. Washington, D.C.

————. 1991b. "Finding Memories in Madagascar." In Kuchler and Melion, *Images of Memory*, 121–40.

Feierman, Steven. 1974. *The Shambaa Kingdom: A History*. Madison, Wis.

————. 1990. *Peasant Intellectuals: Anthropology and History in Tanzania*. Madison, Wis.

————. 1993. "African Histories and the Dissolution of World History." In Bates, Mudimbe, and O'Barr, *Africa and the Disciplines*, 167–212.

————. 1995. "A Century of Ironies in East Africa (c. 1780–1890)." In Curtin, et al., *African History*, 352–76.

Fernandez, James, ed. 1991. *Beyond Metaphor: The Theory of Tropes in Anthropology*. Stanford, Calif.

Fields, Karen. 1994. "What One Cannot Remember Mistakenly." In Fabre and O'Meally, *History and Memory*, 150–63.

Filliot, J.-M. 1974a. *La traite des esclaves vers les Mascareignes au XVIIIe siècle*. Paris.

————. 1974b. "Les établissements français à Madagascar au XVIIIe siècle." In *Perspectives nouvelles sur le passé de l'Afrique noire et de Madagascar*, 67–89. Paris.

Finley, Moses I. 1965. "Myth, Memory, and History." *History and Theory* 4, 3: 281–302.

————. 1968. "Slavery." In *International Encyclopedia of the Social Sciences*, vol. 14, 307–13. New York.

Fischer, David Hackett. 1970. *Historians' Fallacies: Toward a Logic of Historical Thought*. New York.

Fisher, Humphrey. 1988. "A Muslim William Wilberforce? The Sokoto Jihad as Anti-slavery Crusade: An Enquiry into Historical Causes." In Daget, *De la traite à l'esclavage*, III, 537–55.

Flint, John E., ed. 1976. *The Cambridge History of Africa.*, vol. 5. Cambridge, England.

Fontoynont and Raomandahy. 1940. "Les andriana du Vakinankaratra." *Bulletin de l'Académie Malgache* 23: 33–56.

Forbes, Ella. 1992. "African Resistance to Enslavement: The Nature of the Evidentiary Record." *Journal of Black Studies* 23, 1: 39–59.

Foury, B. 1956. *Modave et la colonisation de Madagascar*. Paris.

Freeman, Joseph John, and David Johns. 1840. *A Narrative of the Persecution of the Christians in Madagascar with Details of the Escape of the Six Christian Refugees Now in England*. London.

Freeman-Grenville, G.S.P. 1965. *The French at Kilwa Island: An Episode in Eighteenth-Century East African History*. Oxford.

Fressange, J.B. 1808. "Voyage à Madagascar, en 1802, 1803 par J.B. Fressange, communiqué par M. Péron." *Annales des Voyages, de la Géographie, et de l'Histoire* 2: 3–42.

Friedman, J., and M.J. Rowlands, eds. 1978. *The Evolution of Social Systems*. London.

Frisch, Michael H. 1994. "American History and the Structures of Collective Memory: A Modest Exercise in Empirical Iconography." In Jeffrey and Edwall, *Memory and History*, 33–58.

Froidevaux, Henri. 1934. *Histoire des colonies françaises et de l'expansion de la France dans le monde,* vol. 6, *Madagascar du XVIe siècle à 1811*. Paris.

Fuma, Sudel. 1992. *L'esclavagisme à la Réunion, 1794–1848*. Paris.

Fyfe, Christopher, and David McMaster, eds. 1981. *African Historical Demography*. 2 vols. Edinburgh.

Galenson, David. 1986. *Traders, Planters, and Slaves: Market Behavior in Early English America*. Cambridge, England.

Gamaleya, Clélie. 1984. *Filles d'Heva: trois siècles de la vie des femmes de la Réunion.* St. André, La Réunion.

Gaston-Martin. 1993. *L'ère des négriers (1714–1774): Nantes au XVIIIᵉ siècle.* Paris.

Gemery, Henry A., and Jan S. Hogendorn, eds. 1979a. *The Uncommon Market: Essays in the Economic History of the Atlantic Slave Trade.* New York.

———. 1979b. "The Economic Costs of West African Participation in the Atlantic Slave Trade: A Preliminary Sampling for the Eighteenth Century." In Gemery and Hogendorn, *The Uncommon Market,* 143–61.

Genovese, Eugene D. 1974. *Roll, Jordan, Roll: The World the Slaves Made.* New York.

Gérard, Gabriel, ed. 1984. *Histoire résumée de la Réunion.* Saint Denis, La Réunion.

Gerbeau, Hubert. 1980. "Quelques aspects de la traite illégale des esclaves à l'île Bourbon au XIXᵉ siècle." In *Mouvements de populations dans l'océan Indien,* 273–307. Paris.

———. 1989. "Les traces de l'esclavage dans la mémoire collective des Mascareignes." In Bissoondoyal and Servansing, *Slavery in South West Indian Ocean,* 6–44.

Geschiere, Peter. 1996. "Witchcraft, Kinship and the Moral Economy of Ethnicity: Regional Variations in Cameroon." In la Gorgendière, King, and Vaughan, *Ethnicity in Africa,* 167–92.

Giddens, Anthony. 1979. *Central Problems in Social Theory: Action, Structure, and Contradiction in Social Analysis.* Berkeley, Calif.

Gillis, John. 1992. "Remembering Memory: A Challenge for Public Historians in a Post-National Era." *The Public Historian* 14, 4: 91–101.

Gilroy, Paul. 1993. *The Black Atlantic: Modernity and Double Consciousness.* Cambridge, Mass.

Glassman, Jonathon. 1991. "The Bondsman's New Clothes: The Contradictory Consciousness of Slave Resistance on the Swahili Coast." *Journal of African History* 32, 2: 277–312.

———. 1995. *Feasts and Riot: Revelry, Rebellion, and Popular Consciousness on the Swahili Coast, 1856–1888.* Portsmouth, N.H.

Glazer, Nathan, and Daniel P. Moynihan. 1963. *Beyond the Melting Pot, the Negroes, Puerto Ricans, Jews, Italians, and Irish of New York City.* Cambridge, Mass.

———, eds. 1975. *Ethnicity: Theory and Experience.* Cambridge, Mass.

Gluckman, Max. 1965. "Tribalism in Modern British Central Africa." In Van Den Berghe, *Africa,* 346–60.

Golan, Daphna. 1990. "The Life Story of King Shaka and Gender Tensions in the Zulu State." *History in Africa* 17: 95–111.

Gomez, Michael A. 1998. *Exchanging Our Country Marks: The Transformation of African Identities in the Colonial and Antebellum South.* Chapel Hill, N.C.

Goodall, Norman. 1954. *A History of the London Missionary Society, 1895–1945.* Oxford.

Gow, Bonar A. 1979. *Madagascar and the Protestant Impact: The Work of the British Missions, 1818–1895.* New York.

Grace, John. 1975. *Domestic Slavery in West Africa.* London.

Graeber, David. 1995. "Dancing with Corpses Reconsidered: An Interpretation of Famadihana (in Arivonimamo, Madagascar)." *American Ethnologist* 22, 2: 258–78.

———. 1996a. "Beads and Money: Notes Toward a Theory of Wealth and Power." *American Ethnologist* 23, 1: 4–24.

———. 1996b. "Love Magic and Political Morality in Central Madagascar, 1875–1990." *Gender and History* 8, 3: 416–39.

———. 1996c. "The Disastrous Ordeal of 1987: Memory and Violence in Rural Madagascar." Ph.D. diss., University of Chicago.

———. 1997. "Painful Memories." *Journal of Religion in Africa* 27, 4: 374–400.

Graham, Gerald S. 1967. *Great Britain in the Indian Ocean: A Study in Maritime Enterprise, 1810–1850*. Oxford.

Grandidier, Alfred. 1886. "Des rites funéraires chez les Malgaches." *Revue d'Ethnographie* : 213–32.

———. 1895. "Les Hova de Madagascar." *Revue générale des sciences pures et appliqués* 6ᵉ année, Nᵒ 2 (30 Janvier): 49-53.

———, ed. 1903–1920. *Collection des oeuvrages anciens concernant Madagascar.* 9 vols. Paris.

Grandidier, Guillaume. 1898. "Histoire de la fondation du royaume Betsimisaraka." *Bulletin du Comité de Madagascar* 4: 275–86.

———. 1912. "La mort et les funérailles à Madagascar." *L'Anthropologie* 23: 322–48.

———. 1942. *Histoire Physique, Naturelle et Politique de Madagascar*, vol. 5, *Histoire Politique et Colonial.* Vol. 1, *De la découverte de Madagascar à la fin du règne de Ranavalona Iʳᵉ, 1861.* Paris.

Gray, Richard, ed. 1975. *The Cambridge History of Africa,* vol. 6. Cambridge, England.

Gray, Richard, and David Birmingham, eds. 1970. *Pre-Colonial Trade: Essays on Trade in Central and Eastern Africa before 1900.* London.

Green, Rebecca L. 1996. "Addressing and Redressing the Ancestors: Weaving, The Ancestors, and Reburials in Highland Madagascar". Ph.D. diss., Indiana University.

Greene, Sandra E. 1996. *Gender, Ethnicity, and Social Change on the Upper Slave Coast: A History of the Anlo-Ewe.* Portsmouth, N.H.

Guiart, Jean, ed. 1979. *Les hommes et la mort: rituels funéraires à travers le monde.* Paris.

Guyer, Jane I. 1981. "Household and Community in African Studies." *African Studies Review* 24, 2–3: 87–137.

Hafkin, Nancy J., and Edna G. Bay, eds. 1976. *Women in Africa: Studies in Social and Economic Change.* Stanford, Calif.

Hair, P.E.H. 1965. "The Enslavement of Koelle's Informants." *Journal of African History* 6, 2: 193–203.

Halbwachs, Maurice. 1980. *The Collective Memory.* New York.

———. 1992. *On Collective Memory.* Ed. and trans. by Lewis A. Coser. Chicago.

Hall, Gwendolyn Midlo. 1992. *Africans in Colonial Louisiana: The Development of Afro-Creole Culture in the Eighteenth Century.* Baton Rouge, La.

Hall, Richard. 1996. *Empires of the Monsoon: A History of the Indian Ocean and Its Invaders.* London.

Hallpike, C.R. 1969. "Social Hair." *Man* 4: 256–64.

Hamilton, Carolyn. 1998. *Terrific Majesty: The Powers of Shaka Zulu and the Limits of Historical Invention.* Cambridge, Mass.

Hamilton, Paula. 1994. "The Knife Edge: Debates About Memory and History." In Darian-Smith and Hamilton, *Memory and History in Twentieth-Century Australia*, 9–32.

Hamilton, Ruth Simms, ed. 1990. *Creating a Paradigm and Research Agenda for Comparative Studies of the Worldwide Dispersion of African Peoples*. East Lansing, Mich.

Hardyman, J.T. 1963. "The Madagascar Slave-Trade to the Americas (1632–1830)." *Studia: Revista Semestral* 11: 501–21.

Harms, Robert, Joseph C. Miller, David S. Newbury, and Michelle D. Wagner, eds. 1994. *Paths Toward the Past: African Historical Essays in Honor of Jan Vansina*. Atlanta, Ga.

Harms, Robert. 1981. *River of Wealth, River of Sorrow: The Central Zaire Basin in the Era of the Slave and Ivory Trade, 1500–1891*. New Haven, Conn.

———. 1983. "Sustaining the System: Trading Towns Along the Middle Zaire." In Robertson and Klein, *Women and Slavery in Africa*, 95–110.

———. 1987. *Games Against Nature: An Eco-Cultural History of the Nunu of Equatorial Africa*. Cambridge, England.

Harris, Joseph E. 1968. "Introduction to the African Diaspora." In Ranger, *Emerging Themes*, 147–51.

———. 1971. *The African Presence in Asia: Consequences of the East African Slave Trade*. Evanston, Ill.

———. 1975. "The Black Peoples of Asia." In *World Encyclopedia of Black Peoples*, 264–72. St. Claire Shores, Mich.

———. 1976. "A Comparative Approach to the Study of the African Diaspora." In *Proceedings of a Symposium on The African Dispersal: Expectations and Realities*, 46–56. Boston.

———. 1977a. *Abolition and Repatriation in Kenya*. Nairobi, Kenya.

———. 1977b. *Recollections of James Juma Mbotela*. Nairobi, Kenya.

———. 1982. *Repatriates and Refugees in a Colonial Society: The Case of Kenya*. Washington, D.C.

———. 1992. "The African Diaspora in the Old and New Worlds." In Ogot, *General History of Africa,* vol. 5, 113–36.

———, ed. 1993a. *Global Dimensions of the African Diaspora*. 2d ed. Washington, D.C.

———. 1993b. "Return Movements to West and East Africa: A Comparative Approach." In Harris, *Global Dimensions*, 51–64.

———. 1993c. "Introduction." In Harris, *Global Dimensions*, 3–8.

———. 1996. "The Dynamics of the Global African Diaspora." In Jalloh and Maizlish, *The African Diaspora*, 7–21.

———. 1997. "Diaspora. Overview: The Making of a Global African Presence." In Middleton, *Encyclopedia of Africa South of the Sahara*, vol. 1, 443–53.

Hartwig, Gerald W. 1977. "Changing Forms of Servitude Among the Kerebe of Tanzania." In Miers and Kopytoff, *Slavery in Africa*, 261–85.

Hastie, James. 1903a. "Le voyage de Tananarive en 1817: manuscrit de James Hastie." *Bulletin de l'Académie Malgache* 2, 3: 173–92.

———. 1903b. "Le voyage de Tananarive en 1817: manuscrit de James Hastie." *Bulletin de l'Académie Malgache* 2, 4: 241–69.

Haudrère, Philippe. 1989. *La compagnie française des Indes au XVIIIᵉ siècle (1719–1795)*. 2 vols. Paris.

Hawthorne, Walter. 1998. "The Interior Past of an Acephalous Society: Institutional Change among the Balanta of Guinea-Bissau, c. 1400–c. 1950." Ph.D. diss., Stanford University.

———. 1999. "The Production of Slaves Where There Was No State: The Guinea-Bissau Region, 1450–1815." *Slavery and Abolition* 20, 2: 97–124.

Hébert, Jean-Claude. 1979. "Les tribulations de Lebel, 'négociant-voyageur' sur les hauts plateaux malgaches (1800–1803)." *Omaly sy Anio* 10: 95–143.

———. 1983–1984. "Les Français sur la côte ouest de Madagascar au temps de Ravahiny (1780–1812)." *Omaly sy Anio* 17–20: 235–77.

———. 1989–1990. "Les marchés des hautes terres centrales malgaches avant Andrianampoinimerina." *Omaly sy Anio* 29–32: 71–100.

———. 1996. "Le 'journal du traitant inconnu' en Imerina, en 1808." In mimeographed proceedings of *Fanandevozana ou Esclavage: Colloque international sur l'esclavage à Madagascar* (Antananarivo, Sept. 24–28), 214–48.

———. No date. "La traite des esclaves au temps d'Andrianampoinimerina." Unpublished manuscript in author's files.

Hees, Peter. 1994. "Myth, History, and Theory." *History and Theory* 33: 1–19.

Henige, David. 1982. *Oral Historiography*. New York.

———. 1986. "African History and the Rule of Evidence: Is Declaring Victory Enough?" In Jewsiewicki and Newbury, *African Historiographies*, 91–104.

Hertz, Robert. 1907. "Contribution à une étude sur la représentation collective de la mort." *L'Année Sociologique* 10: 48–137.

Heseltine, Nigel. 1971. *Madagascar*. New York.

Hilliard, Constance. 1985. "Zhur al-Bastin and Ta'rikh al-Turubbe: Some Legal and Ethical Aspects of Slavery in the Sudan as Seen in the Works of Shaykh Musa Kamara." In Willis, *Slaves and Slavery in Muslim Africa*, vol. 1, 160–81.

Hilsenberg, Charles Theodore, and Wenceslaus Bojer. 1833. "A Sketch of the Province of Emerina, in the Island of Madagascar, and of the Huwa, Its Inhabitants, Written during a Year's Residence." *Botanical Miscellany* 3: 246–77.

Hilsenberg, M.C.T. 1829. "Voyage à Madagascar." *Annales des Voyages, de la Géographie, et de l'Histoire* 11: 145–68.

Hiskett, M. 1985. "Enslavement, Slavery and Attitudes Towards the Legally Enslaveable in Hausa Islamic Literature." In Willis, *Slaves and Slavery in Muslim Africa*, vol. 1, 106–24.

Hobsbawm, Eric, and Terence Ranger, eds. 1983. *The Invention of Tradition*. Cambridge, England.

Hoffman, Ronald, Mechal Sobel, and Fredrika J. Teute, eds. 1997. *Through a Glass Darkly: Reflections on Personal Identity in Early America*. Chapel Hill, N.C.

Hogendorn, Jan S., and Henry A. Gemery. 1981. "Abolition and Its Impact on Monies Imported to West Africa." In Eltis and Walvin, *The Abolition of the Atlantic Slave Trade*, 99–115.

Hogendorn, Jan S., and Marion Johnson. 1986. *The Shell Money of the Slave Trade*. Cambridge, England.

Holsoe, Svend E. 1977. "Slavery and Economic Response Among the Vai (Liberia and Sierra Leone)." In Miers and Kopytoff, *Slavery in Africa*, 287–303.

Horowitz, Donald. 1985. *Ethnic Groups in Conflict*. Berkeley, Calif.

Horton, Robin. 1969. "From Fishing Village to City-State: A Social History of New Calabar." In Douglas and Kaberry, *Man in Africa*, 37–58.

Hourani, George. 1963. *Arab Seafaring in the Indian Ocean in Ancient and Early Medieval Times*. Beirut, Lebanon.

House of Commons. 1826. *Papers and Communications Relative to the Slave Trade at the Mauritius and Bourbon, and the Seychelles, from the Time of Their Capture to the Present Time: 1811–1817*. (British Parliamentary Papers, No. 295). London.

Hudson, A.B. 1966. "Death Ceremonies of the Padju Epat Ma'anyan Dayaks." *Sarawak Museum Journal* 13: 341–416.

Humphreys, S.C., and Helen King, eds. 1981. *Mortality and Immortality: The Anthropology and Archaeology of Death*. London.

Hunt, Lynn, ed. 1989. *The New Cultural History*. Berkeley, Calif.

Huntington, Richard. 1973a. "Religion and Social Organization of the Bara People of Madagascar." Ph.D. diss., Duke University.

———. 1973b. "Death and the Social Order: Bara Funeral Customs (Madagascar)." *African Studies* 32: 65–84.

Hunwick, J.O. 1985. "Notes on Slavery in the Songhay Empire." In Willis, *Slaves and Slavery in Muslim Africa*, vol. 2, 16–32.

———. 1992. "Black Slaves in the Mediterranean World: Introduction to a Neglected Aspect of the African Diaspora." *Slavery and Abolition* 13, 1: 5–38.

———. 1999. "Islamic Law and Polemics over Race and Slavery in North and West Africa (16th–19th Century)." In Marmon, *Slavery in the Islamic Middle East*, 43–68.

Hutton, Patrick. 1993. *History As an Art of Memory*. Hanover, N.H.

Iliffe, John. 1979. *A Modern History of Tanganyika*. Cambridge, England.

Inikori, Joseph E., ed. 1982a. *Forced Migration: The Impact of the Export Slave Trade on African Societies*. London.

———. 1982b. "Introduction." In Inikori, *Forced Migration*, 13–60.

———. 1982c. "The Import of Firearms into West Africa, 1750 to 1807: A Quantitative Analysis." In Inikori, *Forced Migration*, 126–53.

———. 1992. "Africa in World History: The Export Slave Trade from Africa and the Emergence of the Atlantic Economic Order." In Ogot, *General History of Africa vol. 5*, 74–112.

———. 1994. "Ideology Versus the Tyranny of Paradigm: Historians and the Impact of the Atlantic Slave Trade on African Societies." *African Economic History* 22: 37–58.

———. 1996. "Slavery in Africa and the Transatlantic Slave Trade." In Jalloh and Maizlish, *The African Diaspora*, 39–72.

Inikori, Joseph E., and Stanley L. Engerman, eds. 1992a. *The Atlantic Slave Trade: Effects on Economies, Societies, and Peoples in Africa, the Americas, and Europe*. Durham, N.C.

———, eds. 1992b. "Introduction: Gainers and Losers in the Atlantic Slave Trade." In Inikori and Engerman, *The Atlantic Slave Trade*, 1–21.

Isaacman, Allen F. 1972. *Mozambique: The Africanization of a European Institution. The Zambesi Prazos, 1750–1902*. Madison, Wis.

———. 1986. "Ex-Slaves, Transfrontiersmen and the Slave Trade: The Chikunda of the Zambesi Valley, 1850–1900." In Lovejoy, *Africans in Bondage*, 273–309.

Isaacman, Allen F., and Richard Roberts, eds. 1995. *Cotton, Colonialism, and Social History in Sub-Saharan Africa*. Portsmouth, N.H.

Isaacman, Barbara, and Allen F. Isaacman. 1977. "Slavery and Social Stratification Among the Sena of Mozambique: A Study of the Kaporo System." In Miers and Kopytoff, *Slavery in Africa*, 105–20.

Isnard, Hildebert. 1953. "Les bases géographiques de la monarchie hova." In *Eventail de l'histoire vivante: hommage à Lucien Febvre*, 195–206. Paris.

Jackson, Kennell. 1976. "The Dimensions of the Kamba Pre-Colonial Past." In Ogot, *Kenya Before 1900*, 174–261.

Jacob, Guy. 1996. "Une expédition coloniale meurtrière: la campagne de Madagascar." In *Australes: études historiques aixoises sur l'Afrique australe et l'océan Indien occidental*, 155–73. Paris.

Jalloh, Alusine, and Stephen E. Maizlish, eds. 1996. *The African Diaspora*. College Station, Tex.

Janzen, John M. 1982. *Lemba, 1650–1930: A Drum of Affliction in Africa and the New World*. New York.

Jeater, Diana. 1993. *Marriage, Perversion, and Power: The Construction of Moral Discourse in Southern Rhodesia, 1894–1930*. Oxford.

Jeffrey, Jaclyn, and Glenace Edwall, eds. 1994. *Memory and History: Essays on Recalling and Interpreting Experience*. Lanham, Md.

Jeffreys, Keturah. 1827. *The Widowed Missionary's Journal*. Southampton, England.

Jewsiewicki, Bogumil, and David Newbury, eds. 1986. *African Historiographies: What History for Which Africa?* Beverly Hills, Calif.

Johns, David. 1835. *Dikisionary Malagasy, Mizara Roa: Ny Faharoa'ny, Malagasy sy English*. Antananarivo, Madagascar.

Johnson, Douglas H. 1992. "Recruitment and Entrapment in Private Slave Armies: The Structure of the *Zarā'ib* in the Southern Sudan." *Slavery and Abolition* 13, 1: 162–73.

Johnson, Marion. 1970. "The Cowrie Currencies of West Africa." *Journal of African History* 11, 1: 17–49 and 11, 3: 331–53.

Johnson, Richard, Gregor McLennan, Bill Schwarz and David Sutton, eds. 1982. *Making Histories: Studies in History-Writing and Politics*. Minneapolis, Minn.

Jones, G.I. 1958. "Native and Trade Currencies in Southern Nigeria During the Eighteenth and Nineteenth Centuries." *Africa* 28: 43–54.

———. 1963. *The Trading States of the Oil Rivers: A Study of Political Development in Eastern Nigeria*. London.

Joseph, Gilbert M., and Daniel Nugent, eds. 1994. *Everyday Forms of State Formation: Revolution and the Negotiation of Rule in Modern Mexico*. Durham, N.C.

Jouannetaud (Lieutenant). 1900. "Notes sur l'histoire du Vakinankaratra." *Notes, Reconnaissances et Explorations* 4, 30: 275–87.

Jourdain, J.P.P. 1839. "Île de Madagascar: notice sur les Ovas." *Annales des Voyages, de la Géographie, et de l'Histoire* 4: 5–27.

Julien, Charles-André, ed. 1977. *Les Africains*, vol. 2. Paris.

Julien, Gustave. 1908. *Institutions Politiques et Sociales de Madagascar*. Paris.

Karp, Ivan, and Steven D. Lavine, eds. 1991. *Exhibiting Cultures: The Poetics and Politics of Museum Display*. Washington, D.C.

Karp, Ivan, Christine Mullen Kreamer, and Steven D. Lavine. 1992. *Museums and Communities: The Politics of Public Culture*. Washington, D.C.

Kea, Ray A. 1982. *Settlements, Trade, and Polities in the Seventeenth Century Gold Coast*. Baltimore.

Keenan, Elinor. 1974a. "Conversation and Oratory in Vakinankaratra, Madagascar." Ph.D. diss., University of Pennsylvania.

———. 1974b. "Norm-Breakers and Norm-Makers: Uses of Speech by Men and Women in a Malagasy Community." In Bauman and Sherzer, *Explorations in the Ethnography of Speaking*, 125–43.

Keim, Curtis A. 1983. "Women in Slavery Among the Mangbetu c. 1800–1910." In Robertson and Klein, *Women and Slavery in Africa*, 144–59.

Kent, Raymond K. 1970. *Early Kingdoms in Madagascar*. New York.

———, ed. 1979. *Madagascar in History: Essays from the 1970's*. Albany, Calif.

Kilekwa, Petro. 1937. *Slave Boy to Priest: The Autobiography of Padre Petro Kilekwa*. London.

Kilmer, Martin. 1982. "Genital Phobia and Depilation." *Journal of Hellenic Studies* 102: 104–12.

Kilson, Martin L., and Robert I. Rotberg, eds. 1976. *The African Diaspora: Interpretive Essays*. Cambridge, Mass.

Klein, Herbert S. 1978. *The Middle Passage: Comparative Studies in the Atlantic Slave Trade*. Princeton, N.J.

———. 1983. "African Women in the Atlantic Slave Trade." In Robertson and Klein, *Women and Slavery in Africa*, 29–38.

———. 1999. *The Atlantic Slave Trade*. Cambridge, England.

Klein, Martin A. 1972. "Social and Economic Factors in the Muslim Revolution in Senegambia." *Journal of African History* 13: 419–41.

———. 1983. "Women in Slavery in the Western Sudan." In Robertson and Klein, *Women and Slavery in Africa*, 67–92.

———. 1988. "Slave Resistance and Slave Emancipation in Coastal Guinea." In Miers and Roberts, *The End of Slavery,* 203–19.

———. 1989. "Studying the History of Those Who Would Rather Forget: Oral History and the Experience of Slavery." *History in Africa* 16: 209–17.

———. 1990. "The Impact of the Atlantic Slave Trade on the Societies of the Western Sudan." *Social Science History* 14, 2: 231–53.

———. 1992. "The Slave Trade in the Western Sudan during the Nineteenth Century." *Slavery and Abolition* 13, 1: 39–60.

———. 1998. *Slavery and Colonial Rule in French West Africa*. Cambridge, England.

Klein, Martin A., and Paul E. Lovejoy. 1979. "Slavery in West Africa." In Gemery and Hogendorn, *The Uncommon Market*, 181–212.

Kling, Blair B., and Michael N. Pearson, eds. 1979. *The Age of Partnership: Europeans in Asia before Domination*. Honolulu, Hawaii.

Knight, Franklin, with Y. Talib and P.D. Curtin. 1989. "The African Diaspora." In Ajayi, *General History of Africa ,* vol. 6, 749–72.

Koelle, Sigismund Wilhelm. 1854. *Polyglatta Africana*. London.

Kohli, Vandana. 1990. "Africans in India." In Hamilton, *Creating a Paradigm*, 61–63.

Kopytoff, Igor, and Suzanne Miers. 1977. "African 'Slavery' As an Institution of Marginality." In Miers and Kopytoff, *Slavery in Africa*, 3–81.

Kottak, Conrad Phillip. 1980. *The Past in the Present: History, Ecology, and Cultural Variation in Highland Madagascar*. Ann Arbor, Mich.

Kottak, Conrad Phillip, Jean-Aimé Rakotoarisoa, Aiden Southall, and Pierre Vérin, eds. 1986. *Madagascar: Society and History*. Durham, N.C.

Kuchler, Susanne, and Walter Melion, eds. 1991. *Images of Memory: On Remembering and Representation.* Washington, D.C.

Kuczynski, Robert René. 1949. *Demographic Survey of the British Colonial Empire.* 4 vols. Oxford.

Kuper, Leo, and M.G. Smith, eds. 1969. *Pluralism in Africa.* Berkeley, Calif.

Kuper, Leo, Hilstan Watts, and Ronald Davies. 1958. *Durban: A Study in Racial Ecology.* London.

Kurin, Richard. 1997. *Reflections of a Culture Broker: A View from the Smithsonian.* Washington, D.C.

Kus, Susan. 1997. "Archaeologist as Anthropologist: Much Ado About Something After All?" *Journal of Archaeological Method and Theory* 4, 3–4: 199–213.

Kus, Susan, and Victor Raharijaona. 1994. "House to Palace, Village to State: Scaling Up Architecture and Ideology." Paper presented at the Society for American Archaeology, Anaheim, CA, Apr. 20–24.

———. 1998. "Between Earth and Sky There Are Only a Few Large Boulders: Sovereignty and Monumentality in Central Madagascar." *Journal of Anthropological Archaeology* 17: 53-79.

Kus, Susan, and Henry Wright. 1986. "Survey archéologique de la région de l'Avaradrano." *Taloha* 10: 49–63.

La Gorgendière, Louise de, Kenneth King, and Sarah Vaughan, eds. 1996. *Ethnicity in Africa: Roots, Meanings and Implications.* Edinburgh.

Lambek, Michael. 1992. "Taboo As Cultural Practice among Malagasy Speakers." *Man* 27, 2: 245–66.

———. 1998. "The Sakalava Poiesis of History: Realizing the Past Through Spirit Possession in Madagascar." *American Ethnologist* 25, 2: 106–27.

Lambek, Michael, and Andrew Walsh. 1997. "The Imagined Community of the Antankaraña: Identity, History, and Ritual in Northern Madagascar." *Journal of Religion in Africa* 27, 3: 308–33.

Lamphear, John. 1970. "The Kamba and the Northern Mrima Coast." In Gray and Birmingham, *Pre-Colonial Trade*, 75–101.

Lanois, Pierre. 1932. *L'état malgache et ses transformations avant le régime français.* Paris.

Larousse du XXᵉ siècle en six volumes. 1930. Paris.

Larson, Pier M. 1987. "Slavery in Central Madagascar: Imerina During the Nineteenth Century". M.A. thesis, University of Wisconsin–Madison.

———. 1992. "Making Ethnic Tradition in a Pre-Colonial Society: Culture, Gender, and Protest in the Early Merina Kingdom, 1750–1822." Ph.D. diss., University of Wisconsin–Madison.

———. 1995. "Multiple Narratives, Gendered Voices: Remembering the Past in Highland Central Madagascar." *International Journal of African Historical Studies* 28, 2: 309–22.

———. 1996. "Desperately Seeking 'The Merina' (Central Madagascar): Reading Ethnonyms and Their Semantic Fields in African Identity Histories." *Journal of Southern African Studies* 22, 4: 541–60.

———. 1997a. "'Capacities and Modes of Thinking': Intellectual Engagements and Subaltern Hegemony in the Early History of Malagasy Christianity." *American Historical Review* 102, 4: 969–1002.

———. 1997b. "A Census of Slaves Exported from Central Madagascar to the Mascarenes Between 1769 and 1820." In Rakoto, *L'esclavage à Madagascar*, 131–45.

———. 1997c. "A Cultural Politics of Bedchamber Construction and Progressive Dining in Antananarivo: Ritual Inversions During the *Fandroana* of 1817." *Journal of Religion in Africa* 27, 3: 239–69.

———. 1999. "Reconsidering Trauma, Identity, and the African Diaspora: Enslavement and Historical Memory in Nineteenth-Century Highland Madagascar." *William and Mary Quarterly,* 3d ser. 56, 2: 335–62.

———. Forthcoming, a. "An Austronesian Mortuary Ritual in History: The Transformation and Politics of Secondary Burial in Highland Madagascar." *Ethnohistory*.

———. Forthcoming, b. "Narrative Bridging: The Art of Popular History in Highland Madagascar."

———. Forthcoming, c. "Royal Power and the Renaissance of Secondary Burial in Highland Madagascar: A Modern History of *Famadihana*."

———. Forthcoming, d. "Vernacular Identity: Rethinking Ethnicity in African History."

Lasalle, Jacques de. 1898. "Mémoire sur Madagascar: Jacques de Lasalle (1797), extrait des Archives de Sainte-Marie et annoté par A. Jully." *Notes, Reconnaissances et Explorations* 3: 557–95.

La Vaissière, Camille de. 1885. *Vingt ans à Madagascar: colonisation, traditions historiques, moeurs et croyances*. Paris.

Law, Robin. 1991. *The Slave Coast of West Africa, 1550–1750: The Impact of the Atlantic Slave Trade on an African Society*. Oxford.

———. 1997a. "Ethnicity and the Slave Trade: 'Lucumi' and 'Nago' as Ethnonyms in West Africa." *History in Africa* 24: 205–19.

———. 1997b. *Sources for the Study of the Slave Trade and the African Diaspora*. Stirling, Scotland.

Law, Robin, and Paul E. Lovejoy. 1997. "The Changing Dimensions of African History: Reappropriating the Diaspora." In Simon McGrath, et al., *Rethinking African History*, 181–200.

Law, Robin, and Kristin Mann. 1999. "West Africa in the Atlantic Community: The Case of the Slave Coast." *William and Mary Quarterly,* 3d ser. 56, 2: 307–34.

Leach, E.R. 1958. "Magical Hair." *Journal of the Royal Anthropological Institute* 88: 147–61.

LeBras, Jean-François. 1971. *Les transformations de l'architecture funéraire en Imerina*. Tananarive, Madagascar.

Le Gentil de La Galaisière, Guillaume Joseph Hyacinthe Jean Baptiste. 1781. *Voyage dans les mers de l'Inde, fait par ordre du roi à l'occasion du passage de Vénus, sur le disque de soleil, le 6 juin 1761, & le 3 du même mois 1769*. 2 vols. Paris.

Le Goff, Jacques. 1992. *History and Memory*. Trans. by Steven Rendall and Elizabeth Claman. New York.

Leguével de Lacombe, B.-F. de. 1840. *Voyage à Madagascar et aux îles Comores (1823 à 1830)*. 2 vols. Paris.

Lejamble, G. 1972. "Les fondements du pouvoir royal en Imerina." *Bulletin de Madagascar* 311: 349–67.

Lescallier, Daniel. 1803. "Mémoire relatif à l'isle de Madagascar, Par le citoyen Lescallier, associé. Lu le 17 fructidor an 9." *Mémoires de l'Institut National des Sciences et Arts: Sciences Morales et Politiques* 4 (Vendemiaire an 11): 1–26.

Levine, Lawrence W. 1977. *Black Culture and Black Consciousness: Afro-American Folk Thought from Slavery to Freedom.* New York.

Levtzion, Nehemia. 1985. "Slavery and Islamization in Africa: A Comparative Study." In Willis, *Slaves and Slavery in Muslim Africa,* vol. 1, 182–98.

Lewis, Bernard. 1979. *Race and Color in Islam.* New York.

———. 1990. *Race and Slavery in the Middle East: An Historical Enquiry.* Oxford.

Leys, Colin. 1975. *Underdevelopment in Kenya: The Political Economy of Neo-Colonialism.* Berkeley, Calif.

Liddell, Henry George, and Robert Scott, eds. 1925-1940. *A Greek–English Lexicon.* New ed. by Sir Henry Stuart Jones. 2 vols. Oxford.

Lindsay, Lisa A. 1994. "'To Return to the Bosom of their Fatherland': Brazilian Immigrants in Nineteenth-Century Lagos." *Slavery and Abolition* 15, 1: 22–50.

Little, Henry William. 1970. *Madagascar, Its History and People.* New York [first published in 1884].

Little, Kenneth, ed. 1959. *Sociological Review* 7, 1: 5–122.

Littlefield, Daniel C. 1981. *Rice and Slaves: Ethnicity and the Slave Trade in Colonial South Carolina.* Baton Rouge, La.

Locke, Lewis. 1835. "An Account of the Ovahs, a Race of People Residing in the Interior of Madagascar: With a Sketch of Their Country, Appearance, Dress, Language, &c." *Journal of the Royal Geographical Society of London* 5: 230–42.

Longmore, Paul K. 1988. *The Invention of George Washington.* Berkeley, Calif.

Lonsdale, John. 1992. "The Moral Economy of Mau Mau: Wealth, Poverty & Civic Virtue in Kikuyu Political Thought." In Berman and Lonsdale, *Unhappy Valley,* 315–504.

Lougnon, Albert. 1958. *Sous le signe de la tortue: voyages anciens à l'île Bourbon (1611–1725).* Paris.

Lovejoy, Paul E. 1974. "Interregional Monetary Flows in the Precolonial Trade of Nigeria." *Journal of African History* 15, 4: 563–85.

———. 1983. *Transformations in Slavery: A History of Slavery in Africa.* Cambridge, England.

———, ed. 1986. *Africans in Bondage: Studies in Slavery and the Slave Trade.* Madison, Wis.

———. 1989. "The Impact of the Atlantic Slave Trade on Africa: A Review of the Literature." *Journal of African History* 30: 365–94.

———. 1994a. "Background to Rebellion: The Origins of Muslim Slaves in Bahia." *Slavery and Abolition* 15, 2: 151–80.

———. 1994b. "The Central Sudan and the Atlantic Slave Trade." In Harms, et al., *Paths Toward the Past,* 345–70.

———. 1997a. "The African Diaspora: Revisionist Interpretations of Ethnicity, Culture and Religion under Slavery." *Studies in the World History of Slavery, Abolition, and Emancipation* [electronic web journal] 2, 1: not paginated.

———. 1997b. "Daily Life in Western Africa During the Era of the 'Slave Route.'" *Diogenes* 178: 1–19.

———. 1997c. "Biography as Source Material: Towards a Biographical Archive of Enslaved Africans." In Law, *Sources for the Study of the Slave Trade,* 119–40.

Lovejoy, Paul E., and Jan Hogendorn. 1993. *Slow Death for Slavery: The Course of Abolition in Northern Nigeria, 1897–1936*. Cambridge, England.

Lovejoy, Paul E., and David Richardson. 1995. "Competing Markets for Male and Female Slaves: Prices in the Interior of West Africa, 1780–1850." *International Journal of African Historical Studies* 28, 2: 261–87.

———. 1999. "Trust, Pawnship, and Atlantic History: The Institutional Foundations of the Old Calabar Slave Trade." *American Historical Review* 104, 2: 332–55.

Lovett, Richard. 1899. *The History of the London Missionary Society, 1795–1895*. 2 vols. London.

Lukacs, John. 1968. *Historical Consciousness; or, The Remembered Past*. New York.

MacCormack, Carol P. 1977. "Wono: Institutionalized Dependency in Sherbro Descent Groups." In Miers and Kopytoff, *Slavery in Africa*, 181–203.

Mack, Beverly B. 1992. "Women and Slavery in Nineteenth-Century Hausaland." *Slavery and Abolition* 13, 1: 89–110.

Mageo, Jeannette Marie. 1994. "Hairdos and Don'ts: Hair Symbolism and Sexual History in Samoa." *Man* 29: 407–32.

Mager, Henri. 1898. *La vie à Madagascar*. Paris.

Mahadi, Abdullahi. 1992. "The Aftermath of the *Jihād* in the Central Sudan as a Major Factor in the Volume of the Trans-Saharan Slave Trade in the Nineteenth Century." *Slavery and Abolition* 13, 1: 111–28.

Malzac, Victorien. 1930. *Histoire du royaume hova depuis ses origines jusqu'à sa fin*. Tananarive, Madagascar.

Mamdani, Mahmood. 1996. *Citizen and Subject: Contemporary Africa and the Legacy of Colonialism*. Princeton, N.J.

Manning, Patrick. 1990. *Slavery and African Life: Occidental, Oriental, and African Slave Trades*. Cambridge, England.

———. 1992. "The Slave Trade: The Formal Demography of a Global System." In Inikori and Engerman, *The Atlantic Slave Trade*, 117–41.

Mannix, Daniel P. 1962. *Black Cargoes: A History of the Atlantic Slave Trade, 1518–1865*. New York.

Mariano, Luis. 1904. *Relação da Jornada e descobrimento da Ilha de S. Lourenço, queo vice Rei da India D. Jeronymo de Azevedo mandou fazer por Paulo Rodrigues da Coast, Capitão e descobridor* [1613–14]. In Grandidier, 1903–1920: vol. 2, 1–64.

Marmon, Shaun E., ed. 1999. *Slavery in the Islamic Middle East*. Princeton, N.J.

Martin, François. 1990. *François Martin: Mémoires, Travels to Africa, Persia and India, 1664–1670*. Trans. by Aniruddha Ray. Calcutta, India.

Martin, Phyllis. 1972. *The External Trade of the Loango Coast, 1576–1870: The Effects of Changing Commercial Relations on the Vili Kingdom of Loango*. Oxford.

Mason, John E. 1990. "Hendrik Albertus and His Ex-Slave Mey: A Drama in Three Acts." *Journal of African History* 31: 423–45.

Mayer, Philip. 1962. *Townsmen or Tribesmen: Conservatism and the Process of Urbanization in a South African City*. Oxford.

Mayeur, Nicolas. 1912a. "Voyage à la côte de l'ouest de Madagascar (pays des Séclaves) par Mayeur (1774), rédigé par Barthélémy Huet de Froberville." *Bulletin de l'Académie Malgache* 10: 79–83.

————. 1912b. "Voyage dans le nord de Madagascar, au Cap d'Ambre et à quelques îles du Nord-Ouest par Mayeur, Novembre 1774-Janvier 1776, Rédigé par Barthélémy de Froberville." *Bulletin de l'Académie Malgache* 10: 93–156.

————. 1913a. "Voyage au pays d'Ancove (1785) par M. Mayeur, Rédaction de M. Dumaine." *Bulletin de l'Académie Malgache* 12: 14–49.

————. 1913b. "Voyage dans le sud et dans l'intérieur des terres et particulièrement au pays d'Hancove, Janvier 1777, Rédigé par Barthélemy de Froberville." *Bulletin de l'Académie Malgache* 12: 139–76.

McGowan, Winston. 1990. "African Resistance to the Atlantic Slave Trade in West Africa." *Slavery and Abolition* 11, 1: 5–29.

McGrath, Simon, Charles Jedrej, Kenneth King, and Jack Thompson, eds. 1997. *Rethinking African History*. Edinburgh.

McPherson, Kenneth. 1993. *The Indian Ocean: A History of People and the Sea*. Oxford.

Meillassoux, Claude. 1971. "Introduction." In Meillassoux and Forde, *The Development of Indigenous Trade and Markets*, 3–86.

————, ed. 1975. *L'esclavage en Afrique précoloniale*. Paris.

————. 1983. "Female Slavery." In Robertson and Klein, *Women and Slavery in Africa*, 49–66.

————. 1986. *Anthropologie de l'esclavage: le ventre de fer et d'argent*. Paris.

————. 1991. *The Anthropology of Slavery: The Womb of Iron and Gold*. Chicago.

Meillassoux, Claude, and Daryll Forde, eds. 1971. *The Development of Indigenous Trade and Markets in West Africa*. London.

Meisner, Maurice. 1977. *Mao's China: A History of the People's Republic*. New York.

Metcalf, Peter. 1982. *A Borneo Journey into Death: Berawan Eschatology from Its Rituals*. Philadelphia.

Metcalf, Peter, and Richard Huntington. 1991. *Celebrations of Death: The Anthropology of Mortuary Ritual*. 2d ed. Cambridge, England.

Middleton, John, ed. 1997. *Encyclopedia of Africa South of the Sahara*. New York.

Middleton, Karen. 1995. "Tombs, Umbilical Cords, and the Syllable Fo." In Evers and Spindler, *Cultures of Madagascar*, 223–35.

————. 1997. "Circumcision, Death, and Strangers." *Journal of Religion in Africa* 27, 4: 341–73.

Miers, Suzanne, and Igor Kopytoff, eds. 1977. *Slavery in Africa: Historical and Anthropological Perspectives*. Madison, Wis.

Miers, Suzanne, and Richard Roberts, eds. 1988. *The End of Slavery in Africa*. Madison, Wis.

Miles, D.J. 1965. "Socio-Economic Aspects of Secondary Burial." *Oceania* 35, 3: 161–74.

Mille, Adrien. 1970. *Contribution à l'étude des villages fortifiés de l'Imerina ancien (Madagascar)*. Tananarive, Madagascar.

Miller, Joseph C. 1976. *Kings and Kinsmen: Early Mbundu States in Angola*. Oxford.

————. 1977. "Imbangala Lineage Slavery (Angola)." In Miers and Kopytoff, *Slavery in Africa*, 205–33.

————, ed. 1980a. *The African Past Speaks: Essays on Oral Tradition and History*. Folkestone, England.

————. 1980b. "Introduction: Listening for the African Past." In Miller, *The African Past Speaks*, 1–59.

———. 1988. *Way of Death: Merchant Capitalism and the Angolan Slave Trade, 1730–1830*. Madison, Wis.

———. 1992. "Muslim Slavery and Slaving: A Bibliography." *Slavery and Abolition* 13, 1: 249–71.

———, ed. 1993. *Slavery and Slaving in World History: A Bibliography*. Millwood, N.Y.

Ministère de l'Economie, du Plan et du Redressement Social (Madagascar). 1993. *Recensement général de la population et de l'habitat, résultats préliminaires, Août 1993*. Antananarivo, Madagascar.

Mintz, Sidney W., and Richard Price. 1992. *The Birth of African-American Culture: An Anthropological Perspective*. Boston.

Mitchell, J.C. 1956. *The Kalela Dance: Aspects of Social Relationships Among Urban Africans in Northern Rhodesia*. Manchester, England.

———. 1957. "Africans in Industrial Towns in Northern Rhodesia." In *H.R.H. The Duke of Edinburgh's Study Conference on the Human Problems of Industrial Communities Within the Commonwealth and Empire*, vol. 2, *Background Papers*, pp. 1–9. London.

———. 1960. *Tribalism and the Plural Society*. Oxford.

———. 1987. *Cities, Society, and Social Perception: A Central African Perspective*. New York.

Molet, Louis. 1962. "Les monnaies à Madagascar." *Cahiers de L'Institut de Science Economique Appliquée*. Série 5, *Humanités, Economie, Ethnologie, Sociologie* 129: 7–48.

———. 1979. *La conception malgache du monde, du surnaturel et de l'homme en Imerina*. 2 vols. Paris.

Moore, Sally Falk. 1986. *Social Facts and Fabrications: "Customary" Law on Kilimanjaro, 1880–1980*. Cambridge, England.

Morgan, Philip D. 1997. "The Cultural Implications of the Atlantic Slave Trade: African Regional Origins, American Destinations and New World Developments." *Slavery and Abolition* 18: 122–45.

———. 1998. *Slave Counterpoint: Black Culture in the Eighteenth-Century Chesapeake and Lowcountry*. Chapel Hill, N.C.

Morrell, Robert, ed. 1996. *Political Economy and Identities in Kwazulu-Natal: Historical and Social Perspectives*. Durban, South Africa.

Morton, Fred. 1994. "Pawning and Slavery on the Kenya Coast: The Miji Kenda Case." In Falola and Lovejoy, *Pawnship in Africa*, 27–54.

Mouser, Bruce L. 1983. "Women Slavers of Guinea-Conakry." In Robertson and Klein, *Women and Slavery in Africa*, 320–39.

Muhammad, Akbar. 1985. "The Image of Africans in Arabic Literature: Some Unpublished Manuscripts." In Willis, *Slaves and Slavery in Muslim Africa*, vol. 1, 47–74.

Mullin, Michael. 1992. *Africa in America: Slave Acculturation and Resistance in the American South and British Caribbean, 1736–1831*. Urbana, Ill.

Munthe, Ludvig. 1982. *La tradition arabico-malgache*. Antananarivo, Madagascar.

Munthe, Ludvig, Charles Ravoajanahary, and Simon Ayache. 1976. "Radama I et les Anglais: les négotiations de 1817 d'après les sources malgaches ('sorabe' inédits)." *Omaly sy Anio* 3–4: 9–102.

Mutibwa, Phares M. 1974. *The Malagasy and the Europeans: Madagascar's Foreign Relations, 1861–1895.* Atlantic Highlands, N.J.

Mutibwa, Phares M., with F.V. Esoavelomandroso. 1989. "Madagascar, 1800–80." In Ajayi, *General History of Africa,* vol. 6, 412–47.

Newbury, Catharine. 1988. *The Cohesion of Oppression: Clientship and Ethnicity in Rwanda, 1860–1960.* New York.

Newbury, Colin W. 1961. *The Western Slave Coast and Its Rulers.* Oxford.

Newbury, David. 1986. "Africanist Historical Studies in the United States: Metamorphosis or Metastasis?" In Jewsiewicki and Newbury, *African Historiographies,* 151–64.

———. 1991. *Kings and Clans: Ijwi Island and the Lake Kivu Rift, 1780–1840.* Madison, Wis.

Nora, Pierre. 1989. "Between Memory and History: Les Lieux de Mémoire." *Representations* 26: 7-25.

Northrup, David. 1978. *Trade without Rulers: Pre-Colonial Economic Development in South-Eastern Nigeria.* Oxford.

Novak, Michael. 1971. *The Rise of the Unmeltable Ethnics.* New York.

Novick, Peter. 1988. *That Noble Dream: The "Objectivity Question" and the American Historical Profession.* Cambridge, England.

Nurse, Derek, and Thomas Spear. 1985. *The Swahili: Reconstructing the History and Language of an African Society, 800–1500.* Philadelphia.

Nwachukwu-Ogedengbe, K. 1977. "Slavery in Nineteenth-Century Aboh." In Miers and Kopytoff, *Slavery in Africa,* 133–54.

Nwulia, Moses. 1981. *The History of Slavery in Mauritius and the Seychelles, 1810–1875.* East Brunswick, N.J.

Ochs, Elinor, and Lisa Capps. 1996. "Narrating the Self." *Annual Review of Anthropology* 25: 19–43.

Ogot, B.A., ed. 1976. *Kenya Before 1900.* Nairobi, Kenya.

———, ed. 1992. *General History of Africa,* vol. 5: *Africa from the Sixteenth to the Eighteenth Century.* Berkeley, Calif.

Olivier de Sardan, Jean-Pierre, ed. 1976. *Quand nos pères étaient captifs: récits paysans du Niger.* Paris.

———. 1983. "The Songhay-Zarma Female Slave: Relations of Production and Ideological Status." In Robertson and Klein, *Women and Slavery in Africa,* 130–43.

Oxford English Dictionary. 1989. 2d ed. 20 vols. Oxford.

Page, Willie F. 1997. *The Dutch Triangle: The Netherlands and the Atlantic Slave Trade, 1621–1664.* New York.

Palat, Ravi, Kenneth Barr, James Matson, Vinay Bahl, and Nesar Ahmad. 1986. "The Incorporation and Peripheralization of South Asia, 1600–1950." *Review, A Journal of the Fernand Braudel Center for the Study of Economics, Historical Systems, and Civilizations* 10, 1: 171–208.

Palmer, Colin A. 1981. *Human Cargoes: The British Slave Trade to Spanish America, 1700–1739.* Chicago.

———. 1996. "Rethinking American Slavery." In Jalloh and Maizlish, *The African Diaspora,* 73–99.

Panikkar, K.M. 1996. *Asia and Western Dominance: A Survey of the Vasco Da Gama Epoch of Asian History, 1498–1945.* 2d ed. New York.

Parry, Jonathan and Maurice Bloch, eds. 1989a. *Money and the Morality of Exchange.* Cambridge, England.

———. 1989b. "Introduction: Money and the Morality of Exchange." In Parry and Bloch, *Money and the Morality of Exchange,* 1–32.

Patterson, K. David. 1975. *The Northern Gabon Coast to 1875.* Oxford.

Patterson, Orlando. 1982. *Slavery and Social Death: A Comparative Study.* Cambridge, Mass.

Payet, J.V. 1990. *Histoire de l'esclavage à l'île Bourbon.* Paris.

Pearson, Michael N. 1976. *Merchants and Rulers in Gujarat: The Response to the Portuguese in the Sixteenth Century.* Berkeley, Calif.

———. 1988. *Before Colonialism: Theories on Asian-European Relations, 1500–1750.* Delhi, India.

———. 1991. "Merchants and States." In James D. Tracy, *The Political Economy of Merchant Empires,* 41–116.

———. 1998. *Port Cities and Intruders: The Swahili Coast, India, and Portugal in the Early Modern Era.* Baltimore.

Peires, J.B. 1982. *The House of Phalo: A History of the Xhosa People in the Days of Their Independence.* Berkeley, Calif.

Perham, Margery, ed. 1963. *Ten Africans.* London.

Petit, Michel. 1967. "Les Zafirabay de la baie d'Antongil (formation et histoire d'un clan, conséquences sur la vie rurale actuelle)." *Annales de l'Université de Madagascar, Série Sciences Humaines* 7: 21–44.

Pfeiffer, Ida. 1981. *Voyage à Madagascar (avril–septembre 1857).* Paris [first published in 1862].

Piersen, William D. 1988. *Black Yankees: The Development of an Afro-American Subculture in Eighteenth Century New England.* Amherst, Mass.

Platt, Virginia Bever. 1969. "The East India Company and the Madagascar Slave Trade." *William and Mary Quarterly* 26, 4: 548–77.

Popovic, A. 1976. *La révolte des esclaves en Iraq au IIIe/IXe siècle.* Paris.

Popular Memory Group. 1982. "Popular Memory: Theory, Politics, Method." In Johnson, et al., *Making Histories,* 205–52.

Postma, Johannes Menne. 1990. *The Dutch in the Atlantic Slave Trade, 1600–1815.* Cambridge, England.

Powdermaker, Hortense. 1962. *Coppertown: Changing Africa.* New York.

Prakash, Om. 1979. "Asian Trade and European Impact: A Study of the Trade from Bengal." In Blair B. Kling and Michael N. Pearson, *The Age of Partnership,* 43–70.

Précis sur les établissements formés à Madagascar imprimé par ordre de l'Amiral Duperré. 1836. Paris.

Prentout, Henri. 1901. *L'Île de France sous Decaen, 1803–1810.* Paris.

Pridham, Charles. 1849. *An Historical, Political, and Statistical Account of Mauritius and Its Dependencies.* London.

Prou, Michel. 1987. *Malagasy un pas de plus: vers l'histoire du "Royaume de Madagascar" au XIXe siècle.* Paris.

Rabedimy, Jean-François. 1979. "Essai sur l'idéologie de la mort à Madagascar." In Guiart, *Les hommes et la mort,* 171–9.

Rabemananjara, Raymond W. 1952. *Madagascar, histoire de la nation malgache.* Paris.

Raharijaona, Victor. 1986. "Reconnaissance archéologique dans la Manandona (Vakinankaratra)." *Taloha* 10: 73–114.

Rainandriamampandry. 1972. *Tantara sy Fomban-dRazana Nangonina sy Nala-ha'dRainandriamampandry*. Tananarive, Madagascar [first published in 1896].

Rainitovo. 1930. *Tantaran'ny Malagasy Manontolo*. Tananarive, Madagascar.

Raison, Françoise. 1976. "Les Ramanenjana, une mise en cause populaire du christianisme en Imerina." *Asie du Sud-Est et Monde Insulindien* 7: 271–93.

Raison, Jean-Pierre. 1972. "Utilisation du sol et organisation de l'espace en Imerina ancienne." In *Etudes de géographie tropicale offertes à Pierre Gouru*, 407–25. Paris.

———. 1976. "Espaces significatifs et perspectives régionales à Madagascar." *L'Espace Géographique* 3: 189–203.

———. 1984. *Les hautes terres de Madagascar et leurs confins occidentaux, enracinement et mobilité des sociétés rurales*. 2 vols. Paris.

Raison-Jourde, Françoise. 1984. "Le travail et l'échange dans les discours d'Andrianampoinimerina." In Cartier, *Le travail et ses representations*, 223–73.

———. 1991. *Bible et pouvoir à Madagascar: invention d'une identité chrétienne et construction de l'état (1780–1880)*. Paris.

Rajaonarimanana, Narivelo. 1979. "Achèvement des funérailles et offrande de linceuls: rites funéraires et commémoratifs des Betsileo du Manandriana." In Guiart, *Les hommes et la mort*, 181–93.

Rajaoson, François. 1969. "Contribution à l'étude du famadihana sur les hauts plateaux de Madagascar." Thèse de troisième cycle. Paris.

Rakoto, Ignace, ed. 1997. *L'esclavage à Madagascar: aspects historiques et résurgences contemporaines*. Antananarivo, Madagascar.

Rakotonirainy, Joseph. 1962. *Principe du fokonolona du temps d'Andrianampoinimerina, 1787-1810*. Antananarivo, Madagascar.

Rakotovololona, Solo. 1986. "Note sur la fouille d'une tombe découverte à Ilafy." *Taloha* 10: 115–32.

Ralaimihoatra, Edouard. 1965. *Histoire de Madagascar*. 2d ed. Tananarive, Madagascar.

———. 1982. *Histoire de Madagascar*. 4d ed. Tananarive, Madagascar.

Randria, Michel. 1942. *Tantaran'i Madagascar sy ny Malagasy*. Tananarive, Madagascar.

Ranger, Terence, ed. 1968. *Emerging Themes of African History*. Nairobi.

———. 1983. "The Invention of Tradition in Colonial Africa." In Hobsbawm and Ranger, *The Invention of Tradition*, 211–62.

———. 1996. "The Moral Economy of Identity in Northern Matabeleland." In la Gorgendière, King, and Vaughan, *Ethnicity in Africa*, 213–35.

Rantoandro, Gabriel. 1983–1984. "Une communauté mercantile du nord-ouest: les Antalaotra." *Omaly sy Anio* 17–20: 195–210.

———. 1995. "Madagascar vue des Pays-Bas depuis les frères de Houtman." In Evers and Spindler, *Cultures of Madagascar*, 101–16.

Raolison, Régis Rajemisa. 1966. *Dictionnaire historique et géographique de Madagascar*. Fianarantsoa, Madagascar.

Raombana. 1980. *Histoires 1*. Fianarantsoa, Madagascar.

———. 1994. *Histoires 2: vers l'unification de l'île et la civilisation nouvelle (1810–1828)*. Fianarantsoa, Madagascar.

Rappaport, Joanne. 1990. *The Politics of Memory: Native Historical Interpretation in the Columbian Andes.* Cambridge, England.

Rasmussen, Susan J. 1999. "The Slave Narrative in Life History and Myth, and Problems of Ethnographic Representation of the Tuareg Cultural Predicament." *Ethnohistory* 46, 1: 67–108.

Rathbone, Richard. 1985. "Some Thoughts on Resistance to Enslavement in West Africa." *Slavery and Abolition* 6, 3: 11–33.

Ratsivalaka, Gilbert. 1977. "Eléments de biographie de Nicolas Mayeur, 1747–1809." *Omaly sy Anio* 5–6: 79–88.

———. 1979. "La traite européene des esclaves en Imerina au début du XIXᵉ siècle." *Tantara* 7–8: 113–35.

———. 1995. *Madagascar dans le sud-ouest de l'Océan Indien (circa 1500–1824): pour une relecture de l'histoire de Madagascar.* 2 vols. Thèse de doctorat d'état, Université de Nice, Sophia Antipolis.

Rawley, James A. 1981. *The Transatlantic Slave Trade: A History.* New York.

Reade, Julian, ed. 1996. *The Indian Ocean in Antiquity.* London.

Reynolds, Edward. 1985. *Stand the Storm: A History of the Atlantic Slave Trade.* London.

Richards, Audrey. 1956. *Economic Development and Tribal Change: A Study of Immigrant Labour in Buganda.* Cambridge, England.

Richardson, James. 1885. *A New Malagasy–English Dictionary.* Antananarivo, Madagascar.

Ricoeur, Paul. 1991. "Narrative Identity." *Philosophy Today* 35, 1: 73–81.

Riesman, David. 1953–1954. "Some Observations on Intellectual Freedom." *American Scholar* 23, 1: 9–26.

Risso, Patricia. 1995. *Merchants and Faith: Muslim Commerce and Culture in the Indian Ocean.* Boulder, Colo.

Roberts, Andrew. 1970. "Nyamwezi Trade." In Gray and Birmingham, *Pre-Colonial Trade*, 39–74.

Roberts, John F. 1997. "Early Modern India and World History." *Journal of World History* 8, 2: 197–209.

Roberts, Richard. 1987. *Warriors, Merchants, and Slaves: The State and the Economy in the Middle Niger Valley, 1700–1914.* Stanford, Calif.

———. 1988. "The End of Slavery in the French Soudan, 1905–1914." In Miers and Roberts, *The End of Slavery*, 282–307.

Roberts, Richard, and Martin A. Klein. 1980. "The Banamba Slave Exodus of 1905 and the Decline of Slavery in the Western Sudan." *Journal of African History* 21, 3: 375–94.

Robertson, Claire C. 1983. "Post-Proclamation Slavery in Accra: A Female Affair?" In Robertson and Klein, *Women and Slavery in Africa*, 220–45.

Robertson, Claire C., and Martin A. Klein, eds. 1983a. *Women and Slavery in Africa.* Madison, Wis.

———. 1983b. "Women's Importance in African Slave Systems." In Robertson and Klein, *Women and Slavery in Africa*, 3–25.

Robinson, David. 1975. "The Islamic Revolution of Futa Toro." *International Journal of African Historical Studies* 8: 185–221.

Rochon, Abe Alexis. 1971. *A Voyage to Madagascar and the East Indies.* New York [first published in 1791].

Rodney, Walter. 1966. "Slavery and Other Forms of Social Oppression on the Upper Guinea Coast in the Context of the Atlantic Slave-Trade." *Journal of African History* 7, 3: 431–47.

———. 1970. *A History of the Upper Guinea Coast, 1545–1800*. Oxford.

———. 1975. "Africa in Europe and the Americas." In Gray, *The Cambridge History of Africa*, vol. 2, 578–651.

———. 1982. *How Europe Underdeveloped Africa*. Washington, D.C.

Ross, Robert. 1983. *Cape of Torments: Slavery and Resistance in South Africa*. London.

Rothchild, Donald, and Victor A. Olorunsola, eds. 1983. *State Versus Ethnic Claims: African Policy Dilemmas*. Boulder, Colo.

Rothermund, Dietmar. 1981. *Asian Trade and European Expansion in the Age of Mercantilism*. New Delhi, India.

Safran, William. 1991. "Diasporas in Modern Societies: Myths of Homeland and Return." *Diaspora* 1, 1: 83–99.

Sahlins, Marshall. 1981. *Historical Metaphors and Mythical Realities: Structure in the Early History of the Sandwich Islands Kingdom*. Ann Arbor, Mich.

Sainte-André, H. Pouget de. 1886. *La colonisation de Madagascar sous Louis XV, d'après la correspondance inédite du comte de Maudave*. Paris.

Saint-Pierre, Bernardin de. 1983. *Voyage à l'Île de France*. Paris [first published in 1773].

Saint-Yves, M.G. 1901. *Madagascar en 1767 et 1768 d'après les papiers du gouverneur Dumas*. Paris.

Samuel, Raphael, and Paul Thompson, eds. 1990. *The Myths We Live By*. London.

Sapir, J. David. 1977. "The Anatomy of Metaphor." In Sapir and Crocker, *The Social Use of Metaphor*, 3–32.

Sapir, J. David, and J. Christopher Crocker, eds. 1977. *The Social Use of Metaphor: Essays on the Anthropology of Rhetoric*. Philadelphia.

Savron, C. 1940. "Les andriana Betsileos (Vakin'Ankaratra)." *Bulletin de l'Académie Malgache* 23: 57–64.

Scherer, André. 1974. *Histoire de la Réunion*. Paris.

Schroeter, Daniel J. 1992. "Slave Markets and Slavery in Moroccan Urban Society." *Slavery and Abolition* 13, 1: 185–213.

Schwartz, Barry. 1987. *George Washington: The Making of an American Symbol*. New York.

Scott, James C. 1985. *Weapons of the Weak: Everyday Forms of Peasant Resistance*. New Haven, Conn.

———. 1990. *Domination and the Arts of Resistance: Hidden Transcripts*. New Haven, Conn.

Scully, Pamela. 1997. *Liberating the Family? Gender and British Slave Emancipation in the Rural Western Cape, South Africa, 1823–1853*. Portsmouth, N.H.

Searing, James F. 1993. *West African Slavery and Atlantic Commerce: The Senegal River Valley, 1700–1860*. Cambridge, England.

Shapin, Steven. 1994. *A Social History of Truth: Civility and Science in Seventeenth-Century England*. Chicago.

Sharp, John, and Emile Boonzaier. 1994. "Ethnic Identity as Performance: Lessons from Namaqualand." *Journal of Southern African Studies* 20, 3: 405–15.

Shaw, Rosalind. 1997. "The Production of Witchcraft/Witchcraft as Production: Memory, Modernity and the Slave Trade in Sierra Leone." *American Ethnologist* 24, 4: 856–76.

———. Forthcoming. *The Dangers of Temne Divination: Ritual Memories of the Slave Trade in West Africa*. Chicago.

Shell, Robert C.-H. 1994. *Children of Bondage: A Social History of the Slave Society at the Cape of Good Hope, 1652–1838*. Hanover, N.H.

Shepperson, George. 1968. "The African Abroad or the African Diaspora." In Ranger, *Emerging Themes*, 152–76.

———. 1976. "Introduction." In Kilson and Rotberg, *The African Diaspora*, 1–10.

———. 1993. "African Diaspora: Concept and Context." In Harris, *Global Dimensions*, 41–49.

Sheriff, Abdul. 1987. *Slaves, Spices & Ivory in Zanzibar: Integration of an East African Commercial Empire into the World Economy, 1770–1873*. London.

Shrimpton, Gordon S. 1997. *History and Memory in Ancient Greece*. Montreal & Kingston, Canada.

Sibree, James. 1880. *The Great African Island*. London.

———. 1896. *Madagascar Before the Conquest: The Island, the Country, and the People*. London.

Simpson, Moira G. 1996. *Making Representations: Museums in the Post-Colonial Era*. London.

Skinner, Elliot P. 1993. "The Dialectic between Diasporas and Homelands." In Harris, *Global Dimensions*, 11–40.

Smith, Mary R. 1981. *Baba of Karo: A Woman of the Muslim Hausa*. New Haven, Conn.

Sobel, Mechal. 1987. *The World They Made Together: Black and White Values in Eighteenth-Century Virginia*. Princeton, N.J.

Solow, Barbara, ed. 1991. *Slavery and the Rise of the Atlantic System*. Cambridge, England.

Soskice, Janet Martin. 1985. *Metaphor and Religious Language*. Oxford.

Southall, Aiden, ed. 1961. *Social Change in Modern Africa: Studies Presented and Discussed at the First International African Seminar, Makerere College, Kampala, January 1959*. London.

Spear, Thomas, and Richard Waller, eds. 1993. *Being Maasai: Ethnicity and Identity in East Africa*. Athens, Ohio.

Steensgaard, Niels. 1974. *The Asian Trade Revolution of the Seventeenth Century: The East India Companies and the Decline of the Caravan Trade*. Chicago.

Stefany, S. 1912. *Fondation du royaume du Vakinankaratra*. Tananarive, Madagascar.

Stein, Robert Louis. 1970. *The French Slave Trade in the Eighteenth Century: An Old Regime Business*. Madison, Wis.

Stern, Steve J. 1982. *Peru's Indian Peoples and the Challenge of Spanish Conquest: Huamanga to 1640*. Madison, Wis.

———. 1988. "Feudalism, Capitalism, and the World-System in the Perspective of Latin America and the Caribbean." *American Historical Review* 93, 4: 829–72.

———. 1995. *The Secret History of Gender: Women, Men, and Power in Late Colonial Mexico*. Madison, Wis.

Stoler, Paul. 1995. *Embodying Colonial Memories: Spirit Possession, Power, and the Hauka in West Africa.* London.

Strobel, Margaret. 1979. *Muslim Women in Mombasa, 1890–1975.* New Haven, Conn.

———. 1983. "Slavery and Reproductive Labor in Mombasa." In Robertson and Klein, *Women and Slavery in Africa,* 111–29.

Stuckey, Sterling. 1987. *Slave Culture: Nationalist Theory and the Foundations of Black America.* Oxford.

———. 1994. *Going Through the Storm: The Influence of African American Art in History.* New York.

Subrahmanyam, Sanjay. 1986. "Aspects of State Formation in India and Southeast Asia, 1500–1600." *Indian Economic and Social History Review* 22, 4: 357–77.

———. 1990. *The Political Economy of Commerce: Southern India, 1500–1650.* Cambridge, England.

Sundiata, Ibrahim K. 1996. *From Slaving to Neoslavery: The Bight of Biafra and Fernando Po in the Era of Abolition, 1827–1930.* Madison, Wis.

Tacchi, Anthony. 1892. "King Andrianampoinimerina, and the Early History of Antananarivo and Ambohimanga." *Antananarivo Annual and Madagascar Magazine* 16: 474–96.

Talib, Y. 1988. "The African Diaspora in Asia." In Elfasi, *General History of Africa,* vol. 3, 704–33.

Taylor, Charles. 1989. *Sources of the Self: The Making of the Modern Identity.* Cambridge, Mass.

Teelock, Vijaya. 1998. *Bitter Sugar: Sugar and Slavery in 19th Century Mauritius.* Moka, Mauritius.

Thomas, Hugh. 1997. *The Slave Trade: The Story of the Atlantic Slave Trade, 1440–1870.* New York.

Thomas, R., and R. Bean. 1974. "The Fishers of Men: The Profits of the Slave Trade." *Journal of Economic History* 34, 4: 885–914.

Thompson, Alvin. 1974. "The Role of Firearms and the Development of Military Techniques in Merina Warfare, c. 1785–1828." *Revue Française d'Histoire d'Outre Mer* 224: 417–35.

Thompson, Paul. 1978. *The Voice of the Past: Oral History.* Oxford.

———. 1994. "Believe It or Not: Rethinking the Historical Interpretation of Memory." In Jeffrey and Edwall, *Memory and History,* 1–13.

Thompson, Richard H. 1989. *Theories of Ethnicity: A Critical Appraisal.* New York.

Thornton, John K. 1980. "The Slave Trade in Eighteenth Century Angola: Effects on Demographic Structures." *Canadian Journal of African Studies* 14, 3: 417–27.

———. 1981a. "An Eighteenth Century Baptismal Register and the Demographic History of Manguenzo." In Fyfe and McMaster, *African Historical Demography,* vol. 1, 405–15.

———. 1981b. "The Demographic Effect of the Slave Trade on Western Africa, 1500-1850." In Fyfe and McMaster, *African Historical Demography,* vol. 2, 693-720.

———. 1983. "Sexual Demography: The Impact of the Slave Trade on Family Structure." In Robertson and Klein, *Women and Slavery in Africa,* 39–48.

———. 1988. "The Art of War in Angola." *Comparative Studies in Society and History* 30, 2: 360–78.

———. 1991. "African Dimensions of the Stono Rebellion." *American Historical Review* 96, 4: 1101–13.

———. 1992. *Africa and Africans in the Making of the Atlantic World, 1400–1680.* Cambridge, England.

———. 1993. "'I Am a Subject of the King of Congo': African Political Ideology and the Haitian Revolution." *Journal of World History* 4, 2: 181–214.

———. 1998. *The Kongolese Saint Anthony: Dona Beatriz Kimpa Vita and the Antonian Movement, 1684–1706.* Cambridge, England.

Tlou, Thomas. 1977. "Servility and Political Control: Botlhanka Among the BaTawana of Northwestern Botswana, ca. 1750–1906." In Miers and Kopytoff, *Slavery in Africa*, 367–90.

Toledano, Ehud R. 1982. *The Ottoman Slave Trade and Its Suppression, 1840–1890.* Princeton, N.J.

———. 1998. *Slavery and Abolition in the Ottoman Middle East.* Seattle.

Tölölyan, Khachig. 1996. "Rethinking *Diaspora*(s): Stateless Power in the Transnational Moment." *Diaspora* 5, 1: 3–36.

Tonkin, Elizabeth. 1992. *Narrating Our Pasts: The Social Construction of Oral History.* Cambridge, England.

Tonkin, Elizabeth, Maryon McDonald, and Malcolm Chapman, eds. 1989. *History and Ethnicity.* London.

Toussaint, Auguste, ed. 1941. *Dictionnaire de biographie mauricienne.* Port Louis, Mauritius.

Toussaint, Auguste. 1954. *Early American Trade with Mauritius.* Port Louis, Mauritius.

———. 1966. *History of the Indian Ocean.* London.

———. 1967. *La route des îles: contribution à l'histoire maritime des Mascareignes.* Paris.

———. 1972. *Histoire des îles Mascareignes.* Paris.

———. 1974. *L'Océan Indien au XVIIIᵉ siècle.* Paris.

Tracy, James D., ed. 1991. *The Political Economy of Merchant Empires.* Cambridge, England.

Trésor de la langue française: dictionnaire de la langue au XIXᵉ et du XXᵉ siècle. 1980. Paris.

Tripathi, D. 1984. *Business Communities of India: A Historical Perspective.* Delhi, India.

Turley, David. 1991. *The Culture of English Antislavery, 1780–1860.* London.

Turner, Jerry Michael. 1975. "Les Brésiliens: The Impact of Former Brazilian Slaves upon Dahomey." Ph.D. diss., Boston University.

Tyerman, Daniel, and George Bennet. 1831. *Journal of Voyages and Travels.* 2 vols. London.

Vail, Leroy, ed. 1989. *The Creation of Tribalism in Southern Africa.* Berkeley, Calif.

Valette, Jean. 1962a. *Etudes sur le règne de Radama Iᵉʳ.* Tananarive, Madagascar.

———. 1962b. *Sainte-Marie et la côte est de Madagascar en 1818.* Tananarive, Madagascar.

———. 1963. "La mission de Chardenoux auprès de Radama Iᵉʳ (1816)." *Bulletin de Madagascar* 207: 657–702.

———. 1965. "Pour une histoire du règne d'Andrianampoinimerina (1787–1810)." *Revue Française d'Histoire d'Outre Mer* 187: 277–85.

———. 1966a. "Le commerce de Madagascar vers les Mascareignes au XVIIIᵉ siècle." *Revue de Madagascar* 33: 35–52.

———. 1966b. "Note sur l'origine du mot Betsileo." *Bulletin de Madagascar* 245: 1006–9.

———. 1966c. "De quelques renseignements sur le commerce à Madagascar à la fin du XVIIIᵉ siècle." *Bulletin de Madagascar* 238: 275–8.

———. 1966d. "Lescallier et Madagascar." *Bulletin de Madagascar* 244: 877–97.

——— 1967. "Note sur une coutume betsimisaraka du XVIIIᵉ siècle: les vadinebazaha." *Cahiers du Centre d'Etudes des Coutumes* 3: 49–55.

———. 1970. "Considérations sur les exportations d'esclaves malgaches vers les Mascareignes au XVIIIᵉ siècle." In *Sociétés et compagnies de commerce en orient et dans l'Océan Indien*, 531–40. Paris.

———. 1972. "Contribution à l'étude de la succession d'Andrianampoinimerina." *Revue Française d'Histoire d'Outre Mer* 214: 113-32.

———. 1979. "Radama I, the Unification of Madagascar and the Modernization of Imerina (1810–1828)." In Kent, *Madagascar in History*, 168–96.

van Binsbergen, Wim. 1992. *Tears of Rain: Ethnicity and History in Central Western Zambia*. London.

Van Den Berghe, Pierre L., ed. 1965. *Africa: Social Problems of Change and Conflict*. San Francisco, Calif.

Vansina, Jan. 1980. "Memory and Oral Tradition." In Miller, *The African Past Speaks*, 262–79.

Vansina, Jan. 1985. *Oral Tradition As History*. Madison, Wis.

Verger, Pierre. 1968. *Flux et reflux de la traite des nègres entre le golfe de Bénin et Bahia de todos os santos du dix-septième au dix-neuvième siècle*. Paris.

Vérin, Pierre. 1975. "Les échelles anciens du commerce sur les côtes nord de Madagascar." Thèse de doctorat d'état, Université de Lille III.

———. 1979. "Le problème des origines Malgaches." *Taloha* 8: 41–55.

———. 1990. *Madagascar*. Paris.

Vig, Lars. 1973. *Les conceptions religieuses des anciens malgaches*. Tananarive, Madagascar.

Villiers, Patrick. 1982. *Traite des noirs et navires négriers au XVIIIᵉ siècle*. Grenoble, France.

Vogel, Claude. 1982. *Les quatre-mères d'Ambohibaho: étude d'une population régionale d'Imerina (Madagascar)*. Paris.

Voll, John Obert. 1994. "Islam as a Special World-System." *Journal of World History* 5, 2: 213–26.

Wallerstein, Immanuel. 1960. "Ethnicity and National Integration in West Africa." *Cahiers d'Etudes Africaines* 1: 129–39.

———. 1987. "The Incorporation of the Indian Subcontinent into the Capitalist World-Economy." In Satish Chandra, *The Indian Ocean*, 222–53.

Walvin, James. 1992. *Black Ivory: A History of British Slavery*. London.

———. 1996. *Questioning Slavery*. London.

Wanquet, Claude. 1980. *Histoire d'une révolution: La Réunion, 1789–1803*. 2 vols. Marseille, France.

―――. 1988. "La traite illégale à Maurice à l'époque anglaise (1811–1835)." In Daget, *De la traite à l'esclavage*, vol. 2, 451–65.

Wanquet, Claude, and Benoit Jullien, eds. 1996. *Révolution française et Océan Indien: prémices, paroxysmes, héritages et déviances*. Paris.

Warner, W. Lloyd, and Paul S. Lunt. 1941. *The Social Life of a Modern Community*. New Haven, Conn.

Weber, Henry. 1904. *La compagnie française des Indes (1604–1875)*. Paris.

Weiner, Annette B., and Jane Schneider, eds. 1989. *Cloth and Human Experience*. Washington, D.C.

White, Geoffrey M. 1991. *Identity Through History: Living Stories in a Solomon Islands Society*. Cambridge, England.

White, Hayden. 1978. *Tropics of Discourse: Essays in Cultural Criticism*. Baltimore.

Williams, Raymond. 1985. *Keywords: A Vocabulary of Culture and Society*. New York.

Willis, John Ralph, ed. 1985a. *Slaves and Slavery in Muslim Africa*. 2 vols. London.

―――. 1985b. "The Ideology of Enslavement in Islam." In Willis, *Slaves and Slavery in Muslim Africa*, vol. 1, 1–15.

―――. 1985c. "Jihad and the Ideology of Enslavement." In Willis, *Slaves and Slavery in Muslim Africa*, vol. 1, 16–26.

Willis, Justin. 1992. "The Makings of a Tribe: Bondei Identities and Histories." *Journal of African History* 33, 2: 191–208.

―――. 1993. *Mombasa, the Swahili, and the Making of the Mijikenda*. Oxford.

Wilmsen, Edwin N., with Saul Dubow and John Sharp. 1994. "Introduction: Ethnicity, Identity and Nationalism in Southern Africa." *Journal of Southern African Studies* 20, 3: 347–53.

Wilson, Monica, and Archie Mafeje. 1963. *Langa: A Study of Social Groups in an African Township*. Cape Town, South Africa.

Wilson, Peter J. 1992. *Freedom by a Hair's Breadth: Tsimihety in Madagascar*. Ann Arbor, Mich.

Wood, Peter H. 1974. *Black Majority: Negroes in Colonial South Carolina from 1670 through the Stono Rebellion*. New York.

Worden, Nigel. 1985. *Slavery in Dutch South Africa*. Cambridge, England.

Worden, Nigel, and Clifton Crais, eds. 1994. *Breaking the Chains: Slavery and Its Legacy in the Nineteenth-Century Cape Colony*. Johannesburg.

Wright, Henry, and Susan Kus. 1979. "An Archaeological Reconnaissance of Ancient Imerina." In Kent, *Madagascar in History*, 1–31.

Wright, John. 1992. "The Wadai–Benghazi Slave Route." *Slavery and Abolition* 13, 1: 174–84.

Wright, John, and Carolyn Hamilton. 1989. "Traditions and Transformations: The Phongolo-Mzimkhulu Region in the Late Eighteenth and Early Nineteenth Centuries." In Duminy and Guest, *Natal and Zululand*, 57–74.

―――. 1996. "Ethnicity and Political Change Before 1840." In Morrell, *Political Economy and Identities*, 15–32.

Wright, Marcia. 1993. *Strategies of Slaves and Women: Life-Stories from East/Central Africa*. New York.

Young, Crawford. 1976. *The Politics of Cultural Pluralism*. Madison, Wis.

―――. 1986. "Nationalism, Ethnicity, and Class in Africa." *Cahiers d'Etudes Africaines* 26, 3: 421–95.

Young, Robert. 1990. *White Mythologies: Writing History and the West*. London.

MANUSCRIPT SOURCES

A. London, England
  1. Public Record Office, Kew
    a. Colonial Office, Series 167 (Mauritius) [PRO/CO/167]
    b. Foreign Office, Series 48 (Madagascar) [PRO/FO/48]

  2. Archives of the London Missionary Society (Council for World Mission Archives), in Library of the School of Oriental and African Studies, University of London, Bloomsbury
    a. Incoming Letters, Madagascar [LMS]
    b. Journals, Madagascar and Mauritius [LMS/J]

  3. British Library, Manuscripts Division
    a. Robert Farquhar Papers, Add. Mss. 18117–18132 [BL/MD/Add.Mss.]

B. Oxford, England
  1. Bodleian Library, Oxford University
    a. "Narrative &c.," a journal of travels in Madagascar in 1825 by Henry Singer Keating, MS.Eng.misc.c.29.

C. Paris, France
  1. Archives Nationales
    a. Série Colonies, Classification C^{5A} [AN/P/COL/C^{5A}]

D. Aix-en-Provence, France
  1. Archives Nationales, Centre des Archives d'Outre-Mer
    a. Archives du Gouvernement Général de Madagascar, sous-séries 1Z and 5(4)D [AN/CAOM/AGGM]
    b. Série Géographique, Madagascar [AN/CAOM/SG/MAD]

E. Caen, France
  1. Archives Départementales de Caen, in Bibliothèque Municipal de Caen
    a. Fonds Decaen, volumes 101 and 102 [ADC/FD]

F. Stavanger, Norway
  1. Archives of the Norwegian Missionary Society, Hjemme Arkiv
    a. Inkomne Brev [NMS]

G. Coromandel, Mauritius
  1. Mauritius National Archives
    a. Series HB (Madagascar) [MNA/HB]
    b. Series IG (Claims for compensation submitted to the Compensation Committee) [MNA/IG]

H. Antananarivo, Madagascar

1. Archives of the République Démocratique de Madagascar, Tsaralalana
   a. Archives Royales, Série IIICC (incoming correspondence from the districts of Imerina and provinces of the empire) [ARDM/AMK/IIICC]

RECORDED INTERVIEWS

Larson Fieldwork Collection, Sound Recordings. In possession of the author. Most of these interviews were conducted in the Vakinankaratra of southwestern Imerina.

Number	Name/Subject	Place	Date
1	Rafaliarivo	Masinandraina	1/9/89
2	Rakotovelo	Soavina	20/9/89
3	*Famadihana* proceedings	Ambohimilemaka	16/9/89
4	Ratsimbazafy	Iavomalaza	23/9/89
5	Fitokanam-pasana	Beromalaza	1/10/89
6	Guitar music	Soavina	20/9/89
7	*Famadihana* proceedings	Manolotrony	23/9/89
8	*Famadihana* music	Beromalaza	1/10/89
9	Hira Gasy	Tsaravazaha	1/10/89
10	Hira Gasy	Soamanandray	11/10/89
11	Razafindrainibe	Morafeno	12/10/89
12	Ralaisolo	Morafeno	12/10/89
13	Raobena Marcelle	Ampilanonana	17/10/89
14	Rafilo	Ambohijato	18/10/89
15	Ratsimba	Ambohijato	18/10/89
16	Rakotomanana	Betafo	20/10/89
17	Ramananjoela	Ambohimanambola	26/10/89
18	Ramarijoela	Betafo	29/10/89
19	Rakotonanahary	Soavina	1/11/89
20	Rakotondravelo	Andramasina	3/11/89
21	Rasamison Parany	Ambalamanga	4/11/89
22	Rakotomamonjy	Ambalamanga	4/11/89
23	Ralaivoay	Mahamavo	4/11/89
24	Rakotoson	Ambohitandraina	9/11/89
25	Ralainjaonina	Antanety-Soamiafara	9/11/89
26	Rakotonirainy	Ambohitrimanjato	9/11/89
27	Rakotovao	Tsiafahy	10/11/89

28	Rakotozafy	Antanety I	26/4/90
29	Hira Gasy	Soavina	2/5/90
30	Rakotondrajoa Alfred	Ambohipihaonana	3/5/90
31	Hira Gasy	Soavina	5/5/90
32	Rasolo Basila	Betafo	17/5/90
33	Rakotonindraina Jean-Pierre	Soanindrariny	26/5/90
34	Rakotomanampy Emile	Soanindrariny	26/5/90
35	Robena Marcelle	Ampilanonana	27/5/90
36	Rafilipo	Nanatonana	29/5/90
37	Ranoarisandy	Nanatonana	29/5/90
38	Andriamampionona Fanja	Ambohimasina	29/5/90
39	Rakotondrainibe Emile	Mahazina	30/5/90
40	Rafrançois	Ambatovaky	30/5/90
41	Rajaofera Daniel	Vatotsara	30/5/90
42	Rakotondradany	Tsarafara-Antohobe	1/6/90
43	Rakotonjanahary	Fiadanana	1/6/90
44	Rakotondrasoa	Ambalamarina-Isandra	6/6/90
45	Rakotojoseph Emile	Tritriva-Vohitsara	6/6/90
46	Rasalamona	Tritriva-Iavomalaza	6/6/90
47	Marriage *kabary*	Morarano	7/6/90
48	Razafinjato Bernard	Mahavoky	8/6/90
49	Rakotoarivelo Joseph	Antoby	12/6/90
50	Ratsimbazafy Philipson	Ambohimasina	12/6/90
51	Rajaofera	Mahavoky-Avaratra	13/6/90
52	Rakotoarinesy Emile	Ambohimirary	13/6/90
53	Rakotonoely Paul	Manandona Ville	15/6/90
54	Reading of Boky Manga	Ambohinomenanahary	15/6/90
55	Rakotoarinesy Emile	Ambohimirary	16/6/90
56	Robena Marcelle	Ampilanonana	17/6/90
57	Rakotondrasoa	Andranomanjaka	18/6/90
58	Rakotondravelo	Vinaninkarena	19/6/90
59	Ramiandrisoa Gilbert	Andratsaimahamasina	20/6/90
60	Rabenarivo Jean	Antsahapetraka	20/6/90
61	Rakotomahenina	Ampandrotrarana	21/6/90

62	Rajoeliarivelo Honorine	Ambohiponana	21/6/90
63	Rakotoarinesy Emile	Ambohimirary	22/6/90
64	Group interview	Ambondrona	23/6/90
65	Rabe Charles	Ambondrona	23/6/90
66	Randriamanantena	Ambarizato	27/6/90
67	Rakotoarisaona	Ambano	27/6/90
68	Rakotomalala Rafaely	Ambohimiarivo	28/6/90
69	Rabarijaona Grégoire	Ambohimiarivo	28/6/90
70	Rabenoro	Ambohimiarivo	28/6/90
71	Rakotondrazaka	Malaza	29/6/90
72	Randrianarivony	Ankazomiriotra	29/6/90
73	Zanadrano	Vohijanahary	1/7/90
74	Ralaimanganivo Antoine	Matieloana	3/7/90
75	Rasoandalana Marceline	Antoabe	3/7/90
76	Raharisoa Jacqueline	Ambondrona	3/7/90
77	Ratolojanahary Sigvald	Ambohitrinibe	4/7/90
78	Randrianarijaona	Ambohitrinibe	5/7/90
79	Rakotondravony	Tsarahafatra	8/7/90
80	Ranaivomanjaka	Tsarahafatra	8/7/90
81	Rakotondrabe Joseph	Mahazoarivo	8/7/90
82	Rabetsilaozana	Antsahamalaza	9/7/90a
83	Rakotondrabe	Antsakarivo	10/7/90
84	Rakotondrazaka	Malaza	11/7/90
85	Rajoda and Razafimahatratra	Miandrarivo	11/7/90
86	Rabemisata	Mandritsara	11/7/90
87	Rakotondrainibe Benoit	Sahatsio	12/7/90
88	Andrianjatovo Franck	Ilaka	13/7/90
89	*Famadihana* proceedings	Soanindrariny	14/7/90
90	Rakotozandry	Antsirabe	15/7/90
91	Razanajatovo	Belazao	15/7/90
92	*Famadihana* proceedings	Soanindrariny	16/7/90
93	Razefasaona	Antanety	17/7/90
94	Randrianabo	Benivary	17/7/90
95	Group interview	Miandrarivo	17/7/90

96	Ralaizafy Gilles	Alakamisy	18/7/90
97	Group interview	Masompieferana	18/7/90
98	Rakotomanana André	Miantsoarivo	18/7/90
99	Rakotondramarolafy	Ambohimanjaka	19/7/90
100	Rakotomandroso	Ambondromisotra	20/7/90
101	Zanadrano	Ambatorangy	22/7/90
102	Ratsimbazafy & son	Alakamisy	23/7/90
103	Razafinjoelina Emile	Ihadilanana-Ambalavory	23/7/90
104	*Famadihana* proceedings	Ihadilanana	23/7/90
105	Ralaimboa Paoly	Ambohipeno	16/10/92
106	Randrianantoavina Samuel	Antsirabe-Ambohimiandrisoa	17/10/92
107	Andrianavalonarivo Razanajatovo	Antsirabe-Ambavahadimangatsiaka	17/10/92
108	Rabadista Joseph	Betafo-Antsitanan-tsena	18/10/92
109	Rakotondrafara Louis	Betafo-Atsinanan-tsena	18/10/92
110	Randriambololona (Pastor)	Ambohitraina	21/10/92
111	Razafindravao Maria Magdalene	Mahamasina-Mahefasoa	22/10/92
112	Ravololondrina Georgette	Manerinerina, Fokontany Ankazobe	22/10/92
113	Razanajatovo Andrianavalonarivo	Antsirabe-Ambavahadimangatsiaka	24/10/92
114	Razafindrazay Thérèse	Betafo-Atsinanan-tsena	25/10/92
115	Rakotondrainibe (Ingahifara) Rakotondrainibe Philippe Rakotondravao Jean Bosco	Andrefan-Andohalo (Ampahatramaha)	28/10/92
116	Ralaizandry Jean-Pierre	Masiniloharano-Ampandrotrarana	29/10/92
117	Raveloson Ranoromalala Bertine	Talata-Andraikiba	29/10/92
118	Rafaralahinjaonina	Anjanapara-Ambohijato	30/10/92
119	Razanadrasoa Julienne (Razily)	Tsarasaotra	30/10/92
120	Rajosefa Emile	Amboromahery	31/10/92
121	Group interview	Atsipilo	31/10/92

122	Ralaivatra Jean-Batiste (Razoany)	Filahoana	11/3/92
123	Rakotondramialy (Razany Dennis)	Avaratanana (Ambohijato-Mandritsara)	5/11/92
124	Rakotonarivo Emmanuel	Ankabahaba-Ambarizato	6/11/92
125	Ralaizandry Emile	Avaratanana (Tsarahasina)	9/11/92
	Razafindrasoa Jeanne-Françoise		
126	Rakotonarivo Emmaneul	Ankabahaba-Ambarizato	9/11/92
127	Rakotondrajoa Jean de Lacroix	Anjanapara-Masitataovana	9/11/92
128	Randrianandraina Ranoël	Betafo	10/11/92
	Julien Dieudoné		
129	Rafidimanana Jean-Luc	Antanamalaza	23/9/96
130	Rakotomalala Louis	Iravoandriana	28/9/96
131	Solofonandrianjary Jean-Richard	Ifandanana-Tsarahasina	27/7/97
132	Iarety	Near Antanety	29/7/97
133	Andriamandrianarivo Jacques-Martileau	Antanety	29/7/97
134	Conversations at Gare Rutière	Andravoahangy-Antananarivo	27/7/97
135	Rakotomalala Louis	Antanamalaza	27/7/97

INDEX

Abercrombie, Thomas, 163
Abolition, of slave trades: by Britain, 61, 225; by France, 225; by Radama, 206, 222–30. *See also* Anglo-Merina alliance
Abortion, 195
Aden, 276
Adultery, 201. *See also* Sex/Sexuality
Africa: ancestors of Malagasy and, 50; enslavement within, 7–23, 32–33, 81, 83–89; forced migrations within, 271–72; slavery within, 123, 273–75; as a source of slaves for the Mascarenes, 50. *See also* African diaspora
African American identity, xix, 269, 270, 277–78. *See also* African diaspora
African diaspora: homelands and, 269, 273; intellectual history of, xxi, 23, 268–71; redefinition of, xv–xvi, 271–77, 289 n.2; several parts of, 9–11, 271–72. *See also* Diaspora
African history: African diaspora and, 269–70, 274; renaissance of, 279
Afrocentrism, 279
Agency: of chiefs and kings, 87, 91–102, 110, 117, 119, 132, 136, 141, 142, 146, 147–56, 166, 176; of commoners and *firenena*, 90, 92, 107–117, 162, 166, 215, 256–57, 286; historical, 33–35; human, 34, 40, 174–75; of

merchants, 70, 72–74, 78–79, 110; of women, 105, 200. *See also* Autonomy; Conflict; Protest; Strategies
Agent commercial, xxvii, 65, 68, 69, 72, 80–81, 120, 152. *See also Régisseur des traites*; Roux, Sylvain
Agriculture: Andrantsay and, 151; Andrianampoinimerina and, 192–94, 196, 238, 261; effects of army and warfare on, 218, 233, 235, 236–38; effects of slave trade on, 63, 126; gender division of labor in, 93, 124–31, 236–38; highland Madagascar and, 124–31; Mascarenes and, 50, 56, 60, 65; need for credit in, 98–99; power of kingdoms and, 93; quest for silver and, 144; *tanety* and, 145; use of cattle in, 145. *See also* Rice
Aix-en-Provence, 33
Ala volo, 178, 244
Alcohol: Andrianampoinimerina, policy of, 197; Radama, consumption of, 249; sale of, 71, 74. *See also* Rum
Algeria, 281
Alliances: between Andrianampoinimerina and *firenena*, 166, 175–83, 191, 203–4, 211–12, 238; among *firenena*, 112; between kings and *firenena*, 7, 109–110, 115–17; between kings and *traitants*, 33, 34,

About the Author

PIER M. LARSON teaches African History at The Johns Hopkins University. Interested in slavery and cultural encounter in Africa and its diasporas, his research is centered on Madagascar, where he grew up.